Undocumented Immigrants in the United States

Undocumented Immigrants in the United States

An Encyclopedia of Their Experience

Volume 2: K–Z

Anna Ochoa O'Leary, Editor

GREENWOOD

AN IMPRINT OF ABC-CLIO, LLC
Santa Barbara, California • Denver, Colorado • Oxford, England

Library of Congress Cataloging-in-Publication Data

Undocumented immigrants in the United States : an encyclopedia of their experience / Anna Ochoa O'Leary, editor.
    pages cm
  ISBN 978-0-313-38424-0 (hardback) — ISBN 978-0-313-38425-7 (ebook)
1. Immigrants—United States—Social conditions.   2. Illegal aliens—United States—Social conditions.   3. United States—Emigration and immigration—Encyclopedias.
I. O'Leary, Anna Ochoa.
 JV6475.U48 2014
  305.9'069120973—dc23   2013024574

ISBN: 978-0-313-38424-0
EISBN: 978-0-313-38425-7

18 17 16 15 14   1 2 3 4 5

This book is also available on the World Wide Web as an eBook.
Visit www.abc-clio.com for details.

Greenwood
An Imprint of ABC-CLIO, LLC

ABC-CLIO, LLC
130 Cremona Drive, P.O. Box 1911
Santa Barbara, California 93116–1911

This book is printed on acid-free paper ∞
Manufactured in the United States of America

Contents

List of Entries   vii

Guide to Related Topics   xi

The Encyclopedia   **409**

Recommended Resources   797

About the Editor and the Contributors   803

Index   811

List of Entries

Acculturation
Acculturation Stress
Activism
Adult Education
Advocacy
Airports
American Civil Liberties Union (ACLU)
American Friends Service Committee
Amnesty
Amnesty International
Arizona
Arizona SB 1070
Assimilation
Asylum
Aztlán
Banking
Barriers to Health
Barrios
Bilingualism
Border Control. *See* U.S. Border Patrol
Border Crossing
Bracero Program
California
Canadian Border
Catholic Church
CC-IME (Consejo Consultivo Instituto de los Mexicanos en el Exterior)
Central American Civil Wars
Childcare
Children
Chinese
Citizenship
Citizenship Education
Civil Rights
Clinton Administration

Colleges and Universities
Community Activism
Community Concerns
Corridos
Counterfeit Documents
Counterterrorism and Immigrant Profiling
Coyotes
Crime
Cubans
Cultural Citizenship
Culture
Day Labor
Death
Deferred Action for Childhood Arrivals (DACA)
Department of Homeland Security. *See* U.S. Department of Homeland Security (DHS)
Deportation
Detention Centers
Devil's Highway
Dillingham Report (1910)
Discrimination and Barriers
Displacement
Domestic Violence
Domestic Work
Dominicans
The DREAM Act
Driver's Licenses
Drug Trade
East Asians
Eastern Europeans
Economics
Education
Elementary Schools

Emergency Quota Act of 1921
Employer Sanctions
Employment
Employment Visas
Enclaves
English as a Second Language (ESL)
  Programs
English Language Learners (ELL)
English-Only Movement
Exclusion
Expedited Removal
Faith-Based Organizations
Families
Family Economics
Family Reunification
Family Structure
Fernandez-Vargas v. Gonzales
Film and Television Representation
Flores-Figueroa v. United States
  No. 08-108
Foreign Consulates
Form I-9
Fourteenth Amendment
Gangs
Garment Industry
Gateways
Gender Roles
Globalization
Governance and Criminalization
Great Lakes Region
Green Cards
Guatemalans
Guestworker and Contract
  Labor Policies
Hart-Celler Act (1965)
Hate Crimes
Head Start
Health and Welfare
High Schools
HIV/AIDS
Homelessness
Home Town Associations
Hondurans
Hospitals
Hotel Industry
Housing
Human Rights Watch

Human Trafficking
Identification Cards
Identity Theft
Illegal Immigration Reform and Immigrant
  Responsibility Act (IIRIRA) (1996)
Illinois
Immigrant Workers Freedom Ride
Immigration Act (IMMACT) (1990)
Immigration and Customs Enforcement
  (ICE)
Immigration and Nationality Act (The
  McCarran-Walter Act) (1952)
Immigration and Naturalization Service
  (INS)
Immigration Reform, 2013–2014
Immigration Reform and Control Act
  (IRCA) (1986)
Inadmissibility
Incarceration
Indians (East). *See* South Asians
Indigenous People
Individual Taxpayer Identification
  Number (ITIN)
Informal Economy
International Students/
  Student Visas
Irish
Japanese. *See* East Asians
Johnson-Reed Act (1924)
Kanjobal Mayans
Koreans. *See* East Asians
Labor Supply
Labor Unions
Landscaping Industry
Lawful Permanent Residents
Laws and Legislation, Post-1980s
League of United Latin American Citizens
  (LULAC)
Legal Representation
Legal Status
LGBT Immigrants without
  Documentation
Limited English Proficiency (LEP)
Literature and Poetry
LULAC. *See* League of United Latin
  American Citizens (LULAC)
Marriage

McCarran-Walter Act. *See* Immigration and Nationality Act (The McCarran-Walter Act) (1952)
Meat Processing Plants
Media Coverage
Mental Health Care Access
Mental Health Issues for Immigrants
Mental Health Issues for Undocumented Immigrants
Mexican American Legal Defense and Education Fund (MALDEF)
Mexicans
Midwest
Migrant Farm Workers
Migration
Military Recruitment and Participation
Minutemen
Mixed-Status Families
Mobility
Mortgages
Morton Memo
Multicultural Education
NAFTA. *See* North American Free Trade Agreement (NAFTA)
National Council of La Raza (NCLR)
National Network for Immigrant and Refugee Rights (NNIRR)
Naturalization
New Jersey
New Mexico
New York
Nicaraguan Adjustment and Central American Relief Act (NACARA)
Nicaraguans
North American Free Trade Agreement (NAFTA)
Nutrition
Obama Administration
Operation Streamline
Operation Wetback
Overstayers
Passports
Patriot Act. *See* USA PATRIOT Act (2001)
Patriotism
Personal Responsibility and Work Opportunity Reconciliation Act (PRWORA) (1996)

Plyler v. Doe
Policies of Attrition
Policy and Political Action
Ports of Entry
Postville, Iowa Raid
Pregnancy and Childbirth
Proposition 187
Prostitution
Protests
Provisional Unlawful Presence (PUP) Waiver
Public Libraries
Racialized Labeling of Mexican-Origin Persons
Racial Profiling
Racism
Refugee Act (1980)
Refugees
Religion
Remittances
Repatriation
Restaurants
Salvadorans
Sanctuary Cities and Secure Communities
Sanctuary Movement
Select Commission on Immigration and Refugee Policy
Seniors
Shadow Population
Single Men
Small Business Ownership
Social Interaction and Integration
Social Security
South Asians
Southern States
Spanish-Language Media
Special Agricultural Workers (SAW)
Sponsors
Sports
State Legislation
Strangers from a Different Shore
Strangers in the Land
Student Visas
Suburbs
Taxes

Temporary Assistance for Needy
  Families (TANF)
Temporary Protected Status (TPS)
Tennessee Immigrant and Refugee Rights
  Coalition (TIRRC)
Texas
Theater
Trafficking Victims Protection
  Reauthorization Act (TVPRA)
Transnationalism
Transportation in the United States
Trauma-Related Symptoms
The "Undocumented" Label
Undocumented Students
United States v. Brignoni-Ponce
United States v. Roblero-Solis
The Uprooted
Urban Life
USA PATRIOT Act (2001)
U.S. Border Patrol

U.S. Census Bureau
U.S. Citizenship and Immigration
  Services (USCIS)
U.S. Customs and Border Protection
  (CBP)
U.S. Department of Homeland Security
  (DHS)
U.S.-Mexico Border Wall
U-Visas
Violence
Violence against Women Act (VAWA)
Wages
Welfare System
Women's Status
Workers' Rights
Workplace Injury
Workplace Raids
Work Visas
Xenophobia
Zapotec People (Oaxaca)

Guide to Related Topics

Following is a list of the entries in this encyclopedia, arranged under broad topics for enhanced searching. Readers should also consult the index at the end of the encyclopedia for more specific subjects.

Advocacy

Activism
Advocacy
American Civil Liberties Union (ACLU)
American Friends Service Committee
Amnesty International
CC-IME
Community Activism
Community Concerns
Faith-Based Organizations
Home Town Associations
Human Rights Watch
Immigrant Workers Freedom Ride
League of United Latin American
    Citizens (LULAC)
Mexican American Legal Defense and
    Education Fund (MALDEF)
Minutemen
National Council of La Raza (NCLR)
National Network for Immigrant and
    Refugee Rights (NNIRR)
Policy and Political Action
Protests
Sanctuary Movement
Tennessee Immigrant and Refugee Rights
    Coalition (TIRRC)

Crime and Violence

Domestic Violence
Drug Trade

Gangs
Human Trafficking
Identity Theft
Violence
Violence against Women Act (VAWA)

Cultural Representation in the United States

Corridos
Devil's Highway
Film and Television Representation
Literature and Poetry
Media Coverage
Spanish-Language Media
Sports
Theater

Culture

Acculturation
Assimilation
Aztlán
Barrios
Central American Civil Wars
Corridos
Cultural Citizenship
Culture
Enclaves
Exclusion
Faith-Based Organizations
Family Reunification

Family Structure
Gateways
Indigenous People
Kanjobal Mayans
Literature and Poetry
Media Coverage
Mixed-Status Families
Patriotism
Remittances
Single Men
Social Interaction and Integration
Sports
Strangers from a Different Shore
Strangers in the Land
Suburbs
Theater
Transnationalism
Urban Life
Zapotec People (Oaxaca)

Discrimination and Barriers

Barriers to Health
Community Concerns
Discrimination and Barriers
English-Only Movement
Film and Television Representation
Hate Crimes
LGBT Immigrants without Documentation
Minutemen
Mobility
Operation Wetback
Racialized Labeling of Mexican-Origin
    Persons
Racial Profiling
Racism
The "Undocumented" Label
Xenophobia

Education

Adult Education
Bilingualism
Children
Citizenship Education
Colleges and Universities
The DREAM Act

Education
Elementary Schools
English as a Second Language (ESL)
    Programs
English Language Learners (ELL)
Head Start
High Schools
International Students / Student Visas
Limited English Proficiency (LEP)
Multicultural Education
Public Libraries
Undocumented Students

Employment and Economics

Banking
Day Labor
Domestic Work
Economics
Employer Sanctions
Employment
Garment Industry
Globalization
Hotel Industry
Individual Taxpayer Identification Number
    (ITIN)
Informal Economy
Labor Supply
Labor Unions
Landscaping Industry
Meat Processing Plants
Migrant Farm Workers
North American Free Trade Agreement
    (NAFTA)
Postville, Iowa Raid
Prostitution
Remittances
Restaurants
Small Business Ownership
Special Agricultural Workers (SAW)
Taxes
Urban Life
Wages
Workers' Rights
Workplace Injury
Workplace Raids
Work Visas

Gender and Family

Childcare
Children
Family Structure
Gender Roles
Marriage
Pregnancy and Childbirth
Single Men
Violence against Women Act (VAWA)
Women's Status

Government Agencies and Administrations

Clinton Administration
Foreign Consulates
Immigration and Customs Enforcement (ICE)
Immigration and Naturalization Service (INS)
Obama Administration
Trafficking Victims Protection Reauthorization Act (TVPRA)
U.S. Border Patrol
U.S. Census Bureau
U.S. Citizenship and Immigration Services (USCIS)
U.S. Customs and Border Protection (CBP)
U.S. Department of Homeland Security (DHS)

Health

Acculturation Stress
Barriers to Health
Death
Health and Welfare
HIV/AIDS
Hospitals
Mental Health Care Access
Mental Health Issues for Immigrants
Mental Health Issues for Undocumented Immigrants
Nutrition
Pregnancy and Childbirth
Trauma-Related Symptoms

History

Barrios
Central American Civil Wars
Dillingham Report (1910)
Flores-Figueroa v. United States
Hart-Celler Act (1965)
Illegal Immigration Reform and Immigrant Responsibility Act (IIRIRA) (1996)
Immigration Act (IMMACT) (1990)
Immigration and Nationality Act (The McCarran-Walter Act) (1952)
Immigration Reform and Control Act (IRCA) (1986)
Plyler v. Doe
Proposition 187
Sanctuary Movement
Strangers from a Different Shore
Strangers in the Land
The Uprooted

Housing

Discrimination and Barriers
Homelessness
Housing
Mortgages
Suburbs
Urban Life

Laws and Policies

Amnesty
Arizona SB 1070
Asylum
Bracero Program
Citizenship
Civil Rights
Counterterrorism and Immigrant Profiling
Crime
Deferred Action for Childhood Arrivals (DACA)
Deportation
Detention Centers
Discrimination and Barriers
Displacement

Emergency Quota Act of 1921
Employment Visas
Expedited Removal
Fernandez-Vargas v. Gonzales
Flores-Figueroa v. United States
Form I-9
Fourteenth Amendment
Governance and Criminalization
Green Cards
Guestworker and Contract Labor Policies
Hart-Celler Act (1965)
Human Trafficking
Identification Cards
Illegal Immigrant Reform and Immigrant
    Responsibility Act (IIRIRA) (1996)
Immigration Act (IMMACT) (1990)
Immigration and Nationality Act (The
    McCarran-Walter Act) (1952)
Immigration Reform, 2013–2014
Immigration Reform and Control Act
    (IRCA) (1986)
Inadmissibility
Incarceration
Individual Taxpayer Identification Number
    (ITIN)
Johnson-Reed Act (1924)
Lawful Permanent Residents
Laws and Legislation, Post-1980s
Legal Representation
Legal Status
Morton Memo
Naturalization
Nicaraguan Adjustment and Central
    American Relief Act (NACARA)
North American Free Trade Agreement
    (NAFTA)
Operation Streamline
Operation Wetback
Passports
Personal Responsibility and Work
    Opportunity Reconciliation Act
    (PRWORA) (1996)
Policies of Attrition
Policy and Political Action
Provisional Unlawful Presence (PUP)
    Waiver
Refugee Act (1980)

Refugees
Repatriation
Sanctuary Cities and Secure Communities
Select Commission on Immigration and
    Refugee Policy
Social Security
Sponsors
State Legislation
Student Visas
Taxes
Temporary Assistance for Needy Families
    (TANF)
Temporary Protected Status (TPS)
The "Undocumented" Label
United States v. Brignoni-Ponce
United States v. Roblero-Solis
USA PATRIOT Act (2001)
U.S.-Mexico Border Wall
U-Visas
Violence against Women Act (VAWA)
Welfare System

Migration

Airports
Border Crossing
Canadian Border
Counterfeit Documents
Death
Devil's Highway
Migration
Mobility
Overstayers
Ports of Entry
Transportation in the United States
Urban Life

Nationalities and Regional Origins

Chinese
Cubans
Dominicans
East Asians
Eastern Europeans
Guatemalans

Hondurans
Indigenous People
Irish
Kanjobal Mayans
Mexicans
Nicaraguans
Salvadorans
South Asians
Zapotec People (Oaxaca)

Religion

Catholic Church
Faith-Based Organizations
Religion
Sanctuary Movement

Social Organization

Childcare
Exclusion
Families
Family Economics
Family Reunification
Family Structure
Housing
Marriage
Military Recruitment and Participation
Mobility
Seniors
Shadow Population

Single Men
Social Interaction
    and Integration
Transportation in the United States
Urban Life
Women's Status

States and U.S. Regions

Arizona
Arizona SB 1070
California
Great Lakes Region
Illinois
Midwest
New Jersey
New Mexico
New York
Southern States
Texas

Transportation

Airports
Coyotes
Driver's Licenses
Human Trafficking
Mobility
Ports of Entry
Transportation in the United States

K

Kanjobal Mayans

The United States' restrictive immigration policy may make immigrant mobility difficult but not impossible. In fact, in response to the stringent immigration policy and hostility toward immigrants, Kanjobal Mayan (also spelled, Q'anjob'al) migrants have established transnational connections in Los Angeles. The Kanjobal Mayan indigenous people are primarily from Guatemala, although a small portion comes from Mexico. At present their Pan-Mayan movement in Guatemala influences the Kanjobal cultural and religious associations in Los Angeles. The involvement of religious and state leaders with these associations assists Kanjobal migrants to reintegrate into the social life of their country of origin. This reintegration enables them to formulate a transnational identity that revitalizes traditional ethnic and cultural ways in what has been referred to as a process of "reactive formation." This means that in the act of reacting culturally in positive ways, immigrants are better able to adjust to their new environment. This ability to use one's ethnic identity and culture in a positive way may be responsible for the sustained transnational relations of migrants that enables their ability to survive the often difficult conditions in the United States (Popkin, 1999: 267).

Transnational migration researchers state that the global market and the reorganization of labor to better respond to fluctuations in the world economy have promoted uneven economic development in less developed areas of the world, contributing to increasing levels of international migration. At the same time, the advancement and availability of technology and affordability of travel have enabled migrants to maintain ties with their countries of origin.

Sassen (1996) claims that in response to international labor movements, migrant-receiving countries attempt to reinforce their immigration policies in efforts to diminish or deter undocumented migration. These efforts work to a large degree to hinder a migrant's ability to move from place to place—an important and historically proven survival strategy.

Research by Popkin (1999), Taylor et al. (1997), and Massey (1998) indicates that stringent U.S. and Mexican immigration policies have created unstable legal situations for the undocumented in the United States, and a considerable increase in the cost of migration. These developments tend to discourage cyclical migration and to encourage extended stays in new destinations. This situation presses migrants to develop ways of coping and surviving in their new destinations. The Mayan Kanjobal community of Los Angeles provides one such example. They have maintained the culture and religion of their country of origin in Santa Eulalia Guatemala by developing a sophisticated support network within a large Latino community in Los Angeles, California. In 1982, Kanjobal Mayans also began arriving in the agricultural community of Indiantown, Florida, to work in the citrus groves. Anthropologist Allan Burns has captured the adaptation, cultural persistence, and survival of this small community of refugees after years of violence, overcoming along the way numerous barriers and outright hostilities, to become a symbol of cultural plurality strategies.

Kanjobal migrants have formed community organizations as a result of the discrimination and social exclusion they face in Los Angeles, in part due to their economic and social status, language, and immigration status (Burns, 2010; Popkin, 1999: 269). In order to cope with these oppressive conditions the Kanjobales strive to reconnect to and strengthen certain aspects of their traditional Guatemalan community. In this example, the Kanjobales of Santa Eulalia who are living in Los Angeles incorporate components of "traditional Mayan culture and religion (*costombre*) into their religious celebrations" (Popkin, 1999: 269). Through these social practices, Kanjobal social organizations reconnect with the social life of their country of origin, bringing a measure of cohesiveness among community members that may become dispersed over time (Burns, 2010). This allows them to maintain their cultural identity, as well as components of their cultural heritage.

As a result of anti-immigrant Latino sentiment in Southern California, the Kanjobales regularly experience discrimination, which predisposes them to further mistreatment and marginalization and social, political and economic inequities within the Los Angeles area where a majority of them reside. However, the Kanjobales identify with their Mayan Indian identity. In addition, for many their first language is their Mayan language; they do not speak fluent Spanish or English. As a result of their Indianness and lack of ability to speak accurate Spanish or English, they are often stigmatized in the form of ridicule from more assimilated Latino groups. This is particularly true in the workplace such as in the garment industry.

Many Guatemalan immigrants do not have legal immigrant documentation, which contributes to their experience of marginalization, relegating them to low-paying jobs in the garment industry where they commonly endure slavelike conditions of working long hours and up to six or seven days per week while only earning below the minimum wage. The Kanjobales also experience the decreased availability of employment in the garment industry due to the competition for jobs by an increasing number of Mexican immigrants relocating to the Los Angeles area. The scholarly literature is replete with evidence of how much of the economic instability in Mexico resulting in greater migration was fueled by the inability of poor landholders to eke out a living after the North American Free Trade Agreement (NAFTA) went into effect. Economic unstable conditions have forced Guatemalans to find additional means of income by finding second part-time jobs, and informal sector activities such as renting rooms to renters out of their residence, or cooking and selling tamales (Popkin, 1999: 273).

Popkin claims that the racial discrimination Mayans face combined with their desire to maintain their cultural identity motivates them to create social organizations in the receiving communities. As a result of this desire to create social organizations, in 1986 a group of Catholic Church parish members along with the aid of a priest from Santa Eulia founded the Fraternidad Eulalense Maya Q'anjobal (FEMAQ) organization, which now comprises eight hundred Kanjobal members and a number of sub-associations located in Los Angeles. Some of the types of cultural traditions that are maintained in this organization consist of: a weekly community prayer service that consists of rituals similar to those practiced during mass in Santa Eulia. Proceeding the prayer session, members dine together and discuss matters occurring in Santa Eulia and Los Angeles. However, other community-building events are also taking place at these social gatherings. Marimba classes are offered to the migrant Santa Eulia youth residing in Los Angeles. Marimba refers to the music and the ancient and traditional musical instrument of Guatemala, similar to a xylophone. The formation of subcommittees that perform service work for the community is also organized, such as a hospital committee that regularly communicates with the immigrant community annually in order to raise funds to pay a doctor who cares for their community members in Santa Eulia. Funds are also collected and used for the return of bodies of Santa Eulia immigrants who have not survived the journey to the United States, to their home communities for burial. Funds generated from these collections also go for the support and construction of *capillas* or small worshipping and meeting sites within the villages of origin of some of the members. Finally, community events and activities are organized in Los Angeles such as the *patronal fiesta* and Mayan soccer team that are fashioned after such events and activities from their communities of origin in Santa Eulia (Popkin, 1999: 277).

The nature of FEMAQ allows for the transference of community traditions and values to the young and old Santa Eulia immigrants. Through their obligations toward their communities of origin, a connection to those communities is strengthened. It allows the Kanjobal to retain, express and share their cultural identity with other Kanjobales who have relocated to Los Angeles, allowing them to create a sense of pride and belonging in an environment that often does not welcome their presence.

Dina Barajas

See Also: Activism; Cultural Citizenship; Culture; Garment Industry; Home Town Associations; Indigenous People; North American Free Trade agreement (NAFTA); Transnationalism.

Further Reading

Burns, Allan F. 2010. *Maya in Exile: Guatemalans in Florida.* Philadelphia, PA: Temple University Press.

Massey, Douglas S. 1998. "March of Folly: U.S. Immigration Policy After NAFTA." *The American Prospect* 37:22–33.

Popkin, Eric. 1999. "Guatemalan Mayan Migration to Los Angeles: Constructing Transnational Linkages in the Context of the Settlement Process." *Ethnic & Racial Studies* 22.2:267–289.

Sassen, Saskia. 1996. *Losing Control? Sovereignty in an Age of Globalization.* New York: Columbia University Press.

Taylor, J. Edward, Philip L. Martin, and Michael Fix. 1997. *Poverty amid Prosperity: Immigration and the Changing Face of Rural California.* Washington: Urban Institute Press.

L

Labor Supply

Unauthorized immigrants come to the United States for a variety of reasons, but their overwhelming motive is economic. Most unauthorized immigrants come in search of work or to join working family members, and employers in the United States have long tapped into immigrant labor supplies to fulfill their labor needs. Currently, there are about eight million unauthorized people in the U.S. work force; they are concentrated in jobs in agriculture, building and grounds maintenance, construction, and food preparation and service.

Immigrants have contributed their low-paid labor to the U.S. economy throughout the nation's history, providing a crucial labor supply in important sectors such as manufacturing, infrastructure, and agriculture from the industrial revolution onward. In fact, immigration to the United States was unrestricted until the end of the nineteenth century in order to help satisfy the high demand for immigrant labor in U.S. industries. The earliest and longest lasting of foreign labor importation systems was a "forced migration," the slave trade, and it brought more than half a million Africans to the United States. Slaves took up residence with the earliest European settlers at Jamestown and, with their descendants, built the foundations of U.S. agriculture for more than two centuries. By the early nineteenth century, as the invention of the cotton gin sparked U.S. industry, unregulated immigration from Europe helped form the industrial labor force in growing cities throughout the north. Different groups of immigrants provided labor to different sectors of the economy: European immigrants staffed factories in cities across the northern United States, Chinese immigrants built thousands of miles of railroad track in the West, Mexican nationals worked the agricultural fields of the U.S. Southwest, and American-born descendants of slaves cultivated cotton and other crops in the South.

Due to the high demand for immigrant workers and the expansionist policy of the early United States, immigration was largely unrestricted throughout the seventeenth, eighteenth, and nineteenth centuries. When restrictive policies were first implemented in 1882, they were explicitly aimed at restricting the immigration of Chinese laborers. Shortly after, the Immigration Act of 1917 curbed immigration of Eastern and Southern Europeans, a main source of labor in the industrial north, and cut off the immigration of all Asians. To ease the demand for labor, Mexican nationals were exempted from numerical restriction, and an unlimited number of visas could be granted to Mexican workers. U.S. businesses sent recruiters deep into the heart of Mexico's populated north-central valleys to tap this labor reserve, and they recruited Mexicans to come north to work in agriculture, construction, and manufacturing. This system came to be known as "*el enganche*" ("the hook") in Mexico, as workers were promised great rewards for their labor but were "hooked" into labor conditions that better resembled indentured servitude.

As immigration from Asia continued to be restricted throughout the first half of the twentieth century, the United States came to rely ever more heavily on labor importation from Latin America, and from Mexico in particular. This reliance was accelerated by World War II, when the working male population of the United States was drastically reduced at the same time that productive output of war materials needed to increase. To help fill labor shortages, women and African American workers were recruited to work in industries throughout the north, while Mexican workers were imported en masse to the U.S. Southwest where they harvested the food that would sustain industrial workers and the families of soldiers abroad. To ensure an unhindered labor supply, the United States and Mexico signed a binational treaty in 1942 that came to be known as the Bracero Program. The Bracero Program was a contract worker program that brought an estimated 5 million workers from Mexico to labor in the agricultural fields, construction sites, and factories across the southwest United States and in cities such as Chicago.

The Bracero Program ended in 1964, and in 1965 the U.S. Congress passed the Immigration and Nationality Act of 1965, or the Hart-Celler Act. The Hart-Celler Act

Mexican laborers apply for temporary employment in the United States in 1943. Here the men are questioned as to their agricultural experience and a preliminary examination is made, such as for calluses on their hands and other outward appearances that would indicate agricultural experience. (Howard R. Rosenberg, "Snapshots in a Farm Labor Tradition," *Labor Management Decisions*, Winter-Spring, 1993)

equalized the national origins quota system, subjecting all nations to the same quota and ostensibly ending the explicitly biased policy of 1924. For the first time in nearly a century, Asians were allowed to immigrate to the United States, and many did so, increasing the Asian population of the United States in the last quarter of the twentieth century. Immigration from Latin America also increased, even though the 1965 law also extended numerical restrictions on immigration to Mexico and other Latin American countries for the first time. Over the next fifteen years, the number of visas available to Latin American workers was reduced from an unlimited number to just twenty thousand per year by 1980. In spite of these new restrictions, the demand for immigrant labor from Latin America has persisted, and Latin American workers continue to shore up the U.S. economy with their low-paid labor. In fact, restrictions imposed by the 1965 Act did not stop, or even slow, the movement of workers from Latin America to the United States. Rather, from the 1970s to the present, increasingly restrictive immigration legislation—combined with a persistent demand for immigrant labor—has converted a century-old labor migration pattern into an unauthorized one.

The reasons for mass labor migration have been long examined by social scientists. The most simple explanation is that migration originates in areas where there are low wages and few job opportunities ("push" factors in "sending" countries), and ends up in areas with higher wages and more job opportunities ("pull" factors in "receiving" countries). That is, people move from poorer countries to richer ones in search of opportunity. However, empirical studies have shown that a host of other factors, including family dynamics, economic development in the sending region, and the relationships between sending and receiving countries, deeply shape migratory patterns. For example, migration from the world's poorest countries is modest, and people who do migrate tend to move to places with which they are familiar, rather than simply to the nearest prosperous nation.

On the other side of the coin, the demand for immigrant labor in receiving areas is often said to be the result of native labor shortages. However, job opportunities for immigrant workers persist even when there are native-born workers available, suggesting that immigrant workers may be preferentially hired for certain jobs that are very low paying, unstable, or socially degraded. This is especially true in the case of unauthorized immigrant workers. The high degree of vulnerability of unauthorized workers makes them less likely to demand higher wages and better working conditions than citizen workers with full rights, and when undocumented workers do organize to improve their conditions, they can be fired by their employers and even threatened with deportation. Thus, many employers have said that they prefer to hire immigrant workers because they are "harder working" and "less demanding" than citizen workers are.

Unauthorized immigrant men in the United States have very high labor force participation rates overall, 94 percent compared to 83 percent for U.S.-born men, and unauthorized immigrant men have higher labor force participation rates than women, 94 percent versus 58 percent. One reason for this is that unauthorized immigrant women are more likely to be at home taking care of children, but unauthorized women are also more likely to work in private residences or in other "informal" economic activities than men are, and may be less likely to be sampled. Even though they are very likely to be in the labor force, unauthorized immigrants have slightly higher unemployment rates than U.S. citizens or legal permanent residents. This is probably at least partially due to the tendency of unauthorized immigrants to work in jobs that are seasonal, temporary, or otherwise unstable, and at least partially due to the difficulties of finding employment without legitimate documentation of employment eligibility.

Unauthorized immigrants also tend to be concentrated in certain industries. Among unauthorized workers, most have jobs in construction (21 percent of unauthorized workers), services, such as janitorial or landscaping services (20 percent), leisure and hospitality, such as food preparation and hotel work (17 percent), and manufacturing (13 percent). Not coincidentally, these industries tend to be low paying, and within each industry unauthorized workers tend to be concentrated in the lowest paid positions. Even though unauthorized immigrant men have higher labor force participation rates than U.S.-born men, the median household income of unauthorized immigrants was $36,000 compared to $50,000 for U.S.-born residents, and unauthorized immigrants are twice as likely to live in poverty as U.S. citizens.

Ruth Gomberg-Muñoz

See Also: Economics; Family Economics; Informal Economy; Labor Unions; Migration; Transnationalism; Wages.

Further Reading

Massey, Douglas, Jorge Durand, and Nolan J. Malone. 2002. *Beyond Smoke and Mirrors: Mexican Immigration in an Era of Economic Integration.* New York: Russell Sage Foundation.

Passel, Jeffrey. 2006. "Size and Characteristics of the Unauthorized Migrant Population in the U.S.: Estimates Based on the March 2005 Current Population Survey." Pew Hispanic Center. http://www.pewhispanic.org/2006/03/07/size-and-characteristics-of-the -unauthorized-migrant-population-in-the-us/.

Passel, Jeffrey, and D'Vera Cohn. 2009. "A Portrait of Unauthorized Immigration in the United States." Pew Hispanic Center. http://pewhispanic.org/files/reports/107.pdf.

Labor Unions

In the height of the struggle between California growers and Latino agricultural workers, the famed leader of the United Farm Workers (UFW), César Chávez, protested the use of undocumented strike breakers, and on a few occasions, even reported undocumented scabs and union dissidents to immigration authorities (Gutiérrez, 1995). The UFW would later change its position on immigration, and Chávez's legacy would go on to be considered synonymous with immigrant rights. However, this perhaps lesser known chapter in history is emblematic of the ambivalent relationship organized labor has had with undocumented immigration throughout history, and the large shifts that have ultimately taken place during the last two decades.

To understand the discomfort unions have had towards immigrants, it is important to understand the political nature of labor organizing. As Hamlin argues, organizing noncitizen workers can be a mixed blessing for labor unions that are not only interested in increasing membership, but also reliant on members' financial contributions and votes in order to maintain political power (Hamlin, 2008: 300). It is under this rationale that in 1986 the AFL-CIO (American Federation of Labor—Congress of Industrial Organizations) lobbied hard to include employers' sanctions in the landmark Immigration Reform and Control Act (IRCA), and in fact, opposed the watershed amnesty that would ultimately grant legal status to over 3 million undocumented immigrants (Parks 2007). This ambivalence would continue until February 2000, when, under the leadership of then-president John Sweeney, the AFL-CIO passed a resolution stating solidarity with immigrant workers and organized labor also called for amnesty for all undocumented workers. This shift was not a spontaneous decree from above, but rather the result of years of grassroots organizing, largely through the efforts of San Francisco Bay Area leaders who referred to themselves as the Labor Immigrant Organizing Network (LION). These labor organizers saw the powerful tool employer sanctions had handed employers in the form of the ominous "No Match Letter" from the Social Security Administration, which in turn facilitated the opportunistic firing of workers sympathetic to union efforts (Hamlin, 2008). This practice would eventually be halted under an injunction prompted by a lawsuit led by many of the same advocates (Leonard, 2009).

While the demographic transformation that propelled organized labor's shift towards its current immigrant-friendly stance has been decades in the making, the actual political shift within union leadership came less than a decade ago.

Undocumented immigrants, in particular, were once assumed to lack any real potential as union recruits. "They were thought to view their situation in relation to their home countries, where conditions were even worse, and they were vulnerable to deportation and thus fearful of any confrontation with authority" (Fantasia and Voss, 2004: 138). Today, immigrants, long considered unorganizable by union leaders, are seen as the future of the labor movement (Milkman, 2006), and an imperative component for its survival (Milkman, 2000). From 1996 to 2006, the share of American workers who are foreign-born increased from 10.6 percent to 15.4 percent, just as the share of American union members who are foreign-born rose steadily from 8.9 percent to 12.3 percent (Fan and Batalova, 2007; Parks, 2007).

Yet, during the same period, union membership fell for both native and foreign-born workers, with an ever widening gap in membership between the two. Many of the industries where undocumented workers can commonly be found are nearly completely isolated from union protection. A mere 1.6 percent of all restaurant and food service workers, 2.2 percent of crop production workers, and 1.1 percent of car washers were union members in 2008 (Hirsch and Macpherson, 2009; Passel and Cohn, 2009). Nonetheless, key service unions, such as the Service Employees International Union (SEIU) and UNITE-HERE (a product of the 2004 merger between the Union of Needletraders, Industrial and Textile Employees and the Hotel Employees and Restaurant Employees union), have waged some of the most public organizing campaigns in recent years, and immigrant workers have certainly played a key role. For example, the now twenty-five-year-old SEIU *Justice for Janitors* campaign has organized 225,000 janitors in more than thirty cities, many of them Latino immigrants (SEIU 2009).

UNITE-HERE's *Hotel Workers Rising* campaign has also launched strikes in cities such as Boston, Chicago, New York, and San Francisco in support of a largely female immigrant workforce (UNITE-HERE 2009). Together, SEIU and UNITE-HERE, along with five other unions—the International Brotherhood of Teamsters, the Laborers' International Union of North America (LIUNA), the United Brotherhood of Carpenters and Joiners, the United Farm Workers of America (UFW), and the United Food and Commercial Workers (UFCW)—would go on to form the breakaway coalition "Change-To-Win" (CTW) in 2005. The split with the AFL-CIO was officially attributed to concerns that the old guard had invested too much on politicking and not enough on organizing (Estreicher, 2006). However, undocumented immigration remained a latent, but substantial, undercurrent of this fissure as well (Hamlin, 2008). In the years following the break, many AFL-CIO central labor councils have signed solidarity charters with their CTW affiliates (AFL-CIO, 2005), and examples abound of collaborations between worker centers (which provide alternative organizing spaces for workers not served by unions, particularly undocumented workers) and central labor councils (Fine, 2006; Turner and Cornfield, 2007).

Despite the split, union leaders from both the Change-to-Win coalition and the AFL-CIO have remained actively engaged over the issue of undocumented immigration and the potential for federal reform. The urgent need for change in federal policy has emerged against a backdrop of several raids that transpired during the latter part of the Bush administration, including the 1,280 beef and pork processing workers arrested at Swift & Co. in Greeley, Colorado, on December 12, 2006, the 361 leather workers arrested at the Michael Bianco Inc. factory in New Bedford, Massachusetts, on March 6, 2007, and the 389 workers arrested at the Agriprocessors kosher meat plant in Postville, Iowa, on May 12, 2008. These actions culminated in the *largest* workplace raid in U.S. history in Laurel, Mississippi, where 592 electronic assembly workers were arrested at Howard Industries on August 25, 2008. Despite drastically low union representation in each of these affected industries, union leaders reacted viscerally to the aggressive campaign launched by the Secretary of Homeland Security Michael Chertoff. In an announcement issued April 14, 2009, leaders from Change to Win and the AFL-CIO issued a joint proposal to pressure Congress to act on immigration reform. Demands included: "1) an independent commission to assess and manage future projections, based on labor market shortages that are determined; 2) a secure and effective worker authorization mechanism; 3) rational operational control of the border; 4) adjustment of status for the current undocumented population; and 5) improvement, not expansion, of temporary worker programs, limited to temporary or seasonal, not permanent, jobs" (Change to Win, 2009). Individual leaders, however, continue to have distinct visions about the particular direction reform should move in, and there is particular disagreement over the viability of a guest worker program (Swarns, 2006).

As prospects for immigration reform linger uncertainly on the horizon, the organizing rights for undocumented workers also remain somewhat constricted. Prior to the 1986 Immigration Reform and Control Act (IRCA), undocumented workers who were active in union organizing efforts had many of the same protections from employer retaliation as did their documented counterparts. (See: *Sure-Tan, Inc. v. National Labor Relations Board,* 1984.) However, in 2002, the Supreme Court handed down the landmark *Hoffman Plastics v. the National Labor Relations Board (NLRB)* decision, which would ultimately absolve employers from the responsibility of rehiring undocumented immigrants they had wrongfully fired for union organizing. In a 5 to 4 decision led by Chief Justice Rehnquist, the court majority argued that IRCA prevented the NLRB from awarding back pay to an undocumented individual who had never been legally authorized to work in the United States in the first place. Legal analysts have denounced this decision as a watershed case that undermines the potency of not only undocumented workers' right to organize, but other protections outside of the union context (Fisk, Cooper and Wishnie, 2005).

However, *Hoffman* has not been the last say on the organizing rights of undocumented workers. Less than two years after being raided in Iowa, the now infamous Agriprocessors was also dealt a blow by the Supreme Court, which refused to rehear its case in *Agriprocessors v. NLRB*. Though the United Food and Commercial Workers (UFCW) had won a 2005 certified election at a smaller Agriprocessors plant in Queens, New York, plant owners had refused to bargain with workers. Owners challenged that seventeen of the twenty-one employees were illegal and thus ineligible to vote for a union. Yet, on November 17, 2008, the Supreme Court upheld the lower D.C. court's decision, ultimately upholding undocumented workers' statuses as employees under the National Labor Relations Act, and thus preserving their right to organize. Neither *Hoffman* nor *Agriprocessors* is likely to be the final word on the role of undocumented workers in union organizing.

Shannon Gleeson

See Also: Hotel Industry; Immigrant Worker Freedom Ride; Labor Supply; Meat Processing Plants; Migrant Farm Workers; Postville, Iowa Raid.

Further Reading

AFL-CIO. 2005. "AFL-CIO Rolls Out Solidarity Charter Program to Reunite Local Labor Movements." *News Archive,* August 26. http://www.aflcio.org/Press-Room/Press-Releases/AFL-CIO-Rolls-Out-Solidarity-Charter-Program-to-Re.

Change to Win. 2009. "Change to Win and AFL-CIO Unveil Unified Immigration Reform Framework." http://www.seiu.org/2009/04/change-to-win-and-afl-cio-unveil-unified-immigration-reform-framework.php.

Estreicher, Samuel. 2006. "Disunity within the House of Labor: Change to Win or to Stay the Course?" *Journal of Labor Research* 27.4:505–11.

Fan, Chuncui Velma, and Jeanne Batalova. 2007. *Foreign-Born Wage and Salary Workers in the US Labor Force and Unions.* U.S. in Focus Washington, D.C.: Migration Policy Institute. http://www.migrationinformation.com/USfocus/display.cfm?id=638.

Fantasia, Rick, and Kim Voss. 2004. *Hard Work: Remaking the American Labor Movement.* Berkeley: University of California Press.

Fine, Janice. 2006. *Worker Centers: Organizing Communities at the Edge of the Dream.* Ithaca, NY: ILR Press.

Fisk, Catherine, Laura Cooper, and Michael J. Wishnie. 2005. "The Story of *Hoffman Plastic Compounds, Inc. v. NLRB:* Labor Rights Without Remedies for Undocumented Immigrants." *Duke Law School Faculty Scholarship Series,* Paper 20.

Gutiérrez, David G. 1995. *Walls and Mirrors: Mexican Americans, Mexican Immigrants, and the Politics of Ethnicity.* Berkeley: University of California Press.

Hamlin, Rebecca. 2008. "Immigrants at Work: Labor Unions and Non-Citizen Members," in *Civic Hopes and Political Realities: Immigrants, Community Organizations, and Political Engagement,* ed. S. Karthick Ramakrishnan and Irene Bloemraad, 300–322. New York: Russell Sage Foundation Press.

Hirsch, Barry T., and David A. Macpherson. 2009. *Union Membership and Coverage Database from the CPS.* Georgia State University and Trinity University. http://www.unionstats.com/.

Leonard, Bill. 2009. "Department of Homeland Security Rescinds Controversial No-Match Rule." Society for Human Resource Management. Oct. 7. http://www.shrm.org/Publications/HRNews/Pages/RescindNoMatch.aspx.

Milkman, Ruth. 2006. *L.A. Story: Immigrant Workers and the Future of the U.S. Labor Movement.* New York: Russell Sage Foundation Press.

Milkman, Ruth. 2000. *Organizing Immigrants: The Challenge for Unions in Contemporary California.* Ithaca, NY: Cornell University Press.

Parks, James. 2007. "Immigrant Union Membership Grew 30 Percent in Last Decade." News: AFL-CIO Now Blog, August 30.

Passel, Jeffrey, and D'Vera Cohn. 2009. "A Portrait of the Unauthorized Migrants in the United States." http://pewhispanic.org/files/reports/107.pdf.

SEIU, Service Employees International Union. 2009. "What Is Justice for Janitors?" http://www.seiu.org/a/propertyservices/property-services-faq.php.

Swarns, Rachel L. 2006. "Union Leader Supporting Guest Worker Proposal." *New York Times,* February 24. http://www.nytimes.com/2006/02/24/politics/24immig.html.

Turner, L., and D. B. Cornfield. 2007. *Labor in the New Urban Battlegrounds: Local Solidarity in a Global Economy.* Ithaca, NY: ILR Press/Cornell University Press.

UNITE-HERE. 2009. "Hotel Workers Rising! About the Campaign." http://www.hotelworkersrising.org/Campaign/.

Landscaping Industry

Landscape workers or paid gardeners, like female domestic workers, represent a valuable labor source for the domestic household economy throughout the United States. While domestic help has historically been a privilege of the affluent, the middle-class, especially after WW II, has also acquired the financial means to hire immigrants and racial minorities to perform traditional household duties. Due primarily to the American obsession with the front lawn, increased influx of low-wage immigrants to U.S. cities since the mid-1960s and major shift from a manufacturing to service economy, the demand for landscape workers has become an integral part of American neighborhoods. In this way, the landscaping industry is integrated into the mainstream suburban economy. These jobs offer workers disadvantaged by their undocumented status opportunities that are not otherwise available to them in the formal economy. The growing need for landscaper and suburban maintenance gardening is indicative of important shifts in service consumption in the United States. Economic restructuring has produced greater income inequality, and busy dual-career families and an aging population have created the demand for labor that undocumented immigrants readily fill (Ramirez and Hondagneu-Sotelo 2009).

Although this mostly immigrant trade provides positive benefits throughout this country (e.g., greener, healthier and aesthetically pleasing communities), Hollywood movies, news reporters and elected officials commonly depict landscape workers as menial workers who occupy low-wage jobs associated with low-social status. They are depicted, for example, as ignorant Latino immigrants who can't speak English and offer no positive benefits to society. As a result, many Latino actors complain of being type-casted in these roles, as if they were playing the role of common criminals. Instead, the landscape industry can be seen as important sites for the construction of masculinity. Thus, by looking closely at the complex nature of this trade and the positive contribution of these honest, hard-working men—mostly from rural Mexico and Latin America—we can better appreciate their labor and efforts to improve the quality of life for all of us.

The landscape trade primarily consists of two social classes: bosses and workers. While the boss is the owner of the small-scale enterprise and handles all business transactions, the worker abides by the wishes of the boss, just as in most companies. As the owner, the boss negotiates a yard maintenance agreement with a homeowner or renter. Instead of legally binding contracts, the boss and client usually establish an oral agreement based on the size of the lot, type of work requested (e.g., mow lawn, water plants and trim bushes), frequency of visits and estimated time to complete job. The mix of informal and formal economic transactions is not uncommon (Ramirez and Hondagneu-Sotelo, 2009).

As independent contractors, bosses mostly charge clients based on the nature of the job, as noted above, versus hourly work. Bosses typically charge from $75 to $100 per month. However, due to the abundance of cheap labor and fierce competition among co-ethnics, owners of landscape businesses charge as little as $50 per month for their services.

Apart from monthly maintenance jobs, however, these individuals can earn well above these monthly rates by performing larger jobs or "extras," such as installing sprinklers or tree trimming, for extra pay during the weekends.

Landscape workers organize themselves in small crews. Depending on the size of the small enterprise, a crew can be from three members to six members. Crews usually consist of the boss, a few workers and a driver. The boss usually accesses his personal social networks to hire workers, which typically includes nuclear family members, extended family members, friends and hometown associates.

In addition, the boss owns all the tools, truck(s) and equipment (e.g., leaf blower, lawn mower, and weed trimmer) and has direct contact with the clients. Moreover, the boss is responsible for covering all business costs, such as equipment maintenance and tool replacements, auto payments, insurance, gasoline and oil. The boss is also responsible for hiring and paying his workers. The boss usually pays the workers in cash on a daily or weekly basis.

Apart from the boss and worker positions, as noted above, crews also include a driver. In addition to his driving duties, this individual also takes on the same duties of a worker. Given that undocumented workers cannot legally obtain driver licenses in states like California—a trend that has extended to other states in the nation—the driver has become a key part of the crew structure and usually gets paid more than the worker.

Moreover, the successful landscape owner has accumulated a good-size route. Usually accumulated over time, the route represents a network of houses regularly serviced by the crew. The route represents the bosses' primary asset. Like any commodity in the formal market, the route has exchange value: it can be sold, traded or gifted. Any exchange of route commonly takes place informally. Both the size and quality (amount being charged per house) of the route determine the boss's monthly earnings and how many workers he can afford to employ.

This trade provides both opportunities and obstacles to Latino immigrants and other groups. On the one hand, Latino immigrants who experience racism and a hostile work environment benefit from this mostly informal trade where workers employ survival strategies and experience limited entry barriers. In this trade, for instance, recent immigrants need not worry about many occupational barriers found in the formal economy, such as providing proof of legal status in this country. Moreover, recent immigrants with limited English skills and lack of formal education can enter this trade without major barriers.

On the other hand, the landscape trade also has its problems. Due to the lack of governmental regulations and protections, many workers experience work-related exploitation. For example, landscape workers (and bosses) lack basic worker protections taken for granted by many U.S. workers, such as minimum wage guarantee, workers' compensation benefits, work site safety rules, health insurance, child labor laws and forty-hour work weeks. Consequently, many landscape workers (and bosses) put in long hours and often work on weekends with little pay and few governmental protections.

However, the case of landscape workers should not be confounded with the abusive practices found in the garment industry, especially since many landscape workers enjoy the opportunity to one day become a boss of their own small landscaping business. Also, many of these small businesses depend on personal strong ties, where kinship and co-ethnic ties from the same hometown bond the crews into family-like units. Finally, the physically hard manual labor embodies masculine toughness that also reflects a specific working-class culture and images consistent with Mexican *machismo*. The concept is intertwined with the performance of masculine "dirty work" occupations, serving to reaffirm daily on-the-job interactions with their fellow workers.

In sum, the landscape trade represents a viable alternative for Latino immigrant workers in this country to survive and thrive. Landscape workers consist of honest, hard-working individuals who deserve respect for making our communities greener, healthier and aesthetically pleasing.

Alvaro Huerta

See Also: Day Labor; Domestic Work; Informal Economy; Labor Supply; Small Business Ownership; Suburbs.

Further Reading

Huerta, Alvaro. 2007. "Looking Beyond 'Mow, Blow and Go': Mexican Immigrant Gardeners in Los Angeles." *Berkeley Planning Journal* 20:1–23.

Huerta, Alvaro. 2010. "The Plight of Paid Mexican Gardeners in Los Angeles' Informal Economy." *Progressive Planning* 183 (Spring):44–49.

Huerta, Alvaro. 2011. "Examining the Perils and Promises of an Informal Niche in a Global City: A Case Study of Mexican Immigrant Gardeners in Los Angeles." Ph.D. dissertation, University of California, Berkeley.

Pisani, Michael J., and David W. Yoskowitz. 2005. "Grass, Sweat, and Sun: An Exploratory Study of the Labor Market for Gardeners in South Texas." *Social Science Quarterly* 86:229–251.

Pisani, Michael J., and David W. Yoskowitz. 2006. "Opportunity Knocks: Entrepreneurship, Informality and Home Gardening in South Texas." *Journal of Borderland Studies* 21.20:59–76.

Ramirez, Hernan, and Pierrette Hondagneu-Sotelo. 2009. "Mexican Gardeners: Entrepreneurs or Exploited Workers?" *Social Problems* 56.1:70–88.

Lawful Permanent Residents

In January 1, 2011, there were an estimated 13.1 million lawful permanent residents (LPRs) living in the United States. LPRs are persons who have been granted lawful permanent "green cards" and who have not yet become U.S. citizens. Mexico was the leading country of origin of the LPR population in 2011 with an estimated 3.3 million or 25 percent of all green card holders in the United States. The top four states where LPRs are most likely to live are California, New York, Texas, and Florida.

The United States Citizenship and Immigration Services (USCIS) office issues the green cards by first approving an immigrant petition, usually filed by an employer or relative. The green card, actually a card that is green, has an "alien" identification number which serves to identify the immigrant. The beneficiaries of a green card, lawful permanent residents, are granted permission to reside and take employment in the United States. Lawful permanent residents possess a social security number, pay state and federal taxes, and contribute toward social security. The holder of a green card must maintain permanent resident status, and can be removed from the United States if certain conditions of this status are not met.

Immigrants who are in the United States without authorization are typically not eligible to apply for an adjustment of their status. Immigrants who are in the United States without authorization are considered "inadmissible" because they have violated U.S. law, and they risk deportation if they apply while in the United States. Moreover, if an immigrant is later to be found inadmissible, it makes it more difficult for relatives who are legal permanent residents or citizens to petition for them to be legally reunited under the family visa program of the Immigration and Naturalization Act. In January of 2013, the Obama Administration announced new rules that will allow thousands of American citizens to avoid long separations from immediate family members who are undocumented and want to initiate the process of becoming legal residents by applying for a Provisional Unlawful Presence (PUP) Waiver. However, this is a very recent development.

Of the total 13.1 million LPRs living in the United States in 2011, an estimated 8.5 million were eligible to naturalize, that is, become citizens (Rytina, 2011). Of all of the categories of immigrants, LPRs have the strongest economic and familial connections and political allegiance to the United States (Wolper, 2010). Many are productive members of society—working, paying taxes, raising children—and may have come to the United States as children. However, in 1996 there were a series of reforms made to the Immigration and Nationality Act (INA) that expanded the range of crimes for which an LPR can be deported. For example, domestic violence may result in the invalidation of the green card and possible deportation of the offender. An LPR who commits a crime and is arrested may end up in immigrant detention centers awaiting a decision on their case. Some of these detention centers are located in remote regions of Arizona, Georgia, and Texas, making it difficult for the detainee to see an immigration lawyer (García Hernández, 2011). The 1996 reforms also provided for the removal of LPRs from the country for committing "crimes of moral turpitude." Although this is a vague term, acts such as fraud and not paying taxes have been interpreted as those that fit the definition of base, vile, or depraved acts that is stated in the INA and have been used against LPRs (Wolper, 2010).

A lawful permanent resident can apply for U.S. citizenship, or naturalization, after five years of being a permanent resident. This period is shortened to three years if the applicant is married to a U.S. citizen, or to four years if permanent residency was received through political asylum. U.S. citizens are entitled to more rights and privileges than lawful permanent residents. Lawful permanent residents do not have the right to vote, the right to be elected in federal and state elections, are not eligible for certain educational fellowships, and are not eligible for federal government jobs. Male permanent residents between the ages of eighteen and twenty-six are subject to registering in the Selective Service System.

Green cards are valid for ten years or two years in the case of a "conditional" resident and must be renewed before the card expires. If the green card holder fails to renew his card, there is the risk of becoming unlawfully present, or "undocumented," and the danger of deportation.

Overview and Process

According to the U.S. Citizenship and Immigration Service website, those who want to become a lawful permanent resident based on the fact that they have a relative who is a citizen of the United States, or a relative who is a lawful permanent resident, must go through a multistep process.

The USCIS must approve an immigrant visa petition, I-130 Petition for Alien Relative, for the person applying. This petition is filed by the relative (sponsor) and must be accompanied by proof of the relationship between the sponsor and the immigrant.

The Department of State must determine if an immigrant visa number is immediately available for the foreign national, even if they are already in the United States. When an immigrant visa number is available, it means they can apply to have an immigrant visa number assigned.

If one is already in the United States, they may apply to change their status to that of a lawful permanent resident after a visa number becomes available, using Form I-485, "Application to Register Permanent Residence or Adjust Status." This is one way one can apply to secure an immigrant visa number. If the applicant is outside the United States when an immigrant visa number becomes available, they must then go to the U.S. consulate servicing the area in which they reside to complete the processing. This is the other way to secure an immigrant visa number. The applicant's relative (sponsor) must prove that they can support the beneficiary at 125 percent above the mandated poverty line, by using Form I-485, "Affidavit of Support" under Section 213A of the Act.

Eligibility

In order for a relative to sponsor an immigrant, they must meet the following criteria: They must be a citizen or lawful permanent resident of the United States and be able to provide documentation proving that status.

If the sponsor is a U.S. citizen, they may petition for the following foreign national relatives to immigrate to the U.S:

Husband or wife
Unmarried child under twenty-one years of age
Unmarried son or daughter over twenty-one
Married son or daughter of any age
Brother or sister, if the sponsor is at least twenty-one years old, or
Parent, if the sponsor is at least twenty-one years old.

If the sponsor is a lawful permanent resident, they may petition for the following foreign national relatives to immigrate to the United States:

Husband or wife
Unmarried son or daughter of any age.

In any case, the sponsor must be able to provide proof of the relationship.

After the petition has been approved, if the applicant holds a conditional residency, he/she is required to undergo an interview to prove the "legitimacy" of the marriage and/or to prove the familial relationship is legitimate. Declarations or affidavits of support from employers or other family members might need to be filed as proof of legitimate relationship and/or to prove the relationship is not fraudulent.

To travel outside of the United States, the lawful permanent resident must obtain a passport from their respective consulate office and travel with their green card at all times.

Judith Flores Carmona

See Also: Citizenship; Inadmissibility; Provisional Unlawful Presence (PUP) Waiver; Sponsors; U.S. Citizenship and Immigration Services (USCIS).

Further Reading

García Hernández, Cesar Cuauhtémoc. 2011. "Due Process and Immigrant Detainee Prison Transfers: Moving LPRs to Isolated Prisons Violates Their Rights to Counsel." *Berkeley La Raza Law Journal* 21:17–60.

Rytina, Nancy, 2011. "Estimates of the Legal Permanent Resident Population in 2011." Office of Immigration Statistics, Policy Directorate, U.S. Department of Homeland Security. http://www.dhs.gov/xlibrary/assets/statistics/publications/ois_lpr_pe_2011 .pdf.

United States Citizenship and Immigration Services (USCIS): http://www.uscis.gov/ portal/site/uscis.

United States Citizenship and Immigration Services (USCIS), overview and process: http:// www.uscis.gov/portal/site/uscis/menuitem.eb1d4c2a3e5b9ac89243c6a7543f6d1a/? vgnextoid=dd346d26d17df110VgnVCM1000004718190aRCRD&vgnextchannel= dd346d26d17df110VgnVCM1000004718190aRCRD.

Wolper, Amy. 2010. "Unconstitutional and Unnecessary: A Cost/benefit Analysis of 'Crimes Involving Moral Turpitude' in the Immigration and Nationality Act." *Cardozo Law Review* 31.5:1907–1942.

Laws and Legislation, Post-1980s

Since the 1980s, United States lawmakers have implemented a number of policies that affect both documented and undocumented immigrants. Most notable are laws emerging from state governments attempting to regulate almost every facet of immigrant life, from health to employment to housing to education. Immigration scholars often refer to California's Proposition 187 in 1994, a law that would have denied welfare benefits to certain classes of legal permanent residents, as a watershed moment in the development of more punitive laws aimed at undocumented immigrants. Although this law failed, two years later (in 1996) the Illegal Immigration Reform and Immigrant Responsibility Act of 1996 (IIRIRA) was passed, which assumed greater controls over employment practices and health programs that impacted undocumented immigrants. The number of laws considered anti-immigrant in nature surged by 2005. Contained within this contemporary history is the public discourse by lawmakers to frame popular notions of immigration as a problem or security threat (Gilbert and Kolnick, 2012). This in turn has provided the impetus for hundreds of legislative responses that have mushroomed in local and state legislatures across the nation (Donnelly, 2012; O'Leary 2009). In 2006, more than 500 anti-immigrant state-level bills were introduced, a trend that peaked in 2007 when the number of bills dealing with immigrants reached 1,562 as every state in the union considered some form of immigration regulation. Many of these replicated existent federal immigration-enforcement responsibilities. These have been referred to as "policies of attrition": laws intended to encourage immigrants to return to their country of origin.

The bulk of the laws since the 1980s have addressed the perception that immigrants overburden the health care system of the United States. A number of laws have thus served to create additional barriers limiting undocumented immigrants' access to regular care providers and programs. Today it is estimated that 60 percent of the nation's approximately 11.2 million undocumented immigrants are uninsured. Lack of a regular provider and lack of insurance are associated with poor health outcomes.

Two policies that benefit the uninsured are the Emergency Medical Treatment & Labor Act (EMTALA) and the advent of Federally Qualified Health Centers (FQHCs). While neither program was designed to accommodate undocumented immigrants, both have come to serve as viable health care options for this population. EMTALA, passed by Congress in 1986, mandates that hospital emergency departments treat all patients, regardless of their ability to pay. Many Americans are familiar with this legislation and believe that a growing undocumented population is contributing substantially to uncompensated health care costs. However, current estimates project that just six percent of undocumented immigrants choose hospital emergency rooms as a regular source of care. A second source of health care for 41 percent of undocumented immigrants is FQHCs. FQHCs are a benefit that was added to Medicare in 1991 with the purpose of providing primary care services to underserved populations, including migrants. Costs for services are free or proportional to the patient's income.

Despite the health care options that are available for undocumented immigrants, 37 percent of these individuals do not have a regular health care provider. Financial limitations and lack of insurance are deterrents for seeking regular care. These factors also apply for many legally residing immigrants due to the Personal Responsibility and Work Opportunity Reconciliation Act of 1996 (PRWORA). This law bars immigrants of less than five years residence from qualifying for public benefits including Medicaid and the State Children's Health Insurance Program (SCHIP). Under the Patient Protection and Affordable Care Act, signed into law in 2010, the statutes dictated by PRWORA remain in place. Also under the health care reform law, undocumented immigrants are not eligible for public benefits.

Another barrier to seeking regular health care for undocumented immigrants is fear of deportation and unfavorable diagnosis. A large percentage of undocumented immigrants express wariness over seeking health care services for fear of deportation. Some FQHCs require documentation from patients for eligibility requirements and record-keeping purposes; however, no-reporting policies are in place to protect patients, regardless of legal status. Other FQHCs collect no data on patients' citizenship status. Many undocumented immigrants are unaware of these protective systems. Due to increased border enforcement, deportation today may result in years of separation from family members and thousands of dollars spent in attempts to return to the United States. Because financial limitations are the primary reason for entering the United States illegally, many undocumented immigrants feel that obtaining regular health care is not worth the risk of deportation.

Fear of unfavorable diagnosis is another health care deterrent for documented and undocumented immigrants. Primary prevention through regular screening is a cost-effective tool that promotes healthier communities and a healthier nation while reducing preventable death. However, preventive screening is underutilized by immigrant populations. For example, as of 2000, Mexican immigrant women were two times more likely to not have a Pap test (a procedure which detects the presence of HPV, the virus that causes cervical cancer) than non-Hispanic white women. Accordingly, data also indicated a disproportionately high incidence of cervical cancer among Latina women in comparison to non-Hispanic white women. Cervical cancer mortality among foreign-born women increased 22 percent between 1985 and 1996. Low screening rates are a direct cause of high cervical cancer mortality among immigrant women. However, the problem is not poor availability of screening; it is poor availability of treatment.

Free cervical and breast cancer screenings are widely available for financially-disadvantaged women. For example, the CDC-sponsored National Breast and Cervical Cancer Early Detection Program (NBCCEDP) was implemented in 1991 to provide breast and cervical cancer screening to low-income, uninsured, and underserved women throughout the United States. However the NBCCEDP did not ensure treatment until the introduction of the Breast and Cervical Cancer Prevention and Treatment Act of 2000. After the Act's implementation, participants with abnormal Pap Tests became eligible for treatment through Medicaid. However, undocumented immigrant women are excluded from both the NBCCEDP and its corresponding treatment act. Thus, some undocumented women claim that they would rather remain ignorant of a condition if affordable treatment for it is unavailable.

Lack of culturally competent care and discrimination are final factors that prevent two percent of documented and five percent of undocumented immigrants from seeking health care services. Prior to 1995, six states were receiving communities for 70 percent of Mexican immigrants. Since 1995, immigrant populations in non-traditional receiving communities such as North Carolina, Nevada, and Kansas have grown by more than 50 percent. The implementation of NAFTA in 1994 and ensuing border enforcement, such as the construction of the border wall, may be important contributors to the growing prevalence of non-traditional receiving communities. These locations are favorable for undocumented immigrants because Border Patrol and Immigration and Customs Enforcement are less likely to patrol them. However, these areas also tend to lack culturally-appropriate resources including bilingual or bicultural health care providers. Non-traditional communities, including health care facilities, may also exhibit stronger discrimination and racism than common receiving communities.

Courtney Waters

See Also: Arizona SB 1070; Barriers to Health; Health and Welfare; Illegal Immigration Reform and Immigrant Responsibility Act (IIRIRA) (1996); Immigration Reform and Control Act (IRCA) (1986); Refugee Act (1980).

Further Reading

Cavazos-Rehg, Patricia A. Luis H. Zayas, and Edward L. Spitznagel. 2007. "Legal Status, Emotional Well-being and Subjective Health Status of Latino Immigrants." *Journal of National Medical Association* 99:1126–1131.

Donnelly, Robert. 2012. "State-Level Immigrant-Related Legislation: What It Means for the Immigration Policy Debate." In *Antimigrant Sentiments, Actions and Policies in North America and the European Union,* edited by Mónica Veréa, 123–136. Mexico City: Centro de Investigación sobre América del Norte (CISAN) de la Universidad Autónoma de México (UNAM).

Gilbert, Liette, and Kathy A. Kolnick. 2012. "Constitutional Failure or Anti-immigrant Success? Local Anti-immigrant Ordinances and Sentiments in the United States." In

Antimigrant Sentiments, Actions and Policies in North America and the European Union, edited by Mónica Veréa, 83–102. Mexico, D.F.: Centro de Investigación sobre América del Norte (CISAN) de la Universidad Autónoma de Mexico (UNAM).

Livingston, Gretchen. "Hispanics, Health Insurance, and Health Care Access." Pew Hispanic Center Web Site. http://pewhispanic.org/files/reports/113.pdf.

O'Leary, Anna Ochoa. 2009. "Arizona's Legislative-Imposed Injunctions: Implications for Immigrant Civic and Political Participation." Mexico Institute at the Woodrow Wilson Center for Scholars Working Paper. www.wilsoncenter.org.

Schleicher, Ellen. 2007. "Immigrant Women and Cervical Cancer Prevention in the United States." Research Brief, Women and Children's Health Policy Center. http://www.jhsph .edu/wchpc/publications/.

League of United Latin American Citizens (LULAC)

The League of United Latin American Citizens, perhaps better known for its acronym, LULAC, was created in the year 1929. LULAC came about through the merger of three Texas organizations: the Order of the Sons of America, the Knights of America, and the League of Latin American Citizens. These united organizations were made up

Nat Klasfeld, 92, of Palm Beach County, Florida, addresses other demonstrators outside the Democratic National Committee headquarters calling for Florida's Democratic primary to be counted April 30, 2008 in Washington, DC. At colleges and universities the youth chapters of LULAC have addressed the challenges faced by undocumented students, and in 2010 LULAC joined MALDEF in the law suit challenging Arizona's SB 1070. (Chip Somodevilla/Getty Images)

of Hispanic American people in the United States who decided to take a stance against racial discrimination in Texas. Particularly this unification came about soon after the United States took over a third of Mexico's territory and thousands of Mexicans became U.S. citizens. These now U.S. citizens were forced to deal with a lot of prejudice, acts of discrimination and segregation in their homes; this frustration was what caused the creation of LULAC.

Since its inception, civil rights, human rights, and education have been at the heart of the organization's mission, which continues today. LULAC's mission is "To advance the economic condition, educational attainment, political influence, housing, health and civil rights of the Hispanic population of the United States." LULAC is today the largest and oldest membership-based civil rights organization in the United States. Originally created in Texas, LULAC now has a membership presence in every state of the country and in Puerto Rico with over seven hundred member councils. Member councils are groups that are made up of individual members and are separated by regions. Up until World War II, LULAC had been primarily a Texas organization, but with the return of Hispanic soldiers from the war who wanted to work towards racial equality in their home states, councils began to emerge throughout the rest of the country.

The first major accomplishment of LULAC was the desegregation of public places like barbershops, beauty salons, pools, restaurants and many others in the state of Texas. In 1946 LULAC was one of the groups working on the case of *Mendez v. Westminster,* which ended over one hundred years of segregation in California schools. This case emerged from the dissatisfaction with the schools that the Mexican children had access to, as they were unequal to those of white students, in terms of the quality of facilities and resources. In 1947, Mendez won the case, ensuring that Mexican children would be allowed to attend the same schools as their white counterparts in California. This win became a major precedent for *Brown v. Board of Education.* Also, in 1954 LULAC won the *Hernandez v. The State of Texas* case, which gave the right to Mexican Americans to serve on juries. In 1957 LULAC also led the formation of what is today the Federal "Head Start Program" for preschool-aged children in the United States. A program that started as an effort to teach preschool-aged children four hundred English words to prepare them for life in an English-speaking country, quickly turned into a federal funded program that reaches every state in the United States.

LULAC members establish councils throughout the country and work in the various programs that LULAC works towards. In 2013, there were over 900 of such councils. Various areas are identified by LULAC as organizational priorities: civic participation, civil rights, economic empowerment, education, health, housing, immigration, public service and technology. LULAC holds various events throughout the year in order to fulfill the above-mentioned organizational priorities, and as a way to gather many of their national members together. The national convention and exposition is a several-day event where members get to participate in various educational seminars, outreach opportunities, career and college fairs as well as several youth-geared initiatives. LULAC also hosts other events such as a legislative gala where they highlight critical legislative issues affecting Hispanic Americans and recognize key leaders who have served the Hispanic community well throughout the year. Additional events include a women's conference, a veterans' summit, a federal training institute and LULAC week.

It should be noted that while LULAC advocates for the rights of minority groups in the United States, the organization itself has historically subscribed to an assimilationist approach, believing that this is the best strategy to combating discrimination. LULAC has also taken a very conservative stance by promoting capitalism and individualism, assuming that if prejudice can be done away with, nothing else in society needs changing. LULAC's promotion of assimilation enforced the idea that Mexican Americans needed to do away with any allegiance to Mexico, stay permanently in the United States, and demonstrate patriotism. These ideals are supported by the organization's official prayer, the "George Washington prayer," and by the league's official song, which is "America the Beautiful." While this organization fights for the rights of immigrants and many disempowered groups in this country who continue to face many of the issues that led to the establishment of the organization in the first place, for many years the organization was sharply criticized for restricting its membership to U.S. citizens only. However, more recently it has come out as vocal advocates of immigrants. For example, in September of 2013, the organization came out in praise of California's Governor Jerry Brown for agreeing to sign into law a bill that would grant undocumented people the right to obtain a driver's license.

Carolina Luque

See Also: Advocacy; Assimilation; Mexican American Legal Defense and Education Fund (MALDEF); National Council of La Raza (NCLR).

Further Reading

League of United Latin American Citizens (LULAC) Website. 2013. http://lulac.org/.
Marquez, Benjamin. 1993. *Lulac: The Evolution of a Mexican American Political Organization.* Austin: University of Texas Press.
Orozco, Cynthia. 2009. *No Mexicans, Women, or Dogs Allowed: The Rise of the Mexican American Civil Rights Movement.* Austin: University of Texas Press, 2009.

Legal Representation

There are many reasons undocumented immigrants may require legal representation. These include needed changes in immigration status (adjustment), legal advice, and relief from wage theft, exploitation, and other criminal violations. There are lawyers and legal aides who provide legal representation at no cost. However, when faced with the likelihood of having to pay for attorney services, many undocumented immigrants, many of whom are underemployed or poorly paid, cannot afford an attorney's legal fees. When this happens, they are essentially denied access to a legal representation.

Legal representation is defined as the legal work that a licensed attorney practices on the behalf of a client. Each lawyer has a designated fee assigned for a range of services. The fees are calculated based on the nature of the case, and its difficulty. Most lawyers charge by the hour, or by flat fee, or retainer, which is a set amount of money, paid up front to retain attorney's services. Lawyers vary in specialties, each with specific knowledge in an area of law. Clients are obligated to provide the lawyer with all true and accurate up-to-date information that affects the case. An attorney may choose to discontinue legal representation if the client lies, asks the attorney to perform unethical or illegal acts or there is a conflict of interest. If an attorney withdraws from a case, they are obligated to protect the best interest of the client such as helping to locate another attorney, reschedule court dates and disclosing papers and documents that are relevant to the case.

Undocumented immigrants may benefit from having legal representation when applying for an adjustment of status, applying for a green card, obtaining a work visa or becoming a naturalized citizen. Though one does not have to obtain an immigration lawyer to handle such cases, when complicated matters of the law arise, it is usually best to have legal representation.

Immigration law can be very challenging to navigate. This difficulty is aggravated if there are language barriers. Having an attorney to help explain legal proceedings and policies can help ease some clients' anxiety of dealing with officials, law enforcement, judges or other professional in matters of immigration law.

Legal representation is often necessary for detainees who have been apprehended by Immigration and Customs Enforcement; however, many undocumented immigrants detained are dissuaded from seeking legal representation. In a national study of detention facilities, the Chicago-based National Immigrant Justice Center found that over half of the immigrant detainees were not offered information regarding their rights and 78 percent were denied private phone calls with their lawyers. Ten percent of detainees were held in facilities that did not offer any kind of legal aid assistance.

Undocumented immigrants facing deportation procedures are not always guaranteed legal services or legal representation. However, there are numerous nonprofit groups, paralegal professionals and attorneys that provide their services at low or no cost for undocumented immigrants. One must use caution when hiring an attorney as research suggests that unethical practices may cause irreversible harm to those seeking immigration benefits or relief if conducted by persons posing as immigration attorneys or "*notarios*," persons not licensed to legally represent a client. The term "*notario*" may confuse immigrants coming from Latin America because in their home country, a similar term refers to persons that are licensed to perform legal services. In the United States, this term is roughly translated as a "notary public," a type of legal authority with limited powers and more commonly associated with witnessing and certifying signatures in matters concerning important documents such as transfers of property, oaths and other affirmations. However, these are not attorneys licensed to practice legal matters. The terms are similar and those looking to falsely represent themselves have been known to take advantage of those who might be confused but hopeful of bringing remedy to their legal problem. Agencies such as the Executive Office of Immigration Review (EOIR), the U.S. Citizenship and Immigration Services (USCIS), the U.S. Department of Justice (DOJ) and the U.S. Department of Homeland Security (DHS) have taken action to address problems posed by the unethical conduct of such notaries.

Operation Streamline provides an example of how criminal prosecution of migrants can place significant strain on legal representation, judges and court resources. Operation Streamline is a program that was enacted in 2005 by the Department of Homeland Security and requires the criminal prosecution of all undocumented border crossers regardless of previous legal history. Magistrate judges are forced to conduct en masse hearings, as many as seventy migrants at a time, in order to process all cases. These large group hearings deprive migrants from obtaining due process of law and do not allow them significant time with an attorney. Due to the en masse hearings, lawyers spend between thirty and sixty minutes explaining legal proceedings, court procedures and the client's case. There is very little time for an attorney to provide quality legal representation in such a small amount of time. Additionally, the high volume of immigration cases generates concerns about morale and burnout among public defenders as the bulk of their cases come from Operation Streamline. The repetitive nature and high volume of cases lead to high turnover rates and make it difficult to recruit new defense attorneys.

Limited access to legal representation drastically increases one's chances of being deported, yet many immigrants who have been detained lack real legal representation. Immigrants with legal representation are five times more likely to win their case than those without. However, unprepared and overworked lawyers may cause more harm than good to a client's case. In New York, a Justice Department Project known as the Legal Orientation Program recently opened and is designed to advise immigrants on their legal rights by lawyers who work pro bono, meaning at no cost. It is also important to note that with increased political will to diminish the rights of immigrants to receive advice from attorneys, the responsibilities of attorneys to represent their clients have also been increasingly challenged. A case in point is the proceedings adopted by programs such as Operation Streamline in various cities along the U.S.-Mexico border, designed to process as many defendants as quickly as possible so they can be immediately deported. The flood of new cases that resulted with the implementation of this program forced federal judges and magistrates to take pleas *en mases* from groups of as many as seventy individuals at once. However, a federal appeals court in the *U.S. v. Arqueta-Ramos* (2013) rejected this procedure. Although it continues today, were it not for the persistence and ethical commitment of attorneys who saw the procedure as an affront to their ability to represent their clients (*U.S. v. Roblero-Solis; U.S. v. Escamilla-Rojas)*, the undermining of immigrants' rights to representation would have gone unchecked.

There is also an increasing need for legal representation in areas of exploitation in the work environment. Criminals and unscrupulous employers use the threat of deportation to withhold wages, force labor, and demand overtime. Undocumented immigrants may be particularly vulnerable to such violations of U.S. labor laws, as they may fear having their immigration status exposed. Employers that are aware of such situations may use it for leverage in order to obtain free or cheap labor from migrants. This system of intimidation and manipulation is known as the deportation threat dynamic (Fussell, 2011). There are four steps in the deportation threat dynamic which include (1) an undocumented migrant locates employment, (2) the employer or criminal presumes that the worker is undocumented, (3) the person takes advantage of the migrant worker either by wage theft or other workplace violations; (4) the migrant does not report crime to law enforcement for fear of being detected (Fussell, 2011). In situations such as these the abuses can take place in a day or over a lengthy period of time. In some instances, migrants have worked months with the promise of a paycheck only to realize that the employer had no intention of paying them. There are legal avenues one can take to recover wages for completed work, though many undocumented workers may not realize what they are nor have knowledge of their legal rights.

In Santa Fe, New Mexico, HB 489, sponsored by Rep. Miguel Garcia, makes it illegal for employers to discriminate against workers who are asking for their wages and extends the statute of limitation, or the length of time one has to pursue a case, for wage claims. Additionally, HB 489 penalizes employers who take advantage of migrant workers and withhold wages. Employers are required to post a notice of wage violations in the work place. Agencies such as Somos Un Pueblo Unido, also located in Santa Fe, New Mexico, provide advocacy and information about civil and workers' rights and a connection to legal representation for workers in New Mexico.

Courtney Martínez

See Also: Asylum; *Fernandez-Vargas v. Gonzales*; *Flores-Figueroa v. United States*; Legal Status; Naturalization; Operation Streamline; *United States v. Roblero-Solis;* Workers' Rights; Workplace Injury.

Future Reading

Dolnick, S. 2011. "Improving Immigrant Access to Lawyers." *New York Times,* May 4.

Fussell, Elizabeth. 2011. "The Deportation Threat Dynamic and Victimization of Latino Migrants: Wage Theft and Robbery." *The Sociological Quarterly* 52:593–615.

HB489 Wage Theft and Somos Un Pueblo Unido website: http://www.somosunpueblounido .org/Documents/HB489English_000.pdf.

Lee, M. M. 2009. "Legal Ethics in Immigration Matters: Legal Representation and Unauthorized Practice of Law." *Congressional Research Service,* 1–14.

Lydgate, J. 2010. "Assembly-Line Justice: A Review of Operation Streamline." The Chief Justice Earl Warren Institute on Race, Ethnicity & Diversity Policy Brief, 1–16.

Legal Status

Legal status is indicated by governmental authorization through some form of documentation that one either possesses or does not possess in order to live and work in a country other than that of one's birth. In the case of the United States, being born in the country provides automatic legal status in the form of birthright citizenship. However, birth is not the only means to legal status in the United States. There also exist forms of temporary authorization granted by visas and other forms of permission to visit the United States as a nonimmigrant. For immigrants, legal permanent residency is a common form of legal status, as well as naturalization, which is citizenship granted to a person who was not a citizen of the country at his or her time of birth.

Legal permanent residency is a form of legal status that grants a person the right to live and work in the United States; while legal permanent residents of the United States are eligible to apply for naturalization after five years of continuous residency in the States, residents may choose, if they prefer, not to become citizens. While legal permanent residents maintain the passport of their home country, they are able to travel abroad and return to the United States by showing their permanent resident card, otherwise known as a green card. There are various ways that one can obtain legal permanent resident status in the United States. It is most commonly gained through a family sponsor or employer sponsor. First, a sponsor (qualifying family member or otherwise) files the petition, and if the sponsor is eligible to apply on behalf of the applicant, he or she moves to the second part of the process, which is called either "adjustment of status" or "visa processing." Adjustment of status is done from within the United States, whereas visa processing is done either from within the United States or from the applicant's home country, at a U.S. consulate. Not all applicants are eligible to become permanent residents, and this is the reason for the adjustment of status process: to determine eligibility. Also, during this time, it is decided whether the applicant is eligible to obtain permanent residency immediately, according to immigration category, or if the applicant will have to wait for a period of time in order to obtain residency.

U.S. citizens may file for their husband or wife, unmarried child under the age of twenty-one, unmarried son or daughter over the age of twenty-one, married son or daughter of any age, brother or sister, or mother or father, to obtain permanent resident status. Permanent residents may file for their husband or wife, unmarried child under the age of twenty-one, or unmarried son or daughter age twenty-one or older. There is a list, however, of relatives who cannot be sponsored for residency. There are other family categories that require special treatment and are not nearly as frequent as the cases previously mentioned. Some examples of these are certain Amerasians, widows and widowers, and battered or abused spouses or children of U.S. citizens or permanent residents.

As previously mentioned, it is possible to obtain legal permanent resident status through employment. In this case, it is the employer who serves as the sponsor instead of the family member. There are several "preference" categories for immigration through employment, assigned importance by United States Citizenship and Immigration Services (USCIS). These include in order: priority workers; advanced degree professionals; skilled, professional, and unskilled workers; special immigrants or religious workers; and foreign investors. Each preference category carries with it its own eligibility requirements and steps that employers must be able to follow in order to sponsor an immigrant.

While it is important to be aware of the paths toward legal status, the concept implies much more than authorization to live and work in a country. It carries with it social and political implications. When a visitor to the United States is without legal status, he or she is most commonly referred to as an "illegal." Other terminology popularly used includes "alien," often used in conjunction with "illegal," which, while considered standard usage in government language to refer to all those born outside of the United States, is only indicative of the otherness of the individual in question. It inspires the image of a nonperson, a stranger, somebody excluded and incapable of being accepted by American society. The term "illegal" creates a binary between those with legal status and those without, but when used to refer to a person, the "illegal" act is equated with the person's identity. In actuality, it is the action of entry without inspection (EWI) that is illegal, or the working without documentation that is illegal; it is not the person that is illegal. The use of "illegal" to refer to persons can be used to identify one's political position on immigration. Those opposed to immigration and nativists predominantly prefer to use the incorrect and more acrimonious use of "illegal" to refer to immigrants. In contrast, those more sympathetic to the plight of immigrants usually prefer to use "undocumented" or "unauthorized" in referring to those who are out of status.

For those without legal status in the United States, it is often quite difficult to obtain valid forms of identification, and therefore one's access to services such as health care, education, housing, among others, is limited. This becomes more complicated as, in the states where anti-immigrant legislation has led to policies of racial profiling such as in the case of Arizona's SB 1070, all people are expected to carry documentation with them at all times to "prove" their status. This applies whether somebody is driving an automobile or whether somebody is shopping in a grocery store, although, according to the law, and upheld by the Supreme Court, the checking of documentation must be done only by law enforcement officers and only when a person under investigation may be breaking some other law. Still, some legal stops can be made for such minor infractions as jaywalking, driving with a broken tail light, and other lesser offenses. Also, it is important to note that regardless of status both undocumented and legal permanent residents can be deported. Those without legal status are limited in political rights in the face of this threat of deportation. Those with legal permanent status are subject to a different legal procedure that provides them more rights to determine if they are to lose their status and be subject to removal from the United States.

The question of how legal status is determined evolves when immigration policy is revised. Currently, this is one of the main discussions in the debate over comprehensive immigration reform. For example, the immigration reform bill offered by the U.S. Senate in June of 2013 proposed to create a new legal status category, Registered Provisional Immigrant, for undocumented immigrants who want to initiate the process of legalization.

Leisha Reynolds-Ramos

See Also: Employment Visas; U.S. Citizenship and Immigration Services (USCIS); "Undocumented" Label; Work Visas.

Further Reading

Anderson, Stuart. 2010. *Immigration.* Santa Barbara, CA: Greenwood.

Bacon, David. 2008. *Illegal People: How Globalization Creates Migration and Criminalizes Migrants.* Boston, MA: Beacon Press.

Johnson, Kevin R. 1996/1997. "'Aliens' and the U.S. Immigration Laws: The Social and Legal Construction of Nonpersons." *The University of Miami Inter-American Law Review* 28.2:263–292.

LeMay, Michael C. 2007. *Illegal Immigration: A Reference Handbook.* Santa Barbara, CA: ABC CLIO.

Lewis, Loida N., Len T. Madlansacay, and Barbara K. Repa. 1999. *How to Get a Green Card: Legal Ways to Stay in the U.S.A.* Berkeley, CA: Nolo.com.

Vasic, Ivan. 2009. *The Immigration Handbook: A Practical Guide to United States Visas, Permanent Residency and Citizenship.* Jefferson, NC: McFarland & Company, Inc, Publishers.

LGBT Immigrants without Documentation

In addition to the common challenges that most undocumented immigrants confront, those who are LGBT (lesbian, gay, bisexual and transgender) face unique stressors that make their immigration experience a more complex one. Among those stressors may be a history of persecution in their homelands and the trauma that may result from this, the lack of legal equality, the need to redefine their sexual identity, and experiences of discrimination and marginalization.

One factor specific to this group is the criminalization of homosexual orientation in immigrants' homelands. Approximately eighty countries around the world continue to criminalize homosexual individuals, including some who impose the death penalty as a punishment for same-sex sexual activity or identity. Among the countries that explicitly criminalize same-sex relationships are Algeria, Belize, Egypt, Jamaica, Malaysia, Pakistan, Singapore, and Uganda, to mention only a few. As a result these countries hold a very negative view of homosexuals and stigmatize this population. However, governments are not the only institutions responsible for the public antipathy and stigma against people who are LGBT. Particular religious institutions have propagated and popularized anti-homosexual messages around the world. For example, the Catholic Church contributed to the fact that many Latin American societies have popular opinions that describe homosexuality as sinful and wrong.

Andre Azevedo poses in New York, 2009. Azevedo, 39, is a transgender man from Brazil who recently won asylum and now lives in New York. In 2011, the "Morton memo" offered binational same-sex couples a level of protection from separation when a partner is undocumented by qualifying same-sex relationships as a "family relationship." (AP Photo/ Mary Altaffer)

As institutional discrimination directly contributes to societal stigma, it is not surprising that there is higher incidence of harassment and violence towards people who are LGBT in those societies where negative messages about homosexuality are endorsed by the majority of the population.

Around the world, people who happen to be lesbians, gay, bisexual or transgender are often victims of disappearance, torture, beatings, rape, threats, unfair arrest and detention, extortion, compulsory psychiatric treatment and numerous other forms of persecution. Facing these possibilities, these individuals may feel the need to conceal their sexual orientation. However, even then they remain at risk of being harassed or harmed for being who they are. They significantly limit their lives and avoid engaging in activities that could identify them as lesbians or gays. For example, congregating with other LGBT people may put these individuals at a high risk of being identified as such. Growing up and living in constant danger can lead to a psychological injury with long-lasting effects, what we also know as psychological trauma.

People who are LGBT who are persecuted or have a well-founded fear of persecution may apply for asylum in the United States under the Immigration and Nationality Act (INA) based on their membership in a particular social group, in this case, sexual orientation. However, the burden is on the applicants to prove their membership in the group and that they experienced past persecution or have a well-founded fear of future persecution. As discussed before, disclosing sexual orientation is not an easy task for LGBT individuals, especially when their lives are in danger. In addition, providing objective evidence of persecution is not an easy task, and at times requires pointing at specific individuals. Notwithstanding these limitations, such development in the U.S. immigration law demonstrates progress in the recognition of human rights of people who are LGBT.

Despite this progress, U.S. immigration policies have historically denied homosexuals the rights that their heterosexual counterparts have. Since 1952, U.S. immigration policy had explicitly prohibited the admission of homosexuals into the United States. Historically, a heterosexual U.S. citizen or permanent resident has been able to sponsor the residency of their undocumented opposite sex partner through marriage. However, until 2013, this right did not apply to same-sex partners, even if these individuals had been married in places where same-sex marriage is legal, such as Mexico City. In part this was due to the 1996 Defense of Marriage Act (DOMA), which stated that federal laws would only recognize marriage when it was between a man and a woman. Until recently, if a lesbian or gay couple applied for residency, it was very likely that this would result in deportation of the undocumented partner. According to the 2000 Census, there were at least thirty-five thousand same-sex bi-national couples in the U.S. Due to this law, such couples faced uncertainty about their future, emotional distress, and economic challenges.

The Uniting American Families Act, sponsored in the Senate by Patrick Leahy (D-VT) and in the House of Representatives by Jerrold Nadler (D-NY), was developed in an effort to advocate for human rights. This bill proposes to amend the INA in order to allow U.S. citizens and permanent residents to sponsor their same-sex partners in the same manner that their heterosexual counterparts can do that. This bill was introduced to the Senate in 2013, where it failed to gain ground.

However, 2012–2013 might be considered a watershed period for the rights of LGBT communities. First, in June 2011, the "Morton memo" was issued by ICE clarifying "family relationships" to include same-sex relationships for qualifying as a family relationship for purposes of prosecutorial discretion in matters of deportation. Hailed as a victory for LGBT communities, this memo made it clear that a legal marriage was not necessary for the relationship to be considered, allowing binational gay couples in the United States that would have been separated with deportation to stay intact.

Subsequently, in the summer of 2013, the U.S. Supreme Court handed down a decision holding Section 3 of the Defense of Marriage Act (DOMA) as unconstitutional. Consequently, Democratic President Obama directed federal departments to ensure the decision and its implication for federal benefits for same-sex legally married couples were implemented.

The impact of these changes in immigration enforcement policy cannot be overestimated. All immigrants face a sense of loss, as they leave people, places, and things behind. Furthermore, the lack of legal endorsement and living under the constant threat of deportation make this experience even more stressful. Undocumented individuals may live day by day in uncertainty and fear, without much control over their future. In addition, immigrants go through acculturation, the process of adapting to a new culture, which can be stressful and challenging. For example, immigrants often struggle to acquire a new language and navigate through new rules and customs.

In addition to the challenges mentioned above, LGBT immigrants face the challenge of simultaneously going through a process of acculturation and sexual identity formation. While they adapt to a new culture and shape their identity as new immigrants, they also are figuring out their identity as LGBT individuals living in a different context. At times immigrating to the United States may be seen as an opportunity to be more open about one's sexual orientation. However, some LGBT immigrants continue to conceal their sexual orientation after immigration for various reasons, including avoiding rejection and internalized stigma. Many LGBT immigrants lead a double life and conceal their sexual identity in their family and work environment, which can become an extreme burden and may prevent them from seeking and receiving much needed emotional support.

Finally, people who are LGBT who immigrate to the United States face multiple forms of discrimination. These individuals often face discrimination by the general society, their own ethnic/racial community, and the homosexual community. Discrimination can take the form of invisibility, marginalization, physical and verbal violence, insults, and other mistreatment, which have a great impact on a person's physical and mental health. Service providers and community agencies dedicated to serve the homosexual community can be a positive source of support and guidance.

Hector L. Torres

See Also: Civil Rights; Exclusion; Hate Crimes; HIV/AIDS; Mental Health Care Access; Mental Health Issues for Immigrants; Sponsors.

Further Reading

Ayoub, L., and S. M. Wong. 2006. *Separated and Unequal.* National Center for Lesbian Rights. http://www.nclrights.org/site/DocServer/immigration_separated_and_unequal.pdf?docID=1141.

Bianchi, F. T., C. A. Reisen, M. C. Zea, P. J. Poppen, M. G. Shedlin, and M. M. Penha. 2007. "The Sexual Experience of Latino Men Who Have Sex with Men Who Migrated to a Gay Epicenter in the USA." *Culture, Health, & Sexuality* 9:505–518.

Ibañez, G. E., B. Van Oss Marin, S. A. Flores, G. Millett, and R. Diaz. 2009. "General Gay-Related Racism Experienced by Latino Gay Men." *Cultural Diversity and Ethnic Minority Psychology* 15.3:215–222.

Midwest Human Rights Partnership for Sexual Orientation and the Lesbian and Gay Immigration Rights Task Force. 2000. *Preparing Sexual Orientation-Based Asylum Claims: A Handbook for Advocates and Asylum Seekers.* http://www.asylumlaw.org/docs/sexualminorities/handbookpart1.pdf.

Perez-Ramirez, L. A. 2002. "Immigration and Trauma: A Study with Latino Gay Men Asylum Seekers." Psy.D. dissertation, Wright Institute.

Limited English Proficiency (LEP)

Widespread consensus is that the United States is a nation of immigrants. Immigrants are credited for major American transformations such as the building of the nation's railroad systems, business enterprises, and tilling the land. For example, in 1868 Chinese and Irish immigrants were employed by the Central Pacific Railroad Company. European, Mexican, and Japanese immigrants were incorporated into this labor force, many of who came to the United States between 1880 and 1900. From this history, a fundamental American attitude has emerged around how it is that one nation has been created out of individuals from many places (Takaki, 1987). In this regard, the politics of language and language use continues to dictate state and national policies, and these in turn guide the educational policies that affect new generations of immigrant children in the areas of English language acquisition and equal opportunities. Many Supreme Court cases have addressed the education of the immigrant children or the children of immigrant families. Among these are *Lau v. Nichols* (1974) addressing bilingual education, *Plyler v. Doe* (1982) addressing the inclusion of undocumented children in public elementary schools, and *Guey Heung Lee v. Johnson* (1971), addressing segregation. In the same way, limited English proficiency has been a policy area that concerns the educational opportunities of immigrant children.

Just as diminished access to education is due to limited English proficiency, so is limited English proficiency a cause of poor health because a barrier to good health care is posed by an immigrant's inability to use health care services in their native language. Health care is important to a society for many reasons, among which is that good health care keeps the costs of insurance down. Older Latino and Asian immigrants with limited English report poorer self-rated health and higher levels of physiological distress. These immigrants experienced challenges meeting with doctors and understanding any written medical information. These immigrant groups are at risk for mental health problems. One study found that Latinos with fair or poor English-speaking abilities reported 22 percent fewer physicians' visits than Latinos whose native language was English. In this study there was a link between limited English proficiency and those with poor health, no health insurance, or no regular source of care. Historical context is important for understanding each Latino subgroup's access to health care, much of which has to do with how each group enters and accesses the health care system (Aguirre-Molina, Molina, and Zambrana, 2001). Health care providers that receive federal funds are required to have medical services translated to their patients in their native language. Medical providers ideally should also be sensitive to both the cultural and linguist components of those in their care.

Historically, states within the United States have demonstrated an unwillingness to provide equal and adequate instruction for English Language Learners (ELLs) that would improve the instruction of limited English proficiency students. Arizona has a long history of being an "English only" state since 1910 when the politicians of then Arizona–New Mexico territory resisted entering the union of U.S. states. At that time, the New Mexico part of the territory was predominantly Spanish-speaking. In fact, Article XIV, Section 10 of New Mexico's state constitution regarding the educational rights of children of Spanish descent explicitly states that: "Children of Spanish descent in the state of New Mexico shall never be denied the right and privilege of admission and attendance in the public schools or other public educational institutions of the state, and they shall never be classed in separate schools and educational institutions of the state, and the legislature shall provide penalties for the violations of this section."

In contrast, in other states there has been marked resistance to providing non-English speakers opportunities equal to those available to English proficient residents. Such opposition has sparked numerous legislative initiatives and countering legal actions over the use of English and its learning. In some cases, high court decisions from these lawsuits have forced the hand of legislators to change state and national policies of today.

For example, one policy that relates to Limited English Proficiency programs is Arizona Proposition 203. Proposition 203 placed restrictions on bilingual education and English as a second language programs and proposed that English only is the language that should be taught. In the state of Arizona all K-12 instruction needs to be conducted in English. In November of 2000 the Arizona voters approved Proposition 203. This legislation replaced bilingual education laws and introduced a new law requiring that classes be instructed in the English language. Teachers in the state of Arizona often need to remind their students to speak English only. Speaking English when an immigrant has limited English proficiency is challenging for both the students and the parents. In the state of Arizona teachers are required to incorporate ELL standards in their lesson plans and their curriculum writing. Teachers in Arizona must write and post their English objectives for their students.

In Arizona, the total number of students classified as English Language Learners in 2004 was 160,666. The majority of these pupils were born outside the United States. According to the Arizona Department of Education (ADE) in 2004, Arizona's public education costs of English language learners totaled $544,109,802 (Gans 2012).

A notable legal case emerged in 1992 when student Miriam Flores sued the Nogales Unified School District for failing to provide her and other English language learners with adequate academic instruction. Flores argued that "appropriate actions" needed to provide educational opportunities for English language learners included funds needed to overcome language barriers for the instruction of English language learners (ELL) in the Nogales Unified School, and to comply with the mandates of the Equal Educational Opportunity Act of 1974. This Act requires school districts in the nation to take action to overcome barriers to students' equal participation in learning. The Flores case moved through the court system for over ten years because the state of Arizona refused to explain how the limited amount of English Language Learner funding related to the amount of services being offered to students. A district court found in favor of Flores, finding that funding provided by the state was inadequate and not based on the actual cost of ELL instruction. However, this decision was appealed by Arizona to the United States Supreme Court in 2009 *(Horne V. Flores),* where the court reversed portions of the previous decision while upholding others. However, in part influenced by the amicus curiae brief prepared by educational policy and finance scholars, the case was remanded back to the lower U.S. district court for further hearings to determine whether the state provided enough education funding to satisfy the mandates under the Equal Educational Opportunity Act (Gándara, 2012). Subsequently, on March 29, 2013, U.S. District Court Judge Raner C. Collins ruled that the state has improved its teaching of ELL students and no longer violated the federal Act requiring states to overcome barriers in schools. As of the writing of this entry (on April 24, 2013), lawyers for Flores had filed a notice that they are appealing the Collins ruling to the U.S. 9th Circuit Court of Appeals.

Senate Bill 1167 (English as the Official Language) was proposed by Arizona legislators in 2005. Although vetoed by then governor Janet Napolitano on May 9, 2005, it passed in 2006. Like its 1988 predecessor, Arizona's "English Only" law, the current law requires all official actions to be conducted in English. However, government representatives can communicate unofficially in another language, as long as the official action is in English. Public safety and emergency medical personnel are excluded from this requirement. The law now also provides residents or businesses protection from civil action arising from any injury that is caused as a result of not being able to comply with the law.

Also in Arizona, Senate Concurrent Resolution 1031, commonly called Proposition 300, affected adult education programs and immigrant students' access to institutions of higher learning beginning in 2007. The adult education provisions restricted eligibility for state-funded services offered by the Arizona Department of Education (ADE) Division of Adult Education. Adult education programs were targeted because of a perception that Spanish-speaking undocumented immigrants were the bulk of the students taking these English classes (O'Leary, 2009). The law now requires state-funded programs in school districts and other institutions and agencies to provide adult education services only to U.S. citizens, legal residents, or people otherwise lawfully present in this country.

According to the United States Department of Education in 2011, the *No Child Left Behind Act* enacted by the administration of President George W. Bush states that school districts have two sets of responsibilities for students with limited English proficiency. States are responsible for ensuring that these students make progress in learning English under Title III of the Act, and that they become proficient in language arts and mathematics under Title I. This impacts undocumented immigrant families because many of their children attend school in the United States. When children enter school they are given a test to assess their English language ability. In the state of Arizona this assessment is called the AZELLA, or the Arizona English Language Learner Assessment. Once a student is identified as an English Language Learner or qualifies for an English Language Development program (ELD), the parents receive notification and a consent form for placement in an ELL program. There is criticism of the assessment. One criticism is that it is not developmentally appropriate for a five-year-old who is entering school. Another criticism is that the assessment is biased against Latino and African American students. A third criticism is that children are labeled as Limited English Proficiency (LEP), English Language Learner (ELL) or English as a Second Language (ESL) student at a young age. The high school's ESL labels include pre-emergent, emergent, basic, intermediate, and proficient. The parent is given a home survey that includes questions about the child's first language and the primary language that is spoken in the home.

The theories that undergird ESL and ELL issues can also be applied to adult education. This impacts adult immigrants as well. In 2009 students from George Mason University in Fairfax, Virginia, launched an ESL bilingual project within a Latino American immigrant community whose members worked as day laborers in construction, service, or domestic work in Northern Virginia. Most of the immigrant ESL students had only obtained a grade school education in their home countries. This was a social learning project. Many labor workers want to learn basic English so that they would be better able to find employment and use basic transportation and find housing (Rabin, Leeman, and Roman-Mendoza, 2011). The project also taught them how to address discrimination and negotiate wages in English.

In order for undocumented immigrants to survive in the United States they need to be able to understand the English language. There is a bilingual advantage based on the geographical location of the immigrants. There are bilingual English and Spanish resources in areas of the United States with large amounts of Latino populations. Mexican and Latino subgroups have an advantage in bordering states to Mexico and in proximity to Cuba and Puerto Rico, such as Arizona, California, Texas, New Mexico, and Florida. Translation is a challenge for undocumented immigrants and U.S. citizens or residents who are not bilingual. Communication is needed between U.S. citizens and migrants in work, housing, healthcare or being a consumer. One benefit of being an undocumented immigrant in the Southwest is that many people are bilingual. Many services are advertised in both English and Spanish. While a benefit to Latino undocumented immigrants it is a disadvantage for an undocumented immigrant from non Spanish-speaking countries.

A language such as English can be very difficult to learn to speak, read, and write, because the words in the English language are made up of many dialects or derivates including Latin, Greek, Anglo Saxon, Old English, and German. ESL classes may be offered throughout the community free of charge in places such as county and city public libraries and community colleges. School districts and public schools may also offer free English classes to parents.

Drew Berns

See Also: Adult Education; Bilingualism; Elementary Schools; English as a Second Language (ESL) Programs; English Language Learners (ELL); English-Only Movement; *Plyler v. Doe.*

Further Reading

Aguirre-Molina, M., C. Molina, and R. Zambrana. 2001. *Health Issues in the Latino Community.* San Franscisco, CA: Jossey-Bass Inc.

Arizona Department of Education. 2012. Arizona English Language Learners Task Force. Available at: http://www.ade.az.gov/ELLTaskForce.

Arizona Secretary of State. 2000. "Proposition 203 Ballot Proposition." Available at: http://www.azsos.gov/election/2000/info/PubPamphlet/english/prop203.htm.

Gándara, Patricia. 2012. "From Gonzales to Flores: A Return to the 'Mexican Room'?" In *Arizona's Firestorm: Global Immigration Realities, National Media & Provincial Politics,* ed. Otto Santa Ana & Celeste González de Bustamante, 121–143. Lanham, MD: Rowman and Littlefield.

Gans, Judith. 2012. "The Economic Impact of Immigrants in Arizona." In *Arizona's Firestorm: Global Immigration Realities, National Media & Provincial Politics,* ed. Otto Santa Ana & Celeste González de Bustamante, 47–72. Lanham, MD: Rowman and Littlefield.

Office of Civil Rights. 2011. Retrieved from U.S. Department of Education, ED.gov. http://www.ed.gov/.

O'Leary, Anna Ochoa. 2009. "Arizona's Legislative-Imposed Injunctions: Implications for Immigrant Civic and Political Participation." Mexico Institute at the Woodrow Wilson Center for Scholars Working Paper. http://www.wilsoncenter.org/publication/arizona%E2%80%99s-legislative-imposed-injunctions-implications-for-immigrant-civic-and-political.

Rabin, L., J. Leeman, and E. Roman-Mendoza. 2011. "Identity and Activism in Heritage Language Education." *The Modern Language Journal* 95. 4.

Takaki, Ronald, ed. 1987. *From Different Shores: Perspectives on Race and Ethnicity in America.* New York: Oxford University Press.

Literature and Poetry

The connection between literature and poetry and immigration has a long history in the United States. Since people have been migrating to the United States, they have also been writing about the experience. Letters, journals, reports, and essays written by Spanish conquistadors, English colonists, French explorers, and Dutch settlers are among those writings that may be considered examples of migrant literature. In their writings they not only scientifically reported in detail what they saw, but they also documented personal accounts of their journeys, including impressions and imaginations of the people, animals, and landscapes they encountered. Although we may not

Alambrista

Literally meaning "wire crosser," *alambrista* is a term used in popular and Latino culture for someone who has crossed or attempted to cross the U.S.-Mexico border by jumping or cutting the wire fence, especially along the California-Mexico border. *Alambrista!* is also the title of a 1977 film written and directed by Robert Young, which follows the fictional journey of an undocumented immigrant from Mexico who crosses into the United States via California. This term has gained importance in Latino culture as the number of undocumented immigrants to the United States increased dramatically during the late twentieth century.

Alambrista is similar to the term *mojado* or "wetback," the latter a pejorative word used for an undocumented immigrant who attempts to enter into Texas by crossing the Rio Grande and thus getting "wet." *Mojado* has come to mean any undocumented worker. *Alambrista,* on the other hand, is used specifically for those who travel across the land border. During the 1960s through the mid-to-late 1980s, many of these *alambristas* made the risky journey to the United States to find agricultural employment, mainly in California.

In the 2006 film *Babel,* another portrayal of the *alambrista* is presented in the character of Amelia, an undocumented Mexican immigrant who is a nanny for the children of a San Diego, California, couple.

The undocumented border crosser is an increasingly visible character in folk tales. The hazardous act of actually crossing the border has come to define the journey of the *alambrista,* with stories of undocumented border crossers often portraying those who successfully cross in a heroic fashion. Also, many stories and tales explain that those *alambristas* who manage to cross safely into the United States are aided by a divine force, normally the Virgin of Guadalupe. Such stories mix traditional characteristics of Latino folk tales (heroic struggles with supernatural forces) with the contemporary problems faced by *alambristas* and debates concerning undocumented immigration in the United States.

Stephanie Reichelderfer

traditionally think of these writers as immigrants, they were indeed moving across continents and oceans, migrating from one space to another. Many of these writings, by individuals such as Spanish conquistadors Hernan Cortes, Francisco Pizarro and Juan de Oñate and English colonists such as John Smith and Samuel Adams are studied today in order to better understand the social, political, religious, and personal factors that motivated people to migrate. Their writings—usually targeted to specific audiences such as kings and queens, business associates, and families—took their stories and reports across the seas, where they influenced laws, attitudes, and actions that helped determine the course of migration to the Western hemisphere.

In 1903, a poem entitled "The New Colossus" written by American national Emma Lazarus (1849–1887) was engraved on a plaque and mounted on the Statue of Liberty at Ellis Island, New York. Originally written in 1883 and auctioned at a fundraiser for the erection of the statue, the poem seemed to foretell the future of the Statue of Liberty as a symbol for American immigration. The poem contains the famous phrase, "Give me your tired, your poor, your huddled masses yearning to breathe free," words which are often heralded as representative of the welcoming and supportive attitudes that should be at the heart of immigration policies in the United States. However, the truth is that attitudes and laws towards immigration have fluctuated throughout American history. Reception of immigrants has depended on a great many factors, including nation of origin, socio-economic status, economic conditions in the United States, and more. The inconsistencies in policies have resulted in a vast array of migration experiences, many of which have been captured in literature and poetry written by immigrants themselves.

In the early twentieth century Chinese immigration to the United States was at a high. Although the federal government had passed the Chinese Exclusion Act in 1882 in order to restrict Chinese immigration, Chinese laborers remained in demand by American businesses, particularly railroad companies. The limitations to Chinese immigration forced many workers to enter the United States illegally, often via western routes through Canada into the states along the West Coast. The government established an immigration station to deal specifically with these immigrants. Located on Angel Island in the bay of San Francisco, California, this center housed immigrants during detainment and deportation. Approximately 175,000 Chinese immigrants passed through the Angel Island Immigration Station between 1910 and 1914. During that time, numerous immigrants wrote poetry reflecting their fears, desires, passions, memories, hopes, and experiences. The poems were written on the walls of the station and remained as a testament to the thousands of individuals who spent time there in the crowded space. The poetry has since been preserved in an anthology and the short film "Island of Secret Memories."

Contemporary literature by immigrant writers and about immigration often focuses on detailing the complexities of immigration. They seek to expose its complicated nature and its role in social and political relations, as well as in the process of globalization. There are a number of fictional writings that focus on the experiences of undocumented immigration. Among them are books written for adults, juveniles, and young readers alike. They tell stories of individuals, families, and communities as they face the daily struggles, joys, and sorrows of living in the United States without documentation. Among these titles are *The Tortilla Curtain* by T. C. Boyle; *Just like Us: The True Story of Four Mexican Girls Coming of Age in America* by Helen Thorpe; *The Crossing* by Gary Paulsen; *Touching Snow* by M. Sindy Felin; and *Return to Sender* by Julia Alvarez. Immigration experiences have also been captured in non-fiction writings by authors such as Luis Alberto Urrea in *The Devil's Highway* and Leo Chavez in *Shadow Lives*. All of these writings serve to demystify immigration issues by humanizing them.

Since the implementation of anti-undocumented immigration laws such as SB 1070 in Arizona and HB 56 in Alabama, poets and writers have responded in great numbers. In 2010, award-winning poet Francisco X. Alarcón created the Facebook page "Poets Responding to SB 1070." The page has over five thousand "friends" and over one thousand poems have been submitted to the website. Submissions have come from around the world, including undocumented immigrants in the United States. Alarcón and members of the moderating panel (also poets, writers, and educators) have shared poems from the page at conferences, festivals, and events in the United States and throughout Latin America. In April 2010, members of the panel gathered for a Press Conference and Poetry Reading/Floricanto on the steps of the Capitol Building in Washington, D.C. There are a number of similar groups using the power of words to illuminate immigrant concerns.

In June 2011, *The New York Times* featured an article by Pulitzer Prize–winning journalist Jose Antonio Vargas. In this article, Vargas admitted to his readership that he is an undocumented immigrant from the Philippines. When he was twelve years old, he came to the United States with his family using a fraudulent visa. Vargas has had a very successful journalism career and has especially been recognized for his work covering the events of September 11, 2001 and the consequent declaration of war against Iraq. Since his revelation, Vargas has devoted his energies and writings to political activism, focusing specifically on issues of immigration.

In this June 28, 2011 photo, Pulitzer Prize-winning journalist and immigration reform activist Jose Antonio Vargas, who revealed that he entered the United States illegally, listens at a Senate Judiciary Subcommittee on Immigration, Refugees, and Border Security hearing regarding immigration reform and the DREAM Act on Capitol Hill in Washington, D.C. Vargas joined other activists on Tuesday, April 23, 2013 in delivering thousands of signatures to the *New York Times* to ask them to stop using the word "illegal" in their articles when referring to immigrants who enter, live or work in the United States without proper legal authorization. (AP Photo/Charles Dharapak)

Jose Antonio Vargas's bold confession helped shed light on a fact that many Americans misunderstand about immigrants. Undocumented immigration is most often associated with unskilled labor forces (agriculture, manufacturing, landscaping, housekeeping, etc.), and many Americans assume that all undocumented immigrants come to the United States to participate in those industries. However, recent findings reveal that undocumented immigrants are present in every professional arena, from agriculture to engineering, computer sciences, academics and—with Vargas's revelation—journalism. His position as an elite writer has afforded Vargas opportunities to bring immigrant issues, particularly those for undocumented immigrants, out of hiding, but also to provide insight into the many layers of immigration.

Migrant writers often use their writing to share their personal experiences with readers, but also to present new perspectives about their countries of origin and countries of destination. Some migrant writers are those who have been exiled from the countries in which they were born. In these cases, the writers are willing to endanger themselves by openly discussing or representing issues that may be politically and socially sensitive. Some exiled writers who have migrated to the United States include Jose Marti of Cuba, Armen Melikian of Armenia, and Chenjerai Hove of Zimbabwe, to name but a few. Oftentimes, exiled writers, artists and scholars are able to receive legal status in the United States and positions that allow them to continue researching and writing, such as academic appointments at American colleges and universities. There are a few nonprofit organizations that assist exiled writers and artists in making the transition to their new circumstances.

Consistent with the use of literature to present the complexities of the immigrant experience, scholarly research and fictional writings have been translated to screen and stage. In 2008, Borderlands Theater in Tucson, Arizona commissioned writer Kara Hartzler to write a play based on the academic work of Anna Ochoa O'Leary of the Binational Migration Institute/University of Arizona. O'Leary conducted fieldwork researching the experiences of women crossing without documentation the Arizona-Sonora sector of the U.S.-Mexico border. In her research, O'Leary learned of the motivating factors for their departure from Mexico, and the treacherous journeys that the women were willing to make in hopes of reaching America. Based on O'Leary's findings, Hartzler created a short play that follows four women on their journey through the Arizona desert. The play is well recognized for its contributions to improving understanding of migrant experiences.

Andrea Hernandez Holm

See Also: Corridos; Devil's Highway; Spanish-Language Media; Theater.

Further Reading

Bacon, David. 2008. *Illegal People: How Globalization Creates Migration and Criminalizes Immigrants.* Boston, MA: Beacon Press.

Hoskins, Gareth. 2005. "A Place to Remember: Scaling the Walls of Angel Island Immigration Station." Institute of Geography and Earth Science.

"Island of Secret Memories: Angel Island Immigration Station, 1910–1940" (video). 1988. Dir. Loni Ding. Center for Educational Telecommunications.

Lai, Him Mark, Genny Lim, and Judy Yung. 1991. *Island Poetry and History of Chinese Immigrants on Angel Island, 1910–1940.* Seattle: University of Washington Press.

Liberty State Park, Liberty Science Center, the Statue of Liberty and Ellis Island Website. www.libertystatepark.com.

O'Leary, Anna Ochoa. 2009. "In the Footsteps of Spirits." In Kathleen Staudt, Tony Payan, and Z. Anthony Kruszewski, eds., *Violence, Security, and Human Rights at the Border,* 91–112. Tucson: University of Arizona Press.

"Poets Responding to SB 1070." 2013. Facebook. https://www.facebook.com/PoetryOfResistance.

"Voices: A Reading List About the New Immigration." October 2008. Family Life Development Center, New York State College of Human Ecology at Cornell for "The Immigrant Child: Past, Present, and Future."

M

Marriage

In immigrant communities around the world, the topic of marriage is a complex one. Although we know a lot about immigration (why people move, where, and how), some topics—like marriage life—remain largely understudied among immigrant populations. Social scientists have documented how marriage life is shaped by out-migration. We know that husbands' role as primary breadwinner pushed men to leave, leaving wives in the country of origin to care for children and in charge of all household responsibilities. In predominantly agricultural societies this entailed that women were not only responsible for the reproductive labor that supported their families, but many had to take on additional wage-earning responsibilities. The Asian American experience is a case in point here. Researchers have documented how labor recruitment practices that favored men, as "sojourners free of family ties," contributed to the separation of families and marriages. In the Chinese experience, men were seen as a source of cheap labor; thus family reunification was not encouraged, creating what sociologists have called the split household family. In the split household, the primary breadwinning responsibilities were separated from the reproductive labor of caring for family. Overall, we know that for split marriages, when husbands fail to maintain economic support after a long period of separation, this has the potential to reshape gendered tasks within families, most prominently pushing women into the labor market.

In the mid-decades of the twentieth century, the Mexican Bracero program, for example, led to the massive recruitment of mostly Mexican men as a source of cheap labor for agriculture and other industries. This labor recruitment contributed to the long-term separation of families and marriages. In fact, social scientists have observed that the separation of married men and women became a key characteristic of Mexican immigration to the United States. Although post-1960 immigration policies have tended to privilege family reunification, for immigrant men and women without documentation, the separation of married couples, parents and children has become a characteristic of contemporary Mexican/Latino immigration. Today, the separation of families is a quality that tends to characterize men and women of the same nationality who cannot come together due to undocumented status or other immigration restrictions. It is also a characteristic that is not unique to the Mexican experience, but to other nationalities across the Americas as well.

Under the auspices of globalization policies, we know that both men and women have been pushed to migrate as primary breadwinners, leading to new family arrangements such as transnational families, husband and wife working abroad, leaving children behind. In some cases, given global labor market demands, it is women who are encouraged to migrate, frequently without documentation, leading to yet a new version of the split household. The migration of working mothers from the Philippines is a case in point. Researchers have documented that for Filipino families separated by restrictive immigration policies the quality of married life has declined a great deal. In a post-9/11 global world, immigration restrictions have exacerbated the problems facing married immigrant families, leading to permanent separations thereby affecting marriage, childcare, and family patterns more permanently.

The reunification of families—a goal of most families that are separated by immigration restrictions—adds significant stressors to married life. In some cases, sexual intimacy between partners declines. Parental authority is difficult to sustain after long periods of separation. Parenting roles are strained by the presence of new siblings competing for attention and support with older children raised in the country of origin. In families where some siblings have documentation and others do not, a new hierarchy of inequality permeates family life with profound consequences for the entire family. In other words, lack of documentation shapes life chances and opportunities for immigrant families in significant ways. Access to education, health care, work, and other community resources impacts the quality of family and married life when lack of documentation excludes some family members from receiving help. Finally, the deportation of a husband and wife is perhaps one of the most serious stressors married couples confront given the current immigration climate.

Married immigrant men and women without documentation face a range of stressors that impact the quality of married life as well. Isolation, the demands of work, lack of extended family support, and health problems have been issues that contribute to marital instability for immigrant couples. Further, once children arrive, the ability to maintain a traditional division of labor is also another stressor for many immigrant families without documentation. Finally, the realization that one pay check may not be sufficient to support their families has pushed undocumented women into the job market, creating a new source of potential stress and tensions for undocumented families. Undocumented immigrant women without family support are less likely to challenge traditional gendered arrangements for fear of causing problems in the marriage and of being subject to deportation. This has also contributed to the double burden of immigrant women's work.

Researchers have documented that the stressors of work impact families across the spectrum. For undocumented men and women work and living in new destinations add stressors to married life that often lead to serious marital problems and frequently dissolution. Husbands' inabilities to support families could lead to a range of psychological and social problems compounding an already stressful married life. Lack of documentation may prevent partners from seeking help, thereby contributing to divorce and marital stress. But, among married undocumented couples, one of the biggest problems causing marital dissolution is intimate partner violence (IPV). Undocumented immigrant women are frequently the subject of intimate partner violence. Research has concluded that immigrant women—with or without documentation—are less likely to seek informal or formal help, thereby becoming an intensely vulnerable population. Undocumented immigrant women in marital arrangements depending on their partners for residence or other forms of legalization are also equally vulnerable. Women who enter the country as a spouse of a U.S. citizen or legal permanent resident are at significant disadvantage if the relationship dissolves prior to obtaining residency status. The undocumented immigrant spouse is left without any recourse and can be subject to deportation. Today, undocumented immigrant women involved in abusive relationships cannot turn to the traditional channels for help such as the police and legal system because these agencies are required to prosecute undocumented immigrants. State and local legal services are also becoming subject to undocumented immigration restrictions. There have also been some initiatives preventing immigrant access to domestic violence services such as shelters and counseling.

Maura I. Toro-Morn

See Also: Childcare; Children; Family Economics; Family Reunification; Family Structure; Mixed-Status Families; Postville, Iowa Raid.

Further Reading

Glenn, Evelyn Nakano. 2000. "The Social Construction and Institutionalization of Gender and Race: An Integrative Framework." In *Revisioning Gender,* ed. M. M. Ferre, J. Lorber, and B. B. Hess. Walnut Creek, CA: Altamira.

Hondagneu-Sotelo, Pierrette. 1994. *Gendered Transitions: Mexican Experiences of Immigration.* Berkeley: University of California Press.

Menjivar, Cecilia. 2000. *Fragmented Ties: Salvadoran Immigrant Networks in America.* Berkeley: University of California Press.

Parrenas, Rachel S. 2001. "Mothering from a Distance: Emotions, Gender, and Intergenerational Relations in Filipino Transnational Families." *Feminist Studies* 27.2:361–390.

Parrenas, Rachel S. 2005. *Children of Global Migration: Transnational Families and Gendered Woes.* Stanford, CA: Stanford University Press.

Meat Processing Plants

The U.S. meatpacking industry has a long history of employing immigrant labor, such as depicted in *The Jungle,* the classic novel by Upton Sinclair published in 1906. This novel depicted the life of immigrants working in the Chicago Stockyards and the terrible working conditions that they were subjected to. More recently, this immigrant workforce has been increasingly filled by unauthorized workers, not the European immigrants of the Sinclair novel, but from Mexico and Central America. With little or no training, many of these workers find jobs in meat processing plants, involving the slaughter, processing, packing and distribution of beef, pork, and poultry products. The state of Texas has one of the highest numbers of meat processing plants in the United States. Throughout the state of Texas there are around 257 meat plants. More than 30 years ago, meatpacking and processing industries were located in the heart of Midwestern cities, including St. Paul, Chicago, and Kansas City. Workers in these

A meat factory worker toils to throw cuts of beef onto a conveyor belt headed for the trim room at Maverick Meats in Denver on Tuesday, March 25, 2008. With little or no training, many undocumented workers find jobs in the meat processing plants, involving the slaughter and packing of beef, pork, and poultry products. Many of these jobs are those with high numbers of occupational injuries. (AP Photo/David Zalubowski)

cities enjoyed salaries comparable to those that workers in the auto and steel industries had. However, by the early 1980s, the industries were gradually relocated to rural parts of the Midwest and South as a cost-cutting measure. In the South, employers could take advantage of right-to-work laws where they did not have to bargain with unions. This allowed these companies to pay workers lower wages and fewer benefits.

Meat processing is one of the most dangerous jobs in the United States. The facilities are full of potentially dangerous machines, levers, stairs, and chemicals. Employees may work long hours and have few breaks. They frequently work under extreme temperatures because meats require constant refrigeration. Very often untrained or un-skilled undocumented workers are hired, and these workers often suffer from serious cuts and crippling repetitive motion injuries such as severe carpal tunnel and tendinitis (Midwest Coalition for Human Rights, 2012). Working in a meat processing plant can cause many illnesses or diseases from exposure to food-borne pathogens and a variety of bacteria from slaughtering the animals. *Listeria monocytogenes* is a micro bacteria that is a leading cause of illness or death from food-borne pathogens. These food-borne pathogens can be prevented by using proper safety and sanitation practices in the processing plants. Unsafe working conditions, no insurance, and lack of medical care can cause serious injuries for the people working in the meat processing plants. Permanent impairments to hands and arms may result from serious cuts and other injuries. In spite of these persistent hazards, there is an underreporting of injury and illness. Workers are often denied any type of medical insurance.

According to a report by the Midwest Coalition for Human Rights (2012), 20 to 50 percent of workers at meat processing industries are immigrants and refugees from Africa, Central America, and Mexico. When the immigrants are hired into the factory, they have to provide legal proof that they have permission to legally work in the United States. The workers provide their information to the employer on the I-9 form. The proof they provide may not be valid, and if the employee's Social Security number does not match the government data base, the Basic Pilot Program (also called E-verify), the employer and the employee may receive a letter stating that both have thirty days to verify the legal status of the employee. If the individual cannot provide this, an immigrant may relocate to find work in other plants in other areas.

Employers also may take advantage of newly arrived immigrants who are undocumented or don't speak enough English. Undocumented immigrants may be less familiar with their rights as employees or may be afraid to complain. Consequently, they fall victims to abuses by their supervisors. Abuse can be based on race, ethnicity, and immigration status, according to the Midwest Coalition for Human Rights report (2012). For this reason, undocumented immigrants can be easily singled out for the worst jobs and lower pay because they are unlikely to complain. In 1980, a skilled butcher could be paid $19 an hour processing meat. With plants moved to rural areas or the South, plant owners were able to pay unskilled, undocumented workers half the amount.

One of the challenges facing meat processing laborers is the raids by Immigration Customs and Enforcement (ICE). These raids have a negative impact on the entire company as well as the workers. The migrants are often abused and deported, the company often needs to shut down its business, and in the case of a meat plant vulnerable meat will be left to spoil. For example, just a few days before Christmas in 2006, Immigration and Customs Enforcement agents raided Swift meat-processing plants in six states throughout the nation: in Greeley, Colorado; Grand Island, Nebraska; Cactus, Texas; Hyrum, Utah; Marshalltown, Iowa; and Worthington, Minnesota, resulting in the arrest of 1,187 undocumented immigrants. In 2007, a Smithfield Foods pork slaughterhouse in Tar Heel, North Carolina, was raided by Immigration Customs and Enforcement. In Postville, Iowa, the meat processing plant, Agriprocessors, was also raided in May 2008, and nearly four hundred undocumented immigrants were arrested. These workers were handcuffed, locked up, and sent to detention centers around the country. Many were charged with identity theft. Workers held in detention centers were separated from families and were frightened and unsure of their legal rights (Capps et al., 2007). The raids can also have an impact on the migrants' family. If there is a raid and a parent is deported or detained, the children often come home from school to be alone. Policy reports (Capps et al., 2007) have pointed to the consequences of these actions by focusing on the fate of the children—many who are U.S.-born—whose parents have been arrested for violations of U.S. laws related to residency and employment without official authorization and were detained and/or deported. These policy briefs have noted that in some cases children of immigrant detainees were left stranded for hours, and many others in the care of friends and relatives. In other cases, families affected by immigration enforcement operations now contend with unemployment and the inability to provide for their families. In yet other cases, school officials have complained that persistent threats or perceived threats of immigration enforcement raids have subjected children to fear and trauma that has disrupted schooling.

Since about 2000, in big cities around the nation, some African Americans, Latinos, and immigrants tried to come together through unions to create better working conditions for all workers. For example in the year 2000 in the state of Mississippi there was an immigrants' Rights Alliance called the Mississippi Immigrant Rights Alliance (MIRA). Together they had a stronger voice and there were some positive changes made within the industry such as hiring directly and not through a contractor.

However, the workers who are located in smaller or more rural areas are less likely to unionize or organize and they may be at a greater risk for injury. When the plants are relocated to rural areas the migrants will follow the jobs. When the migrants relocate, there are transportation issues in the rural areas. The migrants don't have a way to get to work. The towns report higher levels of Latinos within the schools and the communities. Schools are forced to look at curriculum and policies involving bilingual education or structured English immersion programs. Resentment and xenophobia may be exhibited against the undocumented immigrants. There are sometimes high levels of discrimination and racism found in the U.S. Midwest rural areas.

The attitude of the employer can increase or decrease the racism and xenophobia. In the meat processing industry some employers allow the workforce to be an unstable labor force. Migrants report poor relationships with the management of the plants. The workers are paid low wages and there is no room for growth or advancement within the company. There is a high turnover of employees in the food processing industries. The labor turnover has a negative economic effect on the local community. The migrant's poor working conditions and treatment can have an impact on the migrant's family and cause work-family conflict. These additional work-family stressors could have an impact on the overall health and well-being of the immigrant wage-earners who make up part of this essential sector of the U.S. economy.

Drew Berns

See Also: Identity Theft; Immigration and Customs Enforcement (ICE); Labor Supply; Labor Unions; Postville, Iowa Raids; Workplace Raids.

Further Reading

Bacon, David. 2008. *Illegal People: How Globalization Creates Migration and Criminalizes Immigrants.* Boston, MA: Bacon Press.

Capps, R., R. M. Castañeda, A. Chaudry, and R. Santos. 2007. *Paying the Price: The Impact of Immigration Raids on America's Children.* Washington, DC: The Urban Institute/National Council of La Raza (NCLR).

Chasseignaux, E. 2002. "Ecology of *Listeria monocytogenes* in the environment of raw poultry meat and raw pork meat processing plants." *FEMS Microbiology Letters* 210:271–275.

Gouveia, Lourdes. 1997. "Latino Immigrants, Meat Packing and Rural Communities: A Case Study of Lexington, Nebraska." Research Report No. 26, 1–23.

Martin, Phillip. 1998. "Immigration and the Changing Face of Rural America." *Agriculture: Immigrant Port of Entry*. University of California, Davis, 1–12.

Midwest Coalition for Human Rights. 2012. "Always Working beyond the Capacity of Our Bodies: Meat and Poultry Processing Work Conditions and Human Rights in the Midwest." The University of Minnesota, Human Rights Program in the Institute of Global Studies. http://www.midwesthumanrights.org/resources/Meatpacking%20 Report%20v5.pdf.

Media Coverage

Media coverage of undocumented immigration is often of negative in nature. News about immigrants, especially those without official documentation, may be biased and demeaning to immigrants. Analysis of magazine covers and other immigration photographs suggests media discrimination of immigrants has been prominent since at least 1965. Researchers of media coverage seek to make explicit the often coded messages of visual representation of immigrants. Coverage may include explicit negative commentary or convey implicit misrepresentations (through demeaning or disrespectful images) of immigrants, especially those without documentation.

What Should the News Media Call Immigrants Who Are Not Authorized?

Recently the *New York Times* suggested to its reporters and editors that, when appropriate, they find ways other than "illegal alien" to describe immigrants who have arrived in the United States, without legal authorization, but it still allows its use (Haughney, 2013). On April 23, 2013, the *Times* was faced with protesters and seventy thousand signatures on a petition that demanded a ban on "illegal alien" or "illegal immigrant." Among those protesting was Jose Antonio Vargas, a *Washington Post*, Pulitzer prize-winning reporter who had revealed in 2011 after winning the Pulitzer in 2008 that he was an undocumented immigrant from the Philippines. On the other hand, the major news service Associated Press (AP) announced in early April 2013 that it was banning the use of "illegal alien" or "illegal immigrant." According to NPR reporter David Folkenflik, the *Los Angeles Times* has decided to use neither "undocumented immigrant" nor "illegal immigrant," and instead create a "fuller description" of such people, which is a stance taken not only by the *New York Times* but also by NPR. Although Fox News uses the terms "illegal immigrants" and sometimes "illegals," its sister station, Fox News Latino, does not use those terms, citing the fact that most Latinos find them offensive. (Folkenflik, 2013).

References

Folkenflik, David. 2013. "In Newsrooms, Some Immigration Terms Are Going out of Style." *All Things Considered*. NPR News, May 9. http://www.npr.org/2013/05/09/182637402/some-immigration -terms-are-going-out-of-newsroom-style.

Haughney, Christine. 2013. "The *Times* Shifts on 'Illegal Immigrant,' but Doesn't Ban the Use." *New York Times*, April 23. http://www.nytimes.com/2013/04/24/business/media/the-times-shifts-on-illegal -immigrant-but-doesnt-ban-the-use.html?pagewanted=all&_r=0

News media serve to report, but they also create, interpret, and filter social reality. The media are tools of socialization in that they influence how viewers understand immigration, but they are also a reflection of society in general and how the public may already be viewing these issues. Though popular myth suggests that the media are impartial, objective or balanced, news programming and print (as well as "entertainment" programs) have the powerful ability to frame issues and set agendas. Many scholars and observers have written or said at various times that the news media contribute to the reproduction of the status quo, institutional racism, and hegemony. Because most social knowledge has passed through news and even entertainment media, especially with the growing presence of technology in the United States today, the production, distribution, consumption, and perception of media increasingly shape our understanding of the social world, including issues of immigration. Electronic and printed news media provide a filter of both *how* images of certain groups are presented and *which* images of groups receive mass publication. Since media can shift audiences' perception of social phenomena, when the media gives consistently negative coverage of a certain topic, this bias is perpetuated in society. Lack of balanced coverage on immigration and undocumented citizens can lead to inaccurate reflections of social reality.

Immigrants have long been targets of media criticism and labeled as a problem. For immigrants, stereotypes about stealing jobs, taking advantage of systems such as education and welfare, engaging in drug use and smuggling, gangs and other criminal activities often have been one focus of media reporting, particularly in recent history.

This unfavorable media coverage has been measured in multiple ways. Most often, negative stories are defined by the content of the articles being conflict-oriented—as opposed to positive stories that focus on cooperation, conflict resolution, or give sympathetic profiles of immigrants. Negative stories about immigrants occur more often, are consistently longer in length, and are positioned in more prominent places (such as the front page) than positive stories. This results in the reproduction of popular hostile stereotypes about immigrants.

Beginning in the 1970s, media discourse began to equate immigration with illegal passage into the United States, due to more restrictions on immigration from Latin America due to the Immigration and Nationality Act of 1965. Media coverage often contributes to the social construction of the "illegal" as a threat to U.S. citizens. For example, the use of the term "illegal aliens" conjures images of frightening foreigners and criminal strangers. This term has been phased out of more progressive media and replaced with the term "undocumented," but this transformation is still in process. Though some media have framed immigration in more sympathetic terms—the lowly worker stuck in the middle of international disputes about labor, or individuals forced to immigrate for economic reasons over which they have little control—this portrayal tends to be a much less prevalent discourse.

Studies have noted print media's framing of illegal immigration using metaphors of war ("under siege," "invasion," "defending/holding the line," "sneaking in") and natural disasters ("floods of workers," "surges," "opening the floodgates," stemming the "tide"), and references to immigrants using dehumanizing imagery ("round ups," "swarms"). Immigration is not a new issue, but especially in times of economic insecurity, immigration in general, and especially illegal forms of immigration are seen as particularly threatening to so-called American culture and values. Immigration coverage has also been linked with an "us versus them" framing of the issue, emphasizing the "otherness," foreignness, and alienation of immigrants. This criticism is a part of a larger debate about alarmist media in general.

It has been documented that media coverage of undocumented immigrants rarely uses immigrants themselves as sources of information. More often, coverage draws from "official" sources such as the Border Patrol, Immigration and Customs Enforcement (ICE), and politicians. These sources have a stake in dealing with public conceptions of immigration. For instance, the Border Patrol is not a neutral observer of immigration trends. Their purpose as an agency depends on the perception of immigration as a social problem. News stories that rely on the Border Patrol as a resource tend to emphasize agents as patriots, defenders of the homeland, and doing "the best they can" given the "limited support" they receive. Politicians, too, though they may be officials, are not objective in how this issue is presented: frequently they will say what they think will go over best with the public and get them votes.

Undocumented immigration is a complex issue best covered with much nuance, looking at multiple causes and consequences; however, most popular media utilize sound bites, and brief summaries of stories. This usually does not allow for fuller explanations or the showing of multiple angles to a story.

Another argument of media bias suggests that since the majority of immigration articles are written by non-immigrants, journalists who may be predisposed to certain stereotypical conclusions. The social location of a journalist—including the journalist's race, language, and class—can affect the content of the report. Journalists who are closer to the issue may be more sympathetic to undocumented immigrants or at least represent different sides of the immigration story. As an example, many undocumented immigration stories center on Latinos. If reporters do not speak Spanish, they are unlikely to have actual contact with undocumented border crossers, unless they are using translators. These reporters may be therefore too distant from their topic to give details or present balanced descriptions. Without the ability to talk to actual undocumented crossers, these journalists must rely on other accessible data, which may not always be accurate.

Accusations abound that methods of counting undocumented immigrants used by mainstream media are generally not gathered with appropriately sophisticated methods. For some news outlets, there may be a bias towards larger, more sensational numbers that will get more attention. Academics have suggested superior ways of arriving at less biased numbers, hoping to make journalists more accountable to how their information was gathered.

There has been a slight rise in sympathetic profiles and human-interest stories on individual immigrants. The common theme of this discourse is a focus on the hardship of actual crossing: Mexican immigrants in boats crossing the Rio Grande, or large groups huddled in ships or in trucks, and the dangers of smugglers (coyotes) who take advantage of immigrants, especially women and children. Other examples of sympathetic media stories of undocumented include arguments on the creation of a permanent sub-class or undocumented workers: those who have no legal rights and can subsequently be underpaid and/or mistreated and have no hopes of advancement. This underclass status does not dissipate with the second and third generations who are legally in the U.S. Refugees are more often given sympathetic treatment than immigrants in general and especially undocumented immigrants.

In particular, media research that has focused both on general immigration as well as specifically on undocumented immigration suggests there is a special bias against Mexican immigration. Potentially due to being easily identifiable by skin color or language, media discourse specifically on Mexican immigrants is sometimes more often negative, sometimes framed as an "invasion" and portrayed as more threatening. Mexicans are also most commonly associated with "illegal" entry—more than any other immigrating group.

There is also a tendency in the news media to group Mexican immigration with other social problems more serious than seeking employment without authorization. There is a large focus on undocumented immigrants being involved in drugs, gangs, smuggling, rape, murder, violence, and other criminal behavior. The consistent linking of these social problems gives an unbalanced look at the people crossing the border and produces discriminatory ideas. Though there is truth to the claims that these clandestine dealings occur hand in hand with immigration, there is often overemphasis on these criminal issues—making all undocumented crossers seem to be drug mules.

Proposed solutions to correct this media bias include less sensationalized accounts, less demeaning words and images, fewer unbalanced, out of context, biased representations, and fewer stereotypes that may fuel racism, fear and hatred of immigrants. Many suggest that Latino journalists in particular may have more committed advocacy roles, allowing them to better address issues of racism and negative stereotypes in immigration coverage. There has been a growing focus on building a Latino/a elite in journalism, including producers, journalists, and marketers who can help symbolically re-create the representation of Latinos in the news—reclaiming both international heritage and national belonging. This supposed higher sense of social responsibility and obligation to the audience that Latino journalism may have helps to re-focus the media as an assimilation tool for immigrants. Latino journalism may help immigrants reengage with news that they may have sworn off due to the negative images of themselves that they are faced with in U.S. mainstream media.

Jessie K. Finch

See Also: Racialized Labeling of Mexican-Origin Persons; Racial Profiling; Racism; Spanish-Language Media; "Undocumented" Label; Xenophobia.

Further Reading

Chavez, Leo R. 2001. *Covering Immigration: Popular Images and the Politics of the Nation.* Berkeley: University of California Press.

Rodriguez, America. 1999. *Making Latino News: Race, Language, Class.* Thousand Oaks, CA: Sage Publications.

Santa Ana, Otto. 2002. *Brown Tide Rising: Metaphors of Latinos in Contemporary American Public Discourse.* Austin: University of Texas Press.

Mental Health Care Access

Disparities in health, including mental health, are one of the major issues affecting minority ethnic groups in the United States. Immigrants generally, but undocumented immigrants in particular are the most affected. For example, immigrants that cannot provide evidence that they are in the United States lawfully, are not eligible for coverage under the new Affordable Care Act. In addition, they are not allowed to purchase private health insurance, even at full cost, in state insurance exchange(s).

Even though immigrants overall present similar prevalence levels of mental health issues when compared to the levels observed in other population groups, they receive both less and lower-quality mental health care.

Latinos, by far the largest group of immigrants in the United States, exemplify the previous statement. Disparities in accessing care have resulted in patterns of low utilization and frequent dropout from mental health services among Latinos. Research in the 1990s showed that fewer than one in eleven Latinos with a mental disorder contacted a mental health care specialist, and that less than one in five obtained general service for mental health problems. In the case of Latino immigrants (those born outside the United States), the research showed that only one in twenty searched for help. There is no specific data related to undocumented Latino immigrants. But based on empirical information, it seems that the number of those searching for help was substantially lower.

Rates of mental health service usage among Latinos appear to have increased substantially over the past decade, relative to rates reported in the 1990s, particularly for those diagnosed with certain psychiatric disorders. Nevertheless, even after controlling for other predictors of service use, the gap in mental health service utilization between minorities and Caucasians remains substantial. This is particularly acute for Latinos who are foreign-born, more recent immigrants, primarily Spanish speakers, without health insurance coverage, and with no diagnosis of mental illness. Furthermore, among those Latinos who get assistance, only one in four receives adequate treatment.

Several barriers prevent immigrants from seeking, accessing, and continuing to receive mental health services. More research is clearly needed as to whether different types of barriers are significant to access and continue receiving mental health services. Regardless, among the most commonly-mentioned barriers to accessing mental health services are those related to immigration status, lack of health insurance, cost of services or long waiting lists for free services, language differences between clients and providers plus translation issues, location of service providers vs. clients' location, transportation issues including lack of it and/or lack of access to public transportation and/or lack of driver's license, poverty, level of acculturation preventing immigrants from successfully navigating the mental health system of care, lack of childcare, lack of culturally-responsive mental health providers, and social stigma.

It is paramount to take into account the significance and impact of the barriers faced by immigrant parents in the mental health care for their children.

Immigration status is a likely deterrent of mental health care usage in the United States. Current research aimed to estimate the effects of immigration status on mental health care usage among patients with depression or anxiety disorders found that improving immigrants' health care access and health insurance coverage could potentially reduce disparities between U.S.-born citizens and immigrants by 14–29 percent and 9–28 percent respectively (Jie and Vargas-Bustamante, 2011). Even though there is no data available yet, it is anticipated that the enactment of stringent immigration laws in some states, i.e. Arizona and Alabama, will produce the opposite effect of increasing the gap in utilizing mental health services between U.S.-born citizens and immigrants, particularly undocumented immigrants and their children.

Lack of health insurance is a common issue for immigrants and one of the major barriers keeping them from accessing mental health services. Nevertheless, this critical issue is only part of the larger mental health disparities issue. There is often a "domino effect" even for those who have health insurance. It is a common occurrence among immigrants that the person with health insurance makes an appointment, but either cannot find or afford child care or transportation, or does not have money for copayments and prescriptions. The person misses the appointment or does not follow through with the recommendations, the condition worsens, the problems are magnified, and the cycle begins again.

The lack of bilingual, culturally-responsive clinicians has serious implications. For example, based on earlier reports, only twenty-nine Latino mental health professionals existed for every one hundred thousand Latinos. In striking contrast, there were 173 mental health professionals for every one hundred thousand Anglo-Saxons. More current membership characteristics from psychology and social work professional organizations further exhibit the extent of the disproportion between Latino service recipients and Latino practitioners. In 2005, the American Psychological Association reported that 2.1 percent or 1,860 members identified as Hispanics. Data from the National Association of Social Workers Center for Workforce Studies estimated that although Latinos constitute only 4 percent of licensed social workers, approximately 77 percent of all social workers reported having Latino clients on their caseload.

Another commonly mentioned barrier to access mental health services is social stigma. Social stigma is understood as the internalized fear of severe social disapproval by behaving against accepted cultural meaning systems, and norms about mental health issues and treatment. Social stigma, as a mental health services barrier, is rooted in the practice of some cultural values upheld by many immigrants. It is inextricably linked to the sense of embarrassment about discussing personal issues with others. Nearly one-half of minorities report they are embarrassed about discussing their problems with others, a rate nearly four times that of Caucasians (47 percent vs. 12 percent respectively) (Cifuentes 2010).

The design and implementation of mental health strategies and interventions aimed at addressing the needs of a diverse immigrant population—one notably younger than the Caucasian ethnic majority—are essential not only for the immigrants themselves, but for the overall health and productivity of the United States. Beyond its immediate implications, when clients do not receive the mental health services they need, the entire society at large pays a heavy cost, not only financially, but also in terms of social dysfunction and human suffering.

From a financial standpoint, mental health providers expect certain minimum levels of activity and flow of material resources to enable basic levels of care. When this does not happen due to the inability of clients to afford and maintain the recommended regimen of care (including prescription medication and follow-up care) the mental health system becomes compromised, affecting the expedience and effectiveness of services.

When left unaddressed, the personal, marital, and family problems of either would-be clients or those who've dropped out may eventually evolve in dangerous, if gradual downward spirals in well-being, culminating in increased mortality rates through conditions such as depression, family conflict, substance abuse problems, and suicide. In the end, human suffering is not alleviated, and the cost-effectiveness of mental health services delivery decreases.

Mauricio Cifuentes

See Also: Barriers to Health; Health and Welfare; Mental Health Issues for Immigrants; Mental Health Issues for Undocumented Immigrants.

Further Reading

Cifuentes, Mauricio Jose. 2010. "The Impact of Social Stigma on the Therapeutic Relationship for Latino Clinicians: The Elephant in the Room?" Dissertation submitted to the Faculty of the Graduate School of Loyola University, Chicago. http://ecommons .luc.edu/luc_diss/259.

Jie, Ch., and A. Vargas-Bustamante. 2011. "Estimating the Effects of Immigration Status on Mental Health Care Utilizations in the United States." *Journal of Immigrant & Minority Health* 13.4:671–680.

Office of the Surgeon General Center for Mental Health Services National Institute of Mental Health. 2001. "Mental Health: Culture, Race, and Ethnicity: A Supplement to Mental Health: A Report of the Surgeon General." August. Rockville, MD: Substance Abuse and Mental Health Services Administration. Retrieved from http://www.ncbi .nlm.nih.gov/books/NBK44247/.

Smedley, B. D., A. Y. Stith, and A. R. Nelson, eds. 2003. *Unequal Treatment: Confronting Racial and Ethnic Disparities in Health Care.* Washington, D.C.: National Academies Press.

Mental Health Issues for Immigrants

It was believed that new immigrants were at greater risk for mental health problems than those born in the United States, and as they grew accustomed to cultural norms of the United States, the risk of mental health problems would decrease. In part this was expected because many immigrants and refugees have suffered adversity in their native countries, including poverty, war trauma, and persecution. However, research suggests that immigrants have lower rates of mental health disorders than subsequent generations. This relationship is often referred to as the "Immigrant Paradox." It has been hypothesized that this relationship is partly caused by the "healthy immigrant effect" that proposes healthy people are more likely to immigrant and if they become ill, are likely to return to their native country. Research from National Institute of Mental Health Collaborative Psychiatric Epidemiology Surveys has produced some of the most comprehensive assessments on mental health among immigrants. Findings from the surveys indicate that mental health problems affect different groups differently. For instance, risks for specific disorders differ depending on ethnicity, gender, English-language proficiency, number of years living in the United States, and age at the time of immigrating. For example, Caribbean Black men in the United States have a higher rate of mood and anxiety disorders than African American men. Caribbean Black women tend to have lower lifetime rates for anxiety and substance abuse disorders compared with African American women. Among the Latinos, those who reported lower English-language proficiency showed lower rates for mental disorders. In contrast, Asian men who spoke English well were at lower risk for mental disorders over a lifetime; place of birth was the most reliable predictor of mental disorders in Asian women, with foreign-born women reporting fewer lifetime cases than U.S.-born women.

Refugees

Traumatic experiences such as killings, material losses, torture, sexual violence, and harsh detention can have significant long-term effects on a person's psychological well-being. Often compounded with deprivation of basic needs, future uncertainty, and disruption of community and social support, issues for the refugee immigrant not only lead to negative mental health outcomes, but also limit the resources to effectively manage them. Although there is much evidence to demonstrate the adverse impact of such conditions on mental health, leading to problems with physical health, emergency response is typically limited only to food, water, and shelter. Further, most psychological theories and instruments have been developed in Western countries and may be not adequate in attending to the mental health concerns of refugees.

Acculturative Stress

Acculturative stress is the difficulty and stress that occurs during the acculturation process. Some research indicates that immigrants are most likely to experience acculturative stress, but the stress may also be experienced by later generations. Studies on acculturative stress have demonstrated that acculturating toward mainstream U.S. culture may lead to adverse mental health outcomes such as depression, anxiety, and substance abuse. To explain the association between acculturation and stress, researchers often use John Berry's model of acculturative stress. According to this theoretical model there are five factors that influence the relationship between acculturation and acculturative stress: (1) attitudes of the dominant group, (2) type of acculturating group, for instance, is the acculturating individual a refugee or voluntary immigrant, (3) demographic and social characteristics of the individual, the acculturation strategy (e.g., assimilation, integrated, marginalized, and separated), and (5) psychological characteristics of the individual (Berry, 1998).

The influence of acculturation on mental health is also seen in instances when children of immigrant parents acculturate at a faster pace than their parents do, resulting in intergenerational conflict. Often such conflict stems from the parents' difficulty adjusting to the changing family dynamics that may occur as their children acculturate rapidly and become more "Americanized."

Children of immigrants and immigrant adolescents may also face the challenge of having to adopt the cultural expectations of mainstream U.S. culture as well as the culture of origin. Regardless of whether the adolescent was born in the United States, he or she has to accommodate multiple sets of cultural expectations as conveyed by social, familial, community and regional contexts in which he or she resides.

Latinos

Among Latinos, the lower rates of mental health disorders are attributed to strong family and social ties. These ties may serve as protective factors that help individuals effectively cope with mental health problems.

Research indicates that Hispanics who have major depression may present primarily with somatic symptoms and express little negative affect or depressed mood, particularly during initial assessments. Furthermore, Hispanics avoid using the term depression to refer to their depressive symptoms and instead present with complaints of *nervios*. Symptoms of *nervios* include: restless sleep, feelings of desperation, high or low blood pressure, headaches, chest pains, debilitation, and indifference to food, dress and personal hygiene. Not surprisingly, *nervios* has been found to be strongly correlated with depression.

Undocumented Immigrants

Little is known about the mental health status of undocumented immigrants living in the United States. The nature of their immigration status has limited the ability to empirically evaluate the mental health status and needs of this population. A majority of the work on mental health among undocumented immigrants has been conducted with Mexican immigrants; the following have been identified as factors that could affect mental health: (1) the danger associated with crossing the border; (2) limited resources; (3) restricted mobility; (4) social isolation and marginalization; (5) discrimination; (6) fear of detection and deportation; and (7) vulnerability to exploitation.

Seeking Services

Service utilization of mental health services varies among the different groups; however, later generations tend to seek services more frequently than recent immigrants. The discussion of mental health problems or treatment is often perceived as a taboo subject in many cultures. When immigrants opt to seek treatment they often encounter obstacles in access to care. For instance, there are a limited number of service providers who can offer treatment in languages other than English. Further, some mental health providers may lack cultural sensitivity and competence to effectively address the mental health needs of immigrants.

Miguel Angel Cano

See Also: Barriers to Health; Health and Welfare; Mental Health Issues for Undocumented Immigrants.

Further Reading

Berry, J. W. 1998. "Acculturation and Health: Theory and Research." In S. S. Kazarian and D. R. Evans, eds., *Cultural Clinical Psychology: Theory, Research, and Practice,* 39–57. New York: Oxford University Press.

Mental Health Issues for Undocumented Immigrants

Mental health is an integral part of a person's overall health and is more broadly defined than an absence of a mental disorder. Mental health is a state of well-being in which an individual is able to utilize his or her abilities to lead a productive daily life, successfully cope with normal stressors, and be a contributive member of society. There are many determinants of mental health. A multitude of biological, psychological, and social factors influence a person's mental health at any given time. The World

A homeless man tries to rest inside a Tijuana River canal tunnel, in Tijuana, Mexico, 2011. During the day, deportees who find themselves in Tijuana look for work and flee Mexican police, who will jail them for not having papers, just as in the United States. At night they take refuge in the canals, beneath bridges or in shacks; some suffer with mental health problems. (AP Photo/Alejandro Cossio)

Health Organization (WHO) has associated the following conditions with poor mental health: stressful work environment, rapid social change, violation of human rights, discrimination, risk of violence, unhealthy lifestyle, poor physical health, and social exclusion. Undocumented immigrants experience these conditions and more, placing their mental health at extreme risk. Each person is unique in their own vulnerabilities or abilities to cope with mental health threats and their biological predisposition to develop mental illnesses. However, there are common external environmental stressors experienced by undocumented immigrants.

The decision to leave their home countries predisposes immigrants to risk of poor mental health. The decision to emigrate most often stems from experiencing hardships at home and a desire to eliminate or alleviate those stressors. Emotional or psychological tolls are experienced by the person who perceives a sense of failure in being able to make a stable life in their home country. The immigration experience itself is a stressor for any immigrant but for those having to enter a foreign country illegally, the stress and associated risk to mental health greatly increase. Migration trauma or the immigration stress-anxiety experienced is dependent on the conditions under which one goes about entering the country. Crossing the border at designated border crossings utilizing false documentation is stressful but does not pose as much of a threat as having to be smuggled across the border in hiding. The dangers of crossing the U.S.-Mexican border are well documented in the media, resulting in hundreds of fatalities annually. Those that are able to successfully cross the border are often left with the lingering effects of the trauma they endured. These experiences could result in the mental health diagnosis of Posttraumatic Stress Disorder (PTSD).

Once in the host country, undocumented immigrants, compared to their non-immigrant counterparts, are more likely to endure ongoing mental health risk factors such as exploitation and abuse, physical and emotional hardships, lower wages and poor working conditions, limited employment opportunities, poor living conditions, and limited access to health care and other resources. By virtue of their undocumented status, immigrants are not protected by most laws and thus at greater risk for exploitation or abuse especially by employers. Abusive or deplorable working conditions coupled with inability to advocate or speak out about injustices can lead to mental health issues. In the absence of proper mental health care, persons may self-medicate in the form of substance use. This serves to perpetuate mental health problems and increases risk for further complications.

Undocumented immigrants live in a constant state of anxiety due to living a life in hiding for fear of deportation. Chronic stress is known to lead to poor mental health. They either do not seek available resources or do not qualify due to their legal status. Other common mental health conditions or diagnoses experienced by undocumented immigrants include social isolation, depression, and anxiety.

Limited mobility is common among undocumented immigrants. Often having left family and loved ones behind, immigrants often suffer from a longing to be reunited with them. However, due to the hardships and dangers associated with the border crossing they are unable to return to their home countries to visit family and friends. Mobility within the foreign country is also limited due to fear of deportation. Social roles and social status or class often change for undocumented immigrants. Regardless of social position held in their home countries, undocumented immigrants are limited in opportunities in the host culture due to their illegal resident status.

An immigrant's mental health is affected by the receptiveness of the host culture to the particular immigrant's population. They often undergo experiencing marginalization, shame and guilt, and blame or stigmatization. For example, patterns of immigration to the United States have changed throughout the years, and it is these patterns that dictate which group is a target for discrimination and oppression. Undocumented immigrants are currently being targeted in the United States and thus are treated with varying degrees and forms of hostility, oppression, discrimination and racism. Immigrants are considered to be outsiders by citizens of the host country, causing them to be scapegoats on whom to blame social ills such as high unemployment, gangs, criminal activity, and welfare fraud. These accusations are psychologically and emotionally damaging because they are unsubstantiated.

Marcella Hurtado Gómez

See Also: Barriers to Health; Health and Welfare; Mental Health Care Access; Mental Health Issues for Immigrants.

Further Reading

Engstrom, David, and Amy Okamura. 2007. "A Nation of Immigrants: A Call for a Specialization in Immigrant Well-Being." *Journal of Ethnic and Cultural Diversity in Social Work* 16:103–111.

Segal, U. A., and N. S. Mayadas. 2005. "Assessment of Issues Facing Immigrant and Refugee Families." *Child Welfare* 5:63–583.

World Health Organization. http://www.who.int/mediacentre/factsheets/fs220/en/

Mexican American Legal Defense and Education Fund (MALDEF)

The Mexican American Legal Defense and Education Fund, perhaps better known by its acronym, MALDEF, was founded in 1968. MALDEF is one of the leading civil rights organizations for the Latino population in the United States. The organization is made up of a 36-member board of directors which is primarily Hispanics and includes law professors, attorneys, judges, public officials, journalists, businessmen, community leaders and educators. In 1973, just years following its inception, MALDEF won its first court case before the Supreme Court in the case of *White et al. v. Regester et al.* This case challenged state efforts to create multimember voting districts that would have undermined minority representation in Texas and set an example for the larger Texas counties, city councils and school board districts. Single- member districts allow for a stronger connection and accountability measures between the citizens of a given district and the representative looking to represent them. *White et al. v. Regester et al.* was important in bringing Texas eventually into compliance with the Voting Rights Act of 1965. Later in 1982 MALDEF took part in another historic case, *Plyler v. Doe,* which guaranteed tuition-free admission to public K-12 education to all children in the United States regardless of their immigration status, or that of their parents.

The organization's formation emerged from concerns articulated by Mexican American communities living in the United States. MALDEF sought to represent the Mexican American community in civil rights lawsuits, and give voice to the growing Latino community in the United States. Although its inception was in Texas by a small group of individuals, today MALDEF has a nationwide presence. MALDEF has national and regional offices in California, Texas, Illinois, Georgia, and Washington, D.C., and currently works on national-level cases or educational initiatives.

The formation of MALDEF over forty years ago was made possible through a $2.2 million grant from the Ford Foundation. Through this funding MALDEF was able to get to work and establish a team of lawyers who would represent the Latino community in their advocacy pursuits. Through continued support from the Ford Foundation and other donors, MALDEF has been able to provide academic scholarships, hire a staff, and establish many programs to help the Latino community.

MALDEF serves many functions, primarily the promotion of social change through advocacy for issues facing the Latino community. Additionally MALDEF works in litigation in the areas of immigrant rights, employment rights, voting rights, and educational rights of individuals of Mexican American descent. MALDEF has been a supporter of not only the advancement of individuals of Mexican American heritage in the United States, but also one of the biggest advocates for the undocumented community residing in the United States.

Immigration Rights

MALDEF has spoken out against divisive and anti-immigrant measures such as Operation Gatekeeper and other anti-immigrant policy efforts. The staff and lawyers of MALDEF work toward preserving and creating opportunities for the immigrant community in the United States. At the top of MALDEF's policy priorities is working towards a comprehensive immigration reform at the federal level. MALDEF currently does this at the federal, state and local levels to advocate against violations of basic civil rights. Part of this includes the organizing of Hispanic communities around the country to educate them on the consequences of state and federal anti-immigrant legislation. This work is done to empower communities to go out and create change in their communities. MALDEF created the Truth in Immigration project to educate communities about the inaccuracies and stereotypes that exist about immigrants and Latinos in the United States. As part of educating the Latino community, MALDEF also supports efforts by state legislatures and Congress to help in the integration of new immigrants to their communities. MALDEF has led a coalition of national organizations to support investment in programs that provide opportunities for adults and children to learn English. With the number of English language learners in America's public education system growing day by day, MALDEF seeks to increase investment in English as a second language programs in the United States.

Education Rights

Education has also been a major part of their work, including their participation in various lawsuits fighting for bilingual education in public schools and various practices related to the use of standardized exams, which MALDEF believes are unfair measures of a student's academic achievement. A main goal of the organization is to end school segregation that continues particularly in the U.S. Southwest. Another effort that MALDEF works toward is improving the educational access of all students, including undocumented students, particularly in California with the enactment of AB540 (a state version of the proposed DREAM Act) that allows qualified California students to pay the significantly lower in-state tuition at public colleges and universities in the state. MALDEF supports the educational efforts of undocumented students by providing resources on their website, both in English and Spanish, as well as a list of scholarships that students residing outside of the state of California may take advantage of.

Voting Rights

The work of MALDEF with regards to voting rights has been to safeguard the Latino voter's voice. Through work in all levels of government MALDEF strives for the full access of citizens to vote regardless of language ability and national origin. MALDEF has supported the reauthorization of the Federal Voting Rights Act and the *White v. Regester* ruling in which the U.S. Supreme Court struck down attempts by the state of Texas to manipulate redistricting that would have weakened the Latino vote. MALDEF is currently involved in cases challenging other voter suppression laws where certain states have placed unreasonable burdens on U.S. citizens seeking to vote, and where voters have been threated or intimidated.

Employment Rights

Efforts from MALDEF have also affected the employment rights of the Mexican American community. Through litigation efforts MALDEF works to create discrimination-free workplaces, defend against wage abuse, and the denial of opportunities for individuals of Mexican American descent. One of MALDEF's efforts is in working to ensure that Latino families know their financial rights in relation to fraud and foreclosure prevention. Another goal that MALDEF works towards is the understanding that although English is the official language of the law, this is not constructive in working with individuals who do not yet speak the language but instead creates an added barrier to their integration not only in American society but also in their place of work.

Carolina Luque

See Also: Advocacy; Arizona SB 1070; Driver's Licenses; League of United Latin American Citizens (LULAC); National Council of La Raza (NCLR).

Further Reading

MALDEF. 2013. "The Latino Legal Voice for Civil Rights in America." www.maldef.org.
Vigil, Maurilio. 1990. "The Ethnic Organization as an Instrument of Political and Social Change: Maldef, a Case Study." *Journal of Ethnic Studies* 18.1:15–31.

Mexicans

The migration of Mexicans to the United States has been characterized as the world's largest sustained movement of the twentieth and twenty-first century (Overmyer-Velázquez, 2011). Between 1990 and 2005, the increase in the number of migrants in the North America region grew at an average rate of 3.2 per cent per year, faster than in any other in the world, according to *United Nations International Migration Report 2006*. Within this region, the United States was destination to more migrants than any other nation—for an estimated 42.8 million—and three times higher than for any other country in the world, according to the Pew Research Center. Over the past five decades, the single largest group of Latin American immigrants in the United States has been from Mexico, topping out at 30 percent of all immigrants by 2000. According to a Migration Information Source report in September 2013, the United States has about as many immigrants just from Mexico alone (more than 12 million when both legal and undocumented immigrants are counted) as any other country has altogether.

Not surprisingly, the rates of deportation of Mexicans are no less dramatic. According to the Office of Immigration Statistics of the Department of Homeland Security (Hoeffer et al., 2012), in 2011 Mexicans were 59 percent of the 11,510,000 unauthorized immigrants residing in the United States. In 2000, Mexicans represented 55 percent of this population. When the number of undocumented population in the United States peaked at 12 million in 2007, Mexicans accounted for about seven million of this group (Passel & Cohn, 2011). By the same token, Mexicans have constituted the majority of deportations for at least the past decade. In 2009, more than 70 percent of deportees were Mexican (Passel & Cohn, 2011).

The significance of these trends in the migration of Mexicans to the United States is rooted in the history of the relations between Mexico and the United States, and geography. On February 2, 1848, the Treaty of Guadalupe Hidalgo, an agreement between the United States and Mexican governments, officially ceded one third of Mexico's territory to the United States. Between 75,000 and 100,000 Mexicans resided in these seized lands, which span present-day Arizona, California, Colorado, Nevada, and New Mexico, as well as parts of Texas, Utah, and Wyoming. According to the treaty, the United States government granted U.S. citizenship after a year to Mexicans from these territories, unless they declared their intention to remain Mexican citizens. At the time of this historic treaty, the U.S. government had previously granted citizenship only to whites, as stated in the Naturalization Act of 1790. Citizenship status, however, did not necessarily provide equal protection and fair treatment for Mexican Americans. Many Mexicans and Mexican Americans lost political and economic power in the American Southwest. Under the Federal Land Law of 1851, for instance, long-time residents had to present appropriate land-ownership documents to the U.S. government. However, many did not have the required documentation because these papers were no longer available after being handed down over many generations since colonial times.

In the early twentieth century, the U.S. government's economic interests in the Western Hemisphere deferred the imposition of restrictive immigration quotas for Mexicans. Though the U.S. government imposed no limitations on Mexican immigration, it established the U.S. Border Patrol in 1924 to guard national borders, particularly the U.S.-Mexico border. Questions of national belonging repeatedly emerged for both Mexicans and Mexican Americans. During the Great Depression of the 1930s, local, state, and federal agencies in the United States institutionalized massive repatriations and deportations. Immigration and Naturalization Services (INS) officials arrested many Mexicans and Mexican Americans when they went to the corner store, church, or work. Fearing or tiring of these unwarranted raids, some families relocated to Mexico of their own accord. With such a bitter history, many Mexican Americans strongly questioned the legitimacy of their U.S. citizenship during these periods of widespread uncertainty as possession of a U.S. citizenship status provided no protection from discrimination, much less deportation.

During the 1940s, the United States experienced labor shortages as many Americans fought in World War II. Consequently, the United States government instituted a program to officially recruit guest workers. Through a series of agreements between Mexico and the United States, dating from 1942 to 1964, a steady supply of Mexican workers to provide low-cost temporary labor was assured. The series of agreements was popularly known as the Bracero Program, the largest bi-national contracted labor program in the Western Hemisphere. U.S. and Mexican governments pledged to oversee appropriate living and working conditions for braceros, but frequently neglected their supervisory role. This led to poor living and working conditions. After World War II ended, the United States continued to recruit braceros. The implementation of the bracero program fueled a surge in undocumented Mexicans, due to grower and corporate interest in reaping a healthy profit from this vulnerable labor force.

In response to the growing number of undocumented workers, the INS institutionalized Operation Wetback in 1954. This policy resulted in the deportation of hundreds of thousands of Mexicans. Once again, government officials made few, if any, attempts to distinguish citizens from the undocumented. When the deportation campaign ended, the United States and Mexican governments reinstituted the bracero program and extended it until August 31, 1964. It finally ended because the development of modern agricultural equipment lessened the number of workers needed. Also, Lee G. Williams, the government official in charge of the program, characterized it as an exploitative, slave-like labor system that needed to stop. Although the program expired, the United States continued to rely on Mexican workers, this time through informal recruitment. Hearing stories from braceros, for instance, encouraged new generations of Mexican workers to migrate to the United States, sometimes without documentation.

Cold War politics during the postwar era also raised great concern among Mexican and Mexican American communities. They grappled with questions of national security and citizenship. In this climate of cold war politics the United States aimed to protect itself from the threat of communism, largely represented by the Soviet Union. Consequently, the U.S. government implemented tighter control of the national borders. It stiffened the policies for naturalization, to become a U.S. citizen, and for denaturalization, to lose citizenship. Many Mexican American groups, such as the American G.I. Forum and League of United Latin American Citizens, supported these policies. They were concerned with the threat of communism spreading into the United States. At the same time, many Mexican American veterans were disappointed to experience racism at home after having fought fascism abroad. For some, the immigrant presence held back the gains made by Mexican American activists. However, these strict immigration, naturalization, and deportation policies affected many Mexican and Mexican American families, particularly those of mixed-status composition. In sum, the community began to grow aware how these policies reflected a larger problem of racial discrimination.

The second-class treatment that Mexicans and Mexican Americans faced fostered the formation of a Chicana/o identity during the 1960s, especially in the American Southwest. This political identity promoted connections with Aztlán, the symbolic homeland of the ancient Mesoamerican civilization, the Mexicas. It emphasized indigenous and spiritual ties to the territories seized by the United States in the Treaty of Guadalupe-Hidalgo. Chicanas/os emphasized brown pride, community empowerment, and self-determination. The culmination of widespread and diverse grassroots organizing and protests among Chicanas/os is popularly known as the Chicano Movement.

Concerns with a growing influx of Mexican immigration in the 1970s prompted renewed immigrant rights activism. Though the Hart-Celler Immigration and Nationality Act Amendments of 1965 abolished racist quotas, it partly contributed to the production of undocumented Mexican immigration. This act curtailed Mexican immigration to the United States by establishing a Western hemispheric quota, an annual limit of 120,000 immigrants. Thousands more Mexicans were already emigrating from Mexico every year prior to the creation of the act. The quotas reflected a 40 percent reduction from previous levels of immigration, leading to a subsequent rise in undocumented immigration.

The influx of Mexican immigration only continued to increase in the following years. Popular media, the state, and U.S. society at large, used alarmist and dehumanizing language to frame stories about Mexican immigrants. Accordingly, this categorization deflected attention away from structural explanations of immigration, such as policies that maintained inequality and growing global poverty. The Mexican and Mexican American communities mobilized around growing concerns with immigration. By the mid-1970s, many organizations, such as the United Farm Workers, shifted their previous anti-immigrant stance to one supportive of immigrant rights. Resulting from years of activism, the Immigration Reform and Control Act of 1986 (IRCA) provided amnesty for many undocumented people. Yet, it also imposed employer sanctions that would fine employers who knowingly hired undocumented workers. In 1994 California Governor Pete Wilson supported Proposition 187, a failed referendum that banned the government from providing social services—such as public health, education, and welfare services—to the undocumented. It also would have required government employees to report any suspicion of an undocumented person receiving services. In 1999, a federal court found the initiative, popularly known as Save Our State, unconstitutional.

On January 1, 1994, Canada, the United States, and Mexico signed and implemented the North American Free Trade Agreement (NAFTA). NAFTA professed to remove most barriers to trade and investment between the United States, Canada, and Mexico. In doing so, proponents of the agreement promised it would create hundreds of thousands of new high-wage jobs, raise living standards in the United States, Mexico and Canada, and transform Mexico from a poor developing country into a booming export economy. However, such was not the case. Instead, it primarily created poor-paying jobs in border cities, such as Juárez and Tijuana. Moreover, economies in agricultural sectors in the south and central Mexican states were devastated, resulting in greater poverty, unemployment, and economic upheaval as a result of the agreement. The worsening conditions fueled massive immigration to the United States by the late 1990s. This influx of Mexican immigration coupled with economic insecurities once again fueled U.S. xenophobia.

In the twenty-first century, Mexicans and Mexican Americans continue to grapple with questions of national belonging. In the spring of 2006, hundreds of thousands of people participated in marches across the United States to protest House Resolution 4437 (HR 4437), "The Border Protection, Anti-Terrorism, and Illegal Immigration Control Act of 2005." This "enforcement only" bill would have made it a felony to cross the border without authorization and would punish those who aid the undocumented. It failed to advance, but in light of the continued influx of Mexican immigration and economic anxieties, xenophobia flourished. It culminated in April 2010, when Arizona governor Jan Brewer signed one of the harshest anti-immigrant legislation in history, Senate Bill (SB) 1070. This bill authorized local police to investigate, detain, and arrest individuals they suspected did not have proper authorization to live in the United States. It also proposed to make it a state crime to be undocumented. This unleashed widespread public opposition because by mandating that police enforce the law upon penalty of law, racial profiling of Mexicans and Latinas/os would be emboldened. A coalition of civil rights organizations filed a lawsuit in federal court to challenge this legislation, upon which some of the bill's provisions were struck down. Subsequent anti-immigrant legislation under consideration in various states across the nation points to complexities of U.S.-Mexico relations which will continue to have important consequences for generations to come.

Myrna Garcia

See Also: Aztlán; Bracero Program; Hart-Celler Act (1965); Migrant FarmWorkers; Migration; Operation Wetback; Racialized Labeling of Mexican-Origin Persons.

Further Reading

García, Mario T. 1989. *Mexican Americans: Leadership, Ideology, and Identity, 1930–1960.* New Haven, CT: Yale University Press.

Gutiérrez, David G. 1995. *Walls and Mirrors: Mexican Americans, Mexican Immigrants, and the Politics of Ethnicity.* Berkeley: University of California Press.

Hoeffer, Michael, Nancy Rytina, and Brian Baker. 2012. "Estimates of the Unauthorized Immigrant Population Residing in the United States, January 2011." Office of Immigration Statistics, U.S. Department of Homeland Security. Available at http://www.dhs.gov/xlibrary/assets/statistics/publications/ois_ill_pe_2011.pdf.

Menchaca, Martha. 2011. *Naturalizing Mexican Immigrants: A Texas History.* Austin: University of Texas Press.

Overmyer-Velázquez, Mark. 2011. *Beyond la Frontera: The History of Mexico-U.S. Migration.* New York: Oxford University Press.

Passel, Jeffrey, D'Vera Cohn, and Ana Gonzalez-Barrera. 2013. "Population Decline of Unauthorized Immigrants Stalls, May Have Reversed." September 23. Available http://www.pewhispanic.org/2013/09/23/population-decline-of-unauthorized-immigrants-stalls-may-have-reversed/.

Passel, Jeffrey S., and D'Vera Cohn. 2011. "Unauthorized Immigrant Population: National and State Trends, 2010." Washington, DC: Pew Hispanic Center (February 1, 2011). Available at http://www.pewhispanic.org/files/reports/133.pdf.

Ruiz, Vicki. 1998. *From Out of the Shadows: Mexican Women in Twentieth Century America.* Oxford: Oxford University Press.

Midwest

While much of the undocumented immigrant population from Mexico has been concentrated in U.S. border states, a very large percentage has traditionally sought out areas of the American Midwest to settle. The U.S. Census Bureau refers to the Midwest as consisting of 12 states: Illinois, Indiana, Iowa, Kansas, Michigan, Minnesota, Missouri, Nebraska, North Dakota, Ohio, South Dakota and Wisconsin. Illinois is the most populous of the states. Economically, it is a diverse area with industries evenly divided between manufacturing and agriculture. It differs significantly in terms of the region's climate when compared to the climate where immigrants have traditionally settled. Border states such as Texas and California have mild climates and farm work is available all year round. This historically allowed migrant farm workers to follow the crops. However, the Midwest growing seasons are relatively short, necessitating more movement or adapting to other productive activities such as meat processing and factory work. Farm work and food processing involved low-skilled labor and offered poor wages and few benefits. New immigrant arrivals entered these jobs. However, the diversity of the economy has allowed subsequent generations to quickly find better-paying jobs, assimilate, and thrive, and achieve a middle class status (Millard and Chapa, 2001).

Early settlement in the Midwest by Mexican immigrants has been related to the farming crises during the twentieth century. With the labor shortages in the aftermath of World War I and the ensuing Emergency Quota Act of 1921 that prevented more European refugees from coming to the United States, Mexican laborers were recruited to work in agriculture, in the steel mills and meat packing plants. They were recruited by Ford Motor Company in Detroit where they were paid the same as white workers (Gonzalez, 1999). Barrios began to surface in larger urban areas like Chicago.

In Southern Illinois, a Thriving Community of Indigenous Women from Mexico

An excellent example of how immigrant communities have thrived in the Midwest comes from the Tarascan community (an indigenous ethnic group of Mexico) in southern Illinois. The area is known for producing peaches and apples, both of which are labor-intensive, which in turn created a demand for cheap labor that, since the 1970s, has generally been met by a largely undocumented Tarascan migrant population. Here, although undocumented migrant women often find themselves at the very bottom of the social hierarchy in the migrant community as well as the region at large, these same women in the Mexican migrant community have responded by constructing powerful networks of aid and trust that not only offer access to resources that would be otherwise unreachable (health care, education, and so on) but require participation in and civic contributions to that community.

Despite the locals' fears that the migrant population will consume finite resources without returning anything to the community at large, it is well established that the overwhelming majority of these migrants, including the undocumented ones, actively practice what Adelaida del Castillo (2007) calls "social citizenship"; that is, "[t]hey find work, settle, establish viable cultural communities, comply with the law, [and] pay taxes." The women in particular also participate in a strong and well-established tradition of women's volunteer work in rural America, creating strong intercultural social ties as well as contributing to the economic reinforcement and well-being of the community at large.

Reference

del Castillo, Adelaida R. 2007. "Illegal Status and Social Citizenship: Thoughts on Mexican Immigrants in a Postnational World." In *Women and Migration in the U.S.–Mexico Borderlands: A Reader,* edited by Denise A. Segura and Patricia Zavella, 78. Durham, NC: Duke University Press.

In times of labor shortages, employers discovered that the key to retaining workers was to make sure the entire family came along, thus discouraging single male workers from pulling up stakes and changing jobs each time a rumor circulated about a better-paying position elsewhere. Economic upswings were marked by a large movement of Mexican migrant workers to the United States, a significant percentage of whom were drawn to farming communities in the Midwest. Before this post-war period, the Mexican and Mexican American population had remained largely invisible despite the well-documented history of their presence in the area.

However, the 1980s and 1990s saw an unprecedented upswing in the influx of Mexican immigrant men and women to the Midwest, in part attributed to the legalization of many who were formerly undocumented and were able to adjust their status with the Immigration Reform and Control Act of 1986. Legalization allowed immigrants to seek work in places that were considered outside the safety of supportive neighborhoods. No longer constrained by fear and attracted by higher paying jobs elsewhere, there was a significant upswing (from 25 percent to 33 percent) in undocumented immigrants in the Midwest as they moved from what has been referred to as "gateway" cities and states in the U.S. Southwest (Crowley et al., 2006). Additionally, there were assorted economic downturns in places in Latin America that were beginning to emerge as the United States entered a period of postindustrial production and globalization. This set into motion a process of displacement of impoverished populations. The Midwest states of Illinois and Michigan became primary destinations for many immigrants. The better-paying jobs were found in the cities and Chicago and Detroit managed to attract many immigrants. Consequently, Chicago has one of the largest concentrations of undocumented immigrants in the nation outside of the border region. The settlement of immigrants remains uneven in the Midwest, with the largest concentrations in urban areas, and only two percent settling in rural areas (Millard and Chapa, 2001).

The biggest difference between the early and later migrations to the Midwest was that the number of women entering the United States from Mexico—single or married—increased in the 1980s and kept on climbing, to the point that they were crossing the border in nearly equal numbers to Mexican men in 2007. This is referred to as the feminization of migration. However, some of the friction faced by Mexican women migrants upon arrival stemmed from changing gender norms. Gender roles and traditions dictating sexual practices, division of labor, and behavioral norms from Mexico clashed against the modernity of the United States. Most of these women regularly confronted difficulties related to the patriarchy and machismo. However, it is also undeniable that Mexican migrant women have contributed to building community structures for living in the Midwest in ways that insist on establishing their own individuality and agency as well as contributing to the broader community at large.

Poor treatment of recent immigrant arrivals to areas where few immigrants were visible has not been uncommon. The volume by Millard and Chapa (2001) brings together research that illustrates how many places in the rural Midwest continue to be segregated and polarized with the influx of new arrivals. In addition, while the resistance of long-time Midwesterners to newcomers might be expected, Garza points out that some Mexican Americans who arrived with the early immigration in the 1920s and 1930s have voiced strong opinions over the presence of so many new immigrants. Their primary complaint evolved over language and the immigrants' penchant to only speak Spanish and apparent reluctance to assimilate. Other Latino populations, however, cross the cultural divide to work with communities to solve problems. Today, Illinois is considered by many to be a state that is immigrant-friendly, with large urban centers such as Chicago becoming an important locus for advocacy and politics that influence policies to favor immigrants, such as legislated relief for undocumented immigrant students—a state version of the DREAM act.

Anti-immigration discourse in the United States is never steady, but rather ebbs and flows over time, generally following economic trends. That is to say, economic downturns inevitably yield an increase in anti-immigrant discourse, in which immigrants are invariably blamed for the troubles, which then wanes as the economy recovers. Mexican migrant women generally confront a particular form of nativist anxiety fueled by largely inaccurate stereotypes about their "excessive" fertility and sexuality. Due to their status, they are often targeted by the media and nativist groups that accuse them of unearned consumption of local resources without contributing anything in return. While these stereotypes can easily be refuted with existing research, they still have significant psychological traction and weight, the consequences of which may be seen in the dramatic uptick in anti-immigration legislation passed in the last few years, especially those seeking to curtail access to health and education programs.

Sara Potter

See Also: Assimilation; Barrios; Cultural Citizenship; Economics; Emergency Quota Act of 1921; Gateways; Immigration Reform and Control Act (1986); Indigenous People; Postville, Iowa, Raid; Zapotec People (Oaxaca).

Further Reading

Crowley, Martha, Daniel T. Lichter, and Zhenchao Qian. 2006. "Beyond Gateway Cities: Economic Restructuring and Poverty Among Mexican Immigrant Families and Children." *Family Relations* 55.3:345–360.

Del Castillo, Adelaida R. 2007. "Illegal Status and Social Citizenship: Thoughts on Mexican Immigrants in a Postnational World." In *Women and Migration in the U.S.–Mexico Borderlands: A Reader,* edited by Denise A. Segura and Patricia Zavella, 78. Durham, NC: Duke University Press.

Garza, James A. 2007. "The Long History of Mexican Immigration to the Rural Midwest." *Journal of the West* 48.4:89–95.

Gonzalez, Manuel G. 1999. *Mexicanos: A History of Mexicans in the United States.* Bloomington & Indianapolis: Indiana University Press.

Millard, Ann V., and Jorge Chapa. 2001. *Apple Pie and Enchiladas: Latino Newcomers in the Rural Midwest.* Austin: University of Texas Press.

Segura, Denise A., and Patricia Zavella, eds. *Women and Migration in the U.S.-Mexico Borderlands: A Reader.* Durham, NC: Duke University Press.

Migrant Farm Workers

Migrant farm workers are a force that undergirds the nation's food supply. Even so, they continue to be a marginalized and nearly invisible workforce. As a subpopulation of all immigrants present in the United States, migrant farm workers face different challenges than other immigrants who work in other industries. Frequent migration is an unavoidable circumstance of farm worker employment, and inherent in this dynamic are issues associated with social instability of the household unit, and economic uncertainty. It is not unusual for farm workers to move eleven to thirteen times a year in search of work, This industry includes harvesting of crops, field agriculture (including thinning and weeding); reforestation, nursery and greenhouse industries, and food processing (including meat packing).

Historically, U.S. immigration policy has been key to structuring both challenges and opportunities for migrant farm workers through visa programs, such as the Bracero Program and the Seasonal Agricultural Worker (SAW) programs that were especially designed to address the U.S. need for agricultural workers. However, in spite of efforts to provide for the legal authorization to work in the United States through these programs, the unauthorized population continues to grow exponentially. Using data from the National Agricultural Workers Survey (NAWS), a nationally representative dataset

Migrant workers in California pick strawberries, one of the highest valued crops for American farmers, but for migrants one of the lowest-paying and most labor-intensive types of farm work. Many undocumented workers fill jobs in farm work, an industry that undergirds the nation's food supply. Even so, these workers continue to be nearly invisible and unappreciated. (David Butow/Corbis)

of employed farm workers established by the Immigration Reform and Control Act of 1986 and conducted by the U.S. Department of Labor, a study by Peña (2009) found that of the 49,494 respondents whose legal status was recorded since 1988, 20.1 percent were U.S.-born, 4.4 percent were naturalized citizens, 25.0 percent were green card holders, and 7.6 percent had other work authorization. The remaining 43.0 percent reported had no legal authorization to work in the United States. By far, Mexican workers were the majority of all farm workers (72.9 percent), with 54.5 percent of these reporting to be undocumented. Some of the common demographic characteristics among the farm workers reported in this study were that they were generally poorly educated and had poor English language skills.

It is important to note that migrant farm workers are protected by several policies enacted to safeguard fair employment standards for all workers. Among these is the Migrant and Seasonal Agricultural Worker Protection Act. Enacted in 1983, this law provides for basic worker protections that are specific for farm workers. Nonpermanent guest workers legally hired through the federal H-2A guest worker program are also protected by minimum wage legislation, while other migrant farmers are not. Some states have enacted their own minimum wage standards for farm workers, but others (such as Arizona and Texas) elect to abide by the federally mandated minimum wage standards. In terms of the differences between migrant farm workers who are present legally and those that are not, Peña notes that more recent arrivals are more likely to be undocumented and those here legally are more likely to have strong family connections in the United States. Also, undocumented farm workers were more likely to avoid states with high border patrol presence such as Texas, electing instead to go to work in more internal regions of the United States (Peña, 2009).

In North Carolina, the hiring of migrant farm workers through the H-2A program has dramatically jumped from the hiring of 168 workers to 10,500 workers employed during the 1990s, making the state the country's largest user of guest workers (Benson, 2008); and, while most immigrant workers tend to gravitate towards large urban centers in their search for work, over 40 percent of North Carolina's migrant labor force has settled in a handful of rural counties to work in specialized farm industries like tobacco and poultry farms.

The migrant labor camps where workers live while they are harvesting crops come in all shapes and sizes. However, as Benson (2008) notes, they are invariably over-crowded and rundown. He cites a study of farm labor camps conducted in the Eastern United States that showed 10 percent of the units either lacked toilets or had toilets that functioned poorly if at all. The housing units had dysfunctional stoves and structural problems such as damaged windows, leaky and dilapidated roofs, crumbling plaster and peeling paint. State laws in North Carolina specify standards for the housing of migrant farm laborers, requiring that the structures be kept clean and free from garbage, vermin, and insects (Benson, 2008). However, because of their marginalized status, government agencies tend to neglect these housing standards requirements, and non-compliance by agribusiness is the norm. They are rarely penalized for housing code violations, and because many workers speak English poorly and are not likely to know what their rights are, they are less likely to complain. Moreover, a justified fear of de-portation and unemployment results in an underreporting of violations (Benson, 2008). Larson (2001) reports that a high incidence of infectious diseases among farm workers can be attributed to deficient sanitation both at work and at the labor camps and poor-quality drinking water.

A monograph series produced for the National Advisory Council on Migrant Health by the National Center for Farm Worker Health in 2001 reveals that a range of other health issues are associated with living as a migrant farm worker. These include lack of emotional support that comes with long periods of separation from family members and worries about immigration enforcement, poor housing conditions, geo-graphical, social and emotional isolation. Health issues arise from a steady schedule of hard physical toil, long hours at work, and few days off. Many illnesses and injuries stem from the generally arduous farm labor that is compounded by not being able to access medical care (Larson, 2001). These include traumatic injuries such as falls and cuts; musculoskeletal injuries that come with heavy lifting and awkward body posturing, and the repetitive motion tasks, and respiratory problems that come with the constant exposure to breathing in pesticides, dust, plant pollen, and molds. Larson (2001) also reports that there is a high incidence of cancer among farm workers. There are strong but unconfirmed suspicions that a high prevalence of breast cancer, brain tumors, non-Hodgkin's lymphoma, and leukemia within agricultural communities is related to exposure to known cancer-causing chemicals in pesticides and herbicides. Constant unprotected exposure to the sun can also lead to skin cancer, including the more deadly melanoma.

Undocumented farm workers contend with a range of discrimination stressors, which are increasingly linked to health problems and their inability to access health care programs. Research conducted by Carvajal and his colleagues (Carvajal et al., 2013) in the farm worker community near Yuma, Arizona, found that among the most intense stressors were worries about their lack of English language skills and not being able to go to a hospital because of concerns about encountering immigration enforcement authorities. Yuma County in Arizona is known as the lettuce capital of the nation. Other major crops include broccoli, cauliflower, citrus and melons. Yuma County has the largest number of farm workers in the state of Arizona. The Arizona-Sonora border is an important region for the agricultural industry due to the climatic conditions that allow for a vital winter growing season. It is estimated that Yuma employs about half of the Arizona farm worker population. According to the Migrant and Seasonal Farmworker Enumeration Study for Arizona (Larson, 2008), during the winter harvest from November to April there are approximately 41,314 migrant seasonal farm workers; however, estimates vary from 35,000 to 60,000. Yuma's farm worker community can be viewed as a microcosm of the unique issues faced by farm workers wherever they are found.

Anna Ochoa O'Leary

See Also: Bracero Program; Health and Welfare; Meat Processing Plants; Mental Health Care Access; Migration; Shadow Population; Special Agricultural Workers (SAW); Workers' Rights; Work Visas.

Further Reading

Benson, Peter. 2008. "EL CAMPO: Faciality and Structural Violence in Farm Labor Camps." *Cultural Anthropology* 23.4:589–629.

Carvajal, Scott, Cecilia Rosales, Raquel Rubio-Goldsmith, Samantha Sabo, Maia Ingram, Debra McClelland, Floribella Redondo, Emma Torres, Andrea Romero, Anna Ochoa O'Leary, Zoila Sanchez, and Jill de Zapien. 2013. "The Border Community & Immigration Stress Scale and Associations to Health Outcomes." *Journal of Immigrant & Minority Health* 15.2:427–436.

Larson, Alice. 2001. *Environmental / Occupational Safety and Health.* Migrant Health Issues Monograph Series. National Advisory Council on Migrant Health, National Center for Farmworker Health. http://www.ncfh.org/docs/02%20-%20environment .pdf.

Larson, Alice. 2008. Migrant and Seasonal Farmworker Enumeration Study. National Advisory Council on Migrant Health. National Center for Farmworker Health. http:// www.ncfh.org/enumeration/PDF14%20Arizona.pdf.

National Advisory Council on Migrant Health at http://www.ncfh.org/?sid=34

Peña, Anita Alves. 2009. "Locational Choices of the Legal and Illegal: The Case of Mexican Agricultural Workers in the U.S." *International Migration Review* 43.4:850–880.

Migration

Historical Trends

Despite decades of immigration control policy-making, as of March 2012, 11.7 million unauthorized immigrants were living in the United States, according to a Pew Research Center estimate based on U.S. government data. According to Pew Hispanic Research, the number of undocumented migrants increases by approximately five hundred thousand per year, and has more than doubled in the last decade. Approximately 57–70 percent of this population originate from Mexico. The second largest proportion (23–24 percent) comes from Latin America. More than three million—approximately 30 percent of the current population—arrived in the United States between 2000 and 2004. Another 3.6 million undocumented immigrants arrived between 1995 and 1999, and the balance of the population, or 3.5 million immigrants, arrived between 1980 and 1994. Thus, about 65 percent of all undocumented migrants are relatively recent arrivals, having been in the United States for less than a decade. Ancient patterns of migration were relatively fluid, although this is not true today as borders between nations and groups have become increasingly enforced. Recent political developments in the United States offer the opportunity to reexamine migratory trends in a world no longer determined by geopolitical boundaries and the laws and legal frameworks used to regulate them.

Explaining Migration

At the most rudimentary level of understanding, human migration involves the search for resources and better opportunities. One of the most common theories used to explain migration, especially when discussing Hispanic/Latino migration to the United States, is the *neoclassical economic equilibrium theory*. This theory emphasizes economic "push" and "pull" factors as they relate to migration. This theory sees individuals who are beleaguered by poverty and social unrest ("push factors") as rational beings who will seek to migrate to improve their situation. Conversely, destination countries will "pull" these destitute migrants because they fill labor shortages. This theory has been commonly applied to the case of Mexico and its neighbor to the north, the United States, where migration is seen as an escape valve and an answer to problems caused by social inequity in Mexico. Migration is often presented as voluntary although more often than not, it is a matter of economic necessity. A *historical-structuralist* explanation views migration as a result of unfettered capitalism. This view, with its foundations in Marxist thought, holds a predatory capitalist political economy responsible for destabilizing markets and driving down the cost of labor, resulting in migration. In related *migration systems* approaches developed by Latin American theorists such as André Gunder Frank, Raúl Prebisch and Federick Cardoso, "post-colonial" economic developments are critiqued. According to these theorists, efforts to industrialize through economic liberalism have in fact led to the "development of underdevelopment" of third world nations. This structuralist approach promotes the study of migration comprehensively through the examination of the interaction of "macro" and "micro" structures. Macrostructures include large-scale institutional factors (such as neoliberal trade) while microstructures include the local culture and economies of migrants and households.

Contemporary macro-level economic policies have increasingly driven migrants into the international labor market for survival, eventually to migrate to the United States. To be sure, the neoliberal economic philosophies that have worked to disrupt subsistence economies in sending communities in Mexico also underpin the political philosophies that steadily work to undermine migrants' integration in their new destinations. Neoliberalism is a market-driven approach to economic and social policy based on a private enterprise sector that is allowed to operate unfettered by government regulations. Thus, it should not come by surprise that the wide adoption of neoliberal plans such as the North American Free Trade Agreement (NAFTA) by a state such as Mexico in 1994 would adversely impact the economically disadvantaged. Although NAFTA was promoted to the American public as a job creator and an economic development strategy for Mexico, this proved not to be the case. Proponents of the agreement promised it would create hundreds of thousands of new jobs in Mexico, which would raise living standards, transform Mexico from a poor developing country into a booming economy, and reduce the need to migrate. However, the agreement failed to include requirements to protect or increase Mexican workers' wages and workplace standards or human rights, resulting in the abundance of cheap labor for companies to exploit. After NAFTA, Mexican small holders could not compete with U.S.-subsidized corn on the market, and were forced to migrate in search of jobs, resulting in eventual greater migration in general, especially of women. Hence, a decade after NAFTA was signed, 19 million more Mexicans lived in poverty than before the agreement was signed. Indeed, the literature is replete with scholarly analysis of how neoliberal economic changes resulted in the disruption of rural and agricultural-based communities, resulting in the rise in the number of people migrating.

The Process of Migration

With global deterioration of economic conditions, migration has intensified. At the same time, border enforcement in the United States and throughout the world (especially since 9/11) has increased. In 1994, Attorney General Janet Reno announced plans for implementing the *Border Patrol Strategic Plan 1994 and Beyond: National Strategy,* a plan to strengthen enforcement of the nation's immigration laws and to close off the traditional migration corridors along the southwest border. The strategy was an effort to deter illegal entry into the United States and incrementally increase control of the border, making it increasingly complicated and expensive for migrants. It is important to consider that while entry into the United States is an uncomplicated matter for those able to obtain visas, usually by providing a combination of documents that have some proof of economic stability (e.g. wage receipts for the last six months, business tax receipts, retirement income receipts) and material holdings (e.g.

property tax receipts, bank accounts, utility receipts), providing such required documents is nearly impossible for resource-depleted migrants whose movement is largely driven by the economic instability in their communities or place of origin. Not surprisingly, for many migrants who cannot provide such documents (and who are therefore considered to be "undocumented"), central to the process of migration are those activities related to avoiding apprehension for entering the United States "without inspection," meaning crossing in a place other than an official port of entry. Nearly five hundred thousand a year still make their way across well-guarded international borders in this way, eventually to contribute to the transformation of the socioeconomic environment in their destination communities.

With repeat migration, the process of migration is facilitated through migration-specific social capital that leads to the accumulation of useful knowledge and skills (migration-specific human capital). This makes subsequent crossings more efficient, less risky, and more productive. However, migration is increasingly relying on the service of smugglers, known as coyotes, to cross into the United States without authorization. This adds to the cost of migration for many resource-poor migrants. In 2000, the greatest number of migrants to the United States came primarily from Mexico's poorest southern and central states.

Other important factors embedded in the process of transportation to the United States include the outlay of money that may be lost if the migrant is apprehended. The initial costs associated with avoiding apprehension must also be multiplied by the number of times the border crossing is attempted. Far from familial or social support, migrants are often alone when considering the decision to repeat the attempt to cross. They may weigh the price of failure in isolation. They necessarily consider being held in Border Patrol detention for many hours. Routinely, agents force migrants to discard any of the supplies they have. Loss of supplies also means that they would have to re-purchase supplies if they attempt again to cross. Often they are held in custody for many hours or even days. Their want of food while in custody of agents is a frequent complaint. Agents may distribute some crackers and juice, but this is hardly enough for those trekking through the desert for as many as three or four days. Their lack of nourishment may have deadly consequences. With no hope that economic conditions that prompted their migration to begin with will change soon, there are few options except to try to cross again. If they do not succeed in crossing, the initial financial outlay is not only lost, but families in sending communities may need to come up with additional funds to pay for the bus fare home, losing in the process any hope for relief that work in the United States would provide. Moreover, to finance the initial migration journey, many migrants borrow the money and may put up their meager properties as collateral. The loss of personal valuables to corrupt officials and border bandits is necessarily added to the cost of the initial migration journey. The bandits who take advantage of the remote migration routes to rob migrants are also referred to "bajadores" which comes from "bajar," the Spanish verb that means to "pull down," and refers to the tactics these bandits use of forcing victims to pull down their pants at knifepoint or gunpoint to keep them prostrate to facilitate a bodily search for valuables. The loss of valuables adds to the costs associated with migration.

The Impact of Enforcement on Migration

Since 1993, there has been an increase in policies and political action intended to curb illegal immigration. One of these has been the aforementioned *Border Patrol Strategic Plan 1994 and Beyond: National Strategy* implemented by the Immigration and Naturalization Service (INS), which resulted in the increased militarization of the border. This program brought with it additional state resources such as additional surveillance technology, border walls and additional U.S. Border Patrol that force migrants away from urban centers into more remote areas to enter into the United States without being detected. Migration patterns resulted in increased numbers of deaths during migration through the harsh Arizona-Sonora migrant corridor, with more than five thousand men, women, and children dying when attempting to cross the U.S.-Mexico border. The strategy is also known for its localized operations in larger urban centers, known as Operation Hold the Line in 1993 in El Paso, Texas, Operation Gatekeeper in San Diego, California, in 1994, Operation Safeguard in Nogales, Arizona, in 1995, and Operation Rio Grande in Brownsville, Texas, in 1996. The plan assumed that as the urban areas were controlled, the migration traffic would shift to more remote areas where natural barriers including rivers (such as the Rio Grande in Texas), the mountains and subzero winter temperature east of San Diego, and the hostile desert climates in Arizona would act as geographic deterrents to illegal entry. However, the effect was the opposite and a human disaster with the greater poverty that the North American Free Trade Agreement (NAFTA) produced in Mexico that forced larger number of migrants who knowingly assumed greater risks entailed in migration. Moreover, the persistent privation has only aggravated migrants' risk of armed assault, robbery, rape, violence, and other, untold number of physical attacks as they make their way through more remote areas in their search for a better life.

In recent years, the dire conditions have drawn greater political attention of state legislators, especially in Arizona, which is in the center of the Arizona-Sonora migrant corridor, and where greater legislative restrictions have been implemented to curb migration and to discourage migrants from settling in the state. However, some scholars have argued that migration imposes a set of impossible-to-achieve expectations, such as improved social and economic opportunities. An irony is that with greater enforcement, immigrants who successfully reach the United States are more inclined to remain in the United States longer than originally desired, forcing them to assimilate and to create better lives for their families, despite intensified legislative efforts to prevent them from doing so.

However there are other costs in terms of hardships and suffering that come with family separation. These costs necessarily include the time that is expended and are related to "stage migration" of entire families. Stage migration is a term that refers to the piecemeal reunification of families that begins with the initial migration of an adult and continues with the subsequent migration of spouses and each child over a period of time. Scholars, community activists, public school teachers and medical and public health practitioners have recently become alarmed at the consequences of family separation that comes with migration, often pointing out to enforcement officials and policy makers the potential consequences of the amount of suffering that is experienced as a result of increasingly uncompromising policies that remain insensitive to migrant families and children.

The aggressiveness of U.S. deportation policies has forced the repatriation of millions of undocumented migrants, often through programs such as Operation Streamline, Secure Communities, and the 287(g) program (a program that allows federal immigration enforcement agencies to enter agreement with local law enforcement that allows them to enforce immigration law). Although the mass repatriation and deportation efforts focus on recent border crossers and those with a criminal history, many deportees are settled migrants living in the United States, who for many years who have established peaceful and productive livelihoods, lived in obedience to the laws of their host country, and followed established patterns of sending remittances to family members in the country of origin. As a result, the deportation may disrupt previously stable family and household relationships in the United States, who many of them involving children born in the United States who are therefore lawful citizens of the nation as provided by the Fourteenth Amendment of the U.S. Constitution and as such, entitled to equal protection under the law. Parent-child separation amongst undocumented migrants as a result of enforcement politics can have a longstanding impact on the migrant families in both sending and settlement communities. The transitory loss of a parent because of migration can have a profound impact on the healthy developmental course of a child and particularly on the parent-child bond. This is compounded with prolonged separation caused by increased enforcement efforts. A history of mother-child separations has been shown to play a decisive role in weakening the bond between mothers and children and disrupts key parenting practices. Similarly, a father's absence may become a risk factor for the healthy psychological development of his children. Therefore, migrants, perhaps more than any other population in the United States, are more prone to experiencing the long-term negative impact of enforcement policies that come with migration.

For undocumented male migrants, their absence undoubtedly affects traditional family structure and forces a necessary change in gender roles among the remaining females. In communities with a high incidence of migration, male migration as a strategy for supporting the family's goal of financial stability may often result in a weakening of the paternal sense of obligation. The magnitude of fathers' absence due to migration transforms into more familial, social, and labor responsibilities for migrants' wives and children. Not surprisingly, migration as a means for survival (economically and socially) is often achieved at the expense of women, since its costs and benefits are not evenly distributed. As such, women who are left behind in the United States when their husbands are arrested and deported may experience increased levels of stress as their roles shift as primary providers of economic stability for the safety and nourishment of family members, which may include non-productive children and the elderly. Often they are also responsible for cultural reproduction. Changing norms, often compounded with anti-immigrant sentiment, impact how migration transforms both newcomers as well as their destination communities. In this way, migration drives greater social transformation and changes in culture. While culture provides social mechanisms that migrants may use to positively acculturate to their new environments, rapid and unexpected changes may also induce negative outcomes, such as isolation, depression, and anxiety—all of which may have further consequences on the family's physical well-being—changes that will also be experienced in host communities as they too adapt to increased diversity.

Anna Ochoa O'Leary

See Also: Border Crossing; Economics; Family Economics; Globalization; Legal Status; Mobility; North American Free Trade Agreement (NAFTA); Special Agricultural Workers (SAW).

Further Reading

McGuire, S., and K. Martin. 2007. "Fractured Migrant Families: Paradoxes of Hope and Devastation." *Family & Community Health* 30.3:178–188.

Overmyer-Velázquez, Mark. 2011. *Beyond la Frontera: The History of Mexico-U.S. Migration.* New York: Oxford University Press.

Passel, J. S. 2005. Pew Hispanic Center: Unauthorized Migrants: Numbers and Characteristics (June 14, 2005). http://pewhispanic.org/files/reports/46.pdf.

Passel, Jeffrey, D'Vera Cohn, and Ana Gonzalez-Barrera. 2013. "Population Decline of Unauthorized Immigrants Stalls, May Have Reversed." September 23. http://www.pewhispanic.org/2013/09/23/population-decline-of-unauthorized -immigrants-stalls-may -have-reversed/.

United States Government Accountability Office. 2006. Illegal Immigration: Report to the Hon. Bill Frist, Majority Leader, US Senate.

Military Recruitment and Participation

The U.S. Military Selective Service Act of 1948 requires that all males between the ages of eighteen and twenty-five years be registered with the Selective Service and be available for military service. Non-immigrant visitors to the country, such as students, tourists, diplomats, and consular personnel and their families are not included in this mandate. However, all citizens, legal permanent residents, seasonal workers, refugees, dual nations, and undocumented immigrants born after December 31, 1959 are required to register, according to the Selective Service System (www.sss.gov).

The Immigration and Nationality Act permits non-citizens to perform certain types of military service and, as a result, become eligible for an accelerated naturalization process. Non-citizens are immigrants who possess permanent resident visas or green cards and can prove established residency in the United States. These service personnel may ordinarily serve in non-combative positions, but those who do serve in the armed forces for at least one year or in an active combat zone for any length of time may be able to seek citizenship. They may apply for citizenship during duty or within six months of receiving an honorable discharge. Immigrants who have previously served in military conflicts are also eligible to apply. This includes veterans of World War I, World War II, Korea, Vietnam, and the Persian Gulf. Non-citizens who have died in the line of duty may also be eligible for posthumous citizenship. All applicants for citizenship must meet the standards established by the Immigration and Nationality Act, including good moral character, English-language skills, and knowledge of American civics and the U.S. Constitution. All military enlistees must take an oath of loyalty to the United States.

Many people misunderstand the enlistment of non-citizens in the military. They often presume that undocumented immigrants may enlist and become eligible for citizenship through service, but this is not the case. The U.S. military branches must follow strict guidelines regarding active recruitment and enlistment. The laws pertaining to citizenship status of enlistees must be adhered to stringently. Undocumented immigrants are not accepted as enlistees. Non-citizens who do enlist must be documented residents of the country and only they may be eligible for the fast-tracked citizenship offered under certain federal laws. Recruiters are held to high standards regarding misconduct and malpractice in order to prevent any enlistee from being misled about the nature of their participation in the military and to fulfill the requirements of the laws regarding enlistment. Submission or certification of false documents is considered fraud. This is a serious charge that may be tried and punished under the Uniform Code of Military Justice.

In 2003, Executive Order 13269 was issued by President George W. Bush. This order, known as the Expedited Citizenship of Aliens and Non-Citizen Nationals Serving in an Active Duty Status in the War on Terrorism, fast-tracked the naturalization process for non-citizens serving in the military during the War on Terrorism. This war was initiated on September 11, 2001 in response to the terrorism acts against the United States. Under the Executive Order, non-citizen servicemen and women are eligible to apply for citizenship without meeting all of the requirements of the Immigration and Naturalization Act, specifically the requirement of permanent or established residency. Voluntary enlistment and reenlistment of non-citizens into the military increased substantially following the issuance of this order. The Department of Defense reported that approximately three percent of enlisted military personnel were active duty non-citizens—roughly 37,000 of 1.4 million. It anticipated that this number would only continue to grow.

In 2009, the U.S. military announced that it would actively recruit non-citizens with temporary residency status in order to address the shortage of military personnel it was experiencing. It would focus its efforts specifically on "skilled" workers, those with multiple language skills, higher education and professional experience, to fill the growing personnel gaps in medical care, language translation, and intelligence analysis. The military was especially interested in enlisting individuals who spoke Arabic, Chinese, Hindi, Igbo, Kurdish, Nepalese, Pashto, Russian, and Tamil. Spanish speakers were not eligible for this program. Recruits to this program were required to serve for two to six years, depending on their area of specialty. In return for their service, these non-citizen military personnel could qualify for citizenship within six months and have their application fees waived.

Non-Citizen Soldiers

In 2003, the federal government confirmed that the second U.S. casualty of the Iraq War was Marine Lance Corporal José Gutierrez. Gutierrez was a permanent resident who had been living in the United States since he was thirteen years old. He was a citizen of Guatemala, and although he had permanent residency, he had yet to receive U.S. citizenship. It was awarded to him posthumously.

Since the beginning of the Iraq War, the issue of non-citizens serving in the U.S. military has gained great attention. There have been enough cases to suggest a lack of clarity in the policies and a lack of misunderstanding by enlistees. The result has been a number of non-citizen soldiers being deported following their tours of service because of problems with their documentation or legal status.

The primary concern raised by opponents of policies that encourage or even allow non-citizens to serve in the U.S. military is the worry that the government has made it too easy for individuals with ulterior motives to gain access to U.S. security measures. During the 2000s there were a few high-profile cases of non-citizen military personnel who were charged with committing acts of violence against other personnel, attempting to steal military blueprints, and participating in acts of espionage. However, these cases are isolated incidents and pale in comparison to the number of non-citizens who serve the United States honorably, some even sacrificing their lives in the line of duty.

Andrea Hernandez Holm

See Also: Citizenship; Cultural Citizenship; Deferred Action for Childhood Arrivals (DACA); DREAM Act; Lawful Permanent Residents (LPRs).

Further Reading

Military.com. 2013. www.military.com.

Military Times. 2013. www.militarytimes.com.

Preston, Julia. 2009. "US Military Will Offer Path to Citizenship." *The New York Times*, February 14.

Traskey, David. 2003. "The Invisible Warrior: Illegal Immigrants in the Armed Services and the Implications of the Juan Escalante Story." *Immigration and Nationality Law Review* 24:663–685.

Minutemen

Minutemen is a general term used to refer to any of the paramilitary civilian groups organized to protect the border. Although the name is taken from the American militiamen just before and during the Revolutionary War who held themselves in readiness for instant military service—literally men that would be ready "in a minute"—in more recent history these types of groups have formed in the U.S. Southwest in an effort to respond to the U.S. government's inability to secure the U.S.-Mexico border. In most cases, these groups are dressed in military-type clothing and armed with assault weapons and pistols when they patrol the border (Doty, 2009). They are often referred to by migrants as "*casamigrantes*," literally meaning "migrant hunters." The Minutemen and the many other groups who act as a civilian army organized to patrol and defend the U.S.-Mexican border have been categorized as vigilante or hate groups by the

Chris Simcox of the Minuteman Civil Defense Corps speaks during a rally to build a fence along the U.S./Mexican border near Palominas, Arizona, 2006. The Minuteman Project and its chapters have been classified by many organizations as hate groups. (AP/Wide World Photos)

Southern Poverty Law Center, immigrant rights groups, and the Anti-Defamation League.

One of the first and perhaps the most well-known minutemen groups is the Minute Men Project (MMP). The group was organized in 2005 by Chris Simcox, a former teacher from California who moved to Cochise County in the southeast Arizona border region in response to the increase in undocumented immigrants moving through this area, and Jim Gilcrist of the American Border Patrol, another civilian border vigilante group. This region has had a long history of vigilantism, and long before the Minute Men Project was established there. Doty (2009) argues that perhaps because of this history, and the history of impunity under which they operate, minutemen-type groups have been drawn to the area and in fact been inspired by it. For example, in 1976, white ranchers in the area, brothers Patrick and Thomas Hannigan, detained and tortured three Mexican migrants who had crossed the border at Douglas, Arizona, on their way to work in a nearby farm, hanging them from a tree and burning their feet before pistol whipping them back towards Mexico. It took three trials to finally convict one of the brothers. Then in 2006 southern Arizona rancher Roger Barnett was accused of holding 24 undocumented immigrants at gunpoint, assaulting them, and commanding his dog to attack the immigrants. He claimed self-defense although the immigrants were not armed. Although in 2009 a three-judge panel of the Ninth Circuit Court of Appeals in San Francisco upheld charges of beating the four women in the group, and fined

Barnett $87,000, he has openly and publically bragged that he has detained thousands of undocumented immigrants coming through this remote desert area since 1996. Years prior to this case (in 2004), Roger Barnett had been accused and found guilty and fined $100,000 for unlawfully detaining a family of Latino U.S. citizens—including two children—at gunpoint.

Then in April of 2005, The Minute Men Project again captured the nation's attention by announcing a national recruiting drive for the purpose of setting up armed camps along the U.S.-Mexican border in southeastern Arizona because the U.S. government had failed to halt undocumented immigration. For about a month, the group proceeded to set up a series of watch posts along the border. During these undertakings, group members dressed in military-type clothing and armed themselves with assault weapons and pistols (Doty, 2009).

The organization and the project attracted the attention of various other anti-immigrant activists, including those with more extreme views and white supremacist groups. Since the MMP's inception, dozens of similar groups have mushroomed throughout the nation in what is considered to be an exclusionary anti-immigrant movement (Dufort, 2012). With its national recruitment efforts and project to set up armed posts along the border, the MMP overshadowed the operation of a similar and affiliated group, Ranch Rescue, known for its extreme anti-immigrant vigilante tactics in southern Arizona and Texas, and the American Border Patrol. This latter organization had been founded by Glen Spencer in 2002 who, with the blessing of the U.S. Federal Aviation Administration, uses unmanned aerial vehicles equipped with cameras and GPS technology and records immigrant activity along the border. The videos are then uploaded to the American Patrol website. However, some of the tactics that these groups adopt are considered to an infringement of certain rights that Americans take for granted, such as videotaping undocumented immigrant workers or videotaping those employers who hire them.

Some of these strategies received the support of a wide range of individuals, providing some evidence that nativism and the anti-immigration movements work to create more tolerance of those actions that may have previously been considered to be extreme. This shift in attitude makes it easier to overlook some of the actions and views that might lead to hate crimes against immigrants in general. The mainstreaming of such views has worked to support those who have been active in the Save Our State movement in California (Doty, 2009). This movement had been one of the first in recent history to rally public support for anti-immigrant legislation such as California's Proposition 187 (in 1994) and Arizona's Proposition 200 in 2004 (Doty, 2009).

Immigrant and human rights activists and law enforcement groups decry these measures because they embolden others to act in similar ways wherever immigrants are found, not just along the border. Moreover, immigrant rights groups point out that the proliferation of such anti-immigrant tactics is associated with xenophobic rhetoric, resulting in more acts intended to intimidate and threaten immigrants. Inherent in the discourse adopted by these groups are militaristic themes, such as the describing of immigrants as "threats to national sovereignty," the border as a war zone and referring to patrolling actions as "operations." In line with this perspective, those aligned with the movement adopt a military or paramilitary appearance and openly display weaponry.

Prominent individuals and national figures have publically supported such militia groups, such as broadcaster Lou Dobbs, formerly of CNN, former Arizona representative J. D. Hayworth, and former Maricopa County (Arizona) attorney Andrew Thomas (who was later disbarred for abuse of power, among other charges). A major supporter of the Minutemen was the House Immigration Reform Caucus led by then U.S. Congressman Tom Tancredo (Doty, 2009). As a result of these very public displays of support, more people from the U.S. mainstream may have been likely to align themselves with the movement.

However, in addition to patrolling areas along the U.S.-Mexico border in Southern Arizona and Texas, other tactics associated with minutemen types of organizations or individuals have exceeded the boundaries outlined by the U.S. legal framework. These include threatening, detaining suspected undocumented immigrants at gun point, impersonating law enforcement officials, and beating and assaulting suspected immigrants. For example, in 2003, members of the Ranch Rescue organization were charged with assault of two undocumented immigrants from El Salvador near Hebronville in southern Texas. The accused were fined and sentenced. According to the terms of the judgment, a seventy-acre property about two miles from the border belonging to Ranch Rescue leader Casey Nethercott was ordered to be turned over to the two victims.

Anna Ochoa O'Leary

See Also: Exclusion; Hate Groups; Racialized Labeling of Mexican-Origin Persons; *Strangers in the Land*; Violence; Xenophobia.

Further Reading

Cabrera, Luis, and Sonya Glavac. 2010. "Minutemen and Desert Samaritans: Mapping the Attitudes of Activists on the United States' Immigration Front Lines." *Journal of Ethnic and Migration Studies* 30.4:673–695.

Doty, Roxanne Lynn. 2009. *The Law into Their Own Hands: Immigration and the Politics of Exceptionalism.* Tucson: University of Arizona Press.

Dufort, Julie. 2012. "Constructing Security on the U.S.-Mexico Border: An Analysis of the Minutemen Movement." In *Anti-immigrant Sentiments, Actions and Policies in North America and the European Union.* ed. Mónica Verea, 207–228. Mexico City: Centro de Investigación sobre América del Norte (CISAN) de la Universidad Autónoma de Mexico (UNAM).

Holthouse, David. 2005. "Minutemen, Other Anti-Immigrant Militia Groups Stake Out Arizona Border: High-powered Firearms, Militia Maneuvers and Racism at the Minuteman Project." Intelligence Report 2005, issue 118. http://www.splcenter.org/get-informed/intelligence-report/browse-all-issues/2005/summer/arizona-showdown#.UXK-28pXp9U.

Lyall, James Duff. 2009. "Vigilante State: Reframing the Minutemen Project in American Politics and Culture." *Georgetown Immigration Law Journal* 23.2–4:256–291.

Mixed-Status Families

The tenuous and uncertain conditions faced by families with a "mixed" immigration status composition raise many issues about the future of such families, and about how the U.S. legal system will resolve them. Mixed immigration status families—families with a varied legal status of family members within households—is a condition attributed to decades of migration in response to the U.S. demand for labor. Rising poverty in immigrant-sending nations together with increased immigration restrictions has increased the number of immigrants living in the United States without proper residency visas (undocumented immigrants). However, as in many parts of the world, political rhetoric ignores decades of migration from less developed nations in response to the demand for labor in more developed nations.

Changes in U.S. immigration policies have contributed to the development of a complex legal framework designed to accommodate a multitude of immigration-status categories. However, the development of a legal framework is often informed by social and political climates, resulting in one that is disconnected from economic and social realities, and the historical and important role of foreign workers (many of whom are undocumented) to the growth and development of the United States.

With political discourse drawing attention to the lack of a comprehensive plan for immigration reform in 2006 and 2007, contemporary news accounts have highlighted the issue of family separation among immigrant families. Such accounts have focused on the lack of directives for workforce raids by the Immigration and Customs Enforcement (ICE) branch of the Department of Homeland Security (DHS). Subsequent policy reports have pointed out the potential for adverse consequences that such raids may have on children—many of whom are U.S.-born—whose parents have been arrested for violations of U.S. laws related to residency and employment without official authorization and have been detained and/or deported. For example, in 2006, ICE performed a series of workplace raids on the Swift and Co. slaughterhouses in six states resulting in 1,297 arrests—workers separated from their families with little warning or preparation. In March of 2007, ICE arrested three hundred workers at Michael Bianco Inc. leather goods factory in New Bedford, Massachusetts, many of whom were Guatemalan women with children born and living in the United States. Without information about status and detainment of these arrested workers, their children were left stranded for hours, and many others in the care of friends and relatives. Without precedent, ICE flew many detainees to an out-of-state federal detention center before immigrants' advocates had a chance to speak with them about their children. Some detainees were not initially honest with ICE investigators about whether they had children, fearing they, too, would be taken into custody even though some of those children were U.S. citizens.

In light of these conditions, the economic future of U.S.-born children within mixed-status families is especially uncertain. On May 12, 2008, ICE raided the Agriprocessors Inc. kosher meatpacking plant in Postville, Iowa. Most of the 389 workers arrested were charged with using false identification or incorrect Social Security numbers. Authorities reported that some undocumented workers who were sole caregivers for children were allowed to return on humanitarian grounds, but now had to contend with unemployment and inability to provide for their families. Extended family members shouldered the burden of supporting the unemployed workers and the families that depended on them. Educational futures also become uncertain. On May 7, 2008, immigration enforcement arrests at homes in Berkeley and Oakland, California, sent a wave of panic among parents in both cities, as authorities mistakenly believed immigration agents were raiding schools. Although the rumor proved to be false, in Oakland, Mayor Ron Dellums and three school board members converged at the end of the school day at Stonehurst Elementary School along with immigration rights advocates, saying they believed ICE agents would return. "In my view, that is the ugly side of government," Dellums said. "No way children should ever be treated to that kind of harassment and fear."

As U.S. immigration enforcement activity steadily moves towards increased enforcement and the construction of more detention centers to accommodate more detainees, the question of what the future will bring to the children of immigrant parents (many of whom are U.S.-born) is unclear. Failed immigration policy reforms in 2006–2007 heightened public discourse on immigration and pressured individual states such as Arizona to adopt hard-line immigration enforcement measures, and in doing so, neglected to take into account how such measures impact children who by most standards are considered one of the most vulnerable of populations. For example, in 2006, Hazelton, Pennsylvania, passed a city ordinance that prohibited landlords from renting to potential tenants over the age of eighteen who failed to complete an "occupancy permit application," which required the production of identification and proof of the applicant's U.S. citizenship and/or legal residency. Upon review of this ordinance, a number of persons under eleven categories of lawfully present immigrants under federal law were omitted. The ordinance was eventually overturned on the grounds that it made unlawful certain individuals whom the federal government considered to be lawfully present. Because it conflicted with federal law and because both legal and undocumented immigrants were affected even though only undocumented immigrants were targeted, the ordinance was invalidated.

How such anti-immigrant ordinances may violate due process guaranteed by the Fourteenth Amendment of the U.S. Constitution is yet to be resolved. This amendment forbids states from depriving "any person of life, liberty or property, without due process of law." It is important to note that this amendment applies to "persons," and not just citizens or legal residents. As such, the deprivation of due process in which immigrants, because of their legal status, may be erroneously deprived of such rights, may also affect family members who are entitled to certain rights based on the categories of lawful residents, or citizen or noncitizen children. In such cases, Hazelton's "Tenant Registration Ordinance" may not only deny basic housing to immigrants who are unlawfully present, but also to her/his family members who may not be. It is important to note the parallel of Hazelton's anti-immigrant ordinance requiring proof of citizenship with the need to provide proof to access Arizona's healthcare system. The health service restrictions in Arizona also potentially and erroneously deprive immigrants of rights affecting family members who *are* unquestionably entitled to certain rights under any of the categories of lawfully present immigrants under federal law.

Anna Ochoa O'Leary

See Also: Children; Family Economics; Family Reunification; Family Structure; Fourteenth Amendment; Lawful Permanent Residents; Postville, Iowa Raid; Southern States; Workplace Raids.

Further Reading

Capps, Randy, Rosa Maria Castañeda, Ajay Chaudry, and Robert Santos. 2007. "Paying the Price: The Impact of Immigration Raids on America's Children." Washington, DC: Urban Institute and the National Council of La Raza (NCLR). http://www.urban.org/UploadedPDF/411566_immigration_raids.pdf.

Cosentino de Cohen, Clemencia, Nicole Deterding, and Beatriz Chu Clewell. 2005. "Who's Left Behind: Immigrant Children in High and Low LEP Schools." Washington, DC: Urban Institute Program for Evaluation and Equity Research. www.urban.org.

Fix, Michael, and Wendy Zimmermann. 2001. "All under One Roof: Mixed-Status Families in an Era of Reform." *International Migration Review* 35.2:397–419.

Fry, Richard, and Jeffrey S. Passel. 2009. "Latino Children: The Majority Are U.S.-born Offspring of Immigrants." Washington, DC: Pew Hispanic Center. http://www.pewhispanic.org/2009/05/28/latino-children-a-majority-are-us-born-offspring-of-immigrants/.

O'Leary, Anna Ochoa, and Azucena Sánchez. 2011. "Anti-Immigrant Arizona: Ripple Effects and Mixed Immigration Status Households under Policies of Attrition Considered." *Journal of Borderland Studies* 26.1:115–133.

Passel, Jeffrey S., and D'Vera Cohn. 2009. "A Portrait of Undocumented Immigrants in the United States." Washington, DC: Pew Hispanic Center. http://www.pewhispanic.org/2009/04/14/a-portrait-of-unauthorized-immigrants-in-the-united-states/.

Mobility

Mobility describes the ability to move around in space, such as being able to cross borders to visit family (here, the term is not used to mean change in socioeconomic status). The term does not distinguish between the ability to move and the actual behavior of moving; obviously people may be able to travel but may choose not to do so. Nevertheless, ability to move is key to understanding the lives and experiences of undocumented people, because one of the effects of their legal status is the risk to moving around; indeed, they have traveled across borders in the first place to be migrants.

People face many barriers to mobility. These include disabilities, limits placed on women's movement, geographic isolation, lack of geographical knowledge, lack of private vehicles or poor quality of vehicles, and lack of public transportation or poor quality of such transportation. All of these factors may be exacerbated by undocumented status—for example, low incomes caused by working in precarious jobs may result in no vehicles or poorly functioning ones. But the main issue is how undocumented status is directly a barrier to mobility.

First, undocumented status limits movement in and out of the national territory (that is, crossing borders). Even though exit from the United States is little restricted, the difficulty, cost, and risk of arrest upon returning serve as a powerful incentive for undocumented people not to depart, that is, to stay inside the national territory, even if they would prefer to go back and forth (e.g., to visit loved ones in other countries).

Second, undocumented status presents a risk while traveling within the national territory. Within one hundred miles of the U.S. boundaries (land and sea), the Border Patrol can stop people for questioning about legal status, and arrest them. This occurs throughout the transportation system: highways, roads, streets, bus lines, rail lines, stations, and airports. The Border Patrol also operates fixed checkpoints on main highways in the interior of the country (in the border region) that stop and inspect people traveling away from the border. Local and state police often contact undocumented people while they are traveling. Sometimes this is deliberate, as they may operate checkpoints officially or unofficially for the purpose of examining immigration status, as may be done under the 287(g) program of the Immigration and Nationality Act, where states and other localities are able to work with the U.S. Immigration and Customs Enforcement agency (ICE). Other times, this is a byproduct of normal policing of traffic for driving violations, intoxication, etc. The line between unintentional stops and covert profiling of immigrants is often fuzzy. In most but not all states, undocumented status prevents the acquisition of a driver's license, which in turn either means that people do not drive, or that they drive at constant risk of being stopped by local police, which in turn may lead to being identified and deported by the U.S. Department of Homeland Security.

Undocumented people sometimes are trapped by such barriers and risks. They may be literally enclosed by obstacles, and also feel trapped by anxiety and fear. This opposite of mobility is referred to variously as immobilization, enclosure, or entrapment processes. They may be trapped in homes, workplaces, neighborhoods, or short routes between well-known and safe places. And even then, their movement may not actually be fully safe. Surprises may happen because of the policing of roads and transportation routes (as well as other locations, such as workplaces).

But entrapment processes are not complete. Undocumented people are not simply frozen in place or held inside an impenetrable prison. Obviously, they were mobile in the initial act of international migration. Once within the United States, they face a difficult and perilous judgment, often on a daily or at least frequent basis. Take risks? Stay trapped? Is the risk of moving worth the income from going to work? The need to bring a sick child to a health clinic? The moral obligation to help transport a sister or cousin? Likewise, the means of movement involves a complex and risky calculation. Use a car without a license? Hire a guide, transporter, or smuggler? Leave the country and risk never getting back? These considerations form a difficult morality of risk: which reasons for mobility are so morally or practically compelling that undocumented people will put themselves at risk of arrest and deportation in order to travel to obtain that goal?

These barriers to mobility, the complicated choices that surround them, and the anxieties that they induce, have profound effects on the lives of the undocumented. People may not address serious health problems or access preventative care. They may accept less transportation-risky, but more exploitative employment. They may live in marginal, exploitative housing, for lack of ability to move to better locations.

They may be constrained from participating in community activities and networks. Women may be reluctant to travel away from the home, making them more suscepti- ble to domestic abuse and control. The common mixture of citizen, documented, and undocumented people in one single ("mixed status") household means that entrap- ment processes may impact even people with legal status. U.S. citizen children may not access important health and social services because of their undocumented parents' difficulty in travel to provision locations. Other factors, such as fear of au- thorities, may interweave with immobility to create webs of negative effects that are difficult to overcome. And feelings of entrapment may lead to depression and anxiety, harming mental health.

Josiah McC. Heyman

See Also: Acculturation Stress; Mental Health Care Access; Mental Health Care Issues for Undocumented Immigrants; Sanctuary Cities and Secure Communities.

Further Reading

Cunningham, Hilary, and Josiah McC. Heyman. 2004. "Introduction: Mobilities and Enclosures at Borders." *Identities: Global Studies in Culture and Power* 11:289–302.
Migration Policy Institute. 2013. http://www.migrationpolicy.org.
Migration Policy Institute. 2013. "Migration Information Source." http://www.migration-information.org.
Núñez, Guillermina Gina, and Josiah McC. Heyman. 2007. "Entrapment Processes and Immigrant Communities in a Time of Heightened Border Vigilance." *Human Organi- zation* 66:354–365.
Pallitto, Robert, and Josiah McC. Heyman. 2008. "Theorizing Cross-Border Mobility: Surveillance, Security and Identity." *Surveillance & Society* 5:315–333. http://www .surveillance-and-society.org/articles5(3)/mobility.pdf (accessed Oct. 20, 2010).

Mortgages

With the rising number of immigrants arriving in the United States in the mid-1990s, many banks, including the Federal National Mortgage Association (Fannie Mae), took steps to make home ownership easier for recent immigrants (Bradsher, 1994). Since 1992 and for several years, Fannie Mae had conducted its National Housing Survey to find out more about American attitudes toward housing and homeownership. Among the results of the survey was a confirmation of the idea that immigrants come to America because they believed in—and wanted to be a part of—the American Dream. Part of what that notion encompasses is homeownership. In turn, homeownership is correlated to ideas of prosperity and optimism about their new country's prospects, and their own.

However, immigrants' status has a bearing on their relatively low homeownership rates. Immigration and homeownership need to be seen in the context of persistent patterns of racial and ethnic stratification in the country. Immigrants are "doubly" disadvantaged as both an ethnic minority and immigrant and therefore have relatively

Hugo Malara, a 48-year-old immigrant from El Salvador, carries a television set as he packs to move out of his foreclosed home in North Las Vegas, Nevada, 2009. No longer able to make his monthly mortgage payment after losing his job, Malara paid $800 to a former mortgage broker who promised to help him negotiate to keep his home. He later learned that the bank had already sold his home at auction. An untold number of undocumented immigrants lost their homes during the economic downturn in 2007–2008. (AP Photo/Jae C. Hong)

low rates of homeownership (McConnell and Marcelli, 2007). In particular, undocumented immigrants—regardless of how many years they have resided in the United States—live precariously and always in fear that they may be removed from the country. With the prices of homes increasing, mortgage loans are increasingly the only avenue to be a home owner. With job instability and low pay, undocumented immigrants are less likely to apply and receive approval for home loans. Moreover, financial institutions typically require a social security number or driver's license to apply for credit; and proof of citizenship is also typically required for loans. These requirements make it difficult if not impossible for an undocumented immigrant to obtain a mortgage loan. However, in spite of this requirement many still manage to come to own their own home.

Banking practices have changed since the 1980s in part due to their desire to tap into a consumer market fueled by immigration. There is evidence that many banks have been aggressive in recruiting immigrants for mortgage loans (Chanderasekhar, 2004). For example, some banks have allowed immigrants to obtain a home mortgage even if they don't have a social security number. Instead, individual tax identification numbers (ITINs) have at times been used. ITINs are a nine-digit tax-processing number that the Internal Revenue Service began issuing in 1996 to individuals who were required to have a U.S. taxpayer identification number but who did not have one, or were not eligible to obtain a social security number. Since the IRS doesn't require legal residency to obtain an ITIN, many nonresident immigrants or undocumented immigrants use this as a form of identification to pay U.S. taxes and buy homes. Large financial institutions such as Citigroup have accepted ITINs as part of their loan processing. In addition, Citigroup and other financial institutions have accepted an identification card issued by Mexican consulates, called a *matricula consular,* for some bank transactions. Combined with predatory lending practices of some representatives of banking insitutions, consisting of exploitative and fraudulent lending practices, immigrants (including undocumented immigrants) have been able to apply for and be approved for home mortgage loans. In this way, many different categories of immigrants have been able to purchase homes. In a research study by McConnell and Marcelli (2007) in Los Angeles, the relationship between home ownership and different types of immigrants was examined. The results showed that home ownership by type of immigrant status—legal permanent resident, non-immigrant visa holders, and unauthorized immigrant—was not significantly different from that of U.S. citizens. In other words, legal status did not keep undocumented immigrants from buying homes.

Immigrants are strongly committed to achieving homeownership as a symbol of their integration into American life and owning a piece of the American Dream. However, as a general rule they are highly discriminated against in the mortgage-lending process; first because they generally tend to earn less, they are deemed less creditworthy. Credit scores may also overestimate the risk they pose to lending institutions, resulting in higher interest rates. In this way they figure prominently in the discriminatory practices of banks, and constitute discrimination in access to credit.

Anna Ochoa O'Leary

See Also: Banking; Family Economics; Identification Cards; Individual Taxpayer Identification Number (ITIN).

Further Reading

Bradsher, Keith. 1994. "Fannie Mae seeks to ease home buying." *New York Times,* March 10. D1. *Academic Search Complete,* EBSCO*host* (accessed May 2, 2013).

Chanderasekhar, Charu A. 2004. "Can New Americans Achieve the American Dream? Promoting Homeownership in Immigrant Communities." *Harvard Civil Rights–Civil Liberties Law Review* 39.1:169–216.

Johnson, James A. 1995. What immigrants want. "*Wall Street Journal.*" June 20. Retrieved from http://ezproxy.library.arizona.edu/login?url=http://search.proquest.com/docview/398445686?accountid=8360.

McConnell, Eileen Diaz, and Enrico A. Marcelli. 2007. "Buying into the American Dream? Mexican Immigrants, Legal Status, and Homeownership in Los Angeles County." *Social Science Quarterly* 88.1:199–221.

Morton Memo

In June of 2011, a memo was issued by Immigration and Customs Enforcement (ICE) Director John Morton, which outlined new guidelines recommending "prosecutorial discretion" to help immigration enforcement agents determine whether cases for removal are of a high or low priority. Prosecutorial discretion means making decisions that best focus the resources that the government has to carry out its mandates. It is widely understood and accepted that the arrest and removal from the country of more than 11 million undocumented immigrants is neither practical nor feasible. Known as the "Morton Memo," the guidelines recommend that ICE agents are to use their discretion when deciding whom to arrest and remove from the country, encouraging a focus of ICE efforts to find and arrest immigrant fugitives who pose a security threat to society and/or are wanted for committing crimes, and placing on low priority for arrest and removal those immigrants that pose no danger. More specifically, the memo outlined that agents were to use special consideration for not removing undocumented students, undocumented immigrants with longstanding family ties to the United States, undocumented immigrants who have contributed to their communities or served in the military, family members of veterans, those immigrants with serious health issues, caregivers, or victims of crime. The final category of undocumented immigrants that qualified for prosecutorial discretion was the rather vague category of those who "have a strong basis for remaining in the United States."

The memo comes in the wake of the trend towards the greater policing of immigrants. The 1996 Illegal Immigration Reform and Immigrant Responsibility Act (IIRIRA) had significantly expanded enforcement efforts resulting in greater emotional trauma and economic hardship imposed on families when a member of a household, especially if they were primary income earners, was suddenly removed from the country. With IIRIRA, the term used to refer to the process of expelling an undocumented immigrant to their country of origin, deportation, was changed to removal. IIRIRA also provided for expedited removal of immigrants, which accelerates the processing and removal of those immigrants who have entered the country without an immigrant visa or other official entry documents. Moreover, as the study by Hagen and Rodriguez (2002) shows, families of undocumented immigrants include legal resident family members and citizens in what is commonly referred to as mixed immigration status families (Fix and Zimmerman, 2001). The net result is increased policing as mandated by IIRIRA, especially in border states where there has been a historical high concentration of immigrant households, many of which are multigenerational (O'Leary and Sanchez, 2011). With greater policing in these areas, there have been more deportations, more criminalization, and more family separation. Moreover, with immigration enforcement increasingly encompassing areas outside the border region in the more internal parts of the nation, removals have dramatically increased the development of similar conditions elsewhere. More removals have been blamed on the increase in poverty in immigrant communities and growing fear and distrust of authorities, forcing them further into the shadows of U.S. society (Hagen and Rodriguez, 2002).

The Morton Memo also reflects a reversal of the trend of increased prosecution of immigrants living and building communities in the United States. Subsequent to the release of the Morton Memo, on October 5, 2012, another memo was issued by ICE clarifying "family relationships" to include "long-term same-sex partners." Hailed as a victory for LGBT communities, this memo defined same-sex relationships that qualify as a family relationship for purposes of prosecutorial discretion as those in which the individuals:

1. are each other's sole domestic partner and intend to remain so indefinitely;
2. are not in a marital or other domestic relationship with anyone else; and
3. typically maintain a common residence and share financial obligations and assets.

The definition of family relationships set forth in the October 2012 memorandum also made it clear that a legal marriage was not necessary for the relationship to be considered. In this way, same-sex partners became eligible for the exercise of prosecutorial discretion as set forth in the June 2011 "Morton memo." It is estimated that there are 36,000 binational gay couples in the United States and these new policies allow some of these families which would have been separated to stay intact.

Anna Ochoa O'Leary

See Also: Deferred Action for Childhood Arrivals (DACA); Expedited Removal; Families; Family Reunification; Illegal Immigration Reform and Immigrant Responsibility Act (IIRIRA) (1996); LGBT Immigrants without Documentation; Provisional Unlawful Presence (PUP) Waiver.

Further Reading

Fix, Michael, and Wendy Zimmermann. 2001. "All under One Roof: Mixed-Status Families in an Era of Reform." *International Migration Review* 35.2:397–419.

Hagan, Jacqueline, and Nestor Rodriguez. 2002. "Resurrecting Exclusion: The Effects of 1996 U.S. Immigration Reform on Communities and Families in Texas, El Salvador, and Mexico." In Marcelo M. Suarez-Orozco and Mariela M. Páez, eds., *Latinas/os: Remaking of America,* 190–214. Berkeley: University of California Press.

Hoy, Seth. 2012. "DHS Announces Expansion of Prosecutorial Discretion Guidelines." American Immigration Council. http://immigrationimpact.com/2011/08/18/dhs-announces-expansion-of-prosecutorial-discretion-guidelines/.

O'Leary, Anna Ochoa, and Azucena Sanchez. 2011. "Anti-Immigrant Arizona: Ripple Effects and Mixed Immigration Status Households under 'Policies of Attrition' Considered." *Journal of Borderlands Studies* 26.1:115–133.

Multicultural Education

Multicultural education is an approach of teaching that helps students know, value, and respect the diverse languages and culture traditions that enrich the nation, and engages them in learning and maintaining it. Following the Immigration Reform Act of 1965 (also known as the Hart-Celler Act of 1965), the United States has experienced its largest movement of immigrants since the beginning of the twentieth century. This immigration act provided for a greater diversity in the nation's social composition because it allowed those previously restricted by national quotas to enter the United States. This infusion made this country a multicultural one while at the same time challenging its institutions to respond to and to accommodate differences.

One of the institutions where change was to take place was the nation's educational system. Schools became places where students from different backgrounds came together to learn about the American way of life. The challenge for schools and their administrators thus became designing curricula to provide these students with a meaningful curriculum. As such, multicultural education concepts often deal with those human characteristics that celebrate diversity and make it possible. Critical issues that are often raised are those dealing with race, culture, language, social class, gender, and disability. Multicultural education started to be implemented in the United States educational system in 1970 shortly after the Civil Rights Movement. Multicultural education was seen as an answer to tendencies within schooling systems that encouraged assimilation. Assimilation was promoted before the Civil Rights period as a way to "Americanize" foreign students. However, critics pointed out that the effort to Americanize foreign-born students forced them to think of their culture, language, and identity as somehow deficient, un-American, and undesirable, resulting in low self-esteem. As a consequence, students were more likely to feel humiliated and alienated from their schools and teachers, thus impeding learning and higher educational achievement. The results of this were lower earnings and political disenfranchisement and the creation of a semi-permanent underclass made up of mostly minorities and Latinos. For this reason, educators and proponents of multicultural education argue that multicultural education is a human right because it is intricately connected to fundamental human development and self-realization.

For immigrant students, the features of multicultural education have become controversial and highly politicized in the context of growing anti-immigrant sentiment. Although the idea of multicultural education was embraced after the Civil Rights Movement and subsequent research proved that all students regardless of their background stood to benefit from the multicultural approach, critics increasingly began to articulate their nonconformity with students in the school system who were in their view undeserving of public resources. Increasingly so, this view has gained currency among nativists who associate minority youth with more recent immigration trends, namely those coming to the United States from Mexico and Latin American countries.

A case in point comes from the recent efforts in the Republican-dominated state legislature in Arizona to ban ethnic studies curricula in the Tucson Unified School District (TUSD). This effort came on the heels of a notable civic response to dozens of anti-immigrant proposals in the state where in 2006 hundreds of students had walked out of classes in support of immigration reform. Following the demonstration, United Farmworker leader Dolores Huerta was invited to speak at a special assembly for TUSD students where she remarked, "Republicans hate Latinos." Outraged, state Superintendent Tom Horne (later state attorney general) publically blamed the school's Mexican American studies curriculum for inciting civic disobedience and began to push for the dismantling of the program. In 2010, one month after Arizona's SB1070 "Paper Please" law was signed by the state's governor, HB2281, banning ethnic studies from Arizona schools, was also signed into law (O'Leary et al., 2012).

Consistent with the principles of multicultural education, the ethnic studies and Mexican-American studies programs in TUSD had promoted awareness and respect for the presence of all diverse groups, acknowledging and valuing social-cultural differences. The possibility of developing positive racial and language attitudes as well as engaging in inter-group relations was thought to be key to empowering and reaffirming democratic values within the organization or society. For Mexican American, immigrant and Native American students, this approach was seen as necessary to preserve their home cultures and heritage and help them achieve academically, effectively preparing them to live as global citizens in a pluralistic society. This would help students operate and function successfully in multiple cultural contexts. However, in Arizona, State School Superintendent Tom Horne helped craft a legislative measure that eliminated the ethnic studies program in TUSD. In evidence of the connection between undocumented immigration and multicultural education, the bill was proposed as an amendment to a Homeland Security Bill in 2008, first as Arizona Senate Bill 1108, which failed to pass in that year's legislative session. It was re-introduced again in 2010 as HB2281, when it passed. The proposal and the purpose of the law demonstrate how it was strategically linked to the anti-immigrant movement, and further extended this movement to what was portrayed as "immigrant culture."

Today, a dramatic globalization of societies and economies, unprecedented mass movements, as well as the growth of information technology and accessible communication, have transformed older concepts of nationhood and the contributions and role of culture. Multicultural education is thought to help develop the knowledge of students to better enable them to better appreciate world events, situations, and problems from the perspectives and lens of a variety of ethnic and national groups.

Martha Yamilett Martinez-Espinoza

See Also: Assimilation; Cultural Citizenship; Culture; Education; Elementary Schools; English-Only Movement; Globalization; Hart-Celler Act (1965); *Plyler v. Doe.*

Further Reading

Banks, James A. 2006. *Cultural Diversity and Education: Foundations, Curriculum and Teaching.* Pearson.

Kanpo, Barry, and Peter McLaren. 1995. *Critical Multiculturalism: Uncommon Voices in a Common Struggle.* London. Berger and Garvey.

Oakes, Jeannie, and Martin Lipton. 2007. *Teaching to Change the World.* New York: McGraw Hill.

O'Leary, Anna Ochoa, Andrea J. Romero, Nolan L. Cabrera, and Michelle Rascón. 2012. "Assault on Ethnic Studies." In *Arizona Firestorm: Global Immigration Realities, National Media & Provincial Politics,* ed. Otto Santa Ana and Celeste González de Bustamante, 97–120. Lanham, MD: Rowman & Littlefield.

Sleeter, Christine E., and Carl A. Grant. 2009. *Making Choices for Multicultural Education. Five Approaches to Race, Class and Gender.* New York: John Wiley and Sons.

N

National Council of La Raza (NCLR)

The National Council of La Raza (NCLR) is "the largest national Latino civil rights and advocacy organization in the United States" (NCLR, 2013), whose goal is to make the American Dream attainable to the nation's Latino community. This private non-profit organization was established under the mission of improving opportunities and promoting success for Hispanic Americans. To achieve its objectives, NCLR uses a three-pronged approach comprising applied research, policy analysis, and advocacy. The organization focuses its efforts on five areas which include assets and investments, employment and economic status, education, health, and immigration and civil rights. NCLR is based in Washington D.C. and has offices in five major U.S. cities including New York, Chicago, San Antonio, Phoenix, and Los Angeles.

NCLR was founded in 1968 when it became apparent that the Latino community needed an organization to unite and guide it through the numerous movements occurring in and around that period. Despite their participation in the Civil Rights Movement, Latinos, especially Mexican Americans, were unrecognized and underrepresented in the political and civil rights arenas, and no Latino advocacy organization existed at that time. Collaboration among a group of Mexican American leaders led to the establishment of the Southwest Council of La Raza, which was later expanded to reach a broader population of Latinos and renamed to become NCLR.

Currently, NCLR's main clientele is all subgroups of U.S. Latinos. The organization has received criticism for its name, as the literal translation of *raza* is "race," a term that many people find to be exclusionary. However, the true meaning of *raza* is "the people" and it represents the vast array of backgrounds and cultures that characterize Latinos. Furthermore, "the people" extends beyond the Latino community to other demographics that NCLR also serves. In 2006, 20 percent of NCLR's clientele was white and 12 percent black (NCLR, 2013).

A second common criticism of NCLR is that it supports undocumented immigration and encourages amnesty for all. The organization refutes these claims and is in fact a proponent of immigration enforcement. Contrary to some beliefs, the NCLR does not promote *Reconquista,* or the reclamation of the American Southwest by Mexico. Instead, it strongly values the Latino presence in the United States, recognizes the nation's sovereignty, and encourages humane and just border enforcement.

To ensure that justice and humanity are preserved along the border, NCLR advocates for comprehensive immigration reform. The organization recognizes that until significant changes occur within the current immigration system, undocumented immigration will continue. NCLR calls for a solution that supports a more effective path to legal residence and a simpler naturalization process. The organization cites four supporting principles that should guide the solution as

1. "restoring order" by adjusting policies so that undocumented immigrants can feasibly gain legal status, learn English, and support the nation as citizens
2. "cracking down on unscrupulous employers," which would entail penalizing employers who hire and exploit undocumented workers
3. "unclogging legal channels" so that families can be reunited and more immigrants allowed to work legally, and
4. "enacting proactive measures" that will welcome the integration of immigrants into American culture (NCLR, 2013).

NCLR proposes several methods for accomplishing the four outlined solutions. For example, the organization recognizes the sixty-five thousand undocumented high school graduates whose opportunities are limited each year by restrictive legislation. NCLR believes that passage of the Development, Relief, and Education for Alien Minors (DREAM) Act is a step toward citizenship for these young people and an important approach to improving pathways to citizenship for U.S. Latinos as a whole.

NCLR is also a strong proponent of immigrant rights. In 2000, NCLR adopted criminal justice as a new concern within its civil rights category. This area has become critical as anti-immigrant legislation grows more targeted and controversial. The organization is specifically concerned with racial profiling, hate crimes, the juvenile justice system, sentencing reform, and reentry into society post-incarceration. NCLR's website features a number of publications that describe immigrants' rights. However, NCLR critics have argued that these publications teach undocumented people how to avoid law enforcement.

NCLR has made several public efforts to address the noted criticisms and educate the public about the organization's true intentions. NCLR's President and CEO, Janet Murguía, who is also the organization's spokesperson, has appeared on a number of national television broadcasts. She also wrote an open letter to the public which is posted on NCLR's website.

Beyond public outreach, Murguía has been an influential force in other recent NCLR happenings. Under her leadership, NCLR has developed relationships with over three hundred affiliates. This initiative has allowed the organization to expand its reach to forty-one states, the District of Columbia and Puerto Rico, thereby building nationwide support for Latinos.

One of Murguía's priorities since her stepping into the organization's leadership position in 2005 has been strengthening the Latino voice by assisting Latinos with voter registration and applications for citizenship. Through these efforts, NCLR and its partners played an important role in registering over two hundred thousand Latinos for the 2008 election. Indeed, minority participation reached new heights during the 2008 election, and Latinos comprised 7.4 percent of the voters (Hugo Lopez and Taylor, 2009). In the past two decades, the proportion of eligible Latino voters has more than doubled from 4.7 percent in 1988 to 9.5 percent in 2008. Of the population of eligible Latino voters, nearly 50 percent participated in the 2008 election.

Another priority for NCLR is collaborating with representative organizations in other minority communities, such as the National Association for the Advancement of Colored People (NAACP), with the goal of uniting and empowering commonly marginalized populations. NCLR also shows concern for the portrayal of Latinos in the media. Murguía was responsible for reinstalling NCLR's Alma Awards in 2006 which has aired since 2003. The Alma Awards is an NBC broadcast which celebrates the talents and positive portrayals of Latinos in film, music, and television. Prominent Latinos such as Henry Darrow, Zoë Saldaña, Cheech Marin, Christina Aguillera, Antonio Banderas, Jessica Alba, Pitbull, and Demi Lovato have won in recent years.

Courtney Waters

See Also: League of United Latin American Citizens (LULAC); Mexican American Legal Defense and Education Fund (MALDEF).

Further Reading

Hugo Lopez, Mark, and Paul Taylor. 2009. "Dissecting the 2008 Electorate: Most Diverse in U.S. History." Pew Hispanic Center. http://www.pewhispanic.org/2009/04/30/dissecting-the-2008-electorate-most-diverse-in-us-history/.

NCLR. 2013. National Council of La Raza Web Site. http://www.nclr.org/.

USA News Network. 2006, July 13. Lou Dobbs–National Council of La Raza (The Race). YouTube Web Site http://www.youtube.com/watch?v=7kmTLk2Fgas.

National Network for Immigrant and Refugee Rights (NNIRR)

The National Network for Immigrant and Refugee Rights (NNIRR) is an advocacy group focused on the rights of immigrants and refugees in the United States, regardless of immigration status. NNIRR is a network comprising more than 250 different organizations and individuals from several diverse immigrant communities, including labor organizations, religious groups, civil rights activists, and community organizations. The network shares the common mission of promoting migrant and refugee rights as well as economic and social justice.

Established in 1986, NNIRR has implemented many programs designed to empower refugees and immigrants, focusing on human rights as well as labor, environmental, safety, education, welfare, and LGBTQ issues. At the forefront of these programs is their Immigrant Justice and Rights Program. NNIRR maintains the perspective that current U.S. legislation regarding immigration has led to a humanitarian crisis, especially regarding the militarization of the U.S.-Mexico border.

One of their most important accomplishments is the founding of the Human Rights Immigrant Community Action Network or HURRICANE. HURRICANE consists of the aforementioned advocates and organizations, and represents a strategy based on the principles of community-based organization and dialogue. HURRICANE seeks to build a database and publish reports of human rights violations committed against refugees and immigrants. The network seeks to track and document these violations in order to determine the best method of preventing future human rights abuses.

Initiatives have included the "100 Stories Project," reports that contain stories about human rights abuses as well as recommendations for human rights protection, which are usually released on or around International Migrants Day, on December 18.

The third report, entitled "Injustice for All: The Rise of U.S. Immigration Policing Regime," contains several cases of these documented human rights abuses as well as essays from prominent immigrant rights advocates. The 2009–2010 human rights report finds that U.S. immigration control has continued and contributed to an expansion of human rights abuses and violations. According to the report, related trends in the proliferation of human rights violations include increased criminalization of migrants and increased border militarization and police presence. It notes that the number of detainees in U.S. detention centers, the number of deportations, and the amount of migrant deaths at the border have all significantly increased. The report includes 129 documented stories that illustrate a range of human rights abuses, all compiled from individual interviews, reports from members of the HURRICANE network, and outside media reports. The stories contain emotional, physical, and legal accounts of rights violations at the hands of local, county, state, and federal law enforcement officers. More than one-third of the stories discuss abuses against women. Other reports released by the HURRICANE initiative include "Over Raided, Under Siege: Immigration Laws and Enforcement Destroy the Rights of Immigrants" and "Guilty by Immigration Status." HURRICANE has also trained over two hundred community leaders on human rights violation documentation through workshops and webinars.

The network also focuses on community outreach. In addition to the establishment of HURRICANE, NNIRR has created a series of popular educational workshops entitled BRIDGE, or Building a Race and Immigrant Dialogue in the Global Economy. These workshops include information on grassroots legislation, U.S. immigration history, homeland security, human rights, trade policies, and a historical and political perspective of the U.S.-Mexico border. The program also includes the 2001 documentary produced by NNIRR called "Uprooted: Refugees of the Global Economy," which discusses how the current international economy has driven people from their country of origin and focuses on migrants from Haiti, Bolivia and the Philippines. The BRIDGE popular education text has been distributed worldwide and is available in several languages.

Jenna Glickman

See Also: Mexican American Legal Defense and Education Fund (MALDEF); National Council of La Raza (NCLR).

Further Reading

"Injustice for All: The Rise of the Immigration Control Regime." 2010. U.S. Human Rights Network. http://173.236.53.234/~nnirrorg/drupal/sites/default/files/injustice_for_all_-_web_report.pdf.

National Network for Immigrant and Refugee Rights (NNIRR). 2013. http://www.nnirr.org/drupal/.

"The 100 Stories Project." National Network for Immigrant and Refugee Rights. The Human Rights Immigrant Community Action Network. http://www.nnirr.org/~nnirrorg/drupal/programs/immigrant-justice-rights/hurricane.

Naturalization

In the United States, naturalization is the process by which noncitizens become citizens. The process was established by an act of Congress, the Naturalization Act of 1790. This act provided for white immigrants who could also prove they were of good moral character to become citizens. Children under the age of twenty-one who were direct descendants of applicants who successfully obtained citizenship automatically became citizens. Over the years, there were modifications to this initial act: in 1795, 1798, 1870, 1906 and 1952. These modifications addressed the use of race as a criterion for citizenship. For example, in 1868, new alliances between the United States and Mexico flourished in the wake of the American Civil War, which resulted in excellent relations between the two countries and a softening of initial overt racial overtones of the naturalization process. The Naturalization Treaty of 1868 between the new nations allowed Mexican and black immigrants to apply for citizenship. There was strong opposition even then to the agreement by those who saw Mexicans as being of mixed race. Although most were primarily of mixed racial heritage, the result of centuries of intermarriage between Spanish colonizers and Native Americans, there were also many who had black ancestry. At the time of the signing of the treaty, there were no provisions for

Newly naturalized American citizens recite the Pledge of Allegiance. Each year, the U.S. Customs and Immigration Service, the agency responsible for overseeing the process since 2003, welcomes approximately 680,000 citizens during naturalization ceremonies across the United States and around the world. In 2012, the top countries of origin for new naturalized U.S. citizens were (in descending order): Mexico, Philippines, India, Dominican Republic, and China. (PhotoDisc, Inc.)

granting Native Americans in the United States citizenship status. Although many of the racial overtones of citizenship were addressed by the Immigration Act of 1952, immigration scholars continue to maintain today that race, language, and ethnicity continued to shape the process and notions about who is entitled to be a citizen of the United States to the advantage of those coming from western European countries.

The general protocol for naturalization was founded in 1906 and was used until 1952. The applicant was to begin by filling out a declaration of intention. Within this form the applicant was asked to certify that it was his or her own will to become a citizen of the United States. In addition, the applicant was asked to renounce any affiliation or alliance to foreign countries. After the form was filled and a court clerk recorded the applicant's oath, the applicant waited a period varying from two to seven years, in order to petition for U.S. citizenship. The applicant was later asked to appear in court with two witnesses that could validate that they had been residing in the United States for five years and possessed good moral character. A period of investigation would then begin, and a judge would then decide to have a hearing in which the verdict was given. A judge could ask for further investigation or negate the application. If all went well the applicant would be issued an order of citizenship. However, in 1952 the declaration of intent was eliminated from the application process for naturalization.

Currently the general naturalization process requires that the applicant be at least eighteen years old, in addition to being a green card holder for a minimum of five years preceding the date of application. The applicant must also be able to prove residency within the jurisdiction stipulated by the United States Citizenship and Immigration Services. They must also live in the United States continually after the submission of the application up until the point of naturalization. The applicant must be able to speak English in addition to having an understanding of the United States governmental system and history. Finally the applicant must be a person of good moral character in accordance with the United States Constitution.

Each year, the U.S. Customs and Immigration Service, the agency responsible for overseeing the process since 2003, welcomes approximately 680,000 citizens during naturalization ceremonies across the United States and around the world. In 2012, the top countries of origin for new naturalized citizens in descending order were Mexico, Philippines, India, Dominican Republic, and China. However, compared to other groups of immigrants from Latin America and the Caribbean, Mexicans have the lowest rate of naturalization. It is believed that language and other barriers such as financial barriers hinder them from pursuing citizenship. Among those who have not yet naturalized, the desire to do so is great. The surveys show that more than nine in ten (93 percent) Hispanic immigrants who have not yet naturalized say they "would" naturalize if they could. There are also reasons related to history that account for the relatively low rates of Mexicans who apply for citizenship. Greater restriction on immigrants who desire to come to the United States is one. Such restrictions have converged with greater poverty levels in Mexico and thus the need of immigrants to come to the United States to work without authorization. This reduces the number of those who are eligible to become citizens because once having crossed the border without authorization they were no longer qualified, at least until recently when a series of Obama administration memos and directives provided relief for certain undocumented immigrants. For example, in January of 2013, the Obama Administration announced a new rule that will allow thousands of American citizens to avoid long separations from immediate family members who are undocumented and want to initiate the process of becoming legal residents by applying for a Provisional Unlawful Presence (PUP) Waiver. Legal resident status provides a pathway for citizenship.

The articulation of anti-immigrant sentiment also provides for an unwelcoming attitude that discourages many from applying. The proliferation of anti-immigrant legislation in state legislatures attests to this unwelcoming attitude. Contemporary debates over comprehensive immigration reform have also made this attitude clear. The U.S. Congress House Resolution Bill 4427, Border Protection, Antiterrorism, and the Illegal Immigration Control Act of 2005, was an enforcement-only measure that offered no pathway to citizenship for undocumented immigrants. The rather acrimonious debate continued through 2007 when negotiations between legislators broke down and mass demonstrations erupted throughout the country in protest. Although this bill never made it through the Senate, any discussion of the so-called "pathway to citizenship" has raised the ire of many nativists who fear a repeat of any amnesty provision such as that provided by the 1986 Immigration Control and Reform Act (IRCA) and the possibility that it would open the door for more immigration, and not less. Finally, an anti-immigrant sentiment has been harshly articulated in the form of propositions in some states and in the nation's capital to eliminate birthright citizenship for U.S.-born children of undocumented immigrants.

The Immigration and Nationality Act (INA) authorizes U.S. Citizenship and Immigration Services (USCIS) to expedite the application and naturalization process for current members of the U.S. armed forces and recently discharged members. Under special provisions in Section 329 of the INA, signed by a Presidential Executive Order on July 3, 2002, all noncitizens who have served honorably in the U.S. armed forces on or after Sept. 11, 2001 may apply immediately for citizenship. This order also covers veterans of certain designated past wars and conflicts. The authorization will remain in effect until a date designated by a future presidential executive order. Since September 2001, USCIS has naturalized 74,977 members of the military in this way. Spouses and children of noncitizen service members also benefit from this Executive Order. Military Selective Service Act of 1948 mandates under penalty of law that all males residing in the United States (citizens, lawful permanent residents, and undocumented immigrants) ages 18–25 register with Selective Service System (www.sss.gov). Although the Selective Service advertises that it does not collect any information that would indicate whether or not the registrant is undocumented, the military is required to check if any documents used to enlist in the military are false, for which the enlistee may be dishonorably discharged for fraudulent enlistment. There have been several news accounts that suggest that many, in fact, are undocumented immigrants. Many were brought as undocumented children to the United States and may qualify for the military in every other way. Like their native-born counterparts, they too may be drawn to the armed forces for the same reasons, such as finding a steady job with benefits and the respect and dignity that a military lifestyle might provide. Allowing undocumented immigrants to apply for citizenship in conjunction with service in the military has been part of several DREAM Act proposals, but until now, none have garnered enough legislative support to pass both houses of the U.S. Congress.

Anna Ochoa O'Leary

See Also: Citizenship; Citizenship Education; Cultural Citizenship; Immigration Act (IMMACT) (1990); Immigration and Customs Enforcement (ICE); Immigration and Nationality Act (The McCarron-Walter Act) (1952); Immigration Reform and Control Act (IRCA) (1986); U.S. Citizenship and Immigration Services (USCIS).

Further Reading

Gorman, Anna. 2010. "Army veteran, an illegal immigrant, wants citizenship." *Seattle Times,* May 8. Available at http://seattletimes.com/html/nationworld/2011811107_immigarmy09.html.

Menchaca, Martha. 2011. *Naturalizing Mexican Immigrants: A Texas History.* Austin: University of Texas Press.

Ngai, Mae M. 2004. *Impossible Subjects: Illegal Aliens and the Making of Modern America.* Princeton, NJ: Princeton University Press.

Taylor, Paul, Ana Gonzalez-Barerra, Jeffrey Passel, and Mark Hugo Lopez. 2012. "Aging, Naturalization and Immigration Will Drive Growth: An Awakened Giant: The Hispanic Electorate Is Likely to Double by 2030." Pew Research. http://www.pewhispanic.org/2012/11/14/iv-reasons-for-not-naturalizing/.

Zolberg, Aristide R. 2006. *A Nation by Design: Immigration Policy in the Fashioning of America.* Cambridge, MA: Harvard University Press.

New Jersey

According to the Pew Hispanic Center (Passel and Cohn, 2011), New Jersey ranks fifth amongst the states with the largest undocumented immigration population (550,000), accounting for approximately 5 percent of the nation. This statistic is noteworthy since the state is superseded by much larger states (both in the geographic and demographic sense)—California, Texas, Florida, and New York. Despite a decrease in the estimated undocumented population between 2007 and 2010, there has been an estimated gain of at least 400,000 since 1990. Yet, New Jersey ranks fourth among states where undocumented immigrants constitute the largest shares of the overall population (6.2 percent). This statistic highlights the level of concentration that exists in the state. Despite its size, the state of New Jersey ranks high in these demographic dimensions.

An additional finding from the Pew Report (Passel and Cohn, 2011) was that no one national origin group constitutes more than half of the undocumented immigrant population in New Jersey. The population appears to contain much more diversity in terms of country of origin than its larger counterparts like California and Texas. The diversity found among the foreign-born population in the northeastern part of the state (bordering New York City) appears to also exist in the undocumented immigrant population throughout the state (Espenshade, 1997).

Finally, in regards to labor, New Jersey also ranks among the top five states with both the largest number (400,000) and largest share (8.6 percent) of undocumented immigrants in the labor force. This statistic again represents the uniqueness of the state of New Jersey—although smaller than other states (particularly the border states), it contains a high number and concentration of undocumented immigrants in the workforce (amongst the total labor force population).

Polls

Although the state of New Jersey is thousands of miles from the southern border of the United States, polls conducted in the state suggest that immigration, particularly undocumented immigration, is an important issue.

In 2002, soon after the terrorist attacks on September 11, 2001, the Eagleton Institute of Politics at Rutgers University published a poll revealing that 35 percent of state residents believed that legal immigration should be curbed, and 24 percent said it should be halted entirely. Attitudes seemed to have improved in 2006, as another Rutgers-Eagleton poll showed that 65 percent of New Jersey residents believed that undocumented immigrants who have lived and worked in the country for at least two years should be permitted to keep their jobs and eventually seek legal status. While 32 percent of those polled also believed that undocumented immigrants should be deported, those who felt that legal immigration should be curbed or halted in its entirety fell to 29 percent and 5 percent, respectively.

Three years later, those positive attitudes towards undocumented immigrants appeared to have declined in regard to certain rights and privileges. A poll by the Monmouth University Polling Institute in 2009 revealed that 62 percent of New Jersey residents opposed offering undocumented immigrants some type of limited driver's license, whereas only 33 percent favor such a proposal. In addition, only 20 percent would favor a proposal extending in-state college tuition rates to undocumented immigrants residing in the state, compared to 37 percent who believe they should pay higher out-of-state rates. Almost 40 percent felt that undocumented immigrants should not even be allowed to attend public colleges and universities in New Jersey at all. Concerning the children of undocumented immigrants, 32 percent were willing to extend in-state tuition to the children of undocumented immigrants living in the state, 39 percent would charge them out-of-state rates, and 22 percent would bar them from attending state colleges and universities altogether. Finally, 51 percent of state residents consider undocumented immigration to be a very serious problem in New Jersey, while 28 percent consider it somewhat serious, and 18 percent believe it is not serious for the state.

Current Issues

Access to Higher Education

Despite no significant progress of the DREAM (Development, Relief, and Education for Alien Minors) Act in the United States Congress, proposals in the New Jersey State Legislature to allow undocumented immigrants to pay in-state college tuition have existed (with some variation) for years (Semple, 2009). The main stipulation to be eligible for in-state tuition at a publicly supported college or university includes the condition that undocumented immigrant student should have attended a New Jersey high school for at least three years and graduated. Perhaps, reflective of public opinion on the matter (Monmouth, Gannett, 2009) this policy was signed into law on January 7, 2013, by New Jersey Governer Chris Christie.

In turn, individual colleges have led their own initiatives in deliberating whether undocumented immigrant students should be eligible to pay in-state tuition— or be allowed to enroll in a public college or university at all. In February 2011, the County College of Morris reversed its policy to ban undocumented students from enrolling in classes, enacted after the 9/11 attacks on the World Trade Center and Pentagon. Two months later, however, the college partially reversed the decision—now allowing undocumented students to enroll but at twice the in-state tuition cost.

Identification Cards

In an effort to "document the undocumented," three municipalities in New Jersey have begun a program to issue an identification card. These "community cards" do not grant driving or residency privileges, but they ultimately allow individuals to obtain library cards, or to cash work paychecks at the bank. They may also be used for basic municipal and health services in locations such as social service agencies, clinics, and schools. Endorsed in some cases by local and county law enforcement agencies, the municipalities of Asbury Park, Princeton, and the state capital of Trenton have issued their respective Community Cards for a small fee ($10).

David A. Caicedo

See Also: DREAM Act; Identification Cards; New York.

Further Reading

Espenshade, T. J., ed. 1997. *Keys to Successful Immigration: Implications of the New Jersey Experience.* Washington, DC: Urban Institute Press.
Monmouth University/Gannett New Jersey Poll, February 2–8, 2009.
Passel, J. S., and D. Cohn. 2011. *Unauthorized Immigrant Population: National and State Trends, 2010.* Washington, DC: Pew Hispanic Center.
Rutgers-Eagleton Poll, June 14–19, 2006.
Semple, K. 2009. "In New Jersey, Uncertainty for Measures Offering In-State Tuition to Illegal Immigrants." *New York Times,* April 19.

New Mexico

With a little over two million people, New Mexico is one of the nation's less populous states. In 2011, New Mexico had about two hundred thousand foreign-born residents living in the state. As a southwestern state, its integration into the United States begins with the Mexican-American War and Mexico's cessation of a territory that would be

New Mexico, under the Treaty of Guadalupe-Hidalgo of 1848. Since then, the economy of the state has been shaped by movements of migrants from the neighboring Mexican province of Chihuahua, along the historic Camino Real, an ancient route that linked the central valley of Mexico to the area that is now known as New Mexico.

Migrants from Mexico came for farming and mining jobs in the North, bringing with them 150 years of common culture, one that has been until only recently separated from the socioeconomic and political aspects of the rest of Mexico. The Camino Real of pre-Columbian times (turned cattle trail in the nineteenth century) fostered the development of a vaquero culture, cattlemen and some cattlewomen that entailed responsibilities and unique expressions with *corrido* songs romanticizing and capturing the common experiences of those beyond the cattle trade. Common themes of the music include the values, dreams, and ideals of Chihuahua, Mexico, expressed in such musical forms as the *música norteña*.

Increasing numbers of miners later came freely across the U.S.-Mexican border. By 1910 there were about seven hundred thousand working in mines and related businesses, such as factories, road construction, and sharecropping. Female workers could spend time in a variety of manufacturing industries, producing postcards, cigars, and *rebozos* (shawls). Female workers also entered jobs in sewing factories and in office and school janitorial services, and childcare. The majority of these workers were undocumented, which made it difficult to complain about abuses they suffered living "in the shadows." They also often had to suffer from the lack of the social support available in their places of origin.

However, the laws were fraught with contradictions. Business owners, farm owners, and others have encouraged Mexican workers to come work for them. Yet a number of local groups of New Mexicans in 2011 called for tighter immigration enforcement, in this way becoming part of a nativist movement. With increased polarization emerging from debates over increased immigration, even citizen Mexican-Americans who have been present since before 1848 when this former Mexican territory was annexed to the United States have been lumped into a social category assigned to undocumented immigrants.

These hardships have been mediated by a sense of mutual support that, while acknowledging divisions among migrants based on ethnicity, class, and gender issues, instilled the values of mutual cooperation and reciprocal exchange. These social processes have helped cultivate a sense of cultural identity and security within *barrios* in Albuquerque and other urban centers where members are more able to think and express freely themselves in terms of their shared histories, class, and heritage. Historically, this has congealed in the form of organizing and labor unions, which even today continues to uphold experiences that New Mexican immigrants identify with.

Two-term governor and 2008 U.S. presidential candidate Bill Richardson imparted a moderate position towards undocumented immigrants. Of Mexican descent, Richardson supported a controversial New Mexico law allowing undocumented immigrants to obtain driver's licenses for reasons of public safety. He publically denounced immigration raids as dehumanizing and opposed neighboring Arizona's SB1070 legislation. When compared to other border states, New Mexico has a relatively short 180-mile border with Mexico. The border area is very isolated dotted by ranches and small farms in areas, and "colonias" (unregulated housing developments lacking public infrastructure). Because the state's population is so small, the El Paso Sector of the U.S. Border Patrol covers the entire state of New Mexico and the two western most counties in Texas, Hudspeth and El Paso. This vast sector consists of 125,500 square miles, 121,000 square miles in New Mexico and 4,500 square miles in Texas. The number of "aliens" deported by the U.S. Border Patrol in this sector fell dramatically between 1998 and 2009.

Attitudes towards undocumented immigrants appeared to change in 2010, with the election of Susana Martinez as the new governor. Her hard stance against unauthorized immigrants appeared to have helped win support for her campaign, even though nearly half of the New Mexican population identifies as Hispanic or Latino. Her tough stand helped her win votes among Republicans when her primary opponent supported legalization for undocumented immigrants. She also made history by being elected the nation's first Latina governor. However, as a Republican governor, she has promoted more penalties for illegal immigration and eliminated the law allowing undocumented immigrants to obtain driver's licenses, reversing the policy under Democratic Governor Richardson. At that time, there were only two other states in the United States that allowed undocumented immigrants to apply for a license: Utah and Washington. She has argued that by allowing undocumented immigrants to have licenses, New Mexico increasingly encourages them to come for licenses but not to stay. Critics accuse her of ignoring her own heritage as a descendent of Mexican immigrants; but in 2010, 67 percent of Latinos opposed the law allowing licenses for undocumented migrants. In this way Martinez embodies contradiction in the face of rapidly changing attitudes toward undocumented immigrants.

On January 31, 2011 Governor Martinez signed an executive order rescinding sanctuary status for undocumented immigrants in New Mexico. Even so, Susana Martinez has adopted a more moderate attitude towards immigrants compared with other Republican governors. In 2013, she backed a proposal to offer temporary licenses to those who qualify for a two-year reprieve from deportation under President Obama's executive order, the Deferred Action for Childhood Arrivals, or DACA. Those undocumented immigrants who do not qualify under DACA are currently prohibited from obtaining driver's licenses. Unlike Arizona Republican Governor Jan Brewer, who opposes drivers' licenses for all undocumented immigrants, Governor Martinez is making an exception for those granted deferment under DACA.

Ben DuMontier

See Also: Arizona; Driver's Licenses; Texas.

Further Reading

Chew Sánchez, Martha I. 2006. *Corridos in Migrant Memory*. Albuquerque: University of New Mexico Press.

"An Immigration Election Too: The Economy Dominates the Campaign, but People Also Worry about the Border." 2010. *Economist*, October 21. http://www.economist.com/node/17312310.

Mach, Andrew. 2011. "Susana Martinez: Can a Latina Governor be Anti–Illegal Immigration?" *Christian Science Monitor,* Sept. 13. http://www.csmonitor.com/USA/2011/0913/Susana-Martinez-Can-a-Latina-governor-be-anti-illegal-immigration.

Weber, Devra. 1998. "Historical Perspectives on Transnational Mexican Workers in California." In John Mason Hart, ed. *Border Crossings: Mexican and Mexican-American Workers,* 209–233. Wilmington, DE: Scholarly Resources Inc.

New York

The state of New York, especially New York City, has been a destination for immigrants since its inception. Attracting immigrants from all over the world, New York City's character and economy are dependent on vibrant immigrant communities throughout its five boroughs, and extending into the greater New York State area. As immigration has increased drastically over the past twenty years, so has New York seen an increase in immigration, both legal and undocumented.

In 2005, there were an estimated four million immigrants living in New York State and three million living in New York City. Of those four million, close to 645,000 people were undocumented in the state and 535,000 were in New York City. By 2010, 4.7 percent of the state's workforce was made up of undocumented immigrants.

Because of their tenuous legal status, undocumented immigrants are not protected by many U.S. laws, including those that regulate working conditions and safety. Thus, undocumented immigrants are vulnerable to heightened levels of exploitation through lower pay, intimidation tactics, and longer work weeks (one hundred hour weeks are common). Moreover, they have little or no recourse when there is abuse, such as instances of sexual harassment, and often do not have access to information for recovering unpaid wages, or wage theft.

Post-9/11 Changes

While life in New York was never easy for immigrants, undocumented or otherwise, it was possible to receive an education and find a job without the obstacle of one's legal status standing in the way. However, after the attacks on the World Trade Center on September 11, 2001, the cries for stronger national security reaffirmed existing anti-immigrant attitudes and emboldened initiatives to harden the policies towards undocumented immigrants.

For example, before September 2001, all students who lived in New York and had a high school diploma or GED from the state of New York paid in-state tuition at all state and city public universities. However, in the fall of 2001, given national security risks, all students who could not provide the proper legal documentation began paying out-of-state tuition. This was an estimated increase from $1,600 to $3,400 a semester at all public four-year colleges. As a result, the tuition increase placed a university education out of reach for many undocumented immigrants throughout the state, regardless of how many years they have studied in the United States. The trend of restricting in-state tuition to only those students who can verify their legal residency status has been noted in other states as well, such as in Arizona.

The restrictions imposed on undocumented students wishing to attain a post-secondary education helped galvanize support for the Development, Relief, and Education for Alien Minors (DREAM) Act by immigrant service organizations and local trade unions. Although the DREAM Act has failed to gain traction at the federal level, proposed variations of the legislation in general would grant legal residency and a path to citizenship to undocumented immigrants who have studied a minimum of two years in college and/or have served in a branch of the armed forces. As of 2013, the fate of the most recent DREAM Act proposal is linked to the comprehensive immigration reform bill (S. 744) that was considered by the U.S. Congress in the summer and fall of that year.

Both New York City Mayor Michael Bloomberg and Governor Andrew Cuomo have repeatedly stated that undocumented immigrants are vital to New York's economy and have not supported any specific anti-immigrant legislation. They do not support mandating all employers to use E-Verify to check the legal status of their employers, as some other states have. Furthermore, Governor Cuomo opted out of the federal Secure Communities program, citing concerns about the impact of the program on families, immigrant communities and law enforcement. For this reason, New York City and the state have been referred to as sanctuaries. A few months later, President Obama made participation in Secure Communities mandatory for all states, with no option for withdrawal. This program facilitates an increase in detainees and further criminalizes undocumented immigrants in New York.

Officially, eleven towns and cities within New York State (including New York City) have declared themselves to be sanctuary cities where local law enforcement will not aid Immigration and Customs Enforcement (ICE) agents in detaining undocumented immigrants, known as 287(g) agreements. The result is that thousands of undocumented immigrants in New York are deported every year under these agreements. However, in practice this has done little to deter ICE raids and detentions throughout the state and city.

After 2001, the government began to prioritize expanding the militarization of U.S. borders and intensified internal enforcement actions to deport undocumented immigrants. In New York the ICE raids have had a severe impact on immigrant communities, especially Middle Eastern and Southeast Asian communities. Although the practice of racial profiling has been legally sanctioned with the implementation of the 1996 Illegal Immigration Reform and Immigrant Responsibility Act (IIRIRA), growing fears of being arrested, detained and ultimately deported have marginalized undocumented immigrants even further. The effect of the raids and detentions has been to terrorize and criminalize undocumented immigrants, even though the majority have led their lives peacefully and observed the laws of the land.

There have been several ICE raids in New York City where whole neighborhoods have been targeted and terrified as a result. During one such raid in 2007, ICE agents cordoned off several blocks of a primarily Latino neighborhood in Queens and began detaining pedestrians and inhabitants. While the raid was executed in the name of stopping a false documentation operation, agents searched every house in the selected area and detained people just for trying to enter their block to go home. The lack of trust that these types of raids foment has a chilling effect on immigrant integration and civic participation. However, in 2006 after several years of such oppressive tactics, hundreds of thousands of immigrants and their allies came out of the shadows to demonstrate and protest a measure proposed by the U.S. Congress (the Border Protection, Antiterrorism and Illegal Immigration Control Act of 2005 [H.R. 4437]) that would have further criminalized them without a path to legalization for themselves and their families. In May 1, 2006, a mass demonstration brought out thousands of immigrants to the streets of New York.

Detention Centers

The radical increase in the number of undocumented immigrants detained has created a large and profitable business for private detention centers. There are 36 public and private detention centers in the state of New York alone. The Varick Street Detention Center in downtown Manhattan has come under harsh criticism for its treatment of detainees. Although the detention center received a good evaluation by the state, from August 2008 to August 2009 there were 210 grievances filed by 176 separate detainees. The grievances were mostly related to lack of medical attention, abusive treatment and food services.

Afsaneh Moradian

See Also: DREAM Act; Illegal Immigration Reform and Immigrant Responsibility Act (IIRIRA) (1996); Immigration and Customs Enforcement (ICE); Racial Profiling; Sanctuary Cities and Secure Communities; Workplace Raids.

Further Reading

ACLU. 2010. "NYCLU Report Documents Immigration Detainee Grievances at Varick Federal Detention Center." February 24. Available at http://www.aclu.org/immigrants-rights-prisoners-rights-prisoners-rights/nyclu-report-documents-immigration-detainee.

Heyman, Josiah McC., and Jason Ackleson. 2009. "United States Border Security after September 11." In John Winterdyck and Kelly Sundberg, eds., *Border Security in the Al-Qaeda Era,* 37–74. Boca Raton, FL: CRC Press.

Hines, Barbara. 2002. "So Near Yet So Far Away: The Effect of September 11th on Mexican Immigrants in the United States." *Texas Hispanic Journal of Law and Policy* 8.37:37–46.

Huffington Post. 2011. "New York Quits Secure Communities Immigration Enforcement Program, Andrew Cuomo Announces." http://www.huffingtonpost.com/2011/06/01/new-york-quits-secure-communities_n_869969.html.

Romero, Mary. 2008. "The Inclusion of Citizenship Status in Intersectionality: What Immigration Raids Tells Us about Mixed-Status Families, the State, and Assimilation." *International Journal of the Family* 34.2:131–52.

Nicaraguan Adjustment and Central American Relief Act (NACARA)

On November 19, 1997 President Bill Clinton approved the Nicaraguan Adjustment and Central American Relief Act (NACARA). This act emerged after a series of lawsuits and cases regarding U.S. asylum and refugee policy for people from Central America during the 1980s and 1990s. In general, this act was a partial response to the 5 million undocumented individuals residing in the United States in the mid-1990s, many of them Central Americans who fled conflicts in their home countries, in order to help them seek legal permanent resident status. During the 1980s under the 1980 Refugee Act it was very difficult for undocumented people from Central America to gain legal status in the United States. Debates raged about whether or not Central Americans were to be considered political refugees or economic migrants. The results of NACARA were and remain uneven, yet represent a significant policy change with regard to asylum policies for Central Americans fleeing war and violence.

History of NACARA

NACARA was originally called the Victims of Communism Relief Act, and its creation reflects an anti-communist Cold War policy. Under NACARA, Nicaraguans and Cubans are distinguished from Guatemalans, Salvadorans, and people from the former Soviet bloc and given different forms of relief. In the 1980s, Guatemalans and Salvadorans were largely unsuccessful in applying for asylum in the United States, reflecting U.S. foreign policy and Cold War politics under the Reagan administration. Because the U.S. government financially and politically supported the right-wing governments of Guatemala and El Salvador, it would therefore appear contradictory to give asylum to people fleeing political violence in those countries. On the contrary, the U.S. government opposed the leftist governments in Soviet Bloc nations and in Nicaragua under the Frente Sandinista de Liberación Nacional (FSLN) and consequently was more open to people seeking asylum from communist regimes. From 1983 to 1990, less than three percent of people from El Salvador and Guatemala were granted asylum and twenty-five percent of Nicaraguans were granted asylum while seventy-six percent of people from the satellite nations under the former USSR (Union of Soviet Socialist Republics) were granted asylum. During this period, the U.S. government received criticism from the United Nations High Commissioner for Refugees (UNHCR) for its treatment of Central Americans.

In response to the unequal treatment of nationals from different Central American countries, in 1985, immigration advocates and people involved in the sanctuary movement sued the U.S. government in the court case of *American Baptist Churches (ABC) v. Thornburgh*. They claimed the Immigration and Naturalization Service (INS) discriminated against people from Guatemala and El Salvador and wanted to prevent further deportations of these individuals as well as stop prosecutions of those who provided them sanctuary. The case was settled in 1990 in what is known as the ABC settlement.

The ABC settlement formed much of the legal foundation for NACARA. It established that Salvadorans who were in the United States before September 19, 1990 and

Guatemalans who were in the United States before October 1, 1990 had the right to apply for political asylum. However, in September of 1996, the Illegal Immigration Reform and Immigrant Responsibility Act (IIRIRA) was passed, and this legislation tightened the rule for providing relief for hardships that had been used to determine appeals for suspension or cancellation of removal. IIRIRA also put a cap at four thousand people who could apply for suspension of deportation, representing only a fraction of the 240,000 Central American ABC class members. Deportation seemed imminent for many Central Americans in the United States at this time. However, after significant advocacy on the behalf of Central Americans and a trip by President Clinton to Central America in 1997, bi-partisan legislation was introduced by Senators Bob Graham (D) and Connie Mack (R) of Florida and NACARA became law. Although President Clinton was not pleased with the distinction between Central Americans as stipulated in NACARA, he refrained from a presidential veto. It was not until 1999 that the Department of Justice officially recognized that people from Guatemala and El Salvador were fleeing political violence and civil war.

Specifications of NACARA

In general, NACARA allowed Nicaraguans and Cubans to apply for legal permanent residence in the United States and allowed Guatemalans and Salvadorans to apply for "suspension from deportation" or "cancellation of removal." Applicants from Nicaragua and Cuba had to be in the United States before December 1, 1995 to qualify. Individuals from El Salvador and Guatemala had to establish their presence in the United States before 1990 even though the civil wars in these countries did not officially end until 1992 and 1996 respectively. Dependents of NACARA applicants were also eligible to apply.

NACARA is broken into two sections: Section 202, which applies to Nicaraguans and Cubans, and Section 203 which applies to Salvadorans, Guatemalans and nationals of the former Soviet bloc including the nation states that formed the former Soviet Union: Russia, Latvia, Estonia, Lithuania, Poland, Czechoslovakia, Romania, Hungary, Bulgaria, Albania, East Germany, Yugoslavia or any state of the former Yugoslavia.

Under Section 202, Nicaraguans and Cubans who were in the United States before December 1, 1995 were allowed to apply for adjustment of status to legal permanent residence. Their deadline for filing a NACARA application under Section 202 expired on March 31, 2000.

Individuals may still apply to the U.S. Citizenship and Immigration Services for NACARA relief under Section 203. Under Section 203, a Guatemalan who entered the United States on or before October 1, 1990, registered for ABC class benefits on or before December 31, 1991, applied for asylum on or before January 3, 1995 and was not apprehended at entry after December 19, 1990 is eligible to apply. Salvadorans must have entered the United States on or before September 19, 1990, registered for ABC benefits or applied for Temporary Protected Status (TPS) on or before October 31, 1991, applied for asylum on or before February 16, 1996 and not have been apprehended at entry after December 19, 1990. Individuals from former Soviet Bloc countries must have entered the United States on or before December 31, 1990 and applied for asylum on or before December 31, 1991. Guatemalans and Salvadorans with pending asylum applications made on or before April 1, 1990 are also eligible to apply.

Eligible individuals may apply for "suspension of deportation" or special rule "cancellation of removal," otherwise known as "NACARA 203 relief." In addition to the above criteria, individuals must prove seven years of continuous physical presence in the United States, that they have been of "good moral character" during their time in the United States, that deportation would result in extreme hardship to the individual or U.S. citizen family member, and that the individual "deserves the benefit." Additional standards apply to people convicted of crimes. Applications under Section 203 can be adjudicated by a U.S. Customs and Immigration Service (USCIS) asylum officer, an immigration judge or by the Board of Immigration appeals. After some debate, in 1999 it was determined that all members of the ABC class would qualify for meeting the extreme hardship criteria as opposed to this being determined on a case by case basis.

Wendy Vogt

See Also: Central American Civil Wars; Eastern Europeans; Guatemalans; Hondurans; Nicaraguans; Salvadorans; Sanctuary Movement.

Further Reading

Coffino, Eli. 2006. "A Long Road to Residency: The Legal History of Salvadoran and Guatemalan Immigration to the United States with a Focus on NACARA." *Cardozo Journal of International and Comparative Law* 14.1:177–208.

Coutin, Susan Bibler. 2007. *Nations of Emigrants: Shifting Boundaries of Citizenship in El Salvador and the United States.* Ithaca, NY: Cornell University Press.

Garcia, Maria Cristina. 2006. *Seeking Refuge: Central American Migration to Mexico, the United States, and Canada.* Berkeley: University of California Press.

Nicaraguans

According to the U.S. Census Bureau's 2005–2009 American Community Survey, approximately 320,000 people of Nicaraguan origin live in the United States. The community is highly clustered, with most Nicaraguans living in Florida (especially Miami), California, and New York,. While Nicaraguan migration to the United States is long-standing, the vast majority have come over the past three to four decades as a result of the Sandinista uprising, the subsequent U.S.-sponsored Contra counterinsurgency, and several hurricanes. Compared to many other Central American immigrants to the United States during the same period, Nicaraguans have consistently had better luck being granted political asylum and permanent residence. Natural disasters, especially Hurricane Mitch in 1998, have also resulted in many Nicaraguans being granted Temporary Protected Status (TPS). TPS, established by the Immigration Reform Act of 1990, can be granted by the U.S. government to foreign nationals from specific

Nicaraguans in Miami react in jubilation to U.S. District Judge James Lawrence King's decision to block the government's effort to deport as many as 40,000 Nicaraguans and other Latin Americans, 1997. The Refugee Act of 1980 provided Central American refugees fleeing civil war and violence in their homelands the possibility of applying for asylum. (AP/Wide World Photos)

countries affected by armed conflict, environmental disasters, and other extraordinary circumstances.

After years of struggle, the Sandinista National Liberation Front (FSLN) overthrew the U.S.-backed Somoza family dictatorship in 1979, which had been in power since 1934. Under the dictatorship, widespread corruption, inequality and political violence were rampant, and tens of thousands of political opponents were either assassinated or exiled. Under the Carter administration, U.S. policy toward the new Sandinista government was initially friendly. However, shortly after taking office, Carter declared that all aid to Latin American countries was contingent upon their human rights performance and consequently suspended aid to Somoza's Nicaragua. After Somoza was deposed by the Sandinistas, the Carter administration officially recognized Sandinista Nicaragua, quickly restarted aid, and helped renegotiate Nicaragua's foreign debt. This about-face was short-lived. Even before Reagan's 1980 election, the Central Intelligence Agency (CIA) had already started working with anti-Sandinista groups, and Carter cut off aid to Nicaragua in response to its shipping of arms to rebels in El Salvador.

Central American relations became decidedly more hostile under the Reagan administration, which started funding *contra-revolucionarios,* or "Contras," in their fight to overthrow the Sandinistas, and initiated an embargo against Nicaragua. In its zeal to support the Contras, the Reagan administration illegally sold weapons to the Iranian government and sent the profits to the Contras, a scandal whose revelation undermined public support for U.S. policies in Central America. Despite the increased scrutiny, the policies achieved their goal in 1989 when the FSLN was voted out of power amidst increasing economic problems exacerbated by the embargo and ongoing battles with the Contras.

This period of revolution and counter-revolution produced significant out-migration from Nicaragua, with much of it going to the United States and neighboring Costa Rica. According to the 1990 U.S. Census Household Survey, approximately three quarters of the roughly 170,000 Nicaraguans living in the United States when the survey was taken had come after 1980. About 45,000 of those did so with proper documentation, while the majority of the remainder were undocumented and became asylum-seekers upon reaching the United States. With roughly 126,000 applications, Nicaraguans represented 25 percent of all U.S. asylum seekers between fiscal years (FY) 1981 and 1991. Salvadorans were the only nationality with comparable application rates, though they were granted asylum with much lower frequency despite fleeing from a war arguably as vicious as the one Nicaraguans were escaping.

These discrepancies can partially be explained by the U.S.'s divergent political interests in the region: because of its left leanings, the Sandinista government was viewed as an enemy while the Salvadoran and Guatemalan governments were carrying out their brutal military campaigns against leftist insurgents with significant financial and logistical support from the United States. In short, Nicaraguans were fleeing an enemy state and Guatemalans and Salvadorans were fleeing from ally states. The Sandinistas were regularly characterized by the State Department as a repressive regime, while the regular reports of atrocities in El Salvador and Guatemala did not elicit such characterizations, although by all accounts they were also true.

Accordingly, only 2.6 percent of Salvadorans and 1.8 percent of Guatemalans were granted asylum between 1984 and 1990, and the approval rate of Nicaraguans reached a high of 84 percent in FY 1987. Even when they were denied asylum, the Nicaraguan Review Program (NRP), which Attorney General Edwin Meese established in 1987, allowed Nicaraguans to reapply for asylum and provided applicants with work permits as soon as they registered with the Immigration and Naturalization Service (INS). With the end of Sandinista rule in 1990, however, asylum cases became much more difficult to win for Nicaraguans. Indeed, in FY 1990, Nicaraguan asylum approval rates had dropped to just 19 percent. In 1993 Attorney General Janet Reno declared that the electoral defeat of the Sandinistas had rendered the NRP unnecessary and that Nicaraguans would soon have their asylum cases reviewed on the same terms as other applicants.

One of the major changes made by the 1996 Illegal Immigration Reform and Immigrant Responsibility Act (IIRIRA) was a hardening of the requirements for immigrants to suspend their deportation proceedings. Whereas previous legislation required seven continuous years living in the United States and proof that deportation would be an extreme hardship, IIRIRA required ten years and proof of extreme and exceptional hardship. The 1997 Nicaraguan Adjustment and Central American Relief Act (NACARA), however, allowed Nicaraguans, as well as Guatemalans and Salvadorans, to request deportation cancellation under the older terms. With asylum an increasingly unlikely option, NACARA provided an additional and frequently successful means for Nicaraguans to gain legal status.

Following NACARA, avenues open to Nicaraguans and other Central Americans to normalize their immigration status have largely come, tragically, from natural disasters. In 1998 Hurricane Mitch, the second deadliest in the history of the Western Hemisphere, wreaked havoc on Nicaragua, displaced tens of thousands of people, killed almost four thousand, and caused roughly $1 billion in damage. The only silver lining was that the U.S. government granted TPS to all Nicaraguans currently living in the United States through 2007.

Murphy Woodhouse

See Also: Guatemalans; Hondurans; Nicaraguan Adjustment and Central American Relief Act (NACARA); Salvadorans.

Further Reading

García, María C. 2006. *Seeking Refuge: Central American Migration to Mexico, the United States, and Canada.* Berkeley: University of California Press.

Lundquist, Jennifer H., and Douglas S. Massey. 2005. "Politics or Economics? International Migration During the Nicaraguan Contra War." *Journal of Latin American Studies.* 37.1:29–53.

Wasem, Ruth E. 1997. *Central American Asylum Seekers: Impact of 1996 Immigration Law.* Washington, D.C.: Congressional Research Service, Library of Congress.

North American Free Trade Agreement (NAFTA)

The North American Free Trade Agreement (NAFTA) is a free trade agreement signed by the governments of Canada, the United States and Mexico in order to remove barriers to trade between the three countries. In essence, a free trade agreement is a contract that lifts most of the tariffs, quotas, taxes and other impediments to the flow of trade and commerce between countries to allow for greater and faster flow of commodities between them. NAFTA was such an agreement negotiated during U.S. President Clinton's administration. It became effective January 1, 1994. One of the arguments used by the architects of the plan to publically promote the agreement as it was debated in the U.S. Congress, was that the agreement would provide economic development in Mexico and thus curb undocumented immigration into the United States. The idea was that each country would benefit from increased trade between the countries, so that all would prosper, making immigration unnecessary. However, according to legal scholar Kevin Johnson, the agreement itself did not address the issue of immigration (Hing, 2010). Other critics of the agreement argued that the plan would fail to increase wages for Mexican workers. In the United States, organized labor also opposed the agreement, citing the potential loss of American jobs to Mexico.

To be sure, trade did in fact increase significantly between the three countries: as much as eight times over the last twenty years. Already a major trading partner with the United States, by 2001 Mexico became the largest supplier of goods and services to the United States. However, in the end, NAFTA proved to be a bad deal for Mexico's poor subsistence farmers. Largely to blame for this is that the U.S. government subsidizes its corn production to lower its price on the market. With Mexico importing cheap corn from the United States under the free trade principle, Mexican farmers could not get fair prices for their own corn. At the same time, the Mexican government ended its subsidies to its farmers. Unable to sell their corn at a profit, Mexican corn farmers went bankrupt.

Another related factor that contributed to increased poverty in Mexico was the change made to the Mexican constitution regulating communal land tenure laws (the "*ejido* system"). This constitutional change made it easier to sell communal land parcels to foreign business investors, and was advanced by President's Clinton's counterpart in Mexico, Mexican President Salinas de Gortari. Mexican farmers made poor by their inability to sell their corn in a "free" market would thus resort to sell their lands. Once landless, they sought out wage work in large urban cities throughout the republic. When the labor markets in those urban centers were no longer able to absorb the burgeoning influx of landless job seekers, they sought opportunities by migrating north and to the United States in search for work.

It is important to note that the economic philosophy that is fundamental to the concept of "free trade" aims to support private enterprise by allowing it to operate unfettered and free from government regulations. Thus, changing the law in Mexico to allow for the privatization of communal lands is consistent with this economic philosophy. In the end, the changes combined to produce mass displacement of subsistence farmers who were unable to compete with subsidized corn production that would be imported from the United States after NAFTA went into effect. At the same time, the Mexican government withdrew its own subsistence aid to its farmers after NAFTA was enacted. Even with increased trade between nations, subsistence farmers were unable to continue farming. Mexico's labor market was unable to absorb the increased number of migrants moving from rural to urban areas in search for work, and this resulted in a migration to the United States that remains unprecedented to this day

Mexico's agricultural sectors were the hardest hit when NAFTA was implemented because of the disparate economies between the United States and Mexico. Agricultural production in the United States is most advantaged in terms of the latest technology, the scale of its mechanization, and its natural resources that are largely related to its natural topography and geography. Add to this advantage the capacity of the United States to accumulate wealth for investment in research to improve the science behind the development of fertilizers, pesticides, and genetically modified seeds that are more hardy and productive. Returns on this investment come by way of higher prices for the technology and protective patents, which are passed on to potential buyers. In Mexico, only the largest operations were able to afford to purchase or qualify for loans to access these technologies.

In addition, with a U.S. population of 316,668,567, triple the population of Mexico (with about 112.3 million in 2013), the more affluent United States has a tax base that is unrivaled to subsidize its agricultural growers. By far, Mexico's agriculture industry is comparatively less advantaged. Predictably, within ten years of the implementation of NAFTA, Mexico became dependent on the United States for a large percentage of its food. This is especially significant when one considers that Mexico's corn has been historically highly protected and one of its main exports. Estimates suggest that there were close to three million corn farmers in Mexico in the mid-1990s and at the same time, due to high-tech machinery, seventy-five corn farmers in Iowa were able to produce twice as much corn as Mexico at half the cost. Corn, once a highly commoditized food staple, was soon being imported into Mexico at a cheaper rate than Mexican farmers could grow it. This left many Mexican farmers and farm workers without jobs, resulting in the need to migrate.

Most researchers conclude that almost half a million workers in the United States lost their jobs due to NAFTA, primarily due to the production of manufactured goods in Mexico. The best example of this is in the automobile production industry. The former center of automobile production in northern U.S. cities became known as the "rust belt," as more manufacturing was shipped to places in Mexico where labor costs were significantly less than in the United States. A free market approach to the economy includes the deregulation of labor relations. For workers in Mexico, this meant that labor bargaining power would be diminished. For U.S. manufacturers, a less empowered labor force meant lower wages for workers, more worker concessions, and higher profits. Meanwhile, the numbers of jobs lost in manufacturing were offset by job increases in other sectors of the economy. These were primarily in the low-paying service sector, marking an important shift in the U.S. economy. The increase in available low-skilled jobs also meant that those migrating to the United States from Mexico would find greater opportunities to earn better wages than in Mexico. This encouraged more migration to the United States.

Back in Mexico, NAFTA created additional problems. Few people realize that conditions for loans to improve a developing country's infrastructure needed for the influx of large-scale industries set up by the International Monetary Fund and World Bank often include the devaluation of a nation's currency to remain globally competitive (Canales, 2000). Thus, the devaluation of the peso generated by NAFTA also increased migration because Mexican consumers lost their purchasing power. With a currency devaluation of 120 percent in 1994, it was the worst economic crisis in Mexico since the 1930s. This resulted in massive job loss and loss of bank lending soon after NAFTA went into effect, which created a credit crunch and limited economic growth in Mexico.

Another fact largely ignored is that the neoliberal orientation that NAFTA promoted included aggressive cutting of public assistance programs. The conditions for loans set up by the IMF and World Bank resulting in the curtailing expenditures for social welfare programs is referred to as structural adjustment programs (SAPs). Also known as the Washington Consensus (McGuire, 2007), some of these free market–oriented conditions included cutting social safety net programs. In this way, women have been profoundly impacted by NAFTA, resulting in their increased migration, known as the feminization of migration. Many proceeded to migrate north and find employment in *maquiladoras,* also known as "twin plants." *Maquiladoras* are large factories that are set up to take advantage of the free trade agreements between countries, so they are strategically located near borders. Along the U.S.-Mexico border, *maquiladoras* are usually set up by transnational corporations on the Mexican side of the border for the purposes of assembling products, such as clothing and electronics. The parts usually come from the U.S. side of the border. Once the products are assembled by cheap labor on the Mexican side, they are returned to U.S. warehouses of the same company, and prepared for shipping. The majority of workers in *maquiladoras* on the Mexican side of the border have been women. Though *maquiladoras* have been in operation since the 1960s, within the first six years after the implementation of NAFTA, *maquiladora* employment grew 110 percent. The result is that once women are working in northern cities, they are more likely to leave this work in search of better opportunities in the United States. Poor and unsafe working conditions and little to no bargaining power also encourage them to leave for the United States right across the border, and this has resulted in greater numbers of undocumented women immigrants who have found themselves searching for a better life in the United States, even if it means living in the shadows.

Courtney Martínez

See Also: Canadian Border; Clinton Administration; Gender Roles; Globalization; Migration; *The Uprooted.*

Further Reading

Canales, Alejandro I. 2000. "International Migration and Labour Flexibility in the Context of NAFTA." *Social Science Journal* 52.165:409–19.

Hing, Bill Ong. 2010. *Ethical Borders: NAFTA, Globalization, and Mexican Migration.* Philadelphia: Temple University Press.

Gruben, William. 2001. "Was NAFTA Behind Mexico's High Maquiladora Growth?" *Economic and Financial Review* 3:11–21.

McCarty, Dawn. 2007. "The Impact of the North American Free Trade Agreement (NAFTA) on Rural Children and Families in Mexico: Transnational Policy and Practice Implications." *Journal of Public Child Welfare* 1.4:105–23.

McGuire, Sharon. 2007. "Fractured Migrant Families." *Family & Community Health* 30.3:178–88.

Vaughan, Scott. 2004. "How Green Is NAFTA? Measuring the Impacts of Agricultural Trade." *Environment* 46:26–42.

Nutrition

As the number of immigrants in the United States continues to rise, it becomes increasingly important to understand how their diet and nutritional status differ from native-born individuals as well as the major factors that may contribute to those differences. Thus, the following discusses three main factors that strongly influence immigrants' diet and nutrition.

Acculturation

Despite having seemingly healthy dietary habits in their countries of origin, immigrants' adoption of unhealthy dietary practices, such as drinking sugar-sweetened beverages and eating high fat and high calorie fast foods, is positively correlated with their length of stay in the United States (Gregory-Mercado et al., 2006; Ayala et al., 2008). Indeed, acculturation (or the adoption of the host country's cultural norms) seems to be strongly associated with the deterioration of dietary intake among immigrants in the United States. According to a study conducted in Washington State among Hispanic (or Latino) immigrants from Mexico, highly acculturated immigrants had a higher fat intake and ate fewer servings of fruit and vegetables per day compared with those not acculturated (Neuhouser et al., 2004). Immigrants of other ethnicities also exhibit a similar trend. For example, a study conducted in Pennsylvania showed that Chinese immigrants' dietary patterns worsened and fat and sweets consumption increased significantly after immigrating to the United States (Lv and Cason, 2004).

However, the available evidence suggests that acculturation, once understood, can be manipulated and used as a guiding principle to promote and preserve nutrition and the health status of immigrants. The so-called "selective acculturation" concept proposed by the authors of this entry (Yeh et al., 2009) specifically contends that it may be possible to keep the healthful habits of one's culture of origin while adopting the host country's healthful habits and lifestyle.

The Role of Nostalgia in Immigrants' Eating Patterns

As a complementary paradigm to the notion of acculturation, the literature has only recently begun to notice the cultural and emotional significance of familiar foods in supporting immigrants' healthy eating patterns in recipient societies (Koc and Welsh, 2001). The term *nostalgic foods* refers to the familiar food items and recipes prepared, eaten and maintained by immigrant families in the United States, via everyday consumption and generational retention (Viladrich et al., 2008; Viladrich, 2009). Nevertheless, while some aspects of traditional Latino diets may be protective against obesity and chronic disease (e.g., the use of whole grains and legumes), some traditional eating patterns may be harmful, including an excess of fried foods such as chicken and plantains (Viladrich et al., 2008; Viladrich, 2009). A broader understanding of the role of nostalgic foods will help inform public health interventions aiming at slowing, and reversing, the rising obesity trends among immigrants in the United States.

Food Insecurity

Food insecurity is also an important factor influencing immigrants' nutrient intake and health. Due to lack of financial resources or money, many low-income immigrant families worry about obtaining adequate food to feed their families. Instead of fresh produce or other healthy food items, immigrants often do not have a choice but to purchase cheaper calorie-dense and processed foods. This contributes to long-term unhealthy dietary habits and childhood obesity particularly among low-income immigrant households (Kaiser et al., 2002; Rosas et al., 2009). As a result, food insecurity negatively impacts the nutritional status of members of immigrant households, especially among young children.

For families experiencing more severe food access issues, such as adults and children skipping meals, and adults or children going without food for an entire day, their risks extend beyond food and nutrition inadequacy. For instance, immigrants who reported experiencing hunger, the most severe form of food insecurity, also accounted for more days of poor mental and physical health as well as poorer overall health compared with those not experiencing hunger (Hadley et al., 2008).

Anahí Viladrich and Ming-Chin Yeh

See Also: Acculturation; Barriers to Health; Children; Families; Health and Welfare.

Further Reading

Ayala, G. X., B. Baquero, and S. Klinger. 2008. "A Systematic Review of the Relationship between Acculturation and Diet among Latinos in the United States: Implications for Future Research. *Journal of the American Dietetic Association* 108.8:1330–1344.

Dietary Guidelines for Americans. 2013. http://health.gov/dietaryguidelines/.

Gregory-Mercado, K. Y., L. K. Staten, J. Ranger-Moore, C. A. Thomson, J. C. Will, E. S. Ford, J. Guillen, L. K. Larkey, A. R. Giuliano, and J. Marshall. 2006. "Fruit and Vegetable Consumption of Older Mexican-American Women Is Associated with their Acculturation Level." *Ethnicity and Disease* 16.1:89–95.

Hadley, C., S. Galea, V. Nandi, A. Nandi, G. Lopez, S. Strongarone, and D. Ompad. 2008. "Hunger and Health among Undocumented Mexican Migrants in a U.S. Urban Area." *Public Health Nutrition* 11.2:151–158.

Kaiser, L. L., H. R. Melgar-Quiñonez, C. L. Lamp, M. C. Johns, J. M. Sutherlin, and J. O. Harwood. 2002. "Food Security and Nutritional Outcomes of Preschool-age Mexican-American Children." *Journal of the American Dietetic Association* 102.7:924–929.

Koc, M., and J. Welsh. 2001. "Food, Identity and the Immigrant Experience. Ethnocultural, Racial, Religious, and Linguisic Diversity and Identity Seminar." Halifax, Nova Scotia.

Lv, N., and K. L. Cason. 2004. "Dietary Pattern Change and Acculturation of Chinese Americans in Pennsylvania." *Journal of the American Dietetic Association* 104:771–778.

Neuhouser, M. L., B. Thompson, G. D. Coronado, and C. C. Solomon. 2004. "Higher Fat Intake and Lower Fruit and Vegetables Intakes Are Associated with Greater Acculturation among Mexicans Living in Washington State." *Journal of the American Dietetic Association* 104:51–57.

Rosas, L. G., K. Harley, L. C. Fernald, S. Guendelman, F. Mejia, L. M. Neufeld, and B. Eskenazi. 2009. "Dietary Associations of Household Food Insecurity among Children of Mexican Descent: Results of a Binational Study." *Journal of the American Dietetic Association* 109:2001–2009.

USDA MyPlate & Food Pyramid Resources. 2013. http://fnic.nal.usda.gov/dietary-guidance/myplatefood-pyramid-resources/usda-myplate-food-pyramid-resources.

Viladrich, A., D. David, M. Yeh, and N. Bruning. 2008. "Addressing Latinas' Double Jeopardies: The Challenge of Nostalgic Foods in Promoting Healthy Eating Patterns in the U.S." American Public Health Association. APHA 136th Annual Meeting, October 25–29, San Diego.

Viladrich, A. 2009. "Maria's Dilemma: Between Nostalgia and the Saga of Healthy Foods." *Anthropology News* 50.5:45–46.

Yeh, M. C., A. Viladrich, N. Bruning, and C. Roye. 2009. "Determinants of Latina Obesity in the U.S.: The Role of Selective Acculturation." *Journal of Transcultural Nursing* 20:105–15.

Obama Administration

While campaigning, candidate Barack Obama made a push for comprehensive immigration reform (CIR) early in his administration one of his central campaign promises. At a League of United Latin American Citizens (LULAC) meeting on the campaign trail in July of 2008, Obama said, "The system is not working when a young person at the top of her class . . . cannot attend a public college or university. . . . The system isn't working when . . . communities are terrorized by ICE immigration raids. . . . When all of that is happening, the system just isn't working, and we need to change it." Many observers credited strong pro-reform stances like that for winning Obama 70 percent of the Latino vote in 2008.

However, according to Immigration and Customs Enforcement (ICE) numbers, the agency deported more than 392,000 undocumented migrants from the United States in fiscal year (FY) 2010. That figure represented an increase of 23,000 deportations from FY 2008, the last year of the Bush administration, and is indicative of the enforcement-centric approach to immigration policy that has characterized Barack Obama's first term in office. As of September 2011, more than 1 million migrants had been deported under President Obama, and the administration was on pace to deport more in a single term than were deported under both Bush terms.

The disconnect between campaign and administration rhetoric and policy has been explained by many factors, many of which date back to the profound changes wrought by the 9/11 terrorist attacks, which have significantly complicated immigration reform efforts. The Migration Policy Institute's senior policy analyst Marc R. Rosenblum writes that promising immigration negotiations between Mexico and the United States "were derailed by the events of 9/11. . . . [B]order controls immediately became a central topic of concern in the aftermath. The public debates and new policy measures that followed initially conflated antiterrorism measures with immigration control. . . . [S]weeping antiterrorism measures that also affected immigration in critical ways were enacted in the next four years."

The legislative and societal legacy of the terrorist attacks, combined with an increasingly divisive and toxic public debate about immigration, a long history of enforcement-first policies, the 2008 recession, and the prolonged fight over health care reform and other legislative priorities of the Obama administration have pushed immigration reform during Obama's first term to the background, to the chagrin of many of the Latinos who voted for him in 2008.

In a highly publicized speech given in El Paso in May 2011, Obama laid out the chief obstacles to reform efforts and reaffirmed his commitment to comprehensive immigration reform. The speech's rhetoric illustrated the fine line his administration has walked between increased immigration enforcement and continued rhetorical support for significant reforms:

"We define ourselves as a nation of immigrants—a nation that welcomes those willing to embrace America's precepts. . . . Yet at the same time, we are standing at the border today because we also recognize that being a nation of laws goes hand in hand with being a nation of immigrants. . . . [B]ecause these issues touch on deeply held convictions . . . these debates often elicit strong emotions. That's one of the reasons it's been so difficult to reform our broken immigration system."

He went on to tout the doubling of Border Patrol agents since 2004, continued progress on the border fence and the use of unmanned drones in enforcement that his administration has overseen. He also made an economic and humanitarian case for immigration reform and highlighted the fact that his administration has met or exceeded many Republican demands for increased border enforcement measures. The GOP response to the speech focused their criticism on Obama's advocacy for paths to citizenship, foreshadowing the political obstacles to reform that would come during President Obama's second term.

The DREAM Act, or Development, Relief, and Education for Alien Minors Act, was the sole piece of major immigration reform legislation to come up before Congress under Obama's first term, 2008–2012. The president has frequently expressed support for the bill, which would create paths to citizenship for young undocumented migrants who came into the country as children and who have completed two years of college or served in the military. After passing the House of Representatives in late 2010, the bill failed to gain the sixty votes necessary to avoid a filibuster in the Senate on December 18, effectively killing the bill and putting its future in doubt. Shortly after Obama's El Paso speech, Senator Majority Leader Harry Reid reintroduced the bill on May 11, 2011.

Though started toward the end of President Bush's second term, ICE's Secure Communities program has drawn criticism for the Obama administration. The program is basically an information-sharing partnership between ICE and numerous local, state and federal law enforcement organizations in hundreds of jurisdictions. When a participating agency arrests someone, they run their fingerprints against federal databases, and ICE is able to see if the individual is also wanted for immigration violations. If they are, ICE can request that the arrestee be held for an additional forty-eight hours so that they can take custody of them and begin deportation proceedings.

The program has been heavily criticized for resulting in the deportation of migrants with limited or nonexistent criminal records, as well as migrants with significant family ties to the United States. Because of public outcry from immigrants and their allies and advocates, a number of jurisdictions, including the states of Massachusetts, New York and Illinois, have attempted to pull out of the program despite mixed messages from the Department of Homeland Security about whether it is possible to do so.

In terms of immigration enforcement priorities, the Obama administration has recently been pushing for greater prosecutorial discretion on the part of immigration agents. On June 17 of 2011, ICE Director John Morton released an internal memo (later known as "The Morton Memo") that laid out guidelines for agents and directed them to prioritize the deportation of migrants with criminal records and not undocumented migrants with significant family ties to the United States, military service, and higher education, among other criteria. In the memo, Morton wrote that "ICE must prioritize the use of its enforcement personnel, detention space, and removal assets to ensure that the aliens it removes represent, as much as reasonably possible, the agency's enforcement priorities, namely the promotion of national security, border security, public safety, and the integrity of the immigration system."

In an effort to begin implementing this policy, the Department of Homeland Security (DHS) announced in mid-November of 2011 that it would begin a case by case review of all pending deportation cases, of which there are approximately three hundred thousand. Additionally, the department announced that they would begin a training program for field agents and lawyers responsible for enforcing immigration law and prosecuting violations with the goal of significantly reducing the number of deportees with no criminal backgrounds.

Then in June of 2012, through an Executive Order by President Barack Obama, the Deferred Action for Childhood Arrivals (DACA) directed agencies that form part of the U.S. Department of Homeland Security (U.S. Customs and Border Protection, the U.S. Citizenship and Immigration Services, the U.S. Customs Border Protection, and U.S. Immigration and Customs Enforcement) to practice prosecutorial discretion towards those who as children immigrated to the United States without proper authorization. It was widely held that DACA came about only because of the repeated failed attempts to pass the DREAM Act, as many of the requirements to qualify for DACA were modeled from the earlier bipartisan proposals.

In 2012, Barack Obama won the presidential election, earning a second term. What was remarkable in this election was the support from Latinos. Post-election analysis of the vote showed that approximately 71 percent of the Latino electorate voted for him. As if a reward for this support, in January of 2013 the Obama Administration announced a new rule that will allow thousands of American citizens to avoid long separations from immediate family members who are undocumented and want to initiate the process of becoming legal residents by applying for a Provisional Unlawful Presence (PUP) Waiver. The new rule amends the process of acquiring what is called a "provisional unlawful presence waiver," which allows individuals to return to the United States more quickly after immigrant visa interviews in their countries of origin if they can prove that prolonged separation will cause an "extreme hardship" on their U.S.-citizen spouses, children, or parents.

Since his reelection, a tide for support has renewed bipartisan efforts to come up with comprehensive immigration reform, which, if passed, will certainly be a legacy piece of legislation for the Obama administration. To be sure, one of the first issues taken up at the start of his second term, President Obama advanced this goal by distributing a draft of a proposal outlining four "common sense" principles for immigration reform: to create a path towards earned citizenship, strengthen border security, streamline the immigration system, and require business owners to check the immigration status of new hires. The task of developing a proposal for comprehensive immigration reform was subsequently taken up by a bipartisan group of senators, and as of the fall of 2013 had been stalled in the House.

Murphy Woodhouse

See Also: Deferred Action for Childhood Arrivals (DACA); Deportation; Policy and Political Action; Provisional Unlawful Presence (PUP) Waivers; Sanctuary Cities and Secure Communities.

Further Reading

Delahunty, Robert J., and John C. Yoo. 2013. "Dream On: The Obama Administration's Nonenforcement of Immigration Laws, the DREAM Act, and the Take Care Clause." *Texas Law Review* 91.4:781–857.

Gonzales, Alfonso. 2010. "Beyond the Consensus: Oppositional *Migrante* Politics in the Obama Era." *NACLA Report on the Americas* 43.6. *Academic OneFile*. Web. 28 Oct. 2011.

Oulahan, Cain W. 2011. "The American Dream Deferred: Family Separation and Immigrant Visa Adjudications at the U.S. Consulates Abroad." *Marquette Law Review* 94.4:1351–1379.

Rosenblum, Marc R. 2011. *U.S. Immigration Policy since 9/11: Understanding the Stalemate over Comprehensive Immigration Reform.* Washington, DC: Migration Policy Institute.

Operation Streamline

Operation Streamline is a United States Department of Homeland Security (DHS) program with the mission of zero-tolerance enforcement of illegal entry through the Mexico–United States border, by requiring federal criminal prosecution and imprisonment. It was first implemented in 2005 in a limited segment of the Del Rio, Texas, United States Border Patrol sector and has since expanded to seven of the nine southern Border Patrol sectors. It removes migrants from the civil immigration court system and mandates their prosecution on federal criminal charges, most often under 8 U.S.C. 1325, Improper Entry by Alien, a misdemeanor, and/or 1326, Reentry of Removed Aliens, a felony. Operation Streamline proceedings regularly take place in at least eight federal courts in Arizona, New Mexico, and Texas. In each court, Operation Streamline cases are heard *en masse*. In the Federal Courthouse in Tucson, Arizona, every day seventy migrants (most of whom were apprehended by the U.S. Border Patrol in the Tucson Sector) are put through a process in which they have their initial appearance, are advised of the charges, are charged, enter a plea, and then are sentenced for up to 180 days imprisonment, all in a matter of a few hours. The procedure again attracted national attention in April of 2013 by way of a proposal for the comprehensive immigration reform bill that was unveiled by senators who are crafting the legislation, because the bill calls for a tripling of the number of border crossing prosecutions in the U.S. Border Patrol's Tucson sector. The bill calls for the U.S. District Court in Arizona to boost the number of Operation Streamline prosecutions to 210 a day, up from the current 70 and allocates up to $250 million over five years to accomplish that goal (Radnovich, 2013).

Origins

Prior to Operation Streamline, Mexican nationals without a criminal record in the United States who were picked up by the Border Patrol were sent back across the border at the nearest port of entry in a practice called "voluntary return," in which a migrant is allowed to leave the United States without a bar against their seeking readmission in the future. Migrants with no other criminal charges typically did not enter the federal court system until they had several voluntary returns. This practice was set in place to avoid an overburdening of the legal justice system where, such as in the Tucson Border Patrol Sector, as many as 800–1000 apprehensions per day are possible. Moreover, a lack of space in detention centers had become a problem with increased migration. For example, the Del Rio sector saw a higher than average number of OTM ("Other Than Mexican") migrants, especially in the area around Eagle Pass, Texas. The acute shortage of space in detention centers led to a high number of migrants released with a Notice to Appear and word spread about this apparent loophole. By fiscal year 2005, the Del Rio sector released 90.9 percent of apprehended OTM migrants on their own recognizance, for which not all returned, and leading critics of this practice to call it "catch and release."

Operation Streamline was also seen as an answer to the increasing number of formal appearances before a judge. As such, the more formalized proceedings were usually reserved for those migrants who had prior convictions, if their illegal reentry was associated with illegal drugs, or they fled with a Border Patrol agent in pursuit. Non-Mexican migrants were not eligible for voluntary return but were formally deported after appearing before an immigration court judge, after which they would be returned to their country of origin.

The Border Patrol proposed a new plan to the United States Attorney's Office (USAO) for the Western District of Texas in late 2004 and early 2005. A pilot plan proposed prosecuting all OTM migrants apprehended in a one-mile stretch of the Del Rio sector near Eagle Pass not in an immigration court but in the criminal justice system. When the USAO declined to prosecute cases selected by national origin, a discriminatory practice, the Border Patrol proposed prosecuting all migrants apprehended in that area. DHS introduced the final version of Operation Streamline in December 2005.

Procedure

Most Operation Streamline defendants are charged with misdemeanor illegal entry under 8 U.S.C. 1325, with a maximum six-month sentence. Defendants who have previously been deported, either through a formal deportation in civil immigration court or through an expedited departure, or been previously convicted of misdemeanor illegal entry, can be charged with felony reentry, under 8 U.S.C. 1326. Felony reentry generally carries a maximum penalty of two years but a defendant with a criminal record can be sentenced up to twenty years. A conviction on either charge bars the defendant from legally reentering the United States for five years and makes it nearly impossible to ever obtain legal permanent residency in the United States.

Each district court in Operation Streamline sectors has a different capacity to prosecute defendants, from an average of twenty defendants per day in El Paso, Texas, to as many as eighty per day in Del Rio, Texas. Operation Streamline proceedings combine the initial appearance, arraignment, plea, and sentencing in one appearance. Depending on the court, defendants have thirty minutes to an hour to meet with their attorney. In order to cope with the work load, attorneys have been known to meet with as many as six to ten clients at one time, in which they are advised of the charges and their rights, and given advice. During this time, attorneys may make determinations as to whether a client is a minor, is competent, or has special needs (such as not being proficient in Spanish) that would make the client ineligible or unable to proceed with the court appearance.

Until December 2009, all Operation Streamline court magistrates addressed the defendants as a group. The en masse plea hearings involve the judge addressing and asking the group as a whole if they understand the proceedings and if they wish to plead guilty and their recording a "general 'yes' answer." In other words, when the magistrate would address the accused in the courtroom by asking, "Are all of you willing to give up your right to go to trial and plead guilty today?" all of the defendants were expected to answer in unison, *"Si."* ("yes").

However, the United States Court of Appeals for the Ninth Circuit ruled on December 2, 2009, in *United States v. Roblero-Solis,* that en masse plea hearings violated Rule 11(b)1 of the Federal Rules of Criminal Procedure, which outlines the due process requirements of the court in accepting a defendant's plea. It would be difficult to tell if and who of the fifty or more defendants remained silent when addressed, or even answered differently from the rest. It was also possible that, when asked to signify a need for further clarification by standing, a defendant would remain seated and silent, not wishing to draw attention to themselves in such a large group. However, the opinion of the 9th Circuit was that this violation was "harmless." Consequently, there was some modification in the procedure with the Tucson Court addressing defendants in smaller groups of five to six, rather than the entire group of 70. The ruling was only binding upon courts in Tucson and Yuma, within the jurisdiction of the Ninth Circuit resulting in the proceedings taking about one to two hours longer than originally in Tucson. Courts in New Mexico and Texas continue to take en masse pleas.

Effects

Though some of the border district courts prosecuted large numbers of immigration cases prior to Operation Streamline, and though immigration has always meant border district courts have had a heavier caseload than other districts, the implementation of Operation Streamline as a mandatory prosecution program has strained the federal court systems in those jurisdictions. In 2005, the border district courts prosecuted more than one-third of all felonies in the United States. By 2008 they were prosecuting

75 percent of all felonies in the nation. Where nationwide federal criminal case filings increased by 27 percent, filings in the border district courts increased 172 percent. Among the five border district courts, 82 percent of the felony docket is drug and immigration charges, compared to 43 percent of the felony docket in the rest of the nation.

The Southern District of California, the jurisdiction covering the border along the California Border Patrol sectors, does not participate in Operation Streamline. The USAO has retained its prosecutorial discretion and prosecutes only migrants with previous removals or a substantial criminal record. As a result of retaining prosecutorial discretion, the Southern District of California has prosecuted more drug and human smuggling cases per capita than any other district.

Operation Streamline is part of the Department of Homeland Security's consequence program for migrants entering the country without inspection. The agency points to a decline in apprehensions to say that Operation Streamline is an effective deterrent. If Operation Streamline is in fact a deterrent to illegal border crossing, there are a number of possible consequences. The belief that a coyote, or a professional smuggler and guide, would know where and how to avoid apprehension by the Border Patrol has increased their demand as well as the fees they charge. Alternatively, entering through a port of entry with fraudulent identification documents could also become more attractive to migrants, as being arrested by the Border Patrol at an illegal crossing now means almost certain prosecution. Operation Streamline and the increased cost of crossing illegally have also contributed to migrants staying in the United States for longer periods of time after they arrive, taking fewer trips home, resulting in longer periods of separation from family members.

Criticism

It is impossible to determine how much of the decrease in apprehensions is due to Operation Streamline, given that it was implemented in the middle of a decade-long downward trend in migration. The Secure Border Initiative was also implemented in 2005, expanding available technology to border law enforcement agencies, reinforcing border infrastructure, and increasing the number of Border Patrol agents. Mexican census data, federal public defenders and judges, and a recent study all point instead to slow economic growth and high unemployment in the United States as the primary reason for the decrease in migrants. Both federal public defenders and judges also question if Operation Streamline is reaching migrants by word-of-mouth, as DHS claims, and, if it is, if migrants understand the long-term effects of the conviction on their criminal record. It is also questionable how much someone willing to risk their life by crossing a desert is going to weigh the possibility of a minor criminal conviction and a short jail sentence in making the decision. Both San Diego and El Centro Border Patrol sectors, which do not participate in Operation Streamline, have also seen a decrease in apprehensions.

Not knowing whether Operation Streamline has in effect been a deterrent to unauthorized immigration has not thwarted efforts to increase support for it, and this poses problems when financial interests from the private sector interfere with public sector governance. According to a fact sheet compiled by Heather E. Williams, 1st Assistant Federal Public Defender for the District of Arizona, U.S. taxpayers foot the bill for around $1 billion or more a year for housing Operation Streamline defendants from the Tucson sector alone. This figure is based on the fact that typically about half of the defendants receive at least one month sentence, and the rest receive sentences of anywhere between 1 and 6 months in prison. The estimate includes:

$2407.78 per month charged by the Bureau of Prisons to house 1 inmate.
$3458.00 per month charged by the U.S. Marshals to house one inmate at a Corrections Corporation of America facility in Arizona (a private prison company contracted by the federal government), for up to 3,200 inmates.
$2,562,750 cost of 67 Criminal Justice Act (CJA) attorneys for six hours a day, at $125.00/hour for an entire year.

Not included in the estimated one billion in costs to the taxpayer for financing Operation Streamline are associated costs of using the courthouse, courtroom staff, magistrate judges, U.S. Marshals, meals, extra Border Patrol for morning courtroom duty, Special Assistant United States Attorneys, and other incidental costs. The above listed costs also do not include the expenses that come if the number of inmates surpasses 3,200 in the above estimate. For example, the inmate population at Arizona CCAs on September 10, 2012 was 4183. With these costs in mind, it is not difficult to understand how the revenues of the nation's two largest private prison operators, Corrections Corporation of America (CCA) and the GEO Group, doubled from 2005 to 2011. Republican Senator John McCain (R-AZ) reportedly received $32,146 from CCA, and fellow member Marco Rubio (R-FL) of the bipartisan "Gang of Eight" who have been working to draft S.744 (the proposed 2013 comprehensive immigration bill) received a reported $27,300 in contributions from the Florida-based private prison contractor, GEO Group, over the course of his career. Both of these senators also sponsored a bill in 2011 to expand Operation Streamline, which would certainly provide more undocumented immigrant inmates for greater private prison profits (Chavkin, 2013).

What is also important to consider is that the mandatory caseload of petty immigration offenses has taken prosecutorial discretion away from the USAO which has resulted in a decline across the five border district courts in federal prosecution of drug smuggling cases. The USAO in the border district courts now generally declines to prosecute drug charges involving less than five hundred pounds of marijuana unless firearms or a previous criminal record is also involved. Prosecution of white-collar crimes, weapons, organized crime, and public corruption have also declined with the increase in immigration prosecution.

Whether an Operation Streamline defendant is represented by a public defender or a CJA Panel attorney, the time they spend with their counsel is limited. This raises concerns regarding the effective assistance of counsel. The defendant could have a number of issues possibly overlooked by their counsel in their short meeting, including if mental or physical illness is present, if there is a lack of necessary medications, if a case can be made for actual or derivative citizenship, and the level of fluency in English or in Spanish present.

In September of 2013, the 9th Federal Circuit Court of Appeals issued an opinion rejecting the en masse court proceeding used to convict groups of people charged with entering the country illegally, known as Operation Streamline. In *U.S. v. Arqueta-Ramos* (2013), Federal Circuit Judge Richard A. Paez rejected this procedure citing that the court errs by not asking defendants individually and ascertaining whether they understand their rights, under Federal Rule for Criminal Procedures 11(b)1.

On October 11, activists called attention to Operation Streamline by organizing a well-coordinated act of civil disobedience, by impeding buses of immigrant detainees destined for Operation Streamline from arriving at the federal courthouse in downtown Tucson, Arizona. It was the first time in this proceeding's history that the prosecutions were halted. More than 20 activists were arrested.

Lisa Burrell Gardinier

See Also: Deportation; Governance and Criminalization; Incarceration; Repatriation; *United States v. Roblero-Solis*; U.S. Border Patrol.

Further Reading

Burridge, Andrew. 2009. "Differential Criminalization under Operation Streamline: Challenges to Freedom of Movement and Humanitarian Aid Provision in the Mexico-U.S. Borderlands." *Refuge* 26.2:78–91.

Chavkin, Sasha. 2013. "Immigration Reform and Private Prison Cash." *Columbia Journalism Review*. February 20. http://www.cjr.org/united_states_project/key _senators_on_immigration_get_campaign_cash_from_prison_companies .php?page=all.

Lydgate, Joanna Jacobbi. 2010. "Assembly-Line Justice: A Review of Operation Streamline." *California Law Review* 98.2:481–544.

Nazarian, Edith. 2011. "Crossing Over: Assessing Operation Streamline and the Rights of Immigrant Criminal Defendants at the Border." *Loyola Law Review* 57.2:1399–1430.

Radnovich, Connor. 2013. "Immigration bill would triple border-crossing prosecutions in Tucson." Cronkite News (April 19, 2013). http://cronkitenewsonline.com/2013/04/ immigration-bill-would-triple-border-crossing-prosecutions-in-tucson/.

Operation Wetback

Operation Wetback is the name of a program created in 1954 by the U.S. Immigration and Naturalization Service (INS) to remove Mexican immigrants from the country. The use of the term "wetback," used publicly in a derogatory manner, was commonplace for that time. It was used to refer to the condition in which immigrants would be found on the U.S. side of the border after swimming across the Rio Grande River to enter the United States without legal authority to do so.

A group of undocumented Mexican laborers from the northern Indiana and Illinois region walk to board a train in Chicago, to be deported to their native Mexico, July 27, 1951. "Operation Wetback" was the name of a program created in 1954 by the U.S. Immigration and Naturalization Service (INS) to remove Mexican immigrants from the country, although U.S.-citizen family members were also deported. This history is remembered with pain and resentment by Mexico and the descendants of those involved. (AP/Wide World Photos)

The context for this INS operation stems from the World War II context, when the United States suffered from a severe labor shortage, primarily in agriculture. The labor shortage was caused by the war effort that sent hundreds of American workers who could have been working in the fields to the U.S. armed forces. In order to solve its labor shortage, the United States began negotiations with Mexico to come up with an agreement by which Mexico would supply the United States with guest workers. This agreement came to be known as the Bracero program of 1942. Under this guest worker program, primarily Mexican males were hired legally as temporary laborers who would be brought to the United States. The program grew during the World War II years. It is estimated that by 1947, 220,000 Mexican Braceros were contracted to work in the United States through the program, not including those who left the program and worked alongside Braceros as undocumented immigrants.

Although the Bracero program was meant to alleviate a temporary labor shortage during the war, U.S. agricultural employers were unwilling to give it up after it ended. After the expiration of the initial agreement between the United States and Mexico in 1947, there were several versions of the program implemented in different parts of the country, all the way until its formal end in 1964. As a temporary measure, the Bracero program was never meant to provide Mexicans with a legal path to citizenship or permanent residency. Moreover, the harsh conditions of the Bracero program had encouraged many migrant workers to opt out of the program and work instead as undocumented immigrants. A sharp criticism of the Bracero agreement was that it tied workers down to specific employers without the ability to negotiate the conditions of their labor. It also denied them the ability to switch employers in search of better wages, or better treatment. Those workers who elected to stay in the United States fell out of legal status, but this also provided employers the opportunity to hire both undocumented workers as well as Braceros. Those choosing to no longer be confined by the program became more free to negotiate with employers the terms of their employment. They could choose those employers that they would like to work for, and allow the workings of employer fairness, labor market demand, and living conditions to enter into the equation.

An outcome of the Bracero program was that it allowed guest workers the opportunity to create and strengthen social networks and relationships with employers long after they left the program. These networks and relationships allowed both new and established immigrants to continue to come to the United States, and with relative success, and find employment. This accounts for a notable rise of the number of agricultural workers that began to immigrate to the United States, and with it, an increase in undocumented immigration.

The emerging undocumented migration did not go unnoticed by both nativists and policy-makers. With the end of World War II in 1945, the return of U.S. veterans seeking work provided the opportunity for the growing anti-immigrant sentiment to flourish. Mexican immigrants were accused of stealing jobs from more deserving U.S. citizens and veterans of the war. Labor unions also complained that undocumented migration depressed wages and undermined collective bargaining. It became advantageous for politicians and candidates for office to publically denounce the undocumented immigration as the cause of the nation's social economic problems. Political rhetoric aggravated fears about public safety, and nativism and harsh criticism of the program eventually pressured President Eisenhower to end the Bracero program in 1953. By this time, racist attitudes and hostilities had come to define attitudes towards immigrants, and set the stage for the launch of the Operation Wetback program.

In May of 1954, the United States Immigration and Naturalization Service announced that in months to come, the United States would begin implementing Operation Wetback. In addition, U.S. attorney general Herbert Brownell stated that it would be an intense campaign designed to address the growing number of Mexican immigrants in the United States. Operation Wetback was centered primarily in the southwest United States, and in particular, targeted Mexican heritage communities.

The initiation of Operation Wetback took place in the state of California. The effort to deport undocumented Mexican nationals was implemented by the United States Border Patrol, in partnership with local and state level police agencies, establishing a practice that would be used for years to come. Agricultural areas were targeted as locations where high levels of undocumented immigrants could be found living and working. In addition, citizenship checks took place in random places such as bus stops, traffic stops, and supermarkets. Furthermore, while it was not the stated objective to also detain and question U.S.-born Mexican Americans, many were indeed detained by the authorities and were inspected for citizenship status, and although the exact number is unknown, a significant number of U.S. citizens who looked Mexican were also deported, and U.S. citizen children of undocumented immigrants were also deported along with their families. Many Mexican American families were also separated due to immigration raids that came with Operation Wetback. It was common at this time for family members to go missing regardless of citizenship status. For many families composed of mixed status, the threat of being separated was a major concern. In anticipation, many migrant parents chose to leave the United States with their families rather than suffer the grief that came with family separation. Many Mexican American children who were U.S. citizens were in this way forced to leave their country of birth for Mexico.

Several Mexican Americans who possessed United States citizenship pressed charges against the state for civil rights violations. There were many allegations of abuse, which accused Border Patrol and police of racial profiling and police-state tactics in their use of excessive force. Some Mexican Americans had been fully deported, and had returned to the United States with the aid of family members. Most lawsuits were settled, though the verdicts varied from case to case.

The United States went about repatriating Mexican Americans who fit the profile of a Mexican national, who may or may have not been undocumented. One of the most common methods of removing them from the country was by train. In this way, deportees were sent to a variety of states in Central and Southern Mexico. In addition, the deportees were not informed where they were being deported. By intentionally imposing greater hardship, the United States Immigration and Naturalization Services hoped to discourage attempts by deportees to return to the United States. The U.S. government also used ships as a method of transportation, used primarily in the state of Texas. These ships would dock in various ports along the Gulf of Mexico. The anti-immigrant sentiment was also meant to alarm Mexican nationals and draw attention to the harsh treatment that immigrants might expect if they returned to the United States. Although official INS figures have varied through the years, by most estimates about 1 million were formally deported through Operation Wetback. The figure is imprecise because many were known to voluntarily leave the United States out of fear of being apprehended and subjected to the heavy-handed measures used by enforcement agents, and because of desires to remain as family units. In other words, if one family member risked deportation, it was likely that the whole family would leave in order to remain together. Regardless, historical hindsight shows Operation Wetback was not successful in eliminating Mexican immigration which had, after many years, succeeded in part by continuous social processes involving the rekindling of ties to the United States through social and employer relations.

Thalia Marlyn Gómez Torres

See Also: Bracero Program; Guestworker and Contract Labor Policies; Migrant Farm Workers; Special Agricultural Workers (SAW).

Further Reading

Durand, Jorge, and Douglas S. Massey. 2004. *Crossing the Border: Research from the Mexican Migration Project.* New York: Russell Sage Foundation.

Garcia, Juan Ramon. 1980. *Operation Wetback: The Mass Deportation of Mexican Undocumented Workers in 1954.* Westport, CT: Greenwood Publishing Group.

Hernández, Kelly Lytle. 2006. "The Crimes and Consequences of Illegal Immigration: A Cross-border Examination of Operation Wetback, 1943 to 1954." *The Western Historical Quarterly* 37.4:421–444.

Overstayers

When speaking of undocumented immigration, it is most commonly believed that "undocumented" means that the individual in question entered clandestinely, that is, by any means that did not involve crossing with valid documentation through a legal port of entry into the United States. To many people's surprise, official numbers show that as many as 4.4 million of the currently estimated 11 million undocumented immigrants in the United States are thought to have entered the country by legal means on a non-immigrant visa, and to have simply never left (Murray, 2013). This action of remaining in the country after the expiration of one's visa is called "overstay" and understandably, he or she who overstays is called an "overstayer." Another term that could be used for this is "visa violator." Overstaying is often considered the easiest way to take advantage of the American Dream without the risks associated with entering the country clandestinely.

The Center for Immigration Studies, a nonprofit research think tank in Washington, D.C. that analyzes the impacts of immigration on the United States, has expressed that it is difficult to determine exactly how many overstayers are in the United States at any time, who they are, and where they are located. Estimates from the Pew Hispanic Center, a nonpartisan research center with a mission of improving understanding of the Latino community in the United States, show that approximately 40 to 50 percent of the country's 11 million undocumented immigrants entered the country originally with a valid visa. However, the Pew Hispanic Center also recognizes that it is difficult for the government to keep track of both those who enter the country and those who leave the country. As of the present moment, United States authorities do not track exit information to see who should have left the country but did not, and when. Because this exit information is not tracked, it is fairly easy to remain unnoticed by law enforcement agencies in the United States.

Due to the current United States immigration policies that focus heavily on enforcement strategies and securing and controlling the borders, few visa violators are ever caught in comparison to the hundreds of thousands of undocumented immigrants who are apprehended yearly trying to cross clandestinely at the border. Despite the fact that the Border Patrol has doubled the amount of agents stationed along the U.S.-Mexico border in recent years, there has been little to no calling for a crackdown on immigrants with expired visas. However, in recent years and especially after 9/11, there has been increased public discourse around whether or not the ease by which visitors can overstay their visa is a threat to the nation's security.

State Department authorities are unsure as to what type of visa is most commonly overstayed. Studies show that it is not uncommon for those who enter with a student visa to overstay and continue living and working in the country upon completion of their studies. For those who enter on a work visa, it is not uncommon, in the case of losing one's job, for one to stay after the expiration of his or her work authorization visa to simply find work elsewhere. Many work visas are obtained through a specific employer, valid only at that place of employment. Short of controlling the movement of their workers, which is ethically problematic, an existing argument for maintaining greater control over workers seeking employment elsewhere when a work visa has expired is to enforce greater oversight of employers who would hire them. To this end, more than four hundred thousand employers in the United States have begun to utilize E-Verify, an electronic verification system for work authorization managed by United States Citizenship and Immigration Services (USCIS), but its usage is not mandatory in most states. One challenge to this system is that many overstayers turn to borrowing social security numbers already in existence or to obtaining and using falsified documents in order to create "legal identities." This often makes it difficult for employers to identify when someone is authorized to work in the United States or not. It is also common for overstayers to work in the informal sector where documents are often not a requirement for being hired and pay is made "under the table," usually in the form of cash. Such forms of payment lend themselves to employer abuses in the form of paying a lower rate or wage theft. After letting a visa expire, it is common for overstayers to minimize their risk of deportation, contributing to the growing "shadow population." Other overstayers may be encouraged by a hope of reform of the nation's immigration system that might provide a path to legal status and citizenship or of marriage to a U.S. citizen or legal permanent resident that may offer the opportunity to adjust one's status based on close family ties. The consequence of overstaying one's visa is "inadmissibility," making the adjustment of one's status nearly impossible without returning to one's country first. While it was once possible for overstayers to leave the United States and secure or renew a visa in a nearby country, it is now only possible for a visa to be secured in one's home country. Exceptions to this rule are made only in extraordinary circumstances or when no visa-issuing consulate exists in the home country.

Those who enter the United States with non-immigrant visas (as students, tourists, or businesspersons, for instance) are required to complete the I-94 form, used by U.S. Customs and Border Protection (CBP) to indicate their arrival and departure. The CBP Officer then stamps the form and grants final approval of admission to the United States for a specific, authorized period of time. The idea behind the I-94 is that at the time of departure from the United States, it is surrendered to a CBP Officer. In this way, the exit is documented formally. If the form is not surrendered, then it may cause problems the next time the nonimmigrant visitor tries to enter the United States, as it may appear in official records that the visitor has indeed overstayed. Overstaying one's visa complicates future travel to the United States in the event that the visa violator leaves the country and tries to return. Overstaying one's visa for more than 180 days can mean facing removal proceedings—deportation from the United States if caught. If an overstayer remains longer than 180 days over the expiration date of the visa but less than a year, then one is considered "inadmissible" to the United States for three years (called a "bar"), and a period of time of one year or greater makes an overstayer inadmissible for ten years. Immigration experts recommend that all documented nonimmigrant visitors do all they can to make sure they are aware of when their visas expire, and adhere to that date, unless an Extension of Stay or Change of Status is filed within that period of time. They also recommend that departure from the United States be documented by the visa holder, either with a stamp when entering another country, or with a plane ticket or itinerary, or by other such means.

There are certain countries that do not require the use of a visa to enter the United States, called "visa waiver countries." According to statistics from Immigration and Naturalization Services (INS), the INS was reorganized in 2003 and is now known most popularly as the United States Citizenship and Immigration Services, or USCIS. From 1988 to 1992, about 5 to 10 percent of undocumented immigrants who overstayed their visits came from such visa waiver countries. Significant abusers of this system included visitors from France, Sweden, and Italy. While this may not be a great percentage of visa violators, at the very least it shows that Latin American nonimmigrant visa holders are not the only ones to abuse the system. In 2013, an article in the *Wall Street Journal* reported that, of all undocumented immigrants, approximately 40 percent are foreigners who arrived legally but have never returned to their home countries. These overstayers are most likely to have come from African, Asian, and European countries (Murray, 2013).

The difficult thing about a nonimmigrant visa is that in order to receive one, the burden is on the applicant to prove that the ties to one's home country are significant enough to encourage their return. As all nonimmigrant visas must eventually be renewed in order to remain current, those who overstay make it difficult for these ties to be proven. This is another reason why some overstayers simply choose to let their visa expire instead of going through the difficult process of providing the evidence that may no longer exist as they did when the visa was originally applied for and granted. In theory, foreign visitors who are suspected to be likely to overstay their non-immigrant visa are highly scrutinized during the screening process by United States consular officials. In practice, it is quite difficult to determine who will overstay and who will not. This determination is assisted by providing documentation that the applicant has property and wealth in their home country (verified by bank statements and current property tax records) or business operations (verified by business licenses and addresses). The objective is to document the assets of all those who are applying for their nonimmigrant visa by using formal documentation and fees used to pay for the processing of the visa. As such, visa interviews with consular officers are influenced by visual subjective markers of class, wealth, and privilege, tipping the scales of who visa over-stayers are likely to be compared to other undocumented who are more likely to take risks by crossing into the United States through clandestine means, often knowing that any objective assessment by officials is sure to be colored by the subjective, and lead to a denial of the application.

Leisha Reynolds-Ramos

See Also: Employment Visas; Labor Supply; Legal Status; Shadow Population; Work Visas.

Further Reading

Dunn, Ashley. 1995. "Greeted at Nation's Front Door, Many Visitors Stay on Illegally." *New York Times,* January 3.

Edwards, James R., Jr. 2004. "Homeland Security Should Keep Tabs on Visa Overstays." *Insight on the News.*

Gonzalez, Daniel. 2010. "U.S. Not Cracking Down on Immigrants with Expired Visas." *The Arizona Republic.*

Miller, Debra A., ed. 2007. *Illegal Immigration.* Detroit: Thomson Gale.

Murray, Sara. 2013. "Many in U.S. Illegally Overstayed Their Visas." *Wall Street Journal,* April 8. http://online.wsj.com/article/SB10001424127887323916304578404960101110032.html.

P

Passports

A passport is a formal document issued by an authorized official of a country to one of its citizens, to certify the identity of the holder. In the United States, a passport is necessary for exit and reentry into the country if entering via an airport. It also allows a citizen of a country to travel in a foreign country in accordance with visa requirements, and entitles the passport holder certain protection while traveling abroad. Because a passport is a document used by individuals for identification and for proving nationality, the information contained in it is related to the place, date of birth and personal information, as well as next of kin information in case of an emergency. A passport generally has an effective and expiration date, according to the country's issuance policies. A number of pages are included in the document in the form of a booklet, and these pages provide the spaces upon which officials in a foreign country note the entry and exit dates of the passport holder, usually with an official stamp. In this way, the stamps or seals of immigration offices of the countries visited serve to document the international borders crossed during travel for the life of the passport.

For immigrants living outside their country of origin, the loss, theft or expiration of their passport while inside the United States is not a crime, nor does it make them an undocumented immigrant. Such immigrants may contact their Consulate General and apply for a replacement. This standard process prompted non-governmental businesses serving Chinese immigrants in the 1990s to openly advertise "passport replacement services" in Chinese newspapers. A surge in undocumented Chinese immigrants since the early 1990s paralleled a thriving fraudulent passport industry within the travel agency industry that illegally began selling fraudulent passports to unsuspecting undocumented immigrants wishing to return to their homeland. By 1996, U.S. Immigration and Naturalization officials confirmed the arrest of those involved in the sale and distribution of counterfeit Chinese passports. In the United States, possession of false travel documents is a federal crime and punishable by up to five years in prison (Lii, 1996). Only U.S. citizens may apply for a U.S. passport, and only the U.S. Department of State can issue them.

Stricter border security measures in recent years have also placed greater restrictions on immigrants seeking to enter the United States. For impoverished immigrants, the cost of a passport puts this purchase out of reach. In addition to the cost of a passport is the cost of the application for a visa that is required in order to remain inside of a foreign country. In 2004, Western Hemisphere Travel Initiative (WHTI) made it a requirement for all U.S. citizens returning from Canada, Mexico, and the Caribbean to have a passport or related identification card to enter into the United States, although there was a delay in implementing this program. Before then those traveling by land from Mexico to the United States were only required to state their citizenship to the port of entry official, or to provide a state-issued identification (such as a driver's license) to re-enter the country.

For undocumented immigrants already living in the United States, even those who possess a valid passport from their country, travel outside the United States holds the risk of arrest. For those traveling by air, security agents (usually U.S. Customs and Border Protection agents) stationed at airport check points and responsible for inspecting government-issued photo identification against flight tickets before allowing passengers into secure areas are likely to notice that there is no travel visa associated with the passport. Those immigrants who have overstayed their travel visa (and are therefore out of status) are subject to prosecution and detention if they are detected in this manner. Immigrants detained without a valid visa, even though their passport is valid, may be deported, but only after a hearing in an immigration court. This may require imprisonment in a detention facility before the court hearing and a determination is made. An erroneous assumption is that upon being caught trying to leave the United States as an undocumented immigrant authorities will simply let you leave. So while possessing a valid passport from the country of origin will not deter an undocumented immigrant from being detained for immigration hearings and eventual deportation, what matters most is having a valid visa that allowed you to enter the country in the first place. It makes sense to remember this important difference between travel documents. Passports are issued by the country of origin, and visas are issued by the destination country giving permission to enter the destination country. Immigrants who enter the United States without a visa are therefore considered "undocumented" immigrants. It has been argued that the right to return to one's country of origin is a fundamental human right (Liu, 2008). At the same time, by emphasizing concerns over sovereignty and national security, most nations conventionally reserve the right to regulate both who enters and who leaves, in this way effecting more than regulation and control, but its power as well (Meyer, 2009).

Each nation has its own requirements for issuing passports. For example, in the United States of America, the U.S. Department of Homeland Security offers information related to this process on its website. In other countries like Mexico, the Ministry of Foreign Affairs is the office providing the passports to the Mexican citizens. Individuals who live out of the country can obtain a passport at a Mexican embassy or consulate. The validity ranges from one to ten years, depending on other factors such as the amount of the fee that is paid.

Martha Yamilett Martínez-Espinoza

See Also: Airports; Counterfeit Documents; Ports of Entry; U.S. Citizenship and Immigration Services (USCIS); U.S. Customs and Border Protection (CBP).

Further Reading

Lii, Jane H. 1996. "A Passport Quandary for Illegal Immigrants." *New York Times,* December 12. Available at: http://www.nytimes.com/1996/12/12/nyregion/a-passport-quandary-for-illegal-immigrants.html?src=pm.

Liu, Guofu. 2008. "The Right to Return in China." *International Migration* 46.1:191–231.

Lloyd, Martin. 2003. *The Passport: The History of Man's Most Travelled Document.* Sutton Publishing, UK.

Meyer, Karl E. 2009. "The Curious Life of the Lowly Passport." *World Policy Journal* 26.1:71–77.

Patriotism

Patriotism is most commonly defined as a love of or devotion to one's country. It also refers to an attachment to group membership of one's own group as well as an attachment to one's nation. In this way, patriotism fulfills an individual's needs of acceptance by others, sense of belonging, sense of security, and pride and achievement of group accomplishments. Patriotism has an emotional and sentimental aspect when members of the group have a collective nostalgia and fond memories of their country during their formative years and a yearning to preserve that by resisting change.

An influx of immigrants into a country logically initiates change and consequently may pose a challenge to the perceived criteria used to understand belonging and national identity. At the heart of this consternation is whether those wanting to belong are perceived as a threat by those who consider themselves patriotic, and therefore act in repudiation. Moreover, because patriotism has a significant affective quality to its definition and there are implications for involvement and associated civic duty responsibilities, showing one's patriotism lends itself to ideas of exceptionalism. This implies that patriotism involves an individual's conscious sense of duty to be critically engaged and be vigilant of those persons or acts that are perceived as unpatriotic. Perhaps the most acknowledged act of patriotism is serving in any of the nation's branches of the armed forces, and within this, are acts of uncommon valor that might earn a soldier any of the highest symbols of patriotism, such as a Purple Heart, or the Congressional Medal of Honor. All male undocumented immigrants and lawful permanent residents aged 18–25, along with their U.S. citizen peers are required by law to register with the Selective Service System (www.sss.gov) for the military service, if the need should arise. Many descendents of immigrants have served with distinction in the U.S. military. Forty-three Latinos have won our nation's highest award, the Congressional Medal of Honor. As of 2007, 1.1 million Latinos were veterans of the U.S. armed forces, and in fact, were overrepresented among enlisted personnel with 11 percent of newly enlisted in 2006, and in particular in the U.S. Marine Corps. The number of Hispanic army enlistments rose 26 percent between 2001 and 2005, which included a significant gain among Latina women.

In light of increased undocumented migration, the challenge lies in reaching consensus of a definition of patriotism and what constitutes acts of patriotism because patriotism can lead to discrimination against individuals who are not members of the group. Patriotism is often used as the justification for the adoption of negative attitudes or practices against foreign immigrants. Some who have anti-immigrant attitudes justify these attitudes by claiming to be patriotic and to be solely acting out of defense of their nation from foreign influences, or foreign enemies.

In the United States, the more zealous and conservative patriots believe immigrants threaten the norms and values that define what being "American" means. The definition will vary but for many conservatives, the commonly agreed-upon profile excludes those who are not English-speaking, natural-born citizens, and law-abiding. Throughout history, accepted profiles include those who are Anglo Protestant individualists. Undocumented immigrants do not easily match these profile criteria and consequently may not be accepted as Americans by self-proclaimed patriots. Immigrants who more closely fit the common American profile are more readily accepted as American and therefore attain a higher degree of assimilation, and are perceived as more likely to show more loyalty towards the host country.

Undocumented immigrants, being primarily from Latin America, are perceived by many self-defined patriotic Americans to be a threat to America's traditional identity. Immigrants from Latin America are perceived to be significantly different from European immigrants to the United States primarily because of their perceived resistance to assimilation. However, such views are narrow and do not always consider that in fact the process is also shaped by the attitudes of those patriots towards newcomers.

For example, many patriots believe that celebrating diversity and differences poses a threat to establishing common ground and a unified national identity. An expression of love or devotion to one's native country is perceived as a hostile act against patriotism to the host country. Due to the large numbers of immigrants and their geographical proximity to their home country, immigrants from Latin America tend to hold on more tightly to their language and cultural traditions. Undocumented immigrants are seen as less willing to adapt or more resistant to assimilation for two primary reasons:

1. because of their inability to actively participate in many social and political activities; and
2. resentment towards the host culture's hostile attitude.

In addition, undocumented immigrants by virtue of their unauthorized entry into the host country are automatically deemed unpatriotic because they are breaking the law of the land. Unauthorized border crossings have become closely linked with poor moral character. Thus, the automatic impression of undocumented immigrants by patriots is that they are of questionable moral character and come to this country to commit crimes and never intend to become contributing members of society. The scholarly literature in any of these realms counters these claims.

In the United States after the September 11, 2001, terrorist attacks, Americans embraced patriotism and the consequences of this newfound passion had direct negative effects on undocumented immigrants. One of the most significant consequences of the terrorist attacks was that they facilitated suspicion of undocumented immigrants as potential terrorists. Due to the fact that undocumented immigrants enter the country without authorization, records or documentation of their past or future activities is limited. This adds to the heightened concern about their intentions for immigrating and questions to which country their loyalty lies. Apart from attacks and hostility directed toward ethnic minorities, laws were put in place directly aimed at immigrants referring to patriotism in a very direct way. For example, the USA PATRIOT Act gave the federal government new powers to expand surveillance and increase the deportation and detention of foreigners suspected of terrorism. Controversy was raised regarding whether the Patriot Act weakened civil liberties and due process granted under the U.S. Constitution. Another federal level response to the terrorist attacks resulted in matters of immigration moved to the Department of Homeland Security. As the name suggests, the idea of "homeland" inspires loyalty to country.

Most industrialized democratic countries have adopted non-discrimination norms and policies. At the same time, there is an undeniable hostility towards immigrants in these same countries. One observation is that in countries that have established anti-discriminatory laws a person may outwardly or publicly accept these laws but inwardly or privately be in complete opposition to them. Adoption or acceptance of egalitarian laws is not sufficient for group members to internalize egalitarian attitudes. The conjuring of the emotional and affective aspects of patriotism may be the key in understanding this dilemma.

Marcella Hurtado Gómez

See Also: Assimilation; Minutemen; *Strangers in the Land*; Social Interaction and Integration; USA PATRIOT Act (2001).

Further Reading

Depuiset, M. A., and F. Butera. 2005. "On the Relevance of Studying Patriotism and Normative Conflict in Changing Attitudes towards Immigrants." *Psicología Política* 30:71–84.

Schildkraut, D. J. 2007. "Defining American Identity in the Twenty-first Century: How Much 'There' Is There?" *The Journal of Politics* 69:597–615.

Segal, Mady Wechsler, and David R. Segal. (2007). "Latinos Claim Larger Share of U.S. Military Personnel." Population Reference Bureau. http://www.prb.org/Publications/Articles/2007/HispanicsUSMilitary.aspx.

Sinnar, S. 2003. "Patriotic or Unconstitutional? The Mandatory Detention of Aliens under the USA Patriot Act." *Stanford Law Review* 4:1419–1456.

Personal Responsibility and Work Opportunity Reconciliation Act (PRWORA) (1996)

The Personal Responsibility and Work Opportunity Reconciliation Act (PRWORA), signed into law by President Bill Clinton on Aug. 22, 1996, dramatically changed both the country's public welfare system and immigrants' access to it. Chief among the legislation's reforms were the termination of the federal program Aid to Families with Dependent Children (AFDC), which the bill replaced with a heavily curtailed state-administered program called Temporary Assistance to Needy Families (TANF), and the requirement that able-bodied adult recipients of assistance work or participate in work training programs. Additionally, major funding cuts were made to the Food Stamps program, the Supplemental Security Income (SSI) program, and programs aiding documented immigrants. The Department of Agriculture–administered Food Stamp program provides financial assistance to low-income people for the purchase of food, and the Social Security Administration–administered SSI program provides financial assistance to low-income elderly, blind and disabled people. Stricter eligibility requirements for many welfare programs and lifetime caps on assistance were also implemented. According to the Congressional Budget Office (CBO), the cuts and eligibility restrictions were expected to save the federal government $55 billion over the legislation's first six years. Approximately $24 billion of those savings were going to come from the exclusion of previously eligible migrants and refugees from welfare programs.

Major changes to the country's welfare system had been a key policy platform of the Clinton campaign, with the President frequently pledging to "end welfare as we know it." It is important to note, though, that restricting immigrant access to welfare programs was not originally an element of these proposed reforms. With the mild recession of the early '90s and the failure of the 1986 Immigration Reform and Control Act (IRCA) to significantly reduce the number of migrants entering the United States, politicians responded to widespread anxieties about job competition with migrants and their perceived overuse of public services by making such restrictions central to the legislative effort. Supporters of these restrictions often argued that easy access to welfare programs functioned as a "magnet" for potential migrants and that curtailing this access could significantly reduce rates of immigration. Despite his reservations about these restrictions, President Clinton signed them into law.

Prior to the bill's signing, documented migrants and refugees were able to apply for welfare assistance on terms more or less equal to those regulating eligibility for U.S. citizens. Undocumented immigrants were already ineligible for nearly all social services, with the exception of certain medical services, but the law made this exclusion explicit. Though benefits were sharply cut for all recipients, migrants who became naturalized citizens were not affected by the bill's restrictions on immigrant access. After the bill's passage, immigrants were divided up into several broad categories that determined their level of eligibility. As stated above, unrestricted access was granted to naturalized citizens but, with a few exceptions, all other categories experienced significant reductions in access.

Qualified migrants, those in the country with legal documentation, were divided up into those who had attained legal status on or before the day the bill was signed and those who attained legal status afterward. For those who became documented beforehand, access to SSI and Food Stamps was guaranteed for children, the elderly and the disabled, and access to other welfare programs was determined by each state. Post-enactment immigrants were barred from all means-tested welfare programs for their first five years of documented status, after which access to all programs except SSI and Food Stamps was left up to the individual states. Additionally, post-enactment immigrants were barred from SSI and Food Stamps until becoming naturalized U.S. citizens.

Inside each of these categories, exceptions were made for military personnel and their families and immigrants who had worked more than 40 quarters in the United States. For active duty or honorably discharged military personnel and their families, regardless of the date they attained legal status, eligibility for all means-tested welfare programs was guaranteed. For immigrants who had achieved legal status prior to the bill's signing and had worked 40 or more quarters, eligibility was similarly guaranteed. However, those immigrants with 40 quarters of work and legal status attained after passage were barred from all programs for the first five years, after which access was to be determined on a state-by-state basis.

Refugees are a special category and their eligibility, like that of military personnel, is not affected by the date they achieved their status. For all means-tested programs, refugees are allotted five to seven years of access, after which states determine continued eligibility for all programs except SSI and Food Stamps. SSI and Food Stamp eligibility are each capped at a maximum of seven years.

As previously stated, undocumented immigrants were already excluded from nearly all welfare programs before the bill's passage, but language in the legislation created ambiguity about what medical services were legal to provide after its passage. In the October 2003 issue of the *American Journal of Public Health*, Jeffrey Kullgren argued that the bill's "restrictions on undocumented immigrants' access to publicly financed health services unduly burden health care providers and threaten the health of the community at large." Because undocumented immigrants are disproportionately affected by undiagnosed transmittable diseases, PRWORA negatively affected both the care available to undocumented immigrants and endangered the health of everyone around them.

In the years following the bill's passage, several of its exclusions for certain categories of immigrants were amended. Most importantly, the Balanced Budget Act of 1997 increased funding for the SSI program and increased the number of legal immigrants eligible for the program. The Agricultural Research, Extension, and Education Act of 1998 increased funding and immigrant eligibility for the Food Stamp program. Approximately nine hundred thousand migrants were cut from the Food Stamp program following the passage of PRWORA and the latter modification restored food stamps to roughly 250,000 of them.

Murphy Woodhouse

See Also: Barriers to Health; Clinton Administration; Health and Welfare; Laws and Legislation, Post-1980s; Nutrition; Temporary Assistance for Needy Families (TANF); Welfare System.

Further Reading

Inda, Jonathan X. 2006. *Targeting Immigrants: Government, Technology, and Ethics.* Malden, MA: Blackwell Publishing.

Migration Policy Institute. 2001. "Immigrants, Their Families and Their Communities in the Aftermath of Welfare Reform." *Research Perspectives on Migration* 3.1.

Yoo, Grace. 2008. "Immigrants and Welfare: Policy Constructions of Deservingness." *Journal of Immigrant & Refugee Studies* 6.4:490–507.

Plyler v. Doe

In *Plyler v. Doe* (1982), the United States Supreme Court ruled that the State of Texas could not deny to undocumented immigrant children the free public education that it provided to children of U.S. citizens or legal residents. The ruling has ensured that all children residing in the United States, regardless of their immigration status, have access to public education from kindergarten to grade twelve. Beyond its impact on undocumented immigrants' access to public education, the *Plyler* ruling is significant because it established that the Equal Protection Clause of the Fourteenth Amendment of the U.S. Constitution does apply to all persons and thus the protections they are entitled to by law. At the same time, *Plyler* did not circumscribe states' power to discriminate against undocumented immigrants in matters that do not involve education or adversely affect undocumented children.

Plyler evolved from a legal challenge of a 1975 amendment to the State of Texas's education code which allowed public schools to charge undocumented students tuition. In response to the amended code, the Tyler Independent School District adopted a policy of charging every undocumented child $1,000 per year to enroll in any of its schools. In September of 1977, several parents of undocumented children—given the pseudonyms J. and R. Doe to protect their identities and those of their children—sued the school district. James Plyler was the school district's superintendent when the lawsuit was filed. On September 14, 1978, the federal district judge who heard the case, Judge William Wayne Justice, ordered an injunction of the state law and school policy, declaring that both violated the students' rights to equal protection under the law. On October 20, 1980, the Fifth Circuit Court of Appeals affirmed the lower court's finding that the school had violated the equal protection clause. The case then went to the Supreme Court, where arguments were heard on December 1, 1981. On June 15, 1982 the Court ruled, in a decision split 5–4, that the Texas law did in fact violate the Equal Protection Clause of the Fourteenth Amendment of the United States Constitution.

In deciding the case, the Court had to determine whether or not the Equal Protection Clause of the Fourteenth Amendment applied to undocumented immigrants, as well as whether the State of Texas had a "rational basis" for denying undocumented immigrant children opportunities it made available to children of citizens and legal residents. The Equal Protection Clause asserts that no state shall "deny to any person within its jurisdiction the equal protection of the laws." In support of its policy, the State of Texas argued that the Fourteenth Amendment did not apply to undocumented immigrants because even though they are physically present, they are not present *legally,* and therefore are not "persons within the jurisdiction" of the state. Both the majority and minority opinions dismissed Texas's argument, citing previous Supreme Court cases and historical speeches from members of Congress who interpreted the clause to mean persons physically present within a jurisdiction.

While all nine justices agreed that undocumented immigrants should be covered by the Fourteenth Amendment, the Court was divided over whether or not Texas was justified in adopting its policy, argued to promote the general welfare. While the Equal

William Wayne Justice ruled on *Plyler v. Doe,* which gave undocumented immigrant children the right to a free public education in 1982. He considered the ruling the most important in his career. In light of more contemporary efforts of states to legislate harsher immigration control measures, the ruling continues to protect undocumented children's rights to education. (Richard Michael Pruitt/Dallas Morning News/Corbis)

Protection Clause suggests that everyone be treated equally, the Court has permitted states to treat groups of persons differently based upon their different needs and circumstances, and to promote the public good. At the time that Texas adopted its policy of charging undocumented children tuition, the American economy was in a recession and the states along the country's southern border were increasingly engaged in border control—a costly duty they expected to be fulfilled by the federal government. Texas argued that its policy of charging undocumented immigrants tuition was necessary in the face of increasing immigration and a lack of federal assistance with preventing immigration and, consequently, having to meet emerging responsibilities associated with meeting the needs of immigrants. Moreover, the State of Texas argued that charging tuition would provide a deterrent to immigration, which in turn would reduce the numbers of undocumented immigrants. According to the State of Texas, the undocumented immigrants comprised a growing underclass that contributed to crime and burdened the state's welfare programs.

The Court was divided over Texas' policy. Chief Justice Warren Burger, writing the minority opinion, argued that Texas's policy was "rational and reasonable," given the increasing number of immigrants and the state's limited resources. Additionally, Burger and the other three Justices in the minority advocated judicial constraint. While these justices recognized that the Texas policy might have the effect of preventing some youth from being educated, which in turn is undesirable, they argued that education policy should be left to the U.S. Congress and the states. Writing the majority opinion, Justice William Brennan argued that Texas had not provided sufficient evidence that a failure to charge for tuition would significantly burden the state's budget or improve social conditions. Furthermore, the justices in the majority argued that Texas's policy would serve to *expand* the underclass about which Texas expressed concern; that is to say, failure to educate those who lacked legal residency would only add to, rather than reverse, problems like unemployment and crime. Finally, Justice Brennan argued that the Texas policy did in fact create precisely the kind of treatment that the Fourteenth Amendment was designed to abolish since the policy had the effect of punishing undocumented children for circumstances beyond their control—the ability to decide their place of residence.

The *Plyler* decision has remained resilient in the face of local, state and federal efforts to deny undocumented immigrant children access to free public education. One of the most significant challenges to the *Plyler* ruling came in 1994 when Californians approved Proposition 187—a referendum that would have denied undocumented immigrants access to virtually all state-funded services, including education. A trial court struck down many of the provisions of Proposition 187, and citing *Plyler,* the court ruled that the proposition's educational provisions were unconstitutional. The second significant challenge emerged from Congress in 1996 with the Gallegly Amendment— a piece of legislation proposed by Representative Elton Gallegly (R-CA) that would have denied public education benefits to undocumented immigrants. Representative Gallegly proposed this amendment as Congress was drafting federal welfare reform legislation—the Personal Responsibility and Work Opportunity Reconciliation Act (PRWORA)—which barred many noncitizens from receiving public benefits. While PRWORA was passed by Congress and signed by Democratic President Bill Clinton, the Gallegly Amendment drew opposition from members of both parties and President Clinton threatened he would veto legislation that attempted to overturn *Plyler.* Ultimately, the Gallegly Amendment was withdrawn.

In terms of its impact on other areas of the law, *Plyler* is considered to be *sui generis,* or a unique case, as it has not affected many subsequent cases. At the same time, the ruling has been influential in the movement to extend undocumented immigrants' rights to higher education. *Plyler* does not apply to college or other forms of post-secondary education, and as a result, in many states undocumented immigrants who were raised and/or educated in the United States are often banned from attending college or other post-secondary educational institutions. Where they are allowed to attend, they are charged higher out-of-state tuition rates and cannot apply for student aid if they cannot prove that they are legally present in the United States. The *Plyler* decision has influenced those states (such as California and Illinois) that have extended equal access to higher education to undocumented immigrants, and the spirit of *Plyler* is alive in the DREAM Act—federal legislation that if passed would extend higher education access and create a path to citizenship for undocumented immigrants who came to the United States as minors.

Carolyn J. Craig

See Also: Deferred Action for Childhood Arrivals (DACA); DREAM Act; Education; Elementary Schools; High Schools; Personal Responsibility and Work Opportunity Reconciliation Act (PRWORA); Proposition 187; Undocumented Students.

Further Reading

"The 25th Anniversary of *Plyler v. Doe:* Access to Education and Undocumented Children." Berkeley Law Web Site. http://www.law.berkeley.edu/2913.htm.

Soltero, Carolos R. 2006. "*Plyler v. Doe* (1982) and Educating Children of Illegal Aliens." In *Latinos and American Law,* 118–131. Austin, TX: University of Texas Press.

Policies of Attrition

In 2006, a policy paper was produced by the Center for Immigration Studies (CIS), a conservative think tank that outlined a strategy for resolving the growing number of undocumented immigrants in the United States. Entitled "Attrition through Enforcement: A Cost-Effective Strategy to Shrink the Illegal Population," the paper conceded that a deportation of the nearly 12 million undocumented immigrants in the country was unworkable. Furthermore, the cost of such a mass deportation strategy was prohibitive, with an estimated price tag of $206 billion over five years. The author of this paper, Jessica Vaughan (2006), suggested an alternative to both mass legalization and mass deportation, referred to as "Attrition through Enforcement," also known as "Policies of Attrition." In this plan, the size of the undocumented population is reduced at a reasonable cost. It is also reduced in a way that is less radical and less visually offensive than the images on television news programs showing traumatized mothers and children being separated during immigration enforcement raids throughout the United States. Thus the proposed enforcement-through-attrition strategy would concentrate on choking off important avenues to immigrant survival. Among some of the recommendations were to force employers to verify the immigration status of their employees, to crack down on the fraudulent use of social security and tax identification numbers by undocumented immigrants, require the Internal Revenue Service to turn over to the U.S. government information about those taxpayers suspected to be in the country unlawfully, strengthen partnerships between state and local law enforcement officials for policing, increase non-criminal removals, and finally, to promote state and local laws that will discourage settlement by undocumented immigrants. This last point is fundamental for understanding the proliferation of state, county, and municipal laws intended to scrutinize immigrants at every step and every hour of their daily activities.

Essential to the ability of state and local governments to design policies that would quietly but systematically enforce immigration and encourage immigrants to leave the country is the anti-immigrant climate. Negative attention had been fomented by sensationalized media reports and images depicting the border region as a lawless wasteland, rampant with violent drug runners and migrants seeking welfare benefits

(Inda, 2006). Compounded by the nation's post-9/11 fears, a highly charged debate over the nation's outmoded immigration system has encouraged states to impose measures to regulate immigration. As a result, many states throughout the United States have developed laws that have followed the attrition through enforcement strategy.

According to the Conference of State Legislatures website, in 2006, five hundred anti-immigrant state-level bills were introduced that year across the United States, many of which replicated or hardened established federal immigration-enforcement responsibilities. By 2007, the nationwide number of state bills dealing with immigrants tripled to 1,562, as every state in the union considered some form of immigration regulation. For example, in 2006, the town of Hazelton, Pennsylvania proposed two anti-immigrant municipal ordinances. One would have required landlords to ask potential tenants to complete an "occupancy permit application" for which the applicant would produce identification and proof of U.S. citizenship or legal residency (Harnett, 2008). A review of this ordinance showed that it omitted 11 categories of lawfully-present immigrants under federal law. Hazleton's bills became models for other towns like Valley Park, Missouri, and Farmers Branch, Texas, which passed similar ordinances. The Hazelton ordinance has since been invalidated as unconstitutional because it conflicted with federal law and because it impacted not only the undocumented but also immigrants legally present under a range of different visa programs. The other Hazelton ordinance, the "Illegal Immigration Relief Act Ordinance" (similar in principle to the Legal Arizona Workers Act of 2008) prohibited the hiring of unauthorized workers. In 1986, the U.S. Congress already enacted the Immigration Reform and Control Act (IRCA), which created a system for regulating the employment of immigrants and already included employer sanctions for those who knowingly hired undocumented workers. Arizona employer sanctions law has since been upheld by the U.S. Supreme Court.

Another example of a policy of attrition came in 2007, when Virginia's Prince William County Board of Supervisors passed an anti-immigrant "papers please" resolution. This resolution required police officers to check the immigration status of anyone they had probable cause to believe was an undocumented immigrant. Three years later, a similar law, Arizona's SB 1070 would be signed into law, and shortly afterwards, Alabama, Georgia, Indiana, South Carolina and Utah would follow with their own copycat laws. Thus, although the long-term impact of Arizona's well-publicized SB1070 on its immigrant communities has yet to play out, it is important to consider that this law represented only one out of hundreds of state measures focusing on undocumented immigration. In addition, a harsh lesson learned by the community of Prince William County was that by driving immigrants out, such policies invite disarray into local economies, as well as costing taxpayers precious public dollars and resources to enforce the laws.

It is also important to note that anti-immigrant efforts have been part of U.S. history since its inception. Broadly speaking, these efforts can be understood as a way to further hinder immigrants' integration into their host society. Obstacles to this integration occur through legal channels, legislatively mandated means, and also through heated political rhetoric and misinformation that influence social perceptions about immigrants and their descendents in a way that stigmatizes them and marginalizes them socially and politically. Harsh anti-immigrant rhetoric used to win support for these legislative bills foment negative social perceptions that may harm mental well-being as well as general health and potential for human capital development (Kilty & Vidal de Haymes, 2000). In the end, it is questionable whether this multi-pronged approach in fact results in the desired outcome of immigrants leaving the country. The MPI policy paper refers to the "success" of the controversial National Security Entry-Exit Registration System (NSEERS) program that was launched after 9/11 as part of the U.S. war on terrorism. NSEERS is a registration required only for nationals from Middle Eastern countries. This entry-exit system allowed the U.S. Department of Homeland Security to remove about 1,500 *illegally* present Pakistanis, but with the registration requirements of the program, about 15,000 undocumented Pakistani immigrants left the country on their own, according to Vaughan (2006). The policy recommendation in the paper is that Mexican and Canadian immigrants be also required to register under this program, resulting in a way to track and deport "overstayers." Until then, however, what is more certain is the research that shows that harsher retributions against immigrants constitute a recipe for widening health and economic disparities based on race and ethnicity. Both research and conventional wisdom hold that the lack of healthcare and healthcare access has a negative impact on all facets of life: from economic productivity and educational attainment to the prevention of crime and the spread of disease.

Already greater discrimination has been reported as difficulty finding work or housing, difficulty using government services or traveling abroad, and the increased likelihood of being asked to produce documents to prove one's immigration status (Pew Research Center, 2007). The implications of health care access restrictions for immigrants in California is discussed by Marchevsky and Theoharis (2008), who find that because health care service agents are influenced by the public discourse and prejudices, their decisions result in the prevention of eligible applicants from applying and receiving much-needed public benefits. In addition, the public intimidation exhibited by police during immigration raids in Chandler, Arizona in the form of unwarranted stops and searches of presumed undocumented immigrants served to normalize disrespect and contempt for all immigrants, regardless of their status, including U.S. citizen family members. Moreover, although the seeds of legislated health care restrictions for immigrants can be traced to 1994 with California's unsuccessful Proposition 187, more recently, similar approaches have sparked alarm about the effects that such measures will have over time and across a broader base of residents. For example, such policies not only impact undocumented immigrants, but entire families including their U.S. citizen members.

Currently, healthcare, healthcare access, income disparities, and educational attainment are challenges faced by Latino populations. Moreover, undocumented workers are more likely to be engaged in high-risk occupations, such as construction and farm labor, which produces a great need for health care and laws that would make work environments safer. It may very well be that in the long run, policies of attrition will undermine entire subsequent generations—the sons and daughters of immigrants—and in so doing undermine the ability of the United States to maintain its economic advantage.

Anna Ochoa O'Leary

See Also: Arizona; Arizona SB 1070; Exclusion; Laws and Legislation, Post-1980s; Mixed-Status Families; Personal Responsibility and Work Opportunity Reconciliation Act (PRWORA) (1996); Postville, Iowa Raid; Proposition 187; Social Interaction and Integration; Temporary Assistance for Needy Families (TANF); Workplace Raids.

Further Reading

Harnett, H. M. 2008. "State and Local Anti-Immigrant Initiatives: Can They Withstand Legal Scrutiny?" *Widener Law Journal* 17:365–382.

Inda, J. X. 2006. *Targeting Immigrants: Government, Technology, and Ethics*. Malden, MA: Blackwell Publishing.

Kilty, K. M., and M. Vidal de Haymes. 2000. "Racism, Nativism, and Exclusion: Public Policy, Immigration and the Latino Experience in the United States." *Journal of Poverty* 4.1/2:1–25.

Marchevsky, A., and J. Theoharis. 2008. "Dropped from the Rolls: Mexican Immigrants, Race, and Rights in the Era of Welfare Reform." *Journal of Sociology and Social Welfare* 15.3:71–96.

Michelson, M. R. 2001. "The Effect of National Mood on Mexican American Political Opinion." *Hispanic Journal of Behavioral Sciences* 23.1:57–70.

Pew Research Center. 2007. *National Survey of Latinos: An Illegal Immigration Issue Heats Up, Hispanics Feel a Chill*. http://pewhispanic.org/reports/report.php?ReportID=84.

Vaughan, J. 2006. *Attrition through Enforcement: A Cost-Effective Strategy to Shrink the Illegal Population*. Washington, D.C.: Center for Immigration Studies. http://www.cis.org/Enforcement-IllegalPopulation.

Policy and Political Action

An intersecting set of policy flaws in the United States (that loosely parallel those in other prosperous countries) have resulted in a large undocumented population. Two powerful clusters of processes drive migration, whether legally authorized or not. Receiving country drivers include employment and business niches, as well as family unification; sending country drivers include uneven development and violence at various scales; and networks connect the endpoints.

Importantly, U.S. laws are mismatched with these migratory realities. The overall number of legal visas is significantly smaller than the number of people strongly motivated to enter the country as migrants. There are essentially no occupational visas for permanent migration of low-skill workers (unlike the case for high-skill workers), despite the extensive demand for them. There are extensive visas for family reunification, but the specific numbers and rules can pose lengthy delays or insurmountable barriers. Equal quotas for all nations—whether a large nation with high demand or a small one with little demand—put limits on some but not all visas. The overall result is that there are backlogs of years to get some visas, or simply no possibility of migrating legally at all. Furthermore, the last time the United States had a legalization program was over two decades ago (as a result of the 1986 IRCA law), by contrast with several countries that have fairly frequent regularization programs.

The policy scenario facing the United States, which is broadly similar to other prosperous countries, is that there is a strong, continuing urge to "enforce the law," that is, to make socially powerful and dynamic migratory processes conform to an idealized but deeply flawed law. Key decision-makers, including several U.S. Presidents, legislators, and policy experts, would like to achieve a grand bargain. This "comprehensive immigration reform" would include some complex mixture of legalization of the existing undocumented population, reform of future visa numbers and priorities, temporary labor migration, heightened border enforcement, and a fair and just employment enforcement system. The specific details are of great importance in whether this would be humane and would accomplish its policy goals. Nevertheless, comprehensive reform has failed repeatedly in recent years (with legislation dying in 2006 and 2007 and never taking off in 2009 and 2010). In 2013, after a bruising election in 2012 where Latino voters largely rejected the Republican alternative for president, comprehensive immigration reform once again came on center stage with a bipartisan group of eight senators working on immigration in summer 2013. Subsequently, an immigration reform bill passed the Senate, S. 744, but encountered resistance in the Republican-controlled House over provisions making a pathway to citizenship possible for the nearly 11.7 million undocumented immigrants in the country. Articulating this opposition was Republican Bob Goodlatte (R-Va), who as Chair of the House Judiciary Committee would be the first to examine the Senate version of the immigration bill, and reportedly would adopt a piecemeal approach to immigration reform with no special provisions for any class of immigrant hoping to become legal permanent residents.

The politics of potential comprehensive reform can be visualized as a four-sided (quadrangular) struggle. Political elites in the two parties and business elites would like to have immigration reform (though with some policy variation among them) because of two main considerations: adapting the power system to the demographic changes in the future United States, and ensuring a large, inexpensive, and vulnerable labor supply. However, the Republican Party elites and business allies have a challenge from another side, which is right-wing populism with a distinctly xenophobic streak. As this right-wing populist mass is important to the overall conservative policy agenda across a range of issues, the Republican elites have generally abandoned their pro-immigration reform interests and visions in favor of enforcement-only, non-comprehensive measures. Conservative Democrats have been similar, although the 2012 presidential campaign helped distinguish them from more hard-line Republicans. Months of media coverage made it increasingly difficult for Latino voters to ignore acrimonious views from Republican candidates that only promised to bring about harsher treatment of immigrants. For example, Republican presidential candidate Herman Cain became famous for his proposal for border enforcement which was to "electrify the [U.S.-Mexico] fence." Republican governor Mitt Romney's answer to the immigration issue during the primary debates was that by preventing undocumented workers from obtaining a job, they would "self deport." Later news reports divulged that Romney had on his campaign staff as his advisor Kansas secretary of state Kris

Kobach, the architect of Arizona's anti-immigrant "Papers Please Law," SB1070. Post-election analysis intimated that although Latino voters may have been disappointed with the great number of deportations that came with the Obama administration, they most probably feared a worse fate that might have resulted with the election of a Republican candidate for the office (Rodriguez, 2012).

The enforcement-only agenda has been aided by the bureaucratic interests of the enforcement agencies of the state, who benefit in terms of budgets, personnel, equipment, and so forth, allied with a fairly limited but aggressive set of homeland-security industrial contractors (such as Boeing, which received the overall managerial contract for the border wall as well as its failed high-tech component). In addition to more resources, they seek reduction in transparency, oversight, and due process in enforcement. On the other hand, a diverse pro-immigrant network has pushed for both human rights enhancement in enforcement and a wider, more comprehensive immigration reform. Among the elements of this side are labor leadership and activists (but inconsistently membership), ethnic-origin groups, religious leadership and activists (but less so, parishioners), immigration lawyers, liberal Democrats, and people inspired by social justice values. While conceptualized as a four-sided struggle, the failure of comprehensive reform essentially rests with the tactical pandering of the capitalist elite to right-wing masses on this specific issue, within a wider context of resurgent conservatism.

As the grand bargain fails to materialize, political and bureaucratic space opens for the expansion of enforcement of existing laws. The lack of real, lasting adjustments means that the overt theme of "illegality" and a covert racialized imagery of Mexican lawbreakers (incorrect or limited as that analysis may be) will remain. Politicians fear in most cases voting against "law enforcement." This is particularly salient for borders, a powerful symbol attracting enormous efforts at righting the world. In a widespread, though not universal view, the national community is unified and good, and its external boundary protects it from penetration by sources of danger and degradation, which enter from outside. Clearly this is simplistic, and often wrong; but it has responded to the changing demographics of the United States (stemming from Latin American and Asian migration), to the long-term decline of the United States as a completely dominant economic and political power, and to the horrific terrorist attacks of 9/11.

The U.S. border with Mexico has witnessed an enormous and unrelenting increase in immigration law enforcement since late 1993 (interestingly, after a substantial period of Mexican and Central American–origin population growth in the United States, but well before 9/11). Interior enforcement has grown rapidly more recently, since 2005. The fundamental policy assumption of both border and interior enforcement is "deterrence," that potential undocumented migrants will decide not to attempt entry if they face severe risks of arrest, legal punishment, suffering and death, and expensive smuggler fees. However, careful field surveys in Mexico indicate that such forms of deterrence do not work. Migration is affected by the state of the economy, and also the frequency of trips back and forth is reduced (or even halted) by intense border enforcement, resulting in the entrapment of people in the United States.

The single largest change in border policy during the last two-decade massive expansion was the placement of patrol officers directly on the borderline in urban areas.

This displaced undocumented entries to dangerous desert and mountain corridors. The patrol responded with a series of "operations" along the border, following after shifting flows. These operations, in turn, absorbed a vast increase in Border Patrol staffing, going from fewer than four thousand officers in 1993 to more than 21,000 officers in 2011. In addition to frontal operations, all major roads are bottlenecked fifty to seventy-five miles north of the border by interior checkpoints, and public transportation is regularly inspected.

Officers on the ground are still the most important tactical element of the patrol. However, these operations have been reinforced by the construction of eight hundred miles of border wall, by stadium lighting, night vision technology, a dense field of motion sensors, fixed-wing aircraft, helicopters, and other items of technology. The military has been deployed repeatedly to the border, first regular units and then National Guard; military technologies such as surveillance drones are in regular use, and behind-the-scenes operations, such as intelligence gathering and analysis.

The escalation of interior enforcement occurred much later in time, since 2006, but it has resulted in a rapid increase in removals (also known as deportations). These operations include direct raids on houses, public transportation, and places where immigrants congregate. Among the raids are collateral arrests of many non-violator (but undocumented) immigrants when single individuals are being sought by immigration authorities. They also include immediate moves to arrest persons when they arrive at immigration offices to request legal immigration benefits (e.g., undocumented people being petitioned for by legal resident or citizen family members). Workplace raids occur sporadically, but often disrupt whole communities. Recently, the federal government has shifted to a policy of notifying employers of suspected out of status employees, unobtrusively leading to them being fired, known as "silent raids." Employers, except unusually abusive ones, rarely are charged with their law violation, illegal employment. A new database check system for employment, E-Verify, has been deployed sporadically, and so far is flawed and limited; but it represents an important policy trend.

However, the most important mechanism of federal interior enforcement is stops by local and state police, followed by turnovers to immigration authorities. Initially, this was limited to convicted criminals, after their sentences were over, but since 2006 it has shifted to non-convicted persons. Many are simply stopped by police on pretexts, and turned over. Not all jurisdictions allow this, but some encourage it. Others are turned over at the jail, but before conviction, under a new program called Secure Communities. This makes local and state police into extensions of federal immigration police (small numbers are actually deputized in the 287(g) program but most operate informally). This is a matter of considerable contention—it is central to SB 1070 in Arizona—with many police leaders opposing such operations on the grounds that it actually reduces community security by frightening immigrants of all statuses away from the police.

Spread throughout the U.S. interior is an archipelago of immigrant detention and removal officers and facilities. These include federal immigration prisons ("detention centers"), leased private prisons (including leased municipal facilities), short-term hold facilities, and immigration holds, etc., inside local jails. Rapid, secret movement, and lack of traceability, transparency, and accountability leading to complete removal are central policies of this system.

The Illegal Immigration Reform and Immigrant Responsibility Act and the Anti-terrorism and Effective Death Penalty Acts of 1996 removed a wide range of due process and appeal rights from immigrants in removal proceedings and also when petitioning for immigration benefits. They also removed substantial elements of discretion from immigration officers and judges. The remaining elements of officer discretion over arrest and prosecutorial discretion are rarely exercised in favor of deportable immigrants. Within one hundred miles of the land border, and potentially within one hundred miles of all maritime borders, people have reduced protections around search and seizure and can be removed with minimal legal process (known as "expedited removal"). Operation Streamline, applied to some border sectors, charges and in almost every case convicts undocumented border entrants of federal-level criminal charges, and more than one half of all federal prosecutions are now for low-level immigration entry violations. Finally, the immigration enforcement system, both at the border and in the interior, suffers from impunity, lack of oversight, and lack of accountability, not only toward immigrants of all legal statuses, but also to communities where they operate heavily.

State and local legislation has been an important new policy domain and locale of political struggle in recent years. The overall thrust of the legislative proposals is to make the everyday life of undocumented people so difficult that they will move somewhere (undetermined) else (also called policies of attrition). Among the central themes are restrictions for the undocumented on public services (e.g., prenatal health care), state licenses (e.g., to practice occupations), state sanctions on businesses hiring undocumented persons (by regulating business licenses), and state and local police involvement in de facto and sometimes de jure immigration law enforcement. Despite the publicity around them, only a few measures in a limited number of states have actually passed.

In the four-sided model of politics above, the bureaucratic and homeland security coalition in favor of increased enforcement resources is straightforward to understand. The economic and political elite interests in revising immigration policy are more subtle, but not greatly so. Elites see the demographic growth of U.S. citizen Latinos, Asians, and so forth, and politically seek the appearance of identifying with them enough so as to maintain political hegemony. Economically, they want a revised immigration policy that imports to the country a large, well-managed, vulnerable, and easily controlled labor force. These policy preferences are "pro-immigrant," but only in a top-down, domination-oriented manner.

However, as seen in the political model above, the so far politically dominant force has been organized opponents of general immigration reform and increased-level immigration levels. This sector also favors intensified border and interior enforcement. Also, organized proponents of immigration and enforcement reform are important, though not politically dominant. Thus, in order to understand the policy and politics affecting undocumented people, it is important to analyze the perspectives and value commitments of these two mass blocs inside the United States (an analysis that is broadly comparable in other wealthy nations with mass democracies).

Opposition to immigration requires a deep social and cultural analysis. Robust empirical evidence demonstrates that rational economic interests, either in employment competition or government expenditures, do not account for immigration opinions. Rather, negative opinions of immigrants—especially of Mexicans of any status, and of the undocumented—are associated with middle incomes and occupations, older age, being male, and being white. It is part of the wider pattern of political conservatism. One of the challenges in analyzing this is that there are overt positions (e.g., being against illegality) that must be considered, but under conditions of modern "political correctness," where some important positions and emotions are usually denied or unspoken (e.g., racism against Mexicans and Latin Americans generally). It is useful to look back to the history of anti-immigrationism for clues.

Examining past immigration opposition, we note that it reached peaks when the U.S. (or other national) economies were undergoing rapid and disruptive changes, either periods of rapid growth and importation of workers or periods of displacement and job shifts. It also builds up over time, as a political and cultural movement, and is not exactly timed according to economic shifts. Rather, it is a reaction in the strict sense of the word. Dominant political and economic actors and relations force radical changes on the rest of society, parts of which respond by using immigrants as scapegoats. The exclusive possession of "citizenship," not only as a strict legal status but as a notion about who is inside and who is outside, who is deserving and who is unworthy, even risky, is an important theme.

There is a desire for an imagined perfect recent past, and a social-cultural drive to rearrange the world to fit that non-real image. Law enforcement, especially of perfect borders, is a logical (if in reality flawed) response to that desire. One way this is expressed clearly is by viewing immigrants as sources of risk and danger, which was made worse by the external terrorist attacks of 9/11 (although clearly, there are internal sources of risk and danger also, and almost no immigrants are terrorists and very few violent criminals). Also, racism against Mexicans, an enduring theme in U.S. history, makes anti-immigrant sentiment worse; clear evidence is violent attacks on non-Mexican immigrants from Latin America, attacking "Mexicans," and more generally the public confusion between people of Mexican origin, immigrants, and undocumented immigrants specifically. An important reaction to demographic change across the country is a drive to return to an imaginary racial order of the past.

But the pro-immigrant political coalition (enumerated earlier) also has social and cultural roots, as expressed in their desires, images, and ideals. Key ideas about liberal personhood, individual rights, and globalism help explain apparently paradoxical aspects of immigrant advocates. These social justice actors advocate for a free market in labor and greater global engagement. They thus take the ideal capitalist and democratic cultural model of free, liberal personhood as a goal for how migrants should be treated. Taking seriously the ideals of the dominant political-economic system, they critique the status quo for not living up to those ideals. They also hark to the same global awareness of world capitalist and political elites, if differently interpreted.

Looking at the positions of human rights advocates, especially those concerned with borders: all persons should be secure in their bodies, not dying crossing the sea or desert; and should be accorded legal rights of due process and protection from unreasonable search and seizure. But clearly these are minimal standards of liberal justice in a real world that often is below the minimum. Insofar as it breaks with the fundamental assumptions of the status quo, the break is a thoroughgoing rejection of global separation, inequality, coercion, and avoidable death.

Josiah McC. Heyman

See Also: Activism; Advocacy; Exclusion; Governance and Criminalization; Illegal Immigration Reform and Immigrant Responsibility Act (IIRIRA) (1996); Immigration Reform 2013–2014; Operation Streamline; USA PATRIOT Act (2001); U.S. Department of Homeland Security (DHS); U.S.-Mexico Border Wall; Xenophobia.

Further Reading

Andreas, Peter. 2009. *Border Games: Policing the U.S.–Mexico Divide.* 2nd ed. Ithaca, NY: Cornell University Press.

Heyman, Josiah McC. 1998. *Finding a Moral Heart for U.S. Immigration Policy: An Anthropological Perspective.* Washington, D.C.: American Anthropological Association.

Heyman, Josiah McC. 2011. "Constructing a 'Perfect' Wall: Race, Class, and Citizenship in U.S.-Mexico Border Policing." In Pauline Gardiner Barber and Winnie Lem, eds., *Migration in the 21st Century: Ethnography and Political Economy*, chap. 8. New York and London: Routledge.

Massey, Douglas S., Jorge Durand, and Nolan J. Malone. 2002. *Beyond Smoke and Mirrors: Mexican Immigration in an Era of Economic Integration.* New York: Russell Sage Foundation.

Nevins, Joseph. 2010. *Operation Gatekeeper and Beyond: The War on "Illegals" and the Remaking of the U.S. – Mexico Boundary* 2nd ed. New York and London: Routledge.

Rodriguez, Cindy Y. 2012. "Latino vote key to Obama's re-election." CNN. November 9, 2012. http://www.cnn.com/2012/11/09/politics/latino-vote-key-election.

Ports of Entry

Ports of entry are authorized places for people and goods to cross borders. There are air, sea, and land ports. Although they are authorized entrance points, they actually play a significant role in unauthorized migration and the lives of such migrants (this entry uses the term "unauthorized," since many people discussed here actually have documents, and are thus not undocumented).

Many unauthorized migrants enter through ports of entry, although we have no clear handle on what the numbers or proportions are. However, we do have estimates for persons who enter with approved non-immigrant visas (tourists, students, etc.) who violate the terms of those visas by overstaying their expiration dates (that is, not departing when required), working without authorization, and so forth. The Pew Hispanic Center estimated in 2006 that 40 to 50 percent of resident unauthorized migrants are visa overstayers. At the U.S.-Mexico border, a non-immigrant visa (commonly called a border crossing card or laser-visa) allows approved Mexican northern border residents to enter through a U.S. port of entry to visit, shop, etc., but not to work, up to twenty-five miles into the country, for up to thirty days per visit. This visa is sometimes violated, either to commute daily from Mexico to work in the United States, or to reside on the U.S. side of the boundary.

In addition to visa violations, an unknown proportion of migrants enter ports through various sorts of fraud. Entrants through the ports can be U.S. citizens, legal permanent residents, non-immigrant visa holders, or a diverse range of visa holders of other statuses and documentation. These ways of entering can be maneuvered for unauthorized migration—deliberately or inadvertently—in several ways. People can claim falsely to be someone else, presenting that other person's legitimate document. The document itself may be tampered with to alter the identification. Or the document may be counterfeit.

After 9/11, the U.S. government made its documents harder to counterfeit or falsify, and included biometric information on them (e.g., encoded fingerprints). The Western Hemisphere Travel Initiative (WHTI) of 2004 (still being implemented) required all U.S. citizens returning from Canada, Mexico, and the Caribbean to have a passport or related identification card. Previously, people had simply declared U.S. citizenship, and were admitted upon approval of a port inspector. WHTI closed a gap in which some non-citizens entered the United States by falsely claiming citizenship. Although misleading or fraudulent entry through ports has become harder, it has not been altogether prevented. Besides high-quality false/altered/transferred documents, corruption of U.S. inspectors, often by professional smugglers, undermines port controls. Also, some migrants pass through ports physically hidden from inspection (e.g., being built into car false compartments).

Obviously, authorized immigrants and other authorized travelers can come and go through ports of entry, although they are sometimes detained, questioned, and so forth because of suspicious inspectors or unusual documentation and statuses. The boundaries in immigration law between authorized and unauthorized status is not crystal clear, and at ports, people who think they are properly authorized can fall into complicated legal and administrative limbo. U.S. courts have given vast discretionary power and few protections against searches and seizures at ports, making them sites of nearly complete sovereignty of the state.

Asylum seekers often request that status at ports. While asylum should differ from unauthorized migration—asylum is precisely a request for authorization, based on international treaties conveying fundamental human rights—the actual line between asylum and unauthorized migration is often blurred, most of all by the state, which may treat asylum applicants as would-be unauthorized migrants rather than persons fleeing persecution. Such applicants may be vigorously searched, detained, and removed with little or no legal process. Likewise, refugees may appear at ports with travel documents (passports, visas used on the route to get to the port) destroyed, so as not to be easily returned to the countries from which they are fleeing.

The port-crossing experience is a far different experience from undocumented border crossing in places between ports of entry, with people scaling border walls, walking through deserts and mountains, etc. Entrance through ports is physically far easier and safer (except, in some ways, as is the example of people packed into hidden compartments). The port itself stands astride an efficient transportation route, such as roadways or air transport networks. The actual entrance is unquestionably a moment of anxiety if the person intends to do something without authorization. Inspectors target that anxiety, but migrants practice controlling their nerves and being prepared with documents and stories. Port smuggling is usually more expensive and sophisticated (e.g., smugglers who can supply false documents or purchase the services of corrupt officers). Alternatively, legitimate entry on a non-immigrant visa requires a relatively privileged social background (e.g., an apparently fixed residence and good income in the home country are required by the U.S. consular service), even if this is followed by visa violation.

The encounter between entrant and inspector involves a complex and highly unequal sequence of symbolic and material interactions. The inquisitorial representative of the state uses various learned routines and rubrics to sort crossers into legitimate or suspicious. Such sorting may be valid or invalid. The entrants may be fully honest, but they may also hold back aspects of their past histories and future intentions. The inspectorial encounter is thus an attempt by the inspector to attack, crack, penetrate, and assess the inspected in a short period of time (as little as thirty seconds at first encounter).

Behind this immediate interaction are powerful social relations that influence how state officers classify port entrants, how port entrants view the representatives of the state, and how the interactional process proceeds. These key relations include nationality, race, class, gender, age, and sexuality. They are not literally apparent on the surface of the entrant, but rather are processed and performed symbolically in perceptions, communications, and actions. They are not simple in the sense that one such relation exhausts the whole power situation but rather are intersectional, expressing the multiple unequal power orders that converge to make up borders and migrations. As an example, decision-making by U.S. inspectors is not just a matter of racial profiling of Mexicans, though that occurs often, but racial stereotypes are modified by considerations of apparent wealth and power of some Mexicans, and not others.

Because ports are relatively safe and easy, but also more expensive to cross than are borders outside ports, their unauthorized migrant population differs from non-port crossers. Crossers are often more female than non-port populations, and have more small children. They may well be more prosperous in their point of origin, either to have the funds to pay the more sophisticated port smugglers or to obtain legitimate non-immigrant visas. Much remains to be discovered about these distinct populations.

Departure (away from the United States) through ports of entry also matters to unauthorized migrants. Obviously, the best way to leave the country (and in the case of air transport the only way to leave) is via a port. U.S. land ports have relatively modest outbound checks, aimed at contraband money and weapons, not departing migrants. In contrast, air and sea ports do have outbound registration which does record visa violations (e.g., overstays). That record may affect future entry but is not used at the time of departure to arrest people.

Departure, with the intention of return, implies for unauthorized migrants an expensive and/or risky reentrance either via a port or between ports. So why would people depart? Motives may be loved ones, desired health services, visits to familiar places, and so forth. The thought of the peril of future reentry weighs against compelling reasons to depart. Ports thus are, in part, one-way valves that discourage cyclical migration and entrap unauthorized migrants into permanent residence in the new society. There are ways around this, such as the use of friends and relatives with authorized border crossing rights to serve as couriers.

Various "discursive frames" project stereotypes of borders and migration, from xenophobic fears of border invasions to humanitarian concerns with deaths in the desert. On all sides, notions of who is a migrant are dominated by non-port land crossing of the Mexican border: Mexicans, perhaps Central Americans, mostly male, penetrating walls and fences. The U.S. state is envisioned as the Border Patrol, and not the port inspectors. The port of entry side of migration is quite different—more female, more diverse in national origins, facing quite different risks and opportunities. Surprisingly little is known about ports, the people passing through them and working in them.

Josiah McC. Heyman

See Also: Airports; Border Crossing; Deportation; Expedited Removal; Overstayers; Passports; Repatriation; U.S. Border Patrol; U.S.-Mexico Border Wall.

Further Reading

Gilboy, Janet A. 1991. "Deciding Who Gets In: Decisionmaking by Immigration Inspectors." *Law and Society Review* 25:571–99.

Gilboy, Janet A. 1992. "Penetrability of Administrative Systems: Political 'Casework' and Immigration Inspections." *Law and Society Review* 26:273–314.

Heyman, Josiah McC. 2004. "Ports of Entry as Nodes in the World System." *Identities: Global Studies in Culture and Power* 11:303–327.

Heyman, Josiah McC. 2009. "Ports of Entry in the 'Homeland Security' Era: Inequality of Mobility and the Securitization of Transnational Flows." In *International Migration and Human Rights: The Global Repercussions of U.S. Policy,* edited by Samuel Martínez, 44–59. Berkeley and Los Angeles: University of California Press.

Pew Hispanic Institute. 2006. "Modes of Entry for the Unauthorized Migrant Population." May 22. http://pewhispanic.org/files/factsheets/19.pdf.

Postville, Iowa Raid

At around 10:00 AM on May 12, 2008, dozens of Immigration and Customs Enforcement (ICE) agents raided Agriprocessors Inc.'s Postville, Iowa plant, the small town's biggest employer and the country's largest producer of kosher meat. The operation was carried out with the assistance of numerous local, state and federal agents. According to the Department of Homeland Security, the raid was in response to "697 criminal

Supporters of immigration reform walk through downtown Cedar Rapids, Iowa, on Friday, May 10, 2013, to mark the five-year anniversary of the immigration raid at the Agriprocessors plant in Postville. The raids sparked national outrage, resulting in a congressional hearing to examine the heavy-handed methods that ICE used, especially against women and children. (Ryan J. Foley/AP/Corbis)

complaints and arrest warrants against persons believed to be current employees [at the plant]." Most of the warrants and complaints were related to the undocumented status of many of the plant's workers.

The raid resulted in nearly four hundred arrests, of whom 290 were Guatemalan and ninety-three were Mexican. Until the workplace raid several months later at the Howard Industries plant in Laurel, Mississippi, in which nearly six hundred migrants were detained, the Postville, Iowa raid was the largest of its kind in U.S. history. Though the Laurel workplace raid was larger, the Postville raid reignited the national immigration debate and brought renewed scrutiny to the Bush administration's frequent use of the controversial immigration enforcement tactic of workplace raids.

Only ten days after the arrests, 302 undocumented workers had been charged with crimes associated with their use of fraudulent or stolen social security numbers and other forms of identification, and 297 of those charged had pleaded guilty. Most of the migrants who pleaded guilty served five-month sentences and were then deported to their home countries.

The speedy manner in which those arrested were charged and pled guilty raised many eyebrows. In the months after the trial, it was revealed that there had been close collaboration between the prosecutors who brought the cases and the federal court that heard them. The American Civil Liberties Union posted official documents on their website that contained a script of sorts for the migrants' defense attorneys. The scripts detailed the offers that prosecutors would make and the language that judges would use when accepting them, among many other unorthodox procedures that seemed to suggest that the court was aiding prosecutors' attempt to obtain guilty pleas.

A year later, the U.S. Supreme Court ruled unanimously in *Flores-Figeroa v. United States* that prosecutors had inappropriately used the criminal charge of aggravated identity theft to extract guilty pleas to lesser charges from many of the Postville migrants. However, because most of the migrants had already served their sentences and been deported, the ruling had no impact on their cases.

A handful of higher-level employees and managers, including the plant's former owner Aaron Rubashkin and his son Sholom, were also charged with a number of labor, immigration, child labor, and identity fraud crimes. All charges against Aaron Rubashkin were subsequently dropped and he was never convicted of a crime. Similarly, all immigration and child labor charges against Sholom, who was the company's chief executive officer at the time of the raid, were dropped. However, over the course of the investigation a number of financial irregularities were discovered and Sholom was charged with bank fraud and sentenced to twenty-seven years in prison.

Plant supervisors Juan Carlos Guerrero-Espinoza and Martin De La Rosa-Loera were the first two managers to be arrested. Both were charged with helping undocumented employees obtain fraudulent documentation and encouraging them to live in the country illegally. Guerrero-Espinoza pled guilty and was sentenced to 36 months in prison and De La Rosa-Loera was found guilty and sentenced to twenty-three months in prison. Two other plant managers, Hosam Amara and Zeev Levi, fled to Israel shortly after the May 2008 raid. Pending extradition, both face charges of conspiring to harbor illegal immigrants and conspiring to obtain false immigration papers. Several other employees and managers were charged and convicted of similar crimes.

The raid's immediate and long-term effects on the town of Postville were dramatic. The day after the raids, approximately half of all the school district's students, and 90 percent of its Latino students, did not show up for class. Property managers reported sky-high vacancy rates and area businesses quickly started suffering and some closed as a result of the loss of customers in the community. Responding to the severity of the crisis, Postville's city council took the extreme measure of declaring the city a humanitarian and economic disaster area in November 2008, though the federal government did not recognize this designation. Agriprocessor itself went into bankruptcy proceedings six months after the raid. Under the terms of the bankruptcy, the company was sold to the Canadian firm SHF Industries in July of 2009 and the plant reopened shortly thereafter, though with significantly curtailed production levels.

The raid also inspired significant community-organizing efforts. Several months after the raid, Latino immigrants, faith leaders and activists organized a march of about one thousand people through downtown Postville to protest working conditions at the plant and demand immigration reform and legal status for undocumented workers. In

November of 2008, community members and leaders formed the Postville Response Coalition to handle the social and economic fallout from the raid. With conditions in the town improving, especially after the reopening of the plant, the coalition dissolved in 2010. However, annual vigils have been held at the fairgrounds in nearby Waterloo, where migrants were charged and held after the raid.

Workplace raids have continued into the Obama administration, but have been significantly cut back. Whereas well over five thousand undocumented workers were arrested on the job in 2008, fewer than one thousand were arrested in workplace raids in 2010. Under the Obama administration, the Department of Homeland Security has instead focused its resources on auditing employers suspected of employing undocumented workers and fining those who do, known as "silent raids." Overall deportations, however, have significantly increased under the Obama administration.

Murphy Woodhouse

See Also: Governance and Criminalization; Identity Theft; Immigration and Customs Enforcement (ICE); Labor Supply; Policy and Political Action; Workplace Raids.

Further Reading

Argueta, Luis. *AbUSed: The Postville Raid.* 2010. New York: Maya Media. 96 minutes. Video.

McCarthy, A. L. 2010. "The May 12, 2008 Postville, Iowa Immigration Raid: A Human Rights Perspective." *Transnational Law & Contemporary Problems: A Journal of the University of Iowa College of Law* 19.1:293–316.

Peterson, C. L. 2009. "An Iowa Immigration Raid Leads to Unprecedented Criminal Consequences: Why ICE Should Rethink the Postville Model." *Iowa Law Review* 95.1:323–346.

Pregnancy and Childbirth

Pregnancy and childbirth are important topics concerning undocumented immigrant women. In 2008, 340,000 infants were born to undocumented parents (National Public Radio [NPR], 2010). A number of theories have been proposed to explain birth outcomes for immigrant women. There is also public debate over federal and state funding of prenatal care for undocumented pregnant women, often with demeaning and derogatory reference to their children as "anchor babies." Additionally, undocumented pregnant women in police custody face unique challenges.

The "epidemiologic paradox" is a theory that claims that despite greater socioeconomic disadvantage, foreign-born women have surprisingly favorable birth outcomes. This pattern has been demonstrated consistently in Mexican immigrant populations and for this reason is sometimes called the "Latina paradox." Young maternal age, inadequate prenatal care, and low socioeconomic status are factors that typically contribute to poor birth outcomes. However, for low-acculturated Mexican immigrant women who are often under these circumstances, the rates of low birth weight (LBW) and premature birth are similar to those of U.S.-born, non-Hispanic white women, and lower than those for other racial and ethnic groups.

Some cultural factors have been proposed to explain this advantage. For Mexican immigrant women these include traditional diet, low rates of smoking and alcohol use, strong religious beliefs, favorable perceptions of childbearing, and positive family support networks. A "healthy migrant effect" has also been proposed which claims that those individuals who migrate successfully are healthier than people who do not migrate, and therefore, positive birth outcomes are expected.

In a process termed the "acculturation paradox," Latinas' maternal and infant health advantage diminishes over time as they become more accustomed to the American way of life. This shift may be related to a loss of protective cultural factors. The deterioration of birth outcomes over time in the United States has not been demonstrated in all immigrant groups. For example, Korean immigrants experience no difference in birth outcomes with acculturation.

For undocumented immigrant women, the prevalence of LBW and premature birth is higher than documented women, but lower than U.S.-born women. Undocumented immigrants in the state of Colorado had complications during childbirth, inadequate weight gain during pregnancy, and sought late prenatal care. For immigrant women, especially the undocumented, access to prenatal care can be problematic due to lack of insurance, language and cultural barriers, inflexible office hours, transportation issues, and lack of childcare.

Undocumented women cannot be denied care during labor and delivery; these services are covered by Emergency Medicaid. However, for years, there has been debate over public funding for undocumented women's prenatal care. Under the Personal Responsibility and Work Opportunity Reconciliation Act of 1996, undocumented pregnant women are prohibited from receiving federal aid for prenatal care. The law grants states the authority to decide whether to fund prenatal care or to offer nutritional support through the Women, Infants, and Children (WIC) program. If states do decide to support the undocumented, they must enact a new law that verifies this support.

Cost-benefit analyses conducted in California found that denying access to prenatal care would increase costs of postnatal care. This study found that lack of prenatal care for undocumented women is associated with a four times greater risk of LBW and a seven times greater risk of premature birth. Prenatal care costs approximately $702. Meanwhile, hospitalization for infants of mothers who did not receive prenatal care costs approximately $2,341. The difference in costs associated with denial of care would be projected on taxpayers; with each cut in federal dollars, taxpayers would pay $3.33 (Guttmacher Insititute, 2000). Based on these findings, advocates in California support prenatal care for undocumented women.

Another source of debate involving pregnant undocumented women is with regard to so-called "anchor babies." Derogatory in nature, the term is used to describe the practice of entering the United States without documents with the alleged purpose of giving birth to a U.S. citizen child. The supposed advantage of this is that a family can eventually gain legal status through that child. In 2010, there were 5.1 million children in the United States with undocumented parents. Seventy-nine percent of these children were U.S. citizens (NPR, 2010). The Fourteenth Amendment to the Constitution states that all infants born in the United States are granted birthright citizenship. In response to the growing undocumented population, recent legislation proposed mostly by Republicans has moved to revise this amendment but has been met with failure thus far.

Unique challenges can arise for undocumented pregnant women who are in police custody. Numerous cases have been recorded of women being forced to give birth under degrading and often inhumane conditions. In one case, an unidentified woman who goes by "Maria" was detained when her husband was stopped for having an invalid driver's license. Maria's water broke during the confrontation with the law enforcement officer who accused her of faking contractions and told her that she would be having her baby in Nogales. Maria gave birth in the United States, but was not allowed to be with her husband. Instead, an immigration agent remained by her bedside throughout her labor while other agents waited outside. The agent by her side repeatedly reminded Maria that she would be deported to Mexico as soon as the baby was born.

Family members and spouses of pregnant women in custody can be denied admittance to the birthing room and the opportunity to care for the newborn for up to twenty-four hours. In Miriam Mendiola-Martinez's case, she was not allowed to see, hold, or nurse her infant for over two days, and for Alma Chacon it was seventy days. In both instances, the women were shackled before and after the birth.

According to the Bureau of Prisons anti-shackling policy, pregnant women are not allowed to be shackled before, during, or after childbirth while in federal custody. However, state detention centers have their own laws. Fourteen states and U.S. Immigration and Customs Enforcement (ICE) have made it illegal to shackle women during childbirth. However, the remaining thirty-six states allow pregnant women to be handcuffed to their beds if they have received an immigration charge that is considered to be a "criminal offense" (Costantini, 2011).

Courtney Waters

See Also: Barriers to Health; Children; Health and Welfare; Hospitals; Illegal Immigration Reform and Immigrant Responsibility Act (IIRIRA) (1996); Nutrition; Personal Responsibility and Work Opportunity Reconciliation Act (PRWORA) (1996); Policies of Attrition; Policy and Political Action.

Further Reading

Costantini, Cristina. 2011. "Undocumented Women Forced to Give Birth While Shackled and in Police Custody." Huffington Post Latino Voices Web Site. http://www .huffingtonpost.com/2011/09/20/undocumented-pregnant-woman-gives-birth-in -shackles_n_971955.html.

Guttmacher Institute. 2000. "Cutting Public Funding for Undocumented Immigrants' Prenatal Care Would Raise the Cost of Neonatal Care." *Family Planning Perspectives* 32.

National Conference of State Legislatures. 2011. "America's Newcomers, Funding Prenatal Care for Unauthorized Immigrants: Challenges Lie Ahead for States." National Conference of State Legislatures Web Site. http://www.ncsl.org/default.aspx?tabid=13111.

National Public Radio. 2010. "The Debate over 'Anchor Babies' and Citizenship." National Public Radio. http://www.npr.org/templates/story/story.php?storyId=129279863.

Reed, Mary M., John M. Westfall, Carolina Bublitz, Catherine Battaglia, and Alexandra Fickenscher. 2005. "Birth Outcomes in Colorado's Undocumented Immigrant Population." *BMC Public Health* 5:1–7.

Proposition 187

Proposition 187 was a voting initiative proposed in 1994 by the State of California as a response to the U.S. Census findings that the state's Latino population had increased from 19 to 26 percent in just a decade. With 1.3 million undocumented persons living in the state, there was a great concern that the state would become bankrupt economically if measures were not soon taken. Proposition 187, otherwise known as the Save Our State (SOS) Initiative, was written by ten people in the midst of California's economic recession, including former U.S. Immigration and Naturalization Service (INS) agents and local and state representatives. Largely seen as a response to Congress's lack of action taken up to that point regarding mass Latin American immigration to California, it was said that, if passed by voters, it could save California up to $200 million per year. While Proposition 187 was ultimately overturned by the courts as an infringement on powers pertaining to the federal government and as a conflict with federal immigration authorities, it marked the beginning of a trend of state-led attempts to reduce both documented and undocumented immigration, and has been considered a defining moment in American racial politics.

The main idea behind Proposition 187 was that if welfare, medical benefits and educational benefits were "magnets" that were being used to attract migrants across California's borders, as popular state discourse maintained, then these were the services that needed to be made inaccessible to the undocumented population. In this sense, Proposition 187 was directed mostly at women and children, as these were the groups of people most likely to need and use public assistance. If these services were made unavailable, it was thought, it would have two desired effects: it would both discourage undocumented immigrants from entering California, and encourage those already there to leave California.

The most controversial section of Proposition 187 was Section 7, which would have excluded undocumented children from education at the elementary and secondary levels. This portion would require school districts to verify the legal status of all children newly enrolled in public schools in California as well as all those children "reasonably suspected" to be undocumented. This information would then be used to verify the legal status of these children's parents or guardians. After verification of both children and parents, information would be handed over to the State Superintendent of Public Instruction, the Attorney General of California, as well as the Immigration and Naturalization Service (INS). Children would then have a period of ninety days in which they would continue to be provided instruction, and the information would be made available for any government entity to access. As an extension of denial of education to the undocumented, Section 8 called for the exclusion of undocumented immigrants from public colleges and universities. This section required verification of citizenship or legal status of each student at the beginning of each term. Once again, any student reasonably suspected to be undocumented would have their information sent to the INS, this time within forty-five days.

Part of the major concern behind Sections 7 and 8 was that they directly challenged the U.S. Supreme Court's *Plyler vs. Doe* decision from 1982 in which the court granted the right to a free public education for all undocumented children. This case originated in Texas in 1975. Supreme Court Justice William J. Brennan, writing on behalf of the majority, expressed that the denial of free basic education to undocumented children implies a denial of access to existing American civic institutions and to any possibility of their future positive contribution to the progress of the nation. Proponents of Proposition 187 were opposed to the cost of educating undocumented children. Some figures note that for the approximately three hundred thousand to four hundred thousand undocumented children in California in 1994, approximately half of the $1.3 billion annually used toward undocumented persons in the state went directly toward educating undocumented children.

The other largely controversial portions of Proposition 187 were Sections 5 and 6, which excluded all undocumented persons from public social services and publicly funded health care, respectively. The only exception to this would be emergency health care, which is required by federal law to be offered to people in need regardless of income or legal status. Other sections required that the legal status of all persons seeking cash assistance and other benefits be verified, that service providers report suspected undocumented persons to the U.S. Attorney General and to the Immigration and Naturalization Service (INS), and that the making and use of false documents be considered a state felony.

A complicating factor for Proposition 187 was the existence of mixed-status families in California. Any family that includes persons with legal status, meaning U.S. citizens or legal permanent residents, as well as undocumented immigrants, is considered a mixed-status family. The complication lies in the fact that even if a U.S. citizen or legal permanent resident requests state-funded services, there lies a risk that the request could put an undocumented family member in harm's way with immigration authorities. This situation was (and is currently) not at all uncommon for families in California, and in other places with significant sizes of Latino populations and was a point of debate in 1994.

While Proposition 187 never became law, there were still unintended consequences. In one case, an undocumented father chose not to seek public medical care for his twelve-year-old son for fear that they might be turned in to immigration authorities. As a result, the son died. Political involvement around these themes increased, with campuses, communities, and churches raising awareness, holding workshops, and providing speakers discussing the themes of racism that were thought to have motivated the vote for the initiative. Some large conventions to be held in California were cancelled, and efforts to boycott the state went into effect. Many people made pledges of noncompliance. Although Proposition 187 saw its formal death in 1999, today parallels can be made between California's initiative and Arizona's SB 1070, signed into law by Governor Jan Brewer in 2010, where similar anti-immigrant sentiments continue to live on.

Leisha Reynolds-Ramos

See Also: Arizona SB 1070; California; Children; Laws and Legislation, Post-1980s; Mixed-Status Families; Personal Responsibility and Work Opportunity Reconciliation Act (PRWORA) (1996); *Plyler v. Doe;* Policies of Attrition; Policy and Political Action; Women's status.

Further Reading

Jacobson, Robin Dale. 2008. *The New Nativism: Proposition 187 and the Debate over Immigration.* Minneapolis: University of Minnesota Press.

Ono, Kent A., and John M. Sloop. 2002. *Shifting Borders: Rhetoric, Immigration, and California's Proposition 187.* Philadelphia, PA: Temple University Press.

Rosenblum, Karen E. 1999. "Rights at Risk: California's Proposition 187." *Illegal Immigration in America: A Reference Handbook*, ed. David W. Haines and Karen E. Rosenblum. Westport, CT: Greenwood Press.

Wroe, Andrew. *The Republican Party and Immigration Politics: From Proposition 187 to George W. Bush.* New York: Palgrave Macmillan, 2008.

Prostitution

Prostitution is the exchange of sexual relations for money or profit. In the United States, prostitution laws vary from state to state. Currently, prostitution is only legal in select counties in the state of Nevada. Nevada law stipulates that counties with fewer than four hundred thousand residents may choose to allow licensed brothels to operate in the county. Women working at the licensed brothels must submit to weekly medical exams for sexually transmitted diseases. With the exception of Nevada, state laws on prostitution range from classifying it as the lowest class of misdemeanor to a second- or first-degree felony. According to the Federal Bureau of Investigation (FBI), over seventy-five thousand people were arrested on charges of prostitution in 2008. Statistics on prostitution are very unreliable and there is little documentation about the number of undocumented immigrant women working in the sex trade. However, as undocumented women are often unable to obtain jobs in the formal economy, many must work in informal labor markets making them more susceptible to entering prostitution.

Opponents of prostitution argue that it directly leads to the spread of Sexually Transmitted Diseases (STDs), including HIV/AIDS, increased rates of crime, including assault and robbery, and promotes drug use and organized crime. Proponents of prostitution argue that legalizing it will create a better environment to reduce these related crimes. They believe legalizing prostitution would allow mandatory STD testing and promote the safety of prostitutes, making them less vulnerable to robbery and assault.

There are many different forms of prostitution including street prostitution, bar/hotel prostitution, escort or call-in prostitution, and brothel prostitution. Street prostitutes are visible on busy streets and solicit customers who walk or drive by. While this only accounts for ten to twenty percent of all prostitution, it is the most visible form of prostitution. Bar/hotel prostitutes solicit customers at a bar or hotel that is frequented by potential customers. These prostitutes often have an established relationship with the business, and either the manager of the bar or the desk clerk at the hotel refers customers to the prostitute. Because of this, the prostitute must share part of her profits with either the manager or desk clerk. Unlike street and bar/hotel prostitution, escort prostitution is not limited to one location. In this arrangement, potential customers call the escort service that serves as an intermediary between the customer and the prostitute. Brothel prostitution is the only legal form of prostitution in the United States and, again, is limited to some counties in the state of Nevada. Brothels are businesses that are located in a single building and hire multiple prostitutes. Customers come to the brothel where they choose from the available prostitutes for an established fee.

Prostitutes are commonly victims of a wide range of violence and crime. Prostitutes are frequently robbed, assaulted, and raped. Prostitutes working for a pimp are commonly exploited. Brothel prostitutes are offered the most protection as they work in a much more controlled environment, while street prostitutes are the most vulnerable. Most crime against prostitutes goes unreported because of prostitution's illegal status. Prostitutes who are victims of crime fear they will be arrested if they report the crime to the police. Undocumented immigrants working in prostitution face even more fear, as many believe they will be deported if they report the crime. It is unclear how many illegal immigrants work in the sex industry as both the illegal status of both their residence and employment make statistics very difficult to obtain.

There are a number of reasons why undocumented immigrant women are engaged in prostitution. The voluntary prostitution of undocumented immigrant women is frequently a result of economic need. Undocumented immigrants have fewer economic options than other immigrants and often must work in the informal economies of domestic work, day labor, or prostitution. Many other undocumented immigrants working in prostitution are victims of human trafficking. Sex trafficking is defined as the recruitment, harboring, transportation, or obtaining of a person for the purpose of a commercial sex act. Women and children from all over the world are either kidnapped or tricked into believing that they will receive a job and instead are smuggled into the United States and forced into prostitution. It is unclear how many victims of sex trafficking have been smuggled into the United States; however, between 2003 and 2007 307 persons were charged and convicted of human trafficking.

As prostitution law is a state-level issue, federal legislation addresses the connection between immigration, prostitution, and human trafficking. One of the first laws to address the role of immigration and prostitution was the Immigration Act of 1875, more commonly referred to as the Page Law or the Page Act of 1875. Under this law, importing Chinese, Japanese or other Asian women for the purposes of prostitution became illegal. More recently the Trafficking Victims Protection Act of 2000 addressed the issue of the human trafficking of women into forced prostitution. This act extended rights to victims of trafficking who were in the country illegally. This act initiated a special class of visas, the T-visa, to be granted to victims of human trafficking to allow them to remain in the United States.

There are currently groups such as the North American Task Force on Prostitution and the Prostitution Education Network promoting the rights of voluntary sex workers in the United States. These groups believe that the legalization of prostitution is the first step in allowing sex workers to control their own lives. Sex worker advocacy groups also promote health and social services specific to the needs of prostitutes as well as develop support programs to help educate prostitutes on ways to prevent STDs and HIV/AIDS. They are also working to create an avenue for prostitutes to be able to report the crimes committed against them without fear of arrest or harassment from the police.

Kelli Chapman

See Also: Crime; Health and Welfare; Human Trafficking; Informal Economy; Trafficking Victims Protection Reauthorization Act (TVPRA); Women's Status.

Further Reading

Chapkis, Wendy. 2003. "Trafficking, Migration, and the Law: Protecting Innocents, Punishing Immigrants." *Gender & Society* 17.6:923–937.

United Nations Office on Drugs and Crime. 2012. "Global Report on Trafficking in Persons." http://www.unodc.org/unodc/data-and-analysis/glotip.html.

Protests

While voting and running for public office are the most recognized form of political and civic engagement, there are other activities that should be included when considering Latino populations in general, and specifically noncitizens and undocumented immigrants. Some of these activities include signing petitions, wearing buttons with political messages, and encouraging others to become civically engaged. In 2006, for example, both citizens and noncitizens mobilized nationwide in political protest over immigration reform. The demonstrations were inspired by the hope that the nearly 12 million undocumented immigrants in the United States would be offered a path to citizenship, and thus emerge from living in the shadows of society. Scholars are quick to point out that although noncitizen Latinos are less likely to participate openly in political activities, they do engage in activities that can influence political outcomes. In this way, Latinos, who very often include non-citizens, exert political agency in a variety of ways such as contacting elected officials and donating to political causes, with public demonstrations being the most widely used form of civic engagement. (See chart below)

The tradition of protesting as a political means of drawing attention to matters that concern Latino communities has a long history. During the late 1960s and early 1970s, Chicano and Chicana students, along with their teachers, families, and other allies organized and rose to protest, among other things, the structured inequality of the U.S.

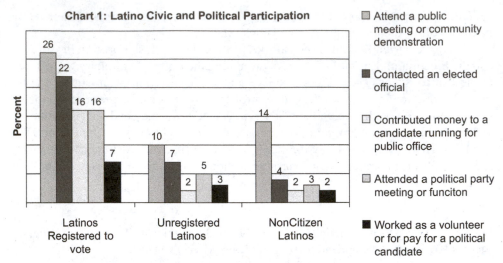

Chart 1: Latino Civic and Political Participation

Adapted from Pew Hispanic Center/Kaiser Family Foundation. (2004). National Survey of Latinos: Politics and Civic Engagement

educational system. Largely influenced by the momentum of the Civil Rights period (1955–1968), voices from these protests helped ignite *El Movimiento,* a national movement that sought political empowerment and social inclusion for Mexican Americans, and Chicanos and Chicanas. El Movimiento was particularly strong at the college level, where there was a large concentration of student activists who formed student organizations and advocated for educational reforms and multicultural curricula that would include Chicano/a Studies.

The extent of Latino immigrant involvement in political protests (including those that may be undocumented) reflects the emergence of hybridized groupings of Latinos that fuse immigrant and nonimmigrant populations, such as mixed immigrant status households and families. This is attributed to deep-seated relational ties between immigrants and permanent U.S. residents that have developed over generations of time. An example of how protests amalgamate different types of Latino groups across legal immigration categories comes from recent protests of students in Tucson, Arizona, over a proposal to eliminate ethnic studies and Mexican-American studies programs from the Tucson Unified School District.

As a result of the U.S. Congress introducing immigration reform proposals in 2005, millions of immigrants and their allies gathered in mass rallies in hundreds of cities across the country during 2006 in what is considered to be the largest civic mobilization since the civil rights era. However, a repressive political and social backlash followed, especially in Arizona, which threatened to further exclude Latinos from the social fabric of the United States. In response, in Tucson, Arizona, thousands of Latinos, immigrants, and their allies filled the streets in protest in one of the city's largest public manifestations in support of immigration reform. Many of those participating were Latino students from local schools. Parents and school administrators expressed concerns after students walked out of classes to participate in the marches in support of immigration reform. Dolores Huerta, cofounder with Cesar Chavez of the United Farm Workers, was invited to speak at a special assembly at Tucson High Magnet School. During her speech, Huerta remarked that "Republicans hate Latinos." Later Huerta explained that her comment was based on the number of anti-immigration bills sponsored by Republicans: "Large numbers of the Republican Party are anti-immigrant or anti-Latino," she said. "I can justify that." The incident came to the attention of Republican Superintendent of Public Instruction Tom Horne who proceeded to reprimand the school for allowing a partisan speech to take place and insisted that equal time be given to Deputy Superintendent Margaret Garcia Dugan, a Latina and Republican, to refute the allegation made by Huerta. However, in an act of civil disobedience (and without prior knowledge by school administrators), students taped their mouths shut with duct tape and turned their backs to the deputy superintendent during this second assembly. Outraged, Superintendent Horne publically blamed the school's Mexican American studies curriculum and its teachers and thereby took up the mission to dismantle the program.

The Dolores Huerta speech at a Tucson School and the subsequent events that led to the 2010 law that cast doubt over the survival of ethnic studies is part of a larger story set within the nation's immigration policy debate and post-9/11 politics. Consistent with its pattern of retooling and reintroducing failed proposals, the Arizona Legislature took up the mantle of eliminating ethnic studies in the years after the Huerta speech. The effort was spearheaded by then State Superintendent Horne who in 2007 appealed to the citizens of Tucson in a letter to pressure the Tucson Unified School District for the elimination of ethnic studies. Having failed in this, Horne helped craft a legislative measure in 2008 that would eliminate ethnic studies programs. It was proposed as an amendment to a Homeland Security Bill in 2008 as Arizona Senate Bill 1108. This "Anti-Ethnic Studies" bill sought to establish that "a primary purpose of public education is to inculcate values of American citizenship" by proposing to eliminate the state's ethnic-studies programs and ethnic-based organizations characterized as "un-American." It would prohibit public tax dollars used in public schools that "denigrate American values and the teachings of western civilization," and prohibit organizations from operating in or around a school campus if they are based in any way on ethnicity or race. Scholars have long noted that generalized anxiety about any and all peoples and activities characterized as non-American has the potential to spill over into the broader Latino community, many of whom are U.S. citizens of Latino and Mexican descent. Empirical research has demonstrated that Latinos' perceptions of discrimination come from negative public discourse about immigrants. These personal experiences of discrimination are also associated with more depressive symptoms among Latino adolescents who cope with denigrating comments on their culture and communities in various forms, the most widely used of which is protests. These forms of civic engagement, together with a positively examined ethnic identity—such as that provided by Chicano/a Studies, Mexican American, or ethnic studies classes—work to buffer adolescents from the negative impact of a political climate that seems to be intolerant of Latinos. Although this bill failed to pass, a similar bill was proposed a year later as SB1069. When this too failed, it was introduced and passed as Arizona House bill 2281 in May of 2010, only a few weeks after Arizona's notorious SB 1070 was passed. The proposed elimination of ethnic studies resulted in a series of protest by students.

Anna Ochoa O'Leary

See Also: Activism; Advocacy; Arizona SB1070; Community Activism; Labor Unions; Policy and Political Action.

Further Reading

Cohen-Marks, Mara, Stephen A. Nuño, and Gabriel R. Sanchez. 2009. "Look Back in Anger? Voter Opinions of Mexican Immigrants in the Aftermath of the 2006 Immigration Demonstrations." *Urban Affairs Review* 44.5:695–717.

Fraga, Luis, John Garcia, Rodney Hero, Michael Jones-Correa, Valerie Martinez-Ebers, and Gary Segura. 2010. *Making It Home: Latino Lives in America.* Philadelphia, PA: Temple University Press.

Kilty, Keith M., and Maria Vidal de Haymes. 2000. "Racism, Nativism, and Exclusion: Public Policy, Immigration and the Latino Experience in the United States." *Journal of Poverty* 4.1/2:1–25.

Leal, David L. 2002. "Political Participation by Latino Non-Citizens." *British Journal of Political Science* 32:353–370.

Michelson, Melissa R. 2001. "The Effect of National Mood on Mexican American Political Opinion." *Hispanic Journal of Behavioral Sciences* 23.1:57–70.

O'Leary, Anna Ochoa, and Andrea J. Romero. 2011. "Chicana/o Students Respond to Arizona's Anti–Ethnic Studies Bill, SB 1108: Civic Engagement, Ethnic Identity, and Well-being." *Aztlán: A Journal of Chicano Studies,* 36.1:9–36.

Pew Hispanic Center/Kaiser Family Foundation. 2004. "National Survey of Latinos: Politics and Civic Engagement." http://pewhispanic.org/reports/report.php?ReportID=33.

Provisional Unlawful Presence (PUP) Waiver

In January of 2013, the Obama Administration announced new rules that will allow thousands of American citizens to avoid long separations from immediate family members who are undocumented and want to initiate the process of becoming legal residents by applying for a Provisional Unlawful Presence (PUP) Waiver. It has been generally a straightforward process for American citizens to obtain green cards for foreign-born spouses or minor children as long as they have not entered the country unlawfully; but this is not the case for those family members who are undocumented. Under a 1996 statute, immigrants who entered the United States illegally must return to their countries of origin to receive their visas from American consulates there. Politicians have referred to this as "going back to the end of the line" when they demand policies that would force immigrants to go back to their country of origin and apply to come back in the legal way. However, once undocumented immigrants leave this country, they are considered "inadmissible," and waiting for the bars to expire before applying for re-entry may take years, depending on how many years the undocumented immigrant has resided in the United States without authorization. The new rule amends the process of acquiring what is called a "provisional unlawful presence waiver," which allows individuals to return to the United States more quickly after attending immigrant visa interviews in their countries of origin if they can prove that prolonged separation would cause an "extreme hardship" on their U.S.-citizen spouses, children, or parents.

Bars are a form of penalty. The longer the undocumented immigrant has lived in the United States without authorization, the more severe the penalty. More specifically, if an unauthorized immigrant had been in the United States for more than 180 days but less than a year, they were barred from applying for admission for three years. If an unauthorized immigrant was in the United States for more than a year, they were barred from applying for admission for ten years. Finally, if an unauthorized immigrant enters the United States in violation of any of the bars, they are permanently inadmissible. With the prospect of being separated from their family members for years or quite possibly indefinitely, these bars had the effect of prolonging family separation if the undocumented immigrant tried to follow the legal path for obtaining a legal resident visa. Even immigrants who did not have any bars to reentry were often stranded abroad while U.S. consulates completed their applications (Oulahan, 2011). Because many children of undocumented parents are minors, leaving them for protracted periods of time would cause unjustified hardships on these children (Menjívar, 2012). Ultimately, this intimidating process dissuaded immigrants, resulting in longer stays in the United States, and contributing to the growing number of undocumented immigrants in the United States.

On March 4, 2013, U.S. Customs and Immigration Services began accepting Form I-601A, Provisional Unlawful Presence Waiver (PUP) applications. The PUP waiver will benefit individuals who have an immediate U.S. citizen relative and have been in the United States unlawfully and wish to apply for an immigrant resident visa, known as a green card. Under the final rule that took effect on March 4, 2013, qualifying individuals may file a provisional unlawful presence (PUP) waiver *before* leaving for their immigrant visa interview abroad to allow for quicker processing and less separation time between them and their families. Family members who wish to apply need to be physically present for six months or longer in the United States to request a PUP waiver before leaving the United States to pick up their visas. In this way, the PUP waiver addresses the inherent problems in the existing law. The critical benefit is that they will not be separated from their citizen family during the application process. In addition, having their waiver in hand before leaving the country should also eliminate the doubts about whether or not they can even come back.

A first stumbling block may be coming up with the $585 application fee for the PUP waiver. Another concern is if the immigrant needs to return to areas blighted by violence. The other hurdle is that applicants must show that it would cause "extreme hardship" to an American citizen if they were deported.

Other requirements include:

1. Be seventeen years of age or older
2. Be an immediate relative of a U.S. citizen (spouse, child or parent of a U.S. citizen)
3. Have an approved Form I-130 (Petition for Alien Relative) or Form I-30 (Petition for Amerasian, widower, or special immigrant)
4. Have a pending immigrant visa case with DOS for the approved immediate-relative petition and have paid the immigrant visa processing fee

5. Not have been scheduled for an immigrant visa interview by a State Department official before January 3, 2013
6. Not be subject to any grounds of inadmissibility other than unlawful presence
7. Not be currently in removal proceedings

There are many indications that this change of policy will have broader benefits for immigrant families and communities. For many years now, legal and immigration scholars have been drawn to research the hardships that come with prolonged periods of family separation as a consequence of harsher measures to enforce immigration laws (Robles and Watkins, 1996). Rosas (2011) examines how the Bracero Program left children to endure the absence of their bracero fathers, while married women transitioned into single motherhood under conditions that were harsh and drove many of them towards undocumented migration to the United States. Children were devastated with the abrupt separation from their parents.

Today, family separation seems to be built into harsher border enforcement policies making short-term, long-term and indefinite separations an inevitable part of the undocumented immigrant experience (O'Leary and Sanchez, 2011). After many years of separation, relations between parents and children across borders may become strained and resentful (Menjívar, 2012). Bitter feelings—often feelings of being abandoned—can take a toll impacting both mental and physical health, and there is still much research that needs to take place to understand how living under legal uncertainty will play out in the long term. Families are the most fundamental units of social organization. At the core of the family unit are the relationships and ideologies of sharing and caregiving that can alleviate tensions and pain among members. If they are unable to visit each other regularly, the relational bond that can help individuals cope with difficulties and uncertainty are weakened and may even disintegrate. Parents stress about and miss their children, worrying about whether the children they may have entrusted with others are safe and being cared for properly. Women have also reported that they may even be made to feel more guilty about leaving children with others (Lahaie et. al., 2009). The new rule is being hailed by many immigrant advocates as a positive step forward in immigration policy. With the PUP waiver available for families of mixed immigration status, there is a positive sign that the U.S. government is moving in the direction of more compassionate and common-sense immigration policies. On the same day that Homeland Security Secretary Janet Napolitano announced the change to the waiver process, it was reported that President Obama would be planning to advocate for immigration reform in the following months.

Anna Ochoa O'Leary

See Also: Children; Deferred Action for Childhood Arrivals (DACA); Deportation; Family Reunification; Green Cards; Immigration Reform, 2013–2014. Inadmissibility; Mixed-Status Familes; Temporary Protected Status (TPS).

Further Reading

Lahaie, Claudia, Jeffrey A. Hayes, Tinka Markham Piper, and Jody Heymann. 2009. "Work and Family Divided across Borders: The Impact of Parental Migration on Mexican Children in Transnational Families." *Community, Work & Family* 12.3:299–312.

Menjívar, Cecilia. 2012 . "Transnational Parenting and Immigration Law: Central Americans in the United States." *Journal of Ethnic & Migration Studies* 38.2:301–322.

O'Leary, Anna O., and Azucena Sanchez. 2011. "Anti-Immigrant Arizona: Ripple Effects and Mixed Immigration Status Households under Policies of Attrition Considered." *Journal of Borderland Studies* 26.1:1–19.

Oulahan, Cain W. 2011. "The American Dream Deferred: Family Separation and Immigrant Visa Adjudications at the U.S. Consulates Abroad." *Marquette Law Review* 94.4:1351–1379.

Robles, Arodys, and Susan Cotts Watkins. 1996. "Immigration and Family Separation in the U.S. at the Turn of the twentieth Century." *Journal of Family History* 18.3:191.

Rosas, Ana Elizabeth. 2011. "Breaking the Silence: Mexican Children and Women's Confrontation of Bracero Family Separation, 1942–64." *Gender & History* 23.2:382–400.

Public Libraries

There are many issues concerning public libraries and immigrants, regardless of the immigrants' status. Many immigrants are unfamiliar with public libraries in the American (and European) concept of the institution, and as a widely available resource to seek help in navigating a wide range of topics ranging from government agencies and institutions to social services and culture. In developing countries, especially in Latin America, public libraries are painfully underfunded, understaffed, and the staff is often undertrained. In addition, the professionalization of librarians in these countries, compared with those in the United States, is much lower. Where well-stocked and well-staffed libraries do exist, they are not likely to be found outside the major metropolitan areas and are often not considered a useful resource. It is thus entirely possible that immigrants may have not used or visited a public library before arriving in the United States, and possibly never even heard of the concept, especially with more recent migrants to the United States who come from rural and agriculturally based societies. Undocumented immigrants in the United States may experience the added burden of fear of using the public library with the increase in scrutiny over undocumented immigrants and their use of public resources. Increasingly, through legislation, they have been denied access to other publically supported institutions based on legal status. The general public debate about undocumented migrants' access to public services further comes into conflict with a central tenet of the professional ethics of librarianship: confidentiality. Just as medical and educational institutions guard patient and student privacy, libraries take patron confidentiality very seriously. From the libraries' perspective, immigration status is nearly always irrelevant to the services provided. Unlike other publically funded services, personnel are not required to verify the legal status of a presumed immigrant and are not responsible for immigration enforcement by reporting those whom they suspect as undocumented. A public library may be limited in its ability to serve multilingual communities. However, if an immigrant

MIke Eitner, a librarian at the Denver Public Library's main branch, stacks copies of Spanish-language newspapers in the El Centro section, catering to Spanish readers. In Denver, where the foreign-born population tripled between 1990 and 2000, largely because of Mexican immigrants, the public library system is considering reorganizing some branches to emphasize bilingual services and material. (Associated Press)

community is new to the area, existing staff may find it difficult to serve the new population and, even if the budget allows for a new hire, it may be difficult to attract staff with the needed language skills. Libraries may also find it difficult to readjust decreasing materials budgets to accommodate a need for foreign language books and media. Library staff and administration; governing boards; and municipal, county, or state governments can all be sources of resistance or support to funding library services for immigrant populations.

Two notable examples of public libraries serving underserved communities, including immigrants, in innovative ways are the San Francisco Public Library (SFPL) and the Pima County Public Library (PCPL), based in Tucson, Arizona. SFPL's staff includes an in-house social worker at the main library and, in 2012, PCPL hired a public health nurse to serve primarily its main library in downtown Tucson and subsequently hired part-time nurses for selected branch libraries. Both programs serve at-risk underserved populations, be they immigrants, homeless, or troubled youth, and are examples of public libraries responding to needs outside their traditional services but of great use to their patrons. Similar to San Francisco, a sanctuary city known for liberal policies towards immigrants, Tucson has declared itself an "immigrant welcoming city," making the two exceptional cases rather than the norm.

Somewhere between providing adequate standard library services and the truly exceptional services provided in San Francisco and Tucson, libraries have begun providing and hosting a variety of other services, such as computer literacy classes, adult education and English as a Second Language (ESL) classes, cultural events, and homework help for students. Immigrant populations would also find these events very useful. Where the public library itself cannot provide the staffing and knowledge within its institution, it has an opportunity to partner with other community organizations, such as educational institutions, social and municipal services, and advocacy and charity groups.

For school-aged children, the public library supplements school libraries. Unfortunately, disadvantaged communities, in which immigrant families are likely to reside, are among the least likely to have school libraries. Library use is a component of academic success, both in grade school and in preparation for using larger and more complex library systems in higher education. For some students, the most basic service provided by libraries—a quiet place to study and access to computers—is the most valuable resource unavailable in an extended family household with competition for the technology at home. Further, the adult educational opportunities increasingly provided by libraries better prepare immigrant parents to help their children through school.

Lisa Burrell Gardinier and Anna Ochoa O'Leary

See Also: Adult Education; Education; Elementary Schools.

Further Reading

Alire, Camila, and Jacqueline Ayala. 2007. *Serving Latino Communities: A How-to-Do-It Manual for Librarians,* 2nd ed. New York: Neal-Schuman.

Burke, Susan K. 2008. "Use of Public Libraries by Immigrants," *Reference & User Services Quarterly* 48.2:164–174.

Cuban, Sondra. 2007. *Serving New Immigrant Communities in the Library*. Westport, CT: Libraries Unlimited.

Luévano-Molina, Susan, ed. 2001. *Immigrant Politics and the Public Library*. Westport, CT: Praeger.

R

Racialized Labeling of Mexican-Origin Persons

Since the early 1800s, persons of Mexican descent in the United States have been the subject of both praise and derision. Within certain time periods and regions of the nation, particularly in times of economic expansion and wartime, Mexican Americans and Mexican migrants have been characterized as important contributors, almost as saviors, to key economic sectors. Through much of the period between 1900 and the 1960s, for example, Mexican labor was seen as indispensable to agriculture, ranching, and mining. Since the 1930s, the construction, light manufacturing, and services sectors have increasingly recruited Mexican labor to assure greater profitability. Though praised by some employers in specific localities, the broader European-descent American community did not necessarily hold the same view of Mexican-origin persons.

Multiple labels have been applied to the ethnic Mexican community over the past two centuries. Some of these, like "greaser," have a long history, dating back to the 1850s, while others are the product of more recent developments. One such development is the close association between the labels "illegal alien," or "undocumented immigrant," and Mexican migrants. They have almost become synonymous. In addition to these, there are a number of racialized labels that have been created and applied, both in English and Spanish, such as "beaner," "*cholo,*" "border bandit," "chili choker," "*mojado,*" and "wetback." Due to the long list of labels, and the unknown etymology of some terms, this entry will focus on some of the labels and metaphors that have been deployed from the 1920s to the present. More specifically, it discusses a U.S. House of Representatives hearing in 1920 regarding the admission of Mexican workers, summarizes the etymology of "wetback," and discusses the application of the "illegal/undocumented" migrant labels.

The U.S. House Committee on Immigration and Naturalization held an important hearing to address the concerns of agricultural interests in the Southwest, particularly the concerns of growers in Arizona and Texas. Members of Congress from the two states, representatives of grower associations, and individual growers participated in the hearing and pleaded for the head tax and literacy requirements of the Immigration Act of 1917 to be waived, as well as the prohibitions in the 1885 Contract Labor Law, for migrants entering from Mexico. Their general argument was straightforward: agricultural interests in the Southwest were facing a significant labor shortage, and without the contribution of Mexican labor their operations would greatly suffer, and there would be dramatic impacts to local economies, as well as the national economy. Mexican labor was urgently needed, and the literacy and head-tax requirements, as well as the restrictions on contracting foreign workers, were major obstacles to economic prosperity—in short, Southwestern interests were asking Congress to "give us our Mexicans."

The characterization of Mexican Americans and Mexican nationals reflected dual and overlapping perspectives. On the one hand, Mexicans were represented as among the best workers available, peaceful, hard working and inoffensive, child-like, law-abiding not criminals, and possessing the qualities of good citizens. They were contrasted with "negroes" or "darkies," "white trash," and "undesirable Orientals." An important element in the labor hierarchy was the perception that Mexicans could live on less, demanded little, had no expectations, were not concerned with the future (caring only for today), had a natural tolerance for the heat, and could work from sunup to sundown. Thus they represented ideal, lower-cost human labor. On the other hand, the positive characterization of Mexican workers was supported by non-human metaphors. Testimony presented at the hearing invoked comparisons to insects (bees that travel to obtain honey, and then leave); animals that hibernate (needing to return to Mexico once it was cold); plants (hot-weather plants that could stand the heat); birds (birds of passage that came and went); as well as goats, horses, and cattle (all needing to be managed and controlled). The characterization of Mexicans at the Congressional hearing made it clear that the very label "Mexican" archived a racialized perspective. Consequently, the label "Mexican" indexes nationality, as well as represents a racialized label. This semantic overlap continues to the present.

Wetback

The label "wetback" is noteworthy in the history of Mexican migration in the United States. Its importance is twofold. First, it is a label that appears to have emerged in the post–Civil War period (a time when much smuggling existed along the Mexico-Texas boundary area), and remains in contemporary usage. Second, its origins and racialized usage are commonly overlooked. Online references and some scholars suggest that the term emerged as part of the implementation of Operation Wetback in 1954, and refers to migrants who swam across the Río Bravo/Rio Grande River and entered the United States without formal authorization. This explanation disregards the noted usage in the 1920s (such as in the hearing noted above), and in scholarly works and popular media prior to 1954.

What is also overlooked in discussions of the label is its dehumanizing element. Several linguists have noted that its origin appears to be an extension of its use in reference to cattle and horses smuggled from Mexico to Texas in the late 1800s. The labels "wet," "wet cattle," "wet ponies," and "wet stock" are said to be the predecessors of the "wet," "wet back," and "wetback" migrant labels. The term is more commonly found in the Mexico-Texas boundary area, and other parts of Texas, than in areas east of the El Paso–Júarez area. And although its use is less common now, it is still invoked by some elected officials and anti-migrant activists to refer to persons of Mexican descent in general, and Mexican migrants more specifically.

Illegals

Between passage of the 1875 Page Law and the 1924 Immigration Act, significant attention turned to the problem of illegal entry. The concern was principally with the illegal entry of Chinese, Japanese, and Europeans through Canada and Mexico. Although periodic concern with the unauthorized entry of Mexican migrants surfaced between 1930 and the 1960s, and the noun form "illegal" began to be applied to Mexican migrants in the 1940s and 1950s, it was not until the early 1970s that U.S. political leaders and the media shifted national attention to Mexican illegal aliens. Consequently, over the past four decades, a strong association has been formed between the term "illegal immigrant" and Mexican migrants.

The near synonymous relationship between "illegal" migrant and Mexican migrant overlooks two important dimensions. First, that the noun form "illegal" was first applied to European Jewish migrants in the 1930s who sought to enter British-controlled Palestine. In the contemporary history of the State of Israel, these migrants are honored as important early pioneers and settlers who made possible the founding of Israel. Second, that the definition of "illegal immigrants" has come to be defined principally as referring to those who entered the country without authorization from Mexico. This has resulted in national and state officials allocating billions of dollars to solving the unauthorized migration, through the use of fences, ground sensors, cameras, other high tech equipment, and personnel to monitor the Mexico-U.S. boundary area. What is disregarded in this policy response is the fact that the population of migrants who enter without authorization may only constitute half, or less, of those who are present without authorization and subject to removal (prior to 1996, subject to deportation). Consequently, the dominant policy approach further cements the association of "illegal immigration" with Mexico, and "illegal immigrants" with Mexican migrants. The significant, though unknown, number of Irish, Polish, and other nationalities represented among those subject to removal, as well as the large number of persons who entered the United States with a visa but have since violated the terms of the visa and thus are also subject to removal, is mostly absent in the national imagination regarding unauthorized migration and migrants.

While many scholars and pro-migrant advocates have observed that the label "illegal immigrant" is a pejorative, dehumanizing term, the label of "undocumented immigrant" has been suggested as a positive or neutral alternative to "illegal" migrant. What is overlooked in the latter term is that it shares certain premises with the former. Both terms place the individual migrant as the principal determining factor. Within the former label, the migrant is framed as an individual who chose to break the law, specifically entry restrictions. On the other hand, migrants who did not obtain the necessary documents for entering the United States are labeled "undocumented" migrants. Under both views, the state (whether Mexico or the United States) remains separate from the actions of the individual. Yet the state is the central entity defining the rules of entry, the exceptions to those rules, and it grants or withholds entry documents. Both perspectives do not factor in that it is the enactment of the law and its implementation that constitutes illegality—thus it creates the boundary between a legal migrant and an illegal or undocumented migrant.

A second common assumption in both perspectives is that migrants are largely characterized as *homo economicus*. Both tend to see migrants not as humans with marital and family aspirations, social expectations of parental and spousal responsibility, and so on, but instead as representing autonomous economic units, persons here simply for jobs. An anti-migrant perspective tends to emphasize their negative economic impact, while a pro-migrant perspective tends to argue for the positive economic contribution to the nation. Thus, both the "illegal immigrant" and "undocumented migrant" labels contribute to the perception of migrants through a prism of economic usurpation and illegality.

In summary, the development and application of racialized labels, as applied to persons of Mexican descent over the past decades, encompass multiple and complex processes. The negative racialization can be direct and explicit (e.g., greaser, wetback, or illegal), as well as involve both overall positive characterization (e.g., among the best workers) and racialized stereotypes. Moreover, U.S. policy actions and the uncritical use of labels can also reinforce the presence and use of racialized labels.

Luis F. B. Plascencia

See Also: Dillingham Report (1910); Guestworker and Contract Labor Policies; Johnson-Reed Act (1924); Operation Wetback; Racial Profiling; Racism; "Undocumented" Label; *U.S. v. Brignoni-Ponce.*

Further Reading

Acuña, Rodolfo. 2004. *Occupied America: A History of Chicanos.* New York: Pearson-Longman.

De León, Arnoldo. 1983. *They Called Them Greasers: Anglo Attitudes Toward Mexicans in Texas, 1821–1900.* Austin: University of Texas Press.

Plascencia, Luis F. B. 2009. "The 'Undocumented' Mexican Migrant Question: Re-Examining the Framing of Law and Illegalization in the United States." *Urban Anthropology* 38.2–4:375–434.

Santa Ana, Otto. 2002. *Brown Tide Rising: Metaphors of Latinos in Contemporary American Public Discourse.* Austin: University of Texas Press.

U.S. House of Representatives, the Committee on Immigration and Naturalization. 1920. "Temporary Admission of Illiterate Mexican Laborers." Sixty-sixth Congress, Second Session. Washington: Government Printing Office.

Racial Profiling

Racial profiling occurs when race or national origin is used as a factor in determining suspicion of wrongdoing. It is most commonly understood to be limited to instances in which individuals or groups of people of color are subject to formal or informal targeting on account of their race, even though race and national origin are not relevant criteria. In immigration matters, racial profiling occurs when law enforcement agents suspect that certain individuals resembling immigrants have violated immigration laws even though there is no evidence that they have done so.

Racial profiling has been a feature of immigration law for more than a century. In the late nineteenth century, Chinese women were effectively prohibited from entering the country under a 1875 law that banned the admission of prostitutes because Chinese women seeking admission into the United States were presumed to be prostitutes. Since the mid-1970s, federal courts have allowed the use of race-based immigration policing to specifically target Latino communities. In *U.S. v. Brignoni-Ponce,* the Supreme Court decided that a person's "Mexican appearance" may be considered in determining whether to stop and question automobile passengers about their immigration status. One year later, in *U.S. v. Martinez-Fuerte,* the Supreme Court affirmed that people "of apparent Mexican ancestry" may be subjected to more in-depth questioning about their immigration status even if nothing else suggested that they had violated any immigration law. Other federal courts have used this argument to include anyone who appears Hispanic or Latino. Most likely acting on this authority, immigration law enforcement officials have considered race and national origin in deciding whether to stop automobiles, raid workplaces, and question individuals who reside in communities, neighborhoods or *barrios* comprised primarily of people of color.

In the aftermath of the September 11, 2001 attacks on the World Trade Center in New York City, tens of thousands of lawful noncitizens from Arab-Muslim countries were required to comply with special immigration registration procedures, in part motivated by fears and belief that these individuals were more likely to be linked to terrorist organizations than individuals from other countries. Though widely criticized by immigrants' rights advocates, federal courts have decided that this racial profiling policy is legal and justified. By relying on immigration regulations, where racial profiling has been litigated and legally sanctioned, law enforcement agencies and government officials are able to use the law to conduct investigation that would otherwise be deemed prejudicial and discriminatory, and therefore unlawful. In light of the signing into law of Arizona SB 1070, the Arizona "Papers Please" law in 2010, immigrant advocates have continued to raise concerns about how this law will embolden the racial profiling of immigrants. Although many provisions of the law were struck down by the U.S. Supreme Court in 2012, certain provisions were allowed to stand, such as the most controversial one that allows members of law enforcement to check the documentation of any person who has been detained for any other violation of the law, including traffic violations.

Georges-Abeyie (2001) is a social theorist and legal scholar who has written on racial profiling based on the mistreatment of blacks in the United States. He argues that the harmful consequences of unmitigated racial profiling are the unseen and unreported acts suffered by racial minorities at the hands of law enforcement agents, who might harbor mores, biases, and norms that condone or encourage their harsh treatment. Insults, roughness, the lack of civility, and other punitive acts work to produce more criminal acts that are attributed to racial and minority groups, while suppressing the rate of criminal acts committed by non-minorities. In other words, where the law allows the policing or enforcing agent any discretion, the tendency is to treat minorities more severely because they are seen as less deserving. This in itself increases the number of minorities who are arrested. Moreover, because more members of minority groups are seen as less deserving, the chance of being denied "fair dealings before the law" is maximized and in this way more "criminals" are ultimately produced (Milovanovic and Russell 2001, xvi). In suspecting that they will not be given fair treatment, racial minorities are also less likely to file complaints against their aggressors. The result is an undercounting of crimes committed against them. Thus, the violations committed against them remain outside the legal system and remain invisible because they go unreported. In other words, what results is a systematic non-reporting of racially biased assaults and "micro aggressions" and even often criminal behaviors committed by law enforcement agents, and this translates into greater suppression of minority groups.

Racial profiling impacts people of color regardless of their immigration status. U.S. citizens and lawful permanent residents—individuals who are legally entitled to live and work in the United States permanently but who are not U.S. citizens—are frequently caught up in immigration law enforcement actions aimed at individuals who are suspected of having violated immigration laws. For example, a 1997 effort to arrest all undocumented individuals in Chandler, Arizona, in which police officers questioned people who appeared to be Mexican or spoke Spanish, resulted in the detention of several U.S. citizens (Romero, 2008). In yet another study, also in Arizona, researchers found that policing authorities were more likely to mistreat barrio residents than their Anglo counterparts because they exhibit more Mexican ethno-racial characteristics, and that citizenship, class, and education level offered them little protection from harassment and intimidating behavior by officials (Goldsmith et. al., 2009)

César Cuauhtémoc García Hernández

See Also: Arizona SB1070; Crime; Governance and Criminalization; Incarceration; Operation Streamline; Racialized Labeling of Mexican-Origin Persons; Racism; *United States v. Brignoni-Ponce.*

Further Reading

Akram, Susan, and Kevin R. Johnson. 2002. "Migration and Regulation Goes Local: The Role of States in U.S. Immigration Policy: Race, Civil Rights, and Immigration Law After September 11, 2001: The Targeting of Arabs and Muslims." *New York University Annual Survey of American Law* 58:295.

Georges-Abeyie, Daniel. 2001. "Foreward: Petit Apartheid in Criminal Justice: 'The More "Things" Change, the More "Things" Remain the Same.'" In *Petit Apartheid in the U.S. Criminal Justice System*, edited by Dragan Milovanovic and Katheryn K. Russell, ix–xiv. Durham: Carolina Academic Press.

Goldsmith, P., M. Romero, R. Rubio Goldsmith, M. Escobedo, and L. Khoury. 2009. "Ethno-Racial Profiling and State Violence in a Southwest Barrio." *Aztlán: A Journal of Chicano Studies* 34.1:93–124.

The Leadership Conference, Executive Summary. N.d. "Wrong Then, Wrong Now: Racial Profiling Before and After September 11, 2001." www.civilrights.org/publications/reports/racial_profiling.

Milovanovic, Dragan, and Katheryn K. Russell. 2001. "Introduction: Petit Apartheid." In *Petit Apartheid in the U.S. Criminal Justice System,* edited by Dragan Milovanovic and Katheryn K. Russell, xv–xxiii. Durham, NC: Carolina Academic Press.

Romero, Mary. 2008b. "The Inclusion of Citizenship Status in Intersectionality: What Immigration Raids Tell Us about Mixed-Status Families, the State, and Assimilation." *International Journal of the Family* 34.2:131–152.

Racism

There is evidence that undocumented immigrants expect to be treated poorly by whites in the United States because of racism (Cleaveland, 2012). Racism is a system of behaviors and practices based on the erroneous principles of racial superiority. Clear examples of racism come with the Jim Crow laws in the South that prevented blacks from advancing in a range of social arenas, from voting to employment. In a racist system, or society, members of the privileged group work to maintain the same system that keeps them in a position of privilege, usually through behaviors and practices aimed to exclude non-dominant group members from power, status, and equal access to resources that would allow them to advance. This also includes the act of repressing knowledge that would refute their misconceptions. Racism should be distinguished from the related term bigotry. To be a bigot is to subscribe to the belief that there is nothing wrong with a social hierarchy based on race. Bigots will accept notions that there are genetic differences that constitute race, which determines an individual's capacity and results in innately superior and inferior groups. According to this hierarchy, individuals from so-called inferior groups are easily identified and categorized by their skin color, language, and physical features. Thus, where racism is a social system or structure that is actively maintained to preserve inequality based on the exclusion and obstacles to advancement of the so-called inferior group, bigotry is the attitude that complements those behaviors—allowing them to proliferate unimpeded or unchallenged. Thus, while not all bigots are racists, all racists are also bigots. Amid the nation's concerns over immigration, both racists and bigots are more likely to accept anti-immigrant policies that reflect their notions (Berg, 2013).

Central to the concept of racism is how it is manifested through attitude (prejudice) and behavior (discrimination). *Prejudice* is the positive or negative attitude, feeling, or judgment about an individual that is based on beliefs held about the group the individual belongs to. Additionally, there is a tendency to hold a fixed view of others by attaching stereotypes to an individual, resulting in a failure to see the diversity within groups and more importantly, the distinctiveness of the individual. Once these attitudes or prejudices are acted upon, the consequences become visible in behaviors known as discrimination. *Discrimination* is a positive or negative behavior toward an individual based on prejudice. In other words, discrimination is the transformation of attitudes and beliefs (often bigoted) that translates prejudice into specific behaviors and acts based on those beliefs. These acts are an expression of an individual's personal prejudices that can lead to legalized acts expressed through institutional policies and laws.

Racism is constituted by three different domains: individual, institutional and cultural. *Individual racism* describes the form of racism that is comprised of the attitudes and behaviors expressing individual prejudices. When individual racism is fed by power and privilege, the resulting acts may be translated into discriminatory policies and laws of an institution, known as *institutional racism.* U.S. history is replete with examples of institutional racism, such as laws that prevented blacks, Native Americans and Mexicans from attending the same schools as whites. By implementing discriminatory policies the prejudicial feelings of the dominant group are expressed and help restrict access of important resources to the dominant group and to the exclusion of all other groups. The last form of racism is *cultural racism,* which is the extension of the dominant group's power to define and establish beliefs, values, and practices such that they become expressions of its culture. No longer just an expression of an individual or an institution but of an entire societal culture, cultural racism creates an environment that allows prejudice and discrimination to seem like a natural part of the social order. An example of this is the depiction of so-called inferior groups as less than human, using racial slurs to publically intimidate and humiliate, so that they are less likely to make demands. A current example of this is to refer to Mexican heritage peoples as "illegals,"

Black slaves were considered to be subhuman, which served to justify the social institution of slavery. Slowly, societies have concluded that racism is wrong, and in 1865 the Thirteenth Amendment to the Constitution was enacted to abolish slavery. Following the legal abolishment of slavery, other amendments and acts were implemented to address issues of discrimination. For example, the Equal Protection Clause of the Fourteenth Amendment prohibited discrimination by state government institutions by granting all people equal protection of the law. Additionally, the Fifteenth Amendment prohibited the denial of voting rights to citizens on the basis of race, color, or previous servitude.

In the United States, the Civil Rights Movement of the 1950s and 1960s was an attempt to dismantle racial discrimination and set into motion a variety of other beneficial institutional changes affecting race relations in the United States. Some examples of institutional change include the Civil Rights Act of 1964, Voting Rights Act of 1965, Immigration and Nationality Services Act of 1965 and Fair Housing Act of 1968. However, despite all of these legal changes executed to eradicate racism, many contend that it still prevails today, albeit in more subtle forms, resulting in unfair treatment for particular ethnic and racial groups in the United States.

Immigration continues to greatly transform the racial demographics of the United States. Not having an expeditious system by which immigrants can come to the United States and fill the nation's demand for labor has been a central issue for many years, raising questions about some of the policies and laws that prevent undocumented immigrants from having the legal right to work and provide for their families. In other words, immigrants are encountering individual, institutional and cultural racism on an everyday basis. Those who come to the United States without documentation experience the even lower status of being judged as "illegal" and "public burdens," and subjected to abuses and stereotypes that ultimately relegate them to poor-paying jobs.

Furthermore, racial discriminatory hiring processes are often underscored by the belief that low-status jobs should go to individuals of low-status races (individuals with darker skin color). Employers may capitalize on these discriminatory hiring practices by taking advantage of undocumented immigrants in offering them jobs that do not provide economic stability or security. Similarly, racial discriminatory unfair housing practices perpetuated by landlords may result in immigrants being subjected to higher fees or denied leases. Many undocumented immigrants have great difficulty accessing healthcare and are forced to obtain care through emergency rooms or inadequate, over-crowded health clinics. Unfortunately, due to the fear of deportation, many undocu-mented and documented immigrants do not go to the police to report any form of abuse or discrimination.

On the interpersonal level, undocumented immigrants usually encounter racism in a more subtle form with some instances of the overt forms. The covert forms of dis-crimination are called *racial microaggressions*. These include the everyday occur-rences of racism that take the form of subtle insults or put downs which are verbal, non-verbal and/or visual in nature. Racial microaggressions are usually automatic and unconscious in the individuals who express them. Microaggressions can include being ignored, excluded, disrespected, denied goods or services, receiving negative remarks regarding immigration, assumed to be poor and/or lazy, and assumed to hold low-status jobs. Other examples of microaggressions include regarding individuals as criminal and therefore undeserving.

Racism still pervades the U.S. society on institutional, cultural and individual levels, though in more covert forms than the past. Racism as manifested through prejudice, ste-reotypes, discrimination, and microaggressions continues to have negative impacts on racial minorities, and society as a whole. The impact from more overt forms of racism such as slavery, Jim Crow laws, the lack of constitutional rights and segregation, can be witnessed through the unequal distribution of resources and access based on race and ethnicity in the United States. Moreover, the effects of racism have been demonstrated to be detrimental to the physical, emotional and mental health of those subjected to its dis-criminatory actions. Increasingly, research has demonstrated that experiences of racism and discrimination have been linked to harmful impacts on racial minorities, such as low self-esteem, depressive symptoms, depression, poor physical health, psychological dis-tress, trauma and lower life satisfaction. The effects of racism have been and continue to be demonstrated to adversely impact the health and well-being of those whom it affects.

Rebecca Rangel and Jillian C. Lyons

See Also: Civil Rights; Dillingham Report (1910); Exclusion; Mental Health Care Access; Racialized Labeling of Mexican-Origin Persons; Racial Profiling; *Strangers from a Differ-ent Shore*; Xenophobia.

Further Reading

Berg, Justin Allen. 2013. "Opposition to Pro-Immigrant Public Policy: Symbolic Racism and Group Threat Opposition to Pro-Immigrant Public Policy: Symbolic Racism and Group Threat." *Sociological Inquiry* 83.1:1–31.

Cleaveland, Carol. 2012. " 'In This Country, You Suffer a Lot': Undocumented Mexican Immigrant Experiences." *Qualitative Social Work* 11.6:566–586.

Franklin, Anderson J., Nancy Boyd-Franklin and Shalonda Kelly. 2006. "Racism and Invisibility: Race-Related Stress, Emotional Abuse and Psychological Trauma for People of Color." *Journal of Emotional Abuse* 6:9–30.

Fredrickson, George M. 1988. *The Arrogance of Race: Historical Perspectives on Slavery, Racism and Social Inequality.* Hanover, NH: Wesleyan University Press.

Yakushko, Oksana. 2009. "Xenophobia: Understanding the Roots and Consequences of Negative Attitudes Toward Immigrants." *Counseling Psychologist* 37:36–66.

Refugee Act (1980)

The United States Refugee Act of 1980 was the first major reform on the admission and resettlement of refugees in several decades, amending the Immigration and Nationality Act. Signed into law by President Jimmy Carter on March 17, 1980, the act sets several objectives as an attempt to increase equity and effectiveness in the processing of refugees. It redefined the meaning of refugee to reflect the definition of the United Nations Convention and Protocol on the Status of Refugees, raised the limitation on refugee admissions from 17,400 to 50,000 each fiscal year, created provisions for emergency procedures if the number of refugees exceeded 50,000, asserted Congressional control of the admission process, established an asylum provision in immigration law, and created several federal programs to assist in the refugee resettlement process as well as the Office of the United States Coordinator for Refugee Affairs and the Office of Refugee Resettlement.

The beginning of the Refugee Act can be traced back to a report in 1969 by the Senate Judiciary Subcommittee on Refugees, in which they urged Congress to reconsider the amount of refugees allowed. However, refugee bills died within the subcommittee and there were no public hearings for another ten years. In 1978, Senator Edward Kennedy began to draft legislation that fundamentally reformed refugee policy; and when he became chairman of the Senate Committee of the Judiciary in 1979, the proposed Refugee Act was introduced in both the Senate and the House of Representatives on March 9 of that year.

There were several concerns regarding the new Refugee Act, one being that the United States was already admitting large amounts of refugees, mostly Soviet Jews and Indochinese refugees. However, the new legislation would assist the incoming refugees in a more efficient and less costly way. Another concern was the "parole authority," or the amount of control wielded by the Attorney General in regards to refugee admission. This concern was shared by a large number of members in Congress, as the authority was eventually eliminated and Congress received greater control in the process. To accommodate for the lost parole authority, emergency provisions were created as another way to respond to international emergencies and crises.

One of the largest problems debated by Congress was the fear of refugees overwhelming the United States after the passing of the Refugee Act, because it would become easier to gain admittance into the country. Therefore a cap was established of 50,000 refugees per fiscal year, with the exception of the admission of refugees during potential emergencies. While this raised the ceiling of refugees considerably from previous legislation, this number was quite small compared to the overall population. The cap signified that there would be just one refugee for every 4,000 Americans, a ratio much smaller in comparison to other countries that annually admit refugees.

Finally, one of the largest concerns regarding the Refugee Act was the overall cost of admittance and resettlement. To demonstrate the effectiveness of the resettlement program, Senator Kennedy reported that the average cost of resettling an Indochinese refugee was

In recognition of the 30th anniversary of the Refugee Act of 1980, the U.S. Citizenship and Immigration Services swears in 27 former refugees and asylees as new citizens on March 30, 2010 in Washington, DC. Since the enactment of the Refugee Act of 1980, the United States has offered protection to approximately 2.5 million refugees. Unlike undocumented immigrants, refugees are those who have left their country of origin due to fear of persecution and violence and are protected and offered assistance in the host countries that have signed on to the UN Convention Relating to the Status of Refugees. (Tim Sloan/AFP/Getty Images)

approximately $4,000, and the majority of refugees were not only able to integrate into the community, but they also were able to pay this money back to the government in the form of federal income taxes within a few years. Furthermore, refugees contributed to American society in noneconomic ways through their diversity and cultural backgrounds.

The Senate successfully and unanimously adopted the bill on September 6, 1979. Eventually, the House of Representatives also adopted the Refugee Bill, but only after several controversial amendments. This resulted in two different versions of the bill, which was resolved by a conference committee, and in this way the provisions of the Refugee Act were set in what is the current form today.

The conferees decided on the definition of refugee, and used the definition set by the United Nations which states: "A refugee is a person having a fear of persecution based on race, religion, political or social group, or nationality." This challenged the previous assertions that refugees were exclusively individuals escaping from communist or Middle Eastern countries and came to include people from all regions of the world. The revision also noted several exclusions to this definition, such as anyone who has participated in the persecution of another person. However, this definition does not include those who leave their country of origin due to economic factors. Those who do are not considered to be refugees, but rather economic migrants.

The committee also agreed that the president could admit additional refugees after the ceiling of 50,000 was reached, but only with the approval of Congress. The act also changes the official title of admittance from "conditional entrants" to permanent resident aliens. However, for the first year of entrance, refugees would be granted a special "refugee" status, after which they could apply for permanent residency. The Refugee Act also creates an asylum provision, allowing for up to 5,000 permanent residencies to those who come to the United States claiming refugee status.

However, the most fundamental change concerned the issue of domestic settlement. Before the Refugee Act, there was no system in place. The largest amount of debate arose from the issue of federal responsibility in refugee resettlement. It was eventually agreed upon that refugees would be allowed a year and a half transition period with a three-year limitation on reimbursement (for items such as medical payments). Additionally, the act allows for $200 million in grants per year for refugee-related programs and services. Finally, it established the new Office of Refugee Resettlement under the Department of Health and Human Services as well as the Coordinator for Refugee Affairs, with the purpose of providing better and more effective coordination of refugee resettlement.

Jenna Glickman

See Also: Central American Civil Wars; Nicaraguan Adjustment and Central American Relief Act (NACARA); Refugees; Salvadorans; Select Committee on Immigration and Refugees.

Further Reading

Kennedy, Edward M. 1981. "Refugee Act of 1980." *International Migration Review* 15:141–156.

LeMay, Michael C. 2007. *Illegal Immigration.* Santa Barbara, CA: ABC-CLIO, Inc., 2007.

Refugee Status Determination: Identifying Who Is a Refugee. Geneva: Office of the United States High Commissioner for Refugees.

Refugees

Refugees are people who reside outside of their own country due to a fear of persecution in their country of origin. According to the formal definition set by the United Nations Convention Relating to the Status of Refugees of 1951 and the 1967 Protocol, a refugee is "any person who, owing to a well-founded fear of being persecuted for reasons of race, religion, nationality, membership of a particular social group or political opinion, is outside the country of his nationality and is unable or, owing to such fear, is unwilling to avail himself of the protection of that country; or who, not having a nationality and being outside the country of his former habitual residence as a result of such events, is unable or, owing to such fear, is unwilling to return to it." If a person is legally recognized as a refugee, he or she is entitled to a certain amount of rights and benefits, also known as international refugee protection. In turn, refugees also have certain obligations, such as following the laws of the host country. At the beginning of 2011, the number of refugees was approximately 10.5 million worldwide, plus an additional 4.8 million refugees in the Middle East that were under the care of the United Nations Relief and Works Administration for Palestinian Refugees (UNRWA). More than half of the world's refugees are from Asia, while another 20 percent are from Africa. Additionally, more than half of all refugees live in urban areas. Living conditions established to accommodate displaced refugees while they await notice about their resettlement in other countries may vary from more elaborate established camps to makeshift centers.

The state in which a person seeks asylum has the primary responsibility of determining if that person fits the refugee definition. This is essential because all states that are party to the 1951 Convention and/or 1967 Protocol are obligated to protect those who meet the stated definition. In particular, a state is not allowed to "return" a refugee to their homeland if they have a well-founded fear of persecution due to the factors mentioned above.

However, in most states, there are provisions for the involvement of the United Nations High Commission for Refugees, also known as the UN Refugee Agency or the UNHCR. Currently, the UNHCR is the only international organization that has a specific mandate to protect refugees. However, several other international agencies also assist with refugee crises and the refugee resettlement process, including the International Committee for the Red Cross, which assists during armed conflicts, the World Food Program, which helps refugees with food aid, the United Nations Children's Fund (UNICEF), which provides aid to women and children, the United Nations Relief and Works Administration for Palestinian Refugees (UNRWA), which provides aid to Palestinians, and the International Organization for Migration, which arranges for the transportation of refugees who end up being resettled overseas.

Refugee status determination can be conducted either individually or with a group. It is preferable to determine refugee status on an individual basis so as to allow for a close examination of details and circumstances in order to know if that person is a refugee. However, in the cases of mass influx from one country to another, individual determination is not practical and many status determinations are conducted in a group. When this occurs, factors of the country of origin are typically examined more so than individual circumstances. An exception is made when there is military conflict, and refugees are mixed in with combatants. Active military combatants do not fall under the refugee definition and therefore are not entitled to receive any international refugee protection. Former combatants could potentially be eligible for refugee status but have to be cleared for the status first; that is, they have to prove that they have renounced all military activities and are now civilians. Former combatants are typically separated from refugees after a mass influx and are then individually examined.

As mentioned, refugees are entitled to certain rights and protections, the most important being non-refoulement, or protection against returning to the country of origin. Essentially, the host country cannot return or deport a refugee to the country in which he or she will be persecuted. Furthermore, refugees do not have to have official refugee status determination in order for the non-refoulement to apply, and those with a pending status also qualify. The exception to the non-refoulement principal is for refugees that pose a serious threat to the security of the host country.

Refugees also qualify for other basic rights, including protection against physical threats in the host country, access to courts in the host country, freedom to move about the host country, with the exception of those that pose a public threat, and reunification with family members who also reside within the host country if possible. They are also given access to primary education for refugee children, and assistance to cover basic needs, such as food, clothing, shelter, and medical assistance.

Depending on the individual situation, there are three options that refugees can pursue in order to establish a permanent living situation. The three solutions available to refugees are voluntary repatriation, local integration, and resettlement. Voluntary repatriation can occur when a refugee voluntarily and safely returns to his or her country of origin. Local integration is a process in which the refugee remains permanently in the host country. Finally, resettlement occurs when the refugee transfers to a third state that is willing to admit him or her with the refugee status.

In addition to the official refugee status, there are several other types of uprooted people. The definition of the 1951 Convention does not include general oppression, insecurity, or victims of economic deprivation. It also does not include those who are displaced within their country of origin, since the definition states that a refugee has to be outside the home country.

Furthermore, as mentioned above, those who leave their country of origin due to economic factors are not considered to be refugees but rather economic migrants. They do not qualify for protection or assistance from the UNHCR. The main difference is that migrants flee to improve their economic standing while refugees flee to save their lives and avoid persecution. However, in many countries, economic hardship is often accompanied by political violence or is the result of a violent political system, and therefore it can be difficult to tell the difference between a refugee and a migrant. An example is Haiti, where, since the 1950s, many Haitians have fled their country due to a corrupt political system and military regime as well as large economic problems.

Jenna Glickman

See Also: Central American Civil Wars; Nicaraguan Adjustment and Central American Relief Act (NACARA); Refugees; Salvadorans; Select Commission on Immigration and Refugee Policy.

Further Reading

Binder, Susanne, and Jelena Tosic. 2002. *Refugee Studies and Politics.* Vienna: Institut für Ethnologie, Kultur-und Sozialanthropologie.

Loescher, Gil, and Ann Dull Loescher. 1994. *The Global Refugee Crisis.* Santa Barbara, CA: ABC-CLIO, Inc.

Refugee Status Determination: Identifying Who Is a Refugee. Geneva: Office of the United States High Commissioner for Refugees.

Sobel, Lester A, ed. 1979. *Refugees: A World Report.* New York: Facts On File, Inc.

UNHCR: The UN Refugee Agency. UNHCR Web Site. http://www.unhcr.org/cgi-bin/texis/vtx/home.

Religion

In general, religion as it exists in Latin American communities is seen as a way to promote social cohesion and very often immigrants in the United States retain their religious-based traditions. Religion is thought to bolster practices of *familialism* as often traditional practice encourages family bonding time, as well as re-establishes the concept of understanding oneself as a part of a large community or a collective that embraces even those outside the family unit. Religiosity has been known to work as a protective factor for youth in situations where family members are involved in drug or alcohol abuse. According to a 2007 Pew Research study, Latinos are transforming the religious landscape of the United States, especially Catholicism, primarily due to the growing numbers of immigrants. In 2007, about a third of all Catholics in the United States were Latinos. According to the study, more than two-thirds of Hispanics (68 percent) identified themselves as Roman Catholics, with the next largest category (at 15 percent) made up of born-again or evangelical Protestants. Nearly one in ten (8 percent) Latinos did not identify with any religion according to the study.

Many studies show that churches and shrines are physical manifestations of religion in both neighborhoods and within households. These structures add to the special aesthetics that religious individuals may find spiritually nourishing, while promoting the positive cultural factors mentioned above. Their presence throughout neighborhoods, *barrios,* and other public spaces represents the influential cultural contributions of Latinos in the community.

It is also very common for unauthorized migrants crossing the border to carry with them various forms of religious paraphernalia. Commonly found with migrants are rosaries, images of the Virgin Mary and other saints, and t-shirts with religious icons, such as the Virgin de Guadalupe. There is also a strong following of the patron saint of migrants among migrant crossers, Saint Toribio Romo Gonzalez. Many have claimed to have seen him and been guided by him in their journey to cross into the United States, an endeavor that may result in injury or death. Saint Toribio Romo Gonzalez was born in 1900 and died at the young age of twenty-seven. He was originally from Jalisco and buried there after his martyred death at the hands of the government that tried to rid strong religious leaders during the Cristero War. Accounts of his appearance and guidance in the border-crossing experience have made this saint a religious attraction wherever shrines are constructed in his honor, as many turn to him for protection in seeking a safe passage for themselves or for family members who cross.

The relationship between religion and immigration is a complex topic. Some scholars see the strength of religious beliefs as a marker for gauging assimilation in new communities. Retention of religious beliefs is thought to lower a migrant sense of loyalty to their adopted country. By the same token, adhering to the religious beliefs of one's birth is thought to reaffirm one's loyalty to one's identity, origin, and nationalism. Catholicism is a religion found throughout the globe, as are Judaism and Islam. Being members of such a global faith allows members of the faith to imagine themselves within communities outside their immediate parishes, and even those beyond any political boundaries. Religious Protestant groups are also said to work in the same way, contributing to the adaptation of newcomers, and to transnationalism.

Religious teachings have played a important part in influencing public attitudes towards immigration. The period of the Mexican Revolution, during the 1910s and through the 1920s, marks one of the largest exoduses to the United States with nearly one million Mexican refugees fleeing violence. Seeing this as demise not only of the Catholic Church but also the greater Mexican community, the Catholic Church began what would be known as a "holy crusade against emigration." This crusade against emigration to the United States was led by the Archbishop of Guadalajara. During Sunday mass, he preached against the dangers that emigration caused the state and church. In particular, there were four main reasons the Church gave to legitimize their opposition to emigration. First was the fact that with family members migrating, others were being left behind, resulting in the disintegration of family and family values. Second, migration and the physical separation from the Church would lead to religious apathy, while leading to potential conversion to Protestantism while in the United States. Thirdly, the migration would inevitably cause a labor shortage on the Mexican side of the border with the absence of workforce in its prime, and in the event of their return, migrants will have become tainted by their stay in the United States, influenced by attitudes of entitlement, and it was predicted that this would result in unproductive and lazy members of the community upon their return. Lastly, the migration was seen as a huge act of disloyalty to the Revolution and an abandonment of the national, hard-fought struggle for justice for *Mexicanos*.

The Archbishop of Guadalajara's prophecy about Catholicism's loss of the faithful to Protestantism has been partially fulfilled as Latino Protestants now mark a powerful presence in the United States. The 2007 Pew Research study shows that many of those who are joining evangelical churches are Catholic converts. In part, this development is related to U.S. politics and political thinking that is highly influenced by religion. In the United States, religious beliefs have been highly influential in shaping the views of the faith community about social issues, including controversial issues concerning abortion, and same-sex marriage. With greater frequency, Latinos are in this way being exposed to how the pulpit is an accepted forum and place to address religious doctrine as well as social and political issues. An example of this comes from the political debate over reproductive choice. The Catholic Church is a promoter of procreation and the idea that all children born are a gift from God. Long advocates against artificial birth control (such as the use of contraceptives, condoms, or abortions) even in developing countries where large portions of the populations are living in poverty, the Catholic Church has refused to promote safer sex practice or contraceptive use for its followers. It is a widely held view that Latinos supported presidential candidate George W. Bush's 2004 bid for the White House because his pro-life views resonated with those of Latinos. In a related issue, in 2011, the Catholic Church announced that condom use to help fight against the AIDS epidemic would be allowed even in sex outside of marriage. However, they still maintained that abstinence is the best solution and that condom use goes against the creation of life. In the end, the Church conceded that in the question of AIDS prevention, if condoms could save lives, then they should be promoted.

One notable example of the convergence of religion and political thought from an intervention by a religious community on behalf of immigrants' rights was the case of Elvira Arellano, a Mexican national working in the United States. Ms. Arellano was working with a false social security number while raising her 7-year-old U.S.-citizen son. She was ordered to appear before an immigration judge on August 15, 2006, and instead found refuge within the Adalberto United Methodist Church in the city of Chicago. She was able to avoid deportation for almost a year while she and her son lived in the church. Eventually and after national media attention, Arellano was deported without her son in August of 2007. Her son would join her later in Mexico.

However, for certain religious organizations, there is a strong tradition of defying laws perceived to be unjust. In the early part of the 1980s, the Sanctuary Movement assisted in the smuggling into the United States of Central American refugees from violence in war-torn nations. This movement was seen as a clear and open defiance of federal laws that prohibited the harboring of what they were calling "illegal aliens." Many of the prominent figures within the movement were arrested, indicted, and even tried for breaking of the law. The movement was led by religious groups and leaders in Tucson, Arizona. However, this movement quickly grew to incorporate various religious groups and cities around the nation. Initially, the movement was trying to provide refugees a place to live, clothes, and food while they tried to navigate the legal process for training and for attaining asylum for hundreds of refugees. At the height of this movement there were as many as five hundred groups around the nation. Some of the major organized religions involved were Catholic, Lutheran, Presbyterian, Baptist, Quaker, and Jewish. In this way, the religious organizations were defying the law but adhering to their religious convictions and "the right of sanctuary." The movement was prominent in the border region but expanded to large cities like Chicago and Philadelphia, as well as states such as California and Texas.

On a less dramatic scale, there have been significant actions on the part of many different denominations of religions that work to provide undocumented migrants with clothes, food, shelter, and other support, despite its being against the law in some places. Due to emerging anti-immigrant legislation being passed in state legislatures in recent years, religious organizations risk being charged with "aiding and abetting" undocumented immigrants. Humane Borders, a group formed from the First Baptist Church in Tucson, Arizona, has been recognized nationally for its work putting out large tanks of water in the desert in an effort to mitigate migrant deaths due to heat exposure and thirst as they attempt to cross the border through the Sonoran desert, which can reach temperatures in excess of 110 degrees F. in the summer. Another organization that was formed to provide humanitarian aid to migrants crossing the desert, No More Deaths, emerged from the South Side Presbyterian Church (also in Tucson, Arizona).

With the signing into law of Arizona's SB 1070 many religious organizations have revitalized the Sanctuary Movement. In particular the Unitarian Universalist Church of Tucson, which in 2010 was the winner of the Bennett Social Justice Award by the Unitarian Universalist Association (UUA) for their work in trying to fight against the anti-immigrant laws and unfair treatment of undocumented migrants on the Arizona border.

The religious organization works with the social justice and immigrant advocacy group No More Deaths.

In this way, religious groups and religion as a framework for action and articulating compassion continued to play an important role in various parts of the country. Churches often provide housing, food, and clothing for those families affected by workforce raids when they are too afraid to return to their home. In Alabama, with the enactment of a slate of anti-immigrant laws, including penalties for people and organizations that aid in "harboring illegal immigrants," religious institutions helped by speaking out against such laws. Many insist that these type of laws go against their religious convictions and freedoms and that regardless of the laws, they will continue to shelter as well as feed, clothe and aid people in need regardless of citizenship status.

Yesenia Andrade

See Also: Advocacy; Catholic Church; Community Concerns; Faith-Based Organizations; Refugee Act (1980); Sanctuary Movement; Transnationalism.

Further Reading

Dahm, Charles W. 2004. *Parish Ministry in a Hispanic Community.* Chicago: Paulist Press.

Fitzgerald, David. 2005. *Emigration's Challenge to the "Nation-Church": Mexican Catholic Emigration Policies, 1920–2004.* eScholarship, University of California. http://www.escholarship.org/uc/item/9nv2t3z9.

Groody, Daniel. 2002. *Border of Death, Valley of Life.* Lanham: Rowman & Littlefield Publishers.

Hagan, Jacqueline, and Helen Rose Ebaugh. 2003. "Calling upon the Sacred: Migrants' Use of Religion in the Migration Process." *The International Migration Review: IMR* 37.4:1145.

Levitt, Peggy. 2002. "Two Nations under God? Latino Religious Life in the United States." In Marcelo M. Suarez-Orozco and Mariela M. Páez, eds., *Latinas/os: Remaking of America*, 150–164. Berkeley: University of California Press.

Pew Research. 2007. *Changing Faiths: Latinos and the Transformation of American Religion.* http://www.pewtrusts.org/our_work_report_detail.aspx?id=20710.

Urrea, Luis Alberto. 2004. *The Devil's Highway: A True Story.* New York: Little, Brown.

Remittances

The vast majority of undocumented immigrants come to the United States because of economic necessity. They usually send remittances to family members left behind, whether wives and children, or aged parents. The economic recession in the United States has had ripple effects among migrant-sending communities in Latin America and the Caribbean. On the local level there has been a decline of remittances to family members left behind. Whereas remittance flows to developing countries around the

Table 1: Migrant Remittances by Selected Trends and Country of Origin

Country	Remittances in millions (USD) in 2011	Percent growth in remittances in 2011 over 2010	Average remittance amount by migrants in the US (in USD)	Deportations in 2010
Mexico	22,731	6	400	282,003
Guatemala	4,377	6	390	29,378
Colombia	4,168	3	222	
El Salvador	3,650	3	321	19,809
Dominican Republic	3,131	4	277	
Honduras	2,862	12	295	24,611
Ecuador	2,673	13	224	
Jamaica	2,025	5		
Nicaragua	1,053	22	125	1,847
Totals	46,670	8.22		

Data adapted from Orozco, 2012. "Future Trends in Remittances to Latin America and the Caribbean." Washington, D.C.: Inter-American Dialogue. Available at http://www.thedialogue.org/PublicationFiles/IAD8642 _Remittance_0424enFINAL.pdf

world increased from $285 billion in 2007 to $328 billion in 2008, in most countries these remittances had declined throughout the course of 2009. The top four migrant remittance-receiving countries in 2011 were India ($63 billion), China ($62 billion), Mexico ($23.6 billion) and the Philippines ($23 billion) (World Bank, 2013). In 2003, 14 percent of adults in Ecuador, 23 percent in Central America, and 18 percent in Mexico received remittances from relatives abroad. It is in Latin America and the Caribbean where decreases in remittances have been most notable. After growing at an average of 19 percent during the 2000–2006 period, the growth rate of remittances fell to just 6.5 percent in 2007 (Ruiz and Vargas-Silva, 2009), with a decline in remittances to Mexico from $26.3 billion in 2008 to $23.6 billion in 2011, (World Bank, 2013). The vast majority of the estimated 11.1 million undocumented immigrants in the United States are senders of these remittances.

It is estimated that one million households in Latin America and the Caribbean that received remittances from migrant family members in the United States, Spain, and elsewhere in 2008 will not receive such remittances in future years until the economy becomes stable, and another four million will receive 10 percent less than previously in the course of the year. The implications of these trends are that these migrant-sending families or households have seen their income reduced in an amount ranging from 7 to 65 percent during the recession of 2007–2008. Remittances are an integral part of the livelihood of many, especially rural, households in the less developed regions of the world.

Table 2: Remittances and GDPs for Selected Countries

Country	Remittances as Percent of GDP in 2011*	Per Capita Remittances Received in USD for 2007**
Mexico	2	255
Guatemala	9.6	319
Colombia	1.3	98
El Salvador	15.9	541
Dominican Republic	6.6	385
Honduras	16.1	369
Ecuador	4.1	232
Jamaica	14.6	790
Nicaragua	9.8	132

*Source: World Bank, 2013
**Source: UN Human Development Report, 2009

The decline in remittances has been partially associated with deportations, and the record numbers of deportations under the Obama administration. Also to blame is the aggressive role taken by states to enforce immigration at more local levels. The rising cost of living in the United States and high unemployment rates, especially in the housing construction sectors, are also factors. During the recession years, a large percentage of migrants stopped remitting and those who continued to do so sent less money (Orozco, 2012).

A notable trend was perceived in the post-recession period suggesting that the dark days of the recession are nearly over. There were greater numbers of migrants who were sending more, as well as a rise in the frequency of sending, from nine times a year in 2008 to 11 in 2010. Remittances to Latin America grew by about 8 percent from 2010 to 2011, almost reaching the pre-recession levels of 2007. Remittances increased to $69 billion (U.S.) in 2011, with the greatest share ($46.670 billion) coming from the nine countries listed in Table 1, and in particular from Mexico, Colombia, and migrants in Central America (Orozco, 2012).

In other notable developments, women are increasingly migrating to high-income countries, and on average, skilled female migrants in the United States send about 6.7 percent more dollars home than their male counterparts. Also, although banks are still the primary way in which remitters transfer funds, more have turned to the Internet and mobile telephone banking (Orozco, 2012). In 2012, migrants from Central America and the Dominican Republic working in the United States also spent approximately 630 million dollars to cover the cost of remittance transfers to family members in their countries of origin (Hayem, 2013).

Remittances form an important part of the Gross Domestic Product (GDP). These are shown for nine selected Latin American and Caribbean countries in Table 2, as is the amount of remittances per capita in U.S. dollars for 2007.

Table 3: Top 10 U.S. Remittance-Sending States

State	Remittances in Millions of USD 2006
California	13,191
Texas	5,222
New York	3,714
Florida	3,083
Illinois	2,853
New Jersey	1,869
Georgia	1,736
Arizona	1,378
North Carolina	1,221
Virginia	1,110

Source: Data taken from Ruiz and Vargas-Silva, 2009. "The Crisis and Migrants' Remittances: A Look at Hispanics in the U.S." International Migration Institute Working Paper No. 18. Oxford, UK. Available at http://www.imi.ox.ac.uk/pdfs/imi-working-papers/working-paper-18-crisis-and-remittances

The majority of remittances are used to cover the recipient household's basic living expense. Remittance flows have contributed to a reduction in poverty within countries and has allowed many families to achieve a higher quality of life by financing the purchase of consumer goods and investments in education, health, housing, and business developments. By most accounts, especially hard hit by the economic decline are rural families that depend on remittances, although urban families have also been affected.

Most remittances in 2006 came from states with large concentrations of immigrants (Ruiz and Vargas-Silva, 2009), as Table 3 shows.

In most Latin American countries, more than 60 percent of remittance receivers are female, and in Guatemala, it reaches 80 percent. More often than not, they are wives or mothers left behind, who serve as caretakers of children and the elderly. Some migrants may be tapping savings in order to continue to send remittances.

Remittances may be sent by individuals or families to family members left behind, or they may be remittances sent from Hometown Associations (HTAs) in the United States for community-wide projects in the home community (Ruiz and Vargas-Silva, 2009). The former, in aggregate, greatly exceed the latter. The greatest proportion of remittances to families go toward meeting basic needs. The vast majority of this money is spent on health care, with smaller portions going toward payments of debts, acquisition of land, tools, or livestock, the purchase of basic consumer goods, or for savings. HTAs, voluntary groups of expatriates from a particular community and residing in a particular destination city, also send remittances, especially for infrastructural and other construction projects. Many of these expatriates are undocumented workers. Although only 4 percent of Mexicans who remit belong to an HTA (as compared to 29 percent for Guyana, 16 percent for Jamaica, and 10 percent for Ecuador and Haiti), Mexico's government has extended greater aid to the HTAs and their home communities than is true of most governments elsewhere. Beginning in 2001 the Mexican government initiated a three-for-one program (superseding an earlier two-for-one program) whereby for every dollar an HTA remits another dollar is contributed by the federal, state, and municipal governments for local development projects. In the case of Mexico, the three-for-one program has funded projects that have provided communities back home with developments such as infrastructure projects to provide water to houses, paving roads and streets, and building schools, plazas, and recreational centers (Ruiz and Vargas-Silva, 2009). Both individual remittances and remittances made through HTAs have declined. An August 2010 article in the newspaper *La Imagen de Zacatecas* reported that HTAs in that state, one of the traditional migrant-sending states, have received 19.6 percent less support in 2009 than they did in 2008. Contributions fell from approximately 63 million pesos to approximately 51 million pesos.

The flow of remittances back to home communities, whether rural villages or cities, has been affected both by the lessening of migration from Mexico to the United States in face of economic recession and by the high rates of unemployment among Mexican immigrants there (Orozco, 2012).

In Mexico, remittances began to decline toward the end of 2007, when the service, low-wage manufacturing, and construction industries began to contract. The decline is due both to outright unemployment (fueling the return of some migrants to Mexico) and reemployment at a lower wage. For example, 152,000 Mexican-born construction workers out of a total of 247,000 Hispanic workers in a workforce of 703,000 lost jobs in the construction sector between 2007 and 2008. In the face of this unemployment Mexican-born workers accepted wage cuts, moved on to take up employment in lower-wage jobs, or returned to Mexico. All three of these phenomena have fed into the cutback in remittances (Ruiz and Vargas-Silva, 2009).

A number of articles in the nation-wide Mexican newspapers, such as *La Jornada, El Universal,* and *La Crónica de Hoy,* as well as in the Los Angeles–based *La Opinión,* have had articles documenting the decline of remittances to Mexico since the beginning of the economic recession in the United States in 2008. In April of 2009, remittances to Mexico had declined 18.7 percent, to 1.8 billion dollars, as compared to April 2008. In May they declined by 19.87 percent or by almost one fifth, as compared to the previous year. In July 2009, remittances were 16.2 percent lower than in July 2009 showing a slight rise from previous months. In November of 2009, remittances to Mexico fell by 14.4 percent compared to November of 2008. The trend continued in 2010. In January of 2010, remittances were even lower than in January of 2009, when they had fallen in comparison to 2008. There was a constant decline, with remittances in January 2010 being 15.34 percent less than remittances in December 2009 and by February 2010, remittances had been falling steadily for the previous fifteen months. In total, 2009 saw a diminution of remittances by 15.7 percent as compared to 2008. In the first six months of 2010, the overall remittance decline, as compared to remittances in 2009, was 4.07 percent. The poorest families in the country—most often those sending undocumented workers to the United States—are most affected.

According to a report by Mexico's Bancomer, the states most affected by the decline of remittances are Guerrero, Hidalgo, Chiapas, Zacatecas, Oaxaca, and Michoacán. The same report points out that workers of Mexican origin in the United

States have lost eight hundred thousand jobs since the beginning of the recession, and 80 percent of the jobs lost were held by immigrants from Mexico, especially in construction, manufacturing, and services (BBVA Bancomer, 2009: 9).

Between the last trimester of 2008 (October to December) and the second trimester of 2009 (April to June), remittances had fallen in the traditional migrant-sending states of Zacatecas, Michoacán, Durango, and Guanajuato, as well as in the newer migrant-sending states of Oaxaca, Puebla, Guerrero, and Chiapas. In August 2009, an article in the prestigious newspaper *La Jornada* reported that sixty-five thousand rural families in the state of Zacatecas were suffering from the absence or decline of remittances due to high unemployment rates among Mexicans in the United States. On the national level, it is estimated that 275 thousand families stopped receiving remittances since 2006.

However, according to a 2012 report by Mexico's largest bank, Bancomer, they expect a downturn in remittances in 2012 between -2.5 percent and -0.5 percent in dollars, compared to 2011. And, although remittances are expected to grow between 1 and 3 percent between 2012 and 2013, they still will not reach the highest remittance levels of 2007 (BBVA Bancomer, 2012).

Tamar Diana Wilson

See Also: Economics; Family Economics; Globalization; Hometown Associations; Labor Supply.

Further Reading

BBVA Bancomer. 2009. "Situación Migración México." http://serviciosdeestudios.bbva .com.

BBVA Bancomer. 2012. "Mexico Migration Outlook, July." https://www.fundacionbbva bancomer.org/imagenes/docs/MigOut_2012Nov.pdf.

Congressional Budget Office. "Remittances: International Payments by Migrants." Washington, D.C. The Congress of the United States Congressional Budget Office. http://www.cbo.gov.

Hayem, Maria Luisa. 2013. "Remittances to Latin America and the Caribbean in 2012." Inter-American Development Bank. http://www5.iadb.org/mif/HOME/Knowledge/ tabid/426/idPublication/78709/language/en-US/Default.aspx.

Kochhar, Rakesh. *Latino Labor Report, 2008: Construction Reverses Job Growth for Latinos.* Washington, D.C.: PEW Hispanic Center. http://pewhispanic.org.

Lowell, B. Lindsay, and Rodolfo O. de la Garza. 2000. "The Developmental Role of Remittances in U.S. Latino Communities and in Latin American Countries." Washington, D.C. Inter-American Dialogue. http://www.thedialogue.org/Publication-Files/Final%20report.pdf.

Orozco, Manuel. 2009. "Migration and Remittances in Times of Recession: Effects on Latin American and Caribbean Economies." Washington, D.C.: Inter-American Dialogue. http://www.oecd.org/dev/americas/42753222.pdf.

Orozco, Manuel. 2009. "Understanding the Continuing Effect of the Economic Crisis on Remittances to Latin America and the Caribbean." Washington, D.C.: Inter-American Dialogue. http://www.thedialogue.org.

Orozco, Manuel. 2012. "Future Trends in Remittances to Latin America and the Caribbean." Washington, D.C.: Inter-American Dialogue. Available at http://www.thedialogue.org/PublicationFiles/IAD8642_Remittance_0424enFINAL.pdf.

Papademetriou, Demetrios G., and Aaron Terazas. "Immigration and the Current Economic Crisis: Research, Evidence, Policy Challenges, and Implications." Washington, D.C. Migration Policy Institute. http://www.migrationpolicy.org.

Passel, Jeffrey S., and D'Vera Cohn. 2012. "Unauthorized Immigrants: 11.1 Million in 2011." Pew Research, Hispanic Center, December 6, 2012. Available at: http://www.pewhispanic.org/2012/12/06/unauthorized-immigrants-11–1-million-in-2011/.

Ratha, Dilip, Sanket Mohapatra, and Ani Silwal. "Outlook for Remittance Flows 2009–2011: Remittances Expected to Fall by 7–20 Percent in 2009." Migration and Development Brief 10. Washington, D.C.: The World Bank. http:siteresources.world bank.org.

Ruiz, Isabel, and Carlos Vargas-Silva. 2009. "The Crisis and Migrants' Remittances: A Look at Hispanics in the U.S." International Migration Institute Working Paper No. 18. Oxford, UK. Available at http://www.imi.ox.ac.uk/pdfs/imi-working-papers/working -paper-18-crisis-and-remittances.

UN Development Report. 2009. "Remittance inflows per capita (USD)." https://mobiledevelopmentintelligence.com/statistics/123-remittance-inflows-per-capita-usd.

World Bank. 2013. "Personal Remittances Received (Percent of GDP)." http://data .worldbank.org/indicator/BX.TRF.PWKR.DT.GD.ZS.

Repatriation

Repatriation commonly refers to the process of returning a person to his or her place of origin. While repatriation is not always a negative process, in recent years with the debate over immigration issues at the nation's center stage, repatriation has increasingly been associated with involuntary return to one's country, and the more formal process of forced deportation or removal of undocumented immigrants from the United States.

Repatriation should be differentiated from the more formalized process of deportation or removal. Repatriation does not always require proceedings before a judge in immigration court where formal charges of "illegal entry" are brought against migrants apprehended at the border. With formal charges, immigrants risk jail time and banishment from the United States. The sentence periods of banishment (called "bars") may vary but usually these get longer for each time that immigrants are caught reentering the United States. Less formalized repatriation procedures that do not involve appearing before a judge in immigration court have been a way of returning individuals to their place of origin without clogging up the judicial system such as in the Tucson Border Patrol sector where hundreds of immigrants may be caught in a single day. Instead, repatriation of immigrants and migrants takes the form of what is commonly called "voluntary return" or "expedited removal" where no formal charges are made.

Because of the increased immigration from Mexico, the United States has sought a means by which a great number of undocumented immigrants can be expeditiously repatriated. Like formal deportation, repatriation involves expulsion from the country. However, unlike deportation, individuals are returned without resorting to the more costly and time-consuming formal deportation proceedings (known as "removal" after the 1996 Illegal Immigration Reform and Immigrant Responsibility Act was passed).

Mexico, too, has actively assisted in the repatriation of its nationals by signing agreements with the United States to guarantee that the process is safe, orderly and implemented with dignity and respect. The agreements are in the form of a Memorandum of Understanding, and usually have the same or similar titles, "Procedures for the Safe and Orderly Repatriation of Mexican Nationals," even though these agreements may be signed by different parties along the border. The agreement is renewed periodically and typically entered into by representatives of the governments of Mexico and the United States who are in some way responsible for executing the procedures for repatriating Mexican nationals. In the Tucson Sector, one of the busiest of the U.S. Border Patrol Sectors in the nation, the most recent instrument was signed in 2010 and was adopted by representatives for the U.S. Border Patrol and the El Instituto Nacional de Migración (INM) and Mexican consular offices for each consular jurisdiction in this part of the border: Nogales, Phoenix, Yuma, Tucson, and Douglas. The instrument is written in both English and Spanish and consists of several paragraphs that address standards for procedures and a timetable for repatriating migrants, and a signatory page. The documents stipulate that every effort will be taken to preserve the safety of women and underage immigrants, and family unity. In this regard, special precautions may be agreed to, such as not repatriating women and children who are more vulnerable at very late hours of the night where they may fall prey to bandits and violent criminals. However, several reports by researchers and humanitarian groups reveal that these standards of practice are frequently ignored or violated. It has been very difficult to hold U.S. officials accountable for their neglect to follow the procedures outlined in these agreements because the Mexican government also does not comply with its responsibilities to assure that its citizens are repatriated to Mexico in a dignified safe and orderly manner. In this way, both governments are at fault. For example, according to these standards, Mexican officials are to verify the physical condition of people being returned and to take appropriate actions in cases where someone alleges mistreatment or a violation of their human rights. In these cases INM officials are required to immediately notify U.S. authorities and the Mexican consulate of any violation of the agreement. A stipulated standard in the agreement between officials along the Arizona-Sonora border is that an INM official be at the port of entry when Mexican nationals are repatriated. The agreement specifies that U.S. officials in Arizona will "make every effort to make timely notifications via telephone (at least thirty minutes) before the actual return" of repatriated individuals. This implies that that an INM official should be at the port of entry to gather data about any abuses, which could then be forwarded to the proper authorities. This raises the question if U.S. officials are in fact calling according to the thirty-minute rule. Without respect for a protocol, little can be concluded with certainty about whether or not Mexican nationals are being repatriated in a dignified, safe, and orderly repatriation and in fact if abuses are taking place.

Another agreement for the repatriation of Mexican nationals is the Mexican Interior Repatriation Program. This program was first implemented in 2004 and has been sponsored jointly by the United States and the Mexican government. This program is intended to send those Mexican nationals who are from the central and southern parts of Mexico back to their communities by plane to the interior of Mexico, rather than to deport them through the northern U.S.-Mexico border. This program has been offered only during the months in which the high temperatures in the Arizona and Sonoran deserts are severe and migrants are at extreme risk of perishing if they attempt to reenter the United States after being repatriated. During the months of July through September, Mexican nationals who volunteer to take part in the program are taken by aircraft to Mexico City. There they are provided a ticket to their community of origin by the Mexican government. The Mexican Interior Repatriation Program is a joint program between the United States and Mexico, but only the United States pays the cost of flying migrants caught in Arizona to the interior of Mexico. Critics of the program have pointed out the high cost of this program to the U.S. government. Humanitarian groups have questioned whether the program is effective. Proponents of the program maintain that it saves lives by discouraging the reentry of migrants who may die in their attempt to cross again into the United States in an area where temperatures in the desert may reach more than 100 degrees. In 2010, 23,384 individuals were repatriated under this program between June and September, with a cost of 14.8 million dollars. During the time that the program was in effect, 12.44 percent of the immigrants arrested trying to cross into the United States (or about 1 in 8) were reentry cases.

In yet another repatriation program, the Alien Transfer Exit Program (ATEP), also known as the lateral repatriation program of the U.S. government, was implemented in 2008. This program was not by agreement with the Mexican government. This type of repatriation is intended to disrupt the cycle of re-entry by migrants who after being repatriated attempt to cross into the United States again, resulting in multiple arrests. This procedure is part of the Department of Homeland Security consequence program intended to deter undocumented migration (another part is Operation Streamline). Therefore, the goal of this program is to repatriate those caught in the Sonora-Arizona migration corridor to areas in Texas, such as McAllen, Laredo, Eagle Pass, El Paso, and Brownsville. Those caught in the San Diego area may be repatriated in Douglas or Nogales, Arizona. The Mexican government has complained to the United States about the lateral repatriation program, citing violation of some of the standards for practice stipulated under the long-standing Procedures for the Safe and Orderly Repatriation of Mexican Nationals. Some of the dangers that its nationals are exposed to when released in areas unknown to them are increased vulnerability that comes from not knowing anyone in the area, and falling prey to smuggling rings and bandits, and isolation and family separation. These conditions expose them to violence and insecurity, especially in places in northern Coahuila and Tamaulipas (across the southern Texas border) where narco traffickers are known to lie in wait hoping to recruit recent deportees knowing that they will have nowhere to turn.

In another example of how Mexican repatriation is dealt with comes from Mexico's response to the signing of Arizona Senate Bill 1070 (SB 1070) by the state's governor, Jan Brewer, in 2010. At that time, the Mexican government braced for the return of what they thought would be thousands of undocumented immigrants fleeing the enforcement of the law. Although these expectations were unrealized, the

Mexican consular network put in place programs to help its nationals return to their country of origin. For those wishing to return, either voluntarily or because they have been ordered to do so by a U.S. authority, consular offices can certify the list of household goods of Mexicans settled abroad, and in this way they avoid paying import taxes upon their return to Mexico. The consular services also include the certification of official U.S. documents before a family returns to Mexico. These include children's school records, diplomas, and other certificates that will be needed once the family returns to Mexico and has need to access services and the public school system.

Other forms of repatriation speak to the undocumented immigrant experience. Many U.S. hospitals are taking it upon themselves to repatriate seriously injured or ill immigrants because they cannot afford to keep and treat patients without insurance who need long-term care. Such repatriations are not undertaken by U.S. officials but by hospitals, via ambulance and commercial planes. The process is often referred to as patient dumping. Although hospital administrators maintain that these cross-border transfers do not occur until the patients are medically stable, critics of the process have expressed concerns that hospitals are repatriating without governmental oversight.

Finally, hundreds of bodies of the deceased lie in facilities in U.S. border counties in any given year, caught in a backlog of investigative work to be identified so that they can be repatriated. The deceased are victims of violence, fatalities resulting from encounters with Border Patrol agents or vigilantes. Others are killed in accidents, drown, or die from injuries while navigating rough desert terrain. Most perish from dehydration and exposure to the elements as they cross the inhospitable desert between Arizona and Sonora. Assuming that the identification of human remains is successful, there is the high cost of processing and transporting these remains to their country of origin. Also, provided that the deceased's family can be located, DNA testing may also be involved. In 2007, the Mexican government spent nearly $3.9 million in repatriating human remains to their families.

Anna Ochoa O'Leary

See Also: Border Crossing; Bracero Program; Death; Deportation; Expedited Removal; Operation Wetback; U.S. Border Patrol.

Further Reading

Gonzalez, Daniel. 2011. "Illegal immigrant repatriation cost, effectiveness questioned." Aug. 21, 2011. *Arizona Republic*. http://www.azcentral.com/news/articles/2011/08/21/20110821illegal-immigrants-repatriation-questioned.html.

O'Leary, Anna Ochoa, 2009. "Mujeres en el Cruce: Remapping Border Security through Migrant Mobility." *Journal of the Southwest*. 51.4:523–542.

Sontag, Deborah. 2008. "Many U.S. hospitals repatriating illegal immigrants." *New York Times*. http://www.nytimes.com/2008/08/03/world/americas/03ihtdeport.4.14970157.html?pagewanted=all.

Vincent, Stefanie. "Medical Repatriation: An Analysis of the International Patient Transferring of Illegal Aliens." *Houston Journal of International Law* 33.1:95–134.

Restaurants

The restaurant industry provides a common livelihood for the immigrant labor force, especially undocumented immigrants. Undocumented immigrants tend to hold the most unfavorable jobs available in restaurants. While some employers prefer undocumented workers, others avoid hiring them. Over the past few years, restaurants have been under scrutiny by immigration enforcement agencies, and hiring and employment policies have changed to limit undocumented employees in the workplace.

Restaurants throughout the United States employ approximately 12.7 million workers, of whom 1.4 million are immigrants, and 700,000 are undocumented (Pew Hispanic Center, 2006). The restaurant industry has shown notable increases in their undocumented labor force over the past decade or so. In New York, a majority of restaurant laborers are male, young, and immigrant, predominately of Asian or Latino descent.

In the restaurant business, undocumented workers tend to fill "back of the house" positions (i.e., chefs, cooks, dishwashers). In 2008, 20 percent of the industry's 2.6 million chefs and cooks and 20 percent of the 360,000 dishwashers were undocumented immigrants. Some sources describe this workforce as "invisible labor" due to their unseen presence in restaurants and their undocumented legal status. "Front of the house" positions such as servers or host/hostesses are practically never granted to undocumented workers. Even among equally qualified applicants of different races, white applicants are more likely to get serving jobs. Similarly, race, language, and immigration status are influential considerations when it comes to promotions.

"Bad" jobs, characterized by low wages, long hours, unfavorable and often unsafe work conditions, and little to no benefits, are traditionally filled by undocumented workers (Restaurant Opportunities Center of New York, 2005). Workers of color, namely immigrants, also report verbal abuse, usually based on race or language. Undocumented workers are in a difficult position because they may face deportation if they complain about wages or poor working conditions. Corrupt employers and the working conditions that they allow are of great concern to immigrant advocate groups.

Employers have mixed reviews regarding undocumented immigrant workers. Some find undocumented workers appealing because they tend to work hard, are willing to learn, and cost less than legally eligible workers. If undocumented workers were removed from restaurants, businesses would have to pay higher wages and taxes, which would increase costs for consumption. Others employers avoid hiring undocumented workers for fear of problems with immigration enforcement, avoiding altogether applicants that "look to be Mexican" (National Council of La Raza, 2011).

Undocumented immigrant employment has been an issue of concern for the Obama administration, which investigated and fined over 2,073 businesses during the first half of the 2010 fiscal year. A tactic that has been observed under the Obama administration that is different from his predecessor is that the nature of workplace raids has become more low-profile investigations that do not get much media coverage. Also called "silent raids," with this tactic businesses receive the brunt of the penalties if found to have violated employment laws.

Ruben Castro, owner of La Fiesta Braval, a Mexican restaurant in Laurel, Mississippi, clears the tables during the lunch rush, August 2008. Castro has had to bring in extra employees to take care of the sudden increase of customers following the immigration raid at nearby Howard Industries electronics plant on Monday. Several Hispanic-run, owned, or staffed businesses, including five of the city's six Mexican food restaurants, were closed as their mainly immigrant employees' feared returning to work after the raid. (AP Photo/Rogelio V. Solis)

For the past two years, the burrito chain Chipotle has been under scrutiny by immigration enforcement in several locations throughout the country including Minnesota, Virginia, and Washington. Raids on restaurants in these states have resulted in the firings of hundreds of undocumented workers. Unlike many other companies, Chipotle paid decent wages and offered opportunities for advancement to its undocumented employees.

In April 2011, 14 Chuy's chain restaurants were raided in California and Arizona through coordinated efforts by immigration enforcement. Forty-two undocumented workers were arrested during the raids. Thirteen of the workers were deported, and the others were permitted to remain in the United States as witnesses or were seeking legal status. The restaurant's owners Mark and Christopher Evenson were charged with tax fraud and harboring undocumented immigrants.

Undocumented employees working in Chuy's restaurants claimed that the owners treated them well and that they liked the company. One employee worked for the company for 14 years at $9.50 per hour for up to 70 hours per week (Preston, 2011). However, many undocumented workers earn minimum wage or less. One study found that

13 percent of restaurant workers earned below minimum wage, though this is likely an underestimate. Accepting low wages is one reason why undocumented workers are appealing to employers.

Deprivation of proper wages can occur by employers withholding wages entirely, paying well below minimum wage, or tampering with an employee's logged time in a practice known as "hour shaving." Fifty-nine percent of workers in one study were not paid for the overtime hours they had worked. In New York, 54 percent of restaurant employees work overtime, 48 percent work more than eight hours per day, and 12 percent work more than sixty hours per week. Furthermore, 90 percent of restaurant workers do not have health insurance. Thus, many individuals are deprived significantly of wages and benefits by dishonest employers.

To avoid cases like Chipotle and Chuy's, many states are requiring that employers use the federal electronic employment verification system, or E-Verify, which checks whether or not potential employees are authorized to work in the United States. The system is known to have several flaws which have proven problematic for immigrants, particularly Latino immigrants who are legally authorized to work. The current system disproportionately issues "tentative confirmation" notices to foreign-born employees, regardless of legal status, compared to native-born (National Council of La Raza, 2011). For example, the rate of database errors for naturalized citizens is thirty times the rate of errors for native-born citizens. Thus, many legally eligible workers are subject to delays in obtaining employment due to the ambiguous verification status assigned to them by the system. It is estimated that problems with E-Verify will impose challenges on more than 20.5 million immigrant Latinos, including workers and small business owners. E-Verify is also financially burdensome on employers.

Another process that the Social Security Administration uses to limit employment of undocumented workers is "no match" letters. These letters inform employers that some of their workers' social security numbers are invalid and that current employees must re-submit their social security numbers.

The National Restaurant Association advocates for immigration reform to make legal status for undocumented workers more attainable.

Courtney Waters

See Also: Domestic Work; Labor Supply; Landscaping Industry; Meat Processing Plants; Workplace Raids.

Further Reading

Kershaw, Sarah. 2010. "Immigration Crackdown Steps into the Kitchen." *New York Times,* September 8. http://www.nytimes.com/2010/09/08/dining/08crackdown.

National Council of La Raza. 2011. "The Impact of E-Verify on Latinos." http://www.nclr .org/images/uploads/pages/NCLRimpactofeverifyonLatinosfactsheet.pdf.

Pew Hispanic Center. 2006. "The Labor Force Status of Short-Term Unauthorized Workers." Fact Sheet. Pew Research Center Web Site. http://www.pewhispanic.org/2006/ 04/13/the-labor-force-status-of-short-term-unauthorized-workers/.

Preston, Julia. 2011. "A Crackdown on Employing Illegal Workers." *New York Times*, May 29. http://www.nytimes.com/2011/05/30/us/politics/30raid.html?pagewanted=all, 2011.

Restaurant Opportunities Center of New York and the New York City Restaurant Industry Coalition. 2005. "Behind the Kitchen Door: Pervasive Inequality in New York City's Thriving Restaurant Industry." http://www.urbanjustice.org/pdf/publications/BKD FinalReport.pdf.

Thompson, Gabriel. 2010. *Working in the Shadows: A Year of Doing the Jobs (Most) Americans Won't Do*. New York: Nation Books.

S

Salvadorans

According to the Pew Hispanic Center, roughly 1.6 million Hispanics of Salvadoran origin live in the United States. Of this 1.6 million, 65 percent were born in El Salvador and only 30 percent are U.S. citizens. Additionally, in a 2012 report the Department of Homeland Security estimated that as of 2011, 660,000 of Salvadorans are unauthorized residents. The Salvadoran population in the United States is fairly clustered, with nearly 40 percent living in California and roughly 14 percent living in Texas.

The remittances of Salvadoran migrants in the United States are a critical part of the Salvadoran economy. According to the country's central bank, Salvadorans working abroad sent home about $3 billion in 2005, a sum equivalent to 15 percent of the country's GDP. Despite the poor economic conditions in the United States and worldwide, the amount of remittances was $3.66 billion in 2011, according to the World Bank (2012). Because of the size and economic importance of the Salvadoran population in the United States, the United States is frequently referred to as El Salvador's Fifteenth Department (or state).

The largest single cause of Salvadoran migration to the United States was the 1980–1992 civil war, which wreaked havoc on the country and cost the lives of roughly seventy-five thousand people. Systematic human rights violations, most infamously the murders of Archbishop Oscar Romero and four U.S. church workers in March and December of 1980 respectively, were extremely common. After the war, the Salvadoran Truth Commission found that government forces and their paramilitary allies had committed 95 percent of these crimes. Despite reports of such human rights violations, the United States provided the Salvadoran government with $6 billion in economic and military aid over the course of the conflict. At the heart of the conflict were massive wealth and land ownership inequalities, features of El Salvadoran society that remain largely unchanged today. At the start of the war, the country's powerful Fourteen Families controlled 60 percent of arable land, all of the banking system, and most industry.

During the twelve-year war, one of the longest in recent Latin American history, more than 1 million Salvadorans fled for the United States. Because the amnesty provisions of the 1986 Immigration Reform and Control Act (IRCA) only applied to migrants who had been living in the country continuously since 1982, asylum was the only option for most Salvadoran refugees to regularize their status. However, most Salvadorans (and Guatemalans) who applied for political asylum status were largely unsuccessful, and they were not granted refugee status by the U.S. government, despite the 1980 Refugee Act that was passed to ease the application process for asylum seekers. Whereas large percentages of applicants from countries with hostile relations to the United States were approved, only 3 percent of Salvadorans were approved for asylum between 1983 and 1986. Scholars and historians point to the United States' active support of the Salvadoran right-wing government's policies as a reason for this high rate of rejection.

This tense situation gave birth to the Sanctuary Movement, a network of religious congregations that openly defied the U.S. government by providing sanctuary to Salvadoran and Guatemalan refugees who fled their countries. Between 1960 and 1996, Guatemala also suffered a long and bloody civil war in which roughly two hundred thousand were killed and tens of thousands disappeared.

The first meeting of the Sanctuary Movement was held by Quakers and Presbyterians living in Tucson in 1980. In 1985, the federal government charged fourteen sanctuary activists in Tucson with alien smuggling and conspiracy. Most of the accused were convicted, but none served prison time. In response, sympathetic lawyers filed a class-action lawsuit on behalf of Sanctuary congregations that was known as *American Baptist Churches v. Thornburgh (ABC)*. The suit demanded an end to prosecution of Sanctuary activists, as well as an end to discriminatory treatment of Central American asylum seekers. The government settled the case in 1991 and as a result, numerous asylum cases were opened or reopened, and the U.S. government pledged to not let foreign policy considerations affect asylum applications.

Shortly before this settlement and partially in response to ongoing human rights abuses in El Salvador and Guatemala, the U.S. Congress passed the Immigration Act of 1990. The bill granted 18-month Temporary Protected Status (TPS) to Salvadorans and approximately 187,000 applied for it. Many of these applicants subsequently applied to have their asylum cases reviewed under the terms of the *ABC* settlement, though extreme backlogs kept many applicants in legal limbo. Because they had pending asylum cases, applicants were unable to apply for family member visas or accrue time in the United States toward becoming naturalized citizens. However, for those Salvadorans covered under the *ABC* settlement, relief came with the 1997 Nicaraguan Adjustment and Central American Relief Act, which allowed them to finally apply for legal permanent residence.

Following the signing of the Peace Accords in El Salvador in 1992, applying for asylum has become much more difficult. Additionally, the mid-1990s saw the passage of numerous restrictive immigration policies, most importantly the 1996 Illegal Immigration Reform and Immigrant Responsibility Act (IIRIRA), as well as increased border and interior immigration enforcement. Following a series of earthquakes in El Salvador in early 2001, TPS was again granted to many Salvadorans through March 2005.

Because of ongoing inequality and other economic and social problems, Salvadorans are still leaving their country in large numbers, though now without the possibility of asylum. While open warfare may have ended, El Salvador remains a very poor and violent country, with intentional homicide rates bested only by neighboring Honduras worldwide.

One of the consequences of increased immigration enforcement has been the deportation of Central American gang members living in the United States. The most famous of these gangs are the Mara Salvatrucha (MS and MS-13) and Barrio 18, both of which started in Los Angeles. Barrio 18 emerged in the 1980s and was largely founded by Mexican-Americans, though open to Central Americans; while MS-13 was formed in the early 1990s by Salvadorans.

Starting in 1992, the Immigration and Naturalization Service (INS) started deporting suspected gang members to their countries of origin, and one of the consequences has been rising gang violence in Central America. Central American governments have responded to gangs with harsh anti-crime measures such as Operation *Mano Dura* (Heavy Hand) in El Salvador.

Murphy Woodhouse

See Also: Central American Civil Wars; Guatemalans; Hondurans; Nicaraguan Adjustment and Central American Relief Act (NACARA); Refugee Act (1980); Refugees.

Further Reading

Coutin, Susan B. 2007. *Nations of Emigrants: Shifting Boundaries of Citizenship in El Salvador and the United States.* Ithaca, NY: Cornell University Press.

García, María C. 2006. *Seeking Refuge: Central American Migration to Mexico, the United States, and Canada.* Berkeley: University of California Press.

Savenije, Wim. 2007. "Las Pandillas Trasnacionales O 'maras': Violencia Urbana en Centroamerica." *Foro Internacional.*

World Bank. 2012. "Migration and Remittances Data." Bilateral Remittance Matrix. http://econ.worldbank.org/WBSITE/EXTERNAL/EXTDEC/EXTDECPROSPECTS/0,contentMDK:22759429~pagePK:64165401~piPK:64165026~theSitePK:476883,00.html#Remittances.

Sanctuary Cities and Secure Communities

Sanctuary cities and the Department of Homeland Security Program are of tremendous relevance to the subject of undocumented immigrants in the United States. Both represent the tension between local and federal governments regarding the enforcement of federal immigration policies and local efforts to integrate immigrants into U.S. communities and increase safety. They also represent the tension between immigrant welcoming policies of some states and cities and increasingly punitive federal immigration policies as a result of the post–September 11, 2001 realignment of the U.S. immigration system to focus on national security and enforcement through intelligence gathering, data sharing, and detention and removal (Mittelstadt et al., 2011).

Sanctuary Cities

Sanctuary cities are municipalities that have policies and /or practices that in general ask city employees to refrain from actions that can contribute to the deportation of

Immigrant Francisco Barranco, right, stands in his bakery La Tapatia, as employee Lorena Vasquez prepares gelatin in the Fair Haven neighborhood in New Haven, Connecticut, 2011. John DeStefano, the 10-term mayor of New Haven, helped undocumented immigrants come out of the shadows five years ago with an ID card program. When he pledged recently to seek authorization for non-citizens to vote in local elections, it endeared him further to the city's large Hispanic population and solidified New Haven's reputation as a sanctuary city. (AP Photo/Jessica Hill)

undocumented immigrants in their community (Kittrie, 2006). Cities with formal sanctuary policies generally instruct city employees and agencies to neither make inquiries about the immigration status of individuals seeking services or the protection of its laws, nor report on the immigration status of the individual to the Department of Homeland Security's (DHS) Immigration and Customs Enforcement (ICE), nor use city resources to enforce federal immigrant legislation. These policies can be adopted at local or state levels and take the form of statutes, ordinances, resolutions or executive orders (Sullivan, 2009). Kittrie (2006) asserts that contemporary sanctuary policies come in three forms: "don't ask," don't inform," and "don't tell." More specifically, Kittrie (2006:1455) states that sanctuary policies generally specify that local law enforcement officers do one or more of the following: "(1) limit inquiries about a person's immigration status unless investigating illegal activity other than mere status as an unauthorized alien ('don't ask'); (2) limit arrests or detentions for violation of immigration laws ('don't enforce'); and (3) limit provision to federal authorities of immigration status information ('don't tell')."

The first local sanctuary policy was established on 1979 in Los Angeles. This policy was a result of the confluence of a number of factors, including growing complexity of federal immigration policy, rising numbers of undocumented immigrants, and increasing sensitivity towards minority communities resulting from the civil rights movement (Sullivan, 2009). The Los Angeles Police Department (LAPD) policy known as Special Order 40 had the goal of improving community relations and cooperation between the LAPD and minority communities and stated that "undocumented alien status itself is not a matter for police action" and that police personnel will not initiate an interaction with the purpose of determining immigration status, nor will they arrest anyone for illegal entry into the United States if their immigration status is revealed. In subsequent years more cities adopted sanctuary policies. This growth has been associated with the sanctuary movement of religious congregations that in the 1980s provided support and protection to Salvadorans and Guatemalans who were fleeing violence and political unrest, but were not granted refugee status by the U.S. government. These congregations offered food, shelter, and support of humanitarian concerns and solidarity with the Salvadoran and Guatemalan immigrants in protest to U.S. policy (Sullivan, 2009).

As the Central American civil wars ended in the 1990s, the Sanctuary Movement was largely inactive from the mid 1990s until the early 2000s when the movement experienced a resurgence in response to the expanded authority offered to local law enforcement following the terrorist attacks of September 11, 2001 (Sullivan, 2009). The majority of the nation's largest cities now have some form of sanctuary policy, a trend that has accelerated rapidly in the last decade (Kittrie, 2006). Presently, there are more than seventy cities and states that have adopted policies that prevent police agencies from asking community residents that have not been arrested to prove their immigration status (Waslin, 2011).

Secure Communities

Currently, the viability of local sanctuary policies is threatened by federal immigration initiatives. The most prominent threat to state and municipal sanctuary policies is the Department of Homeland Security (DHS) Secure Communities initiative launched in 2008 in select jurisdictions. The Secure Communities initiative is the U.S. Immigration and Customs Enforcement (ICE) strategy to increase information sharing between federal agencies and improve the system capacity to identify and remove criminal aliens from the United States. According to the DHS website, the program prioritizes the removal of criminal aliens whose presence poses a threat to public safety, and those that have repeated immigration violations. DHS states that this goal is achieved through the cross-agency sharing of already existing databases. Under the Secure Communities program ICE and the Federal Bureau of Investigation (FBI) form an information-sharing partnership. Since the secure communities program was initiated in 2008 to May 31, 2012, ICE reports that it has identified and deported 147,000 convicted criminal aliens (Department of Homeland Security, 2012).

The ICE website focuses on the federal data sharing and states that the program does not impose new or additional requirements on state and local law enforcement, which routinely share the fingerprints of individuals who are arrested or taken into custody with the FBI to execute criminal background checks. Under Secure Communities, the FBI automatically sends the fingerprints to ICE to check against its immigration databases to identify those that are unlawfully present in the United States or are removable due to a criminal conviction (Department of Homeland Security, 2012). The immigration databases utilized by ICE in this program are the U.S. Visitor and Immigrant Status Indicator Technology Program (US-VISIT), and the Automated Biometric Identification System (IDENT). US-Visit was implemented in 2003 and is one of the most visible post-9/11 travel-control initiatives of the federal government to address security concerns (Mittelstadt et al., 2011). Under US-VISIT, the federal government collects biometric information of all noncitizens entering the country by air or seaports, as well as certain land-border travelers, to deter the entry of those deemed ineligible or a security threat. Under this initiative, ten-fingerprint scans and photographs are taken and stored in IDENT, a database that contains more than 108 million individual records and is interoperable with the FBI's Integrated Automated Fingerprint Identification System, IAFIS (Mittelstadt al., 2011). IAFIS is the world's largest biometric database, containing the fingerprints and criminal histories for more than 70 million individuals in the criminal master file and more than 31 million civil prints.

When the data sharing yields a match, ICE may choose to place a detainer on the individual, a request for the jail to hold that person for up to forty-eight hours beyond the scheduled release date, so that ICE can take custody and initiate deportation proceedings. Immigrants can be subject to a detainer regardless of whether they are in jail for a serious violent crime, for a misdemeanor, a traffic violation or even as victims or witnesses to crimes in situations in which it is unclear who the perpetrator is and the police arrest both.

As of June 5, 2012, the Secure Communities program has been activated in 3,074 jurisdictions in fifty states, four territories and Washington D.C. (Department of Homeland Security, 2012). ICE plans to implement the program in the remaining twenty-six state and local jails across the nation to achieve full participation by 2013. Since the inception of the program, ICE has provided vague, misleading, and even contradictory statements regarding the autonomy of states, cities, and local law enforcement agencies in making decisions regarding participation in the secure communities program. Initially, ICE indicated that localities could opt out or decline participation in the program, thereby respecting sanctuary policies of local communities and states. In its initial implementation, ICE entered into Memoranda of Agreement (MOAs) with State Identification Bureaus, the agency responsible for data sharing between the state and the federal government. It was understood that states had the option to decline entering into a Memorandum of Agreement (MOA), or to terminate the MOA if they no longer wanted to participate in the program. However, ICE has subsequently announced that it had withdrawn all existing MOAs with states, that MOAs are not necessary, and that ICE would unilaterally proceed with the program's expansion to full participation by 2013 (Department of Homeland Security, 2012).

Continuing Controversy

While some localities have voluntarily participated in the Secure Communities program, others have resisted participation. The implementation of Secure Communities presents significant concrete and ethical concerns, as well as legal issues. In particular, cities with sanctuary policies and strong community policing have challenged implementation in their jurisdiction. The legal concern is fundamentally a federalist issue regarding the boundaries between national and local powers and the extent to which Congress can require compliance with its mandates.

In addition to state and local law enforcement agencies, civil liberties groups and immigration advocates have raised a number of practical and ethical concerns with the program. Some of the concerns include: 1) the program encourages racial profiling and pretextual arrests that target immigrants; 2) the program burdens local police and jails; 3) the program may undermine community trust that is essential for community policing and for victims to report crime and help with prosecution; 4) a general lack of congruence with the stated goal of targeting individuals charged or convicted of serious criminal offenses; 5) the lack of oversight and transparency; and 6) the lack of a clear complaint mechanism or redress procedure for individuals erroneously identified by DHS databases or subject to a detainer issued in error (Waslin, 2011).

Maria Vidal de Haymes and Stephen Haymes

See Also: Immigration and Customs Enforcement (ICE); Incarceration; Laws and Legislation, Post-1980s; Policy and Political Action; Racial Profiling; Sanctuary Movement.

Further Reading

Department of Homeland Security Immigration and Customs Enforcement. 2012. "Secure Communities." http://www.ice.gov/secure_communities/.

Kittrie, Orde F. 2006. "Federalism, Deportation, and Crime Victims Afraid to Call the Police. *Iowa Law Review* 91:1449–1508.

Mittlestadt, Michelle, Burke Speaker, Doris Meissner, and Muzaffar Chishti. 2011. "Through the Prism of National Security: Major Immigration Policy and Program Changes in the Decade Since 9/11." Migration Policy Institute, August. http://www.migrationpolicy.org/pubs/FS23_Post-9-11policy.pdf.

Sullivan, Laura. 2009. "Enforcing Nonenforcement: Countering the Threat Posed to Sanctuary Laws by the Inclusion of Immigration Records in the National Crime Information Center Database." 97 *Cal. L. Rev.* 567. http://scholarship.law.berkeley.edu/californialawreview/vol97/iss2/7.

Waslin, Michele. 2011. "The Secure Communities Program: Unanswered Questions and Continuing Concerns." Immigration Policy Institute, November. http://immigration-policy.org/special-reports/secure-communities-program-unanswered-questions-and-continuing-concerns.

Sanctuary Movement

The Sanctuary Movement, a loose network of churches, synagogues, community activists and individuals, emerged in Tucson, Arizona, in the early 1980s to defend Central American refugees fleeing the civil wars in El Salvador and Guatemala.

Organizations already existed in solidarity with the popular forces in Central America and in opposition to United States policy supporting the totalitarian military regimes in power. The open brutality of the assassination of Monsignor Oscar Romero, the Sumpul River massacre and the murder of four American religious women all in 1980 spurred growing discontent with United States policy in Central America. In the same year in July, a group of twenty-four Salvadorans crossed into the Arizona desert from Mexico and twelve died, a tragedy which captured national and international media attention. In Tucson, church and secular groups rallied to provide legal, medical, and material support to the survivors.

About sixty miles from the border with Mexico, migrants crossing into the area historically used the Tucson barrios, Mexican/Chicano neighborhoods clustered in the south and west sides, for safe haven and as a gateway in their journey. The world of undocumented workers was familiar in the barrios for they were neighbors, family members, and a familiar part of the border region experience. Since the early 1970s on, the Westside in Barrio Hollywood, El Concilio Manzo, a grassroots organization, had provided direct services and advocacy for immigrants, focusing especially on the defense of undocumented workers.

After the July 1980 tragedy El Concilio Manzo logically became the center for legal representation and other services for Salvadorans and Guatemalan refugees. Because of limited resources, by the spring of 1981 Manzo sought out other concerned groups and individuals to help and thus the future Sanctuary founding members came together, including participants in Nogales, Arizona, and Sonora, Mexico. Most were from churches, synagogues, Quaker meetings and interested activists. These individuals melded into the faith-based group centered at Southside Presbyterian Church in Tucson that gave form to the Sanctuary Movement.

On March 23, 1982, the Sanctuary Movement was formally announced from Southside Presbyterian Church. Five other churches in California also joined. Sanctuary, according to those who made the call, was based in Judeo-Christian biblical teachings and tradition to provide for "the alien, the stranger." The Sanctuary founders considered their act to stand with the oppressed, the poor, the refugees, as a moral imperative which could only be carried out collectively and where decisions were reached by consensus.

A letter was sent to the Justice Department stating that in summarily deporting Central American refugees, the United States was violating the Refugee Act of 1980 and the international laws regulating the treatment of refugees, persons fleeing for their lives as a result of political, social and/or religious persecutions. Therefore, the simple objective of Sanctuary was to save lives by helping refugees find safe haven from where they would speak truth to power, tell their story(ies) of what was happening in El Salvador and Guatemala. Sanctuary volunteers were asked to 1) interview the refugee(s) in Mexico, 2) make arrangements to have them taken to the border, 3) cross them over, 4) drive them to Tucson, and 5) place them in sanctuary throughout the country.

The national media responded with great interest to the idea of ordinary Americans assisting undocumented persons cross the border and then placing them in sanctuary throughout the United States. The United States government considered Sanctuary volunteers to be law breakers because they were violating specific federal laws to help "illegals" who were simply looking for work, and there was no legal basis for sanctuary. The Sanctuary volunteers saw themselves acting in accordance with the 1980 Refugee Act and international laws. Moreover they believed they were following the law of God. The policy of the Reagan administration was clear: the totalitarian military regimes of El Salvador and Guatemala must be supported at all costs and their opposition had to be eliminated.

As the Sanctuary Movement grew, differing views emerged in which one side, led by the Chicago Religious Task Force, wanted to focus more on the role of the United States and a clear commitment to the popular forces. The Tucson founding group argued that to focus on partisan politics would distort the moral dimensions of sanctuary. The different perspectives were discussed at the Inter-American Symposium on Sanctuary held in Tucson on January 23–24, 1985. Several prominent national and international theologians, scholars, and activists discussed the basis of sanctuary. With the arrests of volunteers in Texas and Arizona throughout 1984, interest heightened and over 1500 persons attended the symposium.

The Reagan administration believed the Sanctuary Movement was simply using religion to advance an entirely political agenda in support of communist subversives. Therefore the government planted informants into the movement and with their gathered information indictments were issued for the arrests of sixteen Sanctuary volunteers in Arizona. Twelve volunteers were brought to trial which lasted from October 22, 1985 to April 17, 1986. The jury returned verdicts of guilty for nine and not guilty for three of the indicted. On July 1, 1986, everyone found guilty was given a suspended sentence ranging from three to five years.

After the trial the Sanctuary Movement continued, but by 1991 the Sanctuary as a social movement had ended. Several events had occurred: immigration reform passed in 1986 and many Central Americans qualified for amnesty, political asylum was granted more frequently by 1987, Temporary Protective Status became available to Central American refugees, and a federal court decision declared that worship services could not be infiltrated. Legal and social service centers for Central Americans run by refugees themselves became established throughout the country.

In the years that followed, several faith-based organizations in Tucson and throughout the United States were established by former Sanctuary volunteers to stop the increasing migrant deaths by direct assistance to migrants at the increasingly militarized U.S.-Mexican border and out in the desert, to stop deportations of families by again providing sanctuary and to provide other services. These efforts have become known as the New Sanctuary Movement, faith-based and committed to civil initiative, the idea of community doing justice, openly, in dialogue and in consensus as was practiced by the Sanctuary Movement. One example is the No More Deaths/*No Mas Muertes* organization, founded by a Unitarian church in Tucson, which continues today.

Guadalupe Castillo

See Also: Activism; Advocacy; Faith-Based Organizations; Guatemalans; Policy and Political Action; Refugee Act (1980); Refugees; Religion; Salvadorans; Sanctuary Cities and Secure Communities.

Further Reading

Corbett, Jim. 1991. *Goatwalking: A Guide to Wildland Living. A Quest for the Peaceable Kingdom.* New York: Viking Penguin.

Corbett, Jim. 2005. *Sanctuary for Life: The Cowbalah of Jim Corbett.* Berthold, CO: Howling Dog Press.

MacEoin, Gary, ed. 1985. *Sanctuary: A Resource Guide for Understanding and Participating in the Central American Refugees' Struggle.* San Francisco, CA: Harper and Row.

Otter, Elna, and Dorothy Pine. 2004. *The Sanctuary Experience: Voices of the Community.* San Diego: Aventine Press.

Select Commission on Immigration and Refugee Policy

The Select Commission on Immigration and Refugee Policy was a special committee established in 1978 by the Congress of the United States to find solutions to the increasing numbers of immigrants to the United States. Its purpose was to analyze existing laws and trends regarding immigrants and refugees and make subsequent recommendations regarding their admissions. The first commission convened in 1978, and on March 1, 1981, the first of its reports was issued. The commission is known for a series of reports on the status of immigrants and refugees in the United States that were influential in determining subsequent policies. The first report, *Restoring Credibility*, was issued in 1981; the second, *Setting Priorities,* was issued in 1995; the third, *Taking Leadership,* and fourth, *Becoming American,* were both issued in 1997. With these four reports, the Commission's work was completed.

Many of the recommendations found in these reports would have direct implications for the lives of refugees and immigrants in the United States for decades to come. Many of the recommendations were incorporated into policy measures as immigration reform and refugee policies were considered. Much of the Commission's efforts to gather information on immigrants and refugees and its subsequent analysis provided important insights that were used by U.S. lawmakers to draft legacy legislation, and in this way they influenced the nation's demographic make-up in the coming years. Some of these recommendations provided the framework for policy matters and in fact found their way into the provisions that appeared later in the Immigration Control and Reform Act of 1986, the Immigration Act of 1990, the Personal Responsibility and Work Opportunity Reconciliation Act (PRWORA) of 1996, and the Illegal Immigration Reform and Immigrant Responsibility Act (IIRIRA) also of 1996 (Ortiz, 1998).

The Commission was largely in response to an increasing number of legal immigrants as well as apprehended undocumented migrants in the 1970s. The number of undocumented migrants had tripled since 1965, with four out of these five migrants coming from Mexico. In 1972, the Immigration and Naturalization Service (now the Department of Homeland Security) published a report stating that unauthorized immigration had increased to over 1 million, which many called "out of control." In 1975, a bill was introduced by the U.S. House of Representatives that imposed sanctions on employers that knowingly hired undocumented immigrants. At that time, President

Gerald R. Ford established the Domestic Council Committee on Illegal Aliens. The council committee then released a report stating that undocumented migrants were the force that drove down wages of low-skilled workers. Furthermore, the council committee recommended increased sanctions for employers who knowingly hired undocumented migrants as well as increased punishments for smugglers that assisted undocumented migrants in crossing the U.S. border. However, Congress was not satisfied with these recommendations and proposals and decided to create another committee to take a look at other possible solutions, and therefore the law was passed in 1978 to create the Select Commission on Immigration and Refugee Policy.

The Commission was comprised of sixteen people, including four members of the U.S. Senate, four members from the U.S. House of Representatives, four members of the general public, and four cabinet members: the Attorney General, the Secretary of Health and Human Services, the Secretary of Labor, and the Secretary of State. Furthermore, staff members, consultants, and witnesses assisted the sixteen members in compiling the report. The interim report released in 1981 concerned three overarching issues—refugees, legal immigration, and illegal immigration.

Portions of the reports that concern refugees mainly addressed the large influx of refugees that had recently been admitted to the United States. The commission considered the issue of mass amounts of asylum seekers and called for a quick and thorough review of any requests for asylum to determine if the individual met the mentioned criteria. Furthermore, it came to the conclusion that the United States should deport all those who do not meet the established criteria for refugee status. This was recommended so that the United States did not appear to accept any form of unauthorized entry. In order to ensure that the process of determining refugee status was fair and expeditious, the Commission called for a body of several agencies to deal with the processing of large numbers of asylum requests in the future, as well as group profiles to help determine refugee status.

The Commission took into account the refugee resettlement process when issuing its final report and recommended that refugees be encouraged to cluster in communities instead of disperse, which had typically proved to be unsuccessful in the past. The report mentioned that the clustering would help ease refugees into the community via more experienced refugees and that it would be more cost-efficient to serve larger and more concentrated refugee populations. However, critics pointed out that this poses a problem if there is large economic competition within that community.

On the topic of legal immigration, the Commission regarded a range of topics. The Commission reviewed the overall impact of undocumented immigration as a whole, including factors such as wages, unemployment, and its cost to social service. Other issues included worksite enforcement, border security, and assimilation and what it meant "to be American" (in its fourth and final report). The Commission warned that there had to be some limits on immigration. The Commission further proposed that legal immigration should be divided by two categories, one for immigrants that were being reunited with family members already residing within the United States and one for immigrants with no family members in the United States. The Commission further agreed on the following categories for exemption from quotas: children, siblings, parents, spouses, and grandparents of U.S. citizens.

The issue of illegal immigration was of primary importance for the Select Commission. The Commission found that, based on public opinion polls, the majority of the public wanted to restrict unauthorized immigration. Finally, the work of the Commission advised against a large-scale temporary guestworker program, recommending instead increased enforcement for unauthorized entrants, while recommending amnesty for certain migrants that entered legally before 1980. The latter was incorporated as part of the 1986 IRCA, where amnesty was provided to qualified undocumented immigrants. As part of these recommendations, it was the Commission's opinion that the enforcement against illegal immigration should include tougher sanctions for employers who knowingly hired undocumented migrants (also adopted in IRCA), a better system for distinguishing workers with and without documents, and more Border Patrol agents, as well as better equipment and training.

Jenna Glickman

See Also: Illegal Immigration Reform and Immigrant Responsibility Act (IIRIRA) (1996); Immigration Act (IMMACT) (1990); Immigration Reform and Control Act (IRCA) (1986); Personal Responsibility and Work Opportunity Reconciliation Act (PRWORA) (1996); Policy and Political Action.

Further Reading

Briggs, Vernon M., Jr. 1982. "Report of the Select Commission on Immigration and Refugee Policy: A Critique." *Cornell Faculty Publication—Human Resource Studies* 36:1–6.
Fragomen, Austin T., Jr. 1981. "The Final Report and Recommendations of the Select Commission on Immigration and Refugee Policy: A Summary." *International Migration Review* 15.4:758–768. http://www.jstor.org/stable/2545523?seq=1.
Martin, Philip L. 1982. "Select Commission Suggests Changes in Immigration Policy—A Review Essay." *Monthly Labor Review Online* 105:31–37.
Ortiz Miranda, Carlos. 1998. "United States Commission on Immigration Reform: The Interim and Final Reports." *Santa Clara Law* 38.3. http://digital-commons.law.scu.edu/cgi/viewcontent.cgi?article=1439&context=lawreview.
Vialet, Joyce. 1980. "A Brief History of U.S. Immigration Policy." *Congressional Research Service* 80–223:28–30.

Seniors

Today people are living longer lives than before. There are elderly immigrants, both legal and undocumented, from many countries living in the United States and the past three decades have seen a dramatic rise in the number of older immigrants. According to the Migration Policy Institute (Batalova, 2012), the number of senior immigrants (those age 65 and over) doubled between 1990 and 2010, from 2.7 million to nearly 5 million. These seniors now account for 12 percent of the 40 million immigrants in the United States. There are two explanations given for this rise in the senior immigrant population. First is that the number of working-age adults who arrived during

Table 1: Top 10 Countries of Origin of Older Immigrants in the United States in 2012.

Country of Origin	Number	Percent of Total
Mexico	735,000	15
Cuba	301,000	6
Philippines	290,000	6
China/Hong Kong	277,000	6
Germany	243,000	5
Canada	204,000	4
Italy	172,000	3
India	165,000	3
South Korea	144,000	3
Vietnam	142,000	3
Total	2,673,000	

Data taken from Batalova, 2012. "Senior Immigrants in the United States." Migration Policy Institute, May, 2012. Available at http://www.migrationinformation.org/usfocus/display.cfm?ID=894#9

the 1980s and the 1990s are just now reaching their senior years. Although there are still not too many in this cohort of immigrants, their numbers are expected to go up in the next several years. Second, immigrants who have become citizens or legal permanent residents have been able to sponsor their parents to come to the United States. According to the Office of Immigration Statistics, U.S. Department of Homeland Security (Hoeffer et al., 2012), of the approximately 11 million unauthorized immigrants living in the United States in 2011, 1.3 million individuals were ages forty-five to fifty-four, and another half million were fifty-five and older. Most of the elderly immigrants in the United States come from Mexico, paralleling general immigration patterns (Table 1).

The elderly undocumented are certain to face challenges in staying healthy while living in the United States. Unauthorized immigrants are currently not eligible for Medicaid, nor will they be eligible under the new Affordable Care Act (also known as Obamacare), but will remain eligible for emergency care under Medicaid. Many of these aging adults live in poverty. In the case of Mexican aging migrants this can affect both sides of the border. It is unknown if Mexico's health care infrastructure would be able to handle all the returning aging seniors from the United States if it needed to. Mexico has no public system of social security or health insurance for the non-wage-earning elderly, leaving it unable to cope with thousands of returning immigrants who spent their working lives in the United States (Porter, 2005).

Because undocumented immigrants are forced to accept jobs that are physically difficult and unsafe, they do not have the life expectancy that U.S.- born citizens have. In 2011, 4,609 workers were killed on the job, of whom 729 were Latino workers. Fatalities in construction—a sector in which Latino immigrants predominate—accounted for 17.5 percent of the total work-related deaths in 2011. Of the 729 fatal work injuries involving Hispanic or Latino workers, 500 (or 69 percent) involved foreign-born workers. Overall, there were 823 fatal work injuries involving foreign-born workers in 2011, of which the greatest share (338 or 41 percent) were born in Mexico (OSHA 2012).

Years toiling as agricultural and construction workers also have a long-term physical impact on both body and health that may result in premature death (Triplett, 2004). In 2003 a fifty-three-year-old farm worker collapsed after picking crops in the San Joaquin Valley, California. His boss did not call for an ambulance or request any medical attention. He told a family member to take him home where he died. Many years of working in the heat can debilitate the overall health of an immigrant. Because of their immigration status, undocumented immigrants are less likely to have health insurance that would prevent and treat many chronic illnesses (e.g. diabetes, high blood pressure, obesity) that if not attended to, can have an impact on their health as they age. The high cost of medical care thus prohibits them from meeting their most basic primary healthcare needs—such as routine checkups and health screens—that might extend life expectancy and improve the quality of life as they age.

Low-skilled, poorly paid immigrants may live in substandard housing, which over time can cause disease and sicknesses to the aging adults. Aging adults may have faced years of fear of deportation, contributing to stress-related illnesses, or in fact may face deportation still. They have not been able to relax and enjoy a sense of retirement as many aging citizens and legal residents can afford to enjoy. They are often living in poverty and cannot afford medical insurances that might provide them with elder care programs and support.

Other challenges to seniors are financial in nature. Many immigrants have worked within the United Stated for many years but economic and financial instability likely results in little wealth accumulation. Many if not most have paid taxes over their working lives to Social Security and Medicare through wage contributions, but under current law, they are not entitled to benefits (Porter, 2005).

In the case of the Mexican immigrant elderly, exposure of younger generations to American culture has weakened Latinos' tendency to care for their family members. One possible explanation for this trend is that those likely to care for the elderly, second and third generations of immigrants, are constrained by poverty, making it necessary for more family members to work. In other words, there may be no one home to care for an aging adult. Thus, even when desiring to care for their elders, adult children caregivers are kept from doing so, significantly distorting cultural norms toward elders (Kao, 2012). Similarly, Yoo and Zippay (2012) found that for elderly Korean immigrants in the U.S., neighbors, senior centers, and public assistance were primary sources of support. Children and spouses were less frequent primary sources of support. Most Korean elderly are first-generation immigrants who adhere closely to traditional cultural beliefs, so they may encounter multiple adjustment problems in the United States, including language barriers, lack of transportation, and isolation. In most cases, regardless of ethnic background, elderly immigrants benefit from social networks in the form of personal acquaintances and organizational affiliations, and social capital that can provide them with access to information, other contacts, and relational ties that are fundamental to emotional and physical well-being.

The inability to invest in a future in the United States foments transnationalism among aging undocumented populations. Transnationalism allows immigrants to be actively connected to both communities of origin and destination. Almost half of Mexican immigrants older than fifty own property in Mexico, and as many as 58 percent of immigrants older than fifty have spouses waiting for them back home (Porter, 2005). Before the hardening of border enforcement, the maintenance of family ties was easier, resulting in more immigrants returning periodically to be reunited with family members in the United States. In the case of Mexican elderly undocumented populations, if they stay in the United States after they are unable to work, there will be a social cost: a burden to be shouldered by family members present in the United States; or they may return home, having spent their youth and productive best days laboring in the United States.

Drew Berns

See Also: Barriers to Health; Culture; Families; Family Structure; Health and Welfare; Social Security; Transnationalism; Workplace Injury.

Further Reading

Batalova, Jeanne. 2012. "Senior Immigrants in the United States." Migration Policy Institute. May, 2012. http://www.migrationinformation.org/usfocus/display.cfm?ID=894#9

Hoeffer, Michael, Nancy Rytina, and Brian Baker. 2012. "Estimates of the Unauthorized Immigrant Population Residing in the United States, January 2011." Office of Immigration Statistics, U.S. Department of Homeland Security. http://www.dhs.gov/xlibrary/assets/statistics/publications/ois_ill_pe_2011.pdf.

Kao, Hsueh-Fen S., and Kyungeh An. 2012. "Effect of Acculturation and Mutuality on Family Loyalty Among Mexican American Caregivers of Elders." *Journal of Nursing Scholarship* 44.2:111–119.

OSHA (Occupational and Safety Health Administration). 2012. "Workplace Injury, Illness and Fatality Statistics." Department of Labor. http://stats.bls.gov/news.release/archives/cfoi_09202012.htm.

Porter, Eduardo. 2005. "Aging Immigrants Could Strain Two Countries." *New York Times,* August 4, 2005. http://www.nytimes.com/2005/08/03/business/worldbusiness/03iht-retire.html?pagewanted=all.

Triplett, William. 2004. "Migrant Farm Workers: Is the Government Doing Enough to Protect Them?" *CQ Researcher* 14:829–852.

Yoo, Jeong Ah, and Allison Zippay. 2012. "Social Networks among Lower Income Korean Elderly Immigrants in the U.S." *Journal of Aging Studies* 26.3:368–376.

Shadow Population

The term "shadow population" has been used by urban planners to refer to non-permanent populations that are unregulated (such as work camps), often near and around cities. However, with greater frequency the term has come to describe the 10 to 12 million undocumented immigrants who because of their undocumented immigrant status are permanently barred from legally residing in the United States. Moreover, because they are always at risk of deportation, they cannot be considered to be permanently settled. Living as a shadow population in this way presents a paradox of sorts. Increased poverty in their country of origin dissuades most from returning. Increased border enforcement also makes cyclical migration more difficult and even deadly. For practical intent and purposes, their settlement in the United States is in fact permanent, while remaining unlawful. This kind of reality has in recent years been the subject of much debate because although the existence of the undocumented population remains outside the legal framework that regulates and governs society—in a way invisible within the legal system—the fact that it continues to exist and in many tangible ways, complicates and obfuscates the legal, social, and economic reality of the nation.

Some immigration scholars trace the emergence of the undocumented immigrant "shadow population" back to the 1986 Immigration Reform and Control Act (IRCA). This measure provided for a path to citizenship for about three million of the five million undocumented immigrants that were present in the country at that time in exchange for harsher measures to restrict their incorporation into the United States. IRCA was notable for its sanctions by way of jail time and fines for employers who knowingly hired undocumented workers. Because of opposition from employers, lawmakers had to modify these enforcement provisions, which made the 1986 law weak. Employers were loath to submit to even the weakest of enforcement measures, and in practice the U.S. government could not enforce the provisions, leaving them largely ignored. At the same time, because of the law, undocumented immigrants became fearful of being arrested, driving them further into the shadows. This development was complicated by the production of false documents to present to potential employers. With this growing trend in the use of fraudulent documents, immigrants assumed greater engagement in unlawful and deportable activity. New identities allowed them to work and pay taxes, but did not legalize their presence. Moreover, the proliferation of fraudulent documents weakened the government's ability to make an accurate accounting of their presence. In this way those not officially authorized to work and therefore not legally in the United States found employment in a host of other low-skilled and low-wage jobs, in restaurants, construction, garment factories, agricultural fields, hotel service industries, and meat packing industries.

Because it is against the law to hire undocumented immigrants, this population remains in the shadows. They are unable to report abuses or unsafe working conditions, so this information is inaccurate at best, and at worse, unknowable. A 2006 Pew Hispanic Center study reports that approximately 2 million undocumented workers are employed in construction where many if not most of the occupational workforce hazards exist. Meat packing jobs in America's slaughterhouses are also notoriously hazardous. However, as long as the injury suffered by these workers remains unreported, any attempt to come up with accurate numbers is thwarted. Employers will not want to expose themselves or their business to legal scrutiny and in this way risk their livelihood. At the same time, unreported hours benefit employers, allowing them to routinely evade payroll taxes because they may be paying undocumented workers "under the table." Unscrupulous employers may also engage in wage theft by issuing paychecks from accounts without the funds. A common practice is for contractors to fire workers who get injured on the job or who complain about working conditions.

Undocumented workers are unlikely to file a law suit, complain, or approach the authorities for help, because they fear arrest or deportation. Again, these figures also remain invisible because of the lack of any safe and accurate way to report them.

In addition, the 1986 law provided for a high-technology automated program—Systematic Alien Verification Entitlements (SAVE)—to identify those immigrants that were ineligible for public welfare benefits—a perceived magnet that was thought to attract immigrants to the country. However, many states refused to use SAVE because of its high cost to operate. Subsequent laws have been enacted to bar undocumented immigrants from receiving federal welfare payments and a range of other benefits, including food stamps and unemployment compensation.

Fearing detection, most do not file for the income-tax refunds owed them. The vast majority are too young to apply for social security benefits if they would be so bold to do so. Because undocumented immigrants come to the United States to work and not to go seek these benefits, all that is left to indicate that they are here, or were here, are traces of their earnings that benefit both their host nation (by way of wage contributions) as well as their sending nation (by way of remittances). Despite average low wages, low education, and the denial of many of the social benefits to which other U.S. workers are entitled, millions of undocumented immigrant workers in the United States are now providing the U.S. economy with a subsidy of as much as $7 billion a year (Porter, 2005). In addition to consumer-related taxes that undocumented immigrants pay while living in the U.S., undocumented workers pay contributions to Social Security and Medicare by way of wage deductions. Porter (2005) reports that these contributions added up to about 10 percent of the revenue surplus in 2004, which is the difference between what the U.S. government currently receives in payroll taxes and what it pays out in benefits. This surplus is seen as a direct benefit of the increase in the use of false documents to gain employment. Starting in the late 1980s, the Social Security Administration received a flood of W-2 earnings. However, because payroll records were inaccurate, the contributions made using false social security numbers were deposited in an "earnings suspense file" until the source of those contributions could be identified. The earnings suspense file had grown to about $189 billion by the 1990s, representing two and a half times the amount of the 1980s. In the 1990s, the earnings suspense file grew on average by more than $50 billion a year, and in 2002 nine million wage statements with incorrect social security numbers, amounting to $6.4 billion in social security taxes, ended up in the suspense file. There is good indication that these earnings correspond to the earnings of undocumented immigrants (Porter, 2005). The distribution of fictitious W-2s was found to fit the distribution of undocumented immigrants in terms of the geographic location of one hundred employers filing the most earnings reports with false social security numbers from 1997 through 2001 and in terms of the employment that they typically engage in: restaurants, construction, and farm operations.

The economic contribution by undocumented immigrants to their sending communities is no less dramatic, significantly reducing poverty there. According to Rempell, in 2003 alone, remittances sent to Mexico by family members working in the United States totaled $13.266 billion. This amount equaled 79 percent of Mexico's oil exports, 71 percent of the *maquiladora* sector surplus, and approximately 2.2 percent of Mexico's gross domestic product.

The fears that undocumented immigrants experience have a lasting effect. From the moment of their crossing into the United States without authorization, undocumented immigrants enter a space of ambiguous existence. Once in the United States and because they are out of status, they are not free to enjoy a life that most Americans take for granted. This existence might be characterized as a space between two worlds, and between what is seen and unseen. This is what it means to be a "shadow population." Moreover, the fear of being revealed—out of the shadows and into the light—has been intensified in recent years. Nativist rhetoric reflects the view that the United States is being overrun and overburdened by immigrant newcomers. Most of the anger has been directed at undocumented immigrants, the majority of whom are Mexicans. This anxiety has resulted in the passing of tougher border security measures and immigration laws. Laws referred to as "policies of attrition" are intended to keep the immigrant population from permanently settling, keeping them "in the shadows." At the same time, such laws have proved to be futile. Due to the extreme poverty that they are fleeing, undocumented immigrants have little option but to take greater risks and suffer appalling hardships to come to the United States and add to the growing number of this population.

Critics of such laws argue that policy of attrition measures only push immigrants further into the shadows and make them more vulnerable to abuse. For example, hate crimes against immigrants have proliferated. Chavez (2012) reports cases in the San Diego area where unknown individuals took sticks to batter Mexican fieldworkers including a Mixtec from Oaxaca walking along a road, leaving one of them paralyzed from the waist down. A message of *"No Mas Aqui"* left at the scene of the crime indicates the xenophobic nature of this attack.

The alternative options to these measures are difficult to conceive and impossible to execute. A police operation such as the one implemented in Postville, Iowa, in 2008 and resulting in the arrest of about four hundred undocumented immigrants, mostly women, sparked outrage among the public and U.S. legislators. Other police actions that would have attempted to identify and expel 10 or 12 million from the United States, known as Operation Endgame, have been proposed and later rejected. In June 2003, the Department of Homeland Security's Office of Detention and Removal released its 2003–2012 Strategic Plan, entitled "Endgame," in which it proposed a goal of developing within ten years the capacity to remove all removable immigrants. The plan included among other things the means for detaining this great number of immigrants by constructing more prisons. However, this plan also identified many significant—perhaps insurmountable—challenges that were beyond the control of the U.S. Department of Homeland Security, including the massive number of immigrants, limited resources, and a lack of political support for the plan.

Whether Americans welcome them or not, once undocumented immigrants are here they have certain rights guaranteed by the Constitution. The equal-protection clause of the Fourteenth Amendment of the U.S. Constitution applies to all, regardless of citizenship status. Undocumented immigrant children have a right to attend school, and all workers, regardless of immigration status, are entitled to the same labor protections and remedies that everyone else is entitled to. At the same time, undocumented immigrants continue to be maligned as outsiders, foreigners, strangers, and transients. They are also accused by nativists of having no commitment to learn the language of the host country and of having divided loyalties between the host and their communities of origin. These labels and perceptions continue to construct the image of the immigrant as an impermanent feature of U.S. society, and push this population further into the shadows.

Anna Ochoa O'Leary

See Also: Barrios; Employer Sanctions; Enclaves; Exclusion; Governance and Criminalization; Identification Cards; Immigration Reform and Control Act (IRCA) (1986); Inadmissibility; Policies of Attrition; Single Men.

Further Reading

Chavez, Leo R. 2012. *Shadowed Lives: Undocumented Immigrants in American Society (Case Studies in Cultural Anthropology).* Fort Worth, TX: Harcourt Brace Jovanovich College Publishers.

O'Brien, Hayden. 2008. "Municipal Overreaching: Federal Preemption as It Applies to Ordinances Outlawing the Rental of Housing to Undocumented Aliens." *Texas Hispanic Journal of Law & Policy* 14.1:69–89.

Porter, Eduardo. 2005. "Illegal Immigrants Are Bolstering Social Security with Billions." *New York Times.* Available at: http://www.nytimes.com/2005/04/05/business/05immigration.html?_r=0.

Rempell, Benjamin. 2005. "Leveraging Migrant Remittances to Mexico: The Role for Sub-National Government." *Journal of Development and Social Transformation.* http://www.maxwell.syr.edu/uploadedFiles/moynihan/dst/rempell8.pdf?n=9442.

Reyes, Augustina H. Peabody. 2010. "The Immigrant Children of Katrina." *Journal of Education* 85.4:443–468.

Single Men

A study of undocumented immigrant single men and how they experience their urban lives is significant because their sense of belonging tends to vary, depending on the cities they live in. The ways that undocumented men acquire a sense of inclusion and belonging depend on the social, cultural, and political dynamics in their urban context. For example, in the border city of El Paso, Texas, undocumented single men working as day workers simply come to understand it as a temporary space, where they need to generate sufficient income, in order to move further into the United States to cities such as Los Angeles, Denver, and Dallas. This viewpoint is expressed mainly because single men understand that in larger urban cities in North America they would earn twice as much as the amount that they would earn in the historically economically disenfranchised city of El Paso.

According to a study reported in the *El Paso Times,* the city experiences much disparity with regard to education, infrastructure, government funding, high levels of unemployment, and underemployment when compared to the rest of Texas and the nation

(*El Paso Times,* 2007). According to the study, El Paso is a border city that is not given much attention when compared to other parts of Texas and the nation, with the result that this border city has lower education rates and higher unemployment rates than many other cities and towns in the country. Up until 1994, half of El Paso's fifty thousand manufacturing jobs were in the apparel and textile industry but with the devaluation of the Mexican currency in 1994, several large apparel manufacturers relocated over the border to Mexico, taking jobs with them. Much like the majority of the cities in the country, the service industry has replaced these manufacturing jobs. What is of interest is that of the seven hundred thousand El Pasoans, Latina/os constitute 80 percent of the total population according to the 2000 census bureau, yet many undocumented Mexican and Central American men prefer to move further north, where they may find it is easier to survive economically. In this regard, the potential of monetary advantage one may find in a given urban location supersedes the social and cultural benefits. Given this context, many of the undocumented migrants understand the U.S. border urbanscape as a site of exploitation which they need to negotiate for a short period of time and ultimately overcome. Thus many of them do not establish a sense of belonging in this city.

For undocumented men, the grim economic prospect of El Paso is not the only element that dissuades them from forming a more permanent relationship with the city. The political dynamics also plays a major role which contributes to their decision to move out of the city. The city of El Paso within U.S. territory is heavily militarized, where Border Patrol agents can be seen driving around in their marked and in some instances in their unmarked vehicles in various parts of the city. Particularly, the downtown area which borders the Mexican city of Juárez has seemingly a higher concentration of Border Patrol men on the look for undocumented migrants. The militarized character of the cityscape consequently serves to limit the men's engagement with the city's commercial and leisure zones. For many men, frequent visits to the corner store, in the downtown area, become a challenge, as the Border Patrol frequents these very same spaces. What many of the men eventually come to know and form links within the city are churches, shelters, and non-profit groups that serve the temporary needs of this population.

In contrast to El Paso, Los Angeles with its diverse population, higher pay rates, and an area free of Border Patrol roaming the streets is perceived as a much easier city to negotiate. Even in the context of economic recession, many undocumented single men who mainly rely on day labor for their source of income and whose jobs came to a sharp decline decided to continue to stay on and weather the economic crisis. Yet many men do make efforts to find work in other areas such as Washington, Wisconsin, and even Iowa only to return to Los Angeles. Several of the men speak of returning to their home countries, only to decide to give it another month or two or perhaps the end of the year, hoping that the economic conditions of this global and formerly affluent city will pick up.

It is in this cosmopolitan city, although with its share of problems of racism, racial profiling, and brutal policing, that many undocumented single men find connections and build panethnic networks. Indeed it is these networks that help them survive the economic downturn. It is in this city that Mexican, Guatemalan, El Salvadoran, Ecuadoran, Peruvian, Nicaraguan men distanced from their families connect speaking a common language with vast variation in their accents. It is in this city that they discuss football (soccer) and go to bars to watch on television live football games being played in their respective home countries.

When the economy comes to a standstill, many of them learn to save and forgo some of the leisure activities. Unable to afford high rents, in this increasingly expensive city, single men begin to share small one-bedroom apartments. It seems a much better option than becoming homeless and sleeping in the city's high crime-ridden parks.

Undocumented single men in times of economic crises in Los Angeles also find church groups, health food stores, bakeries, and the city's food banks and soup kitchens to be a source of moral and practical support. Church groups visit and support single undocumented men waiting on street corners for work and reassure them with prayers, kind words, food, and water. A famous and popular Cuban family bakery helps out by readily donating food to the men who kept the gardens looking beautiful for many Angelinos, to the men who during better economic conditions helped repair roofs of middle-class home owners in this once infinitely fast developing city, to the men who were ever ready to carry and move heavy loads to and from different parts of the city.

Their work allows them to understand the geography of the city. When work is not easily available, the men try out different parts of the city, leaving lower income areas for more middle class and affluent ones. The men also understand how the police system works in the city. They realize that in some parts of the city, the police are less tolerant of undocumented immigrants. Consequently, they learn to avoid such areas. Hence, undocumented single men may experience inclusion more in a particular geographical area than in other locations within the same city.

Finally, undocumented men in some cases become the focus of media attention. For example, as they wait in hope of finding work, a Spanish local news station interviews the men in order to put them on a news program about exploited Latina/o workers. The men agree to be on the program, lend their perspective, and provide accounts of their firsthand experiences. Hence, the experience of undocumented single men becomes visible for five short minutes to the entire city of Los Angeles on a given summer night.

Fazila Bhimji

See Also: Day Labor; Employment; Labor Supply; Ports of Entry; Racial Profiling; Shadow Population; Social Interaction and Integration; Women's Status.

Further Reading

Clawson, Laura. 2005. "Everybody Knows Him: Social Networks in the Life of a Small Contractor in Alabama." *Ethnography* 6:237–264.

Dunn, Timothy. 1997. *The Militarization of the U.S.–Mexico Border 1978–1992: Low Intensity Conflict Doctrine Comes Home.* Austin, TX: CMAS Book.

Purser, Gretchen. 2009. "The Dignity of Job-Seeking Men: Boundary Work among Immigrant Day Laborers." *Journal of Contemporary Ethnography* 38:117–139.

Turnovsky, Carolyn Pinedo. 2006. "A la parada: The Social Practices of Men on a Street Corner." *Social Text* 88:55–72.

Small Business Ownership

Latinos or Hispanics have a long history of involvement with the success of enterprise and commerce in the United States. A Hispanic-owned business is a firm in which Hispanics own 51 percent or more of the equity, interest or stock of the business (U.S. Department of Commerce, 2012). The term Latino, however, is often a term preferred by certain groups and considered to be a broader, more all-encompassing term and is more widely used because it includes those with indigenous roots rather than roots that privilege a European language group (Spanish). The U.S. Census now uses the terms Hispanic or Latino-origin. Hispanic origin can be viewed as the heritage, nationality group, lineage or country of birth of the person or person's parents or ancestors before their arrival in the United States. It should be noted that for the U.S. Census people who identify as Hispanic or Latino or Spanish may choose from any racial category. In other words, Hispanic or Latino is not viewed as a racial category.

The increase in migration from Mexico since the mid-1990s parallels the increased presence of small Mexican businesses and a whole range of other self-employment activities throughout the United States, especially where Mexican immigrant populations are concentrated. In Arizona, for example, the period of population growth paralleled an increase in Mexican-owned firms, an increase of 55.7 percent in the years 2000–2007 (Survey of Business Owners, 2007). The Mexican businesses offer products and services that serve a variety of needs such as for Mexican foods, specialized clothing (e.g. for *quinceañeras* and other religious ceremonies), and Mexican music. However, less researched is how an entrepreneur's immigration status factors into the start, success, or failure of the business. Some examples are found in research by Barros (2009:312) who studied swap meets in San Joaquin, California. She cites a case where the undocumented are prevented from growing a business. Similarly, Valdez (2012:64) finds that for the sometime unauthorized Latinos/as, limited access to market capital hinders their transition into business ownership. Often they are forced to use informal money lenders for the purchases of equipment. In this way, undocumented status is one of several factors that contribute to the social and economically disadvantaged situation experienced by immigrants, and correspondingly, those that are self-employed. Moreover, as a major employer of immigrants, Latino business owners are facing challenges with emerging laws designed to discourage the hiring of undocumented immigrants. For example, in Arizona the tough Legal Workers Act (also known as the Employer Sanctions law) targets businesses that intentionally or knowingly employ unauthorized immigrants. Although the law follows many of the provisions contained in the federal Immigration Reform and Control Act of 1986, the penalties for business owners in Arizona are more punitive. It requires that all employers in Arizona check the employment eligibility of those hired after January 1, 2008, through E-Verify, and if found to be in violation of the law, businesses may lose their licenses to operate. Moreover, the same year that the Legal Workers Act was signed into law, an amendment to Arizona House Bill 2745 made it a requirement for licensing agencies to verify legal residency before granting licenses to businesses in the state. Often, business owners are forced to rely on networks of friends and family to find "straw" purchasers for obtaining operating licenses.

Latino entrepreneurs and business owners are an untapped resource for U.S. economic development (Steinberg et al., 2010). Latino-owned businesses in the United States have demonstrated a steady growth. In 2007, the United States Census reported that 8.3 percent of all businesses in the United States were Hispanic (or Latino)-owned businesses. In the five-year period between 2002 and 2007, Hispanic-owned businesses jumped 43.6 percent to 2.3 million, and receipts from Hispanic-owned businesses in 2007 grew to $350.7 billion, which is up 58 percent from 2002 (U.S. Department of Commerce, 2012), a rate faster than the national average. Clearly, these reported statistics indicate the important role Latino entrepreneurs and business owners play in the American economic landscape.

The value of social networks is also instrumental to the success of more recent Latino immigrant populations and the businesses that they create. A more established Latino business-owner with a longer length of residence in the community will perhaps have a broader set of financial and social networks to draw upon than a more recently arrived immigrant entrepreneur. An individual's social networks are likely to vary by their socioeconomic background, ethnicity, culture and geographic location. In many ethnic communities, including Latino communities, entrepreneurs and business owners have more family members who work for them than do non-ethnic entrepreneurs (Steinberg et al., 2010). Small business owners typically tap into their formal as well as informal networks to achieve success. This further underscores the need for newer and upcoming small-business owners to become a part of networks and groups that can provide the support, knowledge, financial resources, and guidance necessary to achieving long-term business success.

Small business ownership often emerges as an economic option or strategy for Latinos because it is a viable path where business owners can, to a degree, direct and control their own path. For instance, for the Latino immigrant who may possess an education from another country it may be challenging to get employers in the United States to recognize and value that education and experience. Racism in the United States and fear of foreigners may also play a direct role in influencing many Latinos into pursuing their own small business as other potential economic doors close to them based on their immigration status or biased perceptions of Latinos.

Latino-owned small businesses can present more than just a place of business, and in some cases simultaneously serve as a sort of community hub or gathering spot depending upon the services offered. This is especially true in more rural communities where Latinos may live in more clustered communities. In essence, Latino-owned small businesses can serve a central capital or networking function for community members, especially for immigrants. Entrepreneurship through small business ownership may provide an effective self-development asset that ethnic communities can access and harness to create opportunity for their members (Fairlie and Woodruff, 2010; Verdaguer, 2009).

Entrepreneurship manifested through small business ownership is a mode through which Latinos can generate different avenues to economic success and well-being (Steinberg et al., 2010). A successful small business can result in further job creation and opportunity for Latino communities. It is clear that the Latino population in the United States has established itself as a major contributing force to the success of the U.S. economy overall. Ethnic entrepreneurs who own small businesses often rise to meet the needs within their communities. Successful small business owners may serve as community leaders and role models for youth in a community. It is important for any community to have success stories that can be pointed to as a symbol of pride and achievement. Small business ownership often serves this function for Latinos in many communities, both urban and rural, throughout the United States.

Being a small business owner can open the doors to power and success not only for the individual, but also for other members of a community. This occurs through the social networks and reputation that a small business owner establishes. Being able to establish trust with your community members, faith in the product, hard work and consistency are hallmarks of any successful small business. These factors resonate soundly within the many diverse Latino cultures and communities in the United States. In conclusion, Latino small business owners have many strengths and skills to contribute to the U.S. economic system. It is important that Americans recognize these skill sets and make a place for the welcome inclusion of creative Latino entrepreneurs and small business owners at the economic development table.

Sheila Lakshmi Steinberg

See Also: Economics; Employer Sanctions; Enclaves; Family Economics; Landscaping Industry; Social Interaction and Integration.

Further Reading

Barros Nock, Magdalena. 2009. "Swap Meet and Socioeconomic Alternatives for Mexican Immigrants: The Case of the San Joaquin Valley." *Human Organization* 68.3:307–317.

Fairlie, R., and C. M. Woodruff. 2010. "Mexican-American Entrepreneurship." *The B.E. Journal of Economic Analysis & Policy,* Berkeley Electronic Press, 10.1:10.

Steinberg, S. L., S. J. Steinberg, E. Eschker, S. M. Keeble, and J. M. Barnes. 2010. "Rural Ethnic Entrepreneurship: A Spatial Networks Approach to Community Development." California Center for Rural Policy and Institute for Spatial Analysis, Humboldt State University, Arcata, CA. http://www.humboldt.edu/ccrp/sites/ccrp/files/publications/Ford_FINAL%20%282%29.pdf.

U.S. Department of Commerce. 2012. U.S. Census Bureau News. Profile American Facts for Features, CB12-FF.19. "Census Bureau Reports Hispanic-Owned Businesses Increase at More Than Double the National Rate." Washington, D.C. CB10-145. September 21, 2010 and August 6, 2012.

Valdez, Zulema. 2012. *The New Entrepreneurs: How Race, Class and Gender Shape American Enterprise.* Stanford, CA: Stanford University Press.

Verdaguer, M. E. 2009. *Class, Ethnicity, Gender and Latino Entrepreneurship.* New York: Taylor and Francis Press.

Social Interaction and Integration

In general, immigrants arriving in the United States make use of vital social mechanisms to interact with those already settled in destination communities. In this way new arrivals become integrated and acculturated into their new environments. In fact, the escalation of immigration enforcement policies (especially since 9/11) and growing anti-immigrant hostility throughout the nation contribute to immigrants' increased reliance on others for much needed support in order to survive. This is increasingly true for those who are undocumented.

To explain how this social interaction and integration occurs, many scholars often refer to the idea of "social capital." Over the years, this concept has suffered from its many interpretations, but most agree that at its core is the idea that in conditions where individuals are disadvantaged (such as undocumented immigrants who suffer from low wages and exploitation), survival depends on the existence of a strong sense of mutual obligation among those who enjoy better conditions towards those that are less fortunate. In this way, social capital is based on the human relationships that enable actions that lead to immigrants' acceptance into the receiving society, and ultimately to their integration. Social capital is often described simply as access to resources. How this is accomplished depends on a culture where cooperative behaviors, reciprocal exchange, and a deep-seated sense of obligation are fundamental. Throughout the world, less-advantaged communities rely on social capital to compensate for the lack of economic and job stability, or the lack of social service infrastructure. Indeed, social capital is regarded as essential in less developed communities that often lack access to the same resources of their more developed, urban counterparts.

A strong sense of social obligation towards those less fortunate is sometimes manifested symbolically through gift giving and other expressions of care and concern without apparent expectation of economic reward. For some, social interactions and conventions of this nature might appear as wasteful or inefficient. However, for those societies and cultures that observe them, such expressions transmit a sense of belonging to newcomers. A sense of belonging and well-being reduces the stress that newcomers may be experiencing. Periodic relief from acculturation stress helps prevent a wide range of other health problems. Productive and economic development has a better chance of flourishing when principles of social capital are allowed to thrive.

Many studies of immigrant communities living in the United States have used the idea of social capital to describe the kinds of social actions that allow newcomers to overcome obstacles once they arrive in destination communities and eventually become integrated. These actions lead to finding much needed jobs and other opportunities that potentially result in the acquisition of higher levels of human capital. This in turn can lead to higher incomes and influence. This body of research is critical for appreciating the value of social capital in terms of other beneficial outcomes such as the creation and maintenance of social safety nets needed for

Figure 1: A Social Capital Model of Social Interaction and Integration

Types of Resources Ranging from Less to More Tangible Forms (from Coleman, 1988).		
Less Tangible ←	→	More Tangible
Social Capital	Human Capital	Capital
Norms premised on cooperation, social cohesion, and orientations that serve the collective good.	Skills, experience, information	Property, tools, financial wealth

survival. In this way, social networks work to provide new immigrants with new contacts and crucial information used to satisfy daily needs such as for food, transportation, and housing. Social networks may extend over large distances, across international borders, and develop over time through generations of immigrants. Moreover, once networks are established, they tend to become stronger and sustained over time. This assessment flows from one of the best-known theorists of social capital, James Coleman. Coleman (1988) explains that social capital is generated by networks of human relationships. Importantly, the potential of networks to transform social interaction into increasingly tangible resources is what facilitates the eventual desired integration into the host society. Coleman's outline of the process is made clear: Social capital is purposeful and rational, enabling individuals in their active acquisition of human capital (skills, experience), which in turn, enables the acquisition of material capital (property, tools, wealth), as Figure 1 (above) illustrates.

The foregoing model holds in studies about the migration process where migrants are shown to follow this path to acquire additional resources with repeat migration, where migration-specific social capital leads to the accumulation of useful knowledge and skills (migration-specific human capital) that make subsequent crossings more efficient, less risky, and more successful (Singer and Massey, 1998). Once in their destination communities, migrants are likely to acquire jobs, through which they acquire the material assets that may allow them to acquire even more human capital and so on.

In theory, then, the presence of tangible resources within the social network will enable and accelerate the economic integration and well-being of those newcomers who started out as less advantaged. However, social capital is not evenly distributed and can even work to exclude some segments of society from realizing their full potential and therefore less integration. For example, for those who arrive in the United States from humble origins already stigmatized based on ethnicity or color and undocumented, adverse social environments may further or permanently distance them from high-quality human capital and the resources that will lead to full integration. Some scholars have noted that when compared to other immigrants in the United States, such as Cubans, the lack of government policies that protect Mexican immigrants from exploitation and social hostility means that most of them will only find work in the least advantaged areas of the labor market. Furthermore, studies show that immigration authorities behave more violently towards residents of barrios who are perceived as having more Mexican ethnoracial characteristics than those with more Anglo characteristics (racial profiling), and that citizenship and class and education level offer little protection from this mistreatment— all of which keeps them from becoming fully integrated into U.S. society even if they are U.S. citizens. Social hostilities may also work to segregate Mexican immigrants in the least effective schools and in this way arrest their social mobility entirely. Because access to more powerful forms of capital is constrained, sources of social capital for less-welcomed groups will cluster in industries where informal economies and less stable labor market conditions predominate. With integration stifled, disenfranchised and undocumented immigrants will be less able to politically resist the anti-immigrant conditions that keep them from accessing the more empowering forms of capital.

For immigrant women, too, some studies show that social capital (and therefore other means of becoming integrated into their host society) is not always available to them due to gender inequalities and discrimination. Some studies of immigrant women suggest that men accumulate more social capital than women because gender norms allow and even encourage men to have and to develop relationships *outside* the family and neighborhood. These extra-household relationships include more coworkers and members of other social groups, which lead them to other opportunities. In contrast, because women's networks are more likely to be kin-mediated, they may accumulate *less* social capital, and therefore their integration is less assured. Scholars that point out these gender inequities also argue that as long as social capital and the networks it generates are seen as resources, gender patterns of discrimination will insure that women continue to be excluded from accessing the more powerful forms of resources that are available to men. For women that come from more traditional cultures, families and husbands usually exert moral social controls over wives and daughters. By imposing more gender-specific burdens, gender-specific tensions around sexual morality are enforced and thus, women's mobility and self-promoting behaviors that might lead to more integration in an unfamiliar place are constrained, resulting in their exclusion from resources.

Using the same principles of mutual cooperation, social capital has also been used for political empowerment. Political empowerment is a means of achieving social and economic integration. The reaffirmation of feelings of unity among those who have or are suffering similar experiences may thus reflect other commonalities that serve to reaffirm a group's disposition to sympathize with and support individuals who, although strangers, may share similar experiences. A sense of unity can also come from regional origins, such as those who come from the same sending region or state in Mexico. In the United States, some of these regional group affiliations have developed into political and social organizations known as home town associations (HTAs). These operate in principle similar to the mechanisms found in social capital, and in many cases all that is needed for such affiliations to flourish are the common intersections and common fates that bring individuals together—economic hardships and experiences—and that inspire empathy, solidarity, or a charitable disposition towards those less fortunate.

The extent of immigrant political integration also reflects an expansive array of activities of a fusion of immigrant and nonimmigrant social categories in political processes, and the deep-seated affinity between permanent U.S. residents and immigrants that has developed over the more than one hundred years that the United States has depended on immigrant labor to meet its demands. Indeed, inherent within the U.S. Latino population is a historical amalgamation of social groupings (U.S.-born, foreign-born, and naturalized citizens, noncitizens, those with dual citizenship, and the undocumented, all with overlapping ties and interests that have only recently become more visible politically). Distinct categories of political actors and therefore the way that they become integrated into U.S. society have become blurred even further with changes in Mexico's legal framework that grants Mexican citizenship to U.S. citizens of Mexican parentage, including those who were naturalized or born in the United States before 1998. U.S.-Mexican dual nationals may vote in the elections of the two countries and are more likely to turn out to vote than their single-nation counterparts. In fact, dual citizenship has a small but positive effect on U.S. naturalization, thus encouraging the incorporation of new immigrants into the U.S. polity.

At the same time, since 9/11, state legislatures have increasingly become occupied with proposing more restrictive, anti-immigrant voter registration laws. Critics of such laws argue that the undue burden of proving eligibility will fall unequally on the elderly, working poor, disabled, and on the nation's ethnic and linguistic minorities, such as Latinos and Native Americans, leaving them with a diminished voice in matters that most concern them. This is predicted to stifle progressive electoral politics that would improve immigrant integration, given the fusion of political categories that connect Latinos with immigrants. For example, according to Pew Research in 2007, 75 percent of the nation's Latinos disapproved of workplace raids, and 79 percent preferred that local police not take an active role in identifying undocumented immigrants, and more than half (55 percent) disapproved of states checking for immigration status before issuing driver's licenses. Latinos also generally see undocumented immigrants as a plus—both for the Latino community itself and for the U.S. economy in general. Latinos in the United States are feeling a range of negative effects from the increased public attention on illegal immigration and stepped-up enforcement measures. A study by Michelson in 2001 argues that notable political events that shift public attention to immigration issues succeed in altering the "national mood" towards immigrants. Latinos themselves, who more often than not are citizens or legal residents, perceive this national mood as discriminatory and exclusionary. In this manner, Latino political views may prove to be an alternative vision for the United States, which in part may explain the xenophobia that further attempts to exclude them from the country's civic and political life.

However, while voting and running for public office are perhaps the most recognized form of political and civic engagement, privileges denied to immigrants and migrants based on legal status, they exert political agency in other ways. These include attending public meetings, taking part in demonstrations, contacting elected officials, and donating to political causes. Although noncitizen Latinos are less likely to participate in political events, they may engage in activities that can influence political outcomes, such as signing petitions and wearing buttons with political messages. Less direct or less publically visible political activities include voicing concerns to registered voters, social networking, and volunteering to help mobilize communities. Somewhat less researched is consumer behavior that may have political objectives. These less direct forms of civic engagement, such as the buying or boycotting of products and services for political and ethical reasons, can be used by both citizens and noncitizens alike to promote widespread messages of political significance. An example of the success of this strategy was the national/international boycott against of Arizona for passing SB 1070, a notorious law commonly referred to as the "Papers Please Law" that authorized police to ask for immigration papers in the context of another violation.

A broader view of political and civic participation thus recognizes that many Latino families belong to mixed immigration status households—those that consist of individual members who have different legal statuses (citizen, noncitizen legal resident, or undocumented). This accounts for why in 2006 both citizens and noncitizens mobilized nationwide in the largest political protests over immigration reform using this wide range of civic strategies that allow individuals with different immigration status to participate in U.S. politics. This broader view of civic integration will be formidable in considering a future of Latino political participation that is intimately tied to eventual social and economic integration of immigrants. This is especially true as growing number of younger Latinos—sons and daughters of current immigrants—learn and become inspired by older, politically active role models, and become voters. A glimpse of this was visible in the 2012 presidential election where 71 percent of the Latino electorate cast their vote for Barack Obama. Finally, a broader view of political and civic participation will bring to the fore of the nation's attention alternative political approaches that have been historically necessary for democracy. Similar to those engendered by the U.S. Civil Rights movement of the 1960s, membership in organizations based on ethnic, racial, or trans-local identity or values is predicted to advance the development of civic and political voice, greater tolerance, and greater social and economic integration for all.

Ultimately, the resultant, positive outcome of their social interaction and integration is that immigrant newcomers are to varying degrees insured access to more tangible resources needed for survival and adaptation; this process relies on existent attitudes of mutual cooperation, solidarity, and empathy rooted in the ties that connect different categories of Latinos to different categories of immigrants. The real success of both social capital within the realm of economic integration and the political process is the emotional and affective effects that such behaviors will have on those who exercise them in behalf of strangers, where such behaviors become a reward in itself.

Anna Ochoa O'Leary

See Also: Acculturation; Assimilation; Barrios; Culture; Economics; Enclaves; Exclusion.

Further Reading

Ayón, David R. 2006. "Mexican Migrants and Mexican Americans/Latinos: One Agenda or Two?" In *Invisible No More: Mexican Migrant Civic Participation in the United States*, edited by Xóchitl Bada, Jonathan Fox, and Andrew Selee. Washington, D.C.: Wilson Center/Mexico Institute.

Coleman, James S. 1988. "Social Capital in the Creation of Human Capital." *The American Journal of Sociology,* Supplement: *Organizations and Institutions: Sociological and Economic Approaches to the Analysis of Social Structure* S94:S95–S120.

Garcia, Carlos. 2005. "Buscando Trabajo: Social Networking among Immigrants from Mexico to the United States." *Hispanic Journal of Behavioral Sciences* 27.2:3–22.

Granberry, Phillip J., and Enrico A. Marcelli. 2007. "'In the Hood and On the Job': Social Capital Accumulation Among Legal and Unauthorized Mexican Migrants." *Sociological Perspectives* 50.4:579–595.

Goldsmith, Pat, Mary Romero, Raquel Rubio-Goldsmith, Miguel Escobedo, and Laura Khoury. 2009. "Ethno-Racial Profiling and State Violence in a Southwest Barrio." *Aztlán: A Journal of Chicano Studies* 34.1:93–124.

Hagan, Jacqueline, and Nestor Rodriguez. 2002. "Resurrecting Exclusion: The Effects of 1996 U.S. Immigration Reform on Communities and Families in Texas, El Salvador, and Mexico." In *Latinos/os: Remaking America,* edited by Marcelo M. Suarez-Orozco and Mariela M. Páez, 190–201. Los Angeles and London: UC Press.

Kilty, Keith M., and Maria Vidal de Haymes. 2000. "Racism, Nativism, and Exclusion: Public Policy, Immigration and the Latino Experience in the United States." *Journal of Poverty* 4.1/2:1–25.

Michelson, Melissa R. 2001. "The Effect of National Mood on Mexican American Political Opinion." *Hispanic Journal of Behavioral Sciences* 23.1:57–70.

Pew Hispanic Center/Kaiser Family Foundation. 2004. "National Survey of Latinos: Politics and Civic Engagement." http://pewhispanic.org/reports/report.php?ReportID=33.

Pew Research Center. 2007. "National Survey of Latinos: As Illegal Immigration Issue Heats Up, Hispanics Feel a Chill." Available at http://pewhispanic.org/reports/report.php?ReportID=84. Accessed July 25, 2008.

Portes, Alejandro, and Julia Sensenbrenner. 1993. "Embeddedness and Immigration: Notes on the Social Determinants of Economic Action." *American Journal of Sociology* 98.6:1320–1353.

Singer, A., and D. S. Massey. 1998. "The Social Process of Undocumented Border Crossing among Mexican Migrants." *International Migration Review* 32.3:561–592.

Social Security

Social Security and Medicare are so-called "pay as you go" systems in which annual workers' deductions are paid out to existing retirees. Because of a decline in the number of workers relative to retirees that will occur when the Baby Boomers retire, it is thought that the system will develop a massive deficit and collapse. One suggestion is that the social security payments of immigrant workers could keep the system solvent. At the heart of the issue are questions of whether undocumented immigrants should collect that money they have paid into the system through wage contribution if and when they are legalized, and if the United States is prepared to welcome new immigrants with a base of younger workers capable of paying into the system for many years to come to keep it afloat as more seniors retire.

Background

The Baby Boomers form a large demographic group of individuals born in the time of prosperity after World War II (1950–1965). After 1965, Americans stopped having as many children, and this has created a problem for the prospective retirement years of the Baby Boomers. There may not be enough younger workers to pay into the Social Security and Medicare systems, and the public worries that the system might collapse.

In the twenty-first century, the meaning of family has changed as American men and women have become more educated and women have entered the labor force. In this affluent society, like many European countries, there is a negative birth rate (a "baby-bust") among the native-born. The United States achieved zero population growth among the native-born, and then went below the level of population replacement. If it were not for immigrants the United States population would decrease, leaving jobs unfilled and reducing social security payments.

Social security payments depend on the "dependency ratio" of workers- to-retirees. At present, there are enough workers contributing to cover payouts for Social Security and Medicare. However, when the so-called Baby Bust generation is the source of support for retiring Baby Boomers, there will be a shortage of payments into the system unless immigrants contribute to it.

Young immigrants aged eighteen to thirty-four comprised half of those who arrived between 1995 and 2000. Although aging legal immigrants eventually become eligible for social security, it is projected that there will be a payment surplus that can be used to support the native-born. According to projections, the continued growth of the immigrant population will provide payroll taxes to support Boomers; however, if their share of the population begins to diminish, there will be less support for the system.

Undocumented Workers and Social Security

Immigration restriction rhetoric seldom examines the fiscal contributions made by both legal and undocumented immigrants. Restrictionists assume that less or no money goes into the system because immigrants are paid through informal mechanisms, also referred to as "off the books." Despite this belief, many undocumented workers pay into the Social Security system. The Social Security Administration (SSA) receives both legal immigrants' contributions and those that are unlikely to be claimed by undocumented immigrants. This is because they have purchased fraudulent social security numbers (SSN) and cards from criminal document-counterfeiting organizations prior to going to work. If they were to claim benefits using these documents, they risk arrest and removal from the United States.

One might ask if it should not be easy to identify an illegitimate number when the payroll taxation paperwork is reported to the Social Security Administration. It is not. Despite or because of the size of the Social Security Administration bureaucracy, there are thousands of unverified numbers through which money is being deposited. A backlog of investigation into these unverified numbers almost assures that monies will contribute to flow into the system.

When the name and number do not match what the SSA has on record, it issues a written notice to the employer advising them that the name or Social Security number (SSN) reported by the employer for one or more employees may be incorrect. These are called "no match" letters. The letter cautions employers against taking any employment action against an employee based solely on receipt of the letter, and explicitly states that the letter is making no claims about the employee's immigration status. Rather, the letter simply reports the apparent error in either the employer's records or the SSA's records, and requests the employer's and employee's help in correcting the problem.

Immigrant Social Security Tax Surplus

The 2008 Report of the Social Security Administration stated that so-called "other than legal" workers are expected to contribute to the program without ever receiving benefits. These immigrants are living in the United States without legal entry. Since 2000, the SSA has received, on average, more than 9.3 million suspicious wage reports annually (Johnson, 2013). When contributions to social security cannot be matched to individuals' taxpayer identification numbers or social security numbers, they are placed in the Earnings Suspense File (ESF) until the issue can be resolved. The Government Accounting Office (2006) reports that the growing ESF is attributed to payments made by undocumented immigrants. By some estimates, contributions to social security taxes that are in the ESF have grown at an unprecedented pace with cumulative wages since 1990 totalling more than $952.4 billion, unadjusted for inflation (Johnson, 2013).

The Social Security Administration projects that immigrants will cover 15 percent of social security payouts for the anticipated Baby Boomer deficit. In addition, undocumented immigrants, because they tend to be younger and of reproductive age, are expected to have higher fertility rates than the native-born, and their children will become a part of the labor force, legitimately paying into the system over a long period of time. The equivalent would be a 0.3 percent increase in the current Social Security payroll tax. *The New York Times* (2008) asks: "Would the people who want to deport all undocumented workers be willing to make up the difference and pay the taxes that the undocumented are currently paying?" They would probably not, but this is the type of pragmatic question that is not usually addressed in immigration restriction rhetoric.

Are New Immigrants Needed to Support the Baby Boomer Retirement?

The argument that more immigration is needed does not take into account that segments of the new immigrant population have higher fertility rates. The Center for Immigration Studies (CIS) estimates that if net immigration increased to 2.5 million a year, twice the current level, it would only increase the working age population by one percentage point, to 60.5 percent in 2040. In other words, the population would be much larger, but the dependency ratio would not. One suggestion is that, now that people are living longer, the retirement age should be raised.

Another social factor to consider is whether the children of the new immigrant ethnoracial groups will all reach their full potential. Increasing the education and productivity of traditional minorities' children, as well as that of less educated new immigrant groups, would do a great deal to help support the Baby Boomer retirement. On the other hand, many commentators believe that the new immigration increases the worker's social security taxation base, and that their birthrate will compensate for the aging Baby Boom when the "pig in the python," as it has been termed, starts to reach the tail end. It is considered that the new Latino immigration will provide the basis for a new social contract.

In California, the new immigrants are a majority of the state population but a minority of the voting population. Older white voters have repeatedly tried to restrict benefits for the new immigrant population. In this respect, the public is acting against its own interests, because better education for this population would create a better tax base for future social security. By 2015, social security costs will increase from 31 percent of the federal budget to 48 percent. Currently, there are 250 seniors for every one thousand workers; by 2030 this number will increase to 411 for every 1,000 workers.

If U.S. citizen taxpayers are entering a numerical decline, they will need to be replaced by comparably educated workers. Denying an education to the children of unauthorized immigrants will not meet this need. There will be fewer better educated workers to pay into Social Security and Medicare, necessitating drastic cuts. Investing in education for new generations is the best bet. There is a need for better-paid workers, or seniors will not be able to sell their homes to people who cannot afford them. Investing in education for new generations is the best bet.

Conclusion

The social security system is headed for hard times when Baby Boomers retire. Pessimists see it as a failing or ill-designed program to begin with. Optimists view immigrants as a long-term source of support for retirees and the nation's fiscal solvency. Oddly enough, hope lies in a synthesis of these views that will lead to real investment in minority education or investment in minority and new immigrant education that will preserve the economic vitality of the American Dream.

Judith Ann Warner

See Also: Economics; Family Economics; Identity Theft; Individual Taxpayer Identification Number (ITIN); Taxes.

Further Reading

Camarota, S. 2007. "100 Million More: Projecting the Impact of Immigration on the U.S. Population, 2007–2060." Washington, D.C.: Center for Immigration Studies. http://www.cis.org/articles/2007/back707.html.

Government Accountability Office. 2006. "Social Security Numbers: Coordinated Approach to SSN Data Could Help Reduce Unauthorized Work." GAO-06-458T, Feb. 16. Available at: http://www.gao.gov/products/GAO-06-458T.

Johnson, Mary. 2013. "Growth of the Social Security Earnings Suspense File Points to the Rising Potential Cost of Unauthorized Work to Social Security." The Senior Citizens League, February 2013. http://seniorsleague.org/2013/growth-of-the-social-security-earnings-suspense-file-points-to-the-rising-potential-cost-of-unauthorized-work-to-social-security-2/.

Myers, D. 2007. *Immigrants and Boomers: Forging a New Social Contract for the Future of America.* New York: Russell Sage Foundation.

New York Times. 2008. "Editorial: How Immigrants Saved Social Security." April 2. http://www.nytimes.com/2008/04/02/opinion/02wed3.html?ex=1364788800 &...&emc=rss.

South Asians

South Asians prominently include those with ancestry from Bangladesh, Bhutan, India, Nepal, Pakistan, Sri Lanka, and the Maldives. The region is synonymous with the Indian subcontinent. For those immigrating to the United States from South

Raja Muzaffar, left, watches his daughter, Rabia, second left, search for news on Kashmiri earthquake victims as Rabia's brother, Raja Zulqarnain, and mother, Kaneez Fatima, and a cousin, Talat Mahmoud, far right, of Rawalakot, look on at the Muzaffars' home in the Brooklyn borough of New York, November 2, 2005. Many from South Asian nations began to immigrate to the United States relatively recently, after the Immigration and Nationality Act of 1965, also known as the Hart-Celler Act of 1965, ended decades of excluding Asian immigrants. (AP Photo/Kathy Willens)

Asia, like others who come from most all sending countries, their decisions to migrate consider various factors, among which is that their countries encourage leaving for the purpose of temporary work or study abroad, but not to settle. The governments of Pakistan, Bangladesh, and India seek to extend rules and regulations over those who leave the country, because they expect the period of stay to be only temporary. In other words: they expect the return of emigrants so that they can contribute to the home country. This may also encourage those immigrants' efforts to put off completing their documents or to become citizens of the host country. Such sending countries continue to see these citizens as providing large benefits. In 1986 Pakistan received remittances that equaled almost 70 percent of the total merchandise exported. In the same year Bangladesh's second largest sector of foreign exchange was remittances. This was more than what was received from development assistance from institutions like the International Monetary Fund. These policies are cause for some concerns about long-term effects of migration on the economies in South Asia, because their economies may not actually be growing as fast due to the exodus of workers.

In comparison to Latino groups, the immigrant population in the United States that comes from South Asia is small. The majority of South Asians who live in the United States are foreign-born, with over 75 percent of the population born outside of the United States. According to U.S. Census data, foreign-born Indians with a total of 1,855,705 in 2011 represented the second largest of the foreign-born groups. By contrast, the number of foreign-born Pakistanis was 307,855 the same year, followed by those from Bangladesh with 185,275. South Asians possess a range of immigration statuses including undocumented immigrants, student and worker visa holders and their dependents, legal permanent residents, and naturalized citizens.

Many from India have only begun to immigrate to the United State relatively recently, after the Immigration and Nationality Act of 1965, also known as the Hart-Celler Act of 1965, which ended the exclusionary policies that had been in place for decades since the Chinese Exclusion Act of 1882. After Hart-Celler, Indian immigrants came as primarily white-collar professional workers. However, according to Dhingra's 2012 book, *Life Behind the Lobby: Indian American Motel Owners and the American Dream,* Indian immigrants began working in agriculture in northern California before dominating the hotel industry. According to Reuters, Indian immigrants in 2004 owned one half of the hotels in the United States. The Asian American Hotels Owners Association (AAHOA), the largest membership-based Indian business organization in the United States), reports that almost half of all hotel and motels are owned by its members, with a cumulative total of $128 billion in property value.

Some immigration scholars have characterized those coming from the South Asian region as a "model minority" in the United States because of their apparent willingness to assimilate into the culture of the United States, embrace American values of hard work and entrepreneurial acumen, supportive family traditions, independence, and goals for wealth accumulation. According to the 2000 Census, the median household income of Indians was $70,708—far above the national median of $50,046. Indian-American and other scholars contest this characterization, arguing that this group experiences racism and discrimination much like other minorities. They contest the homogenization of this group as having a unified set of political goals or aspirations. In support of this critique, recent reports on human trafficking indicate that the smuggling of undocumented immigrants from parts of India has been on the rise. Human smuggling from India into the United States through Mexico has increased since 2010, with over 1,600 Indians being caught by authorities on the border. In one news report, Indian immigrants paid human smugglers between $12,000 to $20,000 to be smuggled into the United States from India through Mexico. The alarming rise in numbers of undocumented Indian immigrants has been attributed to rising poverty and violence in southeastern Asia, in parts of the Punjab region where Sikhs have been facing religious persecution.

Families are very much affected by the choices immigrants make during the immigration process. Males structure their plans for moving around marriage arrangements, and planning involves issues about having enough funds for couples to meet the costs of travel overseas. Women left behind in India are burdened with the problem of double-time work; they have to deal with both household and work-related activities to support the family. The absence of workers due to emigration especially affects the productivity of families in rural areas of India.

A high percentage of those that do return to their families live for short terms in the United States and do not apply for permanent residency. In 1987, 21 to 40 percent of Indians may have returned to their country. Many are able to return with large amounts of savings. Immigrants in the United States sent $10.84 billion in remittances to India in 2012.

In the United States, traditional festivities are organized as a way to reaffirm some of the values from the old country. However, some who have brought Indian political consciousness with them, including stories of the independence movement and quotes by Mahatma Gandhi, criticize such cultural institutions as perpetuating inequality for some groups. For example, they criticize a double standard that places greater constraints on women, pressuring them to dress in traditional Indian attire, while men can dress in free display of U.S. fashions. The men would not usually be seen as violating traditional Indian values of modesty. Some Indian feminists argue that the images of mother and activist are not incompatible. In this way, these immigrants struggle with negotiating their identities amidst pressures to accept those developed in the host culture.

In other parts of the United States some connect India and a supposed monolithic "Indian culture" to backwardness or worse, competition with their own job and livelihoods. Worse still, they have suffered post-9/11 anti-immigrant sentiment by way of slander and violent attacks, much of which has been perperated by those who mistakenly confuse them with Muslims. The Sikh Coalition is a community-based organization that emerged in New York City in response to a wave of violence and discrimination against the Sikh population following the attacks of September 11, 2001. On that very night of September 11, 2001, an elderly Sikh and two teenagers were violently attacked in Richmond Hill, Queens to avenge the attacks. The coalition called on police to better protect the community and over time, it developed affiliations in other major U.S. cities, including Boston, Washington, D.C., Chicago, Houston, Seattle, San Francisco, and Los Angeles. However, violence erupted in the most visible of ways in August 2012, when six worshippers were murdered in Oak Creek, Wisconsin, by a self-identified neo-Nazi, and later that year, a Sikh man was pushed to his death on a subway platform because the assailant believed he was a Muslim. Since then, in June of 2013, the FBI announced plans to track hate crimes of this nature as an important first step toward designing a policy to help prevent them.

Ben DuMontier

See Also: Assimilation; Hart-Celler Act (1965); Hate Crimes; Lawful Permanent Residents; Small Business Ownership.

Further Reading

Dhingra, Pawan. 2012. *Life Behind the Lobby: Indian American Motel Owners and the American Dream.* Stanford, CA: Stanford University Press.

Fawcett, James, and Benjamin V. Cariño. 1987. *Pacific Bridges: The New Immigration from Asia and the Pacific Islands.* Staten Island, NY: Center for Immigration Studies.

Marosi, Richard, and Andrew Becker. 2011. "Surge of immigrants from India baffles border officials in Texas." *Los Angeles Times,* February 6.

Misir, Deborah N. 2000. "Murder of Navroze Mody: Race, Violence, and the Search for Order." In *Contemporary Asian America: A Contemporary Reader,* edited by Min Zhou and James Gatewood, 501–517. New York: New York University.

Wu, Jean, and Min Song, eds. 2000. *Asian American Studies.* New Brunswick, NJ: Rutgers State University.

Southern States

The Southeastern states in the United States have seen the largest settlement of immigrants since the late twentieth century. The majority come from Latin American countries, although Asian immigrants also began settling in the South in the 1980s. The newcomers have sparked negative perceptions of undocumented immigrants and led to legislation aimed at restricting their immigration and settlement.

Massive immigration at the turn of the twentieth century did not deeply impact the South, since it had high numbers of poor blacks and whites to perform low-wage labor. Moreover, in contrast to other regions of the United States, the South has industrialized more slowly. Therefore, although immigrant labor was important to certain sectors in the South for much of the twentieth century, large-scale immigration did not occur until the late 1980s and early 1990s. Several factors converged to bring about this development. One was the passage of the Immigration Reform and Control Act of 1986 (IRCA) that provided for the legalization of around 2.5 million formerly undocumented immigrants, whose new status gave them freedom to settle in other states and led more women to migrate to the United States, often to join spouses.

Simultaneously, stricter border enforcement discouraged undocumented immigrants from circular migration, leading to more permanent settlement in the United States. Economic recession in traditional immigrant-receiving states, called "gateways," and a resulting anti-immigrant backlash in those places pushed immigrants to new destinations.

New industries in the South made it an appealing destination for immigrants in the 1990s. Although global competition led to the decline of certain industries, Southern states began to appeal to corporations which sought to relocate to more "business-friendly" states, that is, those offering lower taxes, right-to-work policies that weakened unionization efforts, and various other business incentives. These businesses that came to be established in the South soon brought about a demand for low-wage workers. Meanwhile, the North American Free Trade Agreement (NAFTA) increased inequality and economic destabilization in Mexico. The neoliberal restructuring that followed displaced many workers, especially farmers, which stimulated migration to the United States. In addition, continued political unrest in Central American countries like El Salvador and Guatemala in the wake of civil wars and U.S. intervention combined with ensuing economic instability drove many north in search of better opportunities.

The rapidly growing Latino immigrant population in the South faces harsh public perceptions and political rhetoric in the twenty-first century. Negative attitudes toward immigrants are linked to perceptions of undocumented immigrants as responsible for many of the South's economic and social problems and the conflation of undocumented immigrants with criminality. Anti-immigrant sentiments have also been linked to concerns about terrorism after the September 11 attacks on the World Trade Center. Scholars have drawn parallels between the anti-immigrant rhetoric emerging in the South in the early twenty-first century with isolationist ideologies and anxieties about foreigners that at the turn of the twentieth century helped prevent large-scale immigration.

Consequently, anti-immigrant sentiments have ushered in restrictive legislation. In general, these laws seek to discourage undocumented immigrants from coming to a given region while pushing current undocumented residents out (so-called "policies of attrition") though these have been known to impact both legal resident immigrants and unauthorized immigrants. State laws in Georgia, South Carolina, North Carolina, and Alabama have enacted new measures with these goals in mind. Georgia led with the 2006 Georgia Security and Immigration Compliance Act, or Senate Bill 529, which restricts social services to undocumented immigrants, requires that all arrested for DUIs and felonies be checked for legal status, encourages local law enforcement collaborations with Immigration and Customs Enforcement (ICE), and outlaws the hiring of undocumented laborers. North Carolina passed House Resolution 2692 in the middle of 2006, which approves a new immigration court in the state to speed deportations, supports collaborative agreements between local law enforcement officials and Immigration and Customs Enforcement agents, and pressures Congress to make driving while impaired a deportable offense for both legally present and undocumented immigrants. In 2006, North Carolina also restricted driver's licenses to those who can provide a valid social security number. The provision from Georgia's law that officers operating jails in the state verify the immigration status of anyone arrested for a felony or a driving under the influence (DUI) violation took effect in North Carolina in 2008. South Carolina passed H 4400 in 2008, which mandates employment verification, fines delinquent employers, prohibits undocumented people from attending public colleges, and encourages collaboration between local officials and the ICE.

In 2011, Alabama passed perhaps the harshest law in the nation since Arizona's SB1070 was enacted with HB 56. This law was specifically designed to drive out undocumented immigrants as well as to prevent immigrants from taking jobs from Alabamans. In addition to requiring law enforcement to check documentation at any legal stop of an individual, it is also illegal for an undocumented immigrant to apply for work. Some of the provisions of HB 56 were similar to Arizona's SB1070, some of which were rejected in the U.S. Supreme Court decision in June 2012 in *Commerce of the United States of America et al. v. Whiting et al.* Included among the provisions that were rejected was that schools report the number of undocumented students enrolled. The court also struck down the "harboring" provision.

In August 2012, the U.S. Court of Appeals for the Eleventh Circuit blocked the transporting and aiding and abetting provision of the law, basing its decision on the fact that the state law conflicted with federal law. On April 29, 2013, the U.S. Supreme Court, voting 8-1, refused to hear the appeal by Alabama to overturn the ruling by the Appeals Court, thereby allowing that ruling to stay in place and to block punishment for harboring or abetting undocumented immigrants (Savage, 2013).

The Alabama law also had a few unintended consequences, in that farmers and other businesses, mainly meat packing plants, lost huge numbers of workers, and the economy was initially hurt. These businesses, however, eventually had to hire other immigrants who were willing to take on tough and low-paying jobs, negating the argument that the hiring of immigrants took jobs from Alabamans. The businesses also had to spend more on training the new workers (Constable, 2012).

Local (city and county) anti-immigrant ordinances, stemming from frustrations with slow action on the state and federal level to reform immigration laws, have also appeared throughout the South. Anti-congregating ordinances, targeting immigrant day laborers, appeared in Georgia in the late 1990s. Localities have sought to prevent undocumented employment by restricting state governments from conducting business with contractors who had not verified employees' legal status, and prohibiting companies from claiming as tax deductions wages paid to undocumented employees. Ordinances have also aimed to discourage Latino immigrant settlers by requiring landlords to verify legal status, though this and similar anti-immigrant housing ordinances have generally been curtailed by court challenges. English-only ordinances are another widespread, though more symbolic, action taken by localities and states. These ordinances, making English the "official" language, have been passed by twenty-nine states in the United States, including all of the southeastern states.

In addition to state laws and local ordinances, many southern counties have entered into 287(g) agreements between local law enforcement agencies and Immigration and Customs Enforcement, in which local officers are deputized to perform some immigration enforcement functions normally restricted to ICE agents.

Some southern localities have also passed ordinances aimed at accommodating new immigrant neighbors, mainly in the area of education. At the same time, many advocacy groups have organized, as elsewhere in the country, to protect immigrants' rights.

Kathleen Griesbach

See Also: Arizona SB1070; Employer Sanctions; Gateways; Governance and Criminalization; Immigration Reform and Control Act (IRCA) (1986); Incarceration; Meat Processing Plants; Policies of Attrition; Racism; State Legislation.

Further Reading

Constable, Pamela. 2012. "Alabama law drives out illegal immigrants but also has unexpected consequences." *Washington Post,* June 17. http://articles.washingtonpost.com/2012-06-17/local/35462377_1_illegal-immigrants-poultry-workers-alabama-law.

Odem, Mary E., and Elaine Lacy, eds. 2009. *Latino Immigrants and the Transformation of the U.S. South.* Athens, GA: University of Georgia Press.

Savage, David G. 2013. "Supreme Court won't revive Alabama immigration law." *Los Angeles Times,* April 29. http://articles.latimes.com/2013/apr/29/nation/la-na-court-immigration-20130430.

Smith, Heather A., and Owen J. Furuseth. 2006. *Latinos in the New South: Transformations of Place.* Burlington, VT: Ashgate.

Spanish-Language Media

Spanish-language media, the most developed foreign-language broadcast and print media system in U.S history, plays two often-conflicting roles for immigrants: a means of integration into a new society and a connection to their place of origin. As a tool of assimilation, Spanish-language media can contribute to a sense of community and cultural identity for immigrants new to a foreign culture. However, excessive consumption of both news and entertainment programming in a mother language, often about a home country, can potentially impede the acculturation process. Debates continue on the potentially exploitative intentions of Spanish-language media: Do Spanish-language television stations, radio stations, and printed press seek to advocate for and empower immigrants? Or do they seek to reap the benefits of commodifying the largest (and growing) ethnic minority demographic segment of the U.S. population?

Major national demographic shifts (such as those attributed to immigration, legal or otherwise) are important factors in media development and policy. The expansion of Spanish-language media is a product of the growing U.S. Latino population as well as other structural factors. The Telecommunications Act of 1996, which legalized cross-national ownership and ended caps on ownership of media corporations, was supportive of Spanish-language media in terms of growth and capital investments. This allowed Spanish-language stations to expand from traditional Latino Centers (Los Angeles, San Antonio, Miami, etc.) to a nationwide phenomenon. Between 2000 and 2004, there was a 125 percent growth in the number of Spanish-language media outlets. As of 2011, there were more than eight hundred Spanish language daily or weekly newspapers. By the most recent count (fall 2009), there were 1,323 Spanish-language radio stations and 150 Spanish-language TV stations owned by six Spanish-language TV networks. (Currently, Univision, the largest Spanish-language TV network in the United States, ranks fifth in viewers, following the classic "Big Four"—CBS, ABC, NBC, FOX.) Telemundo is the other major Spanish-language TV station.

Growth in the volume of Spanish-language media outlets has been accompanied by consolidation of ownership of these same media. Conglomeration and commercialization are part of larger processes of media globalization, whereby there is increasing domination of Spanish-language media by non-Latino interests. The potential for homogenization (lack of diversity, innovation, and local entertainment or news programming) and depoliticization of Spanish-language media is a growing concern. The concentration of the Spanish-language market includes efforts to standardize Spanish—erasing region-specific dialects, neutralizing different nationalities and moving towards a depoliticized Latino/a identity that is less threatening to potential advertisers. A globalized, pan-ethnic "Latinidad" blurs the unique national histories of a broad number of Latino countries, erasing differences and struggles and instead promoting generic stereotypes of "Latinos." This benefits advertisers who seek to market to Spanish-language speakers more broadly without having to re-record advertisements for each individual national context or cultural group.

Examples of what critics have termed "hegemonic cultural imperialism" are present in all three main media: radio, television and print. In Spanish-language radio, U.S. Latino musicians based primarily in Los Angeles and Miami are consistently privileged over international musicians. In television, the importing of Latin American telenovelas and newscasters has diminished, replaced by U.S.-produced news and entertainment programming. When the largest Spanish language daily newspaper in the mainland United States, *El Diario–La Prensa,* was purchased by Canadian-based CPK Media Holdings, for example, the new owners cancelled a column that was to be written by Fidel Castro.

Though little has been written on how Spanish-language media explicitly ties in with undocumented immigrants, much can be said about these broader debates in terms of how undocumented immigrants utilize and are used by Spanish-language media. There are continued arguments on whether Spanish-language media promotes, endorses, and encourages integration or challenges, opposes, and resists assimilation for recent immigrants who only speak Spanish.

Media deregulation and the subsequent growth in the Spanish-language sector has the potential to reach more disenfranchised sections of the population, especially undocumented immigrants. The Spanish-language itself can be empowering to viewers, who may see it as a form of resistance to dominant American culture. Social movements or state propositions that seek to make English the official language of the United States are examples of ways Spanish-language speakers may feel marginalized. The exclusive access to Spanish-language media shifts some power dynamics for immigrants. Discussions continue as to actual association between Spanish-language media and the increase of opportunities for Latino representation, cultural influence, and subsequent political power or participation. Clearly, Spanish-language media have helped mobilize immigrants to social action over the course of history in the United States, including in 2010 against Arizona's SB1070 law, a highly restrictive immigration law aimed at undocumented immigrants, the majority of whom are Latino, and Mexican more particularly.

Some Spanish-language media are especially immigrant-friendly. Immigrants in general, and specifically those without documentation or those who speak only Spanish, are generally excluded in mainstream media, and many argue that Spanish-language media assures first amendment rights of a free press to Latinos by providing information vital to public life. Many stations focus on the public interest and serving the Latino community by sponsoring political debates, creating and promoting a space for Latino popular culture and advocating for political, economic or cultural empowerment of immigrants. It has been suggested that Spanish-language media may be fairer in coverage of undocumented news issues and in any fictional portrayals of undocumented characters in entertainment programming. In markets where Spanish-language media has a stable footing (Miami, Los Angeles) some media outlets have the resources to take bold stances on issues facing immigrants, especially the undocumented.

However, opponents argue that Spanish-language media prevents immigrant absorption into mainstream culture. Some research suggests that immigrants prefer immigrant-focused publications over general national newspapers and immigrants more often subscribe to cable or satellite in order to access non-local, immigrant-focused programming, connecting them to their home countries. This suggests low levels of integration, but there have been no conclusive studies. These issues figure into larger debates about assimilation (where subordinate cultures take on features of the dominant group) versus pluralism (where subcultures maintain their distinctions and coexist with mainstream culture). Since the 1980s, there has been a growing fear of the "Latinoization" of America. The growth of Spanish-language media can be seen as an example of how Latinos "threaten" traditional American values and thus have met with some resistance. Especially for immigrant groups who are not perceived to be culturally threatened in their home country, host countries may be more resistant to helping protect these groups' cultures.

As noted above, advertising is one of the main impetuses behind the growth of Spanish-language media. Although Spanish-language-media advertising is still much less widespread than its English mainstream counterpart—bringing in $9 billion as opposed to $100 billion—it is growing rapidly. Advertisers make little differentiation between those in the United States legally and those not, as long as they have money to spend on their products. The priority of Spanish-language media as a source of empowerment falls far below the corporate interest of Spanish speakers as a growing consumer demographic. Spanish-language media may help marginalized minorities in the United States to feel a sense of self-worth. However, this may be at the price of self-commodification and as a mechanism of political and social control.

Jessie K. Finch

See Also: Acculturation; Assimilation; Bilingualism; *Corridos;* Culture; English-Only Movement; Film and Television Representation; Media Coverage.

Further Reading

Castanada, Mari. 2008. "Rethinking the U.S. Spanish-Language Media Market in an Era of Deregulation." In *Global Communications: Toward a Transcultural Political Economy,* edited by Paula Chakravartty and Yuezhi Zhao, 201–215. Lanham, MD: Rowman & Littlefield Publishers, Inc.

Center for Spanish Language Media at the University of North Texas. http://www.spanish-media.unt.edu/.

Guskin, Emily, and Amy Mitchell. 2011. "Hispanic Media: Faring Better than the Mainstream Media." In "The State of the News Media 2011: An Annual Report on American Journalism." http://stateofthemedia.org/2011/hispanic-media-fairing-better-than-the-mainstream-media/.

Special Agricultural Workers (SAW)

The 1986 Immigration Reform and Control Act (IRCA) was a sweeping measure that increased employer penalties for the hiring of undocumented migrants, increased the Immigration and Naturalization Service's (INS) budget and expanded its enforcement capabilities, and provided several ways for undocumented migrants currently living in the country to normalize their status. Under IRCA's amnesty provisions, approximately 3 million largely Mexican migrants became legal residents of the United States. Of those 3 million, about 1.3 million applied to become residents under the act's Special Agricultural Worker (SAW) provisions, dramatically exceeding all estimates for turnout. For example, INS had predicted that there would be 210,000 applications in California, Texas, Illinois, New York and Florida, while a little over a million ended up applying. More than 90 percent of applications under SAW were approved and there is evidence of widespread fraud on the part of applicants. The remainder of the 3 million amnesty seekers applied under the Legally Authorized Workers (LAW) program.

To begin the amnesty process under the SAW provisions, which are laid out in Section 302 of IRCA, applicants had to prove that they had worked ninety days in specified seasonal agricultural work in the twelve-month period preceding May 1, 1986. All migrants who could prove this qualified for Group 2 status and immediate temporary residence. Those who could additionally prove that they had worked ninety days in seasonal agriculture in the twelve-month periods prior to May 1, 1985 and May, 1984 and had lived in the United States for a cumulative six months in each of the three twelve-month periods qualified for Group 1 status.

Both Group 1 and Group 2 applicants attained temporary residence upon approval and on equal terms, but permanent residence was granted to Group 1 applicants more quickly; Group 1 applicants who were approved for temporary status prior to November 30, 1988 became permanent residents on December, 1989, or one year after approval for those who attained temporary status after the aforementioned November date. Group 2 applicants, on the other hand, had a two-year wait between approval of temporary status and permanent residency.

Migrants applying for temporary status under the bill's LAW provisions, which are outlined in section 201 of IRCA, had to comply with slightly more stringent requirements. The most important stipulation was that applicants had to prove they had lived continuously in the United States since at least January 1, 1982. Exceptions were made for absences of fewer than forty-five days and cumulative absences of fewer than 180 days. After being approved for temporary status, applicants then had to wait eighteen months to apply for permanent residency. Unlike SAWs, legalization applicants also had to show some English language proficiency, and some knowledge of U.S. history and U.S. government. Approximately 1.7 million undocumented migrants were granted amnesty through this method.

The legalization of 3 million previously undocumented migrants had dramatic consequences, many of them unintended. Having passed in a context of rising anxiety about undocumented immigration, the bill's failure to curb the phenomenon is in part credited with the rise of extreme anti-immigrant sentiment in the mid-1990s, illustrated most strikingly by Proposition 187 in California in 1994. Though border apprehensions declined over the several years following the bill's passage, there is little evidence to suggest that IRCA reduced undocumented immigration over the long term. Additionally, many of the newly legal residents of the United States petitioned to have their family members join them in the United States, a trend that, among other things, provoked rising concern about perceived abuses of social and welfare services on the part of the newly arrived immigrants.

Before IRCA, migrants tended to seek stable employment and remained fairly immobile while working. Freed up by amnesty, however, thousands of migrants left the traditional gateway states of Texas and California. The new networks spread and became established across the country, dramatically changing the human landscape in areas in the United States that had been for the most part isolated from the nation's growing diversity, such as the South. Amnesty also increased concern about wages and working conditions among the newly legalized. Many were less willing to tolerate the exploitative conditions and low wages they had endured before.

Along with amnesty came increased border enforcement, which in part resulted in decreased circularity of migration patterns. The enforcement increases brought on by IRCA were followed by the concentrated enforcement operations, such as Gatekeeper in San Diego, of the mid-nineties. Not wanting to risk capture, many migrants were staying longer than previous generations of migrants had, a trend that has continued and even been exacerbated with increased militarization of the border. To illustrate, in 1992 20 percent of undocumented migrants returned home after six months whereas only 7 percent did so in 2000.

Murphy Woodhouse

See Also: Immigration Reform and Control Act (IRCA) (1986); Migrant Farm Workers.

Further Reading

Baker, Susan G. 1997. "The 'Amnesty' Aftermath: Current Policy Issues Stemming from the Legalization Programs of the 1986 Immigration Reform and Control Act." *International Migration Review* 31.1:5–27.

Cornelius, Wayne A, Philip L. Martin, and James F. Hollifield. 1994. *Controlling Immigration: A Global Perspective.* Stanford, CA: Stanford University Press.

Orrenius, Pia M., and Madeline Zavodny. 2003. "Do Amnesty Programs Reduce Undocumented Immigration? Evidence from Irca." *Demography* 40.3:437–450.

Soblick, Martin D. 1987. "Legalization and Special Agricultural Worker Provisions Under the Immigration Reform and Control Act of 1986." *California Western International Law Journal* 18.1:147–155.

Sponsors

In terms of immigration law, a sponsor refers to someone who petitions for an immigrant to be in the country, usually a family member. Most sponsors consist of a family member who lives in the United States (such as a spouse, parent, or adult child) or employers; but there are many different types of sponsors. A sponsor must be eighteen years of age or older, a U.S. citizen or lawful permanent resident, and live in the United States. A sponsor is responsible for filing an Affidavit of Support Form I-864 with the United States government. In order to be eligible for sponsorship one must complete a petition for the relative, the Office of U.S. Citizenship and Immigration Service (USCIS) must approve the petition, a visa must be available, and the person being sponsored must file an adjustment of status form.

A sponsor must be able to provide proof that they are able to financially support the immigrant who is to be sponsored. If the sponsor's income does not meet the criteria for support, a joint or substitute sponsor may be designated. The same requirements showing financial capability apply for the joint sponsor except that they do not need to be related to the immigrant. The joint or substitute sponsor must meet the 125 percent income requirement alone. Incomes of both sponsors may not be combined in order to meet the requirements. Financial requirements are based on a ratio of income-to-household size. The household size includes the sponsor and all family members living within the same household, including all dependents. The sponsor or joint sponsor is required to submit U.S. federal income tax returns for the three most recent years of employment as proof of financial means of support. In 1996, the Illegal Immigration Reform and Immigrant Responsibility Act (IIRIRA) increased the minimum income requirement for sponsorship. With IIRIRA, the sponsor must provide proof of annual income of at least 125 percent of the poverty income level. Moreover, before IIRIRA went into effect, in lieu of an affidavit of support from a family member, the potential candidate for sponsorship only needed to provide a letter from his employers. Therefore, the hardest hit of the immigrant community were those from the lowest income brackets. As Hagan and Rodriguez (2002) note, the irony of this was that those with the most need of sponsorship to help contribute to household incomes—the most economically needy—were the ones most precluded from being sponsored. Because of this, the authors argue, there was a subsequent increase in the number of immigrants who because of economic need crossed into the United States without authorization in the years following the passage of IIRIRA.

Under IIRIRA, the person who signs the affidavit of support accepts financial responsibility for the sponsored immigrant until they become a U.S. citizen or can be credited with forty quarters of work, about ten years, whichever comes first. Financial responsibility requires that if at any time the immigrant receives any public benefits, or "means-tested public benefit," the financially responsible party is required to repay the debt. If the debt is not repaid, the agency may sue the financially responsible party in court. Examples of federal means-tested public benefits include Temporary Assistance for Needy Families (TANF), Social Security Income (SSI), the State Child Health Insurance Program (CHIP), and food stamps. These new requirements make it more difficult for families in the United States to qualify for sponsorship.

The affidavit of support is required for the petition of all immediate relatives who qualify for immigration into the United States based on family preference. First priority goes to spouses, children and parents, followed by siblings and their spouses. U.S. citizens who are twenty-one years of age or older are eligible to petition for their parents; however, legal permanent residents are not eligible to sponsor their parents to live and work in the United States.

An immigrant may also be sponsored through an employer upon an offer of employment. There are four categories of employment eligibility: EB-1 or Employment-based first preference includes persons who have extraordinary talent in sciences, arts, education, business, and athletics. This includes professors and researchers with at least three years of experience in their chosen field who are recognized internationally. Also included are executives and managers of overseas affiliates who have been employed within three years by a U.S. employer. Second preference of employment-base (EB-2) includes professionals holding advanced degrees, and those with exceptional artistic or scientific abilities. Third preference (EB-3) refers to skilled workers and professionals holding a bachelor's degree. The fourth preference (EB-4) recognizes religious workers, certain overseas employees, members of the U.S. armed forces, and international-organization employees.

Employer-sponsored work-based visas tend to recognize those that have specialized job skills or are in short supply in the United States. Generally, employers prefer to sponsor someone who has received a temporary work-based visa, such as an H-1B. If the employee shows that they are qualified for the job position, employers may later help in the more complex process of helping the beneficiary with a green card application.

In April of 2011, the ACLU called on Congress to pass a bill that would allow sponsorship by one's same-sex partner; it was entitled the United American Families Act. Rep. Jerrold Nadler (D-NY) and Sen. Patrick Leahy (D-VT) sponsored this bill, which would allow gay U.S. citizens the right to petition for and sponsor their same-sex partners for lawful permanent residency. As of June of 2011, the only other option for same-sex partners to apply for permanent legal status was seeking a work-based visa or asylum. Several gay and lesbian couples were able to seek asylum from Pakistan according to the International Gay and Lesbian Human Rights Commission in San Francisco. However, there are term limits on seeking asylum, and the law states that asylum should be sought within one year of entering the United States.

Courtney Martínez

See Also: Families; Family Reunification; Illegal Immigration Reform and Immigrant Responsibility Act (IIRIRA) (1996); Inadmissibility; Provisional Unlawful Presence (PUP) Waiver; Work Visas.

Further Reading

American Civil Liberties Union (ACLU). http://www.aclu.org/immigrants-rights-lgbt-rights/bill-provide-equality-immigration-sponsorship-introduced-congress.

Hagan, Jacqueline, and Nestor Rodriguez. 2002. "Resurrecting Exclusion: The Effects of 1996 U.S. Immigration Reform on Communities and Families in Texas, El Salvador, and Mexico." In *Latinas/os: Remaking of America,* edited by Marcelo M. Suarez-Orozco and Mariela M. Paez, 190–214. Berkeley: University of California Press.

U.S. Citizenship and Immigration Services (UCIS) website: http://www.uscis.gov/portal/site/uscis/menuitem.5af9bb95919f35e66f614176543f6d1a/?vgnextoid=f987a4491c3 5f010VgnVCM1000000ecd190aRCRD&vgnextchannel=b328194d3e88d010VgnVC M10000048f3d6a1RCRD.

Sports

The United States is undergoing a Latinization process as Univision journalist Jorge Ramos writes in his book *The Other Face of America* (2002). Guy Garcia, Ramos's contemporary, states in his book *The New Mainstream* (2004) that ethnic identities, once marginal in the larger scheme of things, will eventually dictate how Americans will eat, work, play, learn, and spend money. It is inevitable that the U.S. sports culture, immigration, and some of the observations found in these two books will converge to explain trends in the sports world for many years to come.

A case in point comes with the reaction to Arizona's SB 1070 in April of 2010, popularly known as the Arizona "Papers Please" or "Show Me Your Papers" law. This piece of legislation—signed into law by its governor, Jan Brewer—provided for broader policing of illegal immigration by state and local law enforcement officials in the state. It also ignited a national firestorm of controversy. At the time, Arizona was home to an estimated 460,000 undocumented immigrants. In response to the law, opponents and immigrant rights advocates began organizing a boycott of the state, and in particular, a call to baseball fans to ask the Major League Baseball Association to pull the 2011 All-Star Game out of Phoenix, Arizona's capital. Protesters began picketing Arizona Diamondbacks games and in Denver, Colorado, there were protests outside of Coors Field on April 28, 2010, and the at Wrigley Field in Chicago to protest the law whenever the Diamondbacks took on these major league teams (Condon, 2010). The result of this boycott effort was mixed, with many Latino fans reluctant to sacrifice their love of the sport for a political cause (Fernández, 2010). There was hope among opponents of the law that Latino players, who make up roughly 30 percent of major leaguers, would refuse to participate in the All-Star game, but it is not clear that this opposition materialized in any real way (Montini, 2011). Although whether or not the boycott of Arizona baseball was truly successful, there was a historical antecedent of a similar boycott that was successful in the 1990s, when Arizona's opposition to instituting Martin Luther King, Jr. Day cost it the 1993 Super Bowl. That year, Arizona lost up to $190 million in revenue when the National Football League decided to move the game from Tempe to Pasadena, California (Fernández, 2010).

In the United States, sports are an important element that adds to community cohesion by bringing people together from all walks of life. William A. Sutton, Mark A. McDonald, George R. Milne, and John Climperman authored an article titled "Creating and Fostering Fan Identification in Professional Sports" (1997) arguing that people in U.S. society are becoming disconnected from a sense of community due to lifestyle and technological changes. Sports activities promote and involve people jointly and provide common symbols and a collective identity.

Latino students in schools across the United States find gyms and fields of play a refuge from the everyday reality regardless of immigration status or socioeconomic status. The sports scene is the one place that being a minority or undocumented or being from a different socioeconomic class holds little bearing on how one competes or how one supports their favorite team or athlete. Sports provide a safe space where everyone is the same. This can be witnessed in three sports Latinos are known to overwhelmingly support: soccer, baseball, and boxing.

It is common knowledge that *fútbol* or soccer is the world's number one sport. For many Latin American immigrants in the United States cheering on one's country every four years during the World Cup reignites national and cultural pride that one can only express twice in a decade. For many Latinos in the United States, this is one time where one is granted license to break out their country's flag or wear their nation's colors in the spirit of athletic nationalism.

Puma's Martin Bravo, left, fights for the ball with Leon's Rafael Marquez during a Mexican soccer league match in Mexico City, Sunday, August 18, 2013. Fútbol or soccer is the world's number one sport, and in the United States, soccer matches offer the opportunity for immigrants to proudly display their nation's colors. Cities like Los Angeles, New York, and Chicago have hosted U.S.-Mexico matches and the vast majority of the spectators have been exuberant Mexico fans. (AP Photo/Christian Palma)

Soccer is a passion for so many Latinos. It can really be exemplified in the rivalry between the United States and Mexico. Mexico has had a history of dominating the Confederation of North, Central America and Caribbean Association Football (CON-CACAF) region. The United States has been challenging that dominance to the chagrin of most Mexicans living in the United States, not to mention those living in Mexico.

When the two countries face off, it is quite literally a blood feud. Mexicans feel their soccer is an extension of themselves and bleed the colors of *El Tri* (short for "El Tricolor," the red, white, and green)—Mexico's moniker derived from the colors of their flag. Americans on the other hand have taken great leaps toward wresting away the number one position in the region, which has historically been Mexican. If one were to Google-search "Mexico-U.S. soccer rivalry" hundreds of posts come up denouncing one country or the other's soccer and fans.

No other sport in the United States can bring Latinos out to U.S. stadiums in droves like a match-up between Mexico and the United States. When the United States plays Mexico on American soil in many major U.S. cities, frenzied Mexican supporters show up in force to the dismay of the U.S. side. U.S. players regularly feel as if they are on foreign soil in their own country. Cities like Los Angeles, New York, and Chicago have hosted U.S.-Mexico matches and the vast majority of the spectators have been rabid Mexico fans.

Latinos are a force in baseball too. Baseball has long been described as the American Pastime. A *New York Times* article reports that the term dates back to the 1850s, according to John Thorn, the author of *Baseball in the Garden of Eden*. However, a Latinization of baseball is taking place and a New Mainstream is emerging. Approximately, one-third of today's Major League Baseball rosters are comprised of Latino ball players. As the game of baseball becomes increasingly global, Latinos are setting the standard of who is playing and dominating the game.

A professional team without Latino ball players would be a team with little hope of being competitive. Latinos have demonstrated at the highest level of the game that they can dominate and excel. Names like Ted Williams, Roberto Clemente, Reggie Jackson, Fernando Valenzuela, Ramon Martinez, and Mariano Rivera are among the game's elite.

The Latino reality is also taking shape at the managerial level as well. Managers like Ozzie Guillen, Lou Pinella, and Felipe Alou have blazed a trail for other Latinos.

Worldwide, soccer is king and in the United States, baseball is America's pastime. There is no doubt about the dominance of these sports on the Latino sports landscape. However, there is one other sport that Latinos dominate pound for pound, and that sport is boxing.

Latinos both in the United States and abroad are a major lifeline to a sport that used to show up regularly on national TV. Newspapers covered it regularly as well. At one time boxing was a mainstream sport. As time has passed and the growth of other sports like American football and basketball took off, boxing's share of the audience has slipped. If not for Latinos, it is conceivable boxing could have disappeared altogether.

Latinos are keeping the sport alive inside the ring and outside as spectators. Oscar de la Hoya, Tito Trinidad, and Julio Cesar Chavez regularly generated millions of pay-per-view dollars while Latinos continue to be the majority of the sport's consumers. Other legends like Roberto Duran, Alexis Arguello, Salvador Sanchez, Wilfredo Gomez, Carlos Monzón, Wilfred Benitez, and Mantequilla Napoles set the standard for Latinos in the squared circle. Today's Latino prize fighters live through those legends and countless other greats.

The impact and impression of Latinos on sports is indelible. By 2050 the Latino population will have tripled in size to 128 million people. Ramos is correct; the United States is going through a Latinization process. So too is the sports landscape; the question is: will America embrace this New Mainstream?

Javier Cervantes

See Also: Arizona SB1070; Culture; Media Coverage; Protests; Social Interaction and Integration.

Further Reading

Condon, Stephanie. 2010. "Arizona Immigration Boycott Zeroes In on Baseball." CBS News. April 29, 2010. http://www.cbsnews.com/8301-503544_162-20003747-503544.html.

Fernández, Valeria. 2010. "Latino Baseball Fans Reluctant to Joint Arizona Boycott." *New America Media.* http://newamericamedia.org/2010/08/latino-baseball-fans-reluctant-to-join-arizona-boycott.php.

Garcia, Guy. 2004. *The New Mainstream: How the Multicultural Consumer is Transforming American Business.* New York: Rayo.

Montini, E. J. 2011. "Not the kind of boycott they wanted." *Arizona Republic,* July 12, 2011. http://www.azcentral.com/arizonarepublic/local/articles/20110712boycott-montini.html#ixzz2RaywCRMq.

Ramos, Jorge. 2002. *The Other Face of America: Chronicles of the Immigrants Shaping Our Future.* New York: Harper Collins.

Sutton, W. A., M. A. McDonald, G. R. Milne, and J. Cimperman. 1997. "Creating and Fostering Fan Identification in Professional Sports." *Sport Marketing Quarterly* 6.1:15–22.

Thorn, John. 2011. *Baseball in the Garden of Eden.* New York: Simon & Schuster.

State Legislation

While Arizona SB 1070 was an example of a state attempting to implement immigration legislation, it was not the first. For many years thousands of laws at state and local levels had been making similar attempts. However, after SB 1070's passage, state governments were emboldened to emulate the extreme effort by Arizona, and by 2011, 1607 bills had been introduced in state legislatures ("State Laws Related to Immigration and Immigrants," 2012). Many of the enacted state laws have in turn been contested or partially blocked by federal courts, and by the U.S. Supreme Court, as has Arizona's. In June of 2012, the U.S. Supreme Court struck down three contested provisions of this law, but kept in place Section 2(B), which obligated law enforcement officials to check the documentation of anyone detained for violation of any other law (including traffic violations) if they had a "reasonable suspicion" that the individual was in the country illegally. Some states had similar laws proposed but awaited the outcome of the lawsuit against Arizona before implementing them, while others—in Mississippi, Texas, and Virginia—were proposed but failed to pass. In 2012, the number of bills to control immigration at the state level appeared to have dropped.

In addition to Arizona, five other states continue to have a version of SB 1070 in force:

In Utah, on March 15, 2011, Republican Governor Gary Herbert signed into law a package of bills that attempt to deal with immigration at the state level, including HB 497, a bill that was inspired by Arizona SB1070. However, Utah's HB 497 also attempted to create a "guest worker" program for undocumented workers currently in Utah. On May 11, hours after HB 497 went into effect, the law was put on hold by the U.S. District Court.

In Indiana, on May 10, 2011, Republican Governor Mitch Daniels signed SB590 over protest by law enforcement agencies and national organizations which threatened to cancel conferences in the state. Although some of the provisions were rescinded, some of the most controversial ones that expanded police authority to enforce federal immigration laws were kept. On June 24, U.S. District Judge Sarah Evans Barker ordered an injunction that blocked the section of Indiana SB 590 that would have increased police arrest authority.

On May 13, 2011, Republican governor of Georgia, Nathan Deal, signed into law House Bill (HB) 87, legislation that allows local state enforcement to question suspects about their immigration status and request documentation to verify. This law also establishes stricter sanctions for businesses hiring undocumented workers and harsher punishment for individuals who hire or harbor undocumented immigrants. Since its passage, numerous news reports have highlighted labor shortages in Georgia's agricultural industry. The law was opposed by the state's Farm Bureau. On June 27, U.S. District Court Judge Thomas Thrash halted two sections of the law dealing with the increased police authority to request proof of citizenship of those detained and the criminalization of those who transported or harbored undocumented individuals.

On June 9, 2011, Republican Alabama governor Robert Bentley signed into law HB 56, also known as the Beason-Hammon Alabama Taxpayer and Citizen Protection Act. It was widely regarded as the harshest immigration law in the country, even more comprehensive than the Arizona law. Like the Arizona law Alabama's HB 56 allows state law enforcement to determine a person's immigration status if "reasonable suspicion" exists in the course of detaining or arresting said individual. The law proposed to prohibit and criminalize business transactions between undocumented immigrants and state agencies and for courts to regard any contract to which an undocumented person is a party as unenforceable. It also proposed to deny bail to detained undocumented immigrants. One of its most controversial proposals would have required schools to ask about the immigration status of every newly enrolled student, and report it to state officials. However, this provision of the law proved unpopular as it led to a vast drop in public school enrollments and a substantial labor shortage in the agricultural sector. It was estimated that the state would lose millions in revenues. By August 1, 2011, a number of civil rights organizations enjoined by the U.S. Department of Justice filed a lawsuit claiming that various provisions of HB 56 conflict with federal immigration law.

On April 29, 2013, the U.S. Supreme Court, voting 8–1, turned down an appeal by Alabama, which had been blocked by the U.S. Court of Appeals for the Eleventh Circuit from enforcing a transporting and assisting provision. This provision would have made it illegal for an Alabama resident to transport, hide, or harbor an undocumented immigrant, but the Supreme Court upheld the U.S. Court of Appeals ruling, noting that the provision conflicted with the federal government's responsibility to prosecute undocumented immigrants (Savage, 2013).

On June 27, 2011, South Carolina followed suit when Republican governor Nikki Haley signed legislation called SB 20, requiring state law enforcement to check the immigration status of anyone they stop or arrest. SB 20 also authorized the creation of a $1.3 million Illegal Immigration Enforcement Unit to serve as a liaison between local police and federal immigration officials. This law was scheduled to take effect in January 2012. It was challenged by a number of groups, and in November 2012, the U.S. District Court for the District of South Carolina in Charleston ruled that, although it allowed the provision for law enforcement to check for legal documentation for immigrants when they were stopped for a violation, as the Supreme Court allows with the

State-level Immigration Legislation Trends
2005-2010

——— Bills Introduced

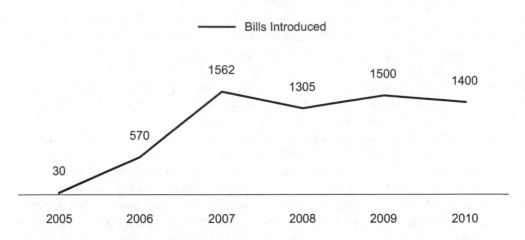

	1562		1305	1500	1400
570					
30					

| 2005 | 2006 | 2007 | 2008 | 2009 | 2010 |

Arizona law, it blocked and invited challenges to other parts of the law, such as making it illegal to give a ride to an unauthorized immigrant.

Long-Term Consequences for Immigrant Populations

Scholars have confirmed that laws like SB 1070 aggravate distrust between Latinos in general and undocumented immigrants in particular and authorities. Research by Trujillo and Paluck (2012) shows that there were higher overall levels of negative affect toward the U.S. government and mistrust of the U.S. Census among Latinos in Arizona compared with two other border states, which was attributed to the environment created by SB 1070 in Arizona. Likewise, an analysis by Lopez (2011) observes that the state's intention to rid itself of immigrant populations has both anticipated and real consequences, not only for those that were uprooted, but also for those left behind, including the loss of friends and family. These laws potentially harbor social and academic problems, anxiety-related health effects, and deepened any mistrust of institutions in immigrant communities. This mistrust in turn disrupts daily routines and discourages civic and social engagement.

Finally, despite the allegations made by various state officials and politicians critical of the federal government's approach to immigration, or maybe because of them, the Obama administration has been proactive in immigration enforcement since assuming office in 2008. Under the Obama administration, U.S. Immigration and Customs Enforcement (ICE) has been consistently active in large-scale raids on businesses hiring undocumented workers as well as responsible for a record number of deportations, surpassing the rates of prior presidential administrations. According to ICE, approximately 400,000 individuals were deported in fiscal year 2011, surpassing the 392,862 deported the prior fiscal year.

Anna Ochoa O'Leary

See Also: Arizona SB 1070; Employer Sanctions; Exclusion; Policies of Attrition; Racial Profiling; Shadow Population; Southern States.

Further Reading

Donnelly, Robert. 2012. "State-Level Immigrant-Related Legislation: What It Means for the Immigration Policy Debate." In *Antimigrant Sentiments, Actions and Policies in North America and the European Union,* edited by, Monica Verea, 123–136. Mexico, D.F.: Centro de Investigación sobre América del Norte (CISAN) de la Universidad Autónoma de México (UNAM).

González de Bustamante, Celeste. 2012. "Arizona and the Making of a State of Exclusion, 1912–2012." In *Arizona Firestorm: Global Immigration Realities, National Media & Provincial Politics,* edited by O. Santa Ana and C. González de Bustamante. New York: Rowman & Littlefield Publisher, Inc.

Lacayo, Elena. 2011. "One Year Later: A Look at SB1070 and Copycat legislation." National Council of La Raza. http://www.nclr.org/images/uploads/publications/AlookatSB1070v3.pdf.

Lopez, Tomas. 2011. "Left Back: The Impact of SB 1070 on Arizona's Youth." University of Arizona. http://www.law.arizona.edu/depts/bacon_program/pdf/Left_Back.pdf.

Savage, David G. 2013. "Supreme Court won't revive Alabama immigration law." *Los Angeles Times,* April 29.

"State Laws Related to Immigration and Immigrants." 2012. National Council of State Legislatures (NCSL). http://www.ncsl.org/issues-research/immig/state-laws-related-to-immigration-and-immigrants.aspx.

Thangasamy, Andrew. 2010. *State Policies for Undocumented Immigrants: Policy-making and Outcomes in the U.S., 1998–2005.* El Paso, TX: LFB Scholarly Pub.

Trujillo, Matthew D., and Elizabeth Levy Paluck. 2012. "The Devil Knows Best: Experimental Effects of a Televised Soap Opera on Latino Attitudes Toward Government and Support for the 2010 U.S. Census." *Analyses of Social Issues & Public* 12.1:113–132.

United States Court of Appeals for the Ninth Circuit. 2010. Amicus Brief. http://www.volokh.com/wp-content/uploads/2010/10/mexicoamicusbrief.pdf.

Strangers from a Different Shore

Strangers from a Different Shore: A History of Asian Americans was written by Ronald Takaki in 1989 and updated and revised in 1998. Ronald Takaki was a third-generation American of Japanese heritage who was born and raised in Hawaii, earned a Ph.D. in history, and taught ethnic studies for years at the University of California, Berkeley. Takaki uses *Strangers from a Different Shore* to highlight historical differences between the ways that immigrants from Asia were treated in the United States compared to immigrants who arrived from Europe. The book does not deal with contemporary undocumented migration from Asia; rather it reminds us that in the past, U.S. immigration policies that determined who could legally migrate and who could naturalize as a citizen were racialized by design, favoring European immigrants and excluding Asians.

Takaki also notes that Angel Island served as the Ellis Island for Chinese immigrants on the West Coast.

Takaki observes that although "Italians, Jews, Irish, and other European-immigrant groups were victims of labor exploitation, social ostracism, and the sharp barbs of intolerant American nativism," or in other words, although they were initially seen as culturally "strange" and treated as "strangers," eventually they were able to physically blend in with "old-stock whites" (1998:12). Regardless of popular attitudes, immigrants from European shores were legally defined as "whites" and thus entitled to naturalize as citizens. In contrast, Asians were "strangers from a different shore." They were not regarded as "white" and could not naturalize, because the Naturalization Law of 1790 only allowed naturalization for "white" persons. This law remained in effect until 1952 (1998:14). Nevertheless, as Takaki documents, several Asians filed lawsuits questioning their racial classification and exclusion from citizenship.

In addition, anti-Asian sentiments particularly on the West Coast resulted in the passage of the Chinese Exclusion Act in 1882. Prior to this, with the Page Law of 1875, the federal government limited access to migration for Chinese women. States like California and cities like San Francisco were passing legislation that restricted Chinese access to gold mining, created dual wage systems, restricted Chinese access to various working-class jobs (which pushed them into opening small businesses such as laundries), required special taxes that only applied to Chinese laundries, restricted access to housing which fostered the creation of ethnic enclaves, and required Chinese men to cut their long hair, usually bound in a long braid and worn hanging down the back of the neck, called a "queue."

In 1908 the United States signed the Gentlemen's Agreement with the Japanese government to restrict Japanese migration. In this agreement, Japan agreed to not issue passports to its citizens, thus eliminating new immigration to the United States. In exchange, the United States agreed to accept the presence of Japanese immigrants already residing there, to permit the immigration of wives, children, and parents, and to avoid legal discrimination against Japanese children in California schools. The agreements were never ratified by the U.S. Congress. In the 1920s xenophobia aimed not only at Asians but at southern and eastern Europeans led to the passage of the National Origins Act in 1924. This law set quotas for future immigration based on each national group's percentage within the existing U.S. population according to the 1910 and later the 1920 census. This law remained in effect until the Immigration Act of 1965 was passed. As Takaki notes, this law excluded Japanese from immigrating to the U.S. mainland (1998:14). In contrast, the law allowed "the annual entry of 17,853 from Ireland, 5,802 from Italy, and 6,524 from Poland" (1998:14). In addition, the quota laws prevented immigrant men from China, Japan, Korea and India who were already in the United States from bringing over wives and forming families, since "aliens ineligible to citizenship" were inadmissible (1998:14). In contrast, the 1924 law not only allowed European-immigrant men to return to bring back wives, but European women who came as wives were not included in the quota limits set for each nationality (1998:14).

Initially the 1924 law did not apply to Filipino immigrants. At the time the Philippines was a territory of the United States, acquired at the end of the Spanish-American War in 1898. However, the Tydings-McDuffie Act of 1934 granted independence to the Philippines, and subsequently the legal restrictions being applied to other Asians also were applied to Filipinos (1998:14).

Takaki discusses efforts by U.S. employers to recruit Asian workers, particularly for agriculture and railroad construction. For example, Chinese immigrants were recruited to work on sugar plantations in Hawaii as early as the 1830s (1998:21). Planters later recruited workers from Japan, Korea, and the Philippines (and other places) to ensure that workers would remain ethnically divided and thus less able to organize strikes to improve salaries and working conditions (1998:24–27). As Takaki describes, to some extent their strategies worked, but eventually workers started forming alliances. Most of the early Asian immigrants were men.

Japanese immigrants were recruited to work in Hawaii as early as the 1860s, but began migrating in larger numbers to Hawaii and the mainland United States after the 1880s (1998:43). As noted earlier, their migration was restricted after 1908. Japanese immigrants on the West Coast began specializing in farming fruits and vegetables, only to see laws passed that prohibited them from owning land. Takaki also describes the internment of Japanese immigrants and U.S.-born Japanese Americans during World War II, as well as their participation as soldiers on the European front.

Between 1903 and 1920 about eight thousand Koreans migrated to the United States, mostly to Hawaii (1998:53). Japanese and Korean women eventually migrated to Hawaii as "picture brides," and also worked in the fields. Takaki describes how Asian women also were recruited to work as prostitutes. Takaki lays out the history of Filipino "manongs" who migrated to Hawaii and the mainland starting in the early 1900s, and Punjabi Sikhs who began migrating to work in agriculture on the West Coast in 1907. In all, only about 6,400 Asian Indians migrated during that time, because U.S. officials started restricting their migration in 1909, and then completely prohibited it by 1917 (1998:62). By comparison, during the late 1800s and early 1900s 430,000 Chinese, 380,000 Japanese, and 150,000 Filipinos immigrated to the United States (1998:65).

Takaki's goal was to revise history to include Asians in the history of America (1998:7). The book provides vivid accounts of everyday life from the perspectives of Asian immigrants from the 1800s through 1965. Takaki also describes Asian migration after 1965, including refugees from Vietnam, Cambodia and Laos. He also deals with the myth of Asians as the "model minority," and discusses Asians within the context of U.S. race relations.

De Ann Pendry

See Also: Chinese; East Asians; Emergency Quota Act of 1921; Johnson-Reed Act (1924); Racism; South Asians; *Strangers in the Land*; Xenophobia.

Further Reading

Espiritu, Yen Le. 2003. *Home Bound: Filipino American Lives across Cultures, Communities, and Countries.* Berkeley: University of California Press.

Hune, Shirley, and Gail M. Nomura. 2003. *Asian/Pacific Islander Women: A Historical Anthology.* New York: New York University Press.

Ngai, Mae. 2004. *Impossible Subjects: Illegal Immigrants and the Making of Modern America.* Princeton, NJ: Princeton University Press.

Ong, Aihwa. 1996. "Citizenship as Subject Making: New Immigrants Negotiate Racial and Ethnic Boundaries." *Current Anthropology* 37.5:737–762.

Takaki, Ronald. 1998. *Strangers from a Different Shore: A History of the Asian Americans,* Updated and Revised Edition. New York: Back Bay Books, Little, Brown and Company.

Strangers in the Land

Strangers in the Land: Patterns of American Nativism, 1860–1925 is widely regarded a seminal text on American nativism. Authored by American historian John Higham and first published in 1955, *Strangers in the Land* provided a groundbreaking systematic analysis of the nature and manifestation of anti-immigrant sentiment and its impact on American political development. The text is an important contribution to the study of American culture, immigration politics, and ethnicity, and influenced scholarship across disciplines within the social sciences. Rutgers University Press published subsequent editions of *Strangers in the Land* that contain minor corrections and new commentary by Higham (1963, 1988, 2002). Higham's introductory and concluding remarks in the later works aim to clarify concepts and address the book's shortcomings, particularly in light of political and intellectual developments that followed publication of the original text. Subsequent editions do not alter in any significant way the fundamental argument of the book.

A key contribution of *Strangers in the Land* is Higham's analysis of American nativism as a distinct kind of American nationalism. The text defines nativism as "intense opposition to an internal minority on the ground of its foreign (i.e., 'un-American') connections" (1963 edition, p. 4). Through his analysis of nativist organizations and their mobilization in America between 1860 and 1925, Higham demonstrates that American nativism is consistently characterized by this opposition, even though the targets of nativists' concerns change over time. Higham differentiates between nativism and other forms of nationalism—in particular, a cosmopolitan form of nationalism that embraces a multi-cultural, multi-ethnic vision of America. Additionally, Higham argues that American nativism is distinct from xenophobia—an intense fear or hatred of foreigners—given that at some times nativists have accommodated particular groups of foreigners, and have been a vehicle for the assimilation of foreigners into American society.

Another important feature of *Strangers in the Land* is Higham's theoretical commitment to the notion that ideas are a powerful force in American society and politics. The examination of ideas—as opposed to institutions or interest groups—was a new area of inquiry at the time *Strangers in the Land* was first published. *Strangers in the Land* demonstrated that while ideas are important, the meaning and influence of ideas change with changes in social, economic, intellectual, and international developments. For this reason, the original publication of *Strangers in the Land* was at the forefront of cultural studies, and in particular the study of rhetoric and symbols as a means by which to understand collective action.

Strangers in the Land focuses on the nativism of the late nineteenth and early twentieth century. To make sense of the political events of these eras, Higham dedicates the first chapter of the book to locating American nativism within the historical record of civilization and American society. Nativism is a distinctly American word, associated specifically with the rise of self-proclaimed nativist political parties in the 1830s and 1840s. At the same time, nativism reflects a long-standing tendency of humans to harbor suspicion, if not hostility, toward those people not part of one's own social group. Higham argues that America has three nativist traditions—anti-Catholic, anti-radical, and anti-immigrant—which are products of conflicts in Europe prior to and during the settlement of the New World, and conflicts that emerged between the European colonizers and the very different indigenous populations they encountered in the Americas. Higham identifies four periods of exceptionally influential nativism: the late 1790s, when nativism gave rise to the Alien Acts; the 1850s, when it contributed to the breakup of the party system; the decade between 1886 and 1896, when nativists succeeded in linking a host of social ills to immigrants; and during World War I, when heightened nativism paved the way for passage of unprecedented restrictions on immigration. In each era, nativists identified threats to the American polity and associated them with the presence and behaviors of particular groups of people—sometimes Irish Catholics, sometimes the Chinese, sometimes Eastern and Southern Europeans.

The nativism that emerged in the late 1800s and early 1900s became increasingly radicalized. Nativist concerns about certain groups of people disseminating bad politics and bad morals merged with new "scientific evidence" produced by eugenics. Eugenics—the study of human traits based on the idea that some races are inherently superior to others—traveled to the United States from Europe at the end of the nineteenth century. Though the eugenics research would later be discredited for its deficiencies as a scientific enterprise, it helped give rise to the notion of a superior "white race" and fueled concerns emerging at the time about the entry of people of inferior races. Growing fears of and hostility toward groups deemed un-American—due to their politics, customs, and race—culminated in increasingly restrictive legislation between the late 1800s and early 1900s.

Federal laws passed in the late 1800s and originating during World War I reflected each of the three traditions of nativism—anti-Catholic, anti-radical, and anti-immigrant—identified by Higham. In 1882, Congress passed the Chinese Exclusion Act, the first major federal law banning a category of people from immigrating. Over the next six decades, Congress would pass more laws explicitly barring certain categories of people from immigrating to the United States. The laws sought to maintain the purity of the nation by excluding people of certain races, criminals, people with disease or disabilities, and people who failed to meet certain moral standards. The Immigration Act of 1924 marked the height of nativism in the early twentieth century, and set the course for increasingly restrictive immigration policy. It established quotas to drastically reduce the number of immigrants from Southern and Eastern Europe, Asia and Africa, and reaffirmed the exclusion of Asians, with the Oriental Exclusion Act of 1924. The 1924 Immigration Act remained the guiding policy on immigration until the 1960s.

While *Strangers in the Land* remains influential and largely unscathed by sustained criticism, Higham himself asserted in later editions that the book's flaws, and changes in American society since its publication, beg for fresh research on American nativism. In particular, *Strangers in the Land* does not adequately explain what, exactly, makes nativism attractive and potent in American society at one time, but not another. For example, Higham contends in *Strangers in the Land* that poor economic conditions were central to the rise of nativism in the late 1800s, and yet the virulent nativism of the early 1900s emerged at a time of economic prosperity. Moreover, Higham's focus on nativist nationalism leaves much to be explained about the power of cosmopolitan ideals. In a review of his own book published in 2000, Higham argues that a more complete treatment of nationalist ideologies—rather than his narrow focus on nativism—would reveal a great deal more about their mobilization and influence on American society and politics. Nothing on nativism paralleling *Strangers in the Land* was published after it until the late 1980s. There are several explanations for this: the widely regarded elegance and sophistication of *Strangers in the Land*; trends in history and other disciplines that privileged the study of particularities of ethnic groups; and a relative decline in nativism and the nation's embrace of multi-culturalism and a more cosmopolitan idea of the nation. Scholars, including Higham, have noted a resurgence in nativism since the early 1980s, and the phenomenon has become a growing area of research within and outside of the United States since.

Carolyn J. Craig

See Also: Chinese; East Asians; Emergency Quota Act of 1921; Minutemen; Patriotism; Racism; *Strangers from a Different Shore;* Xenophobia.

Further Reading

Higham, John. 1955. *Strangers in the Land: Patterns of American Nativism, 1860–1925.* New Brunswick, NJ: Rutgers University Press.
Higham, John. 2000. "Instead of a Sequel, or How I Lost My Subject." *Reviews in American History* 28.2:327–339.
Kwong, Peter. 1997. *Forbidden Workers: Illegal Chinese Immigrants and American Labor.* New York: Free Press.
Lee, Erika. 2003. *At America's Gates: Chinese Immigration During the Exclusion Era, 1882–1943.* Chapel Hill, NC: University of North Carolina Press.
Ngai, Mae. 2004. *Impossible Subjects: Illegal Immigrants and the Making of Modern America.* Princeton, NJ: Princeton University Press.

Student Visas

Since the 1993 and 2001 terrorist attacks on the World Trade Center in New York City, there have been various debates about implementing a system in the United States to better keep track of foreign students who come to the United States on student visas. In 1993, the investigation of the bombing of the World Trade Center revealed that the driver of the Ryder van used to plant explosives was a student who had entered the

American University International Student Services Director Fanta Aw and Special Projects Team Leader Paul Langhan during a news conference on January 8, 2003 in Washington, D.C. American University unveiled its international student tracking system, which is compatible with the INS Student and Exchange Visitor Information System (SEVIS) requirements for tracking international students who have enrolled at the university. (Getty Images)

country on a student visa to attend Wichita State, but later dropped out. After 9/11, it was again discovered that several of the terrorists in the attack of the World Trade Center and other U.S. targets had been granted student visas to enter the United States (Haddal, 2008). Subsequently, there were legislative discussions proposing ways in which such students might be subject to greater surveillance while in the United States (National Review, 2002). The Illegal Immigration Reform and Immigrant Responsibility Act (IIRIRA) of 1996 had provided a mandate for the program, and in 2003, with the enactment of the USA PATRIOT Act, a system was established to keep track of foreign students who have received student visas, known as the Student and Exchange Visitor Information System (SEVIS). Participation in the SEVIS program is now mandatory for all higher education institutions enrolling foreign students (Haddal, 2008). However, critics of the program argue that it is inefficient and impractical (Davis and Oster, 2002).

Currently any foreign-born nonimmigrant student wishing to attend a program of study in the United States must first apply and be approved for a student visa. Before a student applies for a student visa, they must apply to a SEVP-accredited education institution and be accepted into one of their programs. There are three general types of student visas. F-1 visa is the appropriate category for those wishing to study at a university, college, high school, private elementary school, seminary, conservatory, language training program, or other types of academic institutions in the United States. The J-1 exchange visitor visa was developed for individuals wanting to participate in educational and cultural exchanges between the United States and other countries. Those with this visa—such as visiting scholars—are typically part of an exchange program focused on learning, teaching, receiving training, or conducting research. An M-1-visa is generally the classification of visa for individuals looking to attend a vocational or other recognized nonacademic program. Finally, if a potential applicant is going to the United States as a tourist but wishes to take a class that is less than eighteen hours per week, they may apply for a B-type visa. A student visa is required for anyone looking to travel to the United States for seminars, conferences, or an academic program of study.

Nonimmigrant students wishing to apply for a student visa may do so as soon as they have received acceptance into their program of study or school. Embassies are able to issue student visas 120 days prior to the program of study registration date. In order to initiate the application process for a student visa, the school must issue a letter stating that they are responsible for the student at their institution and confirm the student's acceptance. This document is a necessary part of the visa application process. The applying student must also prove that they or their parents have the financial means with which to support the student through the completion of their studies in the United States. The student must also prove that they do not intend to stay in the United States after the completion of their academic program. After submitting the required visa application forms and paying the application and issuance fees the student must go through an interview with the embassy of their home country. During this interview the embassy is essentially looking to see that the student is in fact looking to enter the United States for educational purposes and that they are a serious student.

Once the student has entered the United States, they will be allowed to stay for the duration of their education program. During a student visit to the United States, they may be able to legally work on or off campus, since many universities offer employment opportunities for international visa-holding students. Staying beyond the designated time indicated on the visa document will cause a student to be out of status. Being out of status is a violation of U.S. immigration laws, and the consequences of this may cause one to be ineligible for future visa approvals and thus lose the privilege of returning to the United States. In accordance with the Immigration and Naturalization Act, staying even one day past the date identified in the visa documents results in a voided visa.

Undocumented students are technically not considered international students and unless restricted by their state laws, there is nothing to preclude their admission into U.S. colleges and universities. However, the relationship between undocumented students residing in the United States and their ability to access post-secondary education became part of the national debate with rising expectations for immigration reform and the failure of Congress to pass the Development, Relief, and Education for Alien Minors Act (DREAM Act). Beginning in 2011, the issue of student visas that might be made available to undocumented immigrant students gained national attention with the introduction of the Science, Technology, Engineering and Mathematics (STEM) Visa Act of 2011 in the U.S. Congress by U.S. Senator for Colorado, Michael

Bennet. Bennet, a former Denver school administrator, had responded to the concerns of businesses that America was good at delivering a world-class higher education in these fields only to lose these trained students after they graduate and return to their countries of origin. In 2009, anywhere between one-half and two-thirds of all PhDs were earned by international students at American universities in physics, economics, computer science and other technical fields. The Bennet proposal would have also given undocumented students a student visa if they enrolled in a science, math or technology program as undergraduates (Sherry, 2011). Although the Bennet proposal did not make it to a vote, the issue was taken up again by a group of eight U.S. senators as they grappled with developing a proposal for comprehensive immigration reform in 2013.

Carolina Luque

See Also: Colleges and Universities; Counterterrorism and Immigrant Profiling; Deferred Action for Childhood Arrivals (DACA); DREAM Act; Education; International Students; Student Visas.

Further Reading

Davis, Anne, and Chris Oster. 2002. "Private Eyes Bid to Help the INS Track Students." *Wall Street Journal.* Feb. 11. http://zp9vv3zm2k.search.serialssolutions.com/?sid=EBSCO:Academic+Search+Complete&genre=article&title=Wall+Street+Journal+-+Eastern+Edition&atitle=Private+Eyes+Bid+To+Help+the+INS+Track+Students.&author=Davis%2c+Ann&authors=Davis%2c+Ann%3bOster%2c+Chris&date=20020211&volume=239&issue=29&spage=B1&issn=00999660.

Haddal, Chad C. 2008. Congressional Research Service Report # RL31146. "Foreign Students in the United States: Policies and Legislation." http://www.au.af.mil/au/awc/awcgate/crs/rl31146.pdf.

National Review. 2002. "Border Wars." April 8, 2002. 54 (6):14–15. 4.

Sherry, Allison. 2011. "Bennet Bill Seeks Visas for Illegal Immigrants Studying Math, Science." *Denver Post,* December 14 http://www.denverpost.com/politics/ci_19542420#ixzz2RbIqztr5.

U.S. Department of State. www.travel.state.gov.

Suburbs

A suburb is a type of housing development that emerged primarily in the twentieth century, built in outlying regions of major cities. From World War II onward, suburbs were advertised as self-sufficient communities, a way for those of a growing middle-class to get away from undesirable traits seen in inner cities, such as high population density and traffic congestion, crime, and noise and air pollution. Suburbs have also attracted immigrants and their families with jobs and other opportunities. For example, with more immigrants finding jobs in suburbs, new markets emerge, resulting in the creation of more businesses to cater to the new populations.

Upon their arrival into suburbs, these migrants often must contend with a culture much different than those they are accustomed to, and as a result, they adapt and create differing expressions of identity based on their class and ethnicity. This may result in the emergence of new ethnic enclaves as persons move to suburbs and share in multiple identities with their diverse neighbors. Yet, there are negative characteristics attributed to migrants by others. In some places they have been met with fear, racism, and in some cases, violence. An example of what may happen in such environments comes from the video documentary "9500 Liberty," where the board of supervisors of Prince William County, Virginia, under pressure from voters, enacted an anti-immigrant ordinance in the county (very similar to the later state-wide law enacted in Arizona, SB 1070). Immigrants also contend with physical violence by gangs who commit brutal acts against youth and adults in these areas. However, economic scarcity, racism, and segregation fuel these gangs and increase their numbers. A deeper analysis of historical conditions is necessary to understand the growth of insecurity and increased segregation in suburban neighborhoods.

Suburbs have often been used as a way to avoid living in the interior of cities. Inner cities are perceived as crime-ridden, dirty, and lacking in jobs. Suburbs are built partly from the willingness to pay more to avoid such conditions. Those who could afford to leave became separated from those who had to pay low-rent housing and had no choice but to do short commutes due to lack of personal transportation. Gentrification emerged, with many African-Americans, Latinos, and others being left to the inner cities, but with many more affluent whites moving to such suburbs. Racist attitudes influenced some to attribute the poverty and quality of life to the ethnic makeup of different inner-city neighborhoods.

For example, some residential communities' advertisements featured gates prominently in the pictures. It was made explicit that they were for purchase by "Caucasians" only. Techniques such as redlining implicitly tied the property value to occupation or proximity to families of color, scaring off potential investors. Real estate agencies sometimes sent notices to those families, encouraging them to move elsewhere.

In recent decades, the populations of suburban Latinos have been growing, despite any efforts to restrict their purchase of homes. Due to the legalization efforts of the 1986 Immigration Reform and Control Act more migrants moved to these neighborhoods, including near Garden City in New York and destinations never traveled to before. Their migration networks expanded into aging low-rent housing districts. Suburban migrants began to outnumber inner-city migrants by 18 percent. New areas like the South and West—including cities such as Atlanta, Mobile, and Phoenix—experienced booms in population. News of jobs was spread by employers to rural areas as far away as El Salvador and other countries. Latino immigrant populations have contributed to the growth in diversity in many U.S. states.

Demand for more retail jobs and restaurant services in the late 1980s grew as the economy boomed. There was high demand then for day laborers to work in construction. However, following economic trends dominated by the restructuring of the U.S. economy and reliance on a flexible labor force, this often meant that workers were not given full-time and permanent employment. Instead, the growing trend towards flexible employment resulted in the more precarious underemployment of workers. Contractors preferred these groups because they were less inclined to organize their labor, and they could be paid piecemeal. This was also due to their questionable legal status. Unions among undocumented immigrants and day-laborers were uncommon, as they are still. Many undocumented workers were aware of their precarious position as they gathered in certain places to ask for work with passing employers and construction contractors. These "shape-up sites" were often chosen just because of parking lots for easy transportation, and nearby gas stations provided coffee in the cold mornings. Much construction work was begun to take in the numerous workers, as many could not find full employment due to businesses pressured to reject persons without verifiable work authorizaion. In fact many other suburbs and gated communities have been built due to the ability to employ undocumented workers. Landscaping and concrete pouring for a growing suburbanite population were only some of the tasks they were hired for. Undocumented immigrant women also have found employment as domestic workers and nannies among the more affluent homeowners.

However, established residents of those suburbs began to associate incoming migrants with a rise in gang violence and insecurity of their own homes. Despite the documented drop in nationwide homicide statistics, some suburban residents pushed for tougher enforcement legislation and to boycott local businesses that hired undocumented workers.

One result of the *de facto* segregation was separate funding for schools, based on local distribution of wealth. Some schools in the more affluent areas were able to support more extracurricular and enrichment activities, school testing services, and counseling. Those in the inner cities that had large numbers of Latino, Asian and other migrants were not as endowed. For this reason, and faced with recessionary budget tightening, funds for programs to combat gang activity were slashed. This lack of funding meant some suburbs were even more vulnerable.

The anxiety over increased immigration was also translated into local legislative action. Some city councils broke up those shape-up sites where employers located available undocumented workers. The laws were justified as preserving security for American citizens. In Arizona, for example, a law prohibiting a city, town or county from constructing and maintaining work centers if any part of the center is to facilitate the knowing employment of an alien who is not entitled to lawful residence in the United States (HB 2592) was signed by then-governor Janet Napolitano on May 20, 2005. Ministers and local civil rights advocates have questioned such laws and criticized them on the grounds they were obstructing the First Amendment's guarantee of free assembly.

Arising out of the suburban context, and due to the omnipresence of immigrant women who work as domestics and housekeepers and nannies, in 2008 a "Domestic Workers' Rights" bill was passed in a Washington D.C. district, spearheaded by domestic workers' unions and migrant rights' groups. The bill intended to provide female workers a guarantee of certain employee benefits, such as paid vacation and workers' sick time. This bill was a milestone, and was accomplished by the hard work of legal staff working with immigrant groups in the Washington, D.C. area. Their achievement was meant to be shared with other undocumented workers. More importantly, the great stride towards immigrant workers, rights stood to expand its success in other districts in the area. Domestic workers' unions see these gains as a way to make employers aware of these rights held by all workers regardless of legal status. The passing of this bill has been lauded as a successful example of how a small group of workers, working outside the public eye, were able to craft a participatory role for themselves.

Ben DuMontier

See Also: Day labor's; Domestic Workers; Economics; Landscape Industry; Restaurants; Small Business Ownership; Workers' Rights.

Further Reading

Cantor, Guillermo. 2010. "Struggling for Immigrants' Rights at the Local Level: The Domestic Workers Bill of Rights Initiative in a Suburb of Washington, DC." *Journal of Ethnic and Migration Studies,* 36.7.

Cornelius, Wayne. 1989. "Mexican Migration to the United States: An Introduction." In Wayne A. Cornelius and Jorge A. Bustamante, eds., *Mexican Migration to the United States,* 1–21. Berkeley: University of California Press.

Garland, Sarah. 2009. *Gangs in Garden City: How Immigration, Segregation, and Youth Violence Are Changing America's Suburbs.* New York: Nation Books.

Gottdiener, M., and Leslie Budd. 2005. *Key Concepts in Urban Studies.* Trowbridge, Great Britain: SAGE Publications.

T

Taxes

Taxes are a contribution to both state and local governments either paid automatically for a good or a service, or paid yearly to the Internal Revenue Service (IRS) and to most state governments by those who earn income in the United States. Those who contribute these taxes are called taxpayers. Taxes are significant to the issue of undocumented immigration in the United States because there exists a myth that undocumented immigrants do not pay taxes, and are therefore an even greater strain on the nation's economy. Immigration research institutes and even the IRS have shown that this is not entirely the case. By virtue of being present in the United States and paying sales taxes on goods and services as well as property taxes in rent charges and taxes on gasoline, just like everyone else in the United States, undocumented immigrants contribute to the economy not only in this way, but by paying income taxes, making false the popular notion that the undocumented population does not pay taxes.

Necessary for the declaring of yearly federal income taxes is a Social Security number granted by the Social Security Administration (SSA). Those who are ineligible for a Social Security number for any reason may apply for an Individual Taxpayer Identification Number, or ITIN, which, like a Social Security number, is nine digits long and allows federal income taxes to be declared legitimately. The ITIN was created in 1996 as a way to assure that compliance with United States tax laws is possible for all wage earners in the United States, regardless of legal status. Upon application and acceptance, the ITIN arrives in the form of a letter, not in the form of a card like the Social Security number, and its sole purpose is for ITIN recipients to be able to fulfill their legal obligation of paying their taxes. It is used by foreign nationals as well as some undocumented immigrants. Starting in 2013, however, partly as a result of concern that too many undocumented immigrants were receiving ITINs and possibly illegal tax credits, the application procedures became much stricter, requiring certified copies of passports, driver's licenses, birth certificates, and other forms of documentation.

While many of those who declare taxes paid with ITINs are undocumented, there are also legal residents who use the ITIN who do not qualify for a Social Security number, such as foreign investors and foreign-born students in the United States. Non-immigrants with tourist visas who vacation in the United States may use ITINs to declare prize money that comes from gambling, and subsequent taxes that must be paid on these earnings. The Immigration Policy Center points out that the ITIN does not grant an undocumented individual legal immigration status, nor does it authorize an undocumented individual to work legally in the United States.

Undocumented immigrant, working in the United States, right, looks over his tax return with his tax preparer in California on April 4, 2007. Tax time can be very stressful for many as they file their information with the Internal Revenue Service. The Inspector General for the Social Security Administration estimates, based on taxes paid to Social Security alone, that undocumented immigrants contribute nearly $9 billion per year. (AP Photo/Jeff Chiu)

Part of the success of the ITIN program has been the fact that the United States tax code does not recognize immigration status, and therefore keeps information about immigration status, or lack thereof, private. It is believed that this privacy has helped encourage millions of undocumented immigrants to report their earnings for tax purposes since its initiation in 1996. Between 1996 and 2003, ITINs were issued to more than 7.2 million people, and in just the year 2001 alone, more than $300 million was collected from ITIN filers alone, many of whom were undocumented. Another factor that has encouraged undocumented immigrants to file their taxes yearly, by means of the ITIN, is the popular belief that paying taxes shows good moral character on the immigrant's part. Although vaguely defined, "good moral character" may be one of several attributes that can be used in fulfilling one of many requirements for adjusting one's immigrant status and for gaining legal residency in the United States.

Although the ITIN permits undocumented immigrants to abide by the law in declaring their taxes, usage of an ITIN means the taxpayer is not eligible for the tax and public benefits that are available to those who declare taxes with the use of a Social Security number, United States citizens or otherwise. These include Social Security benefits as well as the Earned Income Tax Credit (EITC), which is a help for low-to-moderate wage earners in that it reduces the amount of taxes owed, and often results in a greater tax refund.

Of importance also to the subject of taxes among the undocumented population in the United States is the fact that labor force participation by many workers takes place in the informal sectors of the economy. The informal economy includes any work in which wages go unregulated. These wages are very often paid in cash and are commonly referred to as "under the table" or "off the books." The government does not tax the wages earned in the informal sector simply because they go unmonitored or unregulated by the government. Women are the workers most commonly found in the informal sector, performing in such capacities as domestic servants and child care providers. Other common examples of informal sector jobs include those engaged in the landscaping industry, those who remove snow from driveways or mow lawns, although none of these jobs are held by undocumented immigrants alone. Many of the workers employed for these jobs are homeowners. Informal sector jobs are also often performed by teenagers for extra spending money, for instance, so in no way does the informal sector pertain only to the undocumented. While it is true that these jobs are untaxed, these jobs are often underpaid to begin with, and the workers are unable to benefit from common formal job sector benefits such as health care, job security, workers' compensation in case of injury on the job, or unemployment insurance when they are laid off. This labor sector in this way remains in the shadow of the regulated workforce, helping define what is commonly known as a "shadow population."

In *They Take Away Our Jobs! And 20 Other Myths About Immigration,* social theorists and public intellectual Noam Chomsky notes that it has been calculated by the Social Security Administration (SSA) that three-fourths of undocumented workers in the formal job sector utilize a false Social Security number, which means that either the name or the number does not match, or the number is fictitious. When the name and number do not match what the SSA has on record, the wage report is held in what is called the Earnings Suspense File (ESF) until the discrepancy can be corrected. Since 2000, the SSA has received, on average, more than 9.3 million suspicious wage reports annually (Johnson, 2013). According to a government Accounting Office report (U.S. GAO, 2006), the SSA uses two relevant files based on earnings records, the Nonwork Alien File and the Earnings Suspense File (ESF). The Nonwork Alien File contains earnings information posted to SSNs issued for nonwork purposes, suggesting that these individuals are working without authorization. The ESF contains earnings reports for which SSA is unable to match the name and SSN of the worker, suggesting employer error, SSN misuse, or unauthorized work activity. The ESF contained about 250 million records as of December 2004, and shows an increasing number of records associated with probable unauthorized work (GAO). Cumulative wages since 1990, after the 1986 amnesty, now total more than $952.4 billion, unadjusted for inflation. Over the years, numerous U.S. Congress subcommittees have also heard testimonies by the Inspector General for the SSA who attributed those payments to undocumented immigrants. By some estimates and based on Social Security taxes alone, the ESF grows at around $9 billion per year, meaning that undocumented immigrants are providing a subsidy of billions to the government when federal income, Social Security and Medicare taxes are combined (Loller, 2008).

Leisha Reynolds-Ramos

See Also: Identity Theft; Individual Taxpayer Identification Number (ITIN); Shadow Population; Social Security; Wages.

Further Reading

Chomsky, Aviva. 2007. *They Take Away Our Jobs! And 20 Other Myths About Immigration.* Boston, MA: Beacon Press 2007.

Immigration Policy Center. 2009. "The Facts About the Individual Taxpayer Identification Number (ITIN)." http://www.immigrationpolicy.org/just-facts/facts-about-individual-tax-identification-number-itin.

IRS. 2013. "General ITIN Information." http://www.irs.gov/Individuals/General-ITIN-Information.

Johnson, Mary. 2013. "Growth of the Social Security Earnings Suspense File Points to the Rising Potential Cost of Unauthorized Work to Social Security." The Senior Citizens League, February 2013. http://seniorsleague.org/2013/growth-of-the-social-security-earnings-suspense-file-points-to-the-rising-potential-cost-of-unauthorized-work-to-social-security-2/.

Loller, Travis. 2008. "Many Illegal Immigrants Pay Up at Tax Time." *USA Today,* April 11. http://usatoday30.usatoday.com/money/perfi/taxes/2008-04-10-immigrantstaxes_N.htm.

U.S. GAO (Government Accountability Office) "Social Security Numbers: Coordinated Approach to SSN Data Could Help Reduce Unauthorized Work." GAO-06-458T, Feb 2006. 16, 2006. http://www.gao.gov/products/GAO-06-458T.

Temporary Assistance for Needy Families (TANF)

Temporary Assistance for Needy Families (TANF) was established in 1997 and is the program that is most commonly associated with the U.S. welfare system. Often undocumented migrants are thought to cross the border with the intent to have children that are American citizens in order to take advantage of this system. This is one of the major arguments used against undocumented immigration. These arguments usually focus on female undocumented migrants. Like their impoverished African American women counterparts, female immigrants suffer demeaning labels like "welfare queens" and are routinely accused of overburdening the welfare system.

However, the reality is that undocumented immigrants, because of their legal status, are not eligible for any benefits that TANF provides. Additionally, immigrants that were admitted into the United States as legal permanent residents after August 22, 1996, are not eligible for any TANF benefits until they have been in the country for more than five years. As such it is no surprise that these regulations are put in place as a reaction to the claims that immigrants are draining the welfare system and justifiy the use of greater scrutiny to ensure that ineligible migrants do not access these social welfare benefits so as to not offer them any incentive to cross the border without proper documentation.

The underlying purpose of this U.S. social welfare system can be explained in four parts.

1. There is a need to assist families in a way that allows for children to be cared for in their own homes.
2. There is a need to reduce the dependency of needy parents by promoting job preparation, work and marriage.
3. There is need to prevent out-of-wedlock pregnancies
4. There is a need to encourage the formation and maintenance of two-parent families.

The welfare system as a whole originally started as a way to support widows and their children financially after the loss of the family breadwinner. The program was originally named Aid to Dependent Children (ADC) but in 1960 the name was changed to Aid to Families with Dependent Children (AFDC). To the country it was an obvious sign that this program was implemented to serve families. However, from the inception, there was an underlying current of resentment towards the beneficiaries of the program when it became increasingly associated with poor, unwed black mothers, resulting in their vilification as so-called "welfare queens." Critics of the program argued that it promoted dependency, rather than a path to self-sufficiency that could only come about with employment. This negative attitude toward single mothers on welfare only progressed into the early nineties, in particular, with overriding notions of women on welfare as "lazy" and "promiscuous." With the prevailing attitude, President Bill Clinton was under great pressure to end a welfare system considered by many political and social conservatives as one that was both wasteful and promoting dependency. The changes that this administration made to the welfare system were significant. No longer would the government provide cash welfare but would instead promote "workfare." Every welfare recipient would be involved in mandatory "workfare" for at least thirty hours a week, and no welfare benefits would exceed five years for any one family. This reform became known as the Personal Responsibility and Work Opportunity Reconciliation Act (PRWORA) of 1996. With this Act, AFDC ended in 1997 and was replaced by TANF.

After the establishment of TANF, welfare departments throughout the country began to undergo drastic changes to discourage the apparent welfare dependency crisis and to make explicit the time limit women would be allowed to stay in the program. For example, the Massachusetts Department of Public Welfare became the Department of Transitional Assistance and other legislative measures worked to move women off welfare and into jobs. Another example is the Job Opportunities and Basic Skills Training (JOBS) implemented in 1992. The difference between the previous vocational opportunities and the newer PRWORA was that PRWORA made participation in these programs mandatory for parents with children over the age of one. The Work Opportunity Reconciliation Act of 1996 embraced similar guidelines of encouraging more responsibility from recipients and lowering dependency on the state. Finally, PRWORA allowed for states take over the administration of the welfare programs, allowing each state to have different application requirements and processes instead of having a national system in place.

At the same time PRWORA was passed, it was established that immigrants who were authorized to work or live in the United States would not be eligible for any welfare benefits for the first five years of their stay in the United States. After this authorized immigrants must become citizens in order to receive benefits or show forty quarters of work history. Again these types of regulations reflected the negative attitudes about immigrants, especially those ideas that those present in the country who were unauthorized only came to the United States to exploit the country's welfare system. In particular, women immigrants became the object of criticism and much scrutiny. The mid-1990s were a time of growing concern over the public costs of undocumented immigrants. During this turbulent time, California's Proposition 187 (1994) was passed. Although it was struck down by a federal court as unconstitutional, public discourse reflected the preoccupation with children of immigrants in the schools and in health clinics. Anti-immigrant discourse drew the public's attention to these children as burdens to public coffers. Johnathan Inda's work (2006), *Targeting Immigrants* documents how cost studies designed to tally the costs of immigrants to the public began reporting the numbers of Medicaid-funded births to undocumented immigrant mothers. This resulted in blame placed on immigrant women as principal abusers of the state welfare system, resulting in its economic troubles. In some sense, the immigrant mothers of 1990s became the "welfare queens" of the time.

Along with TANF, there are other programs available to help support single mothers such as Women, Children, and Infants (WIC) established in 1975 and the Family Support Act of 1988. Women who are eligible for TANF are automatically eligible for WIC. Unlike TANF all immigrants are eligible for WIC regardless of citizenship status. This program provides aid to get the children and mothers the necessary food to stay healthy during the most critical years of a child's development. However, this too has a time limit. Once the child reaches five, they no longer qualify for WIC.

Yesenia Andrade

See Also: Children; Clinton Administration; Families; Family Economics; Health and Welfare; Laws and Legislation, post-1980s; Mixed-Status Families; Nutrition; Proposition 187; Welfare System; Women's Status.

Further Reading

Ehrenreich, Barbara. 2001. *Nickel and Dimed: On (Not) Getting By in America.* New York: Metropolitan Books.

Hombs, Mary Ellen. 1996. *Welfare Reform: A Reference Handbook.* ABC-CLIO Inc.

Inda, Johnathan Xavier. 2006. *Targeting Immigrants: Government, Technology, and Ethics.* Malden, MA: Blackwell Publishing.

Schiller, Bradley R. 2008. *The Economics of Poverty and Discrimination,* 10th edition. Upper Saddle River, NJ: Pearson Education.

Winston, Pam. 1996. "President Clinton Abolishes Welfare as We Know It." *Off Our Backs* 26.9:14.

Wu, Chi-Fang, and Mary Keegan Eamon. 2007. "Public and Private Sources of Assistance for Low-income Households." *Journal of Sociology & Social Welfare* 34.4:121.

Temporary Protected Status (TPS)

Mass exoduses, such as those resulting from natural disasters, warfare, and major political turmoil, confound immigration policies, and U.S. responses have varied widely depending on historical period as well as place of origin and causative factors (Churgin, 1996). Refugee relief acts allowed the admission of more than two hundred thousand people from Europe after World War II. Cubans, by virtue of geographic proximity and the vexing nature of the Cuban-U.S. relationship during the Cold War, also benefited from the extension of preferential treatment, resulting in 370,000 becoming permanent residents by 1978. The fall of Saigon raised the issue again, resulting in the entry of some 750,000 refugees from Southeast Asia by 1990. When dangerous or inhospitable conditions arise, then, and if they persist, humanitarian concerns generally come up against political ones, with rights to safety mixing with those of return (Frelick, 1990).

The executive branch of the U.S. government has responded through refugee policies as well as by creating various categories for temporary status until conditions ameliorate. One of these is Temporary Protected Status (TPS), which grants a stay of removal of those in the country without documents who qualify under the program, plus work authorization to people with non-immigrant visas in the United States who are temporarily unable to return to their homeland because of ongoing armed conflict, environmental disasters, or other extraordinary and temporary conditions. By providing a temporary immigrant status that allows people to remain in the United States, TPS may be viewed as a sound and humanitarian emergency relief measure intended to assist nationals of a given country who are already in the United States at the time of designation. At the same time, with TPS the government may prolong the immigrant's displacement (Mountz et al., 2002).

TPS designation is made when the attorney general, after consultation with appropriate agencies, determines that a country or part of a country is experiencing conditions that would pose a serious hardship or threat to the personal safety of nationals if returned (INA Sec. 244 1A, B). For example, some 82,000 Hondurans and 5,000 Nicaraguans were granted TPS designation to remain and work in the United States in the wake of the devastation of Hurricane Mitch in 1998. TPS may also be granted if a foreign state is unable to handle the return, generally through the deportation of nationals of the state, and officially requests such designation (INA Sec. 244 2C). After El Salvador suffered severe earthquakes in early 2001, undocumented citizens of that country were granted TPS, a designation later extended into 2005. Before the end to the TPS designation period, the secretary of the Department of Homeland Security reviews the conditions in the designated state to determine whether the conditions that led to the TPS designation continue to be met. More recently, the TPS designation for Haitian nationals was extended to 2013 due to the circumstances surrounding the aftermath of Hurricane Sandy in 2012.

The concept of TPS was debated repeatedly in the U.S. Congress in the 1980s before being enacted in 1990 as part of the Immigration Act. Prior to 1990, the only legal way people could remain in the country under such circumstances was by requesting asylum. The need for an intermediate immigration status was recognized as long ago as 1960, when the Department of Justice created the status of Extended Voluntary Departure (EVD), later called Deferred Enforced Departure (DED). In effect, this enabled the attorney general to exercise prosecutorial discretion to not remove nationals from particular countries. Prosecutorial discretion means that administrative agencies (such as the Department of Justice) have discretion in whom they select to prosecute. The impetus for the TPS provision of the 1990 Immigration Act was the desire for some kind of regularized process to avoid having to deport tens of thousands of undocumented immigrants from El Salvador. They had come to the United States during years of conflict for which the United States bore some responsibility through the provision of substantial military aid to successive military-dominated governments. Faced with a potential return of so many to a country already suffering high rates of unemployment and poverty, the president of El Salvador campaigned vigorously with the U.S. government to hold off with such deportations. TPS thus serves, in effect, as a temporary response to humanitarian need for which granting refugee status could be technically or politically difficult.

In 2003, responsibilities for administering the TPS program were transferred to the U.S. Bureau of Citizenship and Immigration Services (BCIS). However, the mechanism for TPS remained essentially unchanged. TPS is usually granted in twelve-to eighteen-month increments but may be renewed at the discretion of the U.S. government, currently through the secretary of the Department of Homeland Security. Once TPS is terminated, people revert to their previous immigration status. An application for TPS does not affect an application for asylum or any other immigration benefit, and people may simultaneously apply for both asylum and TPS. TPS can be a first step in becoming a U.S. citizen (Lowell, 1999). Some, in fact, criticize TPS as being a de facto amnesty or asylum program due to the long lengths of some designations and poor tracking of outcomes.

Refugee status and asylum status are granted in a process similar to the one for TPS. Candidates for TPS are typically unable or unwilling to return to their home country because of fears for their safety or a well-founded fear of persecution on account of their race, religion, nationality, membership in a particular social group, or political opinion. However, refugee and asylum status differ in regard to where the individual is when applying for status: asylum status is obtained within the United States, while refugee status is obtained outside the United States. Asylum and refugee status differ from TPS in that they are seen more as a long-term provision. They allow the individual to live and work in the United States and, after one year, to be able to apply for permanent residency. The goal of TPS is to temporarily provide a safe place for individuals of another nation with the aim of eventually returning the individual to their country.

The TPS program is not without concerns among the beneficiaries of the program and some immigrant rights advocates. For many, a prolonged time away from family may have emotional consequences. They may miss many of the life events important to their communities and worry about those family members who continue to contend with political disorder, displacement, and poverty. The choice to not comply with the conditions of the program, such as returning home, results in a loss of the temporary status, as well as the rights provided by the program such as permission to work, a valid social security number and the hope of some day becoming a permanent resident (Mountz et al., 2002).

When TPS is designated for a particular country, the number of eligible individuals is estimated by the government. In 2006, countries on the list for TPS designation included: Burundi, Liberia, Sierra Leone, Somalia, and Sudan in Africa; El Salvador, Honduras, and Nicaragua in Latin America; and Montserrat in the Caribbean. In 2010, Haiti, was added to the list, and in 2012 those living in the United States from war-torn Syria were given TPS.

Like TPS, Deferred Enforced Departure (DED) is a temporary protection from removal granted to people from a designated country, in this case by the president of the United States as part of the office's constitutional powers to conduct foreign relations. First used in 1990, it appears to provide some flexibility to make adjustments to TPS designations. For example, after El Salvador's TPS ended in 1992, the president still chose not to deport and reverted to Extended Voluntary Departure (EVD), though the name has since been changed to Deferred Enforced Departure (DED). Liberian nationals in the United States were granted DED from 1999 to 2002, after which they were designated under TPS status, due to ongoing armed conflict in their homeland.

Temporary Protected Status has been both praised as a humanitarian relief measure and criticized as an invitation to fraudulent non-immigration visa abuse. It was devised to be a humanitarian response as well as to ease potential deportation burdens on various government agencies. Given incomplete tracking of people with non-immigrant visas, it remains uncertain how many people remain in the United States after their TPS designation ends, how many return to their homelands, who may receive amnesty, and whether some people change their non-immigrant visa status in other ways (Lowell, 1999).

James Loucky

See Also: Expedited Removal; Nicaraguan Adjustment and Central American Relief Act (NACARA); Nicaraguans; Refugee Act (1980); Refugees; Salvadorans; U-Visa.

Further Reading

Churgin, Michael J. 1996. "Mass Exoduses: The Response of the United States." *International Migration Review* 30:310–324.

Frelick, Bill. 1990. "The Right of Return." *International Journal of Refugee Law* 2:442–447.

Lowell, B. Lindsay, ed. 1999. *Foreign Temporary Workers in America: Policies That Benefit the U.S. Economy.* Westport, CT: Quorum Books.

Mountz, Alison, Richard Wright, Ines Miyares, and Adrian J. Bailay. 2002. "Lives in Limbo: Temporary Protected Status and Immigrant Identities." *Global Networks* 2.4:335–357.

U.S. Citizenship and Immigration Services (USCIS). 2013. "Temporary Protected Status. http://www.uscis.gov/.

Tennessee Immigrant and Refugee Rights Coalition (TIRRC)

The Tennessee Immigrant and Refugee Rights Coalition (TIRRC) is one of several immigrant rights organizations in the United States. It was founded as a non-profit organization in 2001. TIRRC's mission has been "to empower immigrants and refugees throughout Tennessee to develop a unified voice, defend their rights, and create an atmosphere in which they are recognized as positive contributors to the state" (Migration Policy Institute, 2011). TIRRC's activities include providing leadership and justice training to immigrants and refugees, organizing lobbying at the local, state, and federal levels, and holding public forums to foster dialogue about immigration and "New Tennesseans." In 2006 TIRRC helped form the Southeast Immigrant Rights Network (SEIRN, www.seirn.squarespace.com) to facilitate cooperation among immigrant rights groups throughout the region. TIRRC also coordinates with national immigrant rights groups, such as National Immigration Law Center (www.nilc.org), the National Immigration Forum (www.immigrationforum.org), and the National Council of La Raza (www.nclr.org).

Tennessee is one of several states that have been characterized as "new destinations" for immigrants and refugees. The foreign-born population in Tennessee grew from 1.2 percent in 1990 to 2.8 percent in 2000 to an estimated 4.2 percent in 2009. This includes immigrants who are undocumented. About half of the foreign-born residents are from Latin America, particularly from Mexico, Guatemala, Honduras, and El Salvador (Migration Policy Institute, 2011; Drever, 2006). Other groups include Iraqi Kurds, Sudanese, Somalians, Russians, Liberians, and Burundians (Pendry, 2011).

TIRRC has advocated for federal immigration reform that would provide a path to legalization for undocumented immigrants. In 2006 when the federal government was considering H.R. 4437, which included some draconian proposals, thousands of people participated in marches across the country to protest those proposals. At that time marches took place in Nashville and in Knoxville. TIRRC also has been active in fostering groups of young people calling for passage of the DREAM Act. In fact, TIRRC was founded after a grassroots campaign that convinced the Tennessee state legislature to pass a law in spring 2001 that enabled residents of the state who could not present a valid social security card to obtain a driver's license. However, since then Tennessee legislators reversed that decision in 2007 and have been proposing laws designed to control "illegal immigration," promote "English only," and in 2011, control Muslim religious practices. Although TIRRC helped immigrants and refugees and their allies organize to lobby against these proposals, at least thirteen anti-immigrant proposals became state law between 2001 and 2011. During that time, in part thanks to the efforts of TIRRC members, Nashville decided not to adopt an "English-only" proposal and at least two favorable state laws were passed. Tennessee is one of several states that have passed anti-immigrant legislation, including Oklahoma, Georgia, Iowa, North Carolina, Arizona, Alabama, and South Carolina (Pendry, 2011). The Tennessee proposals have been directed not only at undocumented immigrants but against legal immigrants. Several scholars have noted that anti-illegal, anti-immigrant and/or anti-Latino sentiments in the United States are not new (e.g., Chavez, 2008).

TIRRC not only has advocated on behalf of undocumented immigrants, they have fostered dialogue between refugees and immigrants of all statuses. For example, they helped taxicab drivers and chicken catchers organize to improve their working conditions. In addition, TIRRC has promoted dialogue with non-immigrants through their "Welcoming Tennessee Initiative." The film *Welcome to Shelbyville* illustrates this work. TIRRC also has sponsored campaigns to help lawful permanent residents apply for citizenship, and help immigrants who are citizens to register to vote. As noted earlier, the goal of the Tennessee Immigrant and Refugee Rights Coalition is to empower its members to speak for themselves.

De Ann Pendry

See Also: Activism; Advocacy; Community Activism; Community Concerns; Driver's Licenses; National Council of La Raza (NCLR); National Network for Immigrant and Refugee Rights (NNIRR); State Legislation.

Further Reading

Ansley, Fran, and Jon Shefner, eds. 2009. *Global Connections, Local Receptions: New Latino Immigration to the Southeastern United States.* Knoxville, TN: The University of Tennessee Press.

Chavez, Leo R. 2008. *The Latino Threat: Constructing Immigrants, Citizens, and the Nation.* Stanford, CA: Stanford University Press.

Drever, Anita. 2006. "New Neighbors in Dixie: The Community Impacts of Latino Migration to Tennessee." In *Latinos in the New South: Transformations of Place,* edited by Heather A. Smith and Owen J. Furuseth, 19–36. Hampshire, England: Ashgate Publishing.

Migration Policy Institute. 2011. "Tennessee: Social and Demographic Characteristics." Washington, D.C. Migration Policy Institute Data Hub. http://www.migrationinformation.org/datahub/state.cfm?ID=TN.

Pendry, De Ann. 2011. "Seeking to Understand the Politics of Immigration in Tennessee," special issue on immigration to the Southeastern United States of the journal *Norteamérica,* published by Centro de Investigaciones sobre América del Norte, Universidad Nacional Autónoma de México, México, D.F. (September 2011).

Welcome to Shelbyville. 2010. Directed and produced by Kim Snyder. Video. www.welcometoshelbyvillefilm.com.

Texas

The state of Texas is located in the geographical region recognized for centuries as a travel corridor for migrants across North America. Beginning as early as the fourteenth century with the Spanish conquistadors, and perhaps earlier than that, people have been traveling paths north and south through routes that cross modern-day Texas and the U.S.-Mexico international border.

Texas was originally a part of North America claimed and colonized by Spain, and later Mexico. In the early nineteenth century American settlers began to move into the region and establish residency. These early Texas settlers were, in fact, there illegally—without permission from the Spanish government. In 1836 the American Texas Congress declared independence from Mexico and became the Republic of Texas. It claimed territory from as far north as the present-day state of Wyoming; west into New Mexico; and east into Oklahoma. It declared the Rio Grande River as its southern border. In 1845 the United States annexed the Republic of Texas and it became the twenty-eighth state of the union. This annexation spurred the Mexican-American War, which was resolved with the Treaty of Guadalupe Hildago in 1848. Through this treaty, Mexico ceded Texas and a vast majority of its northern territories to the United States. The United States agreed to provide U.S. citizenship and protected rights to the Mexican citizens already living there. In 1861 Texas seceded from the United States and joined the Confederate States. It was reinstated to the United States following the Civil War.

The current boundaries of the state of Texas were established by the Compromise of 1850. The U.S. federal government agreed to dissolve the state's debts in exchange for portions of its large territory, and the state was reduced to its present size and shape. Texas is bounded by the states of New Mexico, Oklahoma, Colorado, Mississippi, and Louisiana. Its southern boundary is the Rio Grande, which serves as the international boundary between the United States and Mexico. Parts of Texas also touch the Gulf of Mexico. From the time that Texas became part of the United States its southern border has served as a port of entry for documented and undocumented immigrants.

The Texas border region has had economic value for both the United States and Mexico for a long time. The mining, timber, cattle, railroad, and agricultural industries on both sides of the border have all depended on the exchange of labor and goods between countries. When Texas became a state, Texan ranchers and business owners continued to recruit Mexican laborers for their businesses because there was a shortage of laborers in the state and because Mexicans would accept lower wages. The demand for Mexican laborers in Texas was so great that in 1929 the Emigrant Labor Agency Laws were passed in order to limit the recruitment of Mexican laborers by businesses outside of the state, and in 1934 the Texas Farm Placement Service was established to control the movement of Mexican immigrants.

Despite the demand for Mexican labor, the general attitude towards Mexicans was hostile and the treatment of both immigrants and Mexican Americans was discriminatory and often violent. When the U.S. and Mexican governments created the Bracero Program in the 1940s to secure the temporary employment of Mexican laborers by U.S. agricultural growers, the Mexican government excluded Texas from the agreement, making reference to the conditions Mexican workers were subjected to in that state. These circumstances, however, did not stop the movement of immigrants into Texas.

During the twentieth century, Texas passed a number of laws addressing undocumented immigrants. In 1978 it passed a law prohibiting undocumented children from receiving public education in the state. The law was later overturned (in *Plyler v. Doe* in 1982) by the U.S. Supreme Court as violating the constitutional rights of these children. Provision of public services to undocumented immigrants continues to be a controversial issue in Texas politics. In 1993 the El Paso Border Patrol implemented Operation Blockade, a temporary program that focused on stopping immigrants directly at the border, rather than apprehending and removing them once they entered the country. The program required a massive increase in manpower, from two hundred to four hundred agents working in twenty-four-hour shifts every day of the week. The program was considered so successful that it was made a permanent fixture of the Texas border management, though it was renamed Operation Hold the Line.

According to a report by the Department of Homeland Security, Texas had a population of 1,790,000 undocumented immigrants in 2011 compared with 1,090,000 in 2000 (Hoefer, Rytina, and Baker, 2012). Texas was estimated to have about 14 percent of the country's population of undocumented immigrants. The report indicated that educational, medical, and legal expenditures on undocumented immigrants cost the state of Texas $17.7 billion, but also acknowledged the revenue generated by the same population exceeded that amount.

Movement of undocumented immigrants into the United States through the state of Texas continues to be a controversial issue. When the state passed House Bill 1403 granting undocumented immigrant students residency status that qualified them for in-state tuition costs to state colleges and university, many politicians and residents were outraged. There have been calls for changes to this law, as well implementation of stricter laws prohibiting access to public services for undocumented immigrants, coupled with increased security along the U.S.-Mexico border to deter the movement of immigrants into Texas.

Federal programs such as Operation Hold the Line have worked to redirect immigration traffic away from monitored entry points into the rugged terrains of southern Texas. In addition to the reported escalation of violence in border cities, immigrants experience the perils of crossing across desert spaces that threaten their safety and well-being. In 2012, the national attention turned briefly to reports of 129 bodies, presumably of deceased migrants, found in Brooks County. It is widely believed that they perished from dehydration and exhaustion in their attempt to navigate around the U.S. Border Patrol checkpoint near Falfurrias.

Andrea Hernandez Holm

See Also: Arizona; Bracero Program; California; Labor Supply; Migration; New Mexico; *Plyler v. Doe;* State Legislation.

Further Reading

Acuña, Rodolfo. 2007. "Why Mexicans Moved." In *Corridors of Migration: The Odyssey of Mexican Laborers, 1600–1933*, 1–24. Tucson: University of Arizona Press.
Hoefer, Michael, Nancy Rytina, and Bryan Baker. 2012. "Estimates of the Unauthorized Immigrant Population Residing in the United States: January 2011." http://www.dhs.gov/xlibrary/assets/statistics/publications/ois_ill_pe_2011.pdf.

Montejano, David. 1987. *Anglos and Mexicans in the Making of Texas, 1836–1986.* Austin: University of Texas Press.

"Texas Office of the Comptroller Special Report: Undocumented Immigrants in Texas." 2006. State of Texas.

Texas State Historical Association. The Handbook of Texas Online. www.tshaonline.org/handbook.

Theater

Theater about undocumented immigrants in the United States is part of a larger cultural movement that links artistic practices such as theater, visual arts, film, music, digital arts, and other forms of cultural production to issues of migration, labor, cultural belonging, and identity formation. Through theater, artists provide a range of approaches and perspectives in conveying the complexities of undocumented immigrants' experiences. Relatedly, immigrants regardless of status participate in theater to express themselves culturally as a way to take part in the civic and political life of the United States. Stories of undocumented experiences are present on the stages of contemporary American theater, from individual plays to theater groups to performance festival series focusing on this topic. In works specifically by undocumented immigrants, theater serves as a means of taking control of their own representations, to counter vilified representations of immigrant communities. Immigrants employ theater to raise political awareness about the conditions of their lives. Following a long tradition of political theater in the United States, theater for, by, and about immigrants is practiced to build upon organizing political and cultural movement towards a more just society which values immigrants.

Thematically, theater about undocumented immigrants ranges from shedding light on the particular struggles by this community to providing a nuanced point of view about the debates on immigrant rights in twenty-first-century United States. One production that addressed a matter pertaining to immigrant community and labor is *Los Illegals* created and produced by Los Angeles–based Cornerstone Theater Company. Cornerstone Theater artists partnered with day laborers, domestic workers, various community and justice-organizing groups and individuals to create this theatrical production that was performed in the Armory Northwest in Pasadena in 2007. *Los Illegals* dramatizes the labor conditions for day laborers in the city, in particular the threat of closing the workers' center. This play also depicted the life-threatening journey of people from South America to the United States. *Los Illegals* is a site-specific play, performed outdoors. The parking area for the Armory Northwest was converted to simulate a typical day-laborer center: picnic tables with seats, tarp tent areas, board games, and a trailer office. Audience members were given tickets, similar to the way workers are handed out a ticket and called out for job requests that come through the centers. Reflecting the racial, ethnic, and national diversity of immigrants in Los Angeles, this play portrayed undocumented characters from Mexico, El Salvador, and Korea. The play was written by Michael John Garces and directed by Shishir Kurup. Organizations involved in creating this project included the Institute of Popular

Education of Southern California, the National Day Laborer Organizing Network, the South Asian Network, and the UCLA Downtown Labor Center.

Arizona: No Roosters in the Desert is a play written by Kara Hartzler based on the research by Dr. Anna Ochoa O'Leary on the subject of immigrant women border crossers. This play follows four women, from Mexico and Central America, as they attempt to cross the U.S.-Mexico border. The process of the journey binds the women intimately even though they have no or little connection. Along the way, they share stories with another and make a promise to stand by one another no matter what comes of the journey. It becomes apparent that faced by the numerous perils in their sojourn—bodily injury, hunger, wild animals, and the border police—promises are not easy to keep. The play's world premieres was in El Circulo Teatral, in a Spanish translation. The second world premiere with Borderlands Theater opened on October 2010 in English. *Arizona: No Roosters in the Desert* is published in English by NoPassport Press and by Libros de Godot in Spanish.

In addition to *No Roosters*, Borderlands Theater in Tucson, Arizona, has commissioned and produced other plays depicting the deadly perils of migrants' crossing the border, in *Visitors' Guide to Arivaca* by Evangeline Ordaz. The drama takes place near Arivaca, a remote village just north of the U.S.-Mexico border in southern Arizona. Commissioned by Borderlands Theatre in Tucson, the action brings together characters in the form of undocumented border crossers, humanitarian groups, U.S. Border Patrol, and Native Americans near the remote town of Arivaca. The play was performed by Company of Angels in Los Angeles in 2009. In another play about the border crossing-experience, *Papá está en la Atlántida'* by Javier Malpica, two young Mexican boys take on the quasi adventure of attempting to cross the border on their own in search for their father who reportedly lives in an American city that they only remember as *Atlántida*. However, the mythical allure of this place only leads to tragedy. Resonating in the play is timely social commentary about family separation as a consequence of the migration process, and the realities of migrant deaths as once again the American Dream eludes them.

Other plays explore earlier histories of how immigrants found ways to challenge restrictive immigration laws in the United States. Set in 1915 when the Chinese Exclusion Act was still a law, Genny Lim's *Paper Angels* is a story of a Chinese sojourner attempting to bring his wife to the United States after years of separation. The play explores the complexity of being a paper son. Paper sons and daughters are Chinese men and women who were able to come to the United States by assuming a fake identity as a son or daughter of a Chinese man already living in the United States. When a fire ensued during the 1906 San Francisco earthquake, municipal records were destroyed. Without official records, there was an opportunity to get around the Chinese Exclusion Act that restricted Chinese entry into the United States. At this time, any Chinese who could prove paternal lineage would be allowed to enter. Without access to official records, the process of interrogation was instituted. *Paper Angels* opens with a scene in Angel Island Detention Center in San Francisco Harbor, where thousands of Chinese were detained upon entry under varying duration. This opening scene enacts an interrogation, where an immigration officer forcefully asks questions of a Chinese traveler in order to assess the traveler's identity. Lim wrote this play in 1982 and it has been

Passages: For Lee Ping To by Lenora Lee. Dancer: Marina Fukushima. Theater about undocumented immigrants in the United States is part of a larger cultural movement that links artistic practices to issues of the day. Theater has long served to counter representations of maligned immigrants and to raise awareness about their conditions. (Tim Richards)

produced numerously since. In 2010, the play received a number of production revivals as part of commemorating the tenth-year anniversary of Angel Island. Another performance exploring the similar theme of paper sons is Lenora Lee's *Passages: For Lee Ping To.* It is a multi-media production with dance, poetry, and visual arts inspired by Lee's own family history.

A number of theater works have broached the subject of undocumented migration as it confronts intra-racial, intra-ethnic, and intra-national relations. *Ching Chong Chinaman* by Lauren Yee is a comedic play that depicts how the presence of an undocumented immigrant turns the world of a Chinese American family upside down. The play shows, in a comedic manner, that the politics of migration is not simply between immigrants and white Americans. This Chinese American family who share the same racial identity as the Chinese immigrant grapple with their own views about indentured labor when their own son, who cannot be bothered by his house chores, hires an undocumented Chinese to do the work. The play *Fabric,* written by Henry Ong, dramatizes the plight of Thai garment workers who have been laboring as captives in El Monte, California. Ong was inspired by the 1995 state and federal raid of the apartment complex where 72 Thai nationals were confined. He interviewed some of the Thai nationals, community advocates, and federal and state agents in order to write a play that seeks to foreground the Thai nationals' stories. The play weaves excerpts from court testimonies and Ong's interviews. The Company of Angels, Los Angeles's oldest not-for-profit repertory theater, in association with Thai Community Development Center in 2010, produced *Fabric*. Udaya Kanthi Salgadu's *Letters from My Mother* is a play based on Salgadu's experience as an undocumented domestic from Sri Lanka who was employed by another Sri Lankan. Using the epistolary form, the play narrates the abuses she suffers working and living with her employer through letters between her and her mother who lives in Sri Lanka. The play was developed through the David Henry Hwang Writing Institute of the East West Players. In 2011, a play reading was co-presented by the Coalition to Abolish Slavery and Trafficking, an organization in which Salgadu is a member. Another dance theater piece, Cindy Garcia's *How to Make It to the Dance Floor: A Salsa Guide for Women (Based on Actual Experiences),* confronts intra-Latino racial community hierarchy between citizens and undocumented immigrants. *How to Make It to the Dance Floor* is based on Garcia's ethnographic research on immigrants in Los Angeles nightlife, in particular in salsa dance clubs. Working with dramaturge Lucy Burns, Garcia developed a play about social relations among Latino immigrants, exploring power and gender, and perceived and actual battles between different styles of salsa dancing.

While most theater productions about undocumented immigrants' experiences are created, performed, and viewed by immigrants and non-immigrants, Teatro Jornalero Sin Fronteras (Day Laborer Theater Without Borders) is a theater group made up of day laborers of varying immigrant statuses, including undocumented. This ensemble emerged in 2008 from the collaboration between the Cornerstone Theater and the Workers' Centers in Los Angeles towards the creation of *Los Illegals*. Teatro Jornalero is a performance group dedicated to improving the lives of day laborers through the creation and presentation of plays about the lives of day laborers. The ensemble performs its short plays where day laborers gather, mostly in work centers in Southern California. The group's website reports that Teatro Jornalero has expanded its work in Northern California and El Salvador.

Theater festivals have also featured the subject of undocumented immigrants. In 2011, the New Carpa Theater in Phoenix, Arizona held the "SB 1070 Festival of Plays," conceived by James Garcia, New Carpa Theater's artistic director. The twelve short plays and play excerpts in the festival were selected out of the seventy submissions from the open call for play responses to the Senate Bill 1070 that Arizona state passed, noted by many as the broadest and strictest anti-immigration legislation in the 21st century. The plays performed in the festival, authored by playwrights from all over the United States, variously explored human dignity in the midst of moving across national borders. There were plays that are set in the current period of U.S. immigration sentiments as well as others that portrayed earlier periods in U.S. history such as the era of anti-Irish immigration in the 19th century. The festival was performed in the lawn area of Arizona's state capitol, in Phoenix.

Lucy Burns

See Also: Border Crossing; Chinese; Culture; Death; "Devil's Highway"; Literature and Poetry; Transnationalism.

Further Reading

Camacho, Alicia Schmidt. 2008. *Immigrant Imaginaries: Latino Cultural Politics in the U.S.-Mexico Borderlands.* New York: New York University Press.

Lowe, Lisa. 1999. *Immigrant Acts: On Asian American Cultural Politics.* Durham, NC: Duke University Press.

Ngai, Mai. 2004. *Impossible Subjects and the Making of Modern America.* Princeton, NJ: Princeton University Press.

Román, David. 2005. *Performance in America: Contemporary U.S. Culture and the Performing Arts.* Durham, NC: Duke University Press.

Teatro Jornalero, Cornerstone Theater Company. http://cornerstonetheater.org/teatro -jornalero/about-us/.

Trafficking Victims Protection Reauthorization Act (TVPRA)

Efforts by the United States to combat human trafficking are guided by the Trafficking Victims Protection Act (TVPA) of 2000. This act undergoes reauthorization every two or three years to continue its funding and to strengthen its ability to confront the challenges posed by human trafficking. Each of these reauthorizations can be referred to as the Trafficking Victims Protection Reauthorization Act (TVPRA) of a specified year.

In February 2013, Congress voted to reauthorize the legislation as part of the Violence against Women Act (S. 47), just weeks after the U.S. Senate voted (93–5) to include it as an amendment to S. 47. In 2011, the TVPRA—a bipartisan bill—had been allowed to expire for the first time ("Congress Passes Long-Awaited Anti-Human Trafficking Bill," 2013).

The original TVPA is modeled after the 2000 United Nations Protocol to Prevent, Suppress and Punish Trafficking in Persons especially Women and Children, also known as the Palermo Protocol, which defines trafficking as:

> Trafficking in persons shall mean the recruitment, transportation, transfer, harbouring or receipt of persons, by means of the threat or use of force or other forms of coercion, of abduction, of fraud, of deception, of the abuse of power or of a position of vulnerability or of the giving or receiving of payments or benefits to achieve the consent of a person having control over another person, for the purpose of exploitation. Exploitation shall include, at a minimum, the exploitation of the prostitution of others or other forms of sexual exploitation, forced labour or services, slavery or practices similar to slavery, servitude or the removal of organs.

The Palermo Protocol is the global standard for defining human trafficking. The U.S. TVPA includes the three P's of the Palermo Protocol: prevention, criminal prosecution, and victim protection. The 2000 TVPA focuses on preventing human trafficking abroad, making penalties more severe for traffickers, and protecting victims while helping them rebuild their lives in the United States with federal and state support.

The U.S. Department of State points out that the TVPA defines severe forms of trafficking as sex and labor trafficking. Sex trafficking can result in forced commercial sex acts, sometimes by victims under eighteen years of age, while labor trafficking can result in debt bondage and other forms of involuntary service. The theory underlying the TVPA comes from the Thirteenth Amendment of the U.S. Constitution which prohibits slavery and involuntary servitude except as a consequence of a crime for which an individual has been convicted and sentenced.

Each reauthorization of the TVPA makes existing legislation more effective. For example, the third reauthorization, called the William Wilberforce Trafficking Victims Protection Reauthorization Act of 2008 (WWTVPRA), facilitates the prosecution of sex-trafficking crimes. These prosecutions had proven very difficult because force, fraud, and coercion had to be proven but many victims did not want to testify against the perpetrators. Drawing on the Mann Act, which criminalizes the interstate transport of a person for the purpose of prostitution, the WWTVPRA of 2008 lowered the burden of proof needed to prosecute sex trafficking and made sex tourism a crime. It improved services for trafficking victims and offered them better protection than existed under the original TVPA and the 2003 and 2005 reauthorizations.

2010 marked the tenth anniversary of the enactment of the U.S. TPVA and the Palermo Protocol. Also, it marked the first time that the United States appeared on the U.S. Department of State's Human Trafficking Report. The inclusion of the United States on the list recognized that trafficking occurred not only abroad but also in the United States.

The State Department's annual report on human trafficking divides countries into three tiers with a watch list based on governmental efforts to combat trafficking. A country in Tier 1 recognizes human trafficking exists, takes steps to combat it and meets minimum TVPA standards which include punishing acts of trafficking. For example, in 2010, Canada and the United States got categorized in Tier 1. A country in Tier 2 has not met the minimum standard but is making an effort to do so. For example, in 2010 Mexico and Peru got categorized in Tier 2. A country on the Tier 2 Watch List may have made promises to do better over the next year or is a country with significant trafficking activity that it tries to combat. For example, in 2010 Guatemala and Panama were on the Tier 2 Watch List. A country in Tier 3 has not met the minimum standards and has not made an effort to do so. For example, in 2010 Iran and North Korea got categorized in Tier 3.

One area that gets considered in each TVPRA is the definition of involuntary versus voluntary labor. Undocumented individuals often face labor circumstances which could potentially be considered involuntary service. For example, they could be told that if they do not continue to work they will be reported to immigration officials. However, the courts need to be very cautious when deciding what is voluntary and what is coerced because much contract labor, whether by undocumented or documented laborers, could be construed as voluntary when it is coerced and vice versa. The case of the *United States v. Shackney* (1964) was one of the first cases to raise the issue of coerced and voluntary labor.

In 1963 criminal charges were brought against David Shackney for keeping a Mexican family, the Oroses, in a situation of involuntary servitude. Mr. Shackney had travelled to Mexico to recruit people to work on his chicken farm. The Oroses had signed a contract written in Spanish agreeing to the conditions of the work, including the pay rate and living arrangements. The case against Mr. Shackney did not revolve around the contract but rather around the accusation that he threatened the Oroses with deportation should they stop working and that the Oroses lived in a constant state of fear because of his threats. The complexity of the case revolved around the meaning of coerced work. While the threat of deportation may invoke fear in a worker, it does not mean that the worker cannot leave the job. Instead, it means that the consequence of leaving the job will be potential deportation. This case occurred decades before the original U.S. TVPA but highlights the need for legislation aimed at preventing human trafficking, prosecuting traffickers, and protecting victims as well as the need for adjustments in the form of reauthorizations as knowledge about human trafficking continues to evolve.

Moira A. Murphy-Aguilar

See Also: Coyotes; Human Trafficking; Violence against Women Act (VAWA).

Further Reading

Bales, Kevin, and Ron Soodalter. *The Slave Next Door: Human Trafficking and Slavery in America Today.* Berkeley: University of California Press, 2010.

"Congress Passes Long-Awaited Anti-Human Trafficking Bill." 2013. Polaris Project. http://www.polarisproject.org/media-center/press-releases/743-congress-passes -long-awaited-anti-human-trafficking-bill.

Kotrla, Kimberly. "Domestic Minor Sex Trafficking in the United States." *Social Work* 55:181–187.

Office to Monitor and Combat Trafficking in Persons. U.S. Department of State Web Site. http://www.state.gov/g/tip/.

Transnationalism

Transnationalism as a concept and phenomenon is relatively new to the field of immigration and global studies. This concept emerged in the 1990s and refers to a population that retains a presence in more than one nation, in part because patterns of migration are rooted in the cyclical nature of their movement. In this way, transnational also speaks to the diminishing social importance of political boundaries that separate nations and the people within them.

In practical terms, transnationalism reflects the lives led by immigrants who continue to maintain a connectedness between sending and destination communities. The concept is a break from a traditional view about an immigration process that for the most part seemed to followed a linear direction. In other words, a more traditional view of immigration holds that movement is marked by a beginning, and ends once immigrants arrive at their destinations. Following this traditional view of immigration, once immigrants leave their country of origin, the relations they left behind grow weaker with time to eventually disappear altogether. In this traditional view, immigration to a new country represents a break from the old as they assimilate into the new. This view of the immigration process was modeled after the mass immigration from Europe to the United States at the turn of the twentieth century. In this context, immigrants may have initially worked to maintain bonds with the sending community from their new destinations. However, without basic, regular, and habitual involvement with sending communities, the connectedness to their old ways would inevitably wane (Portes et al., 1999).

Communication and visitations that were needed to maintain relations that would be considered "transnational" by today's standards were complicated when the sending community in Europe was separated from the host community by a vast ocean. Before communication was possible through the phone or internet, maintaining contact required greater effort and cost. As a result, the traditional direction of immigration implied that an immigrant's connectedness to their sending community in Europe would fade, as would any sense of loyalty to the old ways, a past identity, and the language needed to communicate inherent ideas, values, and sentiments. However, it is worth noting that a more modern means of communication does not necessarily lead to transnationalism. With greater geographic distance between immigrants and their sending communities, many are forced to rely less on family members left behind for support. Once in the United States, assimilation processes emphasizing loyalty to the new country and its new ways often prevent that social connectedness between sending and destination communities, and the virtual presence in both worlds that today defines transnationalism.

According to Vertovec, transnationalism involves the study of population movements in a world where improved modes of transportation as well as means of modern telecommunication have shortened the *social distance* between sending and receiving countries. Transnational communities adhere more closely and more constantly to the cultures, ideas, norms, and means of communication of the sending communities in a variety of ways. For this reason, many Latino immigrants continue to speak at least two languages, and many of them have homes and families in two countries. Remittances— one of the most important contributions to Mexico's gross national project—continue to support families in communities of origin, as well as help families there establish businesses and support public works projects. According to Portes, the labor in one country in this way is almost indistinguishable from that in the other.

An ongoing movement between two or more social spaces or locations is at the heart of transnationalism. This is not to say that those social spaces are geographically separated by political boundaries. With greater immigration enforcement measures around them, undocumented immigrants are less unable to move physically across borders without risking arrest. However, within the safety of supportive immigrant communities, they are able to re-create spaces of interaction in ways that evoke the esthetics and culture found in their country of origin. Such transnational spaces are some of the more visible manifestations of transnationalism that reinforces a national identity *in addition to* the identities adopted in the host country. For example, in the United States, Mexican consulate offices may provide spaces for social interaction and celebration of important national holidays, and for bringing together art, music, and food exhibitions to celebrate Mexico's heritage.

For immigrants from Latin America living in the United States, maintaining transnational linkages between two countries has been facilitated by the historic sharing of a common North American land mass. Mexico, in particular, at one time or another, formed part of what is now the continental United States. Consequently, the movement of populations across the border that separates the two nations has been facilitated by social capital formation and the networks of extended family members that have been in the making for hundreds of years. With the border becoming increasingly closed off to the free movement of people by greater border enforcement mechanisms, the cultivation of social networks for support has grown in importance, resulting in an *increase* of family connections, and not less. In this way, transnationalism continues to flourish, even as political borders are hardened.

One of the characteristics within the transnational population living either in the sending or destination country is the maintenance of their families, businesses, and political, religious, and socio-cultural ties through the going back and forth between the two nations, or by using any means of communication. Such transnational connections are often institutionally supported by the government, such as a consulate's office. One of the many services provided by the Mexican consulate that supports transnationalism is providing the certification and transfer of official documentation of educational records for use by educational systems in Mexico upon a family's return. The consulate manages the nation's 3x1 program where funds that home town associations send to their communities of origin for public works projects are matched at a rate of three dollars to every one dollar by municipal, state and federal governments. Other services provided by consulate offices help immigrants in the United States transfer their personal property to Mexico when they decide to return and support the creation of businesses by former immigrants upon their return. In this way, small businesses established during migration are often enlarged after immigrants return home.

Constant communication is a reliable way to gauge transnationalism (Portes et al., 1999). The importance of this is made more visible in light of immigration enforcement. The use of technology has facilitated people's communication; and with the use of the internet and social media, immigrants benefit from real-time communication. These means of communication allow them to have presence in their communities, even though they are physically absent. Moreover, the technology's low cost makes it possible for immigrants from all socioeconomic levels to communicate with each other. In this way, the culture of sending communities also makes its way to the United States via immigrants living there. Conversely, the culture learned from being part of the United States also makes its way to sending communities, known as "social remittances (Levitt, 1998). For both immigrants and those left behind, these activities reaffirm a sense of cultural connectedness and virtual presence in each other's lives in spite of the borders and distances that separate them.

Martha Yamilett Martínez-Espinoza

See Also: Assimilation; CC-IME (Consejo Consultivo Instituto de los Mexicanos en el Exterior); Culture; Hometown Associations; Remittances; Social Interaction and Integration.

Further Reading

Glick Schiller, N., and P. Levitt. 2006. *Haven't We Heard This Somewhere Before? A Substantive View of Transnational Migration Studies by Way of a Reply to Waldinger and Fitzgerald.* The Center for Migration and Development. Working Paper Series.

Levitt, Peggy. 1998. "Social Remittances: Migration Driven Local-Level Forms of Cultural Diffusion." *International Migration Review* 32.4:926–948.

Portes, A., L. Guarnizo, and P. Landolt. 1999. "The Study of Transnationalism: Pitfalls and Promise of an Emergent Research Field." *Ethnic and Racial Studies* 22. Routledge.

Vertovec, Steven. 2006. "Migration and Other Modes of Transnationalism: Towards Conceptual Cross Fertilization." *International Migration Review* 37.3:641–665.

Zuñiga, Victor, and T. Edmond T. Hamman. 2006. "Going Home? Schooling in Mexico of Transnational Children." *Confines* 2.4:41–57.

Transportation in the United States

For undocumented migrants, transportation in the United States has always posed problems, ranging from the threat of a traffic stop by police that may result in apprehension and abuse, to the risk of injury or even death during high speed chases by U.S. Border Patrol agents along the border.

The simple act of obtaining a license to drive is problematic depending on the state in which one lives. With greater frequency, state governments are denying immigrants present in the country without proper authorization the ability to apply for drivers' licenses. Consequently, this limits job prospects if the job requires that they drive a vehicle or need to travel to get to work. It also jeopardizes public safety when immigrants cannot provide proof of having a driver's license to purchase motor vehicle insurance. Consequently, the cost of uninsured drivers on streets and highways raises the costs of automobile insurance for all drivers. The irony of this situation is that while motor vehicle accidents are among the major causes of death of Hispanics, there is some evidence that low-acculturated recent immigrants are relatively safe drivers (Romano et al., 2013).

Transportation within the jurisdiction of the U.S. Border Patrol also poses risks for migrants because of the possibility of being stopped. The Border Patrol has a jurisdiction of about 100 miles inland from the U.S. border with Mexico and Canada. However, most of the surveillance and apprehension activity occurs along the 1,954-mile-long border with Mexico. A primary responsibility of the U.S. Border Patrol is to Perform traffic checks on major highways leading away from the border to detect and apprehend immigrants who have entered into the country without proper inspection and who are attempting to travel further into the interior of the United States. Within the U.S. Border Patrol jurisdiction, it is very common and accepted practice by agents to stop vehicles that have drivers or passengers that could potentially be undocumented immigrants. The USA PATRIOT Act has made it possible for enforcement agents to rely on the proximity to the border to use the "Mexican" appearance of drivers or passengers as just cause for stopping the vehicle and searching it, in the interest of national security. For this reason, undocumented immigrants and legal residents alike are subject to these stops and searches if they appear to be Mexican. As a result of this interaction between officials and undocumented immigrants, there have been several reports and studies documenting cases of abuse by authorities. A report released in 2008 shows that 43 percent of reported stop and search incidents involved abuse by the local police or sheriff's department, and 20 percent of cases reported were attributed to the U.S. Border Patrol (Border Network for Human Rights, 2008).

If stopped, passengers of the vehicle will be questioned to determine their legal status. If the vehicle passenger is found to be present in the country unlawfully, he or she will be detained, processed, and later repatriated or deported. U.S. Border Patrol inspections occur at temporary stationary checkpoints along roadways leading away from the border, or on highways where they may have cause to stop other interior-bound transport vehicles, such as buses, other commercial transport vehicles (such as shuttles), passenger and freight trains, and marine craft. All these modes of transportation are used by undocumented immigrants to reach safe houses or the safety of the final destinations in the interior parts of the country. In attempting to evade U.S. Border Patrol agents, high-speed changes may ensue,

Undocumented immigrants from Mexico sit next to the tractor-trailer they rode across the border into the United States on Interstate 8, east of San Diego on May 3, 2008. The U.S. Border Patrol agents found 61 men packed into the trailer during an attempt to smuggle them into the United States. (AP Photo/U.S. Border Patrol)

putting immigrants at risk of injury or death. Between 1998 and 2005, motor vehicle accidents involving the U.S. Border Patrol were among the leading causes of migrant deaths along the border region, according to a 2006 Government Accountability Office report (GAO, 2006).

Transportation in the United States also involves the very dangerous practice by the human smugglers of leaving people in trunks of cars that are relatively small areas with limited oxygen and in extreme heat for hours at time. Additionally the high number of passengers that smugglers try to move at one time puts passengers at high risk if the vehicle exceeds prudent weight limits and is engaged by a U.S. Border Patrol vehicle in a high-speed chase.

Migrants have reported being victims of abuse by their smugglers during transportation. News reports offer testimonies by migrants recalling having being locked in trailers along the U.S.-Mexico border with little food or water until family members were able to pay off the debt. In one of the most horrifying and famous cases, seventy-four undocumented immigrants were sealed and locked in a trailer in Victoria, Texas, resulting in nineteen deaths from heat exhaustion and suffocation in May of 2003. Although the smuggler later faced charges, the eventual capture and conviction of smugglers is not common because they are rarely identified by those being smuggled. Human smugglers often threaten immigrants with the lives of their families back home if information of their smuggling role is revealed (Lozano, 2006).

Yesenia Andrade

See Also: Border Crossing; Coyotes; Death; Driver's Licenses; Human Trafficking; Racial Profiling; *United States v. Brignoni-Ponce.*

Further Reading

Border Network for Human Rights. 2008. U.S.-Mexico Border Policy Report. http://www .utexas.edu/law/centers/humanrights/borderwall/communities/municipalities-US -Mexico-Border-Policy-Report.pdf.

GAO. 2006. Report No. GAO-06-770, Government Accountability Office Report to the Honorable Bill Frist, Majority Leader, U.S. Senate. "Illegal Immigration Border-Crossing Deaths Have Doubled Since 1995; Border Patrol's Efforts to Prevent Deaths Have Not Been Fully Evaluated." http://www.gao.gov/new.items/d06770 .pdf.

Lozano, Juan A. 2006. "Alleged Smuggler Tells of Frantic Chase." *Boston Globe,* February, 1 http://www.boston.com/news/nation/articles/2006/02/01/alleged_smuggler_tells_of _frantic_chase/?rss_id=Boston.com+%2F+News.

Romano, Eduardo, Scott Tippetts, James Fell, Angela Eichelberger, Milton Grosz, and Connie Wiliszowski. 2013. "Traffic Citation Rates among Drivers of Different Residency Status in the United States." *Accident Analysis & Prevention* 51:215–221.

U.S. Immigration Support. Drivers' Licenses and Social Security Numbers for Illegal Immigrants. http://www.usimmigrationsupport.org/illegalimmigrant-driverslicense .html.

Trauma-Related Symptoms

Human beings are equipped with a complex system to respond to danger which encompasses body and mind. Under threats to life or bodily integrity, or close encounters with violence and death, this complex system can be summarized as the "fight or flight," resistance or escape response. Trauma occurs when the coping mechanisms ordinarily used by an individual to overcome extreme circumstances are not possible. These coping mechanisms become overwhelmed as the individual directly experiences or witnesses horrible events such as those resulting from war, rape, or natural disasters.

Some individuals are exposed not only to one single traumatic event but experience prolonged and/or repeated trauma in their lives such as domestic violence, physical abuse in childhood, or long-term forced captivity. Mostly, prolonged and/or repeated trauma affects the emotion, cognition, memory, and response to danger systems of those impacted by it. As a result, the individual is profoundly and lastingly affected in her sense of control, connection with others, and making meaning of the world around her.

For undocumented immigrants, traumas and symptoms may be related to their border-crossing experiences and the subsequent difficult and harsh experiences associated with living in the United States. A study aimed at understanding several factors related to the health status of undocumented immigrant women shows that dangers involved in undocumented crossings from Mexico into the United States generally are not incorporated into clinical evaluations (Andrews et al., 2002). Those who cross the border on foot in remote locations are commonly victims of robbery, sexual assault, abandonment, isolation, and family separation. The participants in this study reported experiencing extreme danger and life-threatening circumstances. Once in the United States, the women's undocumented status limits employment options, increasing their personal and economic vulnerability to exploitation. When they are working, the women risk deportation and fear that their children will be left behind.

In spite of the predictable psychological harm, for reasons which are not yet clear, some individuals exposed to a single traumatic event or to prolonged and/or repeated traumatic events do not develop any symptoms that are expected to be associated with it. Others develop mild symptoms and yet others are severely affected by the traumatic experience(s). In some cases, the symptoms do not appear until long after the exposure to the traumatic event or experiences ended. Nevertheless, experiencing the symptoms derived from the exposure to traumatic events can be not only a source of extreme difficulty but, paradoxically, also a source of strength and resilience for its survivors.

However, Complex Post-Traumatic Stress Disorder is considered an affliction of the powerless not only because it renders helpless its victims, but because it increases their vulnerability to be harmed repeatedly over the course of their lives. Most undocumented immigrants have suffered historical and cumulative oppression and have been exposed to several traumatic experiences making them highly vulnerable to suffering Complex PTSD. The symptoms of Complex PTSD become engraved in the body and tend to be experienced and expressed independently from their source. As a result, it is very common for survivors of Complex PTSD to constantly complain of physical ailments.

A significant subgroup of youths who are recent immigrants to the United States are at high risk for exposure to violence as part of the conditions they faced in their home country, the border-crossing experience, or subsequent poverty once they settled in the United States (Jaycox et al., 2002). More than 2.2 million school-age children are recent immigrants fleeing poverty, crime, and social unrest in their homeland. In research by Jaycox and colleagues (2002) of recent immigrant children in Los Angeles, 1,004 schoolchildren aged eight to fifteen years old were surveyed about their prior exposure to violence and symptoms of posttraumatic stress disorder (PTSD) and depression. The research shows that while for some the migration journey was uneventful, others experienced violence, assaults and robbery, and even life-threatening events. In this study, 40 percent of children reported that such events had happened to them personally in the previous year, and 63 percent reported having witnessed such events. Very little work has been done to date to examine immigrant children's adjustment to violence exposure which includes depressive symptoms and psychological distress. Thirty-two percent of children reported PTSD symptoms in the clinical range, and 16 percent reported depressive symptoms in the clinical range. Although boys and older children were more likely to have experienced violence, girls reported more PTSD and depressive symptoms.

Motor vehicle accidents due to overcrowded vehicles in part due to the very active criminal enterprise of smuggling undocumented immigrants in the desert of the Southwest are a recent and underrecognized trauma ctiology. A computerized database search from 1990 through 2003 of local newspaper reports of overcrowded motor vehicle crashes along the 281 miles of Arizona's border with Mexico was conducted.

Posttraumatic stress disorder (PTSD) is associated with medical and psychological morbidity. The prevalence of PTSD in urban primary care has not been well described. The objective of the study was to measure the prevalence of PTSD in primary-care patients overall and among those with selected conditions (chronic pain, depression, anxiety, heavy drinking, substance dependence.

The many symptoms associated with Complex PTSD fall into three main categories and are reflected not only in the psyche but also in the body of those afflicted by it. The three categories of Complex PTSD symptoms are: Hyperarousal, Intrusion, and Constriction. Hyperarousal refers to the persistent expectation of danger and it is associated with fear and anxiety; intrusion refers to the reenactment of the sensations and/or images related to the traumatic experiences; constriction refers to the numbing response resulting from the impossibility of using the "fight or flight" response. It relates to dissociation. Sometimes it is expressed as detachment, plain affect, and/or lack of initiative. Other times it is associated with the use of alcohol and/or other drugs to self-induce the dissociative state.

Complex-Post Traumatic Stress Disorder is one of the most common mental health issues found among undocumented immigrant individuals and it affects every single aspect of their lives. Complex Post-Traumatic Stress Disorder among this population is rooted in the multiple traumatic events that undocumented immigrants face. These may begin in early childhood years, such as neglect, abuse (verbal, physical, sexual, emotional), and extreme poverty. It continues with the trauma resulting from making the decision to cross the border and effectively crossing the border. It is perpetuated in the trauma surrounding their lives in a foreign land without knowing how to navigate its multiple systems in the midst of poverty and scarce individual, family and community resources. Undocumented immigrants have to endure some specific, practical, and constant sources of trauma such as the fear of driving without a license or looking for a job without a valid social security number in order to provide for themselves and their families.

Even though the consequences of Complex Post-Traumatic Stress Disorder are pervasive in the lives of its victims and tend to impact them in mostly negative ways, this entity is susceptible of being successfully treated and overcome through different approaches involving not only talk therapy but also spiritual and creative activities such as drawing, acting, active imagination. The ultimate goal for the survivor is to reconnect with herself and her community. Approaches other than talk therapy seem to be necessary in order to reach and heal the imprint left in the brain by the traumatic events. Group therapy seems to be particularly effective for undocumented immigrants dealing with symptoms associated with Complex PTSD because of its emphasis on support and reconnection, the two most significant goals to be achieved for those disconnected from their culture and their fellow human beings.

The spectrum of symptoms resulting from prolonged and/or repeated trauma cannot be understood exclusively under one single disorder and need to be clustered in a broader, more comprehensive category which has not yet been officially recognized. For example, the analysis of the medical screening examinations conducted on the undocumented migrants from Fujian Province of China ($n = 589$) who arrived on four boats on the West Coast of Canada between June 14 and September 9, 1999, showed that abuse by their controllers was rampant (Allan and Szafran, 2005). Migrants indicated they had been threatened, beaten, or raped aboard the boats. Trauma-related symptoms included bruising, which was significantly more common among females. This was especially true of the second of two boats where passengers had significantly more cases of bruising. The authors speculate that because this second boat had been temporarily lost, the social conditions on it may have deteriorated, resulting in the greater abuse of women. The undocumented Chinese migrants were predominantly young, and exhibited evidence of trauma with bruises, scratches, and lacerations. It was suspected that the majority of abuse was perpetrated by the "Snakeheads" (the human smugglers). The researchers note that it was unfortunate they as medical professionals would not be able to follow up on certain psychological trauma or recheck patients as the migrants would only be available for a few short days.

Hence, the categories currently defined by the DSM-V (the manual of diagnostic criteria for mental disorders elaborated by the American Psychiatric Association) such as Depression, Anxiety or Post-traumatic Stress Disorder are incomplete and do not fully encompass the complexities of prolonged and/or repeated trauma. Some of the comprehensive names used to describe the symptoms resulting from prolonged and/or repeated trauma are Complex Post-Traumatic Stress Disorder (Complex PTSD), Post-Traumatic Character Disorder, Complicated Post-Traumatic Stress Disorder, Disorder of Extreme Stress Not Otherwise Specified, and Personality Change from Catastrophic Experience.

Mauricio Cifuentes

See Also: Barriers to Health; Health and Welfare; Mental Health Issues for Undocumented Immigrants; Transportation in the United States; Violence.

Further Reading

Allan, G., and Olga Szafran. 2005. "Health of Chinese Illegal Immigrants Who Arrived by Boat on the West Coast of Canada in 1999." *Journal of Immigrant Health* 7.4:233–238.

Andrews, Tracy J., Vickie D. Ybarra, and Teresa Miramontes. 2002. "Negotiating Survival: Undocumented Mexican Immigrant Women in the Pacific Northwest." *The Social Science Journal* 39.3:431–449.

Herman, Judith. *Trauma and Recovery.* New York: BasicBooks, 1992.

Jaycox, Lisa H., Bradley D. Stein, Sheryl H. Kataoka, Marleen Wong, Arlene Fink, Pia Escudero, and Catalina Zaragoza. 2002. "Violence Exposure, Posttraumatic Stress Disorder, and Depressive Symptoms Among Recent Immigrant Schoolchildren." *Journal of the American Academy of Child & Adolescent Psychiatry* 41.9:1104.

Lumpkin, Mary F., Dan Judkin, John M. Porter, Rifat Latifi, and Mark D. Williams. 2004. "Overcrowded Motor Vehicle Trauma from the Smuggling of Illegal Immigrants in the Desert of the Southwest." *American Surgeon* 70.12:1078–1082.

U

The "Undocumented" Label

Since the 1970s, journalists, elected officials, migrant activists, and social science researchers have been debating a seemingly simple question: what should be the appropriate label for migrants subject to deportation/removal? In other words, what label should be applied to non-citizens residing in the United States who, if discovered by federal migration officials and brought before an immigration judge, might be ordered to be removed from the United States? Although the question appears simple, the situation is not as straightforward as it may appear. The complexity of the matter is due to several reasons. One, there is much confusion regarding the difference between the formal terminology found in the nation's migration statute and the widespread popular terminology used by media, activists, and academics. Two, most discussions of persons subject to removal tend to focus on possible violation of entry restrictions, particularly across the Mexico–United States boundary, thus overlooking the equal or larger number of migrants who also may be subject to removal but whose entry was authorized. Three, there is limited discussion about the linked development of the labels "illegal" and "undocumented" migrant, and the shared limitations of both terms. Four, much of the debate assumes a clear demarcation between "legal" and "illegal/undocumented" migrant status.

Formal v. Popular Terminology

Over the past forty years, an opposition has developed regarding the preferred labels used to refer to migrants who may be subject to removal, specifically those assumed to have entered the United States without formal authorization. On one side, both liberal and conservative segments of society deploy the term "illegal alien," "illegal immigrant," or the grammatically incorrect noun-form "illegal" to refer to such persons—or in Spanish, *"ilegal."* And on the other side, individuals who could be characterized as liberal or progressive tend to evoke the labels "undocumented immigrant," or the also grammatically incorrect noun-form "undocumented"—or *"indocumentado"* in Spanish. Both uses produce oxymorons, and do not have a basis in law. The former, in particular, carries an implied sense that the label is a legal or juridical description of an act; thus it is not surprising that statements such as "Illegal is illegal!" or "What part of illegal don't you understand?" can quickly spread and become part of the contentious debate.

"Illegal immigrant" and "undocumented immigrant" are oxymorons because under the Immigration and Nationality Act, an immigrant is a person who is formally authorized to enter and reside indefinitely in the United States, is designated as a law-ful permanent resident, and granted a permanent resident visa. Neither label exists in the nation's migration statute. The correlate limitation is the limited knowledge of the formal distinction between deportation/removal and "voluntary departure." Subject to removal is the principle that determines who can be ordered removed, or allowed to stay if there are grounds that can be applied in the specific case. What this means is that it is this ultimate judicial decision that determines if a person has a legal right to remain in the United States or not. Apprehension by the Immigration and Customs Enforce-ment (ICE) does not automatically result in removal. Apprehended individuals have the option, though they may not be aware of it, that they can request a removal hearing, or agree to a "voluntary departure" (also known as "return"). A greater number are returned than removed; in Fiscal Year-2009, the most recent complete year reported, there were 393,289 removals, and 580,107 returns. The "voluntary departure" option has historically been the preferred choice for both U.S. migration officials and appre-hended migrants—for the migrant it means a shorter apprehension time, and for the United States it means a reduced cost due to not having to house, feed, and provide medical care to the individual until the removal hearing is held.

The Immigration and Nationality Act contains several concepts that refer to viola-tion of entry or visa requirement: "to be present unlawfully," "alien unlawfully present," "illegal entrant," "not lawfully present," "immigration violator," "criminal alien," and "illegal alien." Even though there is some overlap in the categories, most of these appear in separate provisions of the law and refer to distinct violations. It thus can be observed that the popular labels of "illegal alien/immigrant" and "undocumented im-migrant" do not have a basis in law.

Mexico-U.S. Boundary as the Problem

For the period from the Great Depression to the present, most discussions of the na-tion's migration problems have tended to be framed as concerns related to the unau-thorized entry of Mexican nationals. From the Reagan Administration to the Obama Administration, the overwhelming majority of boundary security resources have been allocated to the two-thousand-mile southern land boundary. The Border Patrol force has grown from 2,444 at the start of the Reagan presidency, to the current force of over 22,000; this ten-fold increase in personnel is in addition to substantial resources allo-cated for ground sensors, steel walls, drones, infrared cameras, and other technology. The four- to five-thousand-mile Canada–United States border has been largely ignored over the last nine decades, though since 2000 it has begun to receive some attention. What this overlooks is the long history of unauthorized migration through the northern boundary, including up to the present.

The framing of the nation's "immigration problem" as an entry-control problem has resulted in an incomplete comprehension of the issue, as well as in limiting the formulation of solutions. Immigration and Naturalization Service and Department of Homeland Security officials have reported to Congress that they estimate that between 30 and 57 percent of persons subject to removal are migrants who have violated the terms of their visas. This points to two important issues that are generally ignored:

(a) that entry violations make up about half of the subject to removal cases, and (b) that the overwhelming majority of resources are being allocated to one half of the "problem." It also points to the inherent problem in the public debate about solving the migration concern, a debate dominated by a concern to "secure the border" as the way to solve the public policy issue. Given the reality of the "immigration violators" issue, even if it were possible to completely stop all unauthorized entries, this would not eliminate the presence of persons who have violated the time or work restrictions of their visas—including migrants from Canada, Ireland, Poland, and other nations—and are thus subject to removal. The absence of concern about the "illegal/undocumented" migrants who entered with authorization but now are subject to removal reinforces the dominant perspective that defines Mexican migration and the Mexico-U.S. boundary as the principal "problem" to be addressed. It is an absence that also fosters a racialized perspective of the issue.

"Illegal" Migrant v. "Undocumented" Migrant

The acrimonious debate on the labels has tended to conceptualize the labels as binary opposites with no common ground. Moreover, their use has become closely associated with opposing political perspectives. Those who prefer the label "illegal immigrant/ alien" tend to take the position that emphasizes the "criminality" and the negative economic and social impact of migrants. And those who prefer to use the "undocumented immigrant" generally assume a more positive view of migrants, and tend to stress the economic contribution of migrants. There are several problems with this dimension of the debate. First, authors commonly fail to provide an explanation for their choice of labels and whom they encompass under the label selected; though, as suggested above, the tendency is to assume that the population is composed of migrants who violated entry restrictions. Second, most authors overlook exploring the co-development of both terms.

The emergence of the application of "illegal alien/immigrant" to Mexican migrants and the oppositional response to this took place in the early 1970s. In response to the debate leading to the passage of California's employer sanctions law in 1971, and the adoption of the label "illegal alien" by the *Los Angeles Times,* Chicano/ Mexican-origin activists began to invoke the labels "*sin documentos*" (Corona, 1972) and later "*indocumentado*" which was translated to "undocumented" migrant. Thus, the label "undocumented" migrant explicitly emerged as an opposition to what was thought to be a pejorative and dehumanizing label: "illegal alien."

What has been overlooked over the past three decades is the common limitation in both terms. Both terms focus on the individual as the determining force, and in so doing obscure the key role of the State in producing the laws and practices that promote the migration, and the categorization of illegality. Both terms also tend to perceive migrants as economic units (*homo economicus*); one stresses the positive economic contribution, the other, the detrimental economic impact. The two perspectives ignore the multiple dimensions of human migrants: as individuals with family and marital aspirations, as persons with social expectations of parental and spousal responsibilities, friendship ties, desires to escape human rights abuses or state-sponsored violence.

Legality v. Illegality

The final limitation in the labeling dilemma is the common assumption that U.S. law and practices adhere to a clear demarcation between a "legal" and "illegal" immigrant. While space does not allow a full discussion of these, the following are some examples of the blurring of the distinction in U.S. law and practices. Since the Civil War, U.S. law has allowed the granting of citizenship to persons performing military work during periods of conflict, even allowing this for migrants unable to prove formal entry into the United States. On July 3, 2002, President Bush signed an Executive Order activating the particular statute, and made it retroactive to September 11, 2001 and to continue during the global war on terrorism. Consequently, non-citizens, including "illegal/undocumented" migrants, who manage to enlist in the military, are granted a path to citizenship for their military work. The U.S. Selective Service System requires that all males between the ages of eighteen to twenty-five must register. Moreover, in the event Congress authorizes a military draft, all persons called upon by the draft are obligated to defend the nation—including "illegal/undocumented" migrants. A final example is the special rules for Cuban migrants. Under the 1995 treaty with Cuba, Cuban nationals apprehended at sea by the U.S. Coast Guard are repatriated to Cuba. However, Cuban migrants who manage to outrun the Coast Guard and "touch" land (acquire "dry foot"), even though they arrived without a visa and did it by evading the Coast Guard, are granted permanent residency and can later be granted citizenship. Because the treaty does not specify where entry has to take place, Cubans entering clandestinely through Mexico at any of the places also commonly used by Mexican migrants, upon successfully entering the United States without documents or without authorization, are also granted permanent residency and placed on a path to citizenship.

Luis F. B. Plascencia

See Also: Deportation; Employment Visas; Governance and Criminalization; Identity Theft; Overstayers; Work Visas.

Further Reading

Corona, Bert. 1972. *Bert Corona Habla del Partido de la Raza Unida y del Alarma en Contra de los 'Ilegales.'* New York: Pathfinder Press.
Coutin, Susan Bibler. 2005. "Contesting Criminality: Illegal Immigration and the Spatialization of Legality." *Theoretical Criminology* 9.1:5–33.
Johnson, Kevin R. 1996–1997. "'Aliens' and the U.S. Immigration Laws: The Social and Legal Construction of Nonpersons. "*Inter-American Law Review* 28.2:263–292.
Plascencia, Luis F. B. 2009. "The 'Undocumented' Mexican Migrant Question: Re-examining the Framing of Law and Illegalization in the United States." *Urban Anthropology* 38.2–4:375–434.
Romero, Mary. 2000–2001. "State Violence, and the Social and Legal Construction of Latino Criminality: From El Bandito to Gang Member." *Denver University Law Review* 78:1081–1118.

Undocumented Students

While the U.S. Supreme Court decision *Plyler v. Doe* assures access to K-12 schooling for undocumented migrants, no such policy exists for higher education. With this in mind, lawmakers in eleven states have created policies providing undocumented students the opportunity to pay resident tuition in state-funded universities and colleges. These fees, while significantly lower than out-of-state or international student fees, are quite expensive and continue to increase on a yearly basis. Therefore, while sixty-five thousand undocumented students graduate from U.S. high schools every year, only a few have the opportunity to continue their studies both because of the limited number of states with policies facilitating access and the cost of tuition where in-state tuition is available. Furthermore, neither the *Plyler v. Doe* decision nor the above-mentioned state policies provide a path to permanent residence or citizenship. This means that students, while able to attend higher institutions, will spend their university years living under precarious conditions. In addition, many students will age out of the possibility of being sponsored through a family member while studying in the university. Therefore, given their immigration status, undocumented students have little possibility to enter the job market in the discipline in which they were trained after completing their degree because they lack a social security number. In the end, the meritocratic ideology of schooling as a means to social mobility can fill undocumented students with hope, but financial difficulty, precarious living conditions, and the knowledge that they may never be able to use their degrees create a sense of hopelessness.

As stated above, eleven states currently have policies in place facilitating access to higher education. These policies stipulate that undocumented migrants can pay resident tuition in state-funded institutions rather than the much higher out-of-state or international student fees. However, the vast majority of these policies do not include a financial aid component, making the reduced resident fees still beyond the reach of many undocumented students. The inability to produce sufficient funds to pay for schooling forces undocumented students to partake in casual enrollment where breaks are created in order to procure the necessary money. These breaks can affect student retention as they have been correlated with reasons why students do not continue their studies. The constant need to pause schooling to procure additional funding can make a degree appear unreachable to an individual who is already living under a large amount of uncertainty.

Although policies creating access to schooling are beneficial for undocumented students, they do not alleviate the effects of their undocumented status. As such, undocumented students are still under constant risk of being apprehended by immigration authorities and being deported. Various studies have shown that such students can experience a number of psychological stresses that affect their studies as well as their daily life. As such, undocumented students must often contend with the knowledge that their investment (in terms of money, time, and psychological stress) can be for naught if they are detained by immigration enforcement.

While many universities have support staff in place to help students (including counselors, psychologists, peer groups, health clinics, staff for student services, etc.)

Nelly Rodriguez, 18, from Wichita, Kansas, holds a sign during a rally in Washington, D.C., April 20, 2004. Roughly 100 students, some facing deportation, staged a mock graduation ceremony on the lawn of the Capitol. They were urging passage of the DREAM Act, a bill which would make it easier for undocumented immigrants to attend college in the United States and eventually take the path to citizenship. (AP Photo/Lawrence Jackson)

many are not trained in immigration policy and cannot provide aid to undocumented students. Often, because of the vast exclusion to social services on the basis of immigration status, undocumented students do not know about their rights to access such services that are paid for through university fees. Furthermore, given the stigma associated with undocumented status as well as the danger of disclosing information about one's status, undocumented students may be wary of accessing such services. This can create a lonely college experience where students may feel as if they are the only undocumented student on campus, thus furthering feelings of hopelessness.

Perhaps the most deflating aspect of attending higher education and being undocumented is the understanding that the awarding of a university degree does not include a path to permanent residence. As such, students continue to live precariously. In addition, given that most jobs requesting a university degree require the furnishing of a social security number, undocumented university students may never qualify for such a position given their immigration status. This means that undocumented students must often determine if the above-mentioned investment to procure a university degree is worth it given that they may never benefit from the labor market possibilities it brings.

Although undocumented students may experience prolonged periods of hopelessness, they are not passive. Many universities today have campus organizations created to act as support groups for undocumented students as well as to advocate in their behalf. These groups enable students to share their stories in safer environments with peers that understand the context of their daily lives as well as the stressors associated with undocumented status. This creates a sense of belonging to the university context as well as a support group to find better coping mechanisms and to navigate the university bureaucracy.

While undocumented university students constantly face hopeless moments in their university careers, there are some support mechanisms in place to help alleviate these feelings. However, the inability for them to attain permanent residence remains the greatest roadblock as it prevents them from finding employment commensurate to their new credentials, and they face the possibility of immigration enforcement detaining and possibly deportation.

Francisco Villegas

See Also: Colleges and Universities; Deferred Action for Childhood Arrivals (DACA); DREAM Act; Education; Elementary Schools; High Schools; *Plyler v. Doe.*

Further Reading

Diaz-Strong, Daysi, and Erica Miners. 2007. "Residents, Alien Policies, and Resistances: Experiences of Undocumented Latina/o Students in Chicago's Colleges and Universities." *Inter Actions: UCLA Journal of Education and Information Studies* 3.2:6.

Dozier, Sandra Bygrave. 1993. "Emotional Concerns of Undocumented and Out-of-Status Foreign Students." *Community Review* 13:33–39.

Madera, Gabriela. 2008. *Undocumented Undergrads: UCLA Undocumented Immigrant Students Speak Out.* Los Angeles: UCLA Center for Labor Research and Education.

Villegas, Francisco. 2010. "Strategic In/visibility and Undocumented Migrants." In *Fanon & Education: Thinking through Pedagogical Possibilities,* edited by George Dei and Marlon Simmons, eds. New York: Peter Lang.

United States v. Brignoni-Ponce

Racial profiling in law enforcement has long been permitted and in fact, was legally affirmed by the case of *United States v. Brignoni-Ponce* in 1975 when the U.S. Supreme Court upheld the use of Mexican appearance as a relevant factor to establish reasonable suspicion of unlawful presence. The Court relied on a statute of the Immigration and Nationality Act that provides any officer of the (then) INS the power without warrant to interrogate ". . . any alien or person believed to be an alien . . ." (Perez, 2011).

The case stemmed from an incident that occurred on the evening of March 11, 1973 when two Border Patrol agents were patrolling an area in a marked patrol car. The patrol car was parked on the shoulder of Interstate 5 north of the city of San Diego, California. As they monitored traffic moving northbound they spotted a car that was being driven by a man who they claimed appeared to be of Mexican ancestry and two passengers whom they also suspected of being of Mexican ancestry. For this reason they decided to follow and eventually pulled the vehicle over. The driver would turn out to be Felix-Humberto Brignoni-Ponce, a legal U.S. citizen of Puerto Rican ancestry; his two passengers were Elsa Marina Hernandez-Serabia a Guatemala national, and Jose Nuñez-Ayala, a Mexican national. As all were speaking Spanish when the Border Patrol agents pulled them over, the agents asked for documentation to prove their lawful status in the United States. When the Border Patrol agents were able to identify that two of the three were undocumented, they arrested all three individuals. In addition to the charges of "illegal entry" by the two undocumented passengers, charges were also brought up against the driver, Brignoni-Ponce, for knowingly transporting undocumented immigrants. For aiding so called "criminals," Brignoni-Ponce was charged with two counts of a federal offense.

A grand jury in the Southern District of California charged and convicted Brignoni-Ponce with two counts of knowingly transporting an alien into the United States. The judge that presided over the case was Judge Howard B. Turrentine, Jr. who denied the motion put forward by Brignoni-Ponce's lawyer to dismiss the testimony of the two passengers on the grounds that all evidence produced by the stop was not valid due to the unlawful nature of the stop. However, the judge dismissed the motion. Brignoni-Ponce was found guilty on both counts and sentenced to four years in prison.

Brignoni-Ponce's appeal to the U.S. Court of Appeals for the Ninth Circuit occurred after the case of *Almeida-Sanchez v. United States*. The importance of this case was that it, too, sought to establish that the tactics used by Border Patrol agents to identify undocumented immigrants were a violation of the Fourth Amendment. Although the court agreed that these tactics were in violation of the Fourth Amendment, they judged them to be valid in the context of the Border Patrol's efforts to use additional information to warrant a stop within close proximity to the border.

In the case that preceded *United States v Brigoni-Ponce, Almeida-Sanchez v. United States* in 1953, the Supreme Court had established that patrol cars could not and would not target and stop vehicles with the intent to question individuals based on their Mexican appearance. However the Immigration and Naturalization Service (INS) insisted that the practice of following and stopping cars in this fashion was "the 'functional equivalent' of the border" (Ong, 2009).

Upon appeal, in *United States v. Brignoni-Ponce,* the U.S. Supreme Court found that the "Mexican appearance" of the driver and passengers was one of several factors that could be used in combination to warrant a stop and question the driver and passengers. The other factors included: proximity of the roving vehicle to the border, traffic patterns of the roadway where the stop occurred, the behavior of the individual of the detained vehicle, the characteristics of the detained vehicle, and the appearance of the passengers in the detained vehicle. The ruling stated that as long as Border Patrol agents could articulate specific attributes of the car or passengers that would warrant suspicion then the stop was permitted. Justice Powell, writing for the majority opinion of the court, stated that trained officers could recognize the appearance of Mexicans, relying on aspects such as clothing and haircuts (Hernández, 2009).

This case presented an important issue concerning the Border Patrol's authority, consistent with the Fourth Amendment, to employ a law enforcement method that is widely used by the Border Patrol for deterring and detecting the unlawful entry and transportation of undocumented immigrants in the country.

The timing of this case happened during a period of a growing budget for the INS. The growing fear of unauthorized workers in particular created fears expressed by citizens of losing their jobs to undocumented workers. This development of the term "'illegal' immigrant" was seen as an outcome of this development in American history—one that institutionalized racism based on immigration status rather than the skin color. It was widely regarded that Mexican-heritage individuals were not being targeted because of their race or color of their skin, but rather by other indicators of unlawfulness, such as a Mexican appearance.

In a related case a year later, *United States v. Martinez-Fuente,* the Supreme Court ruled that checkpoints in the interior of the state were necessary because the continuous and constant movement of undocumented migrants was due to insufficient patrolling on the actual border. As such, the tactics of stopping and searching people in efforts to detain all individuals entering the country "illegally" was seen as an extension of the border patrolling. The case itself involved the right to establish routine checkpoints that would select particular cars to undergo secondary inspection and further questioning. The court upheld these tactics because of the perceived threat of a growing "problem" of "illegal" immigrants in the border region and in the country as a whole. This case also affirmed that no additional facts need to be gathered when stopping vehicles or having them undergo further inspection and questions due to the climate at the time.

Yesenia Andrade

See Also: Arizona SB1070; Deportation; Governance and Criminalization; Racial Profiling; Racism; Repatriation; Transportation in the United States; Xenophobia.

Further Reading

Gowie, Renata Ann. 2001. "Driving While Mexican: Why the Supreme Court Must Reexamine *United States v. Brignoni-Ponce,* 422 U.S. 873." *Houston Journal of International Law* 23.2:233–254.

Hernández, César Cuauhtémoc Garcia. 2009. "La Migra in the Mirror: Immigration Enforcement, Racial Profiling, and the Psychology of One Mexican Chasing Another." *Albany Law Review* 72.4:891–897.

Johnson, Kevin R. 2009. "How Racial Profiling in America Became the 'Law of the Land': *United States v. Brignoni-Ponce* and *Whren v. United States* and the Need for Rebellious Lawyering." June 22. UC Davis Legal Studies Research Paper No. 174. http://ssrn.com/abstract=1424183.

Ong Hing, Bill. 2009. "Institutional Racism, ICE Raids, and Immigration Reform." *University of San Francisco Law Review* 44. http://works.bepress.com/billhing/4.

Perez, Javier. 2011. "Reasonably Suspicious of Being Mojado: The Legal Derogation of Latinos in Immigration Enforcement." *Texas Hispanic Journal of Law & Policy* 17.1:99–123.

United States v. Roblero-Solis

United States v. Roblero-Solis was the first major legal challenge to the controversial federal consequence program known as Operation Streamline. Operation Streamline, started under the Bush administration in 2005, seeks to criminally prosecute and imprison all undocumented border crossers. The 9th Circuit Court of Appeals heard the case in November of 2009 and on December 2nd ruled that, while certain features of Streamline violated federal rules governing criminal cases, the overall practice of trying migrants *en masse* did not constitute a violation of defendants' due process rights. With minor alterations in response to the ruling, Operation Streamline operates today much as it did at when it started.

The program first started in Del Rio, Texas but is now in most Border Patrol sectors and four out of the five federal judicial districts on the border. Streamline's most distinctive feature is the unprecedented number of migrants tried simultaneously in federal courtrooms. In a typical hearing, fifty to seventy handcuffed and shackled migrants hear the charges against them, and, almost without exception, plead guilty to them, and are sentenced. The entire process rarely takes more than two hours.

The program has had dramatic impacts on federal district courts along the border. Between 2002 and 2008, the number of criminal prosecutions of misdemeanor immigration violations increased from 12,411 to 53,697, a rise of 330 percent. Over the same period prosecutions of felony drug and human smuggling cases remained essentially flat. Because of this, the program has been frequently criticized for diverting scarce resources away from serious felonies and toward the prosecution of petty immigration infractions.

At issue in Roblero-Solis was whether these *en masse* hearings, which have no precedent in American courtrooms, violated the defendants' due process rights and Rule 11 of the Federal Rules of Criminal Procedure. Rule 11 governs the terms under which defendants enter their pleas and courts consider them. In Roblero-Solis, two sections of Rule 11 were at issue: 11(b)(1) and 11(b)(2). 11(b)(1) states that, "before the court accepts a plea of guilty or *nolo contendere* (no contest), the defendant may be placed under oath, and the court must address the defendant personally in open court." During this exchange, the judge must determine, among other things, whether the defendant understands the rights they are forfeiting with their plea, such as the right to a jury trial and the right to plead not guilty, and the nature of the charges against them and the penalties they carry. 11(b)(2) states that the court, "before accepting a plea of guilty or *nolo contendere*, . . . must address the defendant personally in open court and determine that the plea is voluntary and did not result from force, threats, or promises. . . ."

In Roblero-Solis, the key word in both sections was 'personally.' In their opinion, the 9th Circuit asked, "Can these mandatory requirements be met when the court addresses a multitude of defendants?" Their answer was no. Prior to this ruling, migrants pled guilty and answered every question simultaneously, resulting in a din of voices in which it would be difficult to discern negative responses or non-responses. Indeed, court stenographers for Operation Streamline cases recorded defendants' responses as "general yes" and "general no." Explaining its decision, the court said, "No judge, however alert, could tell whether every single person in a group of forty-seven or fifty affirmatively answered her questions when the answers were taken at the same time." While recognizing that the procedures, or "shortcuts," that federal courts had adopted in the face of mounting Operation Streamline cases were both "reasonable" and "understandable," the Ninth Circuit held that "we cannot permit [Rule 11] to be disregarded in the name of efficiency nor to be violated because it is too demanding for a district court to observe."

With regard to violations of due process, the Ninth Circuit agreed with lower court rulings that the presence of legal counsel when defendants entered their pleas was sufficient to satisfy due process requirements. However, many legal observers have raised serious questions about the robustness of due process under Operation Streamline. New Mexico District Chief Judge Martha Vázquez summed up some of Operation Streamline's due process issues when she said, "The increase in our criminal caseload . . . has caused us to conduct hearings in a way that we've never had to conduct them before. . . . Our magistrate judges try very hard to conduct their hearings in a way that is understandable to the defendants. But most of our defendants have a first or second grade education in their native countries. . . . And so, we explain to them their constitutional rights in a legal system entirely foreign to them." Additionally, because of the high number of defendants being tried, attorneys are only able to spend limited amounts of time with each of their clients, despite the fact that the consequences of their charges can derail their chances of obtaining legal residence in the United States for years, if not permanently.

Tucson District Assistant Federal Public Defender Jason M. Hannan, who argued Roblero-Solis in front of the Ninth Circuit, brought another case contesting the viability of due process under Streamline in early 2011. In *United States v. Diaz-Ramirez,* Hannan argued that, because of the *en masse* nature of the Streamline hearings, it was impossible to show that his clients were fully aware of the import of the guilty pleas they entered. In 1969 the U.S. Supreme Court ruled in *Boykin v. Alabama* that the official court record must show that a defendant's plea was entered "voluntarily and understandingly." Using *Boykin,* Hannan argued that the "general" yeses and nos entered unto the official court record are insufficient to establish that his clients "voluntarily and understandingly" pled guilty. However, in May the court again ruled that the fact that each defendant had access to legal counsel, among other factors, made it unlikely that they did not understand the nature of their pleas. The decision upheld the U.S. district court ruling that Operation Streamline does not violate the due process rights of migrants.

Murphy Woodhouse

See Also: Deportation; Legal Representation; Operation Streamline; Repatriation.

Further Reading

Chomsky, A. 2011. "Today's Deportees." *Race Ethnicity* 4.2:203–210.
Lydgate, J. J. 2010. "Assembly-line Justice: A Review of Operation Streamline." *California Law Review* 98.2:481–544.

The Uprooted

The Uprooted is a classic book in immigration history, first published in 1951 and written by Oscar Handlin (1915–2011), a leading scholar of American and immigration history. Receiving the Pulitzer Prize for history and offering what was at the time a novel idea, *The Uprooted* proposed an interpretation of American history in which immigrants were an integral part of that history. Rather than focus on how immigrants affected American society, Handlin highlighted the ways American society affected immigrants who were *uprooted* from their traditional way of life by the forces of capitalism and urbanization. Since its publication, *The Uprooted* has served as the original paradigm for studies of immigration history and was one of the first serious studies on immigration in the United States. Even today, scholars of immigration and American history are very familiar with Handlin's work, which attests to its timelessness. The book was published in a second edition in 1973 and there have been numerous reprints since then. It is still in print.

The Uprooted sets up an interpretation of American immigration history based on viewing emigration as an alienating process. Utilizing harsh examples and terminology, Handlin portrays immigrants as individuals who are stripped of their culture, family ties, and traditions due to circumstances out of their control. Caught in an unfamiliar environment, American immigrants spent much of their lives in a state of shock and crisis. Handlin focuses on the mass migrations of southern and eastern Europeans that began in the mid-1800s but does not differentiate by nationality. In *The Uprooted* the story concerns European peasant migrations; thus, according to Handlin, Jews, Italians, and Poles as peasant emigrants all experienced the same negative consequences that resulted from estrangement from the European village.

The Uprooted was published during the 1950s, when there were several legislative attempts by religious and ethnic interests to reform American immigration policy. As the son of Russian Jewish immigrants, Handlin was one of several liberal intellectuals involved in promoting ethnic and religious acceptance by providing historical and sociological arguments on the issue of immigration. In addition to *The Uprooted,* Handlin wrote several articles for the Anti-Defamation League of B'nai B'rith's "Freedom" pamphlet series on antiracism, religious tolerance, and ethnic pluralism. Additionally, Handlin served as a consultant to President Harry Truman's immigration commission where he summarized the committee's criticisms of the 1924 Johnson-Reed Immigration Act that established a quota system based on national origins. While the efforts of Handlin and other liberal intellectuals and politicians were unsuccessful in implementing legislative change in the 1950s, their ideas for immigration reform were recognized in the passage of the Nationality and Immigration Act of 1965 which abolished the quota system.

In writing *The Uprooted* Handlin presented a story of immigration that portrayed all European emigrants as alienated individuals seeking acceptance in American society. Thus the characters in *The Uprooted* were white Euro-Americans who, according to Handlin, deserved formal equality in the United States since, as he states, they were American history. This line of thought, known as pluralism, characterized the liberal politicians of the 1950s, such as New York senator Herbert Lehman. Pluralists espoused formal equality for Euro-Americans but spoke little of Asian Americans or Mexican Americans, though both groups had a long history of immigration to the United States. In the same vein, *The Uprooted* does not devote attention to non-European immigrants.

Since its publication, *The Uprooted* has sparked debate within the field of immigration history but also served as a model for subsequent studies. As early as 1964, Rudolph Vecoli wrote an article for *The Journal of American History* in which he criticized Handlin's overarching interpretation of European peasants and overexaggeration of emigration as an isolating process. However, it was not until 1985, with John Bodnar's book *The Transplanted*, that an interpretation of American immigration was established in direct contrast to Handlin's *The Uprooted*. Consequently, two camps developed among immigration scholars, those who favored the *uprooted* argument and those who supported the *transplanted* argument. *The Transplanted* offered a less harsh view of immigration where immigrants were not violently displaced but simply relocated with traditions, families, and culture intact.

While the *uprooted* and *transplanted* debate continues, immigration historians have communicated other issues with Handlin's work. Ronald Takaki's *Strangers from a Different Shore,* first published in 1989, responds to the way Handlin's *The Uprooted* provided the view of America as white and European. He does so by offering a historical narrative of Asians in the United States who entered not through Ellis Island but through the west coast's Angel Island. Even more recently, historian Mae Ngai's *Impossible Subjects* published in 2004 addresses the historical products of 1950s liberal reformers, such as Handlin, that focused solely on the incorporation of European immigrants into American society. Ngai's paradigm of immigration history concentrates on the origin and prevalence of undocumented immigration, a topic not covered in *The Uprooted* because of its focus on European adaption. When *The Uprooted* was published, European immigrants were still seeking full acceptance into American society; consequently the book is a product of its time and an attempt to portray immigrants sympathetically and as members of the American nation in order to promote legislative reform and American unity.

Modern immigration historians consistently refer back to *The Uprooted* due to its position as one of the first serious studies on U.S. immigration. However, rather than use *The Uprooted* as a model for further research, historians utilize Handlin's interpretation as a marker for where immigration research has been. By challenging the ideas within *The Uprooted* historians are now pursuing studies on non-European immigration, undocumented immigration, and instances of immigrant resistance. Historians may no longer view immigrants as uprooted individuals and no longer emphasize an overarching interpretation of European emigration, but they still read and value *The Uprooted* for being a fundamental work of immigration history.

Ashley M. Zampogna Krug

See Also: Acculturation; Assimilation; Cultural Citizenship Culture Dillingham Report; Emergency Quota Act of 1921; Johnson-Reed Act (1924); Racism; *Strangers from a Different Shore; Strangers in the Land;* Xenophobia.

Further Reading

Handlin, Oscar. 1951. *The Uprooted: The Epic Story of the Great Migrations That Made the American People.* New York: Grosset & Dunlap.

Rothman, David. 1982. *"The Uprooted:* Thirty Years Later." *Reviews in American History* 10:311–319.

Urban Life

Most undocumented immigrants migrate to metropolitan areas in the United States. By 2005 approximately 96 percent of immigrants to the United States settled in metropolitan areas, with over 33 percent of these settling in Chicago, New York, Los Angeles, and Miami. Oftentimes these settlement patterns are a result of relational ties or employment prospects. In many cases, information about employment prospects is derived from the social networks that migrants are embedded within. As a result, it is difficult to disentangle the effects of relational ties from employment prospects when understanding the pull factors that bring undocumented immigrants to urban America. Regardless of motivating factor, the result is that many undocumented immigrants experience their receiving society within an urban environment and, given that almost every estimate of total immigration to the United States concludes that a significant share of that total is undocumented, much of what is known about urban life and migrants in general is applicable to the undocumented. However, there are important distinctions to be made in regard to differential experiences based on legal status. The political and social marginality of the undocumented population creates a unique experience with cities as channels that legal immigrants can access for services are otherwise closed or severely constrained for the undocumented. The following essay discusses urban life in relation to the undocumented and whenever necessary clearly notes those experiences that are differentiated by legal status. In a general way, urban life is similarly experienced by both the documented and undocumented as the concerns of the latter tend to become the concerns of the former due to the fact that their networks and neighborhoods are intertwined .

Undocumented immigrants in cities in the United States settle in what recent urban scholars calls "transnational communities." Major urban areas have become "command and control centers of globalization," one consequence being the creation of transnational communities and identities. Many of these neighborhoods were originally settled by white ethnics during the height of their migration to the United States. In a sense these are intentionally created neighborhoods that migrants settle in for the purposes of ethnic solidarity, just as Poles, Germans, Italians, and others did. These neighborhoods, sometimes referred to as ethnic enclaves, can have both positive and negative effects for the undocumented. They offer support, familiarity, and services provided in their native language, all of which help to ease one's transition into U.S. society. On the other hand, these areas are often isolated and are considered destinations of last resort to most residents of a metropolitan area. As a result, they can restrict incorporation into the mainstream. In the case of poorer migrants, housing in these neighborhoods is often substandard and overcrowded, and it is the combination of financial constraint, a need to preserve ethnic identity, and a lack of knowledge of the housing market across an entire metropolitan region that produces this sort of living arrangement. In addition, the quality of life in these neighborhoods tends to be impacted by environmental degradation (disproportionate exposure to environmental hazards and their associated health risks), insufficient access to open space, a low sense of community as a result of the need to occupy one's time with matters of everyday survival, and a fear of crime. In all of these factors the undocumented tend to be most severely affected as they lack the legal means to seek recourse for their problems.

Oftentimes churches in these neighborhoods are key anchors of community stability and become vital sites through which undocumented immigrants become incorporated into their new society. To an extent, the church, fills the role that the nation-state does for citizens. In other words, with the state refusing to extend assistance and protections to the undocumented, and therefore an alternate structure (the church) serves their needs. Many urban churches are directly involved in championing the rights of immigrants either through protecting them from deportation by creating sanctuaries or by providing access to education about naturalization or asylum process. In short, the church helps immigrants navigate what can be the daunting task of interacting with a large state bureaucracy and provides them with a community space that keeps them linked with their nation of origin and thus allows them to maintain some semblance of their identity.

Many undocumented immigrants move from locations in which local government has not really served their needs and therefore they have little expectation that local government or even a local community in their new society should assist them. As a result, they often do report a low sense of community due to their expectation that local authorities will not help them. In this context some of the social buffers to deviance and crime are not strong; in some cases these communities lack collective efficacy. Combined with the reality that ethnic residential locations are suceptible to problems of crime creates an environment where people come to rely on themselves and family for survival. Being "destinations of last resort" to many native-born city dwellers, these are classic cases of underdeveloped inner-city spaces. They lack sufficient economic investigation by residential seekers and lack sufficient demand from private business capital. In these situations, alternate social structures arise and in some cases these have dangerous consequences–such as gang and drug trafficking activity. All of this is exacerbated for the undocumented. With a heightened sense that their safety might be undermined, they often live in fear, which has significant negative consequences for community dynamics and individual psychology. Many have witnessed themselves, or have knowledge of immigration raids in their neighborhoods, and these can create chaotic results for families.

Undocumented status is at the root of many of the community concerns in urban ethnic enclaves. Nearly every family has someone that is undocumented who is related to them or is an important part of their social network. Communities are often unwilling to deal with the problem of gangs or drugs due to fear that contact with police would result in deportation. They are hesitant to participate in community improvement projects because these often require contact with elected officials, which may lead to the discovery of their undocumented status. A community ethic arises that focuses on self-reliance and not getting into other people's problems or business, which results in decreased quality of life among all residents. Given that many undocumented immigrants in the United States come from more collectivist cultures, it is particularly troubling that they often settle in urban neighborhoods with low levels of community trust and a lack of a sense of community amongst residents. Although some of this results from the fact that these neighborhoods tend to be filled with a transient population, its root causes are in issues of poverty and neglect. It is this reality that prohibits behaviors that cultivate community trust and the development of social capital. Although there are important social and psychological benefits that the undocumented receive from in-group ethnic solidarity that they would not receive if they lived in a neighborhood where there were few co-ethnics, it is also the case that in comparison to their experiences in their home country, urban living in the United States introduces a lack of community trust and erosion of social networks that impact their quality of life. It is important to not romanticize the urban ethnic enclave because this ideal simply masks some of the social problems that these residents experience. It is also important to note that in cities that are just recently experiencing large influx of migrants, there are few options but to settle in an ethnic enclave where they have a better chance of finding employment. In these cases some of the positive social and psychological consequences of in-group solidarity are lessened, if not entirely eliminated. Recent scholarship on new immigrant gateway cities shows that local authorities and residents oftentimes respond with restrictive policy, such as stricter enforcement of housing codes, or passing anti-congregating city ordinances that are directed at day laborers, many of whom are undocumented, as well as laws requiring that English be used in sign and billboards in front of local businesses and offices.

Aaron J. Howell

See Also: Enclaves; Shadow Population; Single Men; Social and Economic Integration Suburbs.

Further Reading

Menjivar, Cecilia. 2000. *Fragmented Ties: Salvadoran Immigrant Networks in America.* Berkeley and Los Angeles, CA: University of California Press.

Menjivar, Cecilia. 2003. "Religion and Immigration in Comparative Perspective: Salvadorans in Catholic and Evangelical Communities in San Francisco, Phoenix, and Washington D. C." *Sociology of Religion* 64:21–45.

Menjivar, Cecilia. 2006. "Liminal Legality: Salvadoran and Guatemalan Immigrants' Lives in the United States." *American Journal of Sociology* 111:999–1037.

Popkin, Eric. 1999. "Guatemalan Mayan Migration to Los Angeles: Constructing Transnational Linkages in the Context of the Settlement Process." *Ethnic and Racial Studies* 22:267–289.

Portes, Alejandro, and Robert L. Bach. 1985. *Latin Journey: Cuban and Mexican Immigrants in the United States.* Berkeley: University of California Press.

Price, Marie, and Lisa Benton-Short. 2008. *Migrants to the Metropolis: The Rise of Immigrant Gateway Cities.* Syracuse: Syracuse University Press.

Singer, Audrey. 2004. *The Rise of New Immigrant Gateways.* Washington, D. C: Brookings Institution Press.

Stodolska, Monika, and Kimberly J. Shinew. 2009. "La Calidad de Vida dentro de La Villita: An Investigation of Factors Affecting Quality of Life of Latino Residents of an Urban Immigrant Residential Enclave." *Journal of Immigrant and Refugee Studies* 7:267–289.

USA PATRIOT Act (2001)

The USA PATRIOT Act is an acronym that stands for Uniting and Strengthening America by Providing Appropriate Tools Required to Intercept and Obstruct Terrorism Act of 2001(Public Law 107–56). It is commonly and simply referred to as "the Patriot Act." The Act was signed into law on October 26, 2001 by President George W. Bush in the aftermath of the 9/11 terrorist attacks. The act was aimed at facilitating law enforcement and immigration authorities' efforts to detain and deport immigrants suspected of terrorism-related acts. It therefore increased their powers in a range of areas. For example, it expanded the power of law enforcement agents to search telephone and e-mail communications, medical, financial, banking, and other records. It also expanded the Secretary of the Treasury's authority to regulate financial transactions, and while this provision impacted everyone, it particularly impacted those involved with foreign individuals and institutions. The act also expanded the definition of terrorism to include domestic terrorism, thus broadening the type and number of activities that would fall under the purview of the Patriot Act.

The events of 9/11 came on the heels of a visit to the United States by Mexico's President Vicente Fox to negotiate a proposal requesting the United States provide for 250,000 work visas exclusively for Mexican nationals each year. In return, Mexico would do its best to provide for the return of its emigrated workers, offer micro-loans to them and educational opportunities for their children. There were other ideas brought to the table that by most standards were viewed as pro-immigrant. For example, under consideration were proposals to allow undocumented immigrants already in the United States to "adjust" their status without having to leave the United States, providing a mechanism by which undocumented immigrants working in the United States could apply for green cards rather than returning to their homelands and applying at foreign consular offices. After the attacks, these proposals were never considered (Linares, 2006).

Since the Patriot Act was made law, legal scholars have been concerned about the nation's anxieties over immigrants in the country bent on inflicting harm on Americans. The 9/11 attacks assured that the lines between immigration and terrorism would become increasingly blurred (ACLU, 2010). The conflation of the two is not new, as Hines (2006) points out. In 1996 when the last anti-terrorism act was passed, the Antiterrorism and Effective Death Penalty Act, the harshest immigration reform bill, the Illegal Immigration Reform and Immigrant Responsibility Act (IIRIRA), was also passed. This trend has been eroding the rights of immigrants in the United States. For example, even before the passage of the Patriot Act and within months after 9/11, FBI

officials acting on tips from the public and other law enforcement officials proceeded to seek out and arrest 1,200 Arab and Muslim immigrants, primarily in the
New York and New Jersey areas, of whom 762 were charged with immigration
violations not connected to terrorism. Many detainees were held for weeks before
being able to appear in immigration court and until the FBI completed its investigation. After 9/11, restrictive release policies were normalized. In addition, because of
the conflation of terrorism and immigration, immigrants are often detained in facilities run by the Department of Homeland Security. These detention centers are often
located in remote areas, making it harder for attorneys working pro bono to help
clients (Hines, 2006).

There is no question that 9/11 fueled fears among Americans about immigrants
in their midst. The Patriot Act responded to those legitimate threats of terrorism.
However, as Adler (2006) points out, there were also those who seemed to take
advantage of those fears to scapegoat immigrants and in this way endeavor to restrict immigration. Massive and very public display of raids to arrest undocumented
immigrants at their work place and neighborhoods by Immigration and Customs
Enforcement (ICE) was a way for the U.S. government to quell the fears of an anx-
ious public and assure it that the United States was winning the war on terror: Televised images of detained immigrants, raids, and a very visible militarized border
helped convey the idea that the government was protecting its constituencies. However, caught in the middle were communities of immigrants whose lives were disrupted in more than one way. Public humiliation and disrespect were just some of
the ways that undocumented immigrants felt the impact of the additional policing
provided by the Patriot Act (Romero, 2008), as well as growing tensions between
groups in ethnic neighborhoods (Adler, 2006). The Patriot Act also facilitated ancil-
lary legislation that provided for more resources to be devoted to border security as
an anti-terrorism effort. This effectively worked to keep undocumented immigrants
within the United States since returning to their homelands became increasingly
difficult if not impossible (Linares, 2006).

Anna Ochoa O'Leary

See Also: Counterterrorism and Immigrant Profiling; Deportation; Governance and Criminalization; Illegal Immigration Reform and Immigrant Responsibility Act (IIRIRA) (1996);
Immigration and Customs Enforcement (ICE); Incarceration.

Further Reading

ACLU (American Civil Liberties Union). 2010. "Surveillance Under the USA PATRIOT
    Act." December 10 http: //www.aclu.org/national-security/surveillance-under-usa
    -patriot-act.
Adler, Rachel H. 2006. "The Interaction of Residency Status, Class, and Ethnicity in a
    (Post-PATRIOT Act) New Jersey Neighborhood." *American Behavioral Scientist*
    50.1:48–69.
Hines, Barbara. 2006. "An Overview of U.S. Immigration Law and Policy since 9/11."
    Texas Hispanic Journal of Law & Policy 12.1:9–28.

Linares, Juan Carlos. 2006. "Hired Hands Needed: The Impact of Globalization and Human Rights Law on Migrant Workers in the United States." *Denver Journal of International Law & Policy* 34.3:321–352.

Romero, Mary. 2008. "The Inclusion of Citizenship Status in Intersectionality: What Immigration Raids Tells Us about Mixed-Status Families, the State, and Assimilation." *International Journal of the Family* 34.2:131–152.

U.S. Border Patrol

The efforts of the U.S. Immigration Service began as early as 1904 and attempted to prevent illegal crossings when resources were available. Between the times of those first patrols and 1924, the U.S. Immigration Service and their mounted patrol canvassed the borders. The Border Patrol was established in 1924 by Congress through the Labor Appropriation Act. At that time, the Border Patrol was charged with protecting the U.S. borders with Mexico and Canada. In 1925, the Border Patrol and its duties were expanded to include the seacoast borders, not just the land borders of Mexico and Canada. The Border Patrol was also under the control of two directors, one based out of Detroit, Michigan for the Canadian border office and one based out of El Paso, Texas for the Mexican border office.

Del Rio Border Patrol inspectors stop a car at a road block near Del Rio, Texas in 1925. The Border Patrol was established in 1924 to control illegal immigration on the U.S.-Mexican border. As the agency's mission shifts toward the war on terror and war on drugs, its budget was estimated to be $3 billion in 2009, for an estimated 16,974 agents. (U.S. Customs & Border Protection)

Originally, the Border Patrol was part of the Bureau of Immigration, but in 1933 the Bureau of Immigration and the Bureau of Naturalization were joined together to form the Immigration and Naturalization Service. In 1940, the Immigration Service was moved from the Department of Labor into the Department of Justice. The Border Patrol grew from 450 officers in the 1920s to over 1,500 in the 1940s. These department shifts and growth indicate a change in understanding of the issue of undocumented immigration as well as being in line with the expansion of government that occurred during the presidency of Franklin D. Roosevelt.

In 1952, the Border Patrol was further expanded and allowed for Border Patrol agents to search for undocumented immigrants anywhere in the United States, not just the limited regions near the borders. As well, the focus of the Border Patrol shifted away from the Canadian border to the Mexican border as illegal immigration from Mexico continued. Until recent years, the Border Patrol was largely a symbolic enforcement agency. The large amount of land area that needed to be patrolled and relatively small force made it difficult for the Border Patrol to truly protect the borders.

Many programs of the Border Patrol were aimed at returning undocumented immigrants to their country of origin. This process, known as repatriation, was often used by the Border Patrol. However, these programs were not very helpful in deterring continued illegal immigration. In 1952, the Border Patrol was able to airlift Mexican immigrants back into the interior of Mexico; but this program was discontinued in the same year because of lack of funds. Other such programs, including boat lifts and train rides back to Mexico, supported by both the U.S. and Mexican government, were also conducted during the early 1950s. These programs were discontinued because of their cost shortly after they began. In the 1960s the Border Patrol was also expanded to accompany domestic airline flights to prevent takeovers and hijackings. Although these processes were meant to discourage future attempts at illegally crossing the border, many immigrants continued to attempt to cross the border and many of them were able to successfully enter the United States.

It its early years, the Border Patrol was largely a mounted horse patrol because of the ruggedness of the land and the need for a quick and quiet mode of transportation. Even with the technological advances experienced since the Border Patrol's creation, horses are still used today patrol some areas of the border. In 1935, the Border Patrol began using motorized vehicles and radios to help in their patrols. During World War II, the Border Patrol used aircraft to help assist in performing their duties and has continued to use aircraft today. Technological advances of the 1980s and 1990s have resulted in transportation changes but also in finding and apprehending undocumented immigrants who cross the U.S. border. Devices such as infrared night-vision scopes and computers have become highly useful devices that help the Border Patrol in locating, arresting, and processing undocumented immigrants.

Government programs and acts during the 1980s and 1990s strengthened the capacity of the Border Patrol. The budget of the Border Patrol increased during this time frame from over $150 million to over $1 billion. At the same time, the number of Border Patrol officers also increased to over ten thousand. The late 1980s and 1990s also sparked a shift in the mindset of the Border Patrol. In the prior years of 1965 through 1986, the Border Patrol operated largely as a catch and release program. Agents would apprehend, or arrest, undocumented immigrants, quickly process them through the system, and have the undocumented immigrant sign a voluntary departure order. Legally, arrested immigrants have a right to a hearing with an immigration judge; but the voluntary departure order waives this right and immigrants are transported back to their home country. In effect, the voluntary departure order allowed for a quick turnaround with undocumented immigrants returning to their home country and then attempting to reenter the United States. The revolving-door policy with the voluntary departure order lost favor and became cause for concern about the effectiveness of the Border Patrol during the 1980s. At the same time, the legal justice system has been able to process all border crossers, which can reach daily totals in hundreds. More recently, many undocumented immigrants caught along the border were subjected to the Department of Homeland Security's consequence program that includes the Alien Transfer and Exit Program (ATEP) (also known as lateral deportation), or Operation Streamline.

In 1986, the Immigration Reform and Control Act (IRCA) was passed. The IRCA increased the budget of the Immigration and Naturalization Service and the Border Patrol also imposed negative sanctions or penalties for employers who knowingly hired undocumented immigrants. In addition, IRCA granted amnesty to long-term undocumented residents of the United States. The IRCA did away with the symbolic enforcement "catch-and-release" system that had been used by the Border Patrol. Years later, the Border Patrol was further expanded by the 1990 Immigration Act. This act allowed the department to hire one thousand more Border Patrol agents, made deportation and criminal procedures easier and more efficient, as well as increased the penalties for immigration violations.

In the more recent decades of the 1980s and 1990s, the Border Patrol has been further expanded and has become more of a militarized enforcement operation rather than the symbolic enforcement that characterized the agency for decades. The IRCA, the 1990 Immigration Act, and changes in strategies of the Border Patrol all demonstrate the more militarized form of the Border Patrol. The Border Patrol also started a targeted enforcement strategy. This targeted enforcement has honed in on major crossing areas such as the areas of San Diego and El Paso. Border Patrol officers became essential to a strategy adopted by the INS that initiated missions such as "Operation Gatekeeper" launched in San Diego in 1994 and "Operation Blockade" launched in El Paso in 1993. These prevention measures included more advanced uses of technology, such as remote camera systems used to scan the border for potential border crossers. These operations routed undocumented immigrants away from urban areas into more remote areas where they were subjected to isolation and harsh environmental conditions, risking life and limb in the process. However, these strategies of prevention by deterrence did not curb illegal immigration as much as cause undocumented immigrants to find different routes to enter the United States and rely more on the services of human smugglers to help them cross the border.

The 1990s also saw the Border Patrol concentrating on other areas of enforcement beyond just the illegal entry of immigrants. The Border Patrol during this time under the Border Security Initiative (BSI) expanded its focus to include search and rescue teams (BORSTAR), and the creation of a joint campaign between the United States and Mexico to make the border more safe and secure. The BSI was put in operation in 1998. It was created with the intention of disrupting smuggling routes and educating potential undocumented immigrants about health and safety concerns such as heat-related deaths. After the events of September 11, 2001, in 2003, the U.S. Border Patrol was reorganized to became a part of the division of U.S. Customs and Border Protection (CBP), under the Department of Homeland Security.

Among the main missions of the Border Patrol as of 2012 is to protect against terrorists and "instruments of terror" from entering the United States ("2012–2016 Border Control Strategic Plan," 2012). The mission of the Border Patrol has changed throughout its many years of existence to fit the problems of the period. Its present-day mission is homeland security, that is, to protect against terrorists after the September 11, 2001 acts. Prior missions of the Border Patrol have ranged from the prevention of drug smuggling during the late twentieth century, to the concern of alcohol smuggling during Prohibition in the 1920s and beginning of the 1930s.

Overall, the Border Patrol has experienced much change. During its years of operating, it has moved to meet the needs of the country including altering the focus from one particular area or border to another, adopting the use of new technologies to be a more efficient and effective operation, and expanding its priorities outside the arena of capturing undocumented immigrants at or near the border.

Amy Baumann Grau

See Also: Border Crossing; Coyotes; Deportation; Expedited Removal; Immigration Reform and Control Act (IRCA) (1986); Repatriation; *United States v. Brignoni-Ponce;* U.S. Customs and Border Protection (CBP).

Further Reading

Massey, Douglas S., Jorge Durand, and Nolan J. Malone. 2003. *Beyond Smoke and Mirrors: Mexican Immigration in an Era of Economic Integration.* New York: Russell Sage Foundation.

"2012–2016 Border Patrol Strategic Plan." 2012. U.S. Customs and Border Protection. http://nemo.cbp.gov/obp/bp_strategic_plan.pdf.

"U.S. Border Patrol." U.S. Customs and Border Protection (CBP). http://www.cbp.gov/xp/cgov/border_security/border_patrol/.

U.S. Census Bureau

The U.S. Census Bureau is the government agency responsible for gathering national demographic and economic data about the population in the country. Demographics are information about a human population such as age, sex, income, marital status, education level, and physical location. The Constitution of the United States mandates that the American population must be counted at least once every ten years. The Census Bureau has conducted a full population count, a census, every ten years since the first census on August 2, 1790. The census consists of two phases of data collection. First, questionnaires are mailed to every household in the country. Second, census employees go to residences that have not returned their questionnaire and collect information for these people.

The 2010 census-collection period directly followed the passage of Arizona's Senate Bill 1070. Arizona SB 1070 was not an isolated event but rather culminated several years of nativist discourse and the production of laws throughout the nation that were intended to drive undocumented immigrants away. Government officials and immigrant advocates expressed concerns about how the political environment would impact the collection of census data from those predicted to be most impacted by the growing acrimony, namely, Latino immigrants who represent the greatest share of all immigrants in the United States. Historically, the census has undercounted Latino populations. For example, the 2000 Census undercounted Latinos by about 1 million. The biggest factor in this failure was determined to be the lack of trust of government and how information will be used. Therefore, in anticipation of 2010, in 2009 the cable television network Telemundo offered to weave census participation messages into one of their popular nationally broadcast Spanish-language soap operas, or *telenovelas,* which would influence audience members' attitudes and promote greater trust and greater understanding of this important process (Trujillo and Paluck, 2012).

Census data are essential to the U.S. government. Census data are used to determine the number of seats each state is allotted in the House of Representatives. Additionally, this data determines the allocation of over $400 billion in federal and state funding for public health, education, transportation, and neighborhood improvements. Census data are crucial for establishing community needs such as elderly services, schools, and roads. For these reasons, the data collected by the Census Bureau comes from the total resident population in the United States at the time of collection. This data includes all citizens and non-citizens regardless of resident status. The Census Bureau does not ask respondents any questions about legal (migrant) status. There is no legislative mandate to collect this information.

The Census Bureau, as well as city and state governments, and nonprofit groups often orchestrate advertising and outreach campaigns to encourage undocumented immigrants and other hard-to-count populations, such as individuals who are poor, homeless, and/or minorities, to participate in the census. These populations typically have high non-response rates. These undercounts can lead to a significant difference in services and funding for these groups. Statisticians argue that a census, which aims to count the whole population, is less effective than statistical sampling in counting frequently undercounted groups. For this reason, the use of statistical sampling in place of the decennial (every ten years) has been politically unpopular. Moreover, in 2010, some Latino leaders called on Latino communities to boycott the census as a means to call attention of the need for immigration reform and to protest the growing policing of immigrants by law enforcement officers. Even when the boycott efforts weakened, many Latinos—particularly those in Arizona—remained apprehensive and hesitant to interact with the process (Trujillo and Paluck, 2012).

The Census Bureau uses different citizenship and nativity definitions when counting the population. The Census Bureau defines a U.S. citizen as an individual who indicates they were born in the United States, Puerto Rico, or a U.S. island area (such as Guam). The Census Bureau also defines individuals who were born abroad to a parent or parents who are U.S. citizens as U.S. citizens. Foreign-born people who indicated that they were U.S. citizens through naturalization, the process of granting citizenship, are also U.S. citizens. In contrast, a non-citizen is an individual who indicates they did not have U.S. citizenship at the time of the survey. This category may include lawful permanent residents, temporary migrants, refuges, asylees, or unauthorized migrants.

The Census Bureau considers foreign-born any person who was not a U.S. citizen at birth. This category includes individuals who indicated that they were a U.S. citizen by naturalization or not a U.S. citizen. Also included in this category are lawful permanent residents (immigrants), temporary migrants (such as foreign students and those with other non-immigrant visas), such as refugees and asylees. The foreign-born category also contains "illegal immigrants," individuals who entered the country surreptitiously or arrived using non-immigrant visas that they then violated by working or staying too long. In contrast, the Census Bureau uses the term native to refer to persons born in the United States or a U.S. island area such as Puerto Rico, or born abroad of a U.S. citizen parent.

Even though the Census Bureau does not ask respondents directly about their own or other household members' legal status, they are still able to collect data about undocumented immigrants in the United States. Beyond the decennial census, the Census Bureau also administers numerous other surveys of the population in the United States. Other bureaus and departments within the U.S. government also sponsor these additional surveys. The Census Bureau continually implements these surveys between the decennial census and throughout the decade. Because these surveys rely on statistical sampling techniques, their data complement the decennial census. Typically, the Census Bureau and those who use this data rely on the decennial census as well as the Current Population Survey (CPS) data for detailed information on the foreign-born population in the United States. The CPS is a monthly employment survey of households.

Additional surveys administered by Census Bureau are less frequently used to gain information about the foreign-born population, but they are, in many ways, just as useful. These surveys include the American Community Survey (ACS), the Survey of Income and Program Participation (SIPP), the National Health Interview Survey (NHIS), the New York Housing Vacancy Survey (NYCHVS), and the American Housing Survey (AHS). These surveys are conducted at different intervals and include interviews as well as long-form survey methods. In addition, the Census Bureau provides national-level projections of the U.S. resident population by nativity through 2100. Further, the Census Bureau is not the only federal government agency that measures international migration. The Immigration and Naturalization Service (INS) and the U.S. Department of State also gather statistics on immigration.

Throughout the existence of the population censuses and surveys in the United States, there have been numerous changes in the measurement of immigrants. In the 1820 and 1830 decennial censuses, census takers "noted" the individuals who were non-naturalized foreigners. However, during these censuses, individuals were not asked specific questions about citizenship status. Then, in 1890, the Census Bureau added explicit measures of citizenship status to the census. With some variations, these measures have been included in the census since, except in 1960. Place of birth questions have appeared on the census since 1850. Parental nativity questions were asked between 1870 and 1970.

Although the 2000 census asked if individuals were born in the United States and, if not, where they were born, the 2010 census did not. Often decennial censuses include a question that asks the year a person born outside of the United States began living in the United States. Notably, the 2000 census asked, "Is this person a citizen of the United States?" This questioned facilitated the categorization of individuals into groups according to claim to U.S. citizenship or into a separate group for non-citizens. Even more notably, however, the 2010 census did not ask if the person was a citizen of the United States, despite efforts of some congressmen to add the question.

The Census Bureau uses the data collected through censuses and surveys to *estimate* the net international migration to states and counties as well as the United States as a whole, since the Census Bureau does not collect information about migrant status, legal or illegal, in any of its survey or census programs. Even though individuals with illegal status may be unwilling to identify themselves and participate in the census, it is likely that unauthorized migrants were included in Census 2000 among the individuals indicating the United States was their usual place of residence at the time of the survey. Thus, while Census Bureau surveys consistently include a large number of undocumented immigrants, the actual concern is an undercount, not an omission. In 2011, a revised analysis of the 2010 census revealed that 11.5 million unauthorized immigrants were living in the United States in January 2011 compared to the estimate of 11.6 million, suggesting little to no change in the unauthorized immigrant population from 2010 to 2011. The larger numbers came during 2000–2004 (3.3 million) and 1995–1999 (3.0 million), which was almost double the number that came between 1990–1994 (1.6 million) (Hoeffer et al., 2012).

The Census Bureau has also made changes to other surveys in order to improve the measurement of the immigrant population. Questions about respondent and parental nativity, citizenship status, and year of arrival in the United States were added to the CPS in 1994. Additionally, the Census Bureau expanded the SIPP by adding in a completely new component devoted to measuring immigration. Beginning in 1984, the Migration History Topical Module has been included on the SIPP. This module asks U.S. natives about their current residence, previous residences, and place of birth. Foreign-born respondents were asked their citizenship status and year of arrival. Previously, the SIPP asked additional questions including parental birthplace and reasons for moving. In 1996, the Census Bureau added more questions to the SIPP Migration Module related to international migration about immigration status, changes in immigration status, and when the status adjustment occurred.

Of all Census Bureau programs, the SIPP contains the most detailed international migration-related questions. Thus, the SIPP is the most extensive Census Bureau data source on the foreign-born population in the United States. However, with a sample size of approximately 14,000 to 37,000 households, the SIPP is a relatively small population survey compared with other Census Bureau programs. The size of the SIPP sample inhibits a detailed analysis of the foreign-born in the United States beyond establishing respondents' nativity and citizenship status.

When investigators use Census Bureau data to study immigrants, they typically consider the individuals who indicate they were foreign-born to be immigrants to the United States. As stated above, the foreign-born category includes multiple kinds of foreigners, causing this assumption to necessarily be inaccurate. However, since the goal of the census and the CPS is to include all people who primarily live in the United States, the actual legal status or likely permanence of these individuals in the United States is unknown.

Amanda Staight

See Also: Lawful Permanent Residents; "Undocumented" Label.

Further Reading

Costanzo, Joseph M., Cynthia J. Davis, and Nolan Malone. 2002. "Guide to International Migration Statistics: The Sources, Collection, and Processing of Foreign-Born Population Data at the U.S. Census Bureau." Population Division, U.S. Census Bureau: Washington, D.C. http://www.census.gov/population/www/documentation/twps0068/twps0068.html.

Hoeffer, Michael, Nancy Rytina, and Brian Baker. 2012. "Estimates of the Unauthorized Immigrant Population Residing in the United States, January 2011." Office of Immigration Statistics, U.S. Department of Homeland Security. http://www.dhs.gov/xlibrary/assets/statistics/publications/ois_ill_pe_2011.pdf.

Trujillo, Matthew D, and Elizabeth Levy Paluck. 2012. "The Devil Knows Best: Experimental Effects of a Televised Soap Opera on Latino Attitudes Toward Government and Support for the 2010 U.S. Census." *Analyses of Social Issues & Public Policy* 12.1:113–132.

United States Census Bureau website. www.census.gov.

United States Census Bureau. 2012. "Foreign Born." http://www.census.gov/population/foreign/.

United States Census Bureau. 2012. "International Migration." http://www.census.gov/population/intmigration/.

U.S. Citizenship and Immigration Services (USCIS)

United States Citizenship and Immigration Services (USCIS) is the federal agency that oversees lawful immigration to the United States. Currently a component of the United States Department of Homeland Security (DHS), USCIS was one of three entities that took the place of Immigration and Naturalization Services (INS) in 2003 in response to the terrorist attacks of September 11, 2001, during which time INS was a part of the U.S. Department of Justice. After the President George W. Bush administration signed the Homeland Security Act on November 25, 2002, this reorganization occurred and DHS became home not only to USCIS, but also to U.S. Immigration and

Customs Enforcement (ICE), as well as U.S. Customs and Border Protection (CBP). The INS ceased to exist officially on March 1, 2003. For a brief moment the agency was named the U.S. Bureau of Citizenship and Immigration Services (BCIS) before being renamed USCIS.

The USCIS Mission Statement states that the agency "will secure America's promise as a nation of immigrants by providing accurate and useful information to our customers, granting immigration and citizenship benefits, promoting an awareness and understanding of citizenship, and ensuring the integrity of our immigration system." USCIS is an agency of eighteen thousand government employees and contractors who work at 250 offices both in the United States and across the world. According to the USCIS official website, the agency's strategic goals include: strengthening the security and integrity of the United States immigration system; providing effective customer-oriented immigration benefit and information services; supporting immigrants' integration and participation in American civic culture; promoting flexible and sound immigration policies and programs; strengthening the infrastructure supporting the USCIS mission; and operating as a high-performance organization that promotes a highly talented workforce and dynamic work culture. Its core values include integrity in the fair administration of the American immigration system, respect in all actions carried out by the agency, ingenuity in finding the most effective ways to carry out USCIS goals, and lastly, vigilance in the face of global threats and national security challenges. This value of vigilance is significant in that, as a component of the Department of Homeland Security, a government body whose main goal is to combat terrorism, the USCIS must also be involved in this effort. For many immigrants, it is understood that the USCIS agents who are interviewing them for their visas work also for the same organization that is responsible for the apprehension and deportation of immigrants and nonimmigrants alike. An extension of this vigilance can be found in the expectation that all foreign-born residents are to report their locations and addresses to USCIS within ten days of relocation within the United States.

One of the principal functions of USCIS is that of processing naturalization petitions. Naturalization is defined on the USCIS website as the process by which U.S. citizenship is granted to a foreign citizen or national after he or she fulfills the requirements established by Congress in the Immigration and Nationality Act (INA). Naturalization is one of two ways in which U.S. citizenship is granted; the second way is by birth.

Foreign nationals who have held permanent resident status in the United States for at least five years, who meet all other eligibility requirements, are eligible for citizenship. Foreign nationals who are spouses of U.S. citizens and originally gained residency through that spouse, after holding permanent resident status for at least three years and meeting all other eligibility requirements, are also eligible for citizenship. USCIS is responsible for helping determine one's eligibility for naturalization. There are many resources on the USCIS website helpful to those who are considering naturalization, and all forms for naturalization as well as other services can be found there. To apply for naturalization, one must complete Form N-400, which is simply called the Application for Naturalization. USCIS processes this application and, if and when approved during a naturalization interview with a USCIC Officer, the applicant is scheduled for a ceremony during which the Oath of Allegiance will be taken. This Oath of Allegiance is a declaration that one's fidelity is now to the United States and not one's country of birth, that one is willing to support and defend the Constitution and laws of the United States, and that one is willing to bear arms or serve otherwise on behalf of the United States, among other declarations. This Oath of Allegiance has been used for over 220 years to lead people to American citizenship. It is during the naturalization interview that the applicant will be asked about their application and background, and the English and civics tests will be given, both in English, unless one qualifies for an exception. The English test consists of reading, writing, and speaking components and the civics test consists of important U.S. government and history topics. Applicants are given up to two opportunities to take and pass both of these tests, within ninety days of each other.

All forms and applications involving immigration to the United States are handled by USCIS. This includes immigration through family petition. U.S. citizens and legal permanent residents may petition for close relatives, or future close relatives as the case may be with a fiancé(e), or with a future adopted child, to immigrate to the United States. The type of status the petitioner holds (as citizen, or as legal permanent resident) determines the immigration benefits that are available to their different family members. Also handled by USCIS are work visas, which are divided between four different employment categories: temporary nonimmigrant worker, permanent immigrant worker, students and exchange visitors, and temporary visitors for business. Each employment category carries with it different requirements, conditions and authorized periods of stay. Green cards, or permanent residency, is another area serviced by USCIS, with possibilities for green cards through many different avenues (through relatives or through a job, for example).

Immigrants are not the only population monitored by USCIS. Non-immigrants are monitored as well, as tourists and other visitors to the United States from foreign countries require visas in order to enter the country. There are many different classes of visas according to the intention of the visit to the United States—for pleasure, business, medical treatment, education, and otherwise. As of January of 2010, there are thirty-five excepted countries that, in most cases, do not require the use of a visa if the duration of the stay in the United States is ninety days or less. These countries are considered Visa Waiver countries and include most European countries, as well as Singapore, South Korea, Australia, and New Zealand. Also, any visitor to the United States who wishes to remain in the country for longer than the period of time that the visa permits must apply for an extension of visit with USCIS. It is then up to the USCIS officer if the extension is to be made or not.

Another responsibility of USCIS is the managing of E-Verify, an electronic program that is used by employers to determine if employees have a legal right to work in the United States, and to stop the employment of unauthorized workers. While participation in E-Verify is not mandatory for employers, more than 409,000 employers are currently using the program to verify the eligibility for employment of their workers, with many more signing up weekly to participate in the program. In some states, however, state law may mandate E-Verify, such as in Arizona and Mississippi.

While the main work of USCIS involves immigration and naturalization services, it also oversees various humanitarian programs and services for those in serious need. Some of these services include: refugee status or asylum for those being persecuted on account of race, religion, nationality, or otherwise; immigration benefits for battered spouses, children, or parents of U.S. citizens; victims of human trafficking or select other crimes; humanitarian parole; temporary protected status (TPS) for those who are temporarily unable to return to their country due to extraordinary circumstances; deferred action for young persons who were brought to the United States illegally by their parents and meet certain other eligibility criteria; and other special situations. International adoptions, approximately 20,000 per year, are also overseen by USCIS, and the agency oversees a Genealogy Program which offers, for fees by service, access to immigration and naturalization records of deceased immigrants.

Leisha Reynolds-Ramos

See Also: Citizenship; Immigration and Customs Enforcement (ICE); Immigration and Naturalization Service (INS); Legal Permanent Residents; Legal Status; Temporary Protected Status (TPS); U.S. Customs and Border Protection (CBP).

Further Reading

Donovan, Thomas W. 2005. "The American Immigration System: A Structural Change with a Different Emphasis." *International Journal of Refugee Law* 17.3:574.

Haynes, Wendy. 2004. "Seeing Around Corners: Crafting the New Department of Homeland Security." *Review of Policy Research* 21.3:369–395.

USCIS. 2009. U.S. Citizenship and Immigration Services: About Us. USCIS Official Website. http://uscis.gov.

U.S. Customs and Border Protection (CBP)

Customs and Border Protection (CBP) is a major operational branch of the Department of Homeland Security. It is one of the largest law enforcement agencies in the United States, with over 44,000 officers and agents. Its main operational subunits are the Border Patrol, Office of Field Operations, Office of Air and Marine Operations, Office of Intelligence and Operations Coordination, and Office of International Trade. The units that are the most relevant to undocumented migration are the Border Patrol and Field Operations. The Border Patrol enforces immigration and contraband laws (especially drugs) on land borders in between ports of entry (it also has some activities on land at maritime borders). Field Operations inspects people, vehicles, and goods entering the nation through land, sea, and airports. Military units (recently National Guard) have periodically been deployed to support CBP, and it is routinely supported by surveillance and control functions of the Joint Task Force-North (JTF-N) at Fort Bliss, Texas.

CBP took shape as a result of the creation of the Department of Homeland Security in 2003 (in the aftermath of 9/11). The Immigration and Naturalization Service, previously in the Department of Justice, contributed the Border Patrol and the immigration

U.S. Customs and Border Protection agent speaks with a driver entering the United States. Under the Western Hemisphere Travel Initiative announced by the Homeland Security and State departments on April 5, 2005, all Canadian, Mexican, and U.S. citizens were required to have a passport to enter or reenter the United States beginning on January 1, 2008. (U.S. Customs & Border Protection)

inspections functions of ports of entry to the new unit. The Customs Service, previously in the Department of Treasury, joined immigration inspectors in the Field Operations division, together with specialists in agricultural and nuclear inspections.

The creation of a unified inspection and enforcement entity for U.S. borders, and its placement in a cabinet level department called "Department of Homeland Security," organizationally and rhetorically signal "borders" as an envisioned security challenge for the nation state. It also acknowledges that borders are means of entry and exit, and not just walls. An interesting way of conceptualizing the magnitude and scale of these operations is that the regulation of commercial and human movement through borders takes roughly as large a workforce (Field Operations) as the barrier function represented by the Border Patrol (each having around 21,000 officers). Administrative practice accords the politically visible Border Patrol more autonomy and resources than Field Operations (ports), demonstrating the higher value placed on the political domain of blockading the border than on enabling movement.

Details of CBP enforcement activities affecting undocumented migrants are found among the responsibilities of the Border Patrol and the management of the ports of entry. A bigger picture starts with the observation that there are actually three border enforcement domains, and it is important to be clear about the differences among these three domains. First, there is prevention of entry from outside threats—of terrorists and terrorist materials (although it is important to acknowledge that not all terrorism enters from outside and in fact may emanate from domestic terrorists). That is rhetorically the dominant justification for U.S. border enforcement, as seen in the CBP mission statement. If this goal does practically matter, it is also heavily symbolic. There have not yet been, for example, any cases of Islamist terrorists crossing the U.S.-Mexico border, though this is plausible. Framing border protection around national security and the U.S. "war on terror" shifts the intensity of 9/11 to issues of drug interdiction and migration.

The second domain is interdiction of illegal drug smuggling into the United States, and related enforcement against cash and arms smuggling into Mexico, all shared with other federal, state, and local law enforcement entities. The discourse that frames drug interdiction operations supports huge budgets and workforces. More recently, the so-called "war" on drugs is seen as the main policy thrust and rhetorical frame of U.S. border enforcement activities.

Unauthorized migration is the third major domain considered. While drug interdiction involves constant surveillance but sporadic enforcement action, immigration enforcement involves constant surveillance and mass arrests and the processing of individuals. Drug-smuggling operations have increasingly converged with undocumented immigration resulting in the movement of shipments through land since this is where migrants are led through by their guides (Andreas, 2009). Moreover, because of the money stakes at hand and the management of the flow of drugs directed by powerful binational cartels, the risk of violence is increasingly present. The vast majority of undocumented migrants are resource-poor who only seek to reach the United States to work. Smuggling organizations take advantage of these and use their force and power of intimidation to move drugs through people. More recently, they have taken control of the human smuggling operations to help the drug smuggling operations. This has presented a conflicting picture of the different branches involved in border security, conflating drug enforcement procedures with migration enforcement.

The officers of CBP interact with people of all types: U.S. citizens and legal residents (especially residents of the borderlands) and undocumented migrants. Officers use a complicated mix of useful practical understandings combined with profiling to sort out who is to be targeted for brief detention, search, and questioning. Such work is only loosely related to constitutional rules ostensibly governing them. Their approach may reflect both their practical and ideological perspectives that may place them anywhere between protectors of a sacred homeland territory and militant xenophobes. Their roles also express fundamental inequalities in the North American power system that are based on race, citizenship, class, gender or ethnicity. Yet officers also understand people they deal with as including many decent migrant workers who may be mixed in with a smaller set of dangerous actors. As a result, they face the daily contradictions of border policy that often escape the wider public. Their work is tiring, often routine and boring, sometimes stressful, and occasionally dangerous. They toil within an unimaginative, authoritarian bureaucracy, though they are generously compensated in material terms.

Josiah McC. Heyman

See Also: Border Crossing; Counterterrorism and Immigrant Profiling; Coyotes; Drug Trade; Immigration and Customs Enforcement (ICE); Passports; Ports of Entry.

Further Reading

Andreas, Peter. 2009. *Border Games: Policing the U.S.-Mexico Divide.* Ithaca, NY: Cornell University Press.

Andreas, Peter, and Thomas J. Biersteker, eds. 2003. *The Rebordering of North America: Integration and Exclusion in a New Security Context.* New York: Routledge.

Heyman, Josiah McC. 1995. "Putting Power into the Anthropology of Bureaucracy: The Immigration and Naturalization Service at the Mexico-United States Border." *Current Anthropology* 36:261–87.

Heyman, Josiah McC., and Jason Ackleson. 2009. "United States Border Security after September 11." In John Winterdyck and Kelly Sundberg, eds., *Border Security in the Al-Qaeda Era,* 37–74. Boca Raton, FL: CRC Press.

Leiken, Robert S., and Steven Brooke. 2006. "The Quantitative Analysis of Terrorism and Immigration: An Initial Exploration." *Terrorism and Political Violence* 18:503–21.

Payan, Tony. 2006. *The Three U.S.-Mexico Border Wars: Drugs, Immigration, and Homeland Security.* Westport, CT: Praeger Security International.

U.S. Customs and Border Protection. 2013. http://www.cbp.gov/.

U.S. Department of Homeland Security (DHS)

The Department of Homeland Security (DHS) controls most immigration functions (with specialized roles for the State Department, the Department of Justice, and the Department of Labor). DHS was founded in 2003 as a response to the September 11, 2001, attacks. The Immigration and Naturalization Service (INS) was folded into it. INS inspections at ports of entry were merged with Customs Inspections and some smaller agencies; these, in turn, were combined with the Border Patrol into a new DHS unit, Customs and Border Protection (CBP). Immigration investigations and detention and deportation were combined with customs enforcement in Immigration and Customs Enforcement (ICE), which enforces immigration law in the U.S. interior and handles immigrants being processed for removal. Immigration and Naturalization Examinations was turned into a new major unit of DHS, Citizenship and Immigration Services (CIS).

From 2003 to 2005, DHS continued many of the previous emphases of the INS, such as extensive Mexican border patrolling. But it also developed a new emphasis on identifying and deporting collective groups, such as men from some Islamic-majority nations, who were out of status according to U.S. laws, as a result of the unfocused wave of national security anxiety after 9/11. It increased the size and intensity of the detention and deportation systems, including many hidden and poorly accounted for facilities. In late 2005, there was a return to focusing on unauthorized migrants without prioritization in terms of terrorism or broader risks to the public. This led to an unprecedented period of expansion of the DHS immigration enforcement units, such as the Border Patrol and ICE. It was also marked by the construction of a 700-mile-long wall-like fence at the Mexican border and unfocused home and job-site raids by ICE.

In some ways, the immigration policies and practices of DHS are a continuation of the patterns set in the era of the INS. The demand for legal immigration and naturalization continues to overwhelm CIS, resulting in long wait times, due to underfunding by the U.S. Congress and a reliance on user fees. CIS is also marked by a poor service ethic and sometimes suspiciousness toward applicants, as well as the attitude that immigration to the United States should be a limited and carefully guarded good. Significantly, the enforcement apparatus is disproportionately focused on Mexican border crossers, and undocumented Mexicans generally, in comparison to what is actually a less border-focused and more diverse population of unauthorized migrants. Employer raids are showy but sporadic and end up penalizing workers more than employers. Enforcement, especially ICE, has serious performance issues in terms of deaths in detention facilities, disregard of constitutional rights, and lack of prioritization in operations and apprehensions. Each of these issues has deep roots in the fear of and social distance from immigrants felt by politically vocal segments of the U.S. public.

At the same time, the inclusion of immigration in Homeland Security has changed important terms of its functioning, specifically by framing it as a matter of national security. Security is a matter of the ultimate survival of the central state (for example, it is a term used for nuclear warfare), and thus to treat a matter as involving security increases the power and discretion of the central state and decreases the ability to check it, or even know what it is doing. The disappearance of people in the U.S. detention system and the general lack of accountability for them is a good example of the increase of state power at the expense of democratic transparency and accountability. However, to simply characterize the immigration elements of DHS as expressions of hostility to immigrants would be wrong, since these organizations served and continue to serve important functions in facilitating the large legal migration and naturalization systems. Rather, DHS reveals the deep ambivalence and anxieties with which Americans view immigration and borders.

Josiah McC. Heyman

See Also: Counterterrorism and Immigrant Profiling; Deportation; Detention Centers; Governance and Criminalization; Immigration and Customs Enforcement (ICE); Immigration and Naturalization Service (INS); Repatriation; U.S. Border Patrol.

Further Reading

Brotherton, David, and Philip Kretsedemas, eds. 2008. *Keeping Out the Other: A Critical Introduction to Immigration Enforcement Today.* New York: Columbia University Press.

Chishti, Muzaffar, Doris Meissner, Demetrios G. Papademetriou, Jay Peterzell, Michael J. Wishnie, and Steve W. Yale-Loehr. 2003. *America's Challenge: Domestic Security, Civil Liberties, and National Unity after September 11.* Washington, D.C.: Migration Policy Institute.

Chiu, Bess, Lynly Egyes, Peter L. Markowitz, and Jaya Vasandani. 2009. *Constitution on ICE: A Report on Immigration Home Raid Operations.* New York: Immigration Justice Clinic, Benjamin N. Cardozo School of Law. http://cw.routledge.com/textbooks/9780415996945/human-rights/cardozo.pdf.

Heyman, Josiah McC. 2008. "Constructing a Virtual Wall: Race and Citizenship in U.S.–Mexico Border Policing." *Journal of the Southwest* 50:305–34.

Heyman, Josiah McC., and Jason Ackleson. 2009. "United States Border Security after September 11." In *Border Security in the Al-Qaeda Era,* edited by John Winterdyck and Kelly Sundberg, 37–74. Boca Raton, FL: CRC Press.

Martínez, Samuel, ed. 2009. *International Migration and Human Rights: The Global Repercussions of U.S. Policy.* Berkeley: University of California Press.

Meissner, Doris, and Donald Kerwin. 2009. *DHS and Immigration: Taking Stock and Correcting Course.* Washington, D.C.: Migration Policy Institute. http://www.migrationpolicy.org/pubs/DHS_Feb09.pdf.

Ngaruri Kenney, David, and Philip G. Schrag. 2008. *Asylum Denied: A Refugee's Struggle for Safety in America.* Berkeley: University of California Press.

Payan, Tony. 2006. *The Three U.S.-Mexico Border Wars: Drugs, Immigration, and Homeland Security.* Westport, CT: Praeger Security International.

U.S. Department of Homeland Security. Website. 2013. http://www.dhs.gov/.

U.S.-Mexico Border Wall

The U.S.-Mexico border wall can be considered both monumental state architecture and a technology for immigration enforcement. The border wall serves as a physical barrier whose technological purpose is to prevent and deter passage across by undocumented people. However, it also serves as a state symbol to visibly signal the political extent of the United States against the political boundary of Mexico.

Starting in 1990, fourteen miles of fence were built south of San Diego. At that time, hundreds of people were found crossing the border on a near daily basis. On the U.S. side, migrants would disappear into the densely populated urban landscape. Three years later, in response to anti-immigrant pressures in California and other border states, the Clinton administration mandated a surge of funding for border enforcement, including the notable shift in materials that were solid and more rigid, therefore, more "wall"-like. Using this funding, the El Paso Sector Border Patrol worked on the same model as California, creating a functional "wall" by parking patrol vehicles at close consecutive intervals along the border in order to prevent people from making unofficial crossings. Because this operation and the early fence in California both initially produced a surge of immigrant arrests and a resultant decline of unauthorized entries into the United States through Mexico, they were deemed successful and became models for enforcement elsewhere across the border. However, these "successes" proved false as later estimates for undocumented passage across the border suggested that after a few months' adjustment period, migrants were circumventing the heavily patrolled enforcement areas. Regardless, these initial border barriers inspired two trends: the use of walls for boundary enforcement, and the predicability of

The border wall between the United States and Mexico a few miles west of the border crossing at Sasabe, Arizona. The U.S.-Mexico border is one of the longest land borders in the world, spanning 1,969 miles from the Pacific Ocean to the Gulf of Mexico. The wall in Sasabe is one of the more recent installments of the rigid border wall system that came with the adoption of the Border Patrol Strategic Plan 1994 and Beyond. (Frontpage/Shutterstock.com)

migrants' efforts to circumvent the barriers, forcing them into increasingly remote, arid and difficult to navigate terrain. Both trends have continued to the present day (2013), cumulatively leading thousands of migrants into perilous conditions, many dying from dehydration and exposure.

The creation of walls was thus subsequently developed by the Immigration and Naturalization Service (INS) in 1994 and known as the Border Patrol Strategic Plan 1994. The stated objective of this plan was "prevention through deterrence" and provided for increased infrastructure such as surveillance equipment and other resources that, in addition to making the boundaries inpenetrable, served to alter traditional migratory routes away from the urban centers where the walls were found. Working with the Department of Defense's Center for Low Intensity Conflict, the INS proceeded to apply the "prevention through deterrence" strategy across those places that were experiencing the most intense border-crossing activity. This led to the construction of fixed border barriers in large urban centers such as El Paso, buttressing the existing fence already erected in San Diego. Other border towns also received lines of primary fencing in this initial wave, including Campo, California; Yuma, Arizona; Nogales, Arizona; Naco, Arizona; and Douglas, Arizona. Added appropriations were legislated in the later Illegal Immigration Reform and Immigrant Responsibility Act of 1996.

In the wake of the attacks on the New York World Trade Center of September 11, 2001, the Department of Homeland Security was founded, and the funding for building walls and enforcing the border divide entered a new era of intensity. The Secure Fence Act of 2006 instructed the Department of Homeland Security to construct an additional 850 miles of border barriers. This act was then amended in 2008 to limit the construction to 700 miles. As of 2012, an estimated 650 miles of fence have been built.

As of the end of 2009, the "wall" at the border consists not only of a wall, but of the infrastructure to support the wall. Such infrastructure includes lines of triple fencing near ports of entry, fencing layers between which Border Patrol vehicles are solely authorized to travel; an increased number of Border Patrol agents working on the ground in the southwest (from 3,555 in 1992 to over twenty thousand agents in 2010), an increase of Border Patrol highway checkpoints, increased measures for screening vehicles at points of entry, the installation of stadium lighting in high traffic smuggling areas and seismic sensors embedded in the ground to detect disturbance surrounding the border wall. The last attribute, part of an array of border support technology known as the Secure Border Initiative Network (SBINet), was installed while equipment was still in development by a number of defense corporations. A number of setbacks with the technology caused the U.S. Government Accountability Office to recommend ending procurement for SBINet in 2010, and funding for the system was officially halted later that same year.

After the erection of the walls in urban areas, the number of undocumented migrant apprehensions recorded by the U.S. Border Patrol equalled those achieved before the wall came to exist. Meanwhile, rates of undocumented migration held steady by all measures, yet the U.S government had quintupled its enforcement budget from a decade previous. In 2004, funding for security along the southern border alone rose to $3.8 billion annually. Since the current strategy of concentrated border enforcement was first rolled out, the annual budget of the U.S. Border Patrol increased tenfold, from $363 million in 1993, to more than $3.5 billion in 2010 (Immigration Policy Center, 2013). However, shortly after the first decade of building walls across the border, the U.S. General Accounting Office (2006) wrote a report documenting that the combination of walls and enforcement was not serving to prevent unauthorized passage over the border, but was instead forcing migrants into remote and dangerous territories and leading to thousands of deaths. This trend has continued to the present (2012).

These facts are strong indications that the technological function of the wall has failed, with migration not being deterred. Meanwhile, enforcement measures have created conditions leading migrants to encounter great physical dangers and expenses in order to evade U.S. border enforcement. In just over a decade, Arizona alone has recorded more deaths of unauthorized migrants (mainly by hypo/hyperthermia and other factors of element exposure) than were recorded along the Berlin Wall in its twenty-eight-year existence.

In 2005, the Deputy Assistant Secretary for Immigration and Customs Enforcement, John P. Clark, stated his protest over expanding the wall in his testimony to Congress. Clark asserted that the proposed expansion sent a negative message to the international community about the United States' decision to continue in the tradition of the Berlin Wall as it related to its southern neighbors.

The above data points to a secondary social purpose of the wall that causes the U.S. government to continue spending billions of dollars on an enforcement strategy that its own Accountability Office (among myriad others) has documented as a failure. In other words, the wall's primary purpose is symbolic (Andreas, 2009). Design of the wall has been a social response to the threat of invasion and terrorism from the outside, especially in the form of increased wall-building legislated in the Secure Fence Acts post-9/11. This form of monumental architecture makes concrete the boundary between the United States and Mexico. However, it also serves a more insidious and symbolic social function to insulate communities and to identify those who do not belong and who have no rights.

Gabriella Soto

See Also: Border Crossing; Policy and Political Action.

Further Reading

Andreas, Peter. 2009. *Border Games: Policing the U.S.-Mexico Divide.* Ithaca, NY: Cornell University Press.

Cornelius, W. 2005. "Controlling 'Unwanted' Immigration: Lessons from the United States, 1993–2004." *Journal of Ethnic and Migration Studies* 31:775–794.

Garcia, M. J., M. M. Lee, and T. Tatelman. 2005. "Immigration: Analysis of the Major Provisions of the REAL ID Act of 2005." *CRS.* Washington, D.C.: Congressional Research Service.

Haddal, C. C., Y. Kim, and M. J. Garcia. 2009. "Border Security: Barriers Along the U.S. International Border." CRS. Washington, D.C.: Congressional Research Service.

Immigration Policy Center. 2013. "The Cost of Doing Nothing: Dollars, Lives, and Opportunities Lost in the Wait for Immigration Reform." http://www.immigrationpolicy.org/just-facts/cost-doing-nothing

Rubio-Goldsmith, R., M. McCormick, D. Martinez, and I. Duarte. 2006. *The "Funnel Effect" and Recovered Bodies of Unauthorized Migrants Processed by the Pima County Office of the Medical Examiner, 1990–2005.* Tucson: University of Arizona.

U.S. Government Accountability Office. "Illegal Immigration: Border-crossing Deaths Have Doubled since 1995; Border Patrol's Efforts to Prevent Deaths Have Not Been Fully Evaluated." Report to the U.S. Senate, GAO--06-770. Washington, D.C.: GAO, 2006.

U-Visas

In 2000, the United States Congress passed the Victims of Trafficking and Violence Protection Act that provided an amendment to the Immigration and Nationality Act (INA) for the creation of a new type of nonimmigrant visa called a U-visa. The reasoning behind this amendment was that a new nonimmigrant visa was necessary to law enforcement agencies in their work of investigating and prosecuting cases where immigrants were victims. Under this program, up to ten thousand three-year U-visas are

Teresa Gomez, photographed from behind, sits in her apartment in Nebraska on May 22, 2009. She is a native of Mexico and a recipient of a U-visa, available for victims of crime, after she had spent nine years helping her now-adult daughter recover from shotgun wounds suffered in a drive-by shooting in Kansas. U-visas are also available to victims of domestic abuse. (AP Photo/Nati Harnik)

issued annually to victims of qualifying crimes in the United States: domestic violence, rape, sexual exploitation, involuntary servitude, murder, attempted murder, and felonious assault. The qualifying crimes are those that might not always be reported due to the lack of trust between authorities and undocumented immigrants. The U-visa was seen as a way of offering protection to victims of such offenses who are otherwise vulnerable to those types of crimes because they may be fearful. Moreover, the list of qualifying crimes included those that are likely to be suffered by those in the course of their migration: kidnapping, murder, and abduction. Without a U-visa, undocumented immigrants have no recourse for denouncing the perpetrators of these crimes against them. When the act was signed into law in 2000, responsibility was passed on to the Immigration and Naturalization service (INS). At that time, the INS was the federal agency responsible for issuing visas. With the act, the INS was charged with creating the regulations that would bring the law into full implementation. The U-Visa in this way became a way to encourage reporting but also aided law enforcement officials in their duties to investigate and prosecute offenders that carry out the crimes. The provision requires that the victim be cooperative with those agents and officials who investigate and prosecute such crimes. Successful applicants were also eligible for work authorization.

In 2003, INS responsibilities were folded into the U.S. Department of Homeland Security (DHS) when it was established, and more specifically, into one of the branches, the United States Citizenship and Immigration Services (USCIS). The USCIS then became the implementing agency of all the visa application processes, including the U-visa. Some legal scholars have noted that with this transition, there was a delay in the implementation of the U-visa program. At the time of the creation of the DHS, memories of the 9/11 attacks were still prominent. These reflected the many concerns over national security and what many perceived to be a faulty system for granting visas to foreigners who had ill intentions. The regulations for U-Visa application under the INS underwent review and this resulted in a delay in the issuance of U-visas.

In response to this delay, in 2005 a class action lawsuit was filed against the DHS on behalf of individual plaintiffs who were likely to be eligible for a U-visa. The lawsuit intended to pressure the DHS to release the new regulations by claiming that the delay was unreasonable and harmful to the plaintiffs. The lawsuit's original complaint was by a petitioner from New Jersey who argued that she had made a good faith effort to obtain a certification from her local police department and the state's district attorney. She was denied certification even though her abuser was prosecuted and convicted. Although the lawsuit was dismissed, the reauthorization of the Violence against Women Act (VAWA) promised to release the new regulations by 2006. When the deadline came and went without regulations being released, a new class action lawsuit was filed (*Catholic Charities CYO v. Chertoff*). This second lawsuit again claimed that the delay hurt eligible U-visa petitioners. Finally, the USCIS released the regulations on September 5, 2007. As per those regulations, applicants can use a USCIS-issued form, the I-918. The I-918 form includes biographical information about the applicant as well as a case history. It also includes two supplements. Supplement A is used to apply for status for the applicant, and the applicant's spouse or children. Supplement B is more complex and has been the center of much controversy.

The instructions for Form I-918 state that Supplement B will be used as evidence that the petitioner was a victim and that the petitioner has information about the criminal activity that occurred in the United States. It requires a certification that the applicant is or is likely to be helpful in the investigation or prosecution of the crime. Although the form may be filled out by the applicant and can be with the help of an advocate, the certifying agency must be a law enforcement agency. The official or supervisor from the agency must follow the instructions for certification, which involves certifying that the applicant was in fact a victim of any of the qualifying crimes. The application is then forwarded to the USCIS. Only the USCIS can review the form and make a determination if the immigrant is eligible for the visa. The law enforcement official's signature also obligates them to notify USCIS if the applicant refuses to cooperate in the investigation. However, what is important to mention is that the filling out of the certification is entirely left to the discretion of the official, and without a completed Form I-918, Supplement B, the applicant is ineligible for a U-visa.

This last point has been the subject of much criticism by those who advocate for immigrants, such as those managing shelters or community-based organizations that help victims of domestic violence. They have pointed out that law enforcement officials often have a range of reactions to the request for certification, with some cooperative while others are resistant to the process. These differences produce different outcomes, and many argue that the use of discretion violates the right to equal protection under the law. A strategy of these advocates has been to promote or strengthen their relationship with the law enforcement agencies which they might ask to sign certifications. The advocates argue that building trusting relationships will go a long way towards making communities safer. A practice among such advocates includes organizing workshops to help educate potential certifying agencies on the regulations and law behind the U-visa. For example, law enforcement agents believe incorrectly that their signature on the certification form grants U-visa status to the petitioner or gives them the authorization to stay in the United States. However, U-visa status can only be granted by the USCIS. The facts that they are certifying—whether the applicant is a victim and helpful—can also suffer from many interpretations. The words "victims" and "helpful" are not clearly defined in the statute, and are thus open to interpretation. Stereotypes of immigrants—often promoted by the media with images of undocumented immigrants as criminals and lawbreakers—may also color the way an official perceive them, potentially resulting in denying them the certification. Many advocates have been quick to point out that law enforcement officials who are not trained in immigration law are more likely to see undocumented immigrants as lawbreakers.

Lack of clarity of what constitutes "being helpful" became obvious in 2004 when fourteen undocumented immigrants who lost family members on 9/11 came forward to apply for a U-visa in exchange for their testimony in the trial of Zacarias Moussaoui who was on trial in an American court in connection with the terrorist attacks. The group of fourteen admitted to a federal official that they were in the United States without documents. After they were all interviewed by authorities, only three with the most useful information were chosen. The eleven other claims for certification were denied. Having exposed their illegal status to a federal official they risked deportation.

In conclusion, the U-visa process is a relatively new one and many questions have yet to be answered. Very few studies exist about the program and the vast majority of the population is not well informed about it. The certification aspect seems to be particularly problematic, but the program has been in existence for too short of a period to assess how it will be resolved.

See Also: Advocacy; Crime; Domestic Violence; Gender Roles; Temporary Protected Status (TPS); Trafficking Victims Protection Reauthorization Act (TVPRA); Violence; Violence against Women Act (VAWA); Women's Status.

Anna Ochoa O'Leary

Further Reading

Bernstein, Nina. 2004. "A Visa Case with a Twist: 9/11; Illegal Immigrants Testified to Try to Stay in the U.S." *NY Times,* Sept 16, 2004. http://query.nytimes.com/gst/fullpage.html?res=9803EEDC1F30F935A2575AC0A9629C8B63.

Farb, Jessica. 2007. "The U Visa Unveiled: Immigrant Crime Victims Freed from Limbo." *Human Rights Brief* 15.1:26–29. http://www.wcl.american.edu/hrbrief/15/151.cfm.

Jensen, Tahja L. 2009. "U Visa 'Certification': Overcoming the Local Hurdle in Response to a Federal Statute." *Idaho Law Review* 45:696–699.

Schuneman, Micaela. 2009. "Seven Years of Bad Luck: How the Government's Delay in Issuing U-Visa Regulations Further Victimized Immigrant Crime Victims." *Journal of Gender Race and Justice* 12:465–491.

Turner, Andrew, et al. 2009. "Case of First Impression: Federal Judge in Civil Case May Certify U Visa Applications of Undocumented Immigrant Human Trafficking Victims." *Clearinghouse Review Journal of Poverty Law and Policy* 42:510–513.

V

Violence

In February 2006 U.S. Border Patrol agents Ignacio Ramos and Jose Compean encountered an alleged drug smuggler along the Texas-Mexico border. During the encounter, Agent Ramos shot the unarmed individual in the backside. Ramos was charged and convicted of causing serious bodily injury, assault with a deadly weapon, discharge of a firearm in relation to a crime of violence, and violation of civil rights. Compean was also convicted of wrongful actions and both men were sentenced to serve over ten years in prison. They appealed the decisions, but their appeals were denied. In 2007, Congress introduced the Ramos and Compean Act. This legislation would pardon the agents, despite the fact that the U.S. Constitution does not grant the right to pardon to Congress. President George W. Bush commuted Ramos's and Compean's sentences in 2009. The agents were released after serving less than two years of their sentence for violent acts against an undocumented immigrant.

The Ramos and Compean cases are indicative of tension between many border agents and the individuals they encounter in the course of their work. More recently, there have been a number of cases throughout the states along the U.S.-Mexico border in which Border Patrol agents are accused of using excessive force against undocumented immigrants. For example, in 2009, an undocumented immigrant from Guatemala filed a lawsuit against the Border Patrol alleging that agents had broken his collarbone while he was in their custody. In Arizona in two separate incidents associated with rock throwing in 2011, agents shot and killed two teens, Ramses Barrón Torres and Carlos LaMadrid. Also in Arizona, on October 10, 2012, during another rock-throwing incident, a Border Patrol agent shot Jose Antonio Elena Rodriguez, another teen, through the fence that divides Nogales, Arizona, from Nogales, Sonora.

According to reports from the humanitarian organization No More Deaths, there were upwards of thirty thousand reported incidents of violence against immigrants in custody of the U.S. Border Patrol between 2008 and 2011 along the Arizona-Mexico border. These types of incidents included physical, mental/emotional, verbal, and sexual violence and were inflicted upon men, women, and children. Such treatment is discounted as exceptional to the standards and values of the Border Patrol, but these incidents have been steadily increasing in number and severity over the last several years. The Department of Homeland Security, which oversees the Border Patrol, has been slow to address this growing problem.

Several issues are involved with the detainment of undocumented immigrants and the prosecution of crimes committed against them. Immigrants may be in the custody of the Border Patrol, Immigration and Customs Enforcement (ICE), or state and local law enforcement agencies, or housed in prisons, detention centers or shelters and impacted by a number of different policies and laws, including whether they have been charged with civil or criminal crimes. In 2003, Congress passed the Prison Rape Elimination Act (PREA), which addressed rape in prisons and applied to immigrants as well. However, the Department of Homeland Security has argued that the PREA does not apply to it and, therefore, its mandates are not extended to immigrants in its custody.

Since the implementation of the Immigration Reform and Control Act of 1986 and the subsequent implementation of the Border Patrol Strategic Plan of 1994 that made possible programs such as Operation Gatekeeper and Operation Hold the Line, civilian participation in border and immigration control has increased as well. In many cases, their participation has been accompanied by the threat of violence. Organizations such as the Minutemen Civil Defense Corps, Minutemen American Defense, and similar groups have taken it upon themselves to assist in the patrolling of the U.S.-Mexico border, even though the Border Patrol has publicly rejected their presence. Members of these organizations make their armed presence known by manning posts along the border, volunteering manpower and materials toward building border fences, and conducting sweeps and searches in areas where immigration and smuggling activity are suspected. In 2011, Shawna Forde and Jason Bush, both members of the Minutemen American Defense, were convicted of killing Raul Flores and his nine-year-old daughter Brisenia in Arivaca, Arizona. According to reports, Forde ordered the invasion of the Flores home on suspicion of illegal drug activity. The attack was not ordered or condoned by any law enforcement agency. Forde and Bush received the death penalty.

Immigrants and Crime

Immigration, and particularly undocumented immigration, is often linked with violence in the minds of many. Drug trafficking and human smuggling are associated with the illegal movement across international borders, and research does suggest that these activities persist along the U.S. international borders. The violence that is involved in maintaining these industries is reported regularly in the American media. However, the number and type of violent acts committed by undocumented immigrants seem to be exaggerated by the media, politicians, and general society. In 2010, Arizona governor Jan Brewer claimed that undocumented immigrants were consistently fighting among themselves in confrontations that often resulted in brutal murders, including decapitation, in Arizona deserts. Former state senator Russell Pearce corroborated her claim, saying that up to five hundred decapitated or dismembered human bodies had been discovered in the border region. Neither politician was able to offer concrete evidence to support these claims, but continued to use them as examples of spillover violence in Mexico that undocumented immigrants bring with them to the United States.

Other claims about immigrant violence include charges of rampant home burglary, trespassing, assault, drunk driving, kidnapping, and rape. In 2011, Arizona Republican senator John McCain claimed that the wildfires ravaging Arizona lands were caused by undocumented immigrants. It was later determined that there was no truth to this statement, but the idea that immigrants were responsible for such destruction had already been disseminated to the public.

Confrontation

As the U.S. states continue to pass restrictive immigrations laws, such as Arizona's SB1070 and Alabama's HB 56, interaction between undocumented immigrants and U.S. law enforcement has seemingly escalated in force. There have been a few high-profile cases, particularly in Arizona, where a Border Patrol agent was killed in the line of duty. Most of these incidents have occurred deep in the deserts of Arizona and involved individuals who were in drug trafficking.

Andrea Hernandez Holm

See Also: Gangs; Hate Crimes; Human Trafficking; Minutemen.

Further Reading

Andreas, Peter. 2005. "The Mexicanization of the US-Canada Border." *International Journal* 60.2:449–462.

Brané, Michelle. 2011. "It's Time to Protect Women and Children in Immigration Detention from Rape." *The Huffington Post,* December 6. www.huffingtonpost.com.

"A Culture of Cruelty: Abuse and Impunity in Short-term U.S. Border Patrol Custody." 2011. No More Deaths. www.culture-cruelty.org.

Hendricks, Tyche. 2005. "On the Border." *The San Francisco Chronicle.* December 5. www.sfgate.com

No More Deaths. No Más Muertes. www.nomoredeaths.org.

Violence against Women Act (VAWA)

The Violence against Women Act (VAWA), passed by the U.S. Congress in 1994, sought to protect undocumented immigrants from domestic violence by allowing victims to self-petition for legal immigration status without having to rely on an abusive U.S. citizen or lawful permanent resident spouse or parent. The act was reauthorized with modifications in 2000; and again, with modifications in 2005; and in 2012, after opposition by conservative Republicans, mainly for provisions for lesbian women and undocumented immigrant women, it finally passed the Senate and House of Representatives and President Barack Obama signed it into law on March 7, 2013.

In crafting VAWA, lawmakers attempted to rectify weak points in existing immigration law which effectively trapped immigrant spouses and children in violent relationships by giving abusive partners control over their and their children's immigrant status. VAWA was instrumental in opening a safe route to legal immigrant status for a battered immigrant spouse who could demonstrate that their spouse had U.S. citizenship or legal permanent resident status, that their marriage was legal, that the abused spouse had entered her marriage in good faith, that they resided together, that she was

House Minority Leader Nancy Pelosi of California, center, accompanied by House Democrats, leads a news conference to discuss the Violence against Women Act on Capitol Hill in Washington, D.C. on January 23, 2013. Under VAWA, undocumented immigrants who are victims of domestic violence may petition for legal status. (AP Photo/Jacquelyn Martin)

subject to battery or extreme cruelty during the marriage, that the self-petitioner was of good moral character, and that deportation would cause extreme hardship for the self-petitioner or his or her family members. Abused children were also eligible under VAWA without the requirement of a good-faith marriage. Confidentiality for the VAWA self-petition was guaranteed. Central to the VAWA legislation were provisions for legal service organizations to assist victims of domestic violence and sexual assault regardless of the victims' immigration status.

Subsequent modifications to the law in VAWA 2000 and its reauthorization in 2005 furthered efforts to redress weaknesses in existing immigration law that placed abused immigrant spouses and children at increased risk of domestic abuse. VAWA 2000 relieved self-petitioners of the burden of having to show extreme hardship, and it also created an exception to the good moral character requirement for crimes that were connected to domestic abuse. For example, law enforcement may routinely make dual arrests when called to a scene of domestic violence. VAWA 2000 extended eligibility for self-petitions to divorced or widowed spouses for up to two years after their divorce or the spouse's death, as well as to abused immigrant spouses whose spouse had lost their lawful permanent resident status due to domestic violence. Additionally, VAWA 2000 created the U-visa, which allowed victims of domestic violence and other crimes who cooperate with law enforcement in investigation or prosecution of that crime to petition for work and residency authorization for four years. A person granted a U-visa may apply for lawful permanent resident status after three years. The U-visa thus serves as a self-petition that provides the successful applicant a pathway to lawful permanent resident status.

In addition to the right to self-petition and the U-visa, VAWA legislation included additional benefits and protections to immigrant victims of domestic violence. Approved VAWA petitioners receive deferred action status which places them on low priority of deportation. VAWA petitioners also are eligible for employment authorization. Immigrants with approved VAWA self-petitions are eligible for public benefits.

The significance of VAWA legislation should be understood as part of the cycle of power and control exerted by abusive partners over their victims. Women and children are disproportionately affected by domestic abuse. Male partner violence is the largest single cause of injury to women in the United States regardless of ethnicity, economic status, or country of origin. Male partners are responsible for 30 percent of all homicidal deaths of women. Women who attempt to leave abusive relationships face substantial physical, economic, emotional and social obstacles.

While domestic violence impacts all women, immigrant women face a disproportionate risk of abuse at the hands of a domestic partner. More than half of married immigrant women experience either physical or sexual abuse. An abusive partner is able to use his power over his spouse's or child's immigration status to control, isolate, harass, and coerce an immigrant victim. Abusers exploit the legal vulnerability of victims by destroying their spouse's legal paperwork, withdrawing their petitions for legal permanent resident status or threatening to contact immigration enforcement. The majority of abusive U.S. citizen or lawful permanent resident spouses never file immigration application for their undocumented spouses. It is for these overlapping and intersecting reasons related to power, gender, and vulnerability compounded by immigration status that undocumented immigrant spouses who are victims of domestic abuse are eligible under VAWA.

The obstacles confronting domestic violence victims in accessing services that would facilitate their ability to leave abusive situations are also exacerbated among the immigrant population. Immigrant women face language barriers, cultural differences, lack of information about their rights and of access to legal employment and public benefits in the U.S. legal system. The majority of undocumented immigrant women are ignorant of protections under VAWA. An immigrant woman relying on her spouse for legal status may be reluctant to file a civil protection order or call the police for fear that engaging the system in any way might bring her moral character into questions or that her spouse, whom she may be economically dependent on, might be deported, thus also endangering her livelihood. Furthermore, in an environment of increased immigration enforcement and border security, the potential consequences of engaging law enforcement or other services are costly, and may result in loss of the custody of children, arrest, and deportation. Immigrant victims of domestic violence are at particular risk of losing their children. According to the Applied Research Center, in 2013 there were an estimated 5,100 children who were living in foster care because their parents were in immigration detention or had been deported.

Beyond these barriers, fear for their children's welfare is the greatest obstacle facing abused immigrant women who are considering seeking assistance outside the home. Immigrant women with children are very likely to have at least one child who is a U.S.-born citizen, increasing anxiety not only of separation, but also that their families will be torn apart because of the mixed status of family members. For immigrant women who want to return to their home country, having a child who is a U.S. citizen provides an abusive U.S. citizen or legal permanent resident spouse with tremendous leverage. The abuser can get a custody order in the United States making it impossible for a woman to leave with her child. If a woman flees her abuser to return to Mexico, her spouse or partner may follow her to her home county and kidnap the child to bring back to the United States where the mother cannot easily follow.

The majority of VAWA self-petitioners are women; however, it is worth noting that the imbalance of power in a mixed-status family, where the documented person is abusive toward any undocumented family members, creates a power and control dynamic that often traps women in abusive relationships.

Immigrants who are victims of domestic violence are practically invisible in society as a result of the abuse, their immigrant status, and increasingly anti-immigrant environment. Policy advocates and victim services providers emphasize that in order for eligible victims to avail themselves of their rights under VAWA, further measures should be taken. These include efforts to increase public awareness of VAWA through informal networks, providing more training for service providers on VAWA and immigrant rights in general as well as training of service providers and community advocates in how to respond to victims in a culturally competent manner, and the establishment of mandatory VAWA training for local law enforcement agencies and immigration officials.

Maia Ingram

See Also: Advocacy; Children; Domestic Violence; Family Economics; Gender Roles; Policy and Political Action; State Legislation; Violence; Women's Status.

Further Reading

Applied Research Center. 2013. "Shattered Families: The Perilous Intersection of Immigration Enforcement and the Child Welfare System." http://arc.org/shatteredfamilies.

Legal Momentum; The Women's Legal Defense and Education Fund. Immigrant Women Program. 2009. http://www.legalmomentum.org/our-work/vaw/iwp.html.

Office on Violence against Women. Department of Justice. 2013. http://www.ovw.usdoj .gov/.

W

Wages

While the wages of unauthorized immigrants in the United States vary widely, as a group unauthorized workers tend to be lower paid than legal residents or U.S. citizens. The average income for an unauthorized worker is about 40 percent less than the income for a legal immigrant or native-born worker. Wages for unauthorized workers also do not rise in correlation with time on the job as much as they do for legal workers, and unauthorized workers are far less likely than legal workers to have employment-based health care coverage or other benefits.

Because of the secretive nature of unauthorized work, it is difficult to get a representative and thorough picture of the labor market characteristics of all unauthorized U.S. workers. However, studies consistently show that unauthorized workers earn less than their legal counterparts, even when characteristics such as educational attainment, fluency in English, time on the job, and industry are controlled for. For example, one study sampled more than two thousand newly legalized immigrants, most of them from Mexico, about their work experiences as unauthorized workers. This study found that unauthorized Mexican immigrants earned about 40 percent less than their legal counterparts; about half of the gap can be explained by factors other than legal status, such as education and English language proficiency, while the other half of the gap is attributable to discrimination based on illegal status itself. This study also found that the wages of immigrants who were able to legalize their immigration status rose substantially, even when other characteristics were controlled for.

Even though unauthorized workers as a group earn less than workers with legal status, there is a great deal of variability among wages earned by undocumented people. In general, unauthorized men earn more than unauthorized women, workers with more skills earn more than less-skilled workers, and workers with higher educational levels earn more than those with less education. One Chicago-area study published in 1992 found that about three quarters of undocumented workers earn wages that are at or slightly above the minimum wage, while ten percent earn less than the minimum wage and thirteen percent earn about twice the minimum wage or higher. In contrast, one third of legal immigrants earn more than twice the minimum wage, while only three percent earn less.

Lower income levels translate into higher poverty rates, and unauthorized immigrants are twice as likely as U.S.-born residents to live in poverty. In addition, the majority of unauthorized immigrant adults lack health insurance and other benefits often associated with employment. There are several possible explanations for the relatively low wages of unauthorized workers.

The first is that unauthorized immigrants tend to have lower levels of education than other U.S. people. Nearly half of all unauthorized adults over the age of twenty-five have not completed high school, compared with only 8 percent of U.S.-born adults over twenty-five. Another 27 percent of unauthorized adults have completed high school but gone no further, and only 15 percent have earned a bachelor's degree or higher. Since jobs that require less education tend to be lower-paying than those that require more education, the low income levels of unauthorized immigrants relative to U.S.-born adults are probably at least partially due to their relatively low levels of educational attainment. However, one Chicago-area study found that unauthorized Latin American immigrants earn 22 to 36 percent less than workers with legal status, even when education, English proficiency, and time on the job are controlled for. These findings were supported by a larger survey of Mexican immigrants who reside mostly in California.

Another factor that likely contributes to low median household incomes for unauthorized immigrants is that relatively few unauthorized immigrant women are in the labor force. About 58 percent of unauthorized women are working or looking for work, compared with 73 percent for U.S.-born women. Unauthorized immigrant women who are in the labor force also suffer from higher levels of unemployment than their male counterparts.

Unauthorized immigrants are also concentrated in certain industries, such as agriculture and construction, in which work is seasonal, or in day-labor occupation, where employment is short-term and precarious. Being out of work for prolonged periods each year reduces the total annual income for seasonal workers and day laborers and also helps explain the income gap.

Another contributing factor to low income levels is a lack of legal status itself. Unauthorized workers tend to be concentrated in low-wage industries in which employers are not scrupulous about checking the employment eligibility of immigrant workers or even preferentially hire unauthorized workers because they expect to pay them less, or in which a high proportion of work is done by subcontracting firms. Subcontracting allows big businesses to pay less for workers while they avoid the responsibility of ensuring employees' work eligibility. In addition, the high degree of vulnerability of unauthorized workers makes them less likely to demand higher wages and better working conditions than workers with legal status. In fact, when undocumented workers do organize to improve their conditions, they may be fired by their employers and even threatened with deportation.

This has led some scholars to theorize that mass unauthorized migration exists precisely because undocumented workers supply a source of low-wage labor in developed countries where native labor is relatively expensive—that is, because undocumented workers will work for less than workers with legal status. According to this perspective, punitive immigration policies do not effectively restrict the entry of immigrants, but they do classify large numbers of immigrants as "illegal," which creates a large pool of relatively powerless workers inside of the United States. The powerlessness of undocumented workers restricts their access to higher-paying jobs, makes them more vulnerable to exploitative employment practices, and leaves them with little recourse in the event of discrimination or abuse. In all, illegal status makes unauthorized workers more likely to work for relatively low wages.

With hopes of comprehensive immigration reform rekindled in 2013, reports about how by allowing undocumented immigrants to emerge from the shadows to access opportunities for employment and thus improve their wage-earning capacity have shown how it would boost the nation's economy. Raúl Hinojosa-Ojeda, founding director of the North American Integration and Development Center at the University of California, Los Angeles, issued a series of reports that predict how in just the first three years following legalization, the earning power of the newly legalized would translate into an increase in net personal income of $30 to $36 billion, generating $4.5 to $5.4 billion in additional net tax revenue. The earning power of this scale would have a multiplier effect enough to stimulate business generated to meet the demand of additional consumer spending, sufficient to support 750,000 to 900,000 jobs.

Ruth Gomberg-Muñoz

See Also: Day Labor; Economics; Employer Sanctions; Employment Visas; Family Economics; Immigrant Workers Freedom Ride; Labor Supply; Labor Unions; Remittances; Work Visas.

Further Reading

De Genova, Nicholas. 2005. *Working the Boundaries: Race, Space, and "Illegality" in Mexican Chicago.* Durham, NC: Duke University Press.

Immigration Policy Center. 2013. "The Cost of Doing Nothing: Dollars, Lives, and Opportunities Lost in the Wait for Immigration Reform." Available at http://www .immigrationpolicy.org/just-facts/cost-doing-nothing.

Mehta, Chirag, Nik Theodore, Iliana Mora, and Jennifer Wade. 2002. "Chicago's Undocumented Immigrants: An Analysis of Wages, Working Conditions, and Economic Contributions." UIC Center for Urban Economic Development.

Passel, Jeffrey, and D'Vera Cohn. 2009. "A Portrait of Unauthorized Immigration in the United States." Pew Hispanic Center. http://pewhispanic.org/files/reports/107.pdf.

Rivera-Batiz, Francisco L. 1999. "Undocumented Workers in the Labor Market: An Analysis of the Earnings of Legal and Illegal Mexican Immigrants in the United States." *Journal of Population Economics* 12:91–116.

Welfare System

Throughout history, immigrants have been socially perceived as outsiders, generally eliciting hostile reactions from U.S. citizens. The result of this is that individuals from the "in-group" will be less likely to want to share resources and will have less-favorable feelings toward the "out-group" (Diaz et al., 2011). Many scholars have applied similar ideas to explain the connection between anti-immigrant debates articulating worries

Gloria Lopez, center, feeds her nephew and son in the kitchen of her apartment in Alamo, Texas on September 6, 2012. The idea that undocumented immigrants get a "free ride" in the welfare system has made it harder for them to receive the assistance needed by eligible immigrants and children, many of whom are U.S.-born. (AP Photo/Eric Gay)

about the costs due to the use of public resources by immigrants and subsequent changes in the U.S. welfare system, and in particular, changes in policies that deprived immigrants of rights many citizens take for granted. King (2007) has argued that myths about immigrants' use of healthcare programs have effectively help garner support for increasing restrictions on immigrant access to healthcare. She lists these myths as:

- U.S. public health insurance programs are overburdened with immigrants.
- Immigrants consume large quantities of limited healthcare resources.
- Immigrants come to the United States to gain access to healthcare services.
- Restricting immigrants' access to the healthcare system will not affect American citizens.
- Undocumented immigrants are "free-riders" in the American healthcare system.

Most scholars agree that legislative proposals such as California's Proposition 187, if allowed to proceed, would have denied welfare benefits to certain classes of legal permanent residents under the Illegal Immigration Reform and Immigrant Responsibility Act of 1996 (IIRIRA), both individual states and the federal government have devalued noncitizens by depriving them of certain basic personal rights granted to citizens (Romero, 2000).

The U.S. welfare system is rooted in the British Poor Laws, which identified individuals who were unable to work because of their physical health. It further granted monetary assistance to the physically impaired and other forms of assistance. In addition, able-bodied unemployed citizens were granted public-service employment. During the 1800s the U.S. government attempted to generate policy surrounding the government's responsibility to the poor. The government was in favor of providing assistance for unemployed individuals that emphasized preparing the poor for the workforce rather than granting cash assistance. A program was passed after the Civil War, which provided aid to war veterans and their dependents.

The U.S. welfare system was created during the 1930s. Welfare was a governmental response to the Great Depression, which assisted those in need. It is estimated that at the lowest point of the Great Depression, one-fourth of the U.S. work force was unemployed. Many families were left with no source of income. It was also during this time that President Franklin Roosevelt drafted the Social Security Act in January of 1935. This act was to provide assistance for the nation's elderly who could no longer work to support themselves. By August of 1935, the act had passed the House and was signed by the president. In 1939 the act was amended in order to include other services to the U.S. populations. Some of these new services were unemployment compensation and Aid to Families with Dependent Children.

In 1964 President Johnson declared the war on poverty. The Johnson administration focused on the low rates of production and the relationship between poverty and the market economy. Thus, under the Johnson administration, there was a trend towards job training and enhancing individual qualifications. In addition, education and hands-on training were emphasized. Assistance was also provided to individuals after completing their job training, in order to facilitate their acquiring jobs and becoming less dependent on public welfare. However, at this time, welfare had a low rate of recipients with an estimated four million.

By the mid-1970s the Nixon administration passed the welfare Food Stamp program. This program provided food coupons to purchase food. The amount was in accordance with the family size, regardless of living arrangements and marital status. Due to a large increase of welfare recipients after the implementation of the Food Stamp program, policy makers came to criticize it as a way to increase dependence on welfare.

In 1996 President Bill Clinton made significant changes to welfare policy, changing it from a federally-run program to a state-administered program. The implementation of the Personal Responsibility and Work Opportunity Reconciliation Act of 1996 placed responsibility on individuals on welfare for finding employment. This act also gave states the federal aid to assist the needy. However, in order for states to receive federal aid, they had to comply with assisting individuals search for employment and holding them accountable for taking responsibility into their own hands. This philosophy and approach was within the broader, emerging attitudes about immigrants as irresponsible and imprudent and incapable of making wise decisions for themselves (Inda, 2006). Thus, the push became increasingly towards reforming the welfare system away from a form of dependency and towards using it as a temporary form of government assistance that was conditional on meeting certain measures of self-sufficiency.

The Temporary Assistance to Needy Families (TANF) program would provide assistance for the needy for two years with the expectation that after that period individuals would be engaged in some form of work. It included the program Job Opportunities and Basic Skills Training Program (JOB), which by some accounts was discriminatory against people of color, eligible immigrants, and especially women (Marchevsky and Theoharis, 2008).

As a result of the 1996 amendments to the welfare system, many legal immigrants in the United States lost their eligibility for public benefits through the U.S. welfare system. Prior to the passage of the 1996 reforms documented migrants were eligible for welfare almost under the same conditions as citizens.

For legal permanent residents who entered the United States prior to August 22, 1996, welfare was still available with the exception of food stamps. Refugees or political asylees admitted to the United States for humanitarian purposes are eligible for aid only within the first five years of their residency in the United States. U.S.-citizen children born to undocumented parents are able to apply for welfare. In this case the undocumented parent would submit a welfare application for their child, and would not be questioned on their own legal status. In this way, households with mixed immigration statues are eligible for federal welfare programs and benefits though U.S.-citizen children. The parent is seen as the administrator of the benefits the citizen child receives.

The 1996 welfare reform law allowed states to design their own programs, giving states the right to determine immigrant's eligibility for state and federal benefits, although neither local, state, nor federal governments were authorized to provide any form of welfare benefits to undocumented immigrants. In addition, the welfare reform act required that welfare employees contact the Immigration and Naturalization Service (INS) if they knew of an individual requesting welfare that was not eligible due to their undocumented status. The only exception made to this regulation was that parents requesting assistance for their U.S.-citizen children were to remain unreported.

The ethnographic research by Marchevsky and Theoharis (2008) shows that when immigrant status became a criterion for making determinations, many eligible immigrants, based on their appearance, language use, and facial characteristics, became more scrutinized by agency personnel. Officials and clerks transmitted generalized impressions that eligible clients were less deserving, and this resulted in their unfair treatment and humiliation. Moreover, there was a systemic lack of efforts to communicate information to eligible immigrant clients, resulting in more obstacles to receiving much-needed public welfare benefits. The authors argue that leaving the interpretation of eligibility criteria and rules in the hands of local welfare officials who may be unwittingly influenced by the public discourse allowed prejudices to impact decisions in a negative way.

Thalia Marlyn Gómez Torres

See Also: Barriers to Health; Health and Welfare; Illegal Immigration Reform and Immigrant Responsibility Act (IIRIRA) (1996); Nutrition; Temporary Assistance for Needy Families (TANF); Women's Status.

Further Reading

Balistreri, Kelly. 2010. "Welfare and the Children of Immigrants: Transmission of Dependence or Investment in the Future?" *Population Research & Policy Review* 29.5:715–743. *Health Business Elite.*

Diaz, Priscila, Delia S. Saenz, and Virginia S. Y. Kwan. 2011. "Economic Dynamics and Changes in Attitudes Toward Undocumented Mexican Immigrants in Arizona." *Analyses of Social Issues & Public Policy* 11.1:300–313.

Inda, Jonathan Xavier. 2006. *Targeting Immigrants: Government, Technology, and Ethics.* Oxford: Blackwell.

King, Meredith L. 2007. "Immigrants in the U.S. Health Care System: Five Myths That Misinform the American Public." Center for American Progress. http://www.americanprogress.org/issues/2007/06/immigrant_health_report.html. Accessed July 21, 2008.

Marchevsky, Alejandra, and Jeanne Theoharis. 2008. "Dropped from the Rolls: Mexican Immigrants, Race, and Rights in the Era of Welfare Reform." *Journal of Sociology & Social Welfare* 15.3:71–96.

Romero, Victor C. 2000. "The Domestic Fourth Amendment Rights of Undocumented Immigrants: On Guitterez [*United States v. Guitterez,* 983 F. Supp. 905]." *Harvard Civil Rights–Civil Liberties Law Review* 35.1:57–101.

Women's Status

Gender constructions and undocumented migration can be considered among a multitude of factors that shape the experiences and the status of women. They also shape the representations of women in the eyes of social and governmental institutions and of scholars of migration and policy.

The Historical Development of Women in Undocumented Migration

Gender is situated in any given historical and socio-cultural context. This makes it an extremely complex subject, particularly in terms of migration and how the migration process impacts the status women may have in a variety of contexts. In particular, the historical, conceptual and political development of "undocumented" migration in the United States during the twentieth and twenty-first centuries hinges on Mexican migration to the United States, and this has parallel impact on how undocumented immigrant women are regarded. The fact that Mexican undocumented immigrants by far make up the largest portion (around 59 percent) of all undocumented immigrants to the United States, racial and xenophobic undertones are also brought to bear. The social contexts surrounding the construct of "undocumented" in this way shape women's participation in Mexican migration over time.

It is generally understood that women have traditionally been a minority in undocumented migration, and that their primary motivation for migrating was to reunite with their husbands. However, over the past two decades, researchers have increasingly noted that women migrate independently in search of employment opportunities in order to financially support themselves and their families. In fact, some pioneering studies on Mexican migration to the United States suggest that women's participation was strong at the early part of the twentieth century. Studies from the 1920s indicate that Mexican migrants of the day were diverse, incorporating not only single men, but women, children, and frequently entire families (Donato and Patterson, 2006). Women also suffer some of the same consequences as all migrants. For example, two-thirds of deported Mexicans between 1931 and 1933 were women (Durand and Massey, 1992). Such historical analyses highlight the formative impact that changing immigration policies have on the demographics of undocumented (and of course, documented) migration, as well as how men and women migrate.

Starting in 1942, the Bracero Program encouraged legal migration of Mexican men to the United States, with the assumption that migration would be temporary and that men would return to their families in Mexico at the end of the season. At the same time, undocumented immigration surged, creating a conceptual dialectic between documented and undocumented immigration. With the start of family reunification policies in the 1970s, women had the option to enter the country legally as wives, putting them in a position of male dependency at least for immigration purposes, if not for economic ones. On the other hand, immigration policies and practices sought to control sexuality at key entry points on the border, with single women (and men) seen as suspect, assumed to be homosexual or otherwise "sexually deviant," and denied entry into the United States on this basis.

Factors That Influence Women's Immigration

Research conducted in the 1980s identified social networks as one of the primary factors influencing women's migration: if the sending community's receiving social network was established in agricultural occupations, women and children more frequently migrated (eventually being legalized) than if it was established in urban occupations. This is attributed to the nature of farm work (and the perceived nature of women), which offers a "range of light and heavy tasks that all family members can undertake to earn income," accessibility of family housing, and more permissiveness of child labor in rural agricultural settings. Migration research generally reinforced women's familial roles in this way. However social networks also play a vital, albeit differential role, in the migration of both men and women. Studies frequently focus exclusively on the importance of migrant women's *kinship* ties, rather than comparing gender constructs in the broader category of social networks within and beyond the family.

Despite the growing feminization of *undocumented* immigration, there has been a reinforcement of male-dominant hierarchical relationships in which Mexican men are more likely to be documented than their female counterparts. This contributes to the undermining of women's status. In part, this may be due to the historically late insertion of legalization on the basis of family reunification compared to men's earlier insertion as documented migrants through agricultural guest worker programs such as the Bracero program of the 1940s, and more recently Special Agricultural Workers program. These tendencies not only affected women migrants' status compared to that of men, but also compounded differences based on class.

Gender-based Violence and Undocumented Migration

Women's relegation to the family and the home, considered private spheres, is a consistently relevant theme both in sending communities and in U.S.-based research and policy. This often compounds the problems and limitations associated with undocumented migration and women's status. Due both to gender norms and immigration policies, undocumented women are often discouraged from leaving their homes in search of work, education, and other opportunities. This puts them at a particular disadvantage for learning English, making them more vulnerable legally and economically.

Beyond family reunification, rape in the country of origin is an alternate way for women to gain access to legal migration through asylum. Women often suffer rape during illegal entry into the United States. Others do not become undocumented migrants of their own free will, but rather are trafficked into the country for sexual exploitation. Although there has been some discussion of extending asylum to women that are victims of domestic violence in their home countries, a generalized disrespect for women and ideas that reflect a normalization of gendered violence for women has muted the voices of marginalized women. This is seen in practice among policing authorities—who generally reflect a hyper-masculine culture—who are reluctant or slow to respond to victims of violence, or worse, blame women for their misfortune. This discourages women from officially denouncing their assailants, resulting in an undercounting of violent acts against women. In this way, the normalization of gendered violence is maintained. Many women are motivated to migrate as a result of diverse forms of gender-based violence that they are subjected to in their places of origin. Lack of policies that reflect a generalized predisposition of violence can be considered another factor in the feminization of undocumented migration.

While one in four women in the United States experiences some form of domestic violence over the course of their lifetime, undocumented migrant women, once in the country, are considerably more likely to experience domestic violence and to endure it for a longer period of time. Regardless of where the abuse takes place or whether the perpetrator is documented or undocumented, the undocumented status of the woman as well as undocumented migration itself can become tools for the perpetrator, who may often threaten to report the woman to immigration authorities and have her deported or to separate her from her children (if in the country of origin, taking them across national boundaries into the United States, where as undocumented individuals without legal identity, they become part of a shadow population that goes undetected). In some cases such abuse can directly motivate women's undocumented migration; they enter the United States illegally in search of children that have been abducted from them by family members.

An undocumented victim of domestic abuse is often unaware that legal options exist to support her in leaving the abusive situation, which leads her to be easily intimidated by the perpetrator's threats to report to immigration authorities and "have her deported." On the condition that they cooperate with authorities in the prosecution of the perpetrator, wives of undocumented spouses can apply for a U-Visa for immigrant victims of serious crimes. Undocumented wives of U.S. citizens or legal permanent residents can file an I-360 petition with immigration, with the possibility of gaining permanent residency or a work permit. The process provides immigration authorities the discretion to halt or delay pending deportation. Despite these resources, reporting a perpetrator of domestic violence to authorities continues to be daunting to undocumented women, as the legal process does not guarantee that they will be able to remain in the country or with their children after their case has been decided.

Migration and Women's Status in Sending Communities

There are many theories on the impact of large-scale migration on women's (presumed) inferior status in relation to men in the developing countries from which the majority of undocumented migrants originate (primarily Mexico and other Latin American countries). As single women increasingly migrate, and even married women migrate completely separate from their spouses, some argue that this gendered "independent" migration reflects improvements in women's status within Mexico, where many communities consist mostly of women, children, and the elderly, since the majority of working-aged men have already migrated to the United States. On the other hand, it also reflects a serious lack of economic and educational opportunity for women in the sending communities and country of origin. At the same time, women's status and roles can be facilitators of their own migration and of men's.Some even have the non-traditional role of people smugglers.

The combination of increased economic responsibilities and unequal gender opportunities that would permit women to fulfill these responsibilities in their place of origin could be considered "push factors" which compel women to seek opportunities elsewhere. Such push factors vary from country to country and from community to community. However, certain "pull factors" in the United States, including changes in U.S. immigration policy over the years, have also shaped whether or not women migrate, which ones migrate, how they migrate, and their motives for doing so.

Female Migration as a Means to Empowerment

Some women migrate believing they will gain improved status and independence through economic opportunity in the United States. Although this is sometimes true, during migration and once in the United States many women continue to be subjected to distinct forms of sexual harassment and gender violence. While some men, women, and couples adopt more "liberal" or "American" ways of relating to one another, others do not, and new forms of submission emerge. Changes in women's status in Mexican-American families that were once believed to be a result of acculturation are now being called into question as similar changes have also been observed in their original communities.

Katherine Careaga

See Also: Culture; Domestic Violence; Domestic Work; Families; Family Reunification; Family Structure; Gender Roles; Human Trafficking; Migration; Violence against Women Act (VAWA).

Further Reading

Donato, Katharine M., and Evelyn Patterson. 2006. "Women and Men on the Move." In *Crossing the Border: Research from the Mexican Migration Project*, edited by Jorge Durand and Douglas S. Massey. New York: Russell Sage Foundation.

Durand, Jorge, and Douglas S. Massey. 1992. "Mexican Migration to the United States: A Critical Review." *Latin American Research Review* 27.2.

Hondagneu-Sotelo, P., ed. 2003. *Gender and U.S. Immigration: Contemporary Trends.* Berkeley: University of California Press.

Hondagneu-Sotelo, Pierrette. 1994. *Gendered Transitions: Mexican Experiences of Immigration.* Berkeley: University of California Press.

Luibheid, Eithne. 2002. *Entry Denied: Controlling Sexuality at the Border.* Minneapolis: University of Minnesota Press.

Simon, Rita J., and Margot DeLay. 1984. "The Work Experience of Undocumented Mexican Women Migrants in Los Angeles." *International Migration Review* 18.4. Special Issue: *Women in Migration.*

Workers' Rights

In 2003 Advisory Opinion OC-18 of the Inter-American Court of Human Rights ruled that the international commitment to nondiscrimination extends into the workplace and that, therefore, undocumented workers may not be discriminated against in the terms and conditions of their work. Federal and state laws reinforced the international ruling, though undocumented workers are not legally permitted to seek employment unless they have work authorization. In the United States, work authorization can be established by providing certain documents to authorities, such as a Native American tribal document, U.S. birth certificate, U.S. passport, U.S. citizen identification (ID) (form I-197), an ID card for the use of a legal permanent resident (a "green card"), Social Security card (unless stamped "not valid for employment"), Certification of Birth Abroad of U.S. Citizen (FS-545 or DS-1350) or a Department of Homeland Security document authorizing employment.

However, workers who are undocumented still have certain rights. Regardless of whether work was obtained legally or illegally, once an employment relationship has been entered into, all workers have the right to equal protection and equal access to recourse if their rights are violated. Equal protection includes equal rights to safe and healthy working conditions, a fair wage, reasonable working hours, judicial and administrative guarantees, protection against discrimination, the prohibition of child labor, access to state health services and workers' compensation, contributions to state pension systems, and freedom of association, the right to collective bargaining and organization to improve working conditions.

An exception to this last principle came with a U.S. Supreme Court decision in 2002 with *Hoffman Plastic Compounds v. National Labor Relations Board (NLRB)*. It is widely regarded that this case marked a trend in the direction of limiting workers' rights. In the *Hoffman* case, a worker without the legal authorization as defined by the

1986 Immigration Reform and Control Act (IRCA) was denied back pay after he was fired by the company for union organizing. Attorneys for the NLRB argued that the undocumented worker was illegally fired because under federal labor law an employer can be held liable for firing an employee who engages in union-organizing activities. In such cases the employers would be liable for any back pay for work not performed due to his termination. However, in *Hoffman,* the U.S. Supreme Court decided that the employee could not collect back pay for work not performed because he was an undocumented worker. The majority opinion argued that awarding back pay to those in the country illegally ran counter to the law set by IRCA that the NLRB had no authority to enforce or administer. They further argued that the award would have condoned prior violations of immigration laws and would have condoned and encouraged future violations. The dissenting opinion argued the exact opposite: that the back pay award would penalize employers for hiring undocumented workers (a violation under IRCA) and in this way deter unlawful activity that immigration laws sought to prevent.

Though by law undocumented workers have equal workplace protections and access to government recourse, the reality is that these workers are the most vulnerable to violations of their rights and the least likely to access administrative and judicial recourse. Undocumented workers are highly vulnerable to workplace abuse, as they tend to have lower English-language skills and little formal education, which limit their access to information on workers' rights and recourse. For example, employers provide health and safety information to workers so they are aware of the risks associated with their work activities, can perform work safely, and file a workers' compensation claim if an accident occurs on the job site. Such written materials and trainings are often provided only in English (although most are also available in Spanish), leaving many workers without the information needed with which to protect themselves. Also, lack of English fluency and education disadvantages workers who are asked to sign a document—such as a contract or disciplinary action—that they are not able to read and understand, but which asks them to provide the signature in order to verify understanding. Undocumented workers also tend to have fewer job skills, which lends to their overrepresentation in low-skilled, low-wage, and often dangerous jobs, where there is high exposure to physical, chemical, and biological hazards. Due to economic need and a lack of social networks, together with a lack of access to the labor market, undocumented workers are forced to accept substandard work conditions, discrimination, endangerment, wage theft, and overall discrimination.

Given their vulnerability, undocumented workers are less likely to complain about the violations of their workplace rights as complaints are often met with employer indifference, retaliation (such as a reduction in hours or pay), or job loss. Furthermore, fear and mistrust of government officials and law enforcement agencies, fear of discovery by immigration officials, apprehension and deportation, and fear of the realization of an employer's threats to their safety or employment all deter undocumented workers from filing complaints or challenging abusive employers. Those who opt to report violations to agencies such as the Occupational Safety and Health Administration (OSHA), Equal Employment Opportunities Commission (EEOC), or Department of Labor (DOL)—government agencies which enforce workers' rights—are met with obstacles such as limited access to translation and materials in the worker's first language, a complex and inflexible U.S. regulatory system, and fear of collaboration between these labor law–enforcement agencies and Immigration and Customs Enforcement (ICE).

Due to the unique vulnerability of undocumented workers, faith-based and other organizations work to advocate for and assist undocumented workers. The worker rights movement historically stems from the work of the following: settlement houses (in the twentieth century, over one hundred settlement houses were established to assist immigrant workers in urban areas by offering educational programs, challenging unjust employers, and advocating for progressive legislative initiatives), labor lyceums and the Jewish Workmen's Circle (in 1900, the Workmen's Circle became a national organization and created labor lyceums, centers where labor unions and workers met for education and to plan campaigns), the Catholic labor schools (between the 1930s and 1960s, the Catholic church sponsored over 100 labor schools in order to strengthen their involvement in the labor movement), and farm worker services centers (religious organizations and farm workers partnered to develop these centers in which they educated farm workers about their rights, connected them with lawyers, organized, and advocated for fair legislation). Today, three networks dominate the advocacy efforts for immigrant workers' rights—the National Day Labor Organizing Network or NDLON (the largest of the networks, which focuses primarily on day laborers), Interfaith Worker Justice or IWJ (known for its mobilization of the faith community around workers' issues), and Enlace (an international network with centers in the United States, Mexico, China, Indonesia, and some European nations). Generally, these organizations educate workers on their workplace rights and organizing skills, provide social services, engage in campaigns that target specific employers and change local, state and national policies, and assist workers in accessing and utilizing government complaint processes, together with developing ally support networks.

There are hundreds of local immigrant-rights organizations that also assist undocumented immigrants by providing information to workers, and assisting them to reclaim unpaid wages or seek redress for employer abuses. For example, the Coalición de Derechos Humanos (CDH), a Tucson, Arizona, community-based immigrant rights organization that since 1998 has assisted undocumented immigrants with complaints regarding a wide range of issues ranging from consumer fraud to harassment by immigration enforcement authorities. Individuals come to CDH to initiate complaints because they trust the organization and feel safe from law enforcement interference. The largest categories of complaints documented by Derechos were those that were related to job dismissals that occurred after workers voiced objections about their treatment, their pay, or about a potential job hazard, or unpaid wages. By maintaining a fear of dismissal, employers silence workers and sustain a systematic undercounting of offenses. The constant threat of unfair dismissal, the incessant and cumulative assaults on their performance and dignity, can take a toll physically, psychologically, and emotionally as confrontations can take weeks and even months to play out. Less is known about the workforce abuses suffered by undocumented women workers. As a subset of the undocumented worker population, women are less likely to engage in legal remedies to address their problems, especially when discriminated against at work, and less likely than the other labor force members to call oppressive treatment an injury or discrimination.

The process of filing a complaint against an abusive employer usually consists of a visit to the CDH office where victims are asked to fill out forms. The initial form collects pertinent personal information. Additional forms help the staff member collect the information that is useful in filing a complaint, e.g. the name of the employer, the employer's contact information, copies of any substantiating documents, and if necessary, a record of hours worked and wages due. Respondents are also asked to provide a narrative of the incident, which can be oral or written. Many times disputes over unpaid wages are readily settled with employers when a staff member calls in behalf of the worker. If not, they might be more willing to come to an agreement with the workers when a staff member informs the employer that wage theft is against the law, regardless of the employee's legal status, and such a complaint may be filed against the employer with the Wage and Hour Division of the Department of Labor. Most employers will be reluctant to have the matter proceed, and in a good percentage of cases, will decide to resolve the matter more amicably. The advocacy and community education work of this organization thus represents the wider struggle taken up by similar organizations across the United States to call attention to the human and economic rights of immigrant workers.

Cristina Sanidad

See Also: Advocacy; Day Labor; Faith-Based Organizations; Immigrant Workers Freedom Ride; Labor Supply; Labor Unions; State Legislation; Wages; Workplace Injury; Work visas.

Further Reading

Bobo, Kim. 2009. *Wage Theft in America: Why Millions of Working Americans Are Not Getting Paid—And What We Can Do about It.* New York: The New Press.

Castro, Arnold, Kaori Fujishiro, Erica Sweitzer, and Jose Oliva. "How Immigrant Workers Experience Workplace Problems: A Qualitative Study. *Archives of Environmental and Occupational Health* 61:249–258.

Cleveland, Sarah. 2005. "Legal Status and Rights of Undocumented Workers. Advisory Opinion OC-18/03." *The American Journal of International Law* 99:460–465.

Gleeson, Shannon. 2010. "Labor Rights for All? The Role of Undocumented Immigrant Status for Worker Claims Making." *Law and Social Inquiry* 35:561–595.

O'Leary, Anna Ochoa. 2007. "Petit Apartheid in the U.S.-Mexico Borderlands: An Analysis of Community Organization Data Documenting Workforce Abuses of the Undocumented." *Forum on Public Policy: A Journal of the Oxford Roundtable.* http://www.forumon publicpolicy.com/papersw07.html#crimjus.

Workplace Injury

Undocumented workers are more likely to be engaged in high-risk occupations, such as construction, farm labor, and meat processing. Very often, these jobs do not include any benefits such as health insurance that they might use for a job-related injury.

Musculoskeletal injuries are the most commonly reported injuries. Farm workers suffer injuries of the skin and chemical exposure, and meat processors may suffer severe cuts to fingers and extremities. Together with job insecurity, undocumented workers may be reluctant to report injuries or seek professional health care for fear of losing their job or deportation; they may ignore or downplay any injury, or if they are medically treated for one, ignore restrictions for returning to work. Employers often prohibit sick leave and work stoppages, and many workers, especially if they are employed in remote locations such as farms and meat processing centers, are not provided transportation to seek medical care for an injury, and may not have enough money to pay for medical care. For all these reasons, workplace injuries go underreported. Instead, workers may seek over-the-counter remedies to deal with their injuries or seek traditional healers (Anthony et al., 2010). The underreporting and disregard of work-related injuries make undocumented workers particularly attractive to employers who are often desperate to find workers and welcome them only as long as they are physically able to work (Correales, 2003).

It is perhaps in acknowledgement that undocumented workers fill a critical and virtually permanent need in the nation's economy that a large number of states have provided some form of workers' compensation for those who have been injured on the job. However, in doing so, they find themselves at odds with the 1986 Immigration Reform and Control Act (IRCA) that prohibits employers from knowingly hiring undocumented immigrants (Correales, 2003). The case *Sanango v. 200 East 16th Street Housing Corp.*, 15 A.D.3d 36 (2004) illustrates this point.

On July 2, 1998 while a laborer on a construction site, Arecenio Sanango was injured when he fell fifteen feet from a ladder. Sanango was an undocumented worker and brought suit against 200 East 16th Street Housing Corporation, which later enjoined Tower Building Restoration Inc., the contractor who employed Sanango. The trial court awarded Sanango $2,452,000 in damages for pain and suffering and $96,000 for lost earnings. The defense objected to the damages of lost earnings due to the fact that Sanango's employment was illegal.

The appellate court conceded that although Sanango was undocumented he was entitled to recover damages for items such as pain and suffering, thus leaving intact the large portion of the award. At issue was whether Sanango could recover damages for his lost earnings. The court weighed the Supreme Court holding in *Hoffman Plastic Compounds v. NLRB*, which held that the Immigration Reform Act explicitly makes it illegal for employers to employ undocumented workers. Thus, awarding back pay to undocumented aliens runs counter to policies outlined by IRCA. The fear was that awarding such damages would be seen as condoning and encouraging future violations of the IRCA. Following the decision in *Hoffman*, the court held that Sanango could not be awarded damages for lost earnings due to his undocumented status. In other words, the undocumented laborer was entitled to damages that occurred due to pain and suffering, but lost earnings could not be recovered because their employment is deemed to be illegal. Overall, *Sanango* should be interpreted as a win for undocumented workers because he was entitled to an award due to injury on the job. In yet another court case, *Balbuena v. IDR Realty*, the New York State appellate court ruled that the employers were held liable for workplace injuries even though the workers were undocumented. In sum, the undocumented status of a laborer does not deprive him of his day in court, and employers are liable for workplace injuries regardless of their employee's legal status.

The court also weighed in with an opinion in a similar case in *Celi v. 42nd Street Development Project, Inc.* (2004). In this case, a New York state court judge upheld a claim filed in behalf of an undocumented worker, Rodolfo Celi. Celi had been seriously injured while performing demolition when he fell through an opening in the basement floor and crashed into the sub-basement. In response to charges that the company was negligent and had violated labor law, company attorneys argued that under *Hoffman,* Mr. Celi's undocumented status prevented him from seeking lost earnings because payment of such wages violated federal immigration law. However, in *Celi,* State Justice David I. Schmidt argued that the *Hoffman* decision did not mandate a change in New York law so as to require the dismissal of the plaintiff's claim to lost earnings. In other words, the state had the right to interpret workman's compensation rules. Celi's claim for award, $26,000 in past lost earnings and $900,000 in future lost earnings, was upheld.

Virginia is illustrative of a state weighing its demand for labor that has recently brought a high number of undocumented immigrants under its workmen's compensation laws. After many years of confusing and internally inconsistent legal holdings denying coverage to undocumented workers, the Virginia general assembly in 2003 amended the workers' compensation statute to include "aliens," regardless of legal status. In yet another state heavily dependent on the work of undocumented immigrants, Nevada, the state readily provides medical coverage and lost wages to undocumented employees under its workers' compensation laws. The popularity of this state as a tourist destination has fueled a dramatic economic growth, especially in industries where the demand for workers in hotel service and construction industries is readily filled by undocumented immigrants. Many of these jobs, such as construction, are physically arduous and often require workers to spend long hours outdoors in extremely high temperatures throughout much of the year. These jobs are not always attractive to legal residents or citizens. An inspection of eighty-nine construction firms in Las Vegas found that 39 percent of the employees appeared to be unauthorized to work in the United States (Correales, 2003).

Often not considered are the long-term effects that a work injury might cause. In *Tarango v. State Industrial Insurance System* in 2001, an undocumented worker sustained a back injury when he fell from an eight-foot ladder while installing sheetrock at a construction site. The worker suffered a permanent partial disability. After receiving medical treatment, the worker was cleared to return to the work, but the treating physician restricted the worker to permanent medium-duty work in which he was to lift no more than fifty pounds. Before his injury, Tarango was a drywall installer, which required him to handle unwieldy sheets of drywall weighing eighty pounds or more. In a normal day a drywall hanger can install between thirty and forty sheets of drywall on walls and ceilings. However, since Tarango's occupation required more activity than the medical clearance allowed, his physician recommended vocational rehabilitation. The employer did not offer the worker a light-duty job. The State Industrial Insurance System (SIIS) awarded payment for a ten percent permanent partial disability, but denied him all vocational rehabilitation benefits, absent proof of a legal right to work. This case illustrates the confusion that can be created by the contradiction between a system designed to assist the worker to return to gainful employment and a largely unenforceable federal statute that prohibits employing undocumented workers.

While several influential states have decided in favor of disabled undocumented workers, others continue to deny them those benefits, even where work related accidents result in life-long disabilities. This compounds the obstacles undocumented workers are likely to face caused by poverty and the lack of access to medical insurance (Brown and Yu, 2002). Although the Affordable Care Act passed during the Obama administration holds promise of insuring millions of individuals who have either been denied access to medical insurance or have not been able to afford it, undocumented immigrants will still be excluded from even purchasing insurance under this new health reform law.

Because of the high cost of private insurance, Latino workers in general are less likely to afford it (Brown and Yu, 2002). Many immigrants work in Latino-owned businesses, which cannot afford to offer employer-based health insurance (EBHI) to their employees. Moreover, a disproportionate number of immigrants work in informal service-sector jobs (domestics, and care-givers), or part-time or seasonal work (construction, agriculture, garment industries, food service), making them ineligible for EBHI. Even when they are eligible for EBHI, such occupations and the low wages they earn are not enough to pay their portion of cost-sharing health insurance plans (Brown and Yu, 2002). Many are thus unable to meet their most basic healthcare needs—regular check-ups, routine immunizations, and necessary medications, much less catastrophic injuries.

Anna Ochoa O'Leary and Alfredo Estrada

See Also: Day Labor; Health and Welfare; Landscaping Industry; Meat Processing Plants; Migrant Farmworkers; Shadow Population; Workers' Rights.

Further Reading

Anthony, Maureen, Evan Martin, Ann Avery, and Judith Williams 2010. "Self Care and Health-Seeking Behavior of Migrant Farmworkers." *Journal of Immigrant & Minority Health* 12.5:634–663.

Brown, E. Richard, and Hongjian Yu. 2002. "Latinos' Access to Employment-based Health Insurance." In *Latinas/os: Remaking of America,* edited by Marcelo M. Suarez-Orozco and Mariela M. Páez, 236–253. Berkeley: University of California Press.

Correales, Robert I. 2003. "Workers' Compensation and Vocational Rehabilitation Benefits for Undocumented Workers: Reconciling the Purported Conflicts between State Law, Federal Immigration Law and Equal Protection to Prevent the Creation of a Disposable Workforce." *Denver University Law Review* 81.2:347–413.

Workplace Raids

Undocumented immigrants face numerous challenges economically. Dire economic conditions in many countries have forced immigrants to come to the United States looking for work. The Immigration Reform and Control Act (IRCA) was implemented in 1986 and prohibited the hiring of undocumented workers. Many employers have reported that they prefer to hire undocumented workers as they work for less than naturalized or U.S. citizens. Employers in factory or agricultural arenas have admitted that it is more cost-efficient to pay a fine and hire undocumented workers, than to hire documented workers. Because of limited employment opportunities, undocumented immigrants tend to hold low-wage positions in areas such as agriculture, factory work, retail, construction, and service industries. Workplace raids tend to adversely impact people who work in these areas and that are in the country without the official work authorization.

Workplace raids have occurred all over the country and have had a significant impact on the communities in which they are conducted. The Department of Homeland Security (DHS), Immigration and Customs Enforcement (ICE), and occasionally Border Patrol have implemented workplace raids in an effort to curb undocumented immigration. ICE was developed in 2003 by the Bush administration. One of the main focuses of ICE became workplace enforcement that resulted in large-scale workplace raids across the United States.

Workplace raids have typically occurred at businesses that are suspected of hiring large number of immigrant laborers, such as in factories and industrial plants. Members of DHS, ICE, and the Border Patrol, as well as local law enforcement, plan raids and implement them without warning. Workplace raids can result in the apprehension and arrest of hundreds of undocumented workers at one time. Typically the undocumented employees are arrested, charged, detained, and put into deportation proceedings.

Contemporary news accounts have highlighted the issue of family separation among immigrant families as a consequence of intensified immigration enforcement raids throughout the United States. Subsequent policy reports have pointed to the consequences of these actions by focusing on the fate of the children—many who are U.S.-born—whose parents have been arrested for violations of U.S. laws related to residency and employment without official authorization and were detained and/or deported. These policy briefs have noted that in some cases children of immigrant detainees were left stranded for hours, and many others in the care of friends and relatives. In other cases, families affected by immigration enforcement operations now contend with unemployment and the inability to provide for their families. In yet other cases, officials have complained that persistent threats or perceived threat of immigration enforcement raids have subjected children to fear and trauma that has disrupted schooling. The magnitude and scale of this phenomenon must be considered in the context of the mounting numbers of deportation of parents who have U.S.-born children. DHS has estimated that between 1998 and 2007, more than 100,000 parents of U.S.-born children were deported from the country. By far, the agency that had the most number of deportation of parents with at least one U.S.-citizen child was ICE, the primary enforcement arm of DHS, responsible for the removal of 46,486 (Department of Homeland Security, 2012).

Some of the largest workplace raids ever conducted occurred on December 12, 2006 and March 6, 2007. Hundreds of ICE agents were involved in three different sites in the cities of Greeley, Grand Island, and New Bedford. Swift and Company meatpacking plants and a military contractor Michael Bianco, Inc. were companies suspected of hiring undocumented immigrants. Approximately 1,600 immigrants in total were questioned, detained and then either released or sent into deportation proceedings. ICE agents obtained a warrant to search the premises for undocumented workers or those using falsified documents (e.g. fake social security cards); they could be charged with identity theft. Those that did not have proper documentation with them were thought to be in the country illegally. Arrestees were held for hours before being allowed to contact their families and inform them of the situation. The large-scale nature of the raids combined with limited communication from ICE officials contributed to a general sense of chaos and fear. Children were not picked up from school and some were left at home because both of their parents had been involved in the raid. Communities began to question the policies of workplace raids, and research supports evidence that the raids may cause irreparable damage to children that have been traumatized and suffer from extreme anxiety related to the raids.

Similar large-scale raids followed suit and became more frequent across the country. In May of 2008 an Agriprocessors plant was raided in Postville, Iowa, where 389 immigrants were arrested, sending the small town into a state of panic. The impact on families and children was significant as families stayed home. One report mentions that half of the schools, six hundred children were absent the day following the raid. Another example includes a factory owned by Howard Industries Inc. in Laurel Mississippi, in August of 2008. At least 350 workers were detained and arrested.

Workplace raids were thought to come to an end with the Obama administration in 2008. Though large-scale raids have dwindled significantly, small-scale local raids persist. In Maricopa County, Arizona, Sheriff Joe Arpaio has spent thousands of tax dollars conducting small-scale raids without permission from the federal government. Sheriff Arpaio faced charges for abuse of power, nurturing a culture of bias, and could have cost the county millions of dollars in federal money. The Department of Justice found evidence of bias against Arpaio's office in a 2011 report after three years of investigation, but the United States declined to prosecute in 2012, and the office was not charged.

New forms of technology are quickly replacing workforce raids with systems such as the E-verify program. The E-verify program is a system that verifies new employees' work eligibility. It is an Internet-based system that compares information from an employee's Form I-9, Employment Eligibility Verification, to data from U.S. Department of Homeland Security and Social Security Administration records to confirm employment eligibility. This system detects if someone is providing a false identification or social security number and prohibits them from working. More than 288,000 employers, large and small, across the United States use E-Verify to check the employment eligibility of their employees. Employers that utilize the E-verify program must display posters in the window of the business advertising that they use it. If an employee's information does not match, they will receive a notification of Tentative Nonconformation or TNC Notice. However, there is a large margin for error within the E-verify system, and an estimated 2.5 million legal residents risk losing their jobs if the errors go undetected. E-verify is not mandatory for all employers; however, federal employees and employers in the states of Arizona and Mississippi are required to use the program. E-verify and the Department of Homeland Security recognize that some employers may violate the program rules and conduct discriminatory practices; thus they request that such practices be reported to DHS in order to protect the rights of the employees.

Despite the efforts made by the government to prevent undocumented immigrants from working, there remains an underground economy. Employment opportunities still exist in the domestic sphere, as well as in agriculture, and day labor sector. Though there are laws and regulations that protect people from employer abuse and exploitation, many undocumented immigrants may be unaware of their rights and afraid of deportation. Having limited options for work may contribute to undocumented workers tolerating employer abuse, loss of wages, and excessive hours of work. Many undocumented workers may be exploited and treated poorly by their employers and fear alerting the authorities because of their undocumented status.

Courtney Martínez

See Also: Governance and Criminalization; Identity Theft; Immigrant Workers Freedom Ride; Immigration and Customs Enforcement (ICE); Labor Supply; Policies of Attrition; Policy and Political Action; Postville, Iowa Raid; Workers' Rights.

Further Reading

Capps, Randy, Rosa Maria Castaneda, Ajay Chaudry, and Robert Santos. 2007. "Paying the Price: The Impact of Immigration Raids on America's Children." *National Council of La Raza,* 1–96.

Department of Homeland Security. 2012. "Deportation of Parents of U.S.-Born Children FY 2011, Second Half." http://www.lirs.org/wp-content/uploads/2012/07/ICE-DEPORT -OF-PARENTS-OF-US-CIT-FY-2011.pdf.

Hsu, Spencer. 2008. "Immigration Raid Jars a Small Town." *Washington Post,* May 18. http://www.washingtonpost.com/wp-dyn/content/article/2008/05/17/ AR2008051702474.html.

Lacey, Marc. 2011. "U.S. Finds Pervasive Bias Against Latinos by Arizona Sheriff." *New York Times,* December 15. http://www.nytimes.com/2011/12/16/us/arizona-sheriffs- office-unfairly-targeted-latinos-justice-department-says.html?pagewanted=all.

Nossiter, Adam. 2008. "Hundreds of Workers Held in Immigration Raid." *New York Times,* August 25. http://www.nytimes.com/2008/08/26/us/26raid.html.

Work Visas

Strategies for controlling immigration that have intensified since the mid-1990s have not necessarily resulted in restricting the demand for immigrant labor. A work visa is a document that proves that a given person is authorized to enter the country to work.

Usually these are issued by the host country to individuals seeking to work outside of their country of citizenship. In the United States, work visas are used to help fill a demand in an industry facing a labor shortage. In 2009, 1,703,697 individuals entered the United States with nonimmigrant work visas. Kretsedemas (2012) argues that in spite of immigration enforcement efforts in recent years, the rate of the number of workers who come legally to the United States using a variety of non-immigrant work visas has expanded. Over the course of the past several decades, the non-immigrant population that has been incorporated into the United States has increased at a rate thirty times the rate of the legal permanent resident (LPR) population. Because these work visas are temporary—often accommodating specialized needs or seasonal work—this estimate may include multiple entries during the space of the same year. These include persons coming to the United States with temporary legal status such as business visitors, suppliers of investment capital, technical experts and other professional skill occupations, as well as low-skill farm workers.

Many of the visas created for the purpose of professional exchange are the result of the North American Free Trade Agreement (NAFTA). Although these work visas are not the same as those given to legal permanent residents (LPRs), some eventually provide many a pathway to permanent residence. The time that work visa holders can spend in the United States varies by visa type. As a general rule, those granted to high-skilled workers can range from a year to six years. On the other hand, H-2 visas for low-skilled guest workers are typically for shorter durations. Moreover, low-skilled migrant workers, such as farm workers, are not granted the type of work visas that give them the option to become legal permanent residents in the United States. The tendency to recruit low-wage migrants as an *ad hoc* labor force that can be easily disposed of when no longer needed—explains why most of these workers become unauthorized migrants. The fact that workers are willing to assume the risks of being likely targets of workforce raids and resultant removal from the country speaks to their poverty and the dire need they have to work and provide for their families. In this way, the policies regulating the issuance of work visas are connected to and work to maintain a social stratification (Kretsedemas, 2012).

There are various types of work visas someone can get in order to work in the United States. One example of a work visa is the H1-B visa, which is for persons in specialty occupations who seek to work temporarily in the United States. According to the Immigration and Nationality Act (INA), in order to be granted this type of visa an individual must possess a highly specialized knowledge requiring the completion of a specific course of higher education. Examples of occupations in this visa category are fashion models and government research and development workers. Seasonal and agricultural worker visas are other examples of temporary workers, for visa type H-2A. This visa program allows for foreign workers to come and work for U.S. employers who need temporary agricultural jobs filled for which U.S. workers are not available. Another example of temporary worker visas available for foreign-born individuals to enter the United States is the O-1 visa. This visa type is for individuals with extraordinary ability or achievement in the sciences, arts, education, business, or athletics, or extraordinary achievements in the motion picture and television field.

Nonimmigrant visas are issued to individuals who wish to only work temporarily in the United States. Depending on the type of temporary work, some visa classifications require the prospective employer to obtain a labor certification from the Department of Labor for the prospective employee. Other forms of approval may also be requested from the Department of Labor.

In addition to labor certification requirements (if applicable), individuals must obtain an approved I-129 form from the United States Customs and Immigration Services before applying for a temporary worker visa at the U.S. embassy or consulate. The I-129 form must be submitted by the prospective employer at least six months in advance of the desired employment start date.

In order to apply for a temporary worker visa, there are specific requirements that must be met. The ultimate decision of whether a person is approved for a visa rests with the corresponding consulate office. These applications must be submitted at the consulate offices of the individual's country of origin. As part of the visa application process, an interview is required. Individuals between the ages of fourteen and seventy-nine must go through an interview with their corresponding contry's consulate. For individuals outside of this age range, interviews are not required unless requested by the consulate or embassy. Processing procedures vary from country to country with some requiring additional processing requirements. Processing requirements include submission of an online nonimmigrant visa electronic application (Form DS-160), a valid passport with a validity date six months beyond the applicant's expected stay in the United States, and one 2x2 photograph. In addition to these requirements, there are mandatory fees that go along with the application process for a work visa. In order to apply for a visa, applicants must pay a nonimmigrant visa application processing fee. If the visa is approved, there is also a mandatory visa issuance fee, and depending on additional specific details, an individual may have to pay additional fees associated with getting their visa.

In relation to families and the children of individuals who seek to come to work in the United States, the spouse and unmarried minor children of an applicant are eligible to apply for the same visa in order to join the main applicant. This has to be supported by documentation proving that the principal applicant will be able to financially support anyone they bring with them into the United States. The spouse or children of a temporary worker who have received visas through the worker are ineligible to work in the United States. There are exceptions if the spouse or children receive an employment authorized endorsement or appropriate work permit.

In order to qualify for a nonimmigrant visa, applicants need to provide proof of "binding ties" to a residence in their home country. This is in a sense to prove that the applicant has no intention of abandoning their home country permanently. This is a requirement for all work-visa types with the exception of the H1B, L-1, and O categories of visas. The misrepresentation of materials or facts, or evidence of other fraud during the visa application process, may result in the permanent refusal of a visa or denial of entry into the United States. Another note worth mentioning is that a visa is not a guarantee of entry into the United States While at the port of entry Customs and Border Protection officials have the authority to allow or deny entry into the United States.

Staying beyond the designated time (overstaying) on the visa documents will cause a person to be out of status. Being out of status is a violation of U.S. immigration laws and the consequences of this may cause one to be ineligible for future visa approvals and thus lose the privilege to return to the United States. In accordance with the Immigration and Naturalization Act, staying even one day past the date identified in the visa documents results in a voided visa.

Carolina Luque

See Also: Employment Visas; Immigrant Workers Freedom Ride; Immigration and Nationality Act (The McCarran-Walter Act) (1952); Lawful Permanent Residents Migrant Farmworkers; Overstayers; "Undocumented," label; U.S. Citizenship and Immigration Services (USCIS).

Further Reading

Kretsedemas, Phillip. 2012. "The Limits of Control: Neo-Liberal Policy Priorities and the US Non-Immigrant Flow." *International Migration* 50 (S-1): e1-e18.
U.S. Citizenship and Immigration Services: www.uscis.gov.

X

Xenophobia

Xenophobia is the unreasonable fears or hostilities towards persons or groups perceived to be foreign or strange. Its existence has been manifested wherever and whenever a cultural or ethnic group comes in contact with another. Many begin with assumptions made by the "in" group about the human qualities of the "out" group. Categorizing people into groups is an adaptive function that simplifies our complex social world, but leads to favorable biases for our own group (the "in-group"), and not for the "out-group." The result of this bias is that generally individuals generate positive ideas (about culture, intelligence, beauty) about their own in-group and formulate negative ones (such as viewing them as inferior) for members of the out-group. This is at the root of xenophobia, ethnocentrism, prejudice, and discrimination (Diaz et al., 2011). Public debates about immigration in the United States not only tend to exacerbate in-group–out-group notions but also translate into actions against the excluded group.

There are numerous examples of how xenophobia has played out in the United States with perhaps one of the most glaring in1882 when the U.S. Congress enacted the Chinese Exclusion Act, which altogether prohibited Chinese immigrants from entry into the United States, and from attaining citizenship. The Emergency Quota Act of 1921 and the subsequent Johnson-Reed Act of 1924 attempted to define, through immigration quotas, an ideal American population based on race and ethnicity. "Out-groups" included Africans, Mexicans, Eastern Europeans, and Asians. "In-groups" were those "ideal immigrants" that were notably from Western Europe. Delgadillo (2011:38) further pinpoints what was typically understood by the ideal in-group as a "hardworking, heterosexual, white ethnic male. . . [who] lifts himself and his family up by virtue of his own efforts, and as a result his descendents enjoy considerable wealth, and privilege."

A step in the opposite direction came with the 1965 Immigration and Nationality Act, which abolished the National Origins formula and provided the means with which the United States became more diverse through immigration, but not before other attempts were made to exclude "out-groups." In 1954, Operation Wetback forcibly deported and repatriated nearly four million undocumented Mexican nationals and their U.S.-citizen children. This last measure illustrates the xenophobic tactic of racialized labeling intended to demean and humiliate out-groups, and followed a long history of attempts to remove Mexicans from U.S. soil by legal means, fear, and violence. These actions against the Mexican "Other" occurred with impunity and without regard to their character, their length of stay in the United States, their work history, nor any familial relationships they may have had to American citizens.

Efforts to make for a more diverse society are threatened by xenophobia and nativism that seeks to portray immigrants as the cause of our social and economic problems. Frustrated by the U.S. Congress's inability to pass comprehensive immigration reform, state legislatures began to adopt measures in an effort to deter immigration, or encourage them to return to their country of origin, known as "policies of attrition." A watershed moment in this trend came with Proposition 187 in California in 1994, which attempted to restrict undocumented immigrants from accessing certain public welfare benefits. Although this law was struck down by a higher court, more laws continued to be proposed and enacted at both the federal and state levels. In Arizona alone, about thirty-seven such policies were proposed in 2006 among the five hundred anti-immigrant state-level bills introduced that year across the United States. In 2007, the number of bills dealing with immigrants peaked at 1,562 as every state in the union considered some form of immigration regulation. Recent state and municipal responses to the "broken" U.S. immigration policy can be understood as a xenophobic backlash that finds support by publically demonizing immigrants.

Since 9/11, the immigration issue has been more firmly linked to questions of national security in the public imagination. Since then, the government has asserted extraordinary controls over both immigrants and citizens that work to stifle the integration of newcomers into society (Delgadillo, 2011). The anti-immigrant fervor reached a new tipping point in the state of Arizona with Senate Bill 1070. This law, like others that came before, was thus not an isolated event but rather one in a long line of attempts to exclude immigrants. Soon after, several copycat bills were passed in other states, such as Alabama's HB 56. Arrocha (2010/2011) argues that by constructing the foreign as the Other and threat, these bills encourage xenophobia and empower groups with a strong anti-immigrant sentiment to become directly involved in the monitoring of immigrants, paralleling the immigration control duties of the U.S. Border Patrol. The results are an increase in racism and segregation. An irrational and often frenzied political rhetoric not only inflames hysteria but misinforms and helps manufacture the idea of a threat to the public posed by groups deemed as not belonging. For those who see such an immigrant group as a threat, integration and assimilation will always be a problem. However, such manifestations also harbor the potential for violence among those all too willing to vent their frustration on innocent victims.

The website of the Southern Poverty Law Center, an organization that tracks hate crimes in the United States, cites Federal Bureau of Investigation (FBI) statistics that show an increase in the number of violent crimes perpetuated against immigrants. As a way to understand xenophobia, the statistics show that the number of hate groups in the United States rose from 602 in 2000 to 888 in 2007. According to the FBI, 819 people were victims of anti-Hispanic hate crimes in 2006, up from 595 in 2003. This is a nationwide 40 percent rise in anti-Latino hate crime violence in three years. Although the majority of the hate crimes have taken place in the border states of California, Arizona, and Texas where immigration has been a contentious political issue since 2004, crimes against immigrants are not limited to the Southwest. Mainstream news outlets have blamed the spike in the violence against Latinos on the anti-immigrant rhetoric from hundreds of nativist groups and politicians. For example, in Shenandoah, Pennsylvania, Mexican immigrant Luis Ramirez, who had been in the country for six years working in agricultural fields and in factories,

Members of the Arizona Rangers stand outside a building while preparing to help the town marshals with crowd control during registration for the Minuteman Project in Tombstone, Arizona on April 1, 2005. At least 100 people registered for the month-long civilian volunteer operation to patrol the border for undocumented immigrants and report them to federal authorities. (AP Photo/Tom Hood)

was beaten to death. Witnesses to such crimes report hearing ethnic slurs as attackers carried out their violent acts. Also among the victims was thirty-eight-year-old Marcelo Lucero, an Ecuadorian immigrant who had been in the United States for six years. His murder came on the heels of Nassau County (New York) ordinances aimed at immigrants and designed to bar their hiring by county contractors. More recently, in December of 2012, a man who was believed to be Muslim or Hindu by his attacker was pushed onto the tracks of an elevated subway station in Queens and crushed by an oncoming train.

Thalia Marlyn Gómez Torres

See Also: Arizona; Arizona SB1070; Hate Crimes; Policies of Attrition; Racialized Labeling of Mexican-Origin Persons; Racial Profiling; Racism; State Legislation; *Strangers from a Different Shore; Strangers in the Land.*

Further Reading

Arrocha, William. 2010/2011. "Arizona's Senate Bill 1070: Targeting the Other and Generating Discourses and Practices of Discrimination and Hate." *Journal of Hate Studies* 9.1:65–92.

Delgadillo, Theresa. 2011. "The Ideal Immigrant." *Aztlán: A Journal of Chicano Studies* 36.1:37–67.

Diaz, Priscila; Delia S. Saenz, and Virginia S. Y. Kwan. 2011. "Economic Dynamics and Changes in Attitudes Toward Undocumented Mexican Immigrants in Arizona." *Analyses of Social Issues & Public Policy* 11.1:300–313.

Kanazawa, Mark. 2005. "Immigration, Exclusion, and Taxation: Anti-Chinese Legislation in Gold Rush California." *The Journal of Economic History* 65.3:779–805.

Leadership Conference on Civil Rights Education Fund. 2009. "Confronting the New Faces of Hate: Hate Crimes in America." Available at http://www.civilrights.org/publications/hatecrimes/escalating-violence.html.

Z

Zapotec People (Oaxaca)

The Zapotecs are an indigenous people who reside in the mountainous state of Oaxaca located in the southern region of Mexico. Research conducted by Lopez and Munro in 1999 shows that the Zapotecs from San Lucas (also known as San Luqueños) have been immigrating to the United States since 1968. Many San Luqueños emigrate out of financial necessity, while others are influenced by the positive experiences expressed by those who have previously journeyed to the United States.

Oaxacans have greatly depended on seasonal agriculture as a means of survival. However, in recent years, they have increasingly suffered the impact of increasing deforestation and soil erosion. Moreover, in the 1980s, they have been adversely impacted by the elimination of governmental funding to help support small farms (Sesia, 1990: 292). Traditionally, the Zapotecs of San Lucas have depended on farming as a primary source of survival, cultivating mainly maize, garbanzo beans, and squash, or they sell livestock such as chickens and goats. Residents increasingly turned to the cultivation of maguey cactus. However, due to the length of time the plant takes to mature, it is not a reliable source of income. The combination of these changes has resulted in increased migration to the United States.

The majority of San Luqueños crossed the United States/Mexico border through the Tijuana border region as undocumented immigrants with the assistance of a coyote, a human smuggler. Like most other immigrants who cross into the United States without proper documents, San Luqueños take a dangerous risk of being abused when relying on a coyote to guide and transport them. In the case of many San Luqueños who have crossed, some experienced no difficulties, while others had been taken advantage of, robbed or abandoned in the mountains by their coyotes. Once in the United States, like many other immigrants with a limited education, they obtain employment in the restaurant industry or other low-skill jobs. However, their full economic integration may be impeded by lack of the ability to speak Spanish or English. For this reason, many of them are initially relegated to low-skilled positions as janitors or dishwashers before eventually being promoted to cooks or waiters.

The initial immigrants from San Lucas were male. However, women have been immigrating since the late 1980s, many of whom were wives accompanied by their children who sought to reunite with their husbands and fathers who had immigrated before them. In addition, data indicates that single women have also begun to immigrate. A number of the initial male San Luqueño immigrants settled with the assistance of a family network, that is, one male family member would immigrate, find employment, then send money to assist other family members such as brothers-in-law and cousins to immigrate. Lopez and Munro (1999) inform us that the San Luqueño immigrants have primarily relocated to Southern California in the cities of Los Angeles, Santa Monica, Venice, Culver City, and the San Fernando Valley.

Although a number of Oaxacans have obtained U.S. citizenship status, the precise number who have obtained this status is unknown. As a result of the Oaxacan Indigenous laws, many Oaxacan who attain U.S. citizenship are still considered as members of their home communities. As for the San Luqueños obtaining U.S. citizenship, status does not alleviate them of their obligations to their communities of origin, namely regarding the *cargo* and *tequio* system (Lopez and Munro, 1999). The *cargo* system is a "hierarchy" of religious community positions. In order to be promoted to a higher position, one must have taken part in a *cargo* at a lower level. Men over the age of eighteen may be required to participate in one of the numerous cargos allocated every one to three years. The *tequio* system is also composed of men over the age of eighteen who provide community service work such as restoring roads or extinguishing fires. Members of these systems are required to maintain their obligations to their communities even if they no longer reside in their home communities (Lopez and Munro, 1999).

The inability of many San Luqueño immigrants to communicate in Spanish or English has made it difficult for them to adjust to their new environment. However, over time an essential social network has developed, which has assisted newer San Luqueño immigrants. These social networks began as a group of men meeting at a park in Santa Monica to play basketball and discuss matters occurring in their home communities, and to inform one another about employment opportunities. In addition, this informal social network provided the way to collect funds needed to return the remains of home community members who died while immigrating to the United States back to San Lucas.

Immigrants from Oaxaca often deny their Oaxacan identity because it is associated with Indigeneity or the status of being "Indian," particularly if you are an Indian or "Indio" (as they are referred to in Mexico and in Central and South America) from Mexico. "Indio" is a term that is often used disparagingly. It is associated with being a second-class citizen in the United States, Mexico and in parts of Central and South America. As a result, many Zapotec immigrants do not speak their Zapotec language for fear of being stigmatized or ridiculed and negatively stereotyped as "Indios." This discrimination against indigenous Oaxacans predisposes them to mistreatment in both Mexico and the United States. As a result of their indigenous as well as undocumented status many Zapotecs experience discrimination by both Caucasian and "Mexican-born," as well as other Latino groups (Lopez and Munro, 1999). The mistreatment that Zapotecs have experienced includes: being paid lower wages, especially in the agriculture industry in California, and particularly harsh exploitative conditions such as having to work long twelve-plus hours per day in the fields and wage theft. Often they are subjected to these abuses because of their inability to communicate in Spanish or English. In addition, they are taken advantage of by unscrupulous employers who know that the workers may be unaware that they are being abused. By comparison, their employment situations in the United States are often better than the opportunities they had in their country of origin. As a result, employers are easily tempted to relax standards of fair employment practices. Thus, immigrants' lack of awareness combined with their inability to communicate in either Spanish or English renders them vulnerable and defenseless against these abuses.

Zapotec children are also subjected to marginalized or unjust and unfortunate experiences such as being placed in bilingual Spanish classes even though they do not speak the language. This is due to California educators not being familiar with their indigenous language and assuming that they speak Spanish since they are from Mexico. However, a majority of the children inevitably learn Spanish and English at the same time as a result of their exposure to them.

Although some San Luqueños have endured and continue to experience challenges in the United States, many have established a home life here. At present there is a considerable population of San Luqueños in the United States, primarily residing in the Los Angeles area. As of 2013, California has close to three hundred thousand Oaxacan Indian migrants, and more than half of them live in Southern California (Quiñones, 2012). These San Luqueños and other Oaxacans have established many small businesses such as restaurants, bakeries, barber shops, and artisan shops selling traditional Oaxacan art (Lopez and Munro, 1999:145). A large proportion of the population have taken jobs in restaurants and some have been able to open their own. In addition, many San Luqueños have completed their education in the United States by graduating from high school and/or attending college. Finally, in 1996 the Organización Quiaviní was developed in Southern California in order to formally unite the San Luqueños and to maintain the social networking created by the initial immigrants.

Dina Barajas

See Also: Culture; Indigenous People; Kanjobal Mayans; Small Business Ownership; Social Interaction and Integration; Transnationalism.

Further Reading

Instituto Nacional de Estadística, Geográfica e Información (INEGI). 1990. *XI Censo General de Población y Vivenda 1990. Estado de Oaxaca.* Aguascalientes, Mexico: INEGI.

Lopez, Felipe H., and Pamela Munro. 1999. "The Zapotec of San Lucas Quiaviní." *Aztlan: A Journal of Chicano Studies* 24.1:129–149.

Programa Nacional de Acción Tercera Evaluación: Mexico y la Cumbre Mundial en favor de la Infancia. 1994. SEP. February.

Quiñones, Sam. 2012. "Bonds of tradition are a financial bind for Oaxacan migrants." *Los Angeles Times*, November 20. http://articles.latimes.com/2012/nov/20/local/la-me-oaxaca-jobs-20121121.

Sánchez, Ignacio Sarmiento. 1992. "*Migración Étnica Oaxaqueñia hacia Los estados Unidos.*" In *Migración Etniciadad en Oaxaca,* ed. Jack Corbett et al., 99–104 Nashville: Vanderbilt University Publications in Anthropology.

Sesia, Paulo. 1990. "*Salud y Enfermedad de Oaxaca.*" *América Indígena* 50.2–3:291–308.

Recommended Resources

Anthologies: Collections of Research Articles on a Broad Range of Issues

Brotherton, David C., and Philip Kretsedemas, eds. 2008. *Keeping Out the Other: A Critical Introduction to Immigration Enforcement Today.* New York: Columbia University Press.

Dowling, Julie A., and Jonathan X. Inda, eds. 2013. *Governing Immigration through Crime: A Reader.* Stanford: Stanford University Press.

Durand, Jorge, and Douglas S. Massey, eds. 2004. *Crossing the Border: Research from the Mexican Migration Project.* New York: Russell Sage Foundation.

Haerens, Margaret, ed. 2006. *Illegal Immigration.* Detroit: Greenhaven Press.

Haines, David W., and Karen E. Rosenblum, eds. 1999. *Illegal Immigration in America.* Westport, CT: Greenwood Press.

López-Garza, Marta C., and David R. Diaz, eds. 2001. *Asian and Latino Immigrants in a Restructuring Economy: The Metamorphosis of Southern California.* Stanford: Stanford University Press.

Massey, Douglasl, ed. 2008. *New Faces in New Places: The Changing Geography of American Immigration.* New York: Russell Sage Foundation.

Millard, Ann V., and Jorge Chapa, eds. 2001. *Apple Pie and Enchiladas: Latino Newcomers in the Rural Midwest.* Austin: University of Texas Press.

Perea, Juan F., ed. 1997. *Immigrants Out! The New Nativism and the Anti-Immigrant Impulse in the United States.* New York: New York University Press.

Verea, Mónica, ed. 2012. *Anti-immigrant Sentiments, Actions and Policies in North America and the European Union.* Mexico City: Centro de Investigación sobre América del Norte (CISAN) de la Universidad Autónoma de Mexico (UNAM).

Monographs That Offer In-Depth Analysis of a Particular Subject

Bacon, David. 2008. *Illegal People: How Globalization Creates Migration and Criminalizes Immigrants.* Boston: Beacon Press.

Castro-Salazar, Ricardo, and Carl Bagley. 2012. *Navigating Borders: Critical Race Theory Research and Counter History of Undocumented Americans.* New York: Peter Lang.

Chavez, Leo R. 1992. *Shadowed Lives: Undocumented Immigrants in American Society*. Fort Worth, TX: Harcourt Brace Jovanovich College Publishers.

Chavez, Leo. 2008. *The Latino Threat: Constructing Immigrants, Citizens, and the Nation*. Stanford: Stanford University Press.

Delgado, Héctor L. 1993. *New Immigrants, Old Unions: Organizing Undocumented Workers in Los Angeles*. Philadelphia: Temple University Press.

Doty, Roxanne Lynn. 2009. *The Law into Their Own Hands: Immigration and the Politics of Exceptionalism*. Tucson: University of Arizona Press.

Ettinger, Patrick. 2009. *Imaginary Lines: Border Enforcement and the Origins of Undocumented Immigration, 1882–1930*. Austin: University of Texas Press.

Gálvez, Alyshia. 2011. *Patient Citizens, Immigrant Mothers: Mexican Women, Public Prenatal Care and the Birth-Weight Paradox*. New York: Rutgers.

Gomberg-Muñoz, Ruth. 2010. *Labor and Legality: An Ethnography of a Mexican Immigrant Network*. Oxford: Oxford University Press.

Hayes, Helene. 2001. *U.S. Immigration Policy and the Undocumented: Ambivalent Laws, Furtive Lives*. Westport, CT: Praeger.

Hing, Bill Ong. 2006. *Deporting Our Souls: Values, Morality, and Immigration Policy*. Cambridge and New York: Cambridge University Press.

Hondagneu-Sotelo, Pierrette. 1994. *Gendered Transitions: Mexican Experiences of Immigration*. Berkeley: University of California Press.

Hondagneu-Sotelo, Pierrette. 2008. *God's Heart Has No Borders: How Religious Activists Are Working for Immigrant Rights*. Berkeley: University of California Press.

Inda, Johnathan Xavier. 2006. *Targeting Immigrants: Government, Technology, and Ethics*. Malden, MA: Blackwell Publishing.

Kanstroom, Daniel. 2007. *Deportation Nation: Outsiders in American History*. Cambridge, MA: Harvard University Press.

Kwong, Peter. 1997. *Forbidden Workers: Illegal Chinese Immigrants and American Labor*. New York: New Press.

Martin, David A., and Peter H. Schuck. 2005. *Immigration Stories*. New York: Foundation Press.

Martinez, Rubén, and Joseph Rodriguez. 2004. *The New Americans*. New York: New Press.

Massey, Douglas S., Jorge Durand, and Nolan J. Malone. 2002. *Beyond Smoke and Mirrors: Mexican Immigration in an Era of Economic Integration*. New York: Russell Sage Foundation.

Massey, Douglas S., and R. Magaly Sánchez. 2010. *Brokered Boundaries: Creating Immigrant Identity in Anti-immigrant Times*. New York: Russell Sage Foundation.

Myers, Ched, and Matthew Colwell. 2012. *Our God Is Undocumented: Biblical Faith and Immigrant Justice*. Maryknoll, NY: Orbis Books.

Ngai, Mae. 2004. *Impossible Subjects: Illegal Aliens and the Making of Modern America*. Princeton, NJ: Princeton University Press.

Orner, Peter, Annie Holmes, Jaykumar Menon, and Tom Andes. 2008. *Underground America: Narratives of Undocumented Lives*. San Francisco: McSweeney's Books.

Pérez, William. 2011. *Americans by Heart: Undocumented Latino Students and the Promise of Higher Education*. New York: Teachers College Press.

Plascencia, Luis F. B. 2012. *Disenchanting Citizenship: Mexican Migrants and the Boundaries of Belonging*. New Brunswick, N.J.: Rutgers University Press.

Rincón, Alejandra. 2008. *Undocumented Immigrants and Higher Education: Sí se puede!* New York: LFB Scholarly Pub.

Sadiq, Kamal. 2009. *Paper Citizens: How Illegal Immigrants Acquire Citizenship in Developing Countries*. Oxford: Oxford University Press.

Sheridan, Lynnaire M. 2009. *"I Know It's Dangerous": Why Mexican Risk Their Lives to Cross the Border*. Tucson: University of Arizona Press.

Stout, Robert Joe. 2008. *Why Immigrants Come to America*. Westport, CT: Praeger.

Suarez-Orozco, Carola, and Marcelo Suarez-Orozco. 2002. *Children of Immigration*. Cambridge, MA: Harvard University Press.

Thangasamy, Andrew. 2010. *State Policies for Undocumented Immigrants: Policymaking and Outcomes in the U.S., 1998–2005*. El Paso, TX: LFB Scholarly Pub.

Tichenor, Daniel J. 2002. *Dividing Lines: The Politics of Immigration Control in America*. Princeton, NJ: Princeton University Press.

Ungar, Sanford J. 1995. *Fresh Blood: The New American Immigrants*. New York: Simon & Schuster.

Yoshikawa, Hirokazo. 2011. *Immigrants Raising Citizens: Undocumented Parents and Their Young Children*. New York: Russell Sage.

Zavella, Patricia. 2011. *I'm Neither Here Nor There*. Durham, NC: Duke University Press.

Zlolniski, Christian. 2006. *Janitors, Street Vendors, and Activists: The Lives of Mexican Immigrants in Silicon Valley*. Berkeley: University of California Press.

Stories about Undocumented Immigrants

Alarcón, Alicia. 2004. *The Border Patrol Ate My Dust*. Houston: University of Houston, Arte Publico Press.

Cull, Nicholas J., and Davíd Carrasco, eds. 2004. *Alambrista and the U.S.-Mexico Border*. Albuquerque: University of New Mexico Press.

Hart, Dianne Walta. 1997. *Undocumented in L.A: An Immigrant's Story*. Wilmington, DE: SR Books.

Hellman, Judith. 2008. *The World of Mexican Migrants: The Rock and the Hard Place*. New York: New Press.

Jiménez, Francisco. *Breaking Through*. New York: Houghton Miflin.

Martinez, Rubén. 2002. *Crossing Over: A Mexican Family on the Migrant Trail*. New York: Picador USA.

Nazario, Sonia. 2007. *Enrique's Journey*. New York: Random House.

Pérez, Ramón (Tianguis). 1991. *Diary of an Undocumented Immigrant*. Houston: Arte Publico Press.

Regan, Margaret. 2010. *The Death of Josseline: Immigration Stories from the Arizona Borderlands*. Boston: Beacon Press.

Tobar, Hector. 2005. *Translation Nation*. New York: Penguin Books.

Documentary Films and Videos

Abandoned: The Betrayal of America's Immigrants. 2000. David Belle and Nicholas Wrathall [Crowing Rooster Arts; Bullfrog Films]. 55 min.

abUSed: The Postville Raid. 2011. Luis A. Argueta [New Day Films; Maya Media]. 70 min.

The Boxer. 2000. Felix Zurita [Television Trust for the Environment; Bulldog Films]. 27 min.

Children in No Man's Land. 2008. Anayansi Prado [Impacto Films]. 42 min.

Immigrant Nation! The Battle for the Dream. 2010. Esau Melendez, Elvira Arellano, and Diego López [New Day Films]. 96 min.

Inocente. 2012. Sean Fine and Andrea Nix Fine [Salty Features]. 40 min.

Letters from the Other Side. Heather Courtney [Front Porch Films; Corporation for Public Broadcasting; New Day Films]. 72 min.

Los Trabajadores/The Workers. 2003. Heather Courtney [New Day Films]. 48 min.

Maid in America. 2004. Kevin Leadingham and Anayansi I. Prado [New Day Films; Impacto films; Women Make Movies]. 60 min.

9500 Liberty. 2010. Annabel Park, Eric Byler, and Jeff Man [Interactive Democracy Alliance]. 80 min.

The Other Side. 2002. Chris Walker [Television Trust for the Environment; Bulldog Films]. 27 min.

Rancho California (por favor). 2003. John Caldwell [Berkeley Media]. 59 min.

Sin País (Without Country). 2010. Theo Rigby [New Day Films]. 19:35 min.

Troubled Harvest. 1990. Sharon Genasci and Dorothy Velasco [Women Make Movies]. 30 min.

The Undocumented. 2010. Marco Williams [Independent Lense/PBS]. 90 min.

Which Way Home. 2009. Rebecca Cammissa [HBO Documentary Films; Mr. Mudd/Documentress Films]. 83 min.

Websites

American Immigration Council. http://www.immigrationpolicy.org/. A non-profit organization providing research and reports aimed at educating the public about most current issues involving immigration today.

Harvard University Library Open Collections Program. http://ocp.hul.harvard.edu/immigration/. A web-based collection of historical materials from Harvard's libraries, archives, and museums that documents immigration to the United States from 1789 to 1930.

The Immigration Policy Center. http://www.immigrationpolicy.org/. The research and policy arm of the American Immigration Council, offering policy research and analysis.

The Mexican Migration Project. http://mmp.opr.princeton.edu/. A database that gathers social and economic data on Mexican-U.S. migration in a comprehensive database that is available to the public free of charge for research and educational purposes.

The Migration Information Source. http://www.migrationinformation.org/. The resource arm of the Migration Policy Institute (below), providing authoritative data from numerous global organizations and governments, and global analysis of international migration and refugee trends.

The Migration Policy Institute. http://www.migrationpolicy.org/. A nonprofit organization providing analysis, development, and evaluation of migration and refugee policies at the local, national, and international levels.

The Pew Charitable Trusts. http://www.pew.org/. A nonpartisan, nonprofit global research and public policy organization that offers reports on a range of issues to inform the public and policy makers, and to stimulate civic life. Includes the Pew Hispanic Center, http://pewhispanic.org, which provides information on Latino immigrant issues.

The U.S. Census Bureau. http://www.census.gov/. The U.S. Census Bureau, a division of the Department of Commerce, offers reports and data on immigration: http://www.census.gov/population/intmigration, on migration within the United States: http://www.census.gov/hhes/migration/, and on foreign-born populations: http://www.census.gov/population/foreign/.

U.S. Department of Homeland Security. http://www.dhs.gov/immigration-statistics. The DHS has information on immigration statistics, forms, and links to related resources.

About the Editor and the Contributors

Editor

Anna Ochoa O'Leary, PhD, is an assistant professor in the Mexican American Studies Department at the University of Arizona, in Tucson. She coordinates the Binational Migration Institute at that institution. She holds a doctorate in cultural anthropology from the University of Arizona. Her published works include *Unchartered Terrain: New Directions in Border Research Method and Ethics* (coedited with Colin Deeds and Scott Whiteford) and *Chicano Studies: The Discipline and the Journey* (2007). Her Fulbright research on border crossings in 2007–2008 are the experiences of repatriated immigrant women has resulted in numerous publications.

Contributors

Yesenia Andrade is a graduate student in Mexican American Studies, University of Arizona, Tucson.

Zeynep Selen Artan is a doctoral candidate at the Graduate Center, City University of New York (CUNY).

Dina Barajas is a doctoral candidate at the University of New Mexico.

Drew Berns is a master's degree candidate in Mexican American Studies at the University of Arizona, Tucson.

Fazila Bhimji, PhD, is a senior lecturer in Film and Critical Media Studies at the University of Central Lancashire, Preston, UK.

Lucy Burns, PhD, is an associate professor in Asian American Studies, University of California at Los Angeles.

David A. Caicedo is a doctoral candidate in social psychology at the Graduate Center, City University of New York.

Maureen Campesino, PhD, RN, is executive director, Southwest Research Consulting, Tucson.

Miguel Angel Cano, PhD, is a postdoctoral fellow in the Department of Health Disparities Research at the University of Texas, M. D. Anderson Cancer Center, Houston.

Katherine Careaga, PhD, is a visiting instructor in Public Health at Fort Lewis College, Durango, Colorado.

Guadalupe Castillo, now retired, was a professor at Pima County Community College, Tucson.

Ricardo Castro-Salazar, EdD, is professor of political science and history at Pima Community College and associate researcher at the Center for Latin American Studies at the University of Arizona, Tucson.

Javier Cervantes has written on Latino American issues.

Kelli Chapman is a doctoral student in sociology at the University of Cincinnati.

Mauricio Cifuentes, PhD, LCSW, is an assistant professor at Augsburg College, Minneapolis, Minnesota.

Carolyn J. Craig, PhD, is a research compliance administrator at the University of Oregon, Eugene.

Ben DuMontier is a master's degree candidate at the Center for Latin American Studies at the University of Arizona, Tucson.

Meaghan Dwyer-Ryan, PhD, teaches at Eastern Connecticut State University, Willimantic.

Kevin Escudero is a doctoral candidate in the Ethnic Studies Department at the University of California, Berkeley.

Alfredo Estrada is a juris doctorate candidate, Valparaiso University School of Law.

Alexandra Filindra, PhD, is an assistant professor in the Department of Political Science at the University of Illinois at Chicago.

Jessie K. Finch is a doctoral candidate, the Department of Sociology, University of Arizona, Tucson.

Judith Flores Carmona, PhD, is an assistant professor in the Honors College and in the Department of Curriculum and Instruction at New Mexico State University, Las Cruces.

Myrna García, PhD, is a visiting assistant professor, Comparative American Studies Program, Oberlin College, Ohio.

César Cuauhtémoc García Hernández, JD, is a lawyer and associate professor of law at Capital University, Columbus, Ohio, whose articles have appeared in several law reviews and magazines.

Lisa Burrell Gardinier is Latin American and Iberian Studies librarian at the University of Iowa Libraries, Iowa City.

Shannon Gleeson, PhD, is an associate professor of Latin American and Latino Studies at the University of California at Santa Cruz.

Jenna Glickman has been a research assistant for the Binational Migration Institute at the University of Arizona, Tucson, and is currently serving in the Peace Corps.

Ruth Gomberg-Muñoz, PhD, is an assistant professor in the Department of Anthropology, Loyola University of Chicago.

Sofía Gómez is a doctoral candidate at the College of Public Health, University of Arizona, Tucson.

Thalia Marlyn Gómez Torres is a doctoral candidate at the University of California at Los Angeles.

Amy Baumann Grau is a doctoral candidate in the Department of Sociology at the University of Cincinnati.

Kathleen Griesbach is a graduate student in Latin American studies at the University of California, San Diego.

Bianca Guzman, PhD, is assistant professor in the Department of Chicano Studies, California State University at Los Angeles.

Stephen Haymes, PhD, is an associate professor in the School of Education, DePaul University, Chicago.

Josiah McC. Heyman, PhD, is chair and professor of anthropology at the University of Texas at El Paso.

Andrea Hernandez Holm is a doctoral student in Mexican American Studies at the University of Arizona, Tucson.

Aaron J. Howell, PhD, is a visiting scholar in the Department of Sociology at Oberlin College and Observatory, Oberlin, Ohio.

Alvaro Huerta, PhD, is a visiting scholar in the Department of Chicano Studies Research Center, and a visiting lecturer at UCLA's César E. Chávez Department of

Chicana/o Studies and Department of Urban Planning, University of California at Los Angeles.

Marcella Hurtado Gómez, PhD, is an internal program evaluator with the LEADER Consortium at Wright State University in Dayton, Ohio.

Maia Ingram, MPH, is deputy director of the Arizona Prevention Research Center at the University of Arizona College of Public Health, Tucson.

Jonathan Xavier Inda, PhD, is an associate professor in the Department of Latina/Latino Studies, University of Illinois, Urbana-Champaign.

Toni Griego-Jones, PhD, is a professor in the Teacher Education Program at the University of Arizona, Tucson.

Daniel Kanstroom, JD, is a professor of law at Boston College Law School.

David Keyes, PhD, is a visiting instructor in the Department of Sociology and Anthropology at Lewis & Clark College in Portland, Oregon.

Caleb K. Kim, PhD, MSW, is associate professor at the School of Social Work at Loyola University, Chicago, Illinois.

Nolan Kline is a doctoral candidate in anthropology at the University of South Florida, Tampa.

Philip A. Kretsedemas, PhD, is an assistant professor of sociology at the University of Massachusetts-Boston.

James Loucky, PhD, is professor of anthropology at Western Washington University, Bellingham.

Carolina Luque, MA, is director of Community Outreach for Scholarships A-Z, Tucson, Arizona.

Jillian C. Lyons is a doctoral candidate at Teachers College, Columbia University, New York.

Gerardo Mancilla is a doctoral candidate in curriculum and instruction at the University of Wisconsin–Madison. He is also a seventh-grade bilingual resource teacher at Cherokee Middle School in Madison, Wisconsin.

Ariana Mangual Figueroa, PhD, is assistant professor of language education at Rutgers, the State University of New Jersey.

Maddalena Marinari, PhD, is an assistant professor at Bonaventure Univerisity, Bonaventure, New York.

Courtney Martínez is a masters graduate from the Department of Mexican American Studies at the University of Arizona, Tucson.

Daniel E. Martínez, PhD, is assistant professor in the Department of Sociology, George Washington University, Washington D.C. and an affiliate of the Binational Migration Institute in the Department of Mexican American Studies at the University of Arizona.

Isabel Martinez, MA, is a doctoral student in Epidemiology & Public Health at the Yale Graduate School of Arts & Sciences, Yale University, New Haven, Connecticut.

Martha Yamilett Martínez-Espinoza is a doctoral candidate in the Teacher Education Program, University of Arizona.

Erika Cecilia Montoya Zavala, PhD, is a professor and researcher at the Universidad Autónoma de Sinaloa, in Culiacán, Sinaloa, Mexico.

Afsaneh Moradian is a doctoral candidate in education at Universidad Autónoma Benito Juarez de Oaxaca, in Oaxaca de Juárez, Oaxaca, Mexico.

Moira A. Murphy-Aguilar, PhD, is professor, Instituto Tecnológico y de Estudios Superiores de Monterrey, and visiting professor, Center for Inter-American and Border Studies, University of Texas at El Paso.

Tamara K. Nopper is adjunct faculty in sociology and Asian American studies at the University of Pennsylvania.

Mariela Nuñez-Janes, PhD, is associate professor of anthropology at the University of North Texas, Denton.

Nancy Ordover is an independent scholar and the author of *American Eugenics: Race, Queer Anatomy, and the Science of Nationalism* (2003). She lives in New York.

De Ann Pendry, PhD, is senior lecturer, Department of Anthropology, University of Tennessee–Knoxville.

Luis F. B. Plascencia, PhD, is an assistant professor of Anthropology, School of Social and Behavioral Sciences at Arizona State University, Tempe.

Suyapa G. Portillo Villeda, PhD, is an assistant professor of Chicano/a-Latino-a Transnational Studies at Pitzer College, Claremont, California.

Sara Potter has written for the Latin American Experience, ABC-CLIO's educational database.

Emily Puhl is a graduate student in Latin American Studies at the University of California, San Diego.

Rebecca Rangel is a doctoral candidate at Teachers College, Columbia University, New York.

Stephanie Reichelderfer is a doctoral candidate in the history department of the University of Maryland, College Park.

Robin Reineke is a doctoral candidate in the School of Anthropology at the University of Arizona, Tucson.

Leisha Reynolds-Ramos is a doctoral student in the Department of Spanish and Portuguese at the University of Arizona, Tucson.

Sarah Elizabeth Ryan, PhD, is assistant professor of communication and adjunct professor of African American and Women's Studies at the University of Texas at El Paso.

Sahar Sadeghi is a doctoral student of sociology at Temple University, Philadelphia, Pennsylvania.

Adrian Sanchez is a Doctor of Psychology (PsyD) candidate, Pacific University School of Professional Psychology, Hillsboro, Oregon.

Cristina Sanidad is a graduate student at Arizona State University, Phoenix.

Cheryl Shanks, PhD, is a professor of political science at Williams College, Williamstown, Massachusetts.

Gabriella Soto is a doctoral student in anthropology at the University of Arizona, Tucson.

Amanda Staight is a research assistant in the Department of Sociology, University of Cincinnati.

Sheila Lakshmi Steinberg, PhD, is a visiting professor at Chapman University, Orange, California.

Ryan Strode is associate director, Arabella Advisors, Chicago Office.

Ramona C. Tenorio, PhD, is associate professor, Department of Anthropology and the Cultures and Communities Program at the University of Wisconsin–Milwaukee.

Maura I. Toro-Morn, PhD, is professor of sociology and director of the Latin American and Latino Studies Program, Illinois State University, Normal.

Hector L. Torres, PsyD, is an assistant professor in the Clinical Counseling Department of the Chicago School of Professional Psychology, and director of the center for Latino/a Mental Health.

Char Ullman, PhD, is associate professor of literacy/biliteracy and educational anthropology, Department of Teacher Education, University of Texas at El Paso.

Maria Vidal de Haymes, PhD, is professor and director of the Institute of Migration and Global Studies at Loyola University, Chicago.

Anahí Viladrich, PhD, is associate professor, departments of Sociology and Anthropology at Queens College, New York, and in the Doctoral Program in Public Health, Graduate Center, City University of New York (CUNY). `

Francisco Villegas is a doctoral candidate in the University of Toronto's Anti-Racism and Cultural Diversity Office Program, Toronto, Canada.

Wendy Vogt, PhD, is assistant professor of Anthropology at Indiana University–Purdue University, Indianapolis.

Judith Ann Warner, PhD, is a professor of sociology and criminal justice in the Department of Sociology at Texas A&M International University, Laredo.

Courtney Waters is a graduate student in Public Health and Mexican American Studies at the University of Arizona, Tucson.

Tamar Diana Wilson is the author of *Women's Migration Networks* (2009) and several other books on immigration issues and on the lives of Latin American women.

Murphy Woodhouse is a graduate student in Latin American studies at the University of Arizona.

Ming-Chin Yeh, PhD, is an associate professor in the Nutrition and Food Science Program at CUNY School of Public Health at Hunter College, New York.

Christopher B. Yutzy is a doctoral candidate in the School of Anthropology at the University of Arizona, Tucson.

Ashley M. Zampogna Krug, PhD, is an instructor in history at Brookdale Community College, Lincroft, New Jersey.

Index

Note: Page numbers in **bold** indicate main entries.

Abbott, Grace, 163
Abuse of Undocumented Immigrants, Asylum Seekers, and Refugees in South America (report), 347
acculturation, **1–4**
  behavioral perspective of, 2–3
  cognitive acculturation, 3
  defined, 1
  discrimination and racism, 3
  familism, 3
  family functioning and, 249
  healthy immigrant effect, 2
  heritage consistency concept, 2
  language and, 4
  language brokering, 249
  Latino/a, 3
  Latino/as, 3
  Latino immigrant health and, 338
  markers of acculturation, 2
  parent-adolescent conflict, 4
  Second Language (ESL) classes, 4
  self-esteem and, 3
  social isolation, 3
  stress, 3
  theory, 1–2
acculturation stress, **5–6**
  defined, 5
  Escobar and Vega (2000) on, 6
  instrumental and/or environmental stress, 5
  isolation and, 5
  migrant farm workers, 6
  signs of, 5–6
  social and/or interpersonal stress, 5
  transmission of culture and, 138
activism, **7–11**

Bay Area Dream Act Coalition (BADAC), 9
California campus organizations, 9–10
civil disobedience, 9
collective action of undocumented university students, 10
Denver march, May 1, 2006, 7 (image)
"Development, Relief and Education for Alien Minors Act" (DREAM Act), 8–9
"Dream 9," 9
forms of, 7–8
Isabel Garcia, 8 (image)
local activism, 11
strategic invisibilization, 10
Underground Undergrads: UCLA Undocumented Immigrant Students Speak Out, 9–10
undocumented university students and, 7, 8, 10
Villegas (2010) on, 10, 11
Adalberto United Methodist Church, Chicago, 607
Addams, Jane, 163
Adler, Rachel H. (2006), 734
adult education, **11–14**
  adult literacy instruction, 12
  Arizona and, 11, 442
  Citizenship Education, 12–13
  Developmental Education, 12
  English to Speakers of Other Languages (ESOL), 12
  Family Literacy Act, 11
  Family Literacy program, 13
  funding of, 11
  GED preparation, 12
  goal of, 11
  hallmark of, 11–12

adult education (continued)
    limited English proficiency (LEP), 443
    naturalization interview and, 13
    prerequisites for naturalization, 13
advocacy, **14–16**
    advocacy organizations, 15–16
    civil rights and, 15
    defined, 14
    e-advocacy, 14
    empowerment and, 14
    immigrant rights and, 15
    impact of, 14–15
    issues needing advocacy, 15
    legislation and, 15
    types of advocacy, 14
    U. S. Bill of Rights, 14
Affordable Care Act (2010), 51, 86, 240,
    427, 635, 781
AFL-CIO, 417, 418
Agricultural Research, Extension, and
    Education Act (1998), 555
Agriculture Job Opportunity Benefits and
    Security Act, xxxv
Agriprocessors kosher meat plant raid, 418,
    493, 571–574
Agriprocessors v. NLRB ruling, 419
Aid to Families with Dependent Children
    (AFDC), 691
airports, **16–18**
    asylum and, 17–18
    biometrics and, 17
    documentation and, 16
    entry denial, 17
    hiding and, 16
    homeland security policy and, 18
    international terrorism and, 18
    irregular migration and, 16
    justification of homeland security, 18
    as a mechanism to trace irregular
        migrants, 17
    as ports of entry, 17
    small plane/small airport entry, 16
    unauthorized entry through, 16, 17
    US-VISIT program, 17
    visa violators, 16, 17
Akin, Jerry, 364–365
Alabama, 212, 238, 446, 790
Alambrista, 445
Alan Simpson (Sen.), 381

Alarcón, Francisco X., 446
Algeria, 437
Alien Contract Labor Law, xxvi
Alien Transfer and Exit Program (ATEP),
    615–616, 737
Allen, Horace, 193
allopathic medicine, 365
Almeida-Sanchez v. United States ruling, 724
Alurista, 44
Amara, Hosam, 573
*American Baptist Churches v. Thornburgh
    (ABC)* ruling, 520–521, 624
American Border Patrol, 490, 491
American Civil Liberties Union (ACLU),
    18–21
    areas of operation, 19
    commitment to the ideal of "free speech
        for all," 20
    date established, 19
    defined, 18
    on detainees, 156, 157
    financial resources, 19
    headquarters of, 19
    history of, 20
    immigrants and immigrant rights, 20
    Immigrants' Rights Project, 18, 20–21
    "Keep America Safe and Free"
        campaign, 20
    legal challenges of, 18–19
    main operations of, 19–20
    Roger Baldwin and, 19 (image)
    size of, 19
American Committee for Protection of
    Foreign Born, 98
American Competitiveness and Workforce
    Improvement Act, xxxv
American Competitiveness in the Twenty-
    first Century Act, xxxvi
American Friends Service Committee
    (AFSC), **21–23**
    beliefs and values, 21–22
    current activities of, 22
    date founded, 21
    headquarters of, 21
    immigrant and refugee rights, 21
    nationwide work of, 23
    "A New Path: Toward Humane
        Immigration Policy" report, 23
    Nobel Peace Prize and, 21

Project Voice, 22–23
Religious Society of Friends (Quaker) and, 21
American Friends Service Committee in Arizona, 149
American G.I. Forum, 473
American Immigration Law Foundation's Immigration Policy Institute, 203
American Immigration Lawyers Association, 377–378
American Indian Movement (AIM), 99
Americanization/100 Percentism campaign, xxviii
American Journal of Public Health, 555
Ammiano, Tom, 389
amnesty, **24–26**
　"chain migration," 25
　Daniel Griswold on, 24
　essence of, 24
　family reunification, 24
　Hispanization and, 24
　Immigration Reform and Control Act of 1986 (IRCA), 24, 25
　legalization program for undocumented immigrants, pros and cons to implementing, 24–25
　Mexican nationals and, 24
　prosperity increase, 25
　rebranding of, 24
　Rivera-Batiz (1999) on, 25, 26
　for undocumented immigrants, 24
　undocumented workers earnings, 25
　wage scale/earnings and, 25
Amnesty International, **26–28**
　activities of, 28
　agenda of, 27
　"Appeal for Amnesty 1961" campaign, 27
　campaigns of, 27, 28
　Cruel. Inhuman. Degrades Us All – Stop Torture and Ill-treatment in the "War on Terror" (report), 27
　date established, 27
　defined, 26
　establishment of, 27
　"Hostile Terrain: Human Rights Violation in Immigration Enforcement in the U. S. Southwest" (report), 27
　human rights of refugees and, 27
　international policies and regulations, 28
　Monthly Postcards to Prisoners Campaign, 27
　Nobel Peace Prize and, 28
　objective of, 26
　Partners in Crime: Europe's Role in US Renditions (report), 27
　political prisoners, 27
　at a rally in Boston, March 27, 2009, 26 (image)
　reports on human rights violations, 27
　Resolution Denouncing Torture—UN Resolution 3059, 28
　United Nations Human Rights prize, 28
　in the United States, 26–27
　on U.S. death penalty, 27
　When the State Kills (report), 27
Anarchist Exclusion Act, 240
Anderson, Benedict, 134
Andreas, Peter (2003), 59, 61, 70
Angeles de la Frontera group, 60, 149
Angel Island Immigration Station, 375, 446
Anti-Coolie Act, xxvi
Anti-Coyote Law (Arizona), 29, 126
　See also coyote (term)
Anti-Discrimination Notice, 273
Anti-Drug Abuse Act, 178
Antiterrorism and Effective Death Penalty Act, 733
"Appeal for Amnesty 1961" campaign, 27
Arellano, Elvira, 288, 607
Arguelles, Lourdes, and B. Ruby Rich (1984), 131, 133
Arizona, **28–32**
　Adult education, 11
　adult education programs, 442
　"Anti-Coyote Law," 29, 126
　Anti-Ethnic Studies bill, 583
　anti-immigrant laws passed in 2005, 29
　anti-immigrant stance of, 28–31
　Arizona English Language Learner Assessment (AZELLA), 233, 443
　Arizona Health Care Costs Containment System (AHCCCS), 29
　ARS 23–901 amendment, 30
　Aztlán, 44
　ban on ethnic studies curricula, 502
　border crossing, deaths from (2005), 60
　Chandler, 38

Arizona (continued)
  community concerns, 111
  day labor and, 143, 144, 145
  Deferred Action for Children Arrivals
    (DACA) program, 31, 35, 152
  Dolores Huerta, 502
  driver's license for undocumented
    immigrants, 185
  economics, 200–201
  employer sanctions, 217, 218
  English as Official Language bill, 29–30
  E-Verify, 30
  FLEA/LAWA law, 217, 218
  HB2281, purpose of, 502, 503
  HB2448, "AHCCCS eligibility for
    services," 30
  House Bill 2281, 583
  House Bill 2745, 644
  human smuggling law, xxxvii
  identity theft laws and immigration, 357
  immigrant health service restrictions, 494
  Jan Brewer, executive order of, 31
  language instruction, 4
  Legal Arizona Workers Act (employers'
    sanctions law), 30–31
  Legal Workers Act, 644
  limited English proficiency (LEP),
    441–442
  Mexican American Legal Defense and
    Education Fund, 29
  Mexican commuters, 307
  Minutemen Project, 111
  Nogales Unified School District suit, 442
  Operation Safeguard, 59, 103, 147,
    254, 376
  Personal Responsibility and Work
    Opportunity Reconciliation Act
    (PRWORA), 30
  Pima County Office of the Medical
    Examiner (PCOME), 148
  Proposition 200 ("Prop 200"), 28–29
  Proposition 203, 232, 441
  Proposition 300 ("Prop 300"), 30, 442
  protest backlash, 582
  Public Programs, Citizenship
    (HB 2030), 29
  racial profiling, 595, 596
  Senate Bill 1167, 29–30, 442
  Senate Concurrent Resolution 1031, 442
  South Side Presbyterian Church,
    Tucson, 245
  Southwest Council of La Raza, xxxi
  "Support Our Law Enforcement and Safe
    Neighborhoods" (SB1070), 31
  Tom Horne, 502
  Tucson Border Patrol sector, 243
  Tucson Unified School District (TUSD),
    502–503
  Valle del Sol v. Whiting et al., 31
  Yuma County, 481
Arizona DREAM Act Coalition, 15
Arizona: No Roosters in the Desert
    (Hartzler), 701
Arizona Rangers, 791 (image)
Arizona SB 1070, 32–36
  boycotts of Arizona and, 34
  Chamber of Commerce of the United States
    of America et al. v. Whiting et al., 35
  citizenship, exclusion of, 92
  controversy of, 32, 33–34
  copycat laws, 33
  date signed into law, xxxviii
  effect of, 285
  formal name of, 32
  hate crimes and, 315
  historical context, 33
  housing and, 344–345
  incarceration, 387
  injunction against, 34–35
  Jan Brewer and, 32, 33
  Janet Napolitano and, 33
  legal status and, 436
  Mexico's response to, 616–617
  national attention to, 33
  new crimes and, 33
  new provisions and greater policing
    powers of, 33–34
  Ninth Circuit Court of Appeals on, 35
  policies of attrition, 560
  portion struck down by Supreme Court, 35
  precursor of, 32
  protests of, 32, 34
  public outcry against, 34
  purpose of, 28, 32
  reputation of, 33
  response to, 34
  results of, 35–36
Sanctuary Movement, 607

Section 2(B), 35
sports, reaction of, 669
U.S. Census Bureau and, 739
U.S. District Judge Susan Bolton on, 34–35
xenophobia, 790
Arpaio, Joe, 783
Arrellano, Elvira case, 114
Arrocha, William (2010/2011), 790, 791
Asian American Hotels Owners Association (AAHOA), 657
Asian Exclusion Act, 309, 405
Asian Exclusion Act (Page Act), 580
assimilation, **36–39**
    anti-terrorism policies and, 37
    Arizona SB1070, 38
    attrition, 37–38
    Chandler, Arizona, 38
    Chandler Raids (1997), 38
    defined, 36
    discrimination and, 37
    Equal Protection Clause of Fourteenth Amendment, 37
    impeded assimilation, 39
    imperialist treatment, 38
    implications of second-class citizenship, 39
    mixed-status Latino families and, 37
    as a negative outcome, 36–37
    paradox of, 129
    post 9/11 immigration policy and, 37
    process of, 36
    state coercion, 38
    War on Drugs and, 38
Associated Press (AP), 457
asylum, **40–42**
    affirmative asylee state populations, 42
    age demographics, 42
    "asylee" status, 40
    asylum application, 40
    Asylum Office Corps, 40
    defined, 40
    denial of, 40
    difference between asylum seeker and refugee, 40
    economic hardship and, 41
    Executive Office of Immigration Review (EOIR), 40
    green card, 41
    number of asylees in the U.S., 41

number of individuals granted asylum affirmatively, 41
    Refugee Act (1980), 40
    refugee privileges, 41
    removal proceedings, 40–41
    requesting asylum, 40
    top ten countries for people granted asylum (2010), 41–42
    United Nations Convention Relating to the Status of Refugees Protocol (1951 and 1967), 40
    United Nations High Commissioner for Refugees, 40
    United States Citizenship and Immigration Services (USCIS), 40
Atkinson, C. S., 162
Atlacatl Batallion, 78
"Attrition through Enforcement: A Cost-Effective Strategy to Shrink the Illegal Population," 559
Aurora Healthcare Walkers Point Clinic, 321
Australian, 367
Aviles-Reyes, Miriam deportation, 338
Aw, Fanta, 681 (image)
Azevedo, Andre, 437 (image)
Aztlán, **42–45**
    anti-immigrant nativists, 42–43
    Aztecs' migratory journey, interpretations of, 43
    "Aztlán" poem (Alurista), 44
    balkanization, 43
    Chicomoztoc, 43
    defined, 42
    Denver Youth Conference, 44
    early scholarship on, 43
    El Movimiento Estudiantil Chicano de Aztlán ("Chicano Student Movement of Aztlán"), 44–45
    "gateway" states, 43
    Jack Forbes on, 44
    La Tira de la Pereginacaion (The Strip of the Pilgrimage) codice, 43
    location of, 43
    Mexica, 42
    Mexican-American War, 44
    Mexicas' migration from, 43
    Mexico City, 43
    poem of, 44

Aztlán (continued)
  separatist movement, 42
  Spanish conquest, 43–44
  Tenochtitlán, 43

Bahamas, 367
Balbuena v. IDR Realty ruling, 220,
  779–780
Baldwin, Roger, 19 (image)
Baltimore Sun, 79
Bancomer, 612, 613
banking, **47–50**
  alternative banking options affects, 49
  avoidance of banking system, 48
  banking fees, 49
  Bank of America, 48
  benefits of informal banking systems,
    48–49
  California Proposition 187, 47–48
  discrimination, 48
  discrimination by appearance, 47
  Federal Reserve Bank of Chicago
    research study, 48
  identification and, 48
  investment, 49
  loans to immigrants, 48
  matricula consular cards, 47
  McConnell and Marcelli (2007) on, 48, 50
  Mexican immigrant community, under
    serving of, 48
  migrant saving accounts, 49
  overcharging of immigrants, 48
  Ruth Horowitz, ethnographic study
    of, 48, 50
  social security numbers, 48
  tanda system, 48
  USA PATRIOT Act, 47
  Virginia study of migrants and banking, 49
Bank of America, 48
Barker, Sara Evans (Judge), 673
Barkin, Elliott R. (2003), 351, 354
Barletta, Lou, 344
Barnett, Roger, 490–491
Barranco, Francisco, 626 (image)
barriers to health, **50–52**
  in access to healthcare services, 51
  Affordable Care Act of 2010, 51
  discrimination, 50
  health disparities, 50–51

interpersonal discrimination, 52
  Juana and son Christian, 50 (image)
  National Institute on Minority Health and
    Health Disparities, 50
  number of undocumented immigrants in
    U.S., 50
  in quality of healthcare services, 51–52
barrios, **53–56**
  Chicano Movement, 54–55
  defined, 53
  expansion of, 55
  history of, 53–55
  importance of, 55
  Latino growth, 55
  Mexican American middle class, 54, 55
  Mexican American reformers, 54
  Movement for Justice in El Barrio,
    53 (image)
  protest and, 55
  relocation, 54
  rural area barrios, 54
  substandard conditions of, 54
  undocumented workers and, 55
  in the U.S., 53
  war refugees and, 54
Barros Nock, Magdalena (2009), 644, 646
Bartholdt, Richard, 161
Baseball in the Garden of Eden (Thorn), 671
Basic Naturalization Act, xxvii
Battalion 316 death squad, 79
Bay Area Dream Act Coalition (BADAC), 9
Beck, Glenn, 314
Belize, 437
Benenson, Peter, 27
Bennett, Michael (Sen.), 377, 682–683
Benson, Peter (2008), 480, 481
Bentley, Robert, 673
Biden, Joe, 173
Bilingual Education Act, xxxi
Bilingual Education Act (BEA), 231
bilingualism, **56–58**
  adult ESL classes, 56
  bilingual education, changes in, 58
  Bilingual Education Act (BEA), 57
  California Proposition 227 and, 57
  categories of bilingual education, 57
  Chicano Movement, 57
  defined, 56
  emergent bilingual population, 57

English-only approaches to bilingual education, 57
language acquisition, 56
in Massachusetts, 57
No Child Left Behind Act (2002) and, 58
options available to learn English, 56
undocumented immigration and, 57
Binational Health Week (*Semana Binacional de Salud*), 269
Binational Migration Institute, 164
Birthright Citizenship Act (2013), 274
Black, Diane (R- Tennessee), 274
Black Panther Party (BPP), 99
Bloomberg, Michael, 518
Boas, Franz, 162
Boeing Company, 564
Bolton, Susan (Judge), 34–35
Border Action Network, 104
Border Angels organization, 149
border crossing, **58–61**
    activist groups, 60
    amnesty, 60
    Andreas (2003) on, 59, 61
    "Border Patrol Strategic Plan 1994 and Beyond," 59
    Clinton administration and, 59
    deaths from, 59, 60
    defined, 58
    demographic changes, 59
    Doris Meissner and, 59
    hate groups, 60
    Janet Reno and, 59
    length of U.S. borders, 59
    militarization of border, 59
    NAFTA, effect on, 59
    nativism and, 59
    number of official U.S. entry points, 58–59
    Operation Gatekeeper, 59
    pre-clearance stations, 58
    ranch owners reaction to, 60
    risks of, 60
    undocumented immigrants contributions to U.S. economy, 60
    vigilantism, 60
    wall-erecting efforts, 59
Border Patrol Strategic Plan 1994 and Beyond: National Strategy, 59, 103, 483, 485

Border Protection, Anti-Terrorism, and Illegal Immigration Control Act (2005), 73, 114, 119, 474, 511
Border Security, Economic Opportunity, and Immigration Modernization Act (S. 744), 377–379, 380
Boykin v. Alabama ruling, 727
Brabeck, Kalina, and Qingwen Xu (2010), 86, 87
Bracero Program, **61–64**
    circumvention of, 63
    controversy, 63
    date ended, 64
    defined, 61
    demand for immigrant labor, 64
    discrimination, 63
    effect of, 61
    ending of, 63
    guestworker and contract labour policies, 305, 306
    immigration quotas, 64
    labor supply, 414
    Mexican laborers and, 62 (image)
    migratory worker patterns, 61
    number of Mexican Braceros, 542
    number of temporary agricultural work visas, 64
    Operation Wetback and, 63, 542–543
    outcome of, 543
    overview of, xxix, 62–63
    purpose of, 62
    unauthorized migration and, 63, 543
    visa, reduction in number, 64
    wages, 63
Bravo, Martin, 670 (image)
Brennan, William (Justice), 558
Brewer, Jan, 31, 32, 33, 185, 516, 760
Brignoni-Ponce, Felix-Humberto, 723–724
British Poor Laws, 769
Brown, Jerry, 67
Brownell, Herbert, 543
Brown versus Board of Education of Topeka, Kansas, 66, 84, 98
Buchanan, Pat, 165
Building a Race and Immigrant Dialogue in the Global Economy (BRIDGE) project, 508
Burger, Warren (Justice), 557
Burns, Lucy, 703
Bush, George H. W., 368

Bush, George W., 120 (image), 166, 488, 733, 759
Bush, Jason, 760

Cable Act, xxviii
Cain, Herman, 379, 563
Calderon, Felipe, 190
California, **65–68**
    Aztlán, 44
    border crossings, 60, 66
    "Border Patrol Strategic Plan 1994 and Beyond," 59
    Calexico, 233
    campus organizations, 9–10
    Chinese/Asian population of, 65
    Chinese Exclusion Act, 65
    De Canas v. Bica ruling, 215
    Dixon Arnet bill, 215
    DREAM Act, 67, 151, 399
    driver's license for undocumented immigrants, 185
    ethnic diversity of, 66
    forced labor, 167
    garment industry in, 282
    Gonzalo Mendez case, 66
    H-1B visas, 222
    history of, 65–66
    Hondurans in, 334
    House Bill 2030, xxxvii
    identity theft laws and immigration, 357, 361
    immigrant population of, 65, 67
    immigrants, influx of, 66
    immigrants, percentage of population of, 67
    incarceration, 389
    indigenous migrants, 392
    influx of undocumented migrants, 361
    laws affecting immigrant population of, 66–67
    Mexican-American War and, 65
    Mexican commuters, 307
    Mexican-heritage population, 9, 43, 55
    migrant contract workers, 305, 307
    Operation Gatekeeper, 254, 376
    Operation Wetback, xxx, 63, 66
    population of, 65
    Proposition 209, 100
    Proposition 227, 57, 232
    school segregation, 66
    Spanish language in, 237, 238
    in-state tuition for undocumented students, 152, 208, 322, 362
    Treaty of Guadalupe Hidalgo, 65, 66
    undocumented immigrant contributions to California's economy, 67
    undocumented university students and, 9
    US Latina/o educational pipeline, 105
    Zapotec people (Oaxaca), 795
    See also Proposition 187
Canadian border, **68–71**
    Alien Contract Labor laws, 69
    Border Crossing Card policy, 69
    the Canadian Agreement, 68
    Canadian laborers and, 69
    Chinese Exclusion Act, 68
    description of, 68
    effect of 9/11 on, 69
    General Order 86, 69
    history of, 68
    illegal activities along, 69, 70
    legality of documentation, 70
    local visitors crossing, 69
    migration to the U.S., 68
    NEXUS program, 70
    Peter Andreas on, 70
    terrorist threat, 69
    unauthorized migration, 718
    U.S. Border Patrol, 69, 736
    U.S.-Canadian trade and, 69–70
Cardoso, Federick, 482
CARECEN (Central American Resource Center), 336
Carter, Jimmy, 523
Carvajal, Scott, Cecilia Rosales et al. (2013), 481
Casa Michoacán (Chicago), 331
Castaneda v. Pickard ruling, 228
Castro, Fidel, 131
Castro, Rubin, 619 (image)
Catholic Church, **71–74**
    Catholic Charities, 74, 245, 246
    Catholic Charities Community Services (NYC), 74
    Catholic Legal Immigration Network Inc. (CLINIC), 71–72
    communion, 72 (image)
    Documented Failures: The Consequences of Immigration Policy on the U.S.-Mexico Border report, 73–74

immigrants and the, 71
on immigration, 71
Irish immigrants and, 71
John Paul II on the illegal migrant, 71
Justice for Immigrants: A Journey of Hope campaign, 72–73
Kino Border Initiative (KBI), 73
legal immigrants and, 71
migrant shelters of, 73
opposition to H.R. 4437, 73
Pedro Pantoja, 73
on the root causes of migration, 72
Strangers No Longer, Together on the Journey to Hope (letter), 72
top immigrant-sending countries and, 71
United States Conference of Catholic Bishops, 72
work of priests and social workers, 73
Catholic labor schools, 777
CC-IME (*Consejo Consultivo Instituto de los Mexicanos en el Exterior*), **74–76**
commissions of, 75
Consejo body, 75
convening of, 75
creation of, 74
date organized, 75
election of *consejeros*, 75
executive committee of, 75
goals of, 74–75
leaders of, 75
meetings of, 75
plenary sessions, 75
recommendations by, 75
Runiones Ordinarias, 75
webpage (www.ime.gov.mx), 75
Celi, Rodolfo, 220
Celi v. 42nd Street Development Project, Inc. ruling, 220, 780
Celler, Emanuel, 311, 312
Center for Immigration Studies (CIS), 38, 545, 559
Central American Civil Wars, **76–80**
Archbishop Oscar Arnulfo Romero, 77
Atlacatl Batallion, 78
Battalion 316 death squad, 79
casualties of, 77
the Cold War and Central America, 77
countries of, 77
El Salvador, 78

Guatemala, 79
history of war and violence in Central America, 77
Honduras, 79
John Negroponte, 79
Nicaragua (Contra War), 77–78
Reagan doctrine, 77
sanctuary movement, 77
School of the Americas, 77
undocumented immigrants and, 76–77
U.S. role in, 77–79
Chacon, Juan, 110
Chae Chan Ping v. United States, xxvii
"chain migration," 25
Chamber of Commerce of the United States of America et al. v. Whiting et al., 35
Chandler Raids (1997), 38
"Change-To-Win" (CTW), 418
Chavez, Cesar, 15
Chávez, César, 416
Chavez, Leo R. (2012), 640, 641
Chertoff, Michael, 418
Chicano Movement
Aztlán studies and, 44, 45
barrios, 54–55
bilingualism, 57
Chicomoztoc, 43
childcare, **80–83**
Adriana D. Kohler on, 82, 83
barriers to good childcare, 80–82
child care arrangements, 80
Edward Zigler on, 81, 83
Gabriella Gonzalez on, 80, 82, 83
Head Start, 81–82
Immigration Reform and Control Act (IRCA), 80
IRA/DHEW report, 81
Lynn Karol on, 80, 82, 83
Mary E. Lang on, 81
Melissa Lazarin on, 82, 83
Migrant and Seasonal Head Start (MSHS), 81–82
number of children of undocumented families in the U.S., 80
poor childcare, 80
programs, increasing access to existing, 82–83
public childcare services, 80

childcare (continued)
  research and politics (1960s–1970s),
    81
  U.S. citizenship of children, 80
children, **83–87**
  Alison Siskin on, 86, 87
  Brown v. Board of Education, 84
  community-based organizations (CBOs),
    86, 87
  D'Vera Cohn on, 84
  Federal Migrant Education Program
    (FMEP), 84
  Frank Ludovina, 84, 85, 87
  Ginny Garcia, 84, 87
  immigration crackdown, 85–86
  impacts of arrest, detention, and
    deportation on children, 85–86
  Jeffrey Passel on, 84
  Kalina Brabeck on, 86
  *League of United Latin American
    Citizens v. Wilson* case, 85
  mixed-status Mexican-American
    undocumented parents and, 84
  number of children living as members of
    undocumented families, 84
  Patient Protection and Affordable Care
    Act of 2010 (PPACA) and, 86
  Plyler vs. Doe case, 84–85
  Qingwen Xu, 86
  SNAP (Supplemental Nutrition
    Assistance Program), 87
  State Children's Health Insurance
    Program (SCHIP), 86
  Susan Morse, 84, 85, 87
  undocumented children (1960s), 84–85
  vulnerabilities along undocumented
    children, 86–87
Chin, Vincent, 112
Chinese, **87–92**
  Chinese Confession Program, 90
  Chinese Exclusion Act (1882), 65, 68,
    88, 90, 193, 676, 679
  Chinese Exclusion Act (1882) and its
    legacy, 89
  Chinese Six Companies, 90
  Chinese workers attacked at Rock
    Springs, 88 (image)
  current undocumented Chinese
    migrants, 91

Development, Relief and Education for
    Alien Minors (DREAM) Act, 91
  economic competition and, 88
  false identities, fabrication of, 89
  Foreign Miners Tax (1850), 88
  Fourteenth Amendment, 89
  Fujian migrants, 90–91
  Golden Venture (ship) and undocumented
    immigrants, 91
  Hart-Celler Act, 89
  Immigration and Nationality Act of 1965
    (Hart-Celler Act), 90
  large-scale migration to the U.S., 87–88
  Magnuson Act (Chinese Exclusion
    Repeal Act of 1943), 92
  methods of unauthorized migration,
    89–90
  "paper sons and paper daughters"
    process, 89
  People's Republic of China (PRC), 90, 91
  smuggling, 90, 91
  Taishanese migrants, 91
  Taiwan, 90
  transcontinental railroad and, 88
  "in transit migrants," 90
  United States v. Wong Kim Ark, 89
  upper-class Chinese migration, 90
  U.S. xenophobia, 789
Ching Chong Chinaman (Yee), 702
Chomsky, Norm, 689
chronology of undocumented immigration
    in the U.S., xxv–xxxix
Cisneros, Henry, 15
Citigroup, 499
citizenship, **92–94**
  African Americans and, 93
  Arizona Senate Bill 1070 and, 92
  Asians and, 93
  benefits of, 96
  birthright citizenship, 93
  Cable Act (1922), 92
  defined, 92
  equality and, 94
  Fourteenth Amendment, 93
  Magnuson Act (Chinese Exclusion
    Repeal Act of 1943), 92
  mainstream media and, 92
  Nationality Act (1870), 92
  Nationality Act (1907), 92

naturalization, 93
Naturalization Law (1790), 92
Operation Wetback, 93
posthumous citizenship, 93
second-class citizenship, 93
Treaty of Guadalupe Hidalgo and, 92
United States v. Wong Kim Ark, 93
U.S. interpretation of, 92
and whiteness, 92, 93
white supremacy and, 92
citizenship education, **94–96**
adult education programs and, 94
answers to the example subjects
questions, 96
benefits of citizenship, 96
the citizenship test, 95
citizenship test, short form of, 96
civics test, 95
disabilities and special exemptions, 96
English test, 95
funding of, 94
naturalization, cost of filing for, 94
naturalization, prerequisites for, 94–95
special considerations, 95–96
undocumented immigrants and, 94
civil rights, **97–101**
American Committee for Protection of
Foreign Born, 98
American India Movement (AIM), 99
anti-communism sentiment, 98
Aspira Consent Decree, 99–100
Black Panther Party (BPP), 99
Brown versus Board of Education of
Topeka, Kansas, 98
California Proposition 209, 100
Civil Rights Act (1964), 99
de facto discrimination, 100
expansion of, 100
Fourteenth Amendment, 100
gender equality, 99
General Brotherhood of Workers or
CASA, 99
groups participating in civil rights
movement, 98
Hart-Celler Immigration and Nationality
Act Amendments (1965), 100
League of Latin American Citizens
(LULAC), 97
Luisa Moreno, 98
Malcolm X, 99
Martin Luther King, Jr., 98
Méndez vs. Westminster School District, 98
Michigan affirmative action ban, 100
National Chicano Moratorium, 99
Paul Robeson, 98
persistent inequalities, 100
philosophies involved in, 97
racial segregation, 98
Rosa Parks, 98
Tlatelolco Massacre, 99
Universal Declaration of Human Rights, 98
U.S. Army soldiers of color and, 98
U.S. contradiction of its principles of
democracy, 97–98
Vietnam War, 99
Voting Rights Act (1965), 99
Young Lords, 99
Civil Rights Act (1964), 99, 227, 228
Clark, John P., 752
Cleveland, Grover, 161
Clinton, Bill, 358, 520, 521, 553, 558, 691
Clinton administration, **101–105**
Amnesty International report, 104
border deaths, 104
Border Patrol Strategic Plan 1994 and
Beyond, 103
border walls, 103–104
conclusion concerning, 104
criticism of, 104
demographic changes, 102
Illegal Immigration Reform and Immigrant
Responsibility Act (1996), 102
immigration, increase in, 101–102
impact on Mexico, 102–103
maquiladoras, 103
militarization of the U.S.-Mexican
border, 103
Native American tribal land, 104
North American Free Trade Agreement
(NAFTA), 102–103
Operation Gatekeeper, 103–104
Personal Responsibility and Work
Opportunity Reconciliation Act
(PRWORA), 337
results of border walls, 104
undocumented immigration and, 101
U.S.-Mexico border wall, 750
vigilantism, 104

Coalición de Derechos Humanos (CDH),
144–145, 148, 777
Cohn, Gary, 79
Cole, J. B. (1980), 131, 133
Coleman, James S. (1988), 648, 651
colleges and universities, **105–108**
Development, Relief and Education for
Alien Minors (DREAM) Act, 107
Hispanic-Serving Institutions (HSIs), 107
Illegal Immigration Reform and
Immigrant Responsibility Act
(IIRIRA), 105
Immigration Reform Bill (S744), 107
marginalization and, 105
Personal Responsibility and Work
Opportunity Reconciliation Act
(PRWORA), 105
Plyler vs. Doe decision, 105
states allowing undocumented students to
pay in-state tuition, 107
states denying undocumented students to
pay in-state tuition, 107
tuition, 106–107
undocumented students and, 105–106
U.S. Latina/o educational pipeline,
105–107
U.S. Latina/o educational pipeline, by
race/eccentricity, subgroup, and
gender (2000), 106 (table)
*Commerce of the United States of America
et al. v. Whiting et al.* ruling, 660
community activism, **108–111**
civil disobedience, 109
defined, 108
deportation, 108, 110
discrimination, 109
"Dream 9," 109–110
forms of, 109–110
immigrant activism, routes of, 110–111
immigration status and deportation, 110
importance of, 110–111
main point about, 108
notion of, 108
occurrence of, 108
peaceful protests, 109
to promote necessary change, 108–109
Salt of the Earth (movie) and, 110
Secure Communities Program, 110
shared experience, 108

social change and, 110
social media and, 109
spontaneous forms of collective
action, 108
sub-communities, 110
community concerns, **111–115**
anti-immigrant legislation, 113
in Arizona, 111
Barack Obama, reelection of, 114
Border Protection, Anti-Terrorism, and
Illegal Immigration Control Act
(2005), 114
Cinthya Felix and, 114–115
criticism, 113–114
deportation, 113
Development, Relief, and Education for
Alien Minors (DREAM) Act, 115
Elvira Arrellano case, 114
hate crimes, 113
Immigration and Customs Enforcement
(ICE), 113, 114
Immigration Reform and Control Act, 112
Latina/o, 113
Plyler v. Doe ruling, 112
political activism, 114
Proposition 187, 112, 113
racial violence, 112
Save Our State initiative, 112
support for immigrants, 112
Tam Tran, 114–115
terrorism, 113
undocumented immigration, 112–113
U.S. Constitution, 114
workplace raids, 114
compadrazgo, 139
Compean, Jose, 759
Complex Post-Traumatic Stress Disorder,
consequences of, 712–714
Conroy, Jeffrey, 314
consular identification cards, 270
Convention on Road Traffic, 185
Coolidge, Calvin, 405
CORE-El Centro, 321
Corker, Bob (Sen.), 377, 390
Corrections Corporation of America (CCA),
389–390
corridos, **115–117**
"*Contrabando y Traición*" (contraband
and betrayal), 116

defined, 115
impact of, 116
"Jaula de Oro" (The Gilded Cage), 117
Los Tigres del Norte, 116–117
parts of, 115
purpose of, 116
roots of, 116
of undocumented immigrants, 116
uses of, 115–116
"The Cost of Immigration" report (Huddle),
    xxxiii
Council of Economic Advisors, 203–204
counterfeit documents, **117–119**
acceptable documents for verifying
    identity for work, 118
black market in, 118
defined, 117
documents most frequently counterfeited,
    117–118
E-Verify, 119
genuine documents, use of, 118–119
Illegal Immigration Reform and
    Immigrant Responsibility Act
    (IIRAIRA), 119
Immigration Reform and Control Act
    (IRCA), 118
individual tax identification number
    (ITIN), 118
"no match" letters, 118
Social Security Administration (SSA), 118
counterterrorism and immigrant profiling,
    119–124
asylum seekers, 122–123
border control defined, 121
Border Protection, Anti-terrorism, and
    Illegal Immigration Control Act, 119
civil liberties and, 120
criticism of, 120, 122, 123
electronic border and counterterrorism, 121
electronic border defined, 121
Enhance Border Security and Visa Entry
    Reform Act (2002), 119
Haitian asylum seekers, 123
legal status expired or revoked, 122
monitoring practices, 120–121
Muehler et al. v. Mena decision, 122
noncitizen removable and terrorism, 120
Operation Tarmac, 122
profiling, 122

raids, 122
screening, 123
security threats, unauthorized migrants
    as, 121–123
September 11 Commission, 120
targeting, 122
US VISIT program, 121
coyote (term), **124–126**
"Anti-Coyote Law" (Arizona), 126
Arizona and, 126
cost of, 125
coyotes comunitarios (coyotes from the
    community), 125
defined, 124
Hondurans, 333
human smuggling and, 124, 126
migrants commodified, 125
pollero, interchangeable term, 124–125
reputation of, 125
undocumented immigrant families
    and, 248
"Creating and Fostering Fan Identification in
    Professional Sports" (Sutton, McDonald,
    Milne, and Climperman), 669
crime, **127–130**
Border Patrol, 127
criminal experiences of immigrants,
    129–130
domestic violence and rape, 129
English language usage, 128
Esequiel Hernandez case, 127
fraud schemes, 128
human trafficking, 129
identity fraud, 128
illegal immigrant label, 127
immigrant crime rings, 128
immigrant reporting of, 129
Immigration and Customs Enforcement, 127
mistaken identity, 127
money laundering, 128
paradox of assimilation, 129
poverty and, 128
smuggling, 127
technological advances and, 128
undocumented immigrants as victims
    of, 128–129
Crisostomo, Flor, 288
The Crossings (Paulsen), 446
Crowley, Joseph, 381

Cruel. Inhuman. Degrades Us All – Stop Torture and Ill-treatment in the "War on Terror" (report), 27
Cuban Refugee Adjustment Act, xxxi
Cubans, **130–133**
  child emigration, 132
  Cuban Revolution, 131
  economic embargoes, 131
  enclaves of, 131
  Fidel Castro, 131
  first-wave migrations, 130–131
  general rule of Cuban immigration
    policy, 131
  "Golden Exiles," 131
  homosexuality, 131, 132
  Johnetta B. Cole (1980), 131, 133
  Lourdes Arguelles and B. Ruby Rich
    (1984), 131, 133
  Mariel Boatlift, 131–132
  Marielitos, 132
  Pedro Zamora example, 132
  Pew Hispanic Center, 130
  political asylees, 131
  as political refugees, 130–131
  population of Cuba, 132
  Priority 2 (P-2) category and, 132
  rafters, 132
  second-wave migrations, 131
  statistics on Cubans in the U.S., 130
  travel restrictions to, 132
  undocumented immigration and,
    130–131
  U.S. Census figures on, 130
  U.S. immigration policies
    toward, 131
cultural citizenship, **133–135**
  assimilation, 134
  citizenship status, 133
  de facto citizens, 134
  defined, 134
  Flores (1997), 133, 135
  focus of, 134
  identity and, 134, 135
  imagined community, 134
  Latinas/os, 134–135
  Renato Rosaldo on, 134, 135
culture, **135–142**
  "Americanization Programs," 137
  ceremonial sponsorship (*compadrazgo*), 139

children and, 139–140
church and community events, 139
confidence and, 137
conformity to cultural norms, 139
corporate-style organization, 140
critical view of, 139–140
cultural change, 140–141
cultural plurality, 138
defining, 135–136
economic instability and poverty,
  persistence of, 136–137
education and, 140–141
ethnic identity and pride, 138
extinction of cultural traditions, 137
George I. Sanchez on, 137
individualism, 140, 141
logic of culture, 137
Octavio I. Romano-V on, 137
ritual celebrations, 139
scholarly notions concerning, 136
social inequalities and, 139
social networks, 138–139
transmission of, 138–139
U.S. Civil Rights Movement, 137–138
wedding, 136 (image)
women and, 139, 140, 141
Cuomo, Andrew, 518
Customs and Border Protection (CBP), 369

Daniels, Mitch, 672
David Henry Hwang Writing Institute, 703
Davis, Gray, 185
Dawnay Day Group, 53
day labor, **143–146**
  abuse education, 144
  abuses of undocumented workers, 144
  in Arizona, 143, 144, 145
  back wages and overtime claims, 145
  communities and, 146
  community education and advocacy, 144
  day labor centers defined, 143
  Day Labor Research Institute, 144
  defined, 143
  employee retaliation, 145–146
  formal day labor centers, 143–144
  informal areas for, 143
  informal economy and, 144
  National Day Laborer Organizing
    Network, 144

National Day Labor Study (Valenzuela), 144, 146
Operation Rollback, 145
voicing complaints, 145–146
wage theft, 144
Wal-Mart case, 145
work centers, 143
Day Labor Research Institute, 144
Deal, Nathan, 673
death, **146–150**
Binational Migration Institute, 148–149
border crossing and, 164
border enforcement and, 146
causes of migrant deaths, 148–149
Coalición de Derechos Humanos (CDH), 148
in detention centers, 157
immigrant rights organizations helping families of missing migrants, 149
market forces, 148
migrant deaths, increase in, 148
migrant fatalities, counting of, 148
Operation Gatekeeper, 147
Operation Rio Grande, 147
Operation Safeguard, 147
Pima County Office of the Medical Examiner (PCOME), 148
segmented enforcement efforts and, 147–148
statistics on immigrant deaths, 146
unidentified remains, missing people, 148, 149
U.S. Border Patrol, Tucson Sector, 148
U.S. immigration policy and, 147
De Canas v. Bica ruling, 215
de facto segregation, 685
Defense of Marriage Act (DOMA), 438, 439
Deferred Action for Childhood Arrivals (DACA), **150–153**
advocacy and, 15
applications for, 150
in Arizona, 31, 35, 152
Barack Obama and, 150, 181
concerns about, 150
criticism of, 151–152
deferred removal action, 150
defined, 150
Delahunty and Yoo (2013), 153
DREAM Act and, 151
driver's licenses, 152, 185
education policy and immigration law, 152–153
explanation of, 150
fee for, 150
importance of, 151
New Mexico, 516
number of applicants, 150–151, 153
number of individuals qualified for (estimate), 151
Plyler v. Doe case, 152
politics of, 151–152, 153
prosecutorial discretion, 150, 153
qualifications for, 150
research on undocumented students, 151
in-state tuition and, 152, 153
Texas Proposition 1403, 153
time period of, 150
Deferred Enforced Departure (DED), 695
Delahunty, Robert J., and John C. Yoo (2013), 153
De La Rosa-Loera, Martin, 573
Delgadillo, Theresa (2011), 789, 791
Dellums, Ron, 494
Denver Youth Conference, 44
Department of Homeland Security (DHS), 154, 368–369
deportable aliens, 385
deportation, **154–155**
appeal of deportation ruling, 155
bond fee, 155
common grounds for, 154
as defined by Department of Homeland Security (DHS), 154
detention, 154–155
historic deportation, 154
Immigration and Customs Enforcement (ICE), 154
individual rights in, 154
lateral, 737
lawful permanent residents and, 154
number of deportations as of fiscal year 2010, 154
Operation Wetback, 154
Order to Show Cause document, 154
process of, 154
"radical" aliens, summary deportation of, xxviii

deportation (continued)
  right to attorney, 155
  variations of, 154
  voluntary departure, 155
detention centers, **155–158**
  ACLU on, 156, 157
  asylum-seekers and, 156
  capacity of U.S. detention system, 157
  costs associated with, 157
  criminality and, 155
  deaths in, 157
  definition of, 155
  detainees in, 155–156
  Detention Watch Network, 157
  gender-based violence in, 165–166
  human costs of, 157
  Kerwin and Lin (2009), 156, 158
  length of detention, 155, 156
  Miriam Lucia Rondona and, 156
  number of detainees in, 156–157
  overcrowding of, 157
  standards for, 156–157
  Transactional Records Access
    Clearinghouse (TRAC), 155
Devil's Highway (Urrea), **158–161**
  Border Patrol, 160
  description of the Devil's Highway, 158
  Edgar Adrian Martinez and, 159
  honors for, 161
  Jesus Mendez, 160
  Luis Alberto Urrea and, 158–161
  NAFTA, 160
  portrayal of the desert, 159
  Sonoran desert, description of, 158–159
  Tohono O'odham oral traditions of, 159
  U.S. immigration policies and, 160
  Yuma 14, 158, 159
Dhingra, Pawan (2012), 657, 658
Diaz-Rico, Lynne T., & Kathryn Weed
    (2006), 231, 234
Dillingham report (1910), **161–164**
  contentious idea in, 162–163
  C. S. Atkinson and, 162
  Daniel Folkmar and, 162
  date printed, 161
  Dillingham Commission, creation
    of, 161
  Franz Boas and, 162
  Grace Abbott on, 163

Immigration Act (1921) and, 163
  Immigration Act (1970) and, 163
  immigration differentiation (old and
    new), 162–163
  immigration policy and, 163
  immigration restriction advocacy, 161
  impact of, 163
  Jane Addams on, 163
  literacy test, 161, 163
  new immigrants flaws, 163
  number of volumes, 162
  purpose of, 161
  quota law, 163
  racial divisions, 162
  recommendations of, 163
  Richard Bartholdt and, 161
  William Paul Dillingham,
    161, 162 (image)
  W. W. Husband and, 162
discrimination and barriers, **164–168**
  barriers to full incorporation into U.S.
    society, 167
  border crossing and death, 164
  criminality, perception of, 165
  defined, 164
  deportation, 166
  deportation and the Obama
    administration, 166
  fear and, 164
  financial burdens, 166–167
  forced labor, 167
  gender-based violence in U.S. detention
    centers, 165–166
  health care services, 167
  human rights, violations of, 165
  immigrants with legal permanent
    status, 166
  Immigration and Customs Enforcement
    (ICE), 165, 166
  immigration reform movement, 167–168
  methods to enforce immigration law, 166
  negativism, 164–165
  Pat Buchanan and, 165
  policymakers and, 165
  prison management and, 165
  privatization and, 165
  racial categorization, 167
  results of strictly enforcement-based
    immigration policy, 166

silent raids, 166
slavery, modern-day, 167
undocumented migrants and community,
    166–167
U.S. economy and the undocumented
    immigrant, 164–165
worksite raids, 166
displacement, **168–172**
blanket TPS for those displaced by
    political strife, 170
dates for DED and TPS issued for those
    displaced by natural disasters (2010),
    169–170
deferred enforced departure (DED), 169
defined, 168
Displaced Persons Act, xxx, 169
economic improvement and, 171
environmental disasters and, 170
examples of blanket TPS, 169
Hurricane Katrina and, 171
identification, lack of, 168–169
inadmissibility, 170
internally displaced persons (IDps), 168,
    171
Liberians, 170–171
NAFTA and, 171
nonrefoulement, 169
refugees and the U.S., 169
refugees defined, 168
stateless, definition of, 169
Temporary Protected Status (TPS), 169,
    170
TPS and natural disasters, 169, 170
TPS hardship, 170
TPS uncertainty, 170
UN High Commissioner for Refugees
    (UNHCR) and, 169
UN Protocol Relating to the Status of
    Refugees, 169
Dixon Arnet bill, 215
Dobbs, Lou, 314, 492
*Documented Failures: The Consequences of
    Immigration Policy on the U.S.-
    Mexico Border* report, 73–74
Domestic Council Committee on Illegal
    Aliens, 633
domestic violence, **172–174**
adjustment of status, petitioning for,
    173–174

alternative names for, 172
characteristics of risk, 172–173
defined, 172
intimate partner abuse, 172
legal rights, 173
T-visa, 173
undocumented immigrants and, 172,
    173–174
U-visa, 173
Victims of Trafficking and Violence
    Protection Act (VTVPA), 173
Violence Against Women Act
    (VAWA), 173
domestic work, **174–177**
advocacy groups, 176
composition of workforce, 175
defined, 174
demand for, 175–176
deportation, 176
"Domestic Workers' Rights in the United
    States" (report), 176–177
Domestic Workers United, 176
live in domestics, 176
recognition of, 175
undocumented domestics, 176
United Domestic Workers of
    America, 176
United Nations Human Rights
    Council, 176
U.S. Census Bureau estimate number
    of, 174
Victims of Trafficking and Violence
    Protection Act (VTVPA), 176
Violence Against Women Act (VAWA), 176
Domestic Workers Rights Bill, 685–686
Dominicans, **177–180**
Anti-Drug Abuse Act, 178
"backdoor pipeline," 178
criminality and, 178
Department of Deportees, 178
deportation, 178
dual citizenship, 179
education, 179
exclusion process, 178
Immigration Reform and Control
    Act, 178
in New York, 179
number of adding to undocumented U.S.
    population, 177–178

Dominicans (continued)
  phenotypic characteristics and
    removal, 178
  racial profiling, 178
  remittances, 178–179
  risk of life, 178
  transnational ties, 178–179
  visa limits, overstaying, 179
  voluntary return, 178
  women and children, 179
Donchak, Derrick, 316
Donnelly, Brian, 402
Doty, Roxanne Lynn (2009), 490, 492
"Dream 9," 9
The DREAM Act, **180–184**
  activism and, 8–9, 182
  advocacy for, 15, 184
  Asian youth and, 91
  candlelight procession for, 181 (image)
  date introduced, xxxvi, 180
  date re-introduced, 180
  date voted on, xxxviii
  Deferred Action for Childhood Arrivals
    (DACA) and, 151
  definition of undocumented alien student,
    181–182
  deportation, 180
  DREAM Act proposals, 183
  DREAMers defined, 182
  eligible population (potential) of, 183
  English Language Learners (ELL)
    and, 233
  explanation of, 180
  formal name of, 180
  high schools and, 323
  issues of undocumented students and,
    181–182
  Legal Permanent Resident (LPR) status,
    183
  National Council of La Raza (NCLR)
    and, 506
  Obama administration and, 534
  Obama administration Executive
    Order, 181
  overview of, 208–209
  Plyler v. Doe ruling and, 558
  pros and cons of, 183–184
  registered provisional immigrant (RPI)
    status, 180

representatives introducing, 180
  Senators introducing, 180
  in-state tuition, 182
Dream Activist, 323
Dred Scott decision (1857), 274
driver's licenses, **184–188**
  9/11 terrorist attacks and, 187
  in Arizona, 185
  authentication measures, 187
  in California, 185
  Convention on Road Traffic, 185
  identification, de facto form of, 186–187
  insurance and, 185
  international driver's license (IDL), 186
  international driving permit (IDP),
    185–186
  international visitors to the U.S. and,
    185–186
  photograph of applicant, 186
  photo identification cards, 186
  Providing for Additional Security States'
    Identification (PASS ID) Act, 188
  public safety vs. privacy, 187
  REAL ID Act, 188
  requirements for obtaining (basic), 186
  undocumented immigrant and, 185, 187
drug trade, **188–191**
  arms trafficking and, 190
  Department of Homeland Security
    and, 190
  drug cartels, 189, 190, 191
  escalation of, 189–190
  Felipe Calderon on, 190
  Michael Hayden on, 189
  militancy, 189
  money laundering and, 190
  Peña Nieto on, 190
  Secure Fence Act, 190
  undocumented immigrants and, 190–191
  undocumented immigration and,
    188–189
  U.S. demand for drugs, 188–189
  U.S.-Mexico border tunnel, 189 (image)
  U.S. national security and, 189
  violence and, 189
  war on drug trafficking (Mexico), 190
  the Zetas, 189
Dugan, Margaret Garcia, 583
Durbin, Dick (Sen.), 377

e-advocacy, 14
Eagleton Institute of Politics at Rutgers
    University, 513
East Asians, **193–196**
    Asian-American scholars on, 195
    Chinese Exclusion Act, 193
    discrimination, 193
    Hart-Celler Act, 193, 194
    in Hawaii, 193, 194
    Hawaiian Sugar Planters' Association, 193
    Horace Allen, 193
    Immigration Act (1965), 194
    interaction of Korean migrants, 195
    Japanese, 193–194
    Japanese-American incarceration, 194
    Japanese and Korean workers
        migration, 193
    Koreans, 193
    Korematsu v. United States, 194
    "model minority" term, 195
    national origin quotas, 194
    organized strikes, 193
    Oriental Exclusion Act, 193
    out-migration of Koreans, 194
    Schedule A visas, 194–195
    U.S. Census estimate of unauthorized
        Korean residents (2010), 193
    U.S. demand for, 194–195
Eastern Europeans, **196–200**
    academics, immigration of, 198
    "brain drain," 197
    Bulgarians, 198
    the Cold War and, 198
    Czechs, undocumented immigrants
        from, 198
    defectors, 197
    discrimination and vulnerability,
        197, 198
    early immigration to the U.S. from, 198
    Eastern bloc nations, 196
    fall of the Berlin Wall, 196
    immigrant sending countries, top ten, 197
    Lautenberg Amendment, 197
    mobility of, 197
    Moscow Parole Program, 197
    Nicaraguan Adjustment and Central
        American Relief Act (1997), 198
    Operation Rollback and, 199
    overstaying work visas, 198

"parole in the public interest," 197
    as percentage of U.S. immigrant
        population, 197
    Poland, undocumented immigrants from, 197
    rate of poverty among total noncitizens
        (2007), 198
    refugee status, denial of, 197
    support networks, 198
    U.S. quota system and, 197
    wakacjusze ("pleasure-seeking
        visitors"), 198
    Wal-Mart, federal racketeering class
        action lawsuit against, 199
    women and children, 198
economics, **200–206**
    affordable housing and immigrant
        construction workers, 204
    agriculture, 201
    business lobby stance on immigration,
        200–201
    conclusion concerning, 205
    economic restructuring, 200, 201–202
    economic restructuring defined, 201
    immigrant entrepreneurs, 204–205
    immigrant labor substitution and native
        job loss, 204
    immigrants as percentage of American
        labor, 201
    immigrants cost to taxpayers, 200
    Immigration Act of 1990 (IMMACT), 200
    immigration of the poor and unskilled, 200
    loss of jobs and immigrants, 200, 201
    low-skilled immigrant work force,
        value of, 201
    low-wage immigrant workers, 203
    New York Times/CBS poll on
        undocumented immigrants and U.S.
        jobs, 203
    non-gateway destinations, 202
    Robert Rector, 203
    service sector industries, 201
    surplus of unskilled immigrant workers,
        effects of, 201–202
    undocumented immigrants and public
        opinion, 202–203
    unionism, 202
    UNITE-HERE, union organizing, 202
    unskilled immigrants–skilled native-born
        complementarities, 203–204

economics (continued)
  U.S. economy and the undocumented
    immigrant, 164–165
education, **206–213**
  adult education, 209
  Bilingual Education Act (BEA), 206, 207
  Bob Goodlatte, 209
  DREAM Act, 208–209
  Dual-Language Bilingual Education, 207
  Head Start, 206
  high school students, 207–208
  Illegal Immigration Reform and
    Immigrant Responsibility Act
    (IIRIRA), 208
  Immigration and Customs Enforcement
    (ICE), 206
  Late-Exit Bilingual Education, 207
  Lau v. Nichols ruling, 207
  levels of, 206–208
  Mexican American Legal Defense and
    Education Fund (MALDEF), 206
  models of English language instruction, 207
  No Child Left Behind (NCLB), 207
  Plyler v. Doe ruling, 208
  in-state tuition, 208
  Structured English Immersion (SEI), 207
  Transitional or Early-Exit Bilingual
    Education, 207
  Two-Way or Dual-Language Immersion
    Bilingual Education, 207
Egypt, 437
Eitner, MIke, 588 (image)
El Concilio Manzo, 630
El Diario–La Prensa, purchase of, 663
Elementary and Secondary Education Act
  (ESEA), 231
elementary schools, **209–213**
  academic curriculum, 212
  Alabama, requirement for documentation
    status, 212
  defined, 210
  deportation, 211
  documentation, 210–211, 212
  English as a Second Language (ESL),
    211–212
  English Language Learners (ELL), 211
  exit level of proficiency in English, 212
  kindergarten, 210
  mixed immigration status, 209

  percentage of Mexican deportees, 211
  Plyler v. Doe ruling, 211
  school completion, 212
  segregation of undocumented students, 211
  states enrolling the most undocumented
    students, 210
  states with increasing undocumented
    student growth, 210
  statistics on undocumented immigrants,
    210
  U.S.-born children and mixed
    immigration families, 209–210
El Grito, 137
Ellis Island, xxvii, xxx, 374, 375
Ellison, Keith, 381
*El Movimiento Estudiantil Chicano de
  Aztlán* ("Chicano Student Movement
  of Aztlán"), 44–45
El Paso Times, 641
El Salvador, civil war, 78
El Universal, 612
Emergency Medical Treatment and
  Active Labor Act (EMTALA),
  337, 427
Emergency Quota Act (1921), **213–215**
  alternative name for, 213
  anti-immigrant sentiment, 214
  cheap labor, 213
  Chinese Exclusion Act, 214
  Chinese immigrant population, control
    of, 213
  date passed by Congress, 213
  ethnicity and race, use of, 214
  explanation of, 213
  Huntington on Mexican immigration,
    214, 215
  objective of, 213
  xenophobia, 789
Emigrant Labor Agency Law (Texas), 698
employer sanctions, **215–218**
  Arizona FLEA/LAWA law, 217, 218
  Arizona SB 1070, 218
  Contract Labor Law (23 Stat. 332), 217
  De Canas v. Bica ruling, 215
  Dixon Arnet bill, 215
  farm labor, 217
  FLCRA law, 217
  Immigration Reform and Control Act
    (IRCA), 215–216

McCarran-Walter Act and, 216
Page Act (18 Stat. 477), 216–217
policy actions predating IRCA, 216–217
Ronald Reagan and, 215
state employer sanction laws, 217
"Texas Proviso," 216
employment, **218–221**
  Balbuena v. IDR Realty, 220
  Celi v. 42nd Street Development Project, Inc., 220
  cheap labor search, 219
  employer responsibilities, 218
  flexible employment arrangements, 219
  Hoffman Plastic Compounds v. National Labor Relations Board (NLRB), 220–221
  immigrant rights, 219
  immigrants, common misperceptions about, 219
  independent contracting, 219
  Operation Rollback, 219
  Porter (2005) on, 221
  Sanango v. 200 East 16th Street Housing Corporation, 220
  undocumented immigrant workers and the U.S. economy, 221
  Wal-Mart case, 219–220
employment visas, **221–224**
  abuses, 222
  biometrics, 224
  employment verification, 224
  E-Verify, 224
  Fifth Preference EB-5 visas, 224
  First Preference EB-1 visas, 223
  Fourth Preference EB-4 visas, 223–224
  H-1B visa, 222
  H-1C visa, 223
  H-2A visas, 222
  H-2B visas, 222
  Immigration Reform and Control Act (IRCA) and, 224
  I-visa, 223
  L-1/L-2 visas, 223
  nonimmigrant NAFTA pro- fessional (TN) visa, 223
  O-1/O-2 nonimmigrant visa, 223
  permanent (immigrant) worker visas, 223
  permanent-based immigrant visa defined, 221

  photo matching, 224
  Q non-immigrant visa, 223
  R-1/R-2 visas, 223
  Second Preference EB-2 visas, 223
  temporary non-immigrant visa defined, 221
  Treaty Trade (E-1) and Treaty Investor (E-2) visas, 222–223
enclaves, **224–227**
  advantages of, 225
  aesthetics and, 225
  Chicago's Ukrainian Village neighborhood, 225 (image)
  Chinatown (New York), 226
  defined, 224–225
  disadvantages of, 226
  ethnic enclaves, examples of, 226
  Little Italy (New York), 226
  native language and, 225
  Pilsner (Chicago), 226
  social comfort and, 225
  social integration and, 226
  social networks and, 225
  undocumented immigrants and, 226
English as a Second Language (ESL) programs, **227–230**
  adult ESL programs, 229–230
  affordable adult ESL classes, 229
  Castaneda v. Pickard ruling, 228
  demand for adult ESL classes, 229
  education level of students in adult ESL classes, 229–230
  English-only laws, 227
  importance of English language, 227
  K-12 ESL programs, 228–229
  Lau v. Nichols ruling, 228
  Limited English Proficient (LEP), 228
  main task of ESL programs, 228–229
  No Child Left Behind Act, 228
  number of U.S. K-12 students classified as Limited English Proficient (LEP), 228
  obstacles to adult ESL classes, 230
  Plyler v. Doe ruling, 227
  right to public education, 227
  suppression of a second language, 227
  Titles VI and VII of the Civil Rights Act (1964), 227, 228
  variations in adult ESL programs, 229

English Language Learners (ELL),
  230–234
  anti-immigrant sentiment, 232–233
  approaches towards Bilingual Education,
    231
  Arizona English Language Learner
    Assessment (AZELLA), 233
  Bilingual Education Act (BEA), 231
  bilingual education programs, 231
  bilingual education standards, 232
  Calexico, California, 233
  DREAM Act and, 233
  Dual Immersion Bilingual Education, 231
  Early Exit Transitional Bilingual
    Education, 231
  Elementary and Secondary Education
    Act (ESEA), 231
  English Only, 232
  explanation of term, 230
  historical context of bilingual education,
    231
  Late Exit Transitional, 231
  Lynne T. Diaz-Rico and Kathryn Weed
    (2006), 231, 234
  motivation, 233
  Proposition 203, 232
  Proposition 227, 232
  Ron Unz on bilingual education, 232
  submodels for teaching English as a
    Second Language, 231
  undocumented students, 233
  World-Class Instructional Design
    Assessment (WIDA), 232
English-only movement, **234–239**
  in Alabama, 238
  constitutional issues involving, 236
  English Language Learners (ELL), 232
  English-only vs. demography, 236–237
  English-only vs. history, 235–236
  English-only vs. the market, 237–238
  explanation of, 234
  Hawaii, 236
  Hispanic population growth, 237
  historical challenges to, 235–236
  interrelated factors influencing, 235
  Louisiana, 236
  New Mexico, 236
  number of languages in the U.S., 235
  political considerations, 238

  political success of, 234–235
  protest against, 234 (image)
  Puerto Rico, 236
  as reactionary, 235
  Spanish and, 235, 236, 237, 238
  Treaty of Guadalupe Hidalgo and,
    235–236
  undocumented immigrant workers and
    the U.S. economy, 237
  U.S. Constitution and, 236
  as a U.S. public language, 237
Equal Educational Opportunity Act (1974),
  442
Escobar, J.I., and W.A. Vega (2000), 6
eugenics, 406
E-verify
  Arizona, 30
  Basic Pilot Program, 455
  counterfeit documents, 119
  employment visas, 224
  identification cards (ID), 353
  identity theft, 355
  overstayers, 546
  restaurants, 620
  U.S. Citizenship and Immigration
    Services, 119, 546, 744
  workplace raids, 783–784
exclusion, **239–241**
  Affordable Care Act and, 240
  Anarchist Exclusion Act, 240
  children and, 240
  Chinese Exclusion Act, 239, 240
  comprehensive immigration reform bill
    (proposed), 239
  core issue in practices of, 240
  examples of exclusion, 240
  grounds for exclusion, 239
  healthcare denial, 240
  of immigrants, 240
  Immigration and Nationality Act (INA),
    239
  Johnson-Reed Act, 240
  nationalism, 240–241
  political borders and, 240
  Proposition 187 (California), 240
  quotas, 240
  removal (formal deportation), 239
  social exclusion, 239, 240
  sociological repercussions of, 239

use of, 239
xenophobia, 239
Executive Office of Immigration Review
 (EOIR), 432
Executive Order 9066 (Roosevelt), xxix
Ex Parte Mitsuye Endo, xxx
Expatriation Act, xxvii
Expedited Citizenship of Aliens and Non-
 Citizen Nationals Serving in an Active
 Duty Status in the War on Terrorism, 488
"Expedited Enforcement Rules" of the
 IIRIRA, xxxiv
expedited removal, **241–244**
 apprehension numbers, 243
 criticism of, 243
 denial of admission, 241
 documentation and, 241
 explanation of, 241
 exponential growth of migrants crossing
  the border, 243–244
 goal of expedited removal process, 242
 Immigration and Naturalization Act
  (INA), 241
 INA, Section 212 (a) 6 (C), 241
 Notice and Order of Expedited Removal
  form, 243
 persons not subject to expedited removal
  proceedings, 242
 relief from expedited removal
  proceedings, 241–242
 resource savings of, 242–243
 U.S. Border Patrol and, 241, 242, 243

Fabric (Ong), 702–703
Faith-based organizations (FBOs), **245–247**
 Casa San Diego, 245
 Catholic Charities, 245, 246
 criticisms of, 247
 defined, 245
 evangelical and Protestant organizations,
  245
 FBOs in the U.S., 246
 Fe y Justicia (Faith and Justice), 245
 in Florida, 246
 Humane Borders, 245–246
 influence of, 246
 international FBOs, 246
 Islamic Center for North American
  Relief, 246

Jesuit Refugee Service (JRS)
 International, 246
Jewish Federation of North America,
 246
No More Deaths/*No Mas Muertes,* 246
Personal Responsibility and Work
 Opportunity Reconciliation Act
 (PRWORA), 246
religious obligation and, 245
Salvation Army, 246
services to marginalized populations, 247
South Side Presbyterian Church, Tucson,
 245
U.S. policies concerning, 246
volunteerism, 246
families, **248–250**
 acculturation, 249
 adult language dependency, 249
 border crossing, 248
 children of immigrant families, 249
 "coyotes," hiring of, 248
 defined, 248
 local laws and, 248
 migration and, 248
 mixed-status, 248
 parental authority, loss of, 249
 separation-reunification dynamic, 248
 social isolation, 249
 stages of migration, 248
 women of immigrant families, 248, 249
family economics, **250–253**
 child labor, 252–253
 globalization and, 251
 immigrant women as primary
  breadwinners, 253
 internal migration (China), 252
 long-term family separation, 252
 Mexican migrant family in desert, 251
  (image)
 migration as a income-generating
  strategy, 251–252
 transnational families, 252
 undocumented working mothers, 252
 vulnerability of undocumented
  immigrant families, 250
family reunification, **253–256**
 border enforcement, 254, 255
 defined, 253
 feminization of migration, 254–255

family reunification (continued)
Illegal Immigration Reform and
Immigrant Responsibility Act
(IIRIRA), 254
internal immigration enforcement
policies, 255
as legal process, 253–254
migration, reasons for, 254
NAFTA, 254
policies (harsh) related to border security,
254
separation-reunification dynamic, 254
support networks, 254
U.S. immigration policies and, 253
family structure, **256–259**
clash/mix of cultures, 257, 258
current trends in migration, 257
defined, 256
deportation, 257
divorce, 258
extended family structures, 256
factors impacting the nuclear family, 257
grandparents, 258
homosexuality, 258–259
migrant process, 257
new realities and, 256
nuclear family, 256–257
patriarchy and machismo, 256, 257, 259
sexuality, 258
social transformation, 256
transnational families, 257–258
types of family structures, 256
women, 258
FBI Integrated Automated Fingerprint
Identification System (IAFIS), 628
Federal Emergency Management
Association (FEMA), 369
Federal Land Law of 1851, 472
Federally Qualified Health Centers
(FQHCs), 427
Federal Migrant Education Program
(FMEP), 84
Federal Reserve Bank of Chicago research
study on immigrant banking, 48
Felix, Cinthya, 114–115
Fernandez-Vargas v. Gonzales, **259–261**
date of, xxxvii
defense argument, 260–261
implications of, 261

Justice David Souter on, 261
legislation involved, 260
overview of, 259–260
Fe y Justicia (Faith and Justice), 245
film and television representation, **261–266**
The Beautiful Country, 265
Borderline, 264
Born in East L.A., 264
Bread and Roses, 265
consequences of narrowly defined
portrayals of undocumented
immigrants, 263
A Day without a Mexican, 263–264
early representations of immigrants, 262
El Norte (The North), 264
Fast Food Nation, 265
fluctuation of media representations of
immigrants, 263
Fun with Dick and Jane, 265
Irish immigrants, 263
Italian immigrants, 263
La misma luna (Under the Same Moon),
266
Latinos, negative portrayal of, 263
Latino stereotype, 264
*Maria Full of Grace (María llena eres de
gracia),* 265
My Family/Mi Familia, 265
My Name Is Earl, 262
Nadine Velazquez, 262 (image)
popular films, portrayals of
undocumented immigrants in,
264–266
popular images of undocumented
immigrants, 262–263
self-image and identity of immigrants,
263
stereotypes, 261–262
*The Three Burials of Melquiades
Estrada,* 265
The Visitor, 265–266
Flake, Jeff (Sen.), 377
Flore, Raul and Brisenia, 315
Flores, Miriam, 442
Flores, W. V., and R. Benmayor (1997),
133, 135
Flores-Figueroa v. United States No. 08–108,
266–267
date and explanation of, xxxviii

Eighth Circuit Court opinion, 266
identity theft, 266, 267, 356
Justice Alito on, 266
Justice Breyer on, 266, 267
Justice Scalia on, 266, 267
Justice Thomas on, 266
Liparota v. United States, 267
overview of, 266–267
steps in government's argument, 267
Supreme Court opinion, 266
United States v. X-Citement Video Inc., 267
Florida, 246, 361, 399
Folkenflik, David, 457
Folkmar, Daniel, 162
Food Stamp program, 554, 769
Forbes, Jack, 44
forced labor, 167
Ford, Gerald R., 633
Forde, Shawna, 315, 760
Ford Foundation, 469
Ford Motor Company, 475
foreign consulates, **268–271**
consular identification cards, 270
consular services, 268–269
cultural programming, 270–271
estimated number of people living
outside country of origin, 268
health assistance, 269
immigrant integration programs, 270–271
importance of, 268
legal assistance, 269
Maintaining Connection with Homeland,
270
number of countries holding a chancery
in Washington D.C., 268
services for migrants in distress,
269–270
Vienna Convention on Consular
Relations (VCCR), 268, 269
"The Forgotton Prisoners" (Benenson), 27
Form I–9, **271–273**
acceptable leaves defined, 272
Anti-Discrimination Notice, 273
contents of, 272
documents needed, 273
formal name of, 271
Immigration Reform and Control Act
(IRCA) and, 271, 272, 382–383
List B, 272

List C, 272–273
mandatory completion of, 272
sections of, 272
Fourteenth Amendment, U.S. Constitution,
273–276
"anchor babies," 575
Arrellano case and, 114
assimilation and, 37
birthright citizenship, 93, 114, 273
Birthright Citizenship Act (2013), 274
California Proposition 187, 275
calls for repeal of, 275–276
Chinese, 89
civil rights and, 100
date adopted, 274
date ratified, xxvi
Dred Scott decision (1857) and, 274
language and, 236
mixed-status families, 494
nativist sentiment and, 274
Plyler v. Doe ruling, 275
Plyler v. Doe ruling violation, 276
purpose of, 274
relevance of, 274
right to equal education, 85
threats to, 273–274, 275–276
undocumented individuals and,
274–275
United States v. Wong Kim Ark and, 89
Fox News, 457
Fox News Latino, 457
Frank, André Gunder, 482
Fraternidad Eulalense Maya Q'anjobal
(FEMAQ) organization, 411
Fremont, Nebraska housing requirements
law, 328
Frente Indígena Oaxaqueño Binacional
(FIOB), 392

Gallegly, Elton (R-CA), 558
gangs, **277–279**
demographics of, 277
deportation, 278
disadvantaged neighborhoods and, 278
females and, 278–279
ICE gang raids, 278
immigrant enforcement laws, 278
Latino gangs, 277
M-18 (*Mara* 18), 277, 278

gangs (continued)
  MS-13 (*Mara Salvatrucha*), 277, 278
  protection for undocumented immigrants,
    279
  racial profiling, 278
Garces, Michael John, 700
Garcia, Cindy, 703
Garcia, Ginny (2011), 84, 87
Garcia, Guy, 668
Garcia, Isabel, 8 (image)
Garcia, James, 703
Garden City, New York, 684
garment industry, **279–283**
  Aguascalientes, Mexico, 279–280
  cheap goods, 281
  employer requirements, 282
  garment industry shops, 279
  globalization, 279, 280–281
  job losses, 281
  in Los Angeles, 279, 281, 282
  NAFTA and, 281
  Seo employees Faviola Munoz and Maria
    Aguirre, 280 (image)
  Soldatenko (1999) on, 279, 282, 283
  Spener and Capps (2001), 279, 281, 283
  "sweat shops," 281–282
  undocumented immigrants and, 279
  unionism in, 282
  U.S. garment shops, 281
  violations of laws regulating fair
    employment standards, 282
  Wal-Mart, 281
  worker displacement, 281
  working conditions, 281–282
gateways, **283–286**
  change in, 283
  Cleveland and Buffalo, 283–284
  continuous gateways, 284
  defined, 283
  effect of Arizona SB1070, 285
  emerging and pre-emerging gateway
    problems, 285–286
  emerging gateways, 284
  English proficiency and, 284
  factors contributing to emergence of
    nontraditional immigrant gateway
    communities, 284
  former gateways, 284
  gateway states, 43, 202, 283, 286

Immigration Reform and Control Act
    (IRCA) and, 284
  labor opportunities, 284–285
  Los Angeles and Miami, 284
  NAFTA, 285
  New York and Chicago, 284
  nontraditional immigrant gateways, 283,
    284, 285
  post–World War II gateways, 284
  re-emerging gateways, 284
  self-repatriation, 285
  social networks, 285
  state laws and immigration, 285
  traditional immigrant gateways, 283, 286
  Washington D.C., Atlanta and Dallas,
    284
Geary Act, xxvii
gender roles, **286–289**
  abuse, 287
  deportation, 287
  domestic labor, hidden costs of, 287
  domestic workers, 287
  Elvira Arellano, example of vulnerability,
    288
  Flor Crisostomo, example of
    vulnerability, 288–289
  globalization, 287
  Hondagneu-Sotelo (2007) on, 287, 289
  immigrant women, study of, 286–287
  Los Angeles research on, 287
  Romero (2002) on, 287, 289
  sanctuary, 288
  sexual harassment, 288
  undocumented immigrant women,
    research on, 287
  vulnerability, triple form of, 287
General Brotherhood of Workers or CASA,
    99
Gentleman's Agreement executive order,
    xxviii, 676
Georges-Abeyie, Daniel (2001), 595, 596
Georgia, 361
Gilcrist, Jim, 490
Gingrich, Newt, 379
globalization, **289–293**
  defined, 289
  family economics and, 251
  garment industry and, 279, 280–281
  gender roles and, 287

immigration and, 291–292
impact on women, 291
investment loans, results of, 291
macro level neoliberal policies, 292
and NAFTA failures, 291
neoliberalism, 290–291
remittance, 290
social welfare program curtailment, 291–292
structural adjustment programs (SAPs), results of, 291
transnational linkages, growth of, 290
Washington Consensus, 291
women, impact on, 291, 292
"Golden Exiles," 131
Golden Venture and undocumented immigrants, 91
Gomez, Teresa, 754 (image)
Gompers, Samuel, 406
Gonzales v. Reno, xxxvi
Goodlatte, Bob (R-Va), 209, 380, 563
Goodlatte, John (R-Va), 367
Good Samaritans, 149
governance and criminalization, **293–296**
anti-immigrant sentiment, 293
comprehensive border control, 294
deportation, 295
forms of governing through crime, 294
gated communities, 293
ICE arrests, number of, 295
ICE interior policing, 294–295
"illegal aliens," 294
illegality and "war on terror," 294
immigration, governing of through crime, 293–296
Jonathan Simon on, 293, 296
manifestations of governing through crime, 293
Paying the Price: The Impact of Immigration Raids on America's Children (report), 295
perception of immigrant criminality, 293
psychological state of U.S. Latinos (survey), 295
raids, 294–295
rating, significance of, 295
rationalization of governing through crime, 293

undocumented migrants resistance to, 296
undocumented migration and, 293
worksite raids, 295
Government Accountability Office (GAO)
on abuses of foreign workers, 222
estimate of immigrants speaking English, 229
report on undocumented immigrants in the U. S., xxxiii
on U.S.-Mexico border wall, 752
Graham, Bob, 521
Graham, Lindsey (Sen.), 273, 377
Grant, Madison, 406
Great Lakes region, **296–298**
agriculture, 297
demographics of, 297
employment opportunities, 297
immigrant networks, 297
migrant self-sufficiency, 298
population growth due to immigration, 297
social services, 297–298
town-hall meetings and undocumented workers, 297
USA PATRIOT Act, results of, 298
U.S. Border Patrol and public transportation, 298
Green, Al, 381
green cards, **298–301**
administration of, 298
Amerasian child of a U.S. citizen, 300–301
asylee/refugee status and, 300
benefits of, 299
children of foreign diplomats, 300
defined, 298
Diversity Immigrant Visa Program, 301
employment green card, 300
family preference category, 299
foreign investors and, 300
formal name of, 298
immediate relatives category, 299
K non-immigrant visa, 299
Legal Immigration and Family Equity Act (LIFE) and, 299–300
limitations on, 299
media family member and, 299
methods to obtain, 299–302

green cards (continued)
  National Interest Waiver, 300
  number of years valid, 301
  programs eligible applicants can use, 301
  renewal of, 301
  replacement of, 301
  responsibilities of, 299
  special categories, 299–300
  special circumstances and programs,
    301–302
  specific skills and qualifications category,
    300
  Violence Against Women Act and, 299
  V nonimmigrant category, 300
  voting, 301
  widows eligibility, 300
Grijalba, Marco, 302 (image)
Grijalva, Raúl, 381
Grijalva, Raúl (Rep.), 380
Griswold, Daniel, 24
Guaman, Maria, 290 (image)
Guatemalan Civil War, 79
Guatemalans, **301–304**
  civil war and, 302, 303
  deportation of, 302
  estimated number of undocumented
    Guatemalan immigrants (2011),
    301–302
  faith-based organizations and, 304
  gang crime, 304
  Guatemala, overview of, 302
  guatemaltecos, 303
  immigration and Guatemala, 302
  journey to the U.S., 303
  Los Angeles and, 304
  Marco Grijalba, 302 (image)
  Phoenix and, 304
  point of destination, 304
  political asylum, 303
  sanctuaries movement, 303
  soldiers and gangs, 303–304
  spiritual communities, 304
  temporary protected status (TPS) and,
    303
Guerrero-Espinoza, Juan Carlos, 573
guestworker and contract labour policies,
  304–308
  agriculture, 306
  Alien Contract Labor law, 305, 306
Bracero Program, 305, 306
commuter "green card" creation,
  306–307
definitional issue in, 305
Department of Labor (DOL) General
  Order 86, 306
Emergency Farm Labor Supply Program,
  305
employment-based visas, 307
geographic dimension, 305
H-2/H-2A visa program, 307
history and experience of migrant
  contract labor, 304
Immigration Act, Section 3 quoted, 306
indentured servants, 306
key issue in examining my current
  contract labor programs, 305
Ninth Proviso, 306
precursor migrant contract labor
  arrangements, 306
principal statutes establishing and
  redefining employment visas, 307
U.S. reliance on migrant contract labor,
  307
World War II contract labor efforts,
  305–306
written work contract, 305
Guey Heung Lee v. Johnson ruling, 440
*Guide To Federal Regulations Concerning
  Public Housing,* 326
Gutierrez, José, 488–489
Gutiérrez, Luis, 381

Hagan, Jacqueline, and Nestor Rodriguez
  (2002), 500, 501, 667, 668
Haley, Nikki, 673
Hamilton, Lee, 120 (image)
Handlin, Oscar, 312
Hannan, Jason M., 388, 727
Hannigan, Patrick and Thomas, 490
Harper, Jim (2012), 354
Hart, Philip, 311
Hart-Celler Act (1965), **309–312**
  accomplishment of, 100
  ad hoc legislation, 310
  Chinese immigrant quota, 89
  Cold War, 310
  cosponsors of, 309, 311
  date signed into law, xxxi, 309

displaced persons, 310
East Asians and, 194
Emanuel Celler and, 311, 312
final votes for, 312
global scope and the Western
    Hemisphere, 310–311
Harry Truman, 310
immediate origins of, 309
Immigration and Nationality Act (The
    McCarran-Walter Act), 373
labor shortages, 311
Lyndon Johnson and, 309
mortgage system, 310
national origins formula, 311
National Origins Quota Act, 311–312
national origins quota system, 90, 401
Oscar Handlin, 312
Philip Hart and, 311
preferences and non-quota immigrants,
    311–312
purpose of, 309
race and refugees, 310
refugee crises, 310
Republican support for, 312
reputation of, 100
Soviet Union and, 309, 310
undocumented Mexican immigration
    and, 473
hate crimes, **312–316**
    anti-immigrant hate groups, activities of,
        313
    anti-immigrant legislation and, 315–316
    anti-immigrant sentiment and, 312, 314
    Arizona SB1070 and, 315
    Bill O'Reilly and, 314
    Border Patrol and, 315
    community concerns, 113
    conspiracy theories in, 313
    criminalization, 315–316
    cultural depictions of morality, 314
    death of Marcelo Lucero, 313 (image),
        314
    examples of, 315, 316
    factors condoning violence against
        undocumented immigrants, 315–316
    FBI definition of, 313
    FBI on the increase in a crimes against
        Latinos, 314
    Glenn Beck and, 314

groups resisting, 316
hate groups, common ideologies of, 313
immigration enforcement, 315
increase in, 314
Jeffrey Conroy, 314
John and Ken Show (KFI AM640) and,
    315, 316
Latinos, rise in hate crimes against, 314
Lou Dobbs and, 314
Mexican American Legal Defense and
    Educational Fund (MALDEF), 316
Minuteman vigilante group, 315
moral integrity, lack of, 314
National Council of La Raza (NCLR),
    316
National Hispanic Media Coalition, 316
National Institute of Justice, 316
nativist mentality, 314
number of hate groups in the U.S., 313
perpetrators of, 316
Pew Research Center, 316
Proposition 187 and, 315
public media outlets and, 314
range of, 313
Shawna Forde, 315
Southern Poverty Law Center (SPLC),
    316
states with highest number of hate
    groups, 313
television personalities and, 314–350
against undocumented and other
    immigrants, 312
welfare system, 315
white nativists and, 313–314
xenophobia, 312
Hawaii, 236
Hawaiian Sugar Planters' Association, 193
Hayden, Michael, 189
Hayworth, J. D., 492
Hazelton, Pennsylvania
    "Illegal Immigration Relief Act
        Ordinance," 560
    ordinance concerning renting to
        undocumented immigrants, 327–328,
        494, 560
Head Start, **317–319**
    American Indian Head Start program,
        317
    benefits of, 317

Head Start (continued)
early childhood development and health
initiatives, 318
Early Head Start program, 317, 318
excess demand services, 317
extent of, 318
family partnerships, objective of, 318
general results, enrollment, and targeted
benefits, 81–82
immigrant children and, 317
in Kentucky, 317
League of United Latin American
Citizens (LULAC) or 400 School, 318
Migrant Head Start program, 317, 318
Migrant Head Start program, cultural
sensitivity of, 319
origins of, 318
programs of, 317
qualifications of, 318
state targeting of, 317
success of, 317
various programs of, 318
health and welfare, **319–321**
allopathic medicine, 319
anti-immigrant rhetoric and policy and,
321
in Arizona, 321
community health clinics, 321
culturally specific health syndromes
treated by Latino lay practitioners,
320–321
curandera, 320
home treatment, 321
huesera, 320
immigrants and healthcare, 320
lay practitioners and undocumented
Latinos, 320–321
local healers, 320
medical pluralism, 319
in Milwaukee, 321
partera, 320
payment, 321
pregnancy, 320
sobada, 320
social networks of undocumented
immigrants, 320
undocumented Latinos and healthcare,
320
Henderson v. Mayor of New York, xxvi

Herbert, Gary, 672
Hernandez, Esequiel case, 127
Hernandez, Luis, 327 (image)
Hernandez v. The State of Texas ruling, 430
Higham, John, 678, 679–680
high schools, **322–324**
"1.5 generation," 322
college affordability, 322
community college, 322
deportation, 323
DREAM Act, 323
Dream Activist, 323
factors affecting undocumented
students's ability to enroll in college,
322
federal financial aid, 322
Immigrant Families and Students in the
Struggle and, 323
incentives and support, 323
job prospects, 323, 324
League of United Latin American
Citizens (LULAC) and, 323
legal barriers to college education, 322
pockets of educational access for
undocumented students, 322
state financial aid, 322
in-state tuition, 322
stigma and fear, 323
support groups, 323
Trail of Dreams walk, 323
undocumented students and, 322
United We Dream Network, 323
University Leadership Initiative and, 323
worth of college education, 324
Hines, Barbara (2006), 733, 734
Hinojosa-Ojeda, Raúl, 767
Hirabayashi v. United States ruling, xxx
Hispanic Association of Colleges and
Universities (HACU), 107
HIV/AIDS, **324–326**
explanation of, 324
HIV risk among heterosexual Latino
migrants, 325
Latinos and, 324–325
living with, 324
transgender immigrants, 325
undocumented immigrants and, 325
undocumented Latino/a immigrants
living with, 325–326

vulnerability of undocumented Latina
   immigrant women, 325
Hoeven, John (Sen.), 377
*Hoffman Plastic Compounds v. National
   Labor Relations Board (NLRB)* ruling,
   220–221, 419, 775–776, 779
homelessness, **326–330**
   advocate groups for undocumented
      youth, 328
   children and, 328
   defined, 326
   discrimination, 328
   fear of detection of undocumented
      immigrants, 327, 328
   Fremont, Nebraska housing requirements
      law, 328
   *Guide To Federal Regulations
      Concerning Public Housing,* 326
   harboring laws, 328
   Hazelton, Pennsylvania ordinance
      concerning renting to undocumented
      immigrants, 327–328
   hidden homeles, 328
   housing assistance, 326
   policies of attrition, 327
   Skid Row, Los Angeles, 327 (image)
   Solid Ground (La Casa Norte) and
      undocumented youth, 328
   undocumented immigrants barriers to
      housing, 326–328
   young immigrants and, 328
Homestead Act, xxvi
home town associations (HTAs), **330–331**
   3x1 program, 330–331
   Casa Michoacán (Chicago), 331
   clubes, 330, 331
   purpose of, 330
   remittances, 611–612
   social interaction and integration, 649
   Zacatecan Federation, 330
Hondagneu-Sotelo, Pierrette (2007), 287,
   289
Hondurans, **331–336**
   adjustment and adaptation, 334–335
   CARECEN (Central American Resource
      Center), 336
   citizenship, path toward, 335
   coup d'éta, 332
   coyotes and, 333

demographic profile, 334
dual citizenship, 335
entrapment and deportation, 335
"expedited Honduran removals"
   agreement, 335
Honduran migration (1990s to present),
   333–334
immigrant rights movement, 333
Immigration Act (1965) and succeeding
   legislation, 332–333
Immigration Act (1965), waves of
   migration up to, 332
Immigration Reform and Control Act
   (IRCA), 333
intermarriage and family petition, 335
male political exiles, 332
public associations and organizations,
   336
rate of migration, 333
rates of Honduran deportees, 335
Sanctuary Movement and, 332
Temporary Protected Status (TPS)
   program, 335, 336
unionism, 333
Honduras, 79
Hoover, Herbert, xxix
Horne, Tom, 502, 583
Horne v. Flores ruling, 442
Horowitz, Ruth. 1983, 48, 50
hospitals, **337–339**
   access to healthcare, 339
   anti-dumping laws, 337
   cost of uncompensated care for hospitals
      and physicians, 338
   cost of undocumented immigrant
      healthcare, 339
   denial of care, 337
   Emergency Medical Treatment and
      Active Labor Act (EMTALA), 337
   health care clinics and undocumented
      immigrants, 338
   Iowa Methodist Medical Center (Des
      Moine), 338
   Latino immigrants, health of, 337
   legal permanent residents and medical
      assistance, 337
   Martin Memorial Medical Center,
      338–339
   Medicaid, 337, 338

hospitals (continued)
Medicare, 338
Miriam Aviles-Reyes deportation, 338
Montejo v. Martin Memorial Medical Center case, 338–339
patient dumping, 337
Personal Responsibility and Work Opportunity Reconciliation Act (PRWORA), 337
repatriations (deportation), 338
repatriation without consent of family or patient, 338
socioeconomic conditions and limited healthcare options, 339
undocumented immigrants and private insurance, 337
undocumented immigrants and uncompensated care, 338
U.S. Border Patrol stakeouts, 338
"Hostile Terrain: Human Rights Violation in Immigration Enforcement in the U.S. Southwest" report, 27
Hotel Employees and Restaurant Employees (HERE) International Union Local 11, 364
hotel industry, **340–342**
English language ability, 341
flexible employment patterns of, 341
Hotel Workers Rising campaign, 342
immigrants replacing blacks in, 341
immigrant women and, 341
inequality patterns, 341
overview of, 340–341
protesters demanding unionization, 340 (image)
soft skills, 341
undocumented workers and, 341
unionism, 341–342
UNITE-HERE, 342
Zamudio and Lichter (2008) on, 341
House Immigration Reform Caucus, 492
House on Mango Street (Cisneros), 363
housing, **342–346**
anti-immigrant sentiment laws, 344–345
anti-stacking ordinances, 344
Arizona Senate Bill 1070, 344–345
children and, 345
churches and charity organizations, 344
group living, 343

Illegal Immigration Relief Act, 344
landlords, 343
living conditions and health outcomes, 343
in Morrison, New Jersey, 343–344
raiding, 345
regulation of, 343–344
undocumented immigrants and, 342–343
Hove, Chenjerai, 448
Howard Industries workplace raid, 572
How to Make It to the Dance Floor: A Salsa Guide for Women (Based on Actual Experiences) (Garcia), 703
H.R. 4437 legislation, 73
Huerta, Dolores, 15, 502, 582–583
Huerta, Saul, 388
Humane Borders organization, 149, 245–246, 607
Human Rights Immigrant Community Action Network (HURRICANE), 507–508
Human Right Watch, **346–347**
"Abuse of Undocumented Immigrants, Asylum Seekers, and Refugees in South America" (report), 347
Americas Watch founding, 347
defined, 346
focus topics of, 347
funding of, 346
headquarters of, 346
Helsinki Watch, establishment of, 346, 347
main objective of, 346
migration and, 347
"naming and shaming," 346
"No Refuge: Migrants in Greece" (report), 347
"No Way to Live: Alabama's Immigration Law"(report), 346
offices of, 346–347
operation areas of, 346
publications of, 347
region-based Watch organizations, 347
World Report, 347
human trafficking, **348–350**
Blue Heart Campaign against Human Trafficking, 350
children as victims, 349
debt bondage, 349–350

defined, 348
estimated number of human trafficking
    victims, 348
females as victims, 349
human smuggling vs. human trafficking,
    348
labor exploitation, 349
methods of traffickers, 349–350
Palermo Protocol, 348
profits, 348
restrictive immigration policies and, 350
statistics on human trafficking worldwid,
    349
Trafficking Victims Protection Act
    (TVPA), 348, 350
U.S. Department of State's Human
    Trafficking Report, 350
victim exploitation, 349–350
William Wilberforce Trafficking Victims
    Protection Reauthorization Act, 348
Huntington, Samuel P., 214, 215
Husband, W. W., 162

I-9 form, 119, 359, 382, 383, 455
I-94 form, 546–547
identification cards (ID), **351–354**
    Barkin (2003) on, 351, 354
    Certificate of Consular Registration, 352
    defined, 351
    driver's licenses, 352
    employment verification, 351
    E-verify program, 353
    falsified ID documents, 353
    features of, 351
    Harper (2012) on, 352, 354
    importance of, 351
    Legal Permanent Resident (LPR) green
        cards, 353–354
    Matricula Consular Card, 352–353
    "REAL ID" act, 351–352
    undocumented immigrants and, 352, 353
    U.S. national ID card, 351
    visas, 353, 354
    Wells Fargo Bank, 352
identity theft, **354–358**
    Arizona prosecution of, 357
    background, 355
    California prosecution of, 357
    costs of, 357

counterfeiting, 355
criminal activities involving, 357
E-verify program, 355
Flores-Figueroa v. United States, 356
fraud, 355
identity numbers, 354
notable cases of, 356–357
prosecution against identity that by
    immigrants, 357
REAL ID Act, 355
Social Security number, 355
*Ignacio Carlos Flores-Figeroa v. United
    States* ruling, 573
Illegal Immigration Reform and Immigrant
    Responsibility Act (IIRIRA), **358–360**
    287g agreements, 359, 360
    asylum, denial of, 386
    border enforcement, 359–360
    Catholic Church and, 72
    Clinton administration and, 102
    date signed into law, 358
    deportation, 359
    education and, 105, 208
    employer sanctions, 359
    E-Verify, 119
    family reunification and, 254
    I-9 form, 359
    impact of cooperation between federal
        authorities and local police, 359, 360
    intention of, 358
    interior enforcement of immigration
        laws, 359
    overview of, xxxiv
    provisions of, 358–359
    "public charges" provision, 386
    racial profiling, 518
    removal of non-citizens, 359
    sponsorship, 359, 667
    Student and Exchange Visitor
        Information System (SEVIS), 681
    voluntary departure, 359
    welfare assistance and, 359
Illinois, **360–364**
    DREAM Act, 399
    Durangnse, 363
    estimated number of undocumented
        migrants in, 361
    false Social Security numbers and, 360
    Illinois Migrant Council v. Pilliod case, 362

Illinois (continued)
  immigration and, 363
  Immigration rally at Grant Park,
    Chicago, 361 (image)
  Mexican immigrants and Chicago, 361,
    362
  Mexican migrant communities, 363
  National Museum of Mexican Art, 363
  PEW Hispanic Center on, 361
  Pilsen neighborhood of Chicago,
    362–363
  population of Chicago and, 362
  in-state tuition for undocumented
    students, 362
  traditional fascination for undocumented
    migrants, 360
  undocumented migrants and, 360
Illinois Migrant Council v. Pilliod ruling,
  362
Immigrant Families and Students in the
  Struggle, 323
immigrant integration programs, 270–271
Immigrant Justice and Rights Program, 507
immigrant right organizations, 149
Immigrants' Rights Project, 18, 20–21
Immigrant Workers Freedom Ride (IWFR),
  xxxvi, **364–366**
  in Arizona, 365
  date of, 364
  Flushing Meadows Park rally, 366
  goals of, 364
  groups supporting, 364
  Hotel Employees and Restaurant
    Employees (HERE) International
    Union Local 11, 364
  Jerry Akin's journal, 364–365
  Mizrahi (2004) on, 366
  "Petition for Academic Visa Reform,"
    365
  riders on, 364–365
  short-term goal of, 364
  in Washington, DC, 365
Immigration Act of 1891, xxvii
Immigration Act of 1917, xxviii
Immigration Act of 1924. *See* Johnson-
  Reed Act (1924)
Immigration Act of 1990 (IMMACT),
  366–368
  date signed into law, xxxiv, 368

deportation, 367
Diversity Immigrant Visa program, 367
economics and, 200
family reunification, 368
family-sponsored visas, 368
"Green Card Lottery," 367
John Goodlatte (Rep. Congressman), 367
Kennedy-Simpson bill, xxxiii
legal immigration, changes to the system
  of, 367
modifications of, 367
purpose of, 366
reallocation of visas, 368
Section 131, 367
visa reallocation, 368
Immigration and Customs Enforcement
  (ICE), **368–372**
  287(g) program, 369, 371
  border control scheme, 294
  children, effect on, 455
  components of operations of, 369
  crime, 127
  Department of Homeland Security
    (DHS), 368–369
  deportation, 154
  deportation goal, 371
  Enforcement and Removal Operations
    (ERO), 369
  formation of, 368
  funding, 370
  government spending on immigration
    enforcement, 370
  at Head Start and Migrant Seasonal
    Headstart Centers, 206
  immigrant rights movement and, 371
  local law enforcement and, 371
  meat processing plants raids, 455
  national security, 370–371
  national security threats, 370
  number of removals (2007–2010), 371
  problems of, 749
  quota system (U.S.), 370
  raids, 294–295
  responsibilities of, 368, 369
  Secure Communities program, 369, 371
  Swift & Company face off, 369 (image)
  unfair detention of American citizens,
    113
  U.S. Border Patrol, 370

violation of basic human rights, 165
workplace raids, 114, 455, 782–783
Immigration and Nationality Act (The McCarran-Walter Act) (1952), **372–374**
aim of, 216
alternative name for, 372
American nativism, 373
Border Patrol, 373
common name of, 372
consequences of, 372–373
deportation, 373
expedited removal, 241
"grounds for exclusion," 239
Hart-Celler Act, 373
ineffectiveness of, 372–373
Johnson-Reed Immigration Act and, 372
military recruitment and participation, 487
nativism, 372
nativist and liberalizing elements of, 372
overview of, xxx, 372
refugees and, 373
"Texas Proviso," 373
"undocumented" label, 717–718
unintentional consequences of, 373
Immigration and Naturalization Service (INS), **374–377**
alarmist preoccupation with national security, 376
Angel Island, 375
Border Patrol, 376
codification of racial profiling, 375
Customs and Border Protection (CBP), 374
date established, xxix
deportation, unjust, 113
disappearance of, 374
Ellis Island, 374, 375
employer penalties, 375–376
enforcement powers of, 375
federal legislation bolstering, 376
governing statute of the Integration Naturalization Act, 375
IIRIRA and, 376
Immigration and Customs Enforcement (ICE), 374
initiatives to hold undocumented immigration, 376
INS agent roles, 376
INS v. Aguirre-Aguirre ruling, xxxv
INS v. Cardoza-Fonseca ruling, xxxiii
INS v. Chadha et al. ruling, xxxii
interior enforcement strategy, 375
militarization of national borders, 376
Operation Gatekeeper, 376
racial profiling, 375
raids, 375
responsibility of, 374
restrictive and exclusionary immigration policies, 375
threat assessments, 375
uneven enforcement of immigration law, 375
United States v. Brignoni-Ponce ruling, 375
U.S. Citizenship and Immigration Service (CIS) and, 374
U.S.-Mexico border wall, 751
U-visas, 754
Immigration Naturalization Act, governing statute of, 375
immigration reform (2013–2014), **377–381**
American Immigration Lawyers Association on S. 744, 377–378
Barack Obama, 379–380
Bob Goodlatte, 380
Border Security, Economic Opportunity, and Immigration Modernization Act (S. 744), 377–379, 380
"border surge" amendment, 377, 380
Comprehensive Immigration Reform for America's Security and Prosperity Act of 2013, 380
Deferred Action for Childhood Arrivals (DACA), 380
Filemon Vela, 380
gang of 8 members, 377
Grijalva-Vela bill, 380
Herman Cain, 379
H.R. 15, 380
Kris Kobach, 379
Latino view of, 379, 380
Mitt Romney, 379
Newt Gingrich, 379
Operation Streamline program, 380
rally and civil disobedience, 381
Raúl Grijalva, 380

immigration reform (continued)
 Republican party view of S. 744, 380
 Rick Perry, 379
 Tea Party view of S. 744, 379
Immigration Reform and Control Act
  (IRCA) (1986), **381–384**
 Alan Simpson, 381
 amnesty, 24, 25, 368, 382, 383, 384, 473
 antidiscrimination provision of, 383
 childcare services, 80
 conflict documents and, 118
 date of first version, xxxii
 detention and removal, 368
 Development, Relief and Education for
  Alien Minors (DREAM) Act, 384
 discrimination in employment practices,
  383
 Dominican deportation, 178
 employer sanctions, 215, 383
 family reunification, 368
 Form I–9, 271, 272, 382–383
 gateway destinations, 284
 human rights violations and, 384
 inadmissible alien, adoption of term, 384
 INS funding, 382, 383
 Legally Authorized Workers (LAW)
  program, 382, 383
 loophole in, 383–384
 and the Midwest, 476
 Peter Rodino, 381
 provisions of, 382
 results of, 112
 Ronald Reagan, 382 (image)
 Secure Communities program, 628
 shadow population and, 638
 Southern states and, 659
 Special Agricultural Workers (SAW)
  provision, 382, 383, 664–665
 Special Counsel for Immigration-Related
  Unfair Employment Practices, 383
 sponsors of, 381
 suburbs and, 684
 U.S. Border Patrol and, 370, 383, 737
 workplace raids, 782
Impossible Subjects (Ngai), 729
inadmissibility, **384–387**
 affidavit of support, 386
 asylum and, 386
 Border Patrol and, 385

 challenge to the criteria for, 386
 conditions for, 385
 deportable aliens, 385
 deportation, 385
 family reunification application, 386
 family visa program and, 386
 grounds for inadmissibility, number of, 385
 inadmissible alien term, 384, 385
 IRCA and, 384
 "public charges," 386
 reasons for denying asylum, 386
 use of term, 384
 waiver of, 385
incarceration, 106 (table), **387–390**
 Arizona SB1070, 387
 Corrections Corporation of America
  (CCA), 389–390
 crackdowns on immigrants, 388
 criminalization of undocumented
  immigrants, 388
 deportation, 388–389
 drug-smuggling, 388
 expedited court hearings, 388
 expedited removal policy, 388
 factors determining to incarceration of
  Latinos/immigrants, 388–389
 GEO Group, 390
 immigrants, misinformation about, 388
 interior policing, 388
 Latinos and felony crimes, 387–388
 Mexican drug cartel presence, 388
 Migration Policy Institute Report (2011),
  389
 Operation Streamline, 388
 policing of minority populations, 387
 post-9/11 political climate and, 388
 prejudice, 388
 private prison industry, 390
 racial profiling, 387
 S.744 proposal, 390
 Section 287(g) agreements, 389
 Secure Communities program, 389
 *Uneven Justice: State Rates of
  Incarceration by Race and Ethnicity*
  (report), 387
 United States v. Roblero-Solis ruling, 388
 U.S. Senators and the private prison
  industry, 390
 visa overstayers, 388

income, median household income of
undocumented immigrants, 416
Inda, Johnathan Xavier (2006), 692
indigenous people, **391–393**
Frente Indígena Oaxaqueño Binacional
(FIOB), 392
indigenous defined, 391
*Instituto Nacional de Estadísticas y
Geografía e Información (INGEI)*
on, 391
the Internet and, 392
language of, 391
Mexican states with largest indigenous
population, 391
Michoacán migration, 392
NAFTA, negative impact of, 391
Oaxaca state, 391
as percentage of Mexico's population,
391
as percentage of U.S. farmworkers, 392
Purépechas from Michoacán, 391
social and political organizations, 392
Triqui from Oaxaca, 391
U.S. destinations for, 392
"Indio" term, 794
Individual Taxpayer Identification Number
(ITIN), **393–394**
benefits of, 394
earnings suspense, 393
"fringe" financial agents, 394
Latinos and, 394
limitations of, 393
new IRS procedures involving, 393
payment of income taxes, 393
purpose of, 393
Social Security and, 393
taxes, 687–688
unauthorized workers tax
payments, 393
informal economy, **394–397**
definitions of, 395
examples of, 395
Hart's (1973) essay on the "informal
sector," 394
importance of, 396
informal activities defined, 395
landscaping and, 396
licit and illicit goods and services, 396
Portes and Castells (1989) on, 395, 397

research and, 395
terminology of, 394–395
"Injustice for All: The Rise of U.S.
Immigration Policing Regime," 508
Institute for Mexicans Abroad, 270
Instituto de los Mexicanos en el Exterior
(IME), 270–271
*Instituto Nacional de Estadísticas y
Geografía e Información (INGEI)*, 391
Inter-American Court of Human
Rights, 775
Interfaith Worker Justice or IWJ, 777
International Brotherhood of Teamsters,
418
international students/student visas,
397–401
access to higher education for
undocumented immigrants, 398
American-born children
as ineligible, 400
DREAM Act and, 399
implications of undocumented migration
for international education, 400
Information System (SEVIS), 398
international student defined, 397
management of student visas, 398
number of international students at U.S.
colleges/universities, 397–398
out-of-state tuition, 398
overstaying, results of, 400
remesas and, 400
in-state tuition, 399
Student and Exchange Visitor Program
(SEVP), 398, 681
student visas, 399–400
tourist visa, 400
types of student visas, 399
Iowa Methodist Medical Center (Des
Moine), 338
Iran, 367
Irish, **401–403**
anti-Irish sentiment, 401
Emerald Isle Immigration Center, 402
emigration, rates of, 401, 402, 403
estimated number of undocumented Irish
immigrants in the U.S., 401
immigration, resurgence of, 402
Immigration Act of 1990, 402
Ireland, prosperity of, 402–403

Irish (continued)
  Irish criticism of the U.S., 402
  Irish Famine and immigration, 401
  Irish Free State, creation of, 401
  Irish Immigration Reform Movement
    (IIRM), 402, 403
  Irish Voice newspaper, 402
  the New Irish, 402
  overstaying, 401
  settlement in the U.S., 402
Islamic Center for North American
    Relief, 246

Jamaica, 437
Jesuit Refugee Service (JRS)
    International, 246
Jewish Federation of North America, 246
Jewish Workmen's Circle, 777
Job Opportunities and Basic Skills Training
    (JOBS), 691
John and Ken Show (radio), 315, 316
John Paul II (Pope), 71
Johnson, Albert (Rep.), 405, 406
Johnson, Lyndon, 309
Johnson-Reed Act (1924), **405–407**
  acts included with, 405
  agribusiness lobby, 406
  Albert Johnson (Rep.), 405, 406
  alternative name of, 405
  Asian Exclusion Act and, 405
  blood relations, 405
  census of 1890 and, 405
  date enacted, xxix
  David Reed (Rep.), 405
  documentation requirements in, 406
  enforcement of, 406–407
  eugenics, 406
  exclusion and, 240
  McCarran-Walter Act and, 372
  Mexican emigration, 406
  Mexican quota debate, 406
  National Origins Act and, 405
  national quota system, 405, 407
  natural origins and, 405
  overview of, xxix
  purpose of, 405
  quoted on quotas, 405
  racial delineations, classifications, 405
  Samuel Gompers and, 406

  sponsors of, 405
  xenophobia, 789
Jordan Commission on Immigration
    Reform, xxxiv
The Journal of American History, 729
Juana and son Christian, 50 (image)
Juan facing deportation, 76 (image)
The Jungle (Sinclair), 453
Justice, William Wayne (Justice), 557 (image)
Justice for Immigrants: A Journey of Hope
    campaign, 72–73
Justice for Janitors campaign, 417–418
*Just Like Us: The True Story of Four
    Mexican Girls Coming of Age in
    America* (Thorpe), 446

Kanjobal Mayan, **409–411**
  alternative spelling for, 409
  community in Indiantown, Florida, 410
  community in Los Angeles, California,
    409–410
  cultural identity, 410
  discrimination and social exclusion, 410
  Florida and, 392
  Fraternidad Eulalense Maya Q'anjobal
    (FEMAQ) organization, 411
  garment industry, 410
  influence of, 409
  international migration, 409
  Kanjobales of Santa Eulalia, 410
  language of, 410
  Marimba classes, 411
  Massey (1998) on, 409, 411
  origins of, 409
  Popkin (1999) on, 409, 410, 411
  reintegration, 409
  Sassen (1996) and, 409, 411
  social organizations, 410–411
  subcommittees, formation of, 411
  Taylor et al. (1997) on, 409, 411
Kansas, 362, 399, 428
Karoly, Lynn A., and Gabriella C. Gonzalez
    (2011), 80, 82, 83
Kean, Thomas, 120 (image)
"Keep America Safe and Free" campaign,
    20–21
Kennedy, Edward (Sen.), 402, 600–601
Kerwin, Donald, and Serena Yi-Ying Lin
    (2009), 156, 158

King, Martin Luther Jr., 15, 98
King, Meredith L. (2007), 768, 771
King, Steve (Rep.), 274
Kino Border Initiative, 104
Kino Border Initiative (KBI), 73
Kittrie, Orde F. (2006), 626, 629
Klasfeld, Nat, 429 (image)
Knights of America, 429
Kobach, Kris, 379, 563–564
Kohler, Adriana D., and Melissa Lazarin
    (2007), 83
Korematsu v. United States, 194
Korematsu v. United States ruling, xxx
Kretsedemas, Phillip (2012), 785, 787
Kullgren, Jeffrey, 555
Kurup, Shishir, 700
Kyl, Jon (Sen.), 273

Laborers' International Union of North
    America (LIUNA), 418
Labor Immigrant Organizing Network
    (LION), 417
labor supply, **413–416**
    Asian immigration, 414, 415
    Bracero Program, 414
    Chinese immigrants, 413
    el enganche (the hook), 414
    factors influencing labor migration, 450
    forced migration (slave trade), 413
    Hart-Celler Act and, 414–415
    history of immigrant labor supply,
        413–415
    immigrant labor demand in U.S. industry,
        413
    industries employing unauthorized
        immigrants (percentage), 416
    labor force participation of unauthorized
        immigrants, 415
    mass labor migration, reasons for, 415
    median household income of
        unauthorized immigrants, 416
    Mexican laborers applying for temporary
        employment, 414 (image)
    number of unauthorized people in U.S.
        workforce, 413
    persistence of demand for Latin
        American workers, 415
    unemployment rates of unauthorized
        immigrants, 415–416

    U.S. reliance on Latin America labor
        importation, 414
labor unions, **416–420**
    AFL-CIO ambivalence toward immigrant
        workers, 417
    AFL-CIO split, 418
    Agriprocessors v. NLRB ruling, 419
    César Chávez, 416
    "Change-To-Win" (CTW), 418
    *Hoffman Plastics v. the National Labor
        Relations Board (NLRB)* ruling, 419
    Hotel Workers Rising campaign, 418
    immigrants and union survival, 417
    Immigration Reform and Control Act
        (IRCA), 418, 419
    industries isolated from union
        protection, 417
    Justice for Janitors campaign, 417–418
    Labor Immigrant Organizing Network
        (LION), 417
    organizing rights of undocumented
        workers, 418–419
    percentage of foreign-born American
        workers, 417
    Service Employees International Union
        (SEIU), 417, 418
    undocumented immigration and,
        416–417
    union membership, decrease of, 417
    United Farm Workers (UFW), 416
    UNITE-HERE, 417
    workplace raids, 418
La Crónica de Hoy, 612
La Jornada, 612, 613
LaMadrid, Carlos, 759
landscaping industry, **420–423**
    demand for landscape workers, 420–421
    depiction of landscape workers, 421
    divisions of labor in, 421–422
    economic transactions in, 421
    incarceration, 421–422
    masculinity and, 422
    opportunities and obstacles to Latino
        immigrants, 422
    positive benefits of, 421, 422
    problems in, 422
    social classes in landscape trade, 421
Lang, Mary E., 81, 83
Langhan, Paul, 681 (image)

La Opinión, 612
La Prensa, 333
Larson, Alice (2001), 480, 481
lateral deportation, 737
Latina/o educational pipeline, by race/
    eccentricity, subgroup, and gender
    (U.S., 2000), 106 (table)
Latino civic and political participation,
    582 (chart)
Latino Outreach, 210
Latinos, psychological state of U.S.
    (survey), 295
Latinos in America (2009) CNN
    documentary, 8
*La Tira de la Pereginacaion (The Strip of
    the Pilgrimage)* codice, 43
Lau v. Nichols ruling, 207, 227
Lau v. Nichols ruling, 440
lawful permanent residents (LPRs),
    423–426
    "crimes of moral turpitude," 424
    detention centers, 424
    eligibility, 425
    family visa program, 423
    Form I-485, "Application to Register
        Permanent Residence or Adjust
        Status," 425
    green cards, 424
    I-130 Petition for Alien Relative, 424
    number of lawful permanent residents in
        the U.S., 423
    number of LPRs eligible to
        naturalize, 424
    overview and process, 424–425
    Provisional Unlawful Presence (PUP)
        Waiver, 424
    rights of, 424
    unauthorized immigrants and, 423
    United States Citizenship and
        Immigration Service (USCIS), 423
    waiting period, 424
laws and legislation, post-1980s, **426–429**
    Emergency Medical Treatment & Labor
        Act (EMTALA), 427
    Federally Qualified Health Centers
        (FQHCs), 427
    Illegal Immigration Reform and
        Immigrant Responsibility Act of 1996
        (IIRIRA), 426

immigrant health care services, barriers
    to, 426–428
Medicaid and the State Children's Health
    Insurance Program (SCHIP), 427
National Breast and Cervical Cancer
    Early Detection Program
    (NBCCEDP), 428
national security, 426
number of bills dealing with immigrants
    (2007), 426
Personal Responsibility and Work
    Opportunity Reconciliation Act of
    1996 (PRWORA) and, 427
policies of attrition, 426
Proposition 187 (California), 426
receiving communities for Mexican
    immigrants, 428
Lazarus, Emma, 445–446
League of United Latin American Citizens
    (LULAC), **429–431**
    assimilation, promotion of, 431
    civil rights, 97
    creation of, 429–430
    events of, 430–431
    first major accomplishment of, 430
    Head Start program and, 318, 430
    Hernandez v. The State of Texas
        ruling, 430
    incarceration, 473
    member councils, 430
    membership, 430
    Mendez v. Westminster ruling, 430
    mission of, 430
    rally, 429 (image)
    undocumented students and, 323
    as vocal advocates of immigrants, 431
*League of United Latin American Citizens
    v. Wilson* ruling, 85
Leahy, Patrick (D-VT), 438, 668
legalization program for undocumented
    immigrants, pros and cons to
    implementing, 24–25
legal representation, **431–434**
    attorney withdrawal, 432
    client-attorney relationship, 432
    defined, 431
    deportation and, 432
    deportation threat dynamic, 433–434
    detainees and, 432

DHS and, 432
en mases pleas, 433
example of criminal prosecution of migrants, 433
Executive Office of Immigration Review (EOIR), 432
fees, 431–432
HB 489 and, 434
immigration law, 432
Legal Orientation Program, 433
limited access to, 433
National Immigrant Justice Center, 432
notaries, unethical conduct of, 432
Operation Streamline and, 433
reasons undocumented immigrants seek, 431, 432
in Santa Fe, New Mexico, 434
unethical practices, 432
USCIS and, 432
U.S. v. Arqueta-Ramos ruling, 433
work environment exploitation and, 433
legal status, **434–437**
absence of, 436
adjustment of status, 435
alien term defined, 435
birthright citizenship, 434
comprehensive immigration reform, 436
defined, 434
documentation, 436
employment and legal permanent residency, 435
entry without inspection (EWI), 436
illegal term defined, 435–436
legal permanent residency, 434–435
legal permanent resident status, application process, 435
passports, 435
preference categories for immigration through employment, 435
racial profiling, 436
Registered Provisional Immigrant status, 436
social and political implications of, 435–436
temporary authorization of citizenship, 434
terminology used in, 435–436
visa processing, 435
Leonardo, Angel, 210 (image)

Letters from My Mother (Salgadu), 703
Levi, Zeev, 573
Lewis, John, 381
LGBT immigrants without documentation, **437–440**
acculturation and sexual identity formation, 439
Barack Obama on, 439
the Catholic Church and, 437
countries commercializing same-sex relations, 437
criminalization of homosexuals, 437
Defense of Marriage Act (DOMA), 438, 439
discrimination, 439
institutional discrimination, 437–438
Morton Memo, 437, 439
persecution of LGBT people, 438
risk of life, 438
same-sex marriage, 438
Uniting American Families Act, 438–439
U.S. asylum and, 438
Libros de Godot publishing, 701
Life Behind the Lobby: Indian American Motel Owners and the American Dream (Dhingra), 657
limited English proficiency (LEP), **440–444**
adult education, 443
adult education programs, 442
Arizona and, 441–442, 443
difficulty of English, 443
education and, 440
English Language Learner (ELL), 443
Equal Educational Opportunity Act (1974), 442
free English classes, 443–444
George Mason University bilingual project, 443
Guey Heung Lee v. Johnson ruling, 440
health care and, 440–441
Horne v. Flores ruling, 442
importance of immigrants in U.S. history, 440
Lau v. Nichols ruling, 440
Limited English Proficiency (LEP), 443
New Mexico and, 441
No Child Left behind Act, 442–443
Nogales Unified School District suit, 442
notable legal case involving, 442

limited English proficiency (LEP) (continued)
  opposition to, 441
  Plyler v. Doe ruling, 440
  segregation, 440
  translation, 443
Liparota v. United States ruling, 267
literature and poetry, **444–449**
  Alambrista, 445
  Anna Ochoa O'Leary, Hartzler's play
    about, 448
  Chinese immigration, 446
  contemporary titles concerning
    immigration, 446
  The Crossings (Paulsen), 446
  Devil's Highway (Urrea), 446
  Emma Lazarus, 445–446
  exiled writers, 448
  Francisco X. Alarcón, 446
  immigrant writers on immigration
    (contemporary), 446
  and immigration (history), 444–445
  "Island of Secret Memories," 446
  Jose Antonio Vargas, 447–448
  *Just Like Us: The True Story of Four
    Mexican Girls Coming of Age in
    America* (Thorpe), 446
  Kara Hartzler, 448
  The New Colossus" (Lazarus), 445–446
  "Poets Responding to SB 1070" (Alarcón
    on Facebook), 446–447
  Return to Sender (Alvarez), 446
  Shadow Lives (Chavez), 446
  The Tortilla Curtain (Boyle), 446
  Touching Snow (Felin), 446
Lodge, Henry Cabot, 161
Lopez, Felipe H., and Pamela Munro (1999),
    793, 794, 795
Lopez, Gloria, 768 (image)
Lopez, Tomas (2011), 674, 675
Los Angeles Times, 457, 719
Los Tigres del Norte, 116–117
Louisiana, 236
Luce-Celler Act, xxx
Lucero, Rosario and Joselo, 313 (image)
LULAC et al. v. Wilson et al. ruling, xxxiv

Mack, Connie, 521
Magnuson Act (Chinese Exclusion Repeal
    Act of 1943), xxx, 92

Maintaining Connection with
    Homeland, 270
Malara, Hugo, 499 (image)
Malaysia, 437
Marchevsky, Alejandra, and Jeanne
    Theoharis (2008), 561, 562, 770, 771
Marquez, Rafael, 670 (image)
marriage, **451–453**
  abusive relationships, 453
  Asian Americans, 451
  children and, 452
  deportation, 453
  dissolution of, 452–453
  documentation, 452
  domestic violence, 453
  family reunification, 451, 452
  Filipinos, 452
  intimate partner violence, 452
  legal recruitment practices and, 451
  migration working mothers, 452
  parenting roles, 452
  separation of families, 451, 452
  stressors to married life, 451–453
  transnational families, 451–452
  vulnerability of undocumented
    immigrant women, 452–453
Marti, Jose, 448
Martinez, Edgar Adrian, 159
Martinez, Juana Garcia, 147 (image)
Martinez, Susana, 516
Martin Memorial Medical Center, 338–339
Maryland, 399
Massey, Douglas S. (1998), 409, 411
matricula consular cards, 47
Matthews v. Diaz ruling, xxxii
Matuz, Dulce, 15
McCain, John (Sen.), 274, 377, 390, 540,
    760–761
McConnell, Eileen Diaz, and Enrico A.
    Marcelli (2007), 48, 50, 499
McConnell, Mitch (Sen.), 273
meat processing plants, **453–457**
  agriprocessors raids, 455
  Basic Pilot Program (E-verify), 455
  cost-cutting relocation, 453
  dangers of, 454–455
  discrimination and racism, 456
  employer attitude, 456
  I-9 form, 455

ICE raids, 455–456
The Jungle (Sinclair), 453
labor turnover, 456
legal proof of permission to work, 455
low-cost labor, 453
Maverick Meats trim room, 454 (image)
medical insurance, 455
Midwest Coalition of Human Rights
   (report), 455
migrant labor and, 453
Mississippi Immigrant Rights Alliance
   (MIRA), 456
racism and xenophobia, 456
in rural areas, 456
Smithfield Foods pork slaughterhouse
   raid, 455
in the South, 454
state of Texas, 453
Swift meat-processing plants raids, 455
unauthorized workers and, 453
undocumented immigrant abuse, 455
unionism, 456
unstable labor force in, 456
working conditions, 453
media coverage, **457–460**
alarmist media, 459
biased numbers in, 459
Border Patrol as a source of
   information, 459
criticism of immigrants, 458
dehumanizing imagery of
   immigrants, 458
discrimination of immigrants, 457
"illegal alien" term debate, 457, 458
immigration equated with illegal
   passage, 458
journalists and, 459
Latino journalism, 460
metaphors of war in, 458
Mexican immigration and social
   problems, 460
negative coverage of undocumented
   immigration, 457, 458
"otherness" in, 459
proposed solutions to correct media bias
   of immigration, 460
social impact of news and entertainment
   media, 458
socialization and, 458

sources of information, 459
special bias against Mexican
   immigration, 460
stereotypes (hostile) about
   immigrants, 458
sympathetic immigrant coverage,
   459–460
"us versus them" in immigration
   coverage, 459
visual representations of immigrants, 457
Medicaid and the State Children's Health
   Insurance Program (SCHIP), 427
Medina, Angelica, 1 (image)
Meissner, Doris, 59
Melendez, Robert (Sen.), 377
Melikian, Armen, 448
Mendez, Gonzalo and school
   segregation, 66
Mendez, Jesus, 160
Méndez vs. Westminster School District, 98
Mendez v. Westminster ruling, 430
Menendez, Robert (Sen.), 132
mental health care access, **461–463**
barriers preventing immigrants from,
   461, 462
children and, 461
clinicians and Latino health care, 462
disparities in, 461
domino effect in, 462
health insurance and undocumented
   immigrants, 461, 462
immigration status and mental health
   care usage, 461–462
Latinos and mental health care, 461
mental health utilization, gap in,
   461, 462
rates of mental health service usage, 461
social stigma and, 462
social workers and Latino health
   care, 462
societal implications of, 462–463
mental health issues for immigrants,
   463–466
acculturative stress, 464–465
children and acculturation, 464–465
comprehensive assessments on mental
   health among immigrants, 464
factors affecting mental health of
   undocumented immigrants, 465

mental health issues for (continued)
Hispanics and depression, 465
Immigrant Paradox, 463–464
Latinos and, 465
National Institute of Mental Health
Col- laborative Psychiatric
Epidemiology Surveys, 464
nervios, 465
refugees and, 464
service utilization, 465
undocumented immigrants
and, 465
mental health issues for undocumented
immigrants, **466–468**
chronic stress, 467
common mental health conditions
experienced by undocumented
immigrants, 467
determinants of mental health, 466
discrimination and oppression, 468
exploitation and abuse, 467
homeless man tries to rest inside a
Tijuana River canal tunnel,
466 (image)
mental health defined, 466
mobility and, 467
posttraumatic stress disorder
(PTSD), 467
psychologically and emotionally
damaging accusations, 468
social roles and social status changes,
467–468
substance abuse, 467
Mexican American Legal Defense and
Education Fund (MALDEF),
468–471
Arizona Proposition 200 and, 29
bilingual education, 470
composition of, 468
date founded, 468
education rights, 206, 470
employment rights, 470
formation of, xxxi, 469
functions of, 469
on hate crimes, 316
immigration rights, 469
inception of, 469
Plyler v. Doe ruling, 469
purpose of, for 69

voting rights, 470
White et al. v. Regester et al. case, 468
Mexican American middle class, 54, 55
Mexican-American War, 44
Mexican Interior Repatriation Program,
615–616
Mexicans, **471–475**
American G.I. Forum, 473
Border Protection, Anti-Terrorism, and
Illegal Immigration Control Act of
2005, 474
Bracero Program, 472
California Proposition 187, 473–474
Chicano Movement, 473
Cold War politics and, 472–473
Federal Land Law of 1851, 472
guest workers recruitment, 472
Hart-Celler Immigration and
Nationality Act Amendments
(1965), 473
historic relations between Mexico and
the U.S., 471–474
immigrant rights activism, 473
Immigration Reform and Control Act of
1986 (IRCA), 473
imposition of restrictive immigration
quotas, 472
League of United Latin American
Citizens, 473
Mexican deportation statistics, 471
Mexican migration statistics, 471
NAFTA and, 474
Operation Wetback, 472
repatriations and deportations, 472
Senate Bill (SB) 1070, 474
stories about Mexican immigrants, 473
structural explanations of
immigration, 473
Treaty of Guadalupe Hidalgo, 471
Mexica people, 42, 43
Michael Bianco Inc., leather goods factory
workforce raid, 418, 493, 783
Michelson, Melissa R. (2001), 650, 652
Midwest, **475–478**
anti-immigrant discourse, 477–478
barrios, formation of, 475
Chicago, 477
community of indigenous women from
Mexico, 476

defined, 475
Detroit, 477
difference between early and later
    migrations to, 477
displacement of impoverished
    populations, 477
diversity of its economy, 475
early Mexican immigrant settlement
    in, 475
farm and food processing work in, 475
Ford Motor Company, 475
Illinois as immigrant friendly, 477
Immigration Reform and Control Act,
    impact of, 476
Mexican women migrants, 477
migrant stereotypes, 477
Millard and Chapa (2001) research,
    477, 478
rural Midwest, 477
settlement of immigrants in, 477
states included in, 475
Tarascan community, 476
upswing in undocumented immigrants in,
    476–477
Midwest Coalition of Human Rights
    (report), 455
Migrant and Seasonal Agricultural Worker
    Protection Act, 479
migrant farm workers, **478–481**
Benson (2008) on, 480, 481
Carvajal et al. on, 481
common demographic characteristics
    among, 479
difference between legal and illegal
    migrant farmworkers, 480
discrimination stressors, 481
health issues of, 480–481
importance of, 478
Larson (2001) on, 480, 481
Migrant and Seasonal Agricultural
    Worker Protection Act, 479
migrant labor camp, 480
migrant workers picking strawberries,
    479 (image)
National Agricultural Workers Survey
    (NAWS), 478–479
National Center for Farm Worker Health
    (2001) on, 480
in North Carolina, 480

Peña (2009) on, 479, 480, 481
statistics on, 479
Texas and, 480
U.S. immigration policy and, 478
visa programs for, 478
work of, 478
Yuma County and, 481
migration, **482–487**
287(g) program and, 486
aggressive U.S. deportation
    policies, 486
Arizona and, 485
"bajadores," 484
Border Patrol detention, 484
Border Patrol Strategic Plan 1994 and
    Beyond: National Strategy, 483, 485
capitalism and, 482
children and, 486
corruption and, 484
costs of, 484
coyotes and, 484
explaining migration, 482–483
family separation costs, 485–486
historical-structuralist explanation
    of, 482
historical trends in, 482
hunger and, 484
impact of enforcement on, 485–487
localized operations concerning, 485
"macro" and "micro" structure
    interaction, 483
migration-specific human capital, 484
migration systems approach to, 482
NAFTA, 483, 485
negative outcomes, 486–487
neoclassical economic equilibrium
    theory, 482
neoliberalism, 483
parent-child separation, 486
process of migration, 483–484
repatriation and deportation, 486
statistics on undocumented
    immigrants, 482
structuralist approach to, 482–483
survival and, 486
theories about, 482
undocumented migrants, 482
visas requirements, 483–484
women and, 486

military recruitment and participation, **487–489**
  accelerated naturalization process, 487
  criticism of non-citizen soldiers, 489
  enlistment of non-citizens, 488
  Expedited Citizenship of Aliens and Non-Citizen Nationals Serving in an Active Duty Status in the War on Terrorism, 488
  Immigration and Nationality Act (The McCarran-Walter Act), 487
  José Gutierrez, 488–489
  of non-citizens, 487–488
  non-citizen soldier deportation, 489
  non-citizen soldiers, 488–489
  non-citizens with temporary residency status recruitment, 488
  posthumous citizenship, 487, 489
  Selected Service registration, 487
  voluntary enlistment and reenlistment of non-citizens, 488
Millard, Ann V., and Jorge Chapa (2001), 477, 478
Minutemen, **489–492**
  American Border Patrol, 490, 491
  Andrew Thomas and, 492
  anti-immigrant legislation and, 491
  armed camps along the border, 491
  as *casamigrantes,* 489
  Casey Nethercott, 492
  caught settlement against, 492
  Chris Simcox of the Minuteman Civil Defense Corps, 490
  civilian border vigilante groups, 490
  defined, 489
  Doty (2009) on, 490, 492
  exclusionary anti-immigrant movement, 491
  Glen Spencer, 491
  hate crimes and, 315, 491
  House Immigration Reform Caucus and, 492
  J. D. Haywood and, 492
  Jim Gilcrist, 490
  Lou Dobbs and, 492
  militaristic themes of, 491–492
  Minute Men Project (MMP), 111, 490, 491
  national recruitment, 491
  Patrick and Thomas Hannigan case, 490
  prominent individuals in national figures supporting militia groups, 492
  public displays of support for militia groups, 492
  Ranch Rescue organization, 491
  Ranch Rescue organization case, 492
  Roger Barnett case, 490–491
  Save Our State movement in California, 491
  tactics (illegal) of, 491, 492
  tolerance for, 491
  Tom Tancredo and, 492
  U.S. Federal Aviation Administration and, 491
  as vigilante or hate groups, 489
  vigilantism and impunity, 492
  xenophobic rhetoric, 491
Minutemen American Defense, 760
Minutemen Civil Defense Corps, 760
Mississippi Immigrant Rights Alliance (MIRA), 456
mixed-status families, **493–495**
  Agriprocessors kosher meat plant raid, 493–494
  children of, 493, 494
  defined, 493
  economic future of U.S.-born children, 493–494
  education, 494
  Fourteenth Amendment and, 494
  Hazelton, Pennsylvania "Tenant Registration Ordinance," 494
  health service restrictions in Arizona, 494
  Immigration and Customs Enforcement (ICE), 493
  Proposition 187 and, 578
  school raids, 494
  U.S.-born children of, 493
  workforce raids, 493
  workforce raids, examples of, 493
Mizrahi, Terry (2004), 366
mobility, **495–497**
  287(g) program and, 496
  barriers to, 495
  Border Patrol, 496
  defined, 495
  entrapment processes, 496

immobility, effects of, 496–497
lack of driver's license, 496
morality of risk and, 496
police profiling, 496
risks to, 496
undocumented status as barrier to,
495–496
Monmouth University Polling Institute, 513
*Montejo v. Martin Memorial Medical
Center* case, 338–339
Monthly Postcards to Prisoners Campaign, 27
Moreno, Luisa, 98
Morrison, Bruce, 402
Morrison, New Jersey, 344
Morse, Susan C., and Frank S. Ludovina
(1999), 84, 85, 87
mortgages, **497–499**
the American Dream and, 497, 499
change in banking practices, 498–499
Citigroup and, 499
Federal National Mortgage Association
(Fannie Mae), 497
homeownership by type of immigrant
status, 499
immigrant disadvantages in, 497–498
immigrant homeownership rates, 497
individual tax identification numbers
(ITINs) and, 498–499
matricula consular identification, 499
McConnell and Marcelli (2007) on, 499
predatory lending practices, 498, 499
recruitment of immigrants for mortgage
loans, 497, 498–499
social security numbers and, 498
Morton Memo, **500–501**
defining same-sex relationships, 501
effects of, 500–501
explanation of, 500
family relations, clarification of, 501
Hagen and Rodriguez (2002) on,
500, 501
IIRIRA expansion of enforcement
efforts, 500
LGBT communities and, 437, 439, 501
prosecutorial discretion, 500
removals, 500
Moussaoui, Zacarias trial, 756
Movement for Justice in El Barrio,
53 (image)

Muehler et al. v. Mena ruling, 122
multicultural education, **501–503**
Arizona ban on ethnic studies
curricula, 502
Arizona HB228, purpose of, 503
Arizona HB2281, purpose of, 502, 503
concepts, 502
criticism of, 502
defined, 501
as a human right, 502
overview of, 501–502
public resources and, 502
Tucson Unified School District (TUSD),
502–503
Murguía, Janet, 506
Murillo, Enrique, 85
Muzaffar, Raja and Rabia, 656 (image)

"NACARA 203 relief," 522
Nadler, Jerrold (D-NY), 668
Napolitano, Janet, 33, 217, 685
National Breast and Cervical Cancer Early
Detection Program (NBCCEDP), 428
National Chicano Moratorium, 99
National Council of La Raza (NCLR),
505–507
about, 505
Alma Awards, 507
criminal justice concern about, 506
criticism of, 505
current main clientele of, 505
Development, Relief, and Education for
Alien Minors (DREAM) Act, 506
founding of, 505
goal of, 505
hate crimes, 316
Janet Murguía and, 506
methods for accomplishing outlined
solutions, 506
mission of, 505
principles of, 506
priorities of, 506–507
public outreach, 506
while registration and applications for
citizenship, 506
National Day Laborer Organizing
Network, 144
National Day Labor Organizing Network or
NDLON, 777

National Day Labor Study, 144
National Hispanic Media Coalition, 316
National Immigrant Justice Center, 432
National Immigration Law Center, 181
National Institute of Justice, 316
National Institute of Mental Health
    Collaborative Psychiatric
    Epidemiology Surveys, 464
National Institute on Minority Health and
    Health Disparities, 50
National Journal, 150
National Museum of Mexican Art, 363
National Network for Immigrant and
    Refugee Rights (NNIRR), **507–508**
    "100 Stories Project," 508
    Building a Race and Immigrant Dialogue
    in the Global Economy (BRIDGE)
    project, 508
    community outreach, 508
    establishment of, xxxiii, 507
    Human Rights Immigrant Community
    Action Network (HURRICANE),
    507–508
    Immigrant Justice and Rights Program, 507
    "Injustice for All: The Rise of U.S.
    Immigration Policing Regime," 508
    overview of, 507
    "Uprooted: Refugees of the Global
    Economy" documentary, 508
National Origins Act (1924), 405, 676
National Public Radio (NPR), 457
National Security Entry- Exit Registration
    System (NSEERS) program, 561
Native American reservations, 70
nativism
    East Asian and, 194
    escalation of border enforcement, 59
    McCarran- Walter Act, 372, 373
    Minutemen, 491
    Operation Wetback, 543
    *Strangers from a Different Shore: A
    History of Asian Americans,* 676
    *Strangers in the Land: Patterns of
    American Nativism, 1860–1925,* 678,
    679, 680
naturalization, **509–512**
    anti-immigrant sentiment, 511
    application for, 510
    black immigrants, 509

Border Protection, Anti-Terrorism, and
    Illegal Immigration Control Act
    (2005), 511
declaration of intent, 510
defined, 509
expediting of, 511
general naturalization process, 510
general protocol for, 510
Mexicans and, 510–511
military naturalization, 511
Native Americans, 509, 510
Naturalization Act (1790), 509
Naturalization Act (1798), xxv
Naturalization Act (1870), xxvi
Naturalization Treaty (1868),
    509–510
number of naturalized citizens
    per year, 510
"pathway to citizenship"debate, 511
prerequisites for naturalization, 13
Provisional Unlawful Presence (PUP)
    Waiver, 511
requirements for, 510
Section 329 of the INA, 511
top countries of origin for, 510
U.S. armed forces and, 511
U.S. Customers and Immigration
    Service, 510
Nebraska, 362, 399
Negroponte, John, 79
neoliberalism, 290–291, 483
Nethercott, Casey, 492
Nevada, 428
"A New Path: Toward Humane Immigration
    Policy" (report), 23
The New Colossus" (Lazarus), 445–446
New Jersey, **512–514**
    access to higher education, 513–514
    "community cards," 514
    diversity of undocumented immigrant
    population, 512
    identification cards (ID), 514
    influx of undocumented migrants, 361
    percentage of labor force
    undocumented, 512
    poll on legal immigration, 513
    poll on undocumented immigrants, 513
    population of undocumented immigrants
    in, 512

in-state tuition, poll on, 513
uniqueness of, 512–513
The New Mainstream (Garcia), 668
New Mexico, **514–517**
  attitude towards undocumented
    immigrants, 516
  barrios in, 515
  Bill Richardson, his position on
    undocumented immigrants, 515
  border with Mexico, 515–516
  Camino Real, 515
  Deferred Action for Childhood Arrivals
    (DACA), 516
  driver's licenses and, 516
  election of Susana Martinez, 516
  employer discrimination, 434
  English-Only Movement, 236
  female workers in, 515
  labor unions, 515
  limited English proficiency (LEP), 441
  mining, 515
  overview of, 514–515
  population of, 514
  sanctuary status in, 516
  in-state tuition, 362, 399
  vaquero culture of, 515
New Sanctuary Movement, 76, 631
New York, **517–519**
  287(g) agreements in, 518
  Andrew Cuomo on undocumented
    immigrants, 518
  detention centers, 519
  DREAM Act, 518
  education, 517–518
  estimated number of immigrants living
    in, 517
  ICE raids in New York City, 518–519
  immigration and, 517
  influx of undocumented migrants, 361
  Michael Bloomberg on undocumented
    immigrants, 518
  percentage of workforce undocumented, 517
  post-9/11 changes, 517–518
  protests against oppressive tactics in, 519
  racial profiling, 518
  sanctuary cities in, 518
  in-state tuition, 362, 399, 517
New York City Immigrant Rights
  Coalition, 366

New York Times, 157, 447, 457, 654, 671
New York Times/CBS poll on undocumented
  immigrants and U.S. jobs, 203
Nicaragua (Contra War), 77–78
Nicaraguan Adjustment and Central
  American Relief Act (NACARA),
  520–522
  American Baptist Church (ABC) v.
    Thornburgh ruling, 520–521
  cancellation of removal, 521, 522
  effect of, 521
  history of NACARA, 520–521
  NACARA 203 relief, 522
  original name of, 520
  purpose of, 520
  Section 202, 521
  Section 203, 521
  sections of, 521
  specifications of, 521–522
  sponsors of, 521
  suspension of deportation, 521, 522
  Temporary Protected Status (TPS), 521
Nicaraguans, **522–525**
  application rates of, 524
  asylum, 524
  contra-revolucionarios, 523–524
  deportation cancellation, 525
  illegal sale of weapons, 524
  in Miami reacting to court decision on
    deportation, 523 (image)
  Nicaraguan Adjustment and Central
    American Relief Act (NACARA),
    524–525
  number of Nicaraguans living
    in U.S., 522
  overview of, 522–523
  Temporary Protected Status (TPS), 522
  U.S. foreign policy and, 523–524
Nieto, Peña, 190
Nigeria, 367
Ninth Circuit Court of Appeals, xxxix, 30, 35
"no match" letters, 118, 620, 653
No More Deaths/*No Mas Muertes*
  organization
  assistance to families and migrants in
    distress, 60, 149
  faith-based organizations and, 246
  New Sanctuary Movement, 631
  on U.S. Border Patrol, 104, 759

non-gateway destinations, 202
nonrefoulement, 169
NoPassport Press, 701
"No Refuge: Migrants in Greece"
(report), 347
North American Free Trade Agreement
(NAFTA), **525–528**
automobile production industry and, 527
Clinton Administration and, 102–103
corn subsidies and, 526
date signed into law, xxxiii, 525
defined, 525
devaluation of peso, 527
displaced persons and, 171
effect on agriculture, 526–527
effect on Mexican workers, 527
effect on migration, 527
effect on U.S. manufacturers, 527
effect on U.S. workers, 527
failures of, 291
family reunification, 254
garment industry, 281
gateways and, 285
globalization, 291
impact on Mexico, 59, 102–103, 410,
474, 527–528
indigenous people and, 391
maquiladoras, 527–528
migration and, 483
poverty, exasperation of, 384
privatization of communal lands, 526
purpose of, 525
Southern states and, 659
structural adjustment programs
(SAPs), 527
subsistence farming and, 526
work visas, 785
xenophobia, 474
North American Task Force on Prostitution,
581
North Carolina, 428
Northern California DREAM Mobilizing
Summit, 9
"No Way to Live: Alabama's Immigration
Law"(report), 346
nutrition, **528–531**
acculturation, 529
childhood obesity, 530
food insecurity, 529–530

nostalgic foods, 529
role of nostalgia in immigrants' eating
patterns, 529
"selective acculturation" concept, 529

Oath of Allegiance, 744
Obama, Barack
Deferred Action for Childhood Arrivals
(DACA), 150, 195
federal benefits for same-sex marriage
couples, 439
Latino vote, 379, 651
Morton Memo, 379
reelection of, 114
Secure Communities mandatory
participation, 518
Obama administration, **533–536**
"common sense" principles for
immigration reform, 535–536
on comprehensive immigration reform
(CIR), 533
criticism of Secure Communities
program, 534
Deferred Action for Childhood Arrivals
(DACA), 181, 535
deportation and, 166, 533, 534, 535, 674
disconnect between campaign and
administration rhetoric and policy, 533
DREAM Act and, 534
El Paso speech, 534
GOP response to, 534
immigration enforcement priorities of,
534–535
Latino support for, 535
LULAC meeting speech, 533
The Morton Memo, 535
Provisional Unlawful Presence (PUP)
Waiver, 424, 511, 535
workplace raids and, 574
Office of Refugee Resettlement, 602
O'Leary, Anna Ochoa, 448, 701
Operation
Blockade, 699, 737
Endgame, 640
Gatekeeper, 59, 103–104, 147, 254,
376, 485
Gateway, 737
Hold the Line, 103, 147, 254, 376, 485
Rio Grande, 147, 376, 485

Rollback, 145, 199, 219–220
Safeguard, 59, 103, 147, 254, 376, 485
Tarmac, 122
Operation Streamline, **536–541**
actions against, 541
comprehensive immigration reform bill,
536–537
cost to taxpayers, 540
criticism of, 539–540
decline in USAO prosecution of drug
smuggling case, 540
Del Rio border sector, 536, 537
Department of Homeland Security
on, 539
deportation, 737
detention center space and, 537
effective assistance of counsel, 540
effects of, 538–539
en masse plea hearings, 538
explanation of, 536
first implementation of, 536
Heather E. Williams on, 540
Immigration Reform, 2013–2014
and, 380
Improper Entry by Alien law, use of, 536
incarceration and, 388, 390
Jason M. Hannan on, 727
John McCain (Sen.), 540
legal representation and, 433
Marco Rubio (Sen.), 540
migration and, 486
origins of, 537
OTM migrants, 536
private prison operators profits and, 540
procedure of, 537–538
purpose of, 536
Reentry of Removed Aliens law,
use of, 536
sector capacities to prosecute, 538
Tucson border sector, 536
United States v. Roblero-Solis ruling,
538, 725–726
U.S. v. Arqueta-Ramos ruling, 541
Operation Wetback, **541–545**
American labor shortage and, 542
anti-immigrant settlement, 544
Border Patrol and police-state
tactics, 544
Bracero program, 542–543
California, 544
children and, 544
citizenship checks, 544
civil rights violations, 544
context of, 542–543
date institutionalized, xxx, 543
deportation, 66, 154, 542 (image)
deportation methods, 544
excessive force, use of, 544
failure of, 544–545
family separation, 544
Herbert Brownell on, 543
Hold the Line, 699
hypocrisy in, 63
repatriating Mexican Americans, 544
results of, 472
second-class citizenship, 93
targets of, 543, 544
U.S. citizen deportation, 544
voluntary return, 544
wetback term, 63, 541
Order of the Sons of America, 429
O'Reilly, Bill, 314
Oriental Exclusion Act (1924), 88, 193,
309, 679
The Other Face of America (Ramos),
668–669
"otherness," 435, 459, 789
overstayers, **545–548**
Center for Immigration Studies on, 545
consequence of visa overstaying, 546
employer abuses, 546
estimating number of, 545
E-Verify, 546
I-94 form, 546–547
inadmissibility and, 546, 547
informal sector employment, 546
overstay defined, 545
overstaying 180 days, 547
Pew Hispanic Center on, 545
"shadow population," 546
visa application process, 547–548
visa expiration, 546
visa renewal, 547
visa waiver countries, 547
Wall Street Journal on, 547

Paez, Richard A. (Judge), 540
Page Act (18 Stat. 477), 216

Paisanos al Rescate, 149
Pakistan, 437
Pakistanis, 561
Pantoja, Pedro, 73
Papá está en la Atlántida (Malpica), 701
Paper Angels (Lim), 701
Parks, Rosa, 98
Partners in Crime: Europe's Role in US Renditions (report), 27
Passages: For Lee Ping To (Lee), 702
Passel, Jeffrey S., and D'Vera Cohn (2009), 87
The Passing of the Great Race (Grant), 406
passports, **549–550**
    defined, 549
    fraudulent, 549
    loss/expiration, 549
    overstayers and, 550
    requirements for issuing, 550
    right of return argument, 550
    risk of arrest, 550
    stamps and seals, 549
    in the U.S., 549
    valid visa and, 550
    Western Hemisphere Travel Initiative (WHTI), 549–550
Patient Protection and Affordable Care Act of 2010 (PPACA) and, 86
patriotism, **551–553**
    acculturation of Latin America immigrants, 552
    affective quality of, 551
    after September 11, 2001, 552–553
    anti-immigrant attitudes and, 552
    definition of, 551
    hostility towards immigrants, 553
    immigrant threat to being "American," 552
    military service and, 551
    national identity and, 551
    undocumented immigrants as threat, 552
    USA PATRIOT Act, 553
Paying the Price: The Impact of Immigration Raids on America's Children (report), 295
Peña, Anita Alves (2009), 479, 480, 481
People's Republic of China (PRC), 90
Perry, Rick, 379
Personal Responsibility and Work Opportunity Reconciliation Act (PRWORA), **553–557**

Agricultural Research, Extension, and Education Act (1998), 555
    amendments to, 555
    Arizona and, 30
    date signed into law, 553
    documented migrants and refugees, 554
    effects of, 553–554
    estimated national savings from, 554
    faith-based organizations, 246
    Food Stamp program, 554, 555
    hospitals, 337
    laws and legislation, post-1980s, 427
    levels of welfare assistance eligibility for immigrants, 554–555
    major funding cuts of, 554
    medical services, 554, 555
    military personnel and their families, 555
    refugees, 555
    Supplemental Security Income program (SSI), 554, 555
    Temporary Assistance for Needy Families (TANF), 554, 691
    undocumented immigrants, 554, 555
    U.S. Latina/o Educational Pipeline, 105
Pew Hispanic Center
    on Cubans, 130
    on Illinois, 361
    on immigrant labor substitution and native job loss, 204
    on Latino vote (2012), 379
    on net migration from Mexico to U.S. (2012), xxxviii
    on New Jersey, 512
    on number of children in undocumented families, 80
    on overstayers, 545
    on ports of entry, 568
    on the psychological state of U.S. Latinos, 238
    on Salvadorans, 645
    on second-generation English usage, 238
    on undocumented children, 82, 84, 86
    on undocumented construction workers, 638
Piekarsky, Brandon, 316
pluralism, 728
Plyler v. Doe ruling, **556–559**
    arguments presented, 556
    California Proposition 187, 558

college education and, 558
date of, xxxii
the DREAM Act and, 558
elementary schools and, 211
English-language instruction, 227
Equal Protection Clause, 556–557
Fourteenth Amendment and, 275, 556
Gallegly Amendment, 558
impact of, 558
majority opinion, 558
MALDEF and, 469
overview of, 556
public education as a legal right, 206
reasoning of the Court, 556–558
significant challenges to, 558
Texas argument, 556, 557
undocumented school children and,
    84–85, 105, 112
as unique (sui generis), 558
Warren Burger on, 557
William Brennan on, 558
William Wayne Justice on, 557
"Poets Responding to SB 1070" (Alarcón
    on Facebook), 446–447
policies of attrition, **559–562**
anti-immigrant climate, 559–560
anti-immigrant state-level bills, 560
Arizona SB 1070, 560
"Attrition through Enforcement: A Cost-
    Effective Strategy to Shrink the Illegal
    Population," 559
cost of mass deportation, 559
economic disparities, 561
examples of, 560
Hazelton, Pennsylvania "Illegal
    Immigration Relief Act Ordinance," 560
Hazelton, Pennsylvania ordinance
    concerning renting to undocumented
    immigrants, 560
health care access restrictions, 561
immigrant integration and, 560–561
Jessica Vaughan (2006), 559, 562
Marchevsky and Theoharis (2008) on,
    561, 562
National Security Entry-Exit Registration
    System (NSEERS) program, 561
"papers please" resolution of Prince
    William County, Virginia, 560
policy recommendations, 559

public intimidation by police, 561
Vaughan (2006) on, 561, 562
xenophobia, 790
policy and political action, **562–568**
Bob Goodlatte (R-Va), 563
Border Patrol operations, 565
border policy, largest change in, 564–565
central themes of restriction, 566
comprehensive immigration reform, 563
due process and appeal rights, 566
economic and political elite interests
    in, 566
enforcement-only agenda, 564
family reunification visas, 562
Herman Cain, 563
human rights advocate, positions of,
    567–568
and the imagined perfect recent past, 567
immigrant advocates, paradoxical aspects
    of, 567
immigrant detention and removal officers
    and facilities, 565–566
immigration law enforcement, 564
immigration opposition analysis, 567
interior enforcement, 565
Kris Kobach, 563–564
legalization program, 562–563
local and state police stops, 565
migration, processes driving, 562
migration policy flaws, 562
Mitt Romney, 563
occupational visas, 562
policies of attrition, 566
policy scenario, 563
political correctness at, 567
politics of potential comprehensive
    reform, 563–564
racism, 567
state and local legislation on, 566
visas, 562
Popkin, Eric (1999), 409, 411
Porter, Eduardo (2005), 221, 639, 641
Portes, Alejandro, Manuel Castells, and
    Lauren A. Benton, eds. (1989), 395, 397
Portes, A., L. Guarnizo, and P. Landolt
    (1999), 707, 709
ports of entry, **568–571**
defined, 568
departure, with the intention of return, 571

ports of entry (continued)
    departures, 570
    modification of racial stereotypes, 570
    port inspectors, 571
    racial profiling, 570
    stereotypes of borders and migration, 571
    unauthorized migrant population
        difference, 570
    unauthorized migration, 568
posttraumatic stress disorder (PTSD),
    467, 713
Postville, Iowa raid, **571–574**
    Aaron and Sholom Rubashkin, 573
    American Civil Liberties Union on, 573
    charges in, 572, 573
    community-organizing efforts, 573–574
    date of, 571
    Department of Homeland Security
        (DHS) on, 571–572
    effects on Postville, 573
    Hosam Amara, 573
    incarceration, 573
    Juan Carlos Guerrero-Espinoza, 573
    Martin De La Rosa-Loera, 573
    national concern for, 572–573
    number of arrests, 572
    protests of, 572 (image)
    purpose of (stated), 571–572
    results of, 572
    workplace raids and the Obama
        administration, 574
    Zeev Levi, 573
Powell, Lewis F. (Justice), 724
Prebisch, Raúl, 482
pregnancy and childbirth, **574–577**
    abuses of undocumented pregnant
        women, 576
    an, 575
    "anchor babies," 574, 575–576
    Emergency Medicaid, 575
    epidemiologic paradox theory, 574–575
    Fourteenth Amendment, U.S.
        Constitution, 575
    "healthy migrant effect," 575
    Latina paradox, 574–575
    number of infants born to undocumented
        parents (2008), 574
    prenatal care, access to, 575
    prenatal care, cost of, 575

prenatal care, refusal of, 575
    rates of low birth weight (LBW) and
        premature birth, 574–575
    undocumented pregnant women in police
        custody, 576
    Women, Infants, and Children (WIC)
        program, 575
Prince William County, Virginia anti-
    immigrant ordinance, 32–33, 560
Prison Rape Elimination Act (PREA), 760
Procedures for the Safe and Orderly
    Repatriation of Mexican Nationals, 615
Project Voice, 22–23
Proposition 187, **577–579**
    alternative name for, 112
    banking and, 47–48
    children and, 85
    community activism and, 108, 578
    consequences of (unintended), 578
    constitutionality of, 275
    controversial portions of, 578
    date past, xxxiii
    discrimination and hate, 315
    "Exclusion of Illegal Aliens from
        Public Elementary and Secondary
        Schools," 85
    explanation of, 577
    *League of United Latin American
        Citizens v. Wilson* ruling, 85
    LULAC et al. v. Wilson et al. on, xxxiv
    main idea behind, 67, 577
    mixed-status families and, 578
    nativist anxieties in, 102
    parallel with Arizona's SB 1070,
        578–579
    percentage of California voters
        approving, 275
    Plyler v. Doe ruling and, 558, 578
    as protection from the undocumented, 112
    purpose of, 113, 240
    racism, 578
    results of, 285
    Section 7 of, 577–578
    Sections 5 and 6 of, 578
    Temporary Assistance to Needy Families
        (TANF), 692
    welfare system, 768
    xenophobia, 790
prosecutorial discretion, 150, 153

prostitution, **579–581**
 arguments for/against, 579
 Asian Exclusion Act (Page Act), 580
 bar/hotel prostitution, 580
 brothel prostitution, 580
 defined, 579
 escort prostitution, 580
 FBI statistics on, 579
 federal legislation on, 580–581
 forms of, 580
 HIV/AIDS, 579, 581
 immigration and prostitution, 580–581
 legality of, 579
 North American Task Force on
  Prostitution, 581
 Prostitution Education Network, 581
 sex trafficking, 580
 Sexually Transmitted Diseases (STDs),
  579
 street prostitution, 580
 Trafficking Victims Protection Act
  (2000), 580–581
 undocumented immigrant women, 580
 violence and crime, 580
protests, **581–584**
 adolescents and, 583
 Anti-Ethnic Studies bill, 583
 Arizona and, 582
 Arizona House Bill 2281, 583
 Dolores Huerta speech in Tucson,
  Arizona, 582–583
 ethnic studies, elimination of, 583
 extent of Latino immigrant involvement
  in political protests, 582
 hybridized groupings of Latinos, 582
 Latino civic and political participation,
  582 (chart)
 Latino tradition of protesting, 581–582
 "Republicans hate Latinos" remark, 583
Provisional Unlawful Presence (PUP)
  Waiver, **584–587**
 application fee, 585
 bars defined, 585
 benefits of, 585, 586
 children, 585, 586
 concerns in, 585
 critical benefit of, 585
 explanation of, 584–585
 family separation, 585, 586

"going back to the end of the line"
  reference, 584
 green card application, 585
 immigrant advocates reaction to, 586
 inadmissible undocumented
  immigrants, 584
 lawful permanent residents (LPRs), 424
 naturalization, 511
 Obama administration and, 424, 511,
  535, 584
 requesting PUP waiver, 585
 requirements, 585–586
Public Law 78, xxx
public libraries, **587–589**
 adult education and, 589
 basic services of, 589
 Denver Public Library's El Centro
  section, 588 (image)
 immigrants and, 587
 patron confidentiality, 587
 Pima County Public Library (PCPL), 588
 San Francisco Public Library (SFPL), 588
 school-aged children and, 589
 services of, 589
 staffing, 588
 undocumented immigrants and, 587
 value of, 589
Puerto Rico, 236

racialized labeling of Mexican origin
  persons, **591–594**
 agricultural interests and migrant label,
  591–592
 characterization of Mexican Americans
  and Mexican nationals r, 592
 illegal alien label, 591
 illegal immigrant label, 593
 illegals, 593–594
 multiple labels applied to the ethnic
  Mexican community, 591
 praise and derision of Mexican
  Americans and Mexican migrants,
  591, 592
 summation of, 594
 undocumented immigrant label, 591, 593
 wetback label, 592–593
racial profiling, **594–597**
 ACLU, 19
 in Arizona, 595, 596

racial profiling (continued)
   Arizona SB1070, 31, 34, 474, 595
   assimilation and, 37
   defined, 594
   Dominicans and, 178
   federal courts on, 595
   gangs and, 278
   Georges-Abeyie (2001) on, 595, 596
   harmful consequences of, 595
   "Hostile Terrain: Human Rights
      Violation in Immigration Enforcement
      in the U.S. Southwest" report, 27
   Illegal Immigration Reform and
      Immigrant Responsibility Act
      (IIRIRA), 518
   Illinois Migrant Council v. Pilliod
      ruling, 362
   immigration law and, 595
   impact of, 596
   incarceration and, 387
   "Keep America Safe and Free"
      campaign, 20
   law enforcement and, 595–596
   legal status and, 436
   National Council of La Raza (NCLR), 506
   New York and, 518
   Operation Wetback, 544
   ports of entry and, 570
   Secure Communities program, 629
   social interaction and integration, 648
   United States v. Brignoni-Ponce ruling,
      595, 723
   unjust deportation, 375–376
   U.S. v. Martinez-Fuert ruling, 595
racism, **597–600**
   bigotry vs. racism, 597
   Cubans and, 131
   cultural racism, 598
   defined, 597
   discrimination and, 597, 598
   East Asians and, 195
   education, 7
   effects of, 599
   on fair housing, 598–599
   healthcare, 599
   hiring processes, 598
   homelessness, 328
   immigrants and, 598–599
   immigration status, 725

   individual racism, 597–598
   institutional racism, 598
   interpersonal level racism, 599
   manifestations of, 597
   meat processing plants, 456
   policy and political action, 567
   prejudice and, 597
   Proposition 187, 578
   racial discrimination, 598–599
   racial microaggressions, 599
   self-esteem of children and, 3
   small business ownership, 645
   suburbs and, 684
   undocumented immigrants expectation
      of, 597
   U.S. soldiers of color and, 98
   xenophobia and, 790
Ramírez, Luis, 112
Ramos, Ignacio, 759
Ramos, Jorge, 668
Ramos and Compean Act, 759
Ranch Rescue organization, 491, 492
Rangel, Charles, 381
rape, 60, 129, 173, 287, 288, 714, 760, 773
Reagan, Ronald, 24, 77, 78, 215, 382
      (image), 523
Reagan doctrine, 77
REAL ID Act (Border Protection, Anti-
      Terrorism and Illegal Immigration
      Control Act), xxxvii
Rector, Robert, 203
Reed, David (Rep.), 405
Refugee Act, xxxii
Refugee Act (1980), **600–602**
   30th anniversary of the Refugee Act
      (1980), 601 (image)
   asylum, 600, 602
   cap on refugees, 600
   concerns about, 600–601
   cost of admittance and resettlement
      resettlement, 600–601
   definition of refugee, 601
   domestic settlement, 602
   Edward Kennedy (Senator), 600–601
   exclusions to definition of
      refugee, 601
   history of, 600
   objectives of, 600
   Office of Refugee Resettlement, 602

official title of admittance, 602
special "refugee" status, 602
refugees, **602–604**
  asylum, 603
  basic rights for, 604
  defined, 602
  economic hardship and refugee status, 604
  formal definition of, 602
  international organizations assisting, 603
  international refugee production, 602
  local integration, 604
  military combatants and refugee
    status, 603
  non-refoulement principle, 603
  number of (2011), 603
  obligations of, 603
  resettlement, 604
  status determination, 603
  types of uprooted people, 604
  UN Refugee Agency (UNHCR), 603, 604
  voluntary repatriation, 604
Reid, Harry, 534
religion, **605–608**
  Archbishop of Guadalajara, 606
  Catholic, 605, 606
  churches and shrines, 605
  condom use, 606
  Elvira Arellano case, 607
  evangelical, 605, 606
  familialism, 605
  as a framework for action, 608
  "holy crusade against emigration," 606
  Humane Borders group, 607
  influence on social issues, 606
  Latinos and, 605
  No More Deaths advocacy group, 608
  political thought and, 607
  Protestant, 605, 606
  refuge, 607
  relation between immigration and, 605–606
  religious paraphernalia, 605
  reproductive choice, 606
  Saint Toribio Romo Gonzalez, 605
  Sanctuary Movement, 607
  undocumented migrant aid, 607, 608
  Unitarian Universalist Church of Tucson,
    607–608
Religious Society of Friends (Quaker)
  and, 21

remittances, **608–614**
  Bancomer on, 612, 613
  benefits of, 611
  Central America/Dominican Republic
    cost of remittance transfers, 610
  decline in, 608–609, 612–613
  deportation and, 610
  economic recession and, 608, 609
  El Universal on, 612
  female migrant remittances, 610
  Gross Domestic Product (GDP) and, 610
  growth of (2010 to 2011), 610
  home town associations (HTAs),
    611–612
  Internet and mobile telephone
    banking, 610
  La Crónica de Hoy on, 612
  La Jornada on, 612, 613
  La Opinión on, 612
  livelihood and, 609
  Mexican government and HTAs,
    611–612
  Mexican states, effect of decline in, 612
  remittance receivers, 611
  remittances and GDPs for selected
    countries, 610 (table)
  top 10 U.S. remittance-sending states,
    611 (table)
  trends in, 608–609, 610
  use of, 611
Rempell, Benjamin (2005), 639, 641
Reno, Janet, 59
repatriation, **614–617**
  Alien Transfer Exit Program (ATEP),
    616
  defined, 614
  deportation/removal and, 614, 615
  El Instituto Nacional de Migración
    (INM), 615
  formal charges, 614
  human remains, 617
  Mexican consular services for, 617
  Mexican Interior Repatriation Program,
    615–616
  Mexican-U.S. agreements concerning,
    615–616
  Mexico's response to Arizona Senate Bill
    1070, 616–617
  patient dumping, 617

repatriation (continued)
  Procedures for the Safe and Orderly
    Repatriation of Mexican Nationals, 615
  Tucson Border Patrol sector, 614, 615
  U.S. hospitals and, 617
  voluntary return/expedited removal, 614
In re Rodriguez, xxvii
resources recommended
  anthologies, 797
  documentary films and videos, 800
  monographs, 797–799
  stories about undocumented immigrants,
    799–800
  websites, 800–801
restaurants, **618–621**
  "back of the house"positions, 618
  bad jobs classification, 618
  Chipotle burrito chain, 619
  Chuy's chain restaurants, 619–620
  electronic employment verification
    errors, 620
  employers reviews of undocumented
    immigrants, 618
  E-Verify, 620
  "front of the house" positions, 618
  immigrant labor force and, 618
  National Restaurant Association on, 620
  "no match" letters, 620
  Ruben Castro, owner of La Fiesta Braval,
    619 (image)
  tentative confirmation notices, 620
  undocumented workers and, 618
  wages, deprivation of, 618
  workplace raids/silent raids, 618
Return to Sender (Alvarez), 446
Revueltas, Rosaura, 110
Richardson, Bill, 515
Rivera-Batiz, F. L. (1999), 26
Roberts, Demetress, 210 (image)
Robeson, Paul, 98
Rodino, Peter (Rep.), 381
Rodriguez, Jose Antonio Elena, 759
Rodriguez, Nelly, 722 (image)
Romano-V, Octavio I., 137
Romero, Mary (2002), 287, 289
Romero, Oscar Arnulfo (Archbishop), 77
Romney, Mitt, 379, 563
Rondona, Miriam Lucia, 156 (image)
Roosevelt, Franklin Delano, 194, 769

Rosaldo, Renato, 134, 135
Rosenblum, Marc R., 533
Rubashkin, Aaron and Sholom, 573
Rubio, Marco (Sen.), 132, 377, 390, 540

Salgadu, Udaya Kanthi, 703
Salsbury, Jessica, 175 (image)
Salt of the Earth (movie), 110
Salvadorans, **623–625**
  *American Baptist Churches v.
    Thornburgh (ABC)* ruling, 624
  asylum, 623–624
  Barrio 18, 625
  Central American gang violence,
    624–625
  civil war and migration to the U.S., 623
  Immigration Act (1990), 624
  Mara Salvatrucha (MS and MS-13), 625
  Nicaraguan Adjustment and Central
    American Relief Act (1997), 624
  number of Salvadorans in the U.S., 623
  Operation *Mano Dura* (Heavy Hand), 625
  remittances of, 623
  Sanctuary Movement, 624
  Temporary Protected Status (TPS), 624
Salvation Army, 246
Samaritans group, 60
*Sanango v. 200 East 16th Street Housing
  Corp.* ruling, 220, 779
Sanchez, George I., 137
sanctuary cities and secure communities,
  625–629
  DHS on the Secure Communities
    initiative, 627
  FBI and the Secure Communities
    program, 627, 628
  first local sanctuary policy, 626
  forms of contemporary sanctuary
    policies, 626
  Francisco Barranco and La Tapatia
    bakery, 626 (image)
  ICE and the Secure Communities
    program, 627, 628
  Integrated Automated Fingerprint
    Identification System (IAFIS), 628
  Kittrie (2006) on, 626, 629
  LA Police Department Special
    Order 40, 627
  sanctuary cities, 625–627

Sanctuary Movement, 627
Secure Communities controversy,
  628–629
Secure Communities program, 627–629
U.S. Visitor and Immigrant Status
  Indicator Technology Program (US-
  VISIT), 628
Sanctuary Movement, **629–632**
  actions of volunteers, 630
  Arizona's SB 1070 and, 607
  arrest of volunteers, 631
  basis of, 630
  Central American civil wars, 77
  Chicago Religious Task Force, 631
  date formally announced, 630
  El Concilio Manzo, 630
  Honduras, 332
  impact of, 631
  Inter-American Symposium on
    Sanctuary, 631
  letter to the Justice Department, 630
  New Sanctuary Movement, 76, 631
  No More Deaths/*No Mas Muertes*
    organization, 631
  objective of, 630
  origins of, 629–630
  Reagan administration on, 631
  religion and, 607
  Salvadoran/Guatemalan refugees, 624
  Sanctuary volunteers, 630, 631
  Southside Presbyterian Church,
    Tucson, 630
  terrorist attacks, September 11, 2001, 627
  U.S. government view of, 630–631
Sassen, Saskia (1996), 409, 411
Save Our State initiative, 112
Save Our State movement in California, 491
Schakowsky, Jan, 381
Schmid, David I., 220
School of the Americas (Western
  Hemisphere Institute for Security
  Cooperation), 77
Schumer, Charles (Sen.), 377
Schwarzenegger, Arnold, 185
Science, Technology, Engineering and
  Mathematics (STEM) Visa Act (2011),
  682–683
Seasonal Agricultural Worker (SAW)
  program, 478

Secure Border Initiative Network
  (SBINet), 752
Secure Communities Program, xxxvii, 110
Secure Fence Act, 190
Secure Fence Act (2006), 752
Select Commission on Immigration and
  Refugee Policy, **632–634**
  on asylum, 633
  Becoming American report, 632
  composition of, 633
  date established, 632
  date of initial report, 633
  deportation, 633
  Domestic Council Committee on Illegal
    Aliens, 633
  effect of, 632
  Gerald R. Ford and, 633
  illegal immigration, 634
  legal immigration, 633
  purpose of, 632
  reason for, 632
  recommendations, 633
  recommendations, effect of, 632, 634
  refugee resettlement process, 633
  Restoring Credibility report, 632
  Setting Priorities report, 632
Semana Binacional de Salud (Binational
  Health Week), 269
seniors, **634–637**
  10 countries of origin of older
    immigrants in the U.S. (2012),
    635 (table)
  Affordable Care Act and elderly
    undocumented, 635
  caregivers, 636
  family ties and, 637
  financial challenges to undocumented
    immigrants, 636
  Korean elderly, 636
  life expectancy of undocumented
    immigrants, 635–636
  Medicare and elderly undocumented, 635
  as Mexican property owners, 637
  Mexico's healthcare infrastructure, 635
  number of senior immigrants in the
    U.S., 634
  premature death, 636
  senior immigrant population, growth of,
    634–635

seniors (continued)
  social cost of, 637
  transnationalism, 636–637
  Yoo and Zippay (2012) on, 636, 637
The Sentencing Project, 387
September 11 Commission, 120
Service Employees International Union
    (SEIU), 417, 418
Sessenbrenner bill, 120
sex trafficking, 580
Shadow Lives (Chavez), 446
shadow population, **637–641**
  Chavez (2012), 640, 641
  constitutional rights of, 640
  consumer-related taxes and, 639
  definitions of, 637–638
  earnings suspension file of Social
    Security, 639
  employer abuses of, 638–639
  fraudulent documents, 638
  hate crimes, 640
  Immigration Reform and Control Act
    (IRCA), 638
  income tax refunds and, 639
  meatpacking jobs and, 638
  nativists accusations, 640–641
  Operation Endgame, 640
  paradox of, 638
  Pew Hispanic Center study on, 638
  police actions against, 640
  policies of attrition, 640
  Porter (2005) on, 639, 641
  public welfare benefits and, 639
  remittances, amounts of, 639
  Rempell (2005) on, 639, 641
  Systematic Alien Verification
    Entitlements (SAVE), 639
  U.S. revenue surplus and, 639
  W-2 earnings of, 639
Sikhs, 658
Simcox, Chris, 490
Simon, Jonathan (2007), 293, 296
Sinclair, Upton, 453
Singapore, 437
single men, **641–643**
  border militarization, 642
  in El Paso, Texas, 641–642
  Latina/os and El Paso, Texas, 642
  in Los Angeles, California, 642–643

Siskin, Alison (2011), 86, 87
slavery, modern-day, 167
small business ownership, **644–646**
  Arizona House Bill 2745, 644
  Barros (2009:312) on, 644, 646
  benefits of, 646
  community and, 645
  definition of Hispanic-owned
    business, 644
  entrepreneurship, 645
  growth of Latino-owned businesses, 645
  Hispanic origin defined, 644
  increase in Mexican-owned firms in
    Arizona, 644
  Latino term, 644
  Legal Workers Act (Arizona), 644
  racism and fear of foreigners, 645
  social networks, 645
  statistics on Hispanic (or Latino)-owned
    businesses, 645
  U.S. Census terms for racial
    category, 644
  Valdez (2012:64) on, 644, 646
SNAP (Supplemental Nutrition Assistance
    Program), 87
social interaction and integration, **646–652**
  Coleman (1988) on, 648, 651
  election of Barack Obama, 651
  extra-household relationships, 649
  hometown associations (HTAs), 649
  immigrant women and social capital, 649
  Latino political views, 650
  Latino view of undocumented
    immigrants, 650
  Michelson (2001) on, 650, 652
  mixed immigration status household,
    650–651
  mutual cooperation, 649
  Pew Research (2007) on, 650, 652
  political and civic engagement, 650
  political empowerment, 649
  political participation, 651
  positive outcome of, 651
  racial profiling, 648
  segregation of Mexican immigrants, 648
  social capital, 647
  social hostilities and exploitation, 648
  social networks, 648
  social obligation, 647

types of resources ranging from less to more tangible forms, 647 (table)
U.S. Latino population amalgamation of social groupings, 649
U.S.-Mexican dual nationals, 649–650
Social Security, **652–655**
  Baby Boomer retirement and new immigrants, 654–655
  Baby Boomers, 652
  Baby Bust generation, 653
  background information, 652–653
  conclusion concerning, 655
  contributions to, 653
  "dependency ratio" of workers-to-retirees, 653
  Earnings Suspense File (ESF), 654
  education of immigrants, 654, 655
  explanation of, 652
  immigrant Social Security tax surplus, 653–654
  immigration effect on Social Security fund, xxxv
  increase costs of (2015), 654
  legal immigrants and, 653
  Medicare, 652, 653
  need for immigration argument, 654
  New York Times on, 654
  "no match" letters, 653
  "pig in the python" concept, 654
  social factors in, 654–655
  Social Security Act, 769
  taxes paid by immigrants, 654
  undocumented workers and, 653
  young immigrants and, 653
Solares (mother and daughter), 136 (image)
Soldatenko, María Angelina (1999), 279, 283
Solid Ground (La Casa Norte) and undocumented youth, 328
South Asians, **655–659**
  anti-immigrant sentiment, 658
  Asian American Hotels Owners Association (AAHOA), 657
  Bangladesh, 656, 657
  in comparison to Latino groups, 657
  defined, 655
  Dhingra (2012) on, 657, 658
  Hart-Celler Act (1965) and, 657
  hate crimes, 658
  human smuggling from India, 657
  immigrant choices, 657
  immigration statuses, 657
  India, 656
  Indian migration, 657–658
  median household income of Indians, 657
  "model minority" characterization, 657
  Pakistan, 656, 657
  percentage of population born outside the U.S., 657
  remittances, 656, 658
  sending countries on migration, 656
  Sikhs, 658
  traditional festivities of, 658
  undocumented Indian immigrants, 657
Southeast Immigrant Rights Network (SEIRN), 696
Southern Poverty Law Center (SPLC), 316, 790
Southern states, **659–661**
  287(g) agreements, 661
  anti-congregating ordinances (Georgia), 661
  anti-immigrant ordinances, 661
  anti-immigrant sentiments in, 660
  Commerce of the United States of America et al. v. Whiting et al. ruling, 660
  education, 661
  English-only ordinances, 661
  factors influencing immigration to, 659
  H 4400 (North Carolina), 660
  harboring or abetting undocumented immigrants, 660
  HB 56 (Alabama), 660–661
  House Resolution 2692 (North Carolina), 660
  immigrant labor, 659
  Immigration Reform and Control Act (IRCA) effect on, 659
  large-scale immigration, 659
  Latino immigrant population, 659–660
  migration to, 659
  NAFTA, 659
  restricted driver's licenses (North Carolina), 660
  Senate Bill 529 (Georgia), 660
  verification of immigration status, 660
Southside Presbyterian Church, Tucson, 630
South Side Presbyterian Church, Tucson, Arizona, 245

Southwest Council of La Raza, xxxi
Spanish-language media, **662–664**
    acculturation process and, 662
    advertising, 662, 664
    assimilation and, 664
    conflicting roles of, 662
    consolidation of ownership of, 662
    El Diario–La Prensa, purchase of, 663
    hegemonic cultural imperialism, 662–663
    homogenization, 662
    immigrant-friendly, 663
    immigrant integration and, 663
    "Latinidad," 662
    "Latinoization" of America, 664
    as nationwide phenomenon, 662
    social action and, 663
    Spanish-language TV networks, 662
    standardize Spanish, 662
    statistics concerning, 662
    Telecommunication Act (1996), 662
    undocumented immigrants and, 663
Special Agricultural Workers (SAW),
    664–666
    amnesty, 664
    amnesty, effects of, 665–666
    amnesty process, 665
    anti-immigrant sentiment and, 665
    border enforcement, 666
    California Proposition 187, 665
    Group 1/Group 2 status, 665
    Immigration Reform and Control Act
        (IRCA), 664–665
    Legally Authorized Workers (LAW)
        program, 665
    militarization of border, consequence
        of, 666
    temporary status application, 665
Spencer, Glen, 491
Spener, David, and Randy Capps (2001),
    279, 281, 283
sponsors, **666–668**
    Affidavit of Support Form I-864, 666
    defined, 666
    eligibility for sponsorship, 666
    employment eligibility, categories of,
        667–668
    examples of, 666
    family preference, 667
    financial requirements, 667

    financial responsibility, 667
    Hagan and Rodriguez (2002), 667, 668
    Illegal Immigration Reform and
        Immigrant Responsibility Act
        (IIRIRA), effects of, 667
    income requirements for sponsorship, 667
    income-to-household size, 667
    means-tested public benefits, 667
    requirements for, 666–667
    same-sex partner sponsor, 668
    United American Families Act, 668
sports, **668–672**
    baseball, 671
    boxing, 671
    "Creating and Fostering Fan
        Identification in Professional Sports"
        (Sutton, McDonald, Milne, and
        Climperman), 669
    Latinization of U.S. sports, 668–669, 671
    Mexico-U.S. soccer rivalry, 670–671
    reaction to Arizona's SB 1070, 669
    soccer, 669–671
    value of, 669
State Children's Health Insurance Program
    (SCHIP), 87
state legislation, **672–675**
    in Alabama, 673
    Arizona SB 1070, 672
    court action against, 672, 673
    in Georgia, 673
    in Indiana, 672
    Indiana SB 590, 673
    long-term consequences for immigrant
        populations, 674
    Lopez (2011) on, 674, 675
    Obama administration deportations, 674
    in South Carolina, 673–674
    state-level anti-immigrant legislative
        trend (2005-2010), 674 (fig.)
    Trujillo and Paluck (2012) on, 674, 675
    in Utah, 672
in-state tuition, states allowing
    undocumented students to pay, 107
in-state tuition, states denying
    undocumented students to pay, 107
Strangers from a Different Shore (Takaki),
    675–678
    Asian Indian migration, 677
    Asian migration after 1965, 677

Chinese Exclusion Act (1882), 676
European immigrant groups, 676
Filipino immigrants, 676–677
Filipino "manongs," 677
Japanese migration, 676
Korean migration, 677
National Origins Act (1924), 676
overview of, 675–676
prostitution, 677
quota limits, 676
recruitment of Asian workers, 677
Ronald Takaki, 675, 676, 677
Tydings-McDuffie Act (1934), 676–677
The Uprooted (Handlin) and, 729
Strangers in the Land (Higham), **678–680**
American nativism, 678, 679, 680
areas of operation, 678
Chinese Exclusion Act (1882), 679
criticism of, 679–680
date first published, 678
Immigration Act of 1924, 679
importance of, 678
influence of, 678
John Higham on, 678, 679–680
nativist concerns, 679
Oriental Exclusion Act of 1924, 679
Rutgers University Press and, 678
traditions of nativism, 679
Strangers No Longer, Together on the Journey to Hope (letter), 72
strategic invisibilization, 10
structural adjustment programs (SAPs), 291
student visas, **680–683**
application for, 682
B-type visa, 682
Illegal Immigration Reform and Immigrant Responsibility Act (IIRIRA), 681
interview for, 682
J-1 exchange visitor visa, 682
M-1-visa, 682
Michael Bennett (Sen.) on, 683
necessity of, 682
PhDs loss, 683
requirements for, 682
Science, Technology, Engineering and Mathematics (STEM) Visa Act (2011), 682–683
Student and Exchange Visitor Information System (SEVIS), 681

terrorist attacks and, 680–681
types of, 681–682
undocumented students have, 682
voided visa, 682
suburbs, **683–686**
"9500 Liberty" (documentary), 684
day laborers, 684–685
de facto segregation, 685
defined, 683
Domestic Workers Rights Bill, 685–686
fear of migrants, 685
gang violence, 684
Garden City, New York, 684
gated communities, 684
gentrification, 684
immigrants and, 683–684
Immigration Reform and Control Act (1986) and, 684
inner cities and, 684
local legislative action against immigrants, 685
migration networks, 684
redlining, 684
"shape-up sites," 685
suburban Latino population growth, 684
unionism, 685
Supplemental Security Income program, 554
Sutton, W. A., M. A. McDonald, G. R. Milne, and J. Cimperman (1997), 669, 672
Swift and Co. workforce raid, 85, 418, 493, 783
Systematic Alien Verification Entitlements (SAVE), 639

Taiwan, 90
Takaki, Ronald, 675
Tancredo, Tom, 492
Tarango v. State Industrial Insurance System ruling, 780–781
Tarascan community, 476
Targeting Immigrants (Inda), 692
taxes, **687–690**
dollar amount collected from ITIN filers, 688
Earned Income Tax Credit (EITC), 688
Earnings Suspense File (ESF), 689
explanation of, 687
false Social Security numbers, 689
good moral character and, 688

taxes (continued)
  Individual Taxpayer Identification
    Number (ITIN), 687–688
  informal economy and, 689
  limitations of ITIN permits, 688
  Nonwork Alien File, 689
  Norm Chomsky on, 689
  sales taxes, 687
  Social Security numbers, 687
  They Take Away Our Jobs! And 20 Other
    Myths About Immigration
    (Chomsky), 689
  undocumented immigrant contribution to
    Social Security, 688, 689
  undocumented immigrant contribution to
    U.S. economy, 687
  undocumented immigrants and, 687
  women and, 689
Taylor, J. Edward, Philip L. Martin, and
  Michael Fix (1997), 409, 411
Telecommunication Act (1996), 662
Telemundo, 662, 739
Temporary Assistance to Needy Families
  (TANF), **690–692**
  Aid to Families with Dependent Children
    (AFDC), 691
  Clinton administration, 691
  criticisms of the U.S. welfare system, 691
  date established, 690
  eligibility for, 690
  establishment of, 691
  female immigrants, 690
  female immigrants, labeling of, 690, 692
  Job Opportunities and Basic Skills
    Training (JOBS), 691
  origins of U.S. welfare system, 691
  Personal Responsibility and Work
    Opportunity Reconciliation Act
    (PRWORA), 691–692
  Proposition 187 (California), 692
  public costs of undocumented
    immigrants, 692
  Targeting Immigrants (Inda), 692
  underlying purpose of U.S. social
    welfare system, 691
  undocumented migrants and, 690
  U.S. welfare system, 690, 691
  "welfare queens," 690, 691, 692
  welfare system, 770

Women, Children, and Infants (WIC), 692
Work Opportunity Reconciliation Act
  (1996), 691
Temporary Protected Status (TPS),
  693–695
  asylum status and, 694
  candidates for, 694
  characterization of, 693
  citizenship and, 694
  concerns among the beneficiaries of, 694
  countries on the list for TPS
    designation, 695
  criticism of, 695
  Deferred Enforced Departure (DED),
    694, 695
  determination of, 693
  displacement and, 169, 170
  El Salvador and, 693, 694, 695
  explanation of, 693
  Extended Voluntary Departure (EVD), 694
  goal of, 694
  Guatemalans, 303
  Haitians, 693, 695
  Hondurans, 335, 336, 693
  Immigration Act of 1980, 693
  increments of, 694
  Liberian nationals and, 695
  Nicaraguans, 521, 522, 693
  penalties in, 694–695
  praise of, 695
  refugee status and, 694
  Salvadorans, 624
Tennessee Immigrant and Refugee Rights
  Coalition (TIRRC), **696–697**
  advocacy of, 696, 697
  foreign-born population in Tennessee, 696
  founding of, 696
  mission of, 696
  "new destinations" characteristic, 696
  Southeast Immigrant Rights Network
    (SEIRN) and, 696
  Tennessee anti-immigrant proposals, 696
  Welcome to Shelbyville (film), 697
  "Welcoming Tennessee Initiative," 697
Tenochtitlán, 43
Texas, **697–700**
  attitude toward Mexicans, 698
  Bracero Program, 698
  Casa San Diego, 245

demand for Mexican laborers, 698
DREAM Act, 399
economic by of Texas border, 698
Emigrant Labor Agency Law (1929), 698
Fe y Justicia (Faith and Justice), 245
forced labor, 167
House Bill 1403, 699
identity theft laws and immigration, 361
influx of undocumented migrants, 361
migrant farm workers and, 480
Operation Blockade, 699
Operation Hold the Line, 103, 147, 254, 376
Operation Hold the Line, consequences of, 699
overview of, 697–698
Proposition 1403, 153
in-state tuition for undocumented students, 152, 153, 208, 322, 362, 699
Texas Farm Placement Service, 698
undocumented immigrant laws, 698–699
undocumented immigrant population, 699
undocumented immigrants, expenditures on, 699
undocumented immigrants, revenues generated by, 699
"Texas Proviso," 216, 373
Thai Community Development Center, 703
theater, **700–704**
    Arizona: No Roosters in the Desert (Hartzler), 701
    Borderlands Theater, Tucson, Arizona, 701
    Ching Chong Chinaman (Yee), 702
    Company of Angels, 703
    Cornerstone Theater Company, 700, 703
    David Henry Hwang Writing Institute of the East West Player, 703
    Fabric (Ong), 702–703
    festivals, 703
    How to Make It to the Dance Floor: A Salsa Guide for Women (Based on Actual Experiences) (Garcia), 703
    Letters from My Mother (Salgadu), 703
    Los Illegals (Garces), 700, 703
    Papá está en la Atlántida (Malpica), 701
    Paper Angels (Lim), 701
    Passages: For Lee Ping To (Lee), 702
    "SB 1070 Festival of Plays," 703

Teatro Jornalero Sin Fronteras (Day Laborer Theater Without Borders), 703
    undocumented immigrants and, 700
    Visitors' Guide to Arivaca (Ordaz), 701
They Take Away Our Jobs! And 20 Other Myths About Immigration (Chomsky), 689
Thomas, Andrew, 492
Thompson, Ginger, 79
Thorn, John, 671
Thrash, Thomas (Judge), 673
Tlatelolco Massacre, 99
Toribio Romo Gonzalez (Saint), 605
Torres, Ramses Barrón, 759
The Tortilla Curtain (Boyle), 446
Touching Snow (Felin), 446
Trafficking Victims Protection Reauthorization Act (TVPRA), **704–706**
    definition of involuntary vs. voluntary labor, 705
    expiration of, 704
    forced prostitution, 580
    legal theory underlying, 705
    original bill, 704
    Palermo Protocol, 704
    reauthorization of, 704, 705
    sex trafficking, 705
    trafficking defined, 704
    T-visas, 581
    United States v. Shackney ruling, 705–706
    U.S. State Department's annual report on human trafficking, 705
Tran, Tam, 114–115
Transactional Records Access Clearinghouse (TRAC), 155
transnationalism, **706–709**
    3x1 program, 708
    communication, 707, 708
    concept of, 706–707
    defined, 706
    documentation of educational records, 708
    Mexican consulate support, 708
    networks of extended family members, 708
    Portes (1999) on, 707, 709
    remittances, 707
    social capital formation, 708

transnationalism (continued)
    social distance, 707
    social remittances, 708
    social spaces/locations, 707
    technology, use of, 708
    Vertovec (2006) on, 707, 709
    virtual presence, 707
The Transplanted (Bodnar), 729
Transportation and Security Administration
    (TSA), 369
transportation in the United States, **709–711**
    abuses of Mexicans, 710
    human smugglers, 711
    jurisdiction of U.S. Border Patrol, 709
    license to drive, 709
    motor vehicle accidents involving U.S.
        Border Patrol, 711
    proximity to the border and national
        security, 709
    risk to immigrants, 710–711
    stop and search incidents, 710
    U.S. Border Patrol and, 709–711
    use of Mexican appearance, 710
trauma-related symptoms, **712–715**
    categories of Complex PTSD
        symptoms, 713
    Complex Post-Traumatic Stress Disorder,
        consequences of, 712–714
    Complex Post-Traumatic Stress Disorder,
        undocumented immigrants and,
        713–714
    comprehensive names used to describe,
        714–715
    constriction, defined, 713
    DSM-V categories, 714
    hyperarousal, defined, 713
    immigrant youths and, 713
    intrusion, defined, 713
    motor vehicle accidents, 713
    posttraumatic stress disorder (PTSD), 713
    prolonged and/or repeated trauma, 712
    "Snakeheads" (human smugglers), 714
    symptoms, spectrum of, 714
    trauma defined, 712
    undocumented immigrants and, 712
    undocumented immigrant women
        and, 712
Treaty of Guadalupe Hidalgo (1848), xxv,
    44, 65, 66, 92, 235–236, 471

Treaty of Paris (1793), 68
Trujillo, Matthew D., and Elizabeth Levy
    Paluck (2012), 674, 675
Truman, Harry S., 310
Tubman, Harriet, 15
Turrentine, Howard B. Jr. (Judge), 724
T-visa, 173
Tydings-McDuffie Act (1934), 676–677

Uganda, 437
Ukraine, 367
*Underground Undergrads: UCLA
    Undocumented Immigrant Students
    Speak Out*, 9–10
undocumented immigrants in U.S., number
    of, 50
undocumented immigrant workers and the
    U.S. economy, 60, 221, 237
"undocumented" label, **717–720**
    Canada–United States border,
        unauthorized migration across, 718
    complexity in, 717
    Cuban migrants, special rules for, 720
    debate concerning, 717
    "dry foot" rule, 720
    formal v. popular terminology, 717–718
    "illegal" migrant v. "undocumented"
        migrant, 719
    Immigration and Nationality Act,
        717–718
    indocumentado label, 719
    legality v. illegality, 720
    Mexico-U.S. boundary as the problem,
        718–719
    military draft and, 720
    oxymorons, "illegal alien/immigrant"
        and "undocumented immigrant,"
        717–718
    sin documentos label, 719
    subject to removal principle, 718
    violation of entry or visa requirement
        concepts, 718
    visa violations, 718–719
undocumented students, **721–723**
    DREAM Act rally, 722 (image)
    effects of undocumented status, 721–722
    financial aid, 721
    job market and, 721, 722
    Social Security number, 722

in-state tuition, 721
support groups for, 722
university services and, 721–722
value college education to, 722
Uneven Justice: State Rates of Incarceration by Race and Ethnicity (report), 387
unionism, 202, 282, 333, 341–342, 456, 685
United Adalberto Methodist Church, 288
United American Families Act, 668
United Brotherhood of Carpenters and Joiners, 418
United Farm Workers, 473
United Farm Workers (UFW), 416
United Food and Commercial Workers (UFCW), 418
United Nations
  Convention and Protocol on Refugees, xxxi
  Convention Relating to the Status of Refugees Protocol (1951 and 1967), 40
  High Commissioner for Refugees (UNHCR), 40, 169
  Human Rights Council, 176
  Protocol Relating to the Status of Refugees, 169
  Protocols on Human Trafficking and Immigrant, xxxvi
United States Bill of Rights, 14
United States Chamber of Commerce, 216
United States Coast Guard, 369
United States Department of State's Human Trafficking Report, 350
United States economy and the undocumented immigrant, 221
United States Federal Aviation Administration, 491
United States Military Selective Service Act (1948), 487
United States role in Central American civil wars, 77–79
United States v. Arqueta-Ramos ruling, 433, 541
United States v. Brignoni-Ponce ruling, **723–725**
  Almeida-Sanchez v. United States ruling, 724
  Border Patrol, authority of, 724
  Border Patrol tactics, 724, 725

factors involved in, 724
"illegal' immigrant" term, 724
Immigration and Naturalization Service (INS), 375
Justice Powell on, 724
overview, 723–724
proximity to the border, 724
racial profiling, 595, 723
United States v. Martinez-Fuente ruling, 725
use of Mexican appearance, 723, 724, 725
United States v. Diaz-Ramirez ruling, 727
United States v. Martinez-Fuente ruling, 595, 725
United States v. Roblero-Solis ruling, 725–727
  9th Circuit Court of Appeals ruling on, 726–727
  Boykin v. Alabama ruling, 727
  due process violation, 726, 727
  en masse hearings, 726
  incarceration, 388
  at issue in, 726
  Jason M. Hannan on Operation Streamline, 727
  Martha Vázquez on, 727
  Operation Streamline, 538, 725–726, 727
  Rule 11 of the Federal Rules of Criminal Procedure, 726
  United States v. Diaz-Ramirez ruling, 727
United States vs. Bhagat Singh Thind ruling, xxix
United States v. Shackney ruling, 705–706
United States v. Wong Kim Ark ruling, xxvii, 89, 93
United States v. X-Citement Video Inc. ruling, 267
United We Dream Network, 323
UNITE-HERE, 203, 342, 417, 418
Uniting American Families Act, 438–439
Uniting and Strengthening America by Providing Appropriate Tools Required to Intercept and Obstruct Terrorism (USA PATRIOT Act), 47
Universal Declaration of Human Rights, 98
University Leadership Initiative, 323
Unz, Ron, 232
The Uprooted (Handlin), **727–730**
  criticism of, 729

The Uprooted (Handlin) (continued)
  importance of, 729
  Impossible Subjects (Ngai) and, 729
  influence of, 729
  Oscar Handlin, 727–728
  overview of, 728
  pluralism, 728
  Pulitzer Prize, 728
  Rudolph Vecoli on, 729
  Strangers from a Different Shore
    (Takaki), 729
  The Transplanted (Bodnar), 729
  uprooted vs. transplanted debate, 729
"Uprooted: Refugees of the Global
  Economy" documentary, 508
Urban Institute, 86
urban life, **730–733**
  churches and the undocumented, 731
  cities attracting immigrants, 730
  collective efficacy, 731
  community ethnic, 732
  community trust and development, 732
  crime, 731
  environmental degradation, 731
  ethnic enclaves, 730–731
  ethnic solidarity, 730
  immigration raids, 731
  local government, local community
    services, 731
  new immigrant gateway cities reaction to
    immigration, 732
  percentage of immigrants in metropolitan
    areas, 730
  transnational communities, 730
  underdeveloped space in capitalism, 731
  undocumented status and community
    problems, 731–732
Urrea, Luis Alberto, 158–161
  awards of, 160–161
  Devil's Highway, 158–161
  other works of, 160–161
  poetry of, 160–161
USA PATRIOT Act, **733–734**
  Adler (2006) on, 734
  Antiterrorism and Effective Death
    Penalty Act, 733
  Arab and Muslim immigrants, 734
  attorney privilege, 734
  banking and, 47

border security, 734
conflation of terrorism and immigration,
  733, 734
date signed into law, 733
detainment, 298
detention centers, 734
effect on foreign students, visiting
  professors, 298
erosion of immigrant rights in the U.S.,
  733–734
formal name of, 733
Hines (2006), 733, 734
immigration restriction and, 734
impact on undocumented immigrants, 734
powers of, 298, 553
purpose of, 733
restrictive release policies, 734
U.S.-Mexico negotiations, 733
workplace and neighborhood raids, 734
U.S. Border Patrol, **735–738**
  abuses of, 22, 74, 104
  Alien Transfer and Exit Program
    (ATEP), 737
  authority of, 724
  Border Security Initiative (BSI),
    737–738
  budget of, 736
  Canadian border, 69, 736
  catch and release program, 737
  crime and, 127
  deaths, 148
  Del Rio Border Patrol inspectors stop a
    car (1925), 735 (image)
  The Devil's Highway (Urrea), 158,
    159–160
  duties of, 127, 154, 735, 738
  establishment of, xxix, 154, 370, 375
  exclusion and, 239
  expansion of, 735, 736, 737
  expedited removal, 241, 242, 243
  in film and television, 264
  funding of, increased, 370, 736
  Great Lakes region, 298
  growth of, 736
  hate crimes and, 315
  hospital stakeouts, 338
  Illegal Immigration Reform and
    Immigrant Responsibility Act
    (IIRIRA) and, 358

"Illegal" Migrant v. "Undocumented" Migrant, 718
Immigration Act (IMMACT), 367
Immigration and Customs Enforcement (ICE) and, 370
Immigration and Naturalization Service (INS), 375, 376
inadmissible alien and, 385
IRCA effect on, 737
Johnson-Reed Immigration Act and, 375
jurisdiction of, 709
McCarran-Walter Act and, 373
media coverage and, 459
migrant deaths, 148, 164
militarization of, 737
mindset of, 736–737
missions of, 738
No More Deaths reports on, 759
Operations Gateway and Blockade, 737
Operation Wetback, 544
original organization of, 736
purpose of, 69, 127, 735
record apprehensions of, xxxiv
reorganization of, 738
repatriation, 736
as symbolic, 736
targeted enforcement strategy, 737
technological advances, 736
terrorism and, 127
Tucson Sector, 148, 164, 536, 540, 615
United States v. Brignoni-Ponce ruling, 723–724
U.S.-Mexico border wall, 752
violence and, 759–760
U.S. Census Bureau, **738–742**
Arizona SB 1070, 739
census data, necessity of, 739
citizenship and nativity definitions of, 739–740
composition of decennial census, 738
constitutional mandate, 738
Current Population Survey (CPS), 740
decennial census, 738–739, 740
definition of foreign-born person, 740
definition of non-citizen, 740
definition of U.S. citizens, 739–740
foreign-born category, 740, 742
international migration, 741
Latino boycott of, 739

Latino population undercounted, 739
legal migrant status and, 739
measurement of citizenship status, 740–741
measurement of immigrant population, improvements to, 741
Migration History Topical Module, 741
naturalization, 740
net international migration, 741
outreach campaigns, 739
participation in, 739
purpose of, 738
statistical sampling, 739
Survey of Income and Program Participation (SIPP), 740, 741
surveys of, 740
undercounting, 739
undocumented immigrants and, 740
U.S. Citizenship and Immigration Services (USCIS), **742–745**
Application for Naturalization (Form N-400), 743–744
asylum and, 40
citizenship test, 95
duties of, 369
employment visas, 222, 223
E-Verify system, 119, 546, 744
forms and applications handled by, 744
green card, issuing of, 423, 744
green cards, 423
humanitarian programs and services, 745
I-130 Petition for Alien Relative, 424
immigration through family petition, 744
incarceration, 744
Mission Statement of, 743
"NACARA 203 relief," 522
national security and, 743
naturalization and, 511, 743
Oath of Allegiance, 744
"preference" categories for immigration, 435
problems of, 749
prosecutorial discretion, 535
reorganization, 742
Section 203 application, 521
sponsors petition and, 666
strategic goals of, 743
Temporary Protected Status (TPS) program, 694

U.S. Citizenship and Immigration (continued)
   U.S. military naturalizations, 511
   visas, issuing of, 744
   visa waiver countries, 547, 744
   work visas, 744
U.S. Customs and Border Protection (CBP),
   745–748
   border enforcement domains, 746–747
   Border Patrol, 738, 745, 746
   drug interdiction, 747
   enforcement activities affecting
     undocumented migrants, 746–747
   Field Operations, 745, 746
   human smuggling, 747
   I-94 form, 546
   interdiction of smuggled goods, 747
   officers of, 242 (image), 746 (image), 747
   operational subunits, 745
   outside threats prevention, 747
   responsibilities of, 369, 374
   structuring of, 745–746
   unauthorized migration, 747
U.S. Department of Homeland Security
   (DHS), **748–750**
   CIS, problems of, 749
   collective groups, identifying and
     deporting, 748
   components of, 748
   date founded, 748
   detention and deportation systems, 748
   disappearance of people and, 749
   emphasis of, 748
   enforcement apparatus failures, 749
   expansion of immigration enforcement
     units, 748–749
   ICE, problems of, 749
   immigration in Homeland Security, 749
   immigration policies and practices of, 749
   national security, 749
   organization of, 748
U.S.-Mexico border wall, **750–753**
   Berlin wall analogy, 752
   Border Patrol and, 752
   Border Patrol Strategic Plan, 751
   Clinton administration and, 750
   cost to taxpayers, 752
   date started, 750
   effects of, 752
   failure of, 750, 752, 753

   infrastructure of, 752
   INS and, 751
   John P. Clark on, 752
   length of (as of 2012), 752
   objective of, 751
   photograph of, 751
   "prevention through deterrence"
     strategy, 751
   purpose of, 750, 753
   Secure Border Initiative Network
     (SBINet), 752
   Secure Fence Act (2006), 752
   social purpose of, 753
   towns receiving primary fencing, 751
   uses of (trends), 750–751
   U.S. General Accounting Office (2006)
     on, 752
U.S. military Joint Task Force Six, 127
U.S. Visitor and Immigrant Status Indicator
   Technology Program (US-VISIT), 17,
   121, 628
Utah, 362, 399
U-visas, **753–757**
   advocates strategy concerning,
     755–756
   certification, 755
   class action lawsuits, 755
   conclusion concerning, 756
   criticism of, 755–756
   definition of terms involved
     in, 756
   delay in issuance of, 755
   domestic violence and, 173
   eligibility, 754, 755
   Form I-918, 755
   INS and, 754
   lack of clarity in, 756
   number of, 753
   provisions of, 754
   purpose of, 754
   qualifying crimes for, 754
   reporting of crime, 754
   Supplement B form, 755
   USCIS and, 755
   victim cooperation, 755
   Victims of Trafficking and Violence
     Protection Act (VTVPA), 753
   work authorization, 754
   workshops for, 756

Valdez, Zulema (2012), 644, 646
Valenzuela, Abel, Jr. et al., 144, 146
Valle del Sol v. Whiting et al., 31
Vargas, Jose Antonio, 447–448, 457
Vaughan, J. (2006), 559, 561, 562
Vázquez, Martha (New Mexico District
 Chief Justice), 727
Vecoli, Rudolph, 729
Vela, Filemon (Rep.), 380
Velazquez, Nadine, 262 (image)
Venezuela, 367
Ventanilla de Salud program, 269
Vertovec, Steven (2006), 707, 709
Victims of Trafficking and Violence
 Protection Act (VTVPA), 173, 753
Vienna Convention on Consular Relations
 (VCCR), 268, 269
Villegas, Francisco (2010), 10, 11
violence, **759–761**
 Border Patrol Strategic Plan (1994), 760
 Carlos LaMadrid, 759
 civilian participation in border and
  immigration control, 760
 confrontation, 760–761
 detention, 760
 examples of, 759
 gender-based violence, 773
 Ignacio Ramos, 759
 immigrant custody, 760
 immigrants and crime, 760–761
 Jan Brewer, 760
 Jason Bush, 760
 John McCain (Sen.), 760–761
 Jose Antonio Elena Rodriguez, 759
 Minutemen American Defense, 760
 Minutemen Civil Defense Corps, 760
 No More Deaths on U.S. Border Patrol, 759
 Prison Rape Elimination Act (PREA), 760
 Ramos and Compean case, 759
 Ramses Barrón Torres, 759
 of ranch owners, 60
 Shawna Forde, 760
 types of violent incidences, 759
 U.S. Border Patrol agents and, 759
Violence Against Women Act (VAWA),
 761–764
 abused children and, 762
 benefits and protections, 763
 confidentiality, 762

date reauthorized, 173
 date signed into law, 761
 domestic violence, 763
 eligibility under, 763
 Joe Biden and, 761–786
 mixed-status family and, 764
 modifications in 2000, 762
 obstacles confronting domestic violence
  victims, 763–764
 provisions of, 761–762
 purpose of, 173, 761
 reauthorizations of, 761
 self-petition, 763
 U-visa, 762–763
 women with children, 763–764
Violent Crime Control and Law
 Enforcement Act ("Smith Act"), xxxiv
Visitors' Guide to Arivaca (Ordaz), 701
Voting Rights Act (1965), 99

wages, **765–767**
 agriculture and construction work, 766
 education and, 766
 explanations for lower wages of
  unauthorized workers, 766
 health insurance and other benefits,
  765–766
 Latin American immigrants and, 766
 legal status and, 766
 low-wage labor and mass unauthorized
  migration, 766–767
 poverty, 765
 Raúl Hinojosa-Ojeda on, 767
 report on earning power, 767
 unauthorized workers and, 765
 variability among wages earned by
  undocumented people, 765
 women, unauthorized immigrant women
  in the labor force, 766
Wall Street Journal, 547
Wal-Mart, 145, 199, 219–220, 281
Washington (state), 362, 399
Washington Consensus, 291
Water Station in California, 149
Webster-Ashburten Treaty (1842), 68
Welcome to Shelbyville (film), 697
welfare system, **767–771**
 asylum-seekers, 770
 Bill Clinton and, 769

welfare system (continued)
   British Poor Laws and, 769
   California Proposition 187, 768
   communication of information about, 771
   ethnographic research concerning, 771
   Food Stamp program, 769
   Franklin Roosevelt and, 769
   the Great Depression and, 769
   historical overview of, 769–770
   historical reactions to, 767–768
   immigrant status and, 770
   King (2007) on, 768, 771
   legal immigrants, lost eligibility, 770
   legal permanent residents and, 770
   Lyndon Johnson and, 769
   Marchevsky and Theoharis (2008) on,
      770, 771
   myths about immigrants' use of
      healthcare programs, 768
   Personal Responsibility and Work
      Opportunity Reconciliation Act
      (1996), 769–770
   refugees, 770
   Social Security Act, 769
   state design of, 770
   Temporary Assistance to Needy Families
      (TANF) program, 770
   unfair treatment and humiliation in, 771
   U.S.-citizen children, 770
Wells Fargo Bank, 352
Western Hemisphere Institute for Security
   Cooperation (School of the
   Americas), 77
Western Hemisphere Travel Initiative
   (WHTI), 549–550
When the State Kills (report), 27
White et al. v. Regester et al. case, 468
*Who Are We? The Challenges to America's
   National Identity* (Huntington), 214
Williams, Heather E., 540
Williams, Lee G., 472
Wilson, Pete, 473
woman's status, **771–775**
   domestic violence, 773–774
   factors influencing women's
      immigration, 772–773
   family reunification policies, effect
      of, 772
   farm work, 772

   female migration as a means to
      empowerment, 774
   gender-based violence, 773–774
   gender-based violence and
      undocumented migration, 773–774
   historical deportation rates of women, 772
   historical development of women in
      undocumented migration, 771–772
   male dependency, 772
   migration and women's status in sending
      communities, 774
   rape, 773
   "sexually deviant" label, 772
   social networks, 772
   Special Agricultural Workers program,
      772–773
   U-Visa, 774
Women, Infants, and Children (WIC)
   program, 575, 692
Wong Kim Ark v. United States, xxvii, 89, 93
Wong Wing vs. United States, xxvii
workers' rights, **775–778**
   abusive employer, e process of filing a
      complaint against, 770
   Advisory Opinion OC-18 (2003), 775
   advocacy efforts for immigrant workers'
      rights, 777
   Catholic labor schools, 777
   Coalición de Derechos Humanos
      (CDH), 777
   dangerous jobs, 776
   English fluency and lack of education, 776
   equal protection under the law, 775
   *Hoffman Plastic Compounds v. National
      Labor Relations Board (NLRB)* ruling,
      775–776
   Interfaith Worker Justice or IWJ, 777
   Jewish Workmen's Circle, 777
   National Day Labor Organizing Network
      or NDLON, 777
   rights of undocumented workers, 775
   undocumented workers and, 775–776
   violations of workplace rights, 776–777
   vulnerability of undocumented
      workers, 776
   women and, 777
   workplace abuse, 776
Work Opportunity Reconciliation Act
   (1996), 691

workplace injury, **778–781**
Affordable Care Act (2010), 781
Balbuena v. IDR Realty ruling, 779–780
Celi v. 42nd Street Development Project, Inc. ruling, 780
disabled undocumented workers, 781
employer-based health insurance (EBHI) and, 781
Hoffman Plastic Compounds v. National Labor Relations Board (NLRB) ruling, 779
medical insurance, 781
musculoskeletal injurie, 779
Sanango v. 200 East 16th Street Housing Corp. ruling, 779
Tarango v. State Industrial Insurance System ruling, 780–781
Virginia Workmen's Compensation laws, 780
workplace raids, **782–784**
Agriprocessors plant raid, 783
bias in, 783
children and, 782, 783
employer reaction to, 72
E-verify, 783–784
family separation and, 782
ICE and, 782–783
Immigration Reform and Control Act (IRCA), 782
impact on communities, 782
Joe Arpaio, Sheriff and, 783
large-scale raids, 783
Michael Bianco, Inc. raid, 782
results of, 782
small-scale local rates, 783
Swift and Company raid, 782
Tentative Nonconformation or TNC Notice, 783
underground economy and, 784
U.S.-born children, 782
work visas, **784–787**
defined, 784–785
fraud, 786
H1-B visa, 785
H-2A visa, 785
I-129 form, 786
Kretsedemas (2012) on non-immigrant worker visas, 785, 787
labor certification requirements, 786

labor shortages and, 785
length of time involved in, 785
low-wage migrants, 785
mandatory fees, 786
NAFTA and, 785
nonimmigrant visas, purpose of, 786
number of nonimmigrant work visas (2009), 785
O-1 visa, 223, 785
overstaying, 787
permanent resident status, 785
processing procedures, 786
processing requirements, 786
professional exchange and, 785
spouse or children of applicant, 786
temporary worker visa requirements, 786
types of, 785
World-Class Instructional Design Assessment (WIDA), 232
Worthington Daily Globe, 85

X, Malcolm, 99
xenophobia, **789–792**
Alabama, 790
American nativism as distinct from, 678
Arizona and, 790
Arizona Rangers, 791 (image)
Arrocha (2010/2011) on, 790, 791
bias, 789
California Proposition 187, 790
categorizing people, 789
Chinese Exclusion Act (1882), 789
crimes against immigrants, 791–792
defined, 789
Delgadillo (2011) on, 789, 791
Emergency Quota Act (1921), 789
exclusion and, 239
FBI statistics on violent crimes against immigrants, 791
"in" group mentality, 789
hate crimes, 312, 790–791
Immigration and Nationality Act (1965), 789
immigration regulation and, 790
Johnson-Reed Act (1924), 789
Latino political views and, 650
NAFTA and, 474
National Origins Act (1924), 676
national security, 790

xenophobia (continued)
"otherness," 789
policies of attrition, 790
political rhetoric and, 790
racialized labeling, 789
racism, segregation and violence,
791–792
root of, 789

Yick Wo v. Hopkins, xxvi
Yoo, Jeong Ah, and Allison Zippay (2012),
636, 637
Young Lords, 99
Yuma 14, 158

Zamora, Pedro, 132
Zamudio, Margaret M., and Michael I.
Lichter (2008), 341, 342
Zapotec people (Oaxaca), **793–795**
alternative name for, 793
in California, 795
cargo system, 794
children of, 795

coyotes and, 793
description of, 793
discrimination and barriers, 794
employer treatment of, 794–795
family network of, 793–794
farming and, 793
financial necessity immigration, 793
"Indio" term, 794
language barrier of, 793, 794, 795
Lopez and Munro (1999) on, 793,
794, 795
mistreatment of, 794
Oaxacan identity denial, 794
Organización Quaviní, 795
relocation cities (primary), 794
San Luqueños women migration, 793
social networks, 794
tequio system, 794
Tijuana border crossing, 793
Zavala, Luis Eduardo Ramirez, 316
Zigler, Edward, 81
Zigler, Edward, and Mary E. Lang, 199,
81–82